# Tibet: When the Gods Spoke
## India Tibet Relations (1947-1962)
### Part 3

# Tibet: When the Gods Spoke
## India Tibet Relations (1947-1962)

### Part 3

### (July 1954 - February 1957)

## Claude Arpi

(Established 1870)

United Service Institution of India

New Delhi

Vij Books India Pvt Ltd

New Delhi (India)

**Tibet: When the Gods Spoke**
This book is Part 3 of the series on India Tibet Relations (1947-1962). Other books in the series are:
Part 1: Tibet: The Last Months of a Free Nation
Part 2: Will Tibet Ever Find Her Soul Again

Published by

**Vij Books India Pvt Ltd**
(Publishers, Distributors & Importers)
2/19, Ansari Road
Delhi – 110 002
Phones: 91-11-43596460, 91-11-47340674
Fax: 91-11-47340674
e-mail: vijbooks@rediffmail.com

Copyright © 2019, United Service Institution of India, New Delhi

ISBN: 978-93-88161-56-5 (Hardback)
ISBN: 978-93-88161-57-2 (Paperback)
ISBN: 978-93-88161-58-9 (ebook)

All rights reserved.

No part of this book may be reproduced, stored in a retrieval system, transmitted or utilised in any form or by any means, electronic, mechanical, photocopying, recording or otherwise, without the prior permission of the copyright owner. Application for such permission should be addressed to the publisher.

# Contents

| | | |
|---|---|---|
| *Acknowledgements* | | vii |
| Introduction | | 1 |
| 01 | The First Incursions: the Case of Barahoti | 7 |
| 02 | The First Months after the Agreement and Zhou's Visit to India | 34 |
| 03 | Nehru's Important Visit to Beijing | 61 |
| 04 | Cartographical Aggression: the Implications for India | 78 |
| 05 | No Escort Anymore: the Earlier the Better | 97 |
| 06 | Winding-up is Not Easy | 108 |
| 07 | Tibet's Slow Incorporation Starts | 133 |
| 08 | Tibet's Assimilation Continues July – December 1955 | 161 |
| 09 | Developments in Tibet: Implications for Sikkim | 188 |
| 10 | The Foreign Secretary in Tibet | 218 |
| 11 | India's Relations with Bhutan | 231 |
| 12 | The Foreign Secretary's Visit to Bhutan | 256 |
| 13 | Pressure is Mounting on the Borders | 274 |
| 14 | The Advance in the Subansiri Sector of NEFA | 295 |
| 15 | The Uprising in Eastern Tibet | 325 |
| 16 | The Changes in Western Tibet | 338 |

| 17 | On the Indian Side of the Himalaya: The Situation in Tawang | 363 |
| 18 | Kushok Bakula's Tour in Tibet | 385 |
| 19 | The Life of the Consul General of India in Lhasa | 417 |
| 20 | The Preparatory Committee of the Tibetan Autonomous Region | 442 |
| 21 | Will the Dalai Lama Visit India? | 453 |
| 22 | In the Land of the Buddha | 478 |
| 23 | A Milestone in the Relations Between India and Tibet? | 497 |
| 24 | When Men Become Desperate they Consult the Gods | 520 |
| 25 | Some Conclusions: Hoping Against Hope | 549 |
| Annexure | | 554 |
| *Index* | | 559 |

# Acknowledgements

I am indebted to the United Service Institution of India (USI) for offering me the Field Marshal KM Cariappa Chair of Excellence for this research on "The relations between India and Tibet between 1947 and 1962."

I am particularly grateful to the USI Director, Lt Gen PK Singh, PVSM, AVSM (Retd), who has always encouraged me and supported my endeavour.

My thanks too to Maj Gen BK Sharma, AVSM, SM** (Retd), the Deputy Director (Research) and Head of the CS3, under which this research is conducted. I have to also mention his colleague, Dr Roshan Khaniejo, who is coordinating my research for the USI.

Maj Gen PK Goswami, VSM (Retd), Deputy Director (Adm) at the USI has always made it easy for me.

It has been a pleasure to work with all at USI.

I am deeply indebted to Maj Gen PJS Sandhu (Retd) my 'guide' for this work. Though he has now retired, he very much remains part of the USI family. Despite his numerous activities as a 'retired' general, he has taken time to painstakingly go through the manuscript and has made valuable 'strategic' suggestions. I deeply appreciate his kindness and help, which has greatly enriched the manuscript.

My gratitude to my publishers, Brig PK Vij (Retd) and his son, Rohan. It is a pleasure to work with them.

Thank you to Tony Meakin for accepting to go through the manuscript and correct my English and to Nirmala for typing hundreds of the cables, telegrams, reports, from the National Archives of India and the Nehru Memorial Museum & Library.

My appreciation to the entire staff of the National Archives for their readiness to cope with my recurring demands.

My niece Lisa worked on the cover and made the photo publishable. Merci.

Thank you to Uma and Deepti for helping in the proofreading of this volume.

My gratitude to my daughter Smiti who is always supportive.

Finally, I have to express my great appreciation to Abha my wife, for her constant support. She has been my daily counselor for this volume. I really appreciate the hours she has spent reading through the manuscript and commenting on it.

# Introduction

This is the third volume of our study on the relations between India and Tibet (1947-62), undertaken under the Field Marshal KM Cariappa Chair of Excellence of the United Service Institution of India.

**Volume 1**

The first volume recounted the tragedy that befell Tibet; not only had the Dalai Lama and his people lost their country, which had lived blissfully ignorant of the great revolutions reshaping the rest of the world, but it became a tragedy for India too, who lost a peaceful neighbour. Suddenly India had to share a border with Communist China whose ideology was the opposite of Buddhist values. At that time Delhi did not realise it, but when a few years later, India understood that it had lost a secure border, it would be too late.

Some wiser Indian officials and politicians immediately saw the implications in the change of neighbour, but their views were not heard.

Letters, cables, telegrams and notes accessed by us, showed that two factions emerged during the tumultuous months of November/December 1950: on one side were Prime Minister Jawaharlal Nehru and KM Panikkar, his ambassador in Beijing, both obsessed by an imaginary friendship with New China and fixated on the 'larger implications for World Peace'; the other side feared the strategic implications for India.

In a way, the fate of Tibet and India's borders with Tibet was sealed once Sardar Patel, who articulated the dangers of the Chinese invasion for the Indian frontiers, passed away on December 15, 1950; it was hardly two months after the entry of the People's Liberation Army (PLA) in Eastern Tibet. Nehru's policy would have disastrous consequences which can still be felt today on the Indian borders, whether in Ladakh or Arunachal Pradesh.

**Volume 2**

In the second volume, we studied the consequences of the signature of the 17-Point Agreement in May 1951; the Tibetan delegates had no alternative but to accept that "the Tibetan people shall return to the family of the Motherland of the People's Republic of China" and "drive out imperialist aggressive forces from Tibet."

A two-phase operation was meticulously planned by Mao Zedong; the first part culminated in the Battle of Chamdo which saw the Tibetan forces being decimated; the Great Helmsman's second step was 'diplomatic', the weak Tibetan State was forced to put its thumbprint on an agreement allowing Communist China to take over the Land of Snows.

This period also saw the beginning of the *Hindi-Chini-Bhai-Bhai* honeymoon between Delhi and Beijing. Over the next months and years, the Indian officials posted on the Roof of the World would discover the true objectives of the Communists; but nobody in Delhi or the Indian Embassy in Beijing was ready to listen.

The second volume went in depth into the slow break-down and deterioration of the age-old Indo-Tibet relations, gradually being replaced by a cruder relation with the new occupiers of Tibet.

It ended with the signature of the so-called Panchsheel Agreement to which the Tibetans were not even invited to participate. India's long border with Tibet (now China) was wishfully deemed settled in the process.

**Volume 3**

The third volume studies the Chinese consolidation on the plateau after having secured the Indian withdrawal from Tibet through the April 1954 Agreement.

# Introduction

Paradoxically or ironically, this period witnessed the first Chinese intrusions in Barahoti, a small flat grazing ground located in today's Chamoli district of Uttarakhand. Though the first two of the Five Principles (Panchsheel) spoke of 'Mutual respect for each other's territorial integrity and sovereignty and Mutual non-aggression', the Chinese troops walked into the Indian Territory, before the ink on the treaty had dried.

During the period under study, many such intrusions took place in the Central Sector of the Indo-Tibet border, now Sino-Tibet border.

In the next chapters, we look at the diplomatic front, which began with Premier Zhou Enlai's visit to Delhi in June 1954 and followed by Jawaharlal Nehru's trip to Beijing in October; it culminated a year later in the Bandung Conference. Hardly any words about Tibet were exchanged during the encounters between Nehru and Zhou; for the Indian and Chinese leaderships, it was a settled issue …except for the border. The Tibetans were nowhere in the picture.

At that time, the Indian Government started noticing some cartographical aggression by Beijing. One chapter goes into the details of Delhi's handling of the issue and the 'misunderstanding' about what Beijing called 'old maps'.

In Tibet itself, it was time for India to wind-up her presence on the plateau; the negotiations would take many more months than expected, particularly for the dak-bungalows, but early 1955, an agreement would be finally found. A few photos in chapter 6 show the extent to which some of these guest houses were really valuable buildings, but the political decision had been taken to simply hand them over to China. A similar fate awaited the military escort in Gyantse and Yatung; in a rather discreet manner, it was soon withdrawn. Delhi was probably ashamed to have even a scarce military presence in Tibet.

With the passing months, the consolidation of the Chinese presence in Tibet continued; it translated into the construction of several roads leading to Lhasa …and to the Indian borders. The two main axes (Tibet-Sichuan and Tibet-Qinghai) reached the Tibetan capital in December 1954, this would adversely affect the bilateral trade; suddenly, the PLA no longer needed Indian grain and other commodities.

A few chapters are consecrated to Tibet's tiny neighbours, Sikkim and Bhutan which were deeply worried about their own future, while watching the development taking place in the North. Delhi had to work out new policies for these States, as well as for her own border areas. The visit of India's Foreign Secretary RK Nehru to Sikkim, Tibet (Chumbi Valley) and Bhutan was an important event in this new political context; it is covered in three separate chapters.

The changes in NEFA[1], particularly in Subansiri and Tawang Frontiers are studied in some detail. The leadership in Delhi did not understand the strategic issues triggered by the occupation of the Tibetan plateau for her borderlands. It translated into, for example, sending the anthropologist Verrier Elwin on a mission to Tawang, which, though interesting in itself, neglected the military and strategic aspects which were systematically overlooked by the Indian State. It would have disastrous consequences a few years later, though intrepid officers such as Maj SM Krishnatry and Capt L R Sailo clearly described the 'imperiled' border of India.

On the other side of the plateau, in Western Tibet, life continued as usual; Indian traders continued to carry their goods from the Himalayan region and while the Chinese presence was still at a minimum, the PLA focused mainly on building new roads. However, the attention of the Communists was brought by the Tibetans, to the borders areas such as Barahoti or Nilang Valley; this would have long-term consequences for India, the Chinese intrusions still today become active every summer.

The visit to China of Kushok Bakula Rinpoche of Ladakh was an important event which unfortunately did not make the Chinese reconsider their policies or make the Indian Government realize that something was going wrong in Tibet.

It was also the time of the first uprisings in Kham province of Eastern Tibet; the revolt was followed by a violent repression by the Chinese Army. Though not directly related to India-Tibet relations, we look into this momentous event as well as the creation of the Preparatory Committee of the Tibetan Autonomous Region, which was to bring new 'reforms', often unwanted, to the Tibetan 'masses'.

---

1  North East Frontier Agency.

# Introduction

Incidentally, it is the Tibetan 'masses' known as *Mimang*, the People's Association, which revolted first against the occupation of their land, while the clergy and many aristocrats accepted the new situation, for their own interests.

In many ways, the Indian government could only be a silent spectator to the happenings triggered by the signature of the two agreements (the 17-Point Agreement with the Tibetan representatives in 1951 and the so-called Panchsheel Agreement signed with India three years later); both legalized the Chinese presence on the plateau.

The four last chapters are consecrated to the visit of the Dalai Lama and the Panchen Lama to India on the occasion of 2500$^{th}$ anniversary of the birth of the Buddha. What is striking is that at no point in time were the Tibetan Lamas involved in the acceptance of the invitations.

At the last minute, after months of reluctance, Beijing agreed to the visit. It was a risk for Beijing, which knew that many Tibetans were keen that the Dalai Lama should take refuge in India. The Chinese Premier Zhou Enlai visited Delhi thrice in less than three months between November 1956 and January 1957; he wanted to make sure that the Tibetan leader would return to Tibet. In the process, he promised to postpone the Communist 'reforms' for a few years.

Eventually, the two Lamas returned to their homeland, to give a 'last chance' to the Communists to respect their promises. Those final years will be the subject of the last volume of our quadrilogy.

Could India have played a more proactive role? However, for many Indian officials, reforms were necessary and the Chinese presence was not entirely a bad thing for Tibet.

In the process, they forgot to take into account the repercussions of the Chinese occupation of the plateau for the Indian border.

To conclude, an annexure tells us the true story of the Aksai Chin road cutting across the Indian territory in Ladakh.

# 01

# The First Incursions: the Case of Barahoti

India would not have long to wait to see the consequences of The 'Panikkar doctrine', which can be resumed thus, "let us not speak of a border which is settled, if it were not settled China would have brought the issue to the negotiating table".

The former Indian Ambassador to China had managed to convince the Indian Prime Minister of the validity of his views despite the words of Premier Zhou Enlai: "we are prepared to settle all such problems as are ripe for settlement."[1]

It is interesting to study the historical background of the 'disputed' area called Barahoti by India and Wu-Je by China.[2]

In his Monthly Report for August 1955, Apa Pant, the Political Officer in Sikkim wrote: "Only small parties of Chinese are seen constantly moving between Gartok and Taklakot in Western Tibet. Plenty of tinned stores, wireless equipment and furniture are reported to be arriving in Gartok from Lhasa. …Census is still reported to be in progress in Changtan[3]. The *Garpons*[4] helped by two Chinese officers are conducting this census."[5]

---

1　See Volume 2, Chapter 20 of our study, *Will Tibet Ever Find her Soul Again? India Tibet Relations 1947-1962*.

2　See map 1, page 573.

3　Changthang.

4　The Governors of Western Tibet.

5　*Political situation reports on Sikkim from the political officer in Sikkim Gangtok,*

Census also meant the survey of the frontiers; the Indo-Tibet border had become the Sino-Indian border, with consequences still visible as these lines are written over six decades later.

**The Traditional Boundary**

On November 20, 1950, during the question hour in the Parliament, Prime Minister Jawaharlal Nehru was asked: "Will the Prime Minister be pleased to state whether India has got any well-defined boundary with Tibet?"[6]

His answer was: "The border from Ladakh to Nepal has probably not been the subject of any formal agreement between India, Tibet and China but it is well established by custom and long usage. The Historical Division[7] are investigating if there are any formal agreements. There have been a few boundary disputes in this area, but they have been peacefully settled."

It is a historical fact that the Indo-Tibet frontier had been peaceful. It is probably why the Indian diplomats who negotiated the Panchsheel Agreement foolishly 'avoided' mention of the frontiers during the talks (and in the final text). India would pay dearly for this monumental lapse.

Over the years, China kept changing the posts, claiming new areas, often without knowing the coordinates of the places. Barahoti is one such place, but there were others; in the course of the meetings of the Officials of India and China in 1960, which followed the visit of Chinese Premier Zhou Enlai to India in April, both parties presented their claims for the Central Sector.[8]

The Indian report mentioned that the Nilang-Jadhang area and Barahoti, Sangchamalla and Lapthal were clubbed together for discussion.

---

Ministry of External Affairs, Branch NEF, 1955; Ref: File No. 30(3)-NEF/55. Available in the National Archives of India, New Delhi.

6 All other documents in this chapter, except specifically mentioned, are from the Nehru Papers (JN Collection) held at the Nehru *Memorial* Museum and Library in Delhi. The 'papers' are not indexed.

7 Of the Ministry of External Affairs.

8 Today's Uttarakhand State.

On July 18, 1960, during the 15th meeting of the bilateral commission in Beijing, while answering the question of the Indian side, the Chinese side stated that Barahoti (Wu-je), Sangchamalla and Lapthal formed one composite area on the Chinese side of the alignment claimed by them, and there was no Indian territory wedged between these three pockets. This was a new claim to the Indian territory, put forward for the first time, it was contradicting China's previous official positions.

On September 8, 1959, in a letter to Jawaharlal Nehru, Chinese Premier Zhou Enlai had treated Wu-Je, Sangchamalla and Lapthal as three separate areas. A year later however, the Chinese side included these areas of some 300 square miles which belonged to India into the Tibetan territory.

This is just an example of how the posts started to change after India acquired a new neighbour …and the Dalai Lama took refuge in India.

**A Historical Background Prepared by the Intelligence Bureau**

In July 1952, in a note[9] 'Border Disputes and Collection of Taxes by Tibetans in Garhwal District'[10], the Intelligence Bureau (IB) described the topography of the Himalaya in this area which belongs to today's Chamoli district: "The Garhwal-Tibet border can only be crossed through the Mana and Niti Valleys where there are open places and habitation, while the rest of the border area consists of snow-covered mountains studded with glaciers. In the Mana Valley, the last village on the Indian side is Mana which is situated 26 miles from Mana Pass, which lies on the boundary of Tibet and India. From Mana the route to Tibet follows along Saraswati river and there are no grazing grounds or other places of habitation on the way which could be occupied or claimed by the people of Tibet. There is no border dispute in this Valley, although some rumours have been heard, that the Tibetans claim territory upto Kanchanganga, which is situated about one mile South

---

9 *Intelligence Bureau (M.H.A.), Border Disputes and Collection of Taxes by Tibetans in Garhwal District*; External Affairs, Branch NEF, 1952; File No. N/52/1814/1201. Available at the National Archives of India.

10 *Note addressed by Waryam Singh of IB to NR Pillai of the Ministry of External Affairs. Note sent through the Ministry of Home Affairs*; D.I.B. No. 24/76/52(4) dated July 21, 1952.

of Badri Nath[11]. There are no grounds for attaching any importance to such rumours.

This probably referred to the Nilang-Jadhang dispute[12] which will be studied separately. There is no doubt that Delhi was aware of these old Tibetan claims in areas South of Tsangchok-la pass.

The IB Report continued its descriptions of the area: "There are four Passes between Niti Valley and Tibet, namely: Gothing Pass [Niti], Damjin [Tunjun] Pass, Hoti Pass and Ghirti Pass. Niti, the Northern most village in the Indian territory, is situated 11 miles from Gothing Pass and Damjin Pass. There are few plains situated near these passes in the Indian territory."

The Intelligence note admitted that there was an old boundary dispute about Hoti Plain, which in fact consisted of two plains called Bara Hoti and Chhota Hoti, both situated near the Chor Hoti Pass.

The historical background of the 'dispute' was then explained: "About the end of the last century, the Tibetans had established a Customs Post at Hoti Plain. To stop this practice, the British Govt.[13] had to send out a detachment of Gurkhas along with Shri Dharma Nand Joshi, Deputy Collector in 1890. This had a salutary effect and the Tibetans removed their post. It appears that for some time past the Tibetans have again been establishing a Police-cum-Customs post at Hoti during the trading season."

The access to the place was difficult, making it hard to keep a tab on the area. It must be noted that the access is much easier from the Tibetan side than from the Indian. Over the years, this would make it easier for the Chinese to intrude.

The Intelligence Bureau continued: "It is quite possible that if the Tibetans are not stopped from establishing their post at Hoti Plain, they might eventually claim it to be their own territory. Since there is no habitation or cultivation in this area, the Garhwal authorities hardly

---

11 Also written Badrinath.
12 See Chapter 13.
13 Government.

ever visit the area or take any action to denote that it lies within their jurisdiction."

Along the Himalaya watershed, there were many areas where Tibetan authorities tried to change the border for the convenience of their traders and shepherds. The IB report further remarked: "It may be mentioned that last year [1951] when some Indian traders established their trade at Hoti Plain for buying wool, from the Tibetans living near the border, the *Dzong-Pon*[14] of Dhapa[15] [county] (in Tibet) sent his *Serjis*[16] ('messengers') to Hoti Plain to serve notices on the Indian traders to appear before him."

The IB recommended to the Government of India that it was essential that Delhi "should make it clear to the Govt. of Tibet and its *Dzongpon* that the Hoti Plain is Indian territory and the Tibetans have no right to establish any customs post there; nor can they exercise any authority in the area."

The report added: "We understand that the Deputy Commissioner Garhwal has already suggested to the U.P. Govt.[17] that he and the Supdt.[18] of Police should visit Hoti with a detachment of Garhwal Rifles and Armed Police, and that they should hoist the Indian flag there in order to establish their own authority and stop the Tibetans from establishing their Customs post."

It is what the Indo-Tibetan Border Police[19] (ITBP) still does every year, though now they often encounter Chinese troops patrolling the high-altitude plain.

---

14 Dzongpon or Dzongpen (District Commissioner).

15 Daba.

16 Or *Sarjis,* Tibetan emissary-cum-enumerator.

17 Tehri and Garhwal were then under the Government of the United Province.

18 Superintendent.

19 ITBP is a police force. Presently Battalions of ITBP are deployed on Border Guarding Duties from Karakoram Pass in Ladakh to Jachep La in Arunachal Pradesh, covering 3,488 KM of the India China Border. They are manning Border Outposts at an altitude ranging from 9,000 ft to 18,500 ft in the Western, Middle and Eastern Sectors of the India China Border. ITBP is basically a mountain trained force and most of the officers and men are professionally trained mountaineers and skiers.

The Bureau concluded: "A number of Indian traders from Niti and Mana Valleys visit Tibet every year for purposes of trade. They have to pay certain taxes inside Tibet. However, in case of Mana Valley, the *Serjis* of the *Dzong-Pon* of Chaprong[20] realize Rs. 22 from the people of Mana as *Singthal* i.e. Land Tax. This collection is made in Indian territory when the *Serji* comes to announce that the pass is open. The *Serjis* are also provided with free food and fuel. It is reported that in the records of the *Dzongpon* this levy is entered as Land Tax and not as Trade Tax. No such collection is made from the villagers of Niti Valley. We feel that the Tibetan tax-collectors should not be allowed to collect taxes inside the Indian territory. The traders could pay this amount which is really a Trade Tax, when they visit the Tibetan markets."

As we shall see, a similar situation had arisen in Nilang-Jadhang area.

On April 24, 1952, the Ministry of External Affairs received the Ministry of Defence (MoD) views: "the guiding principle in the new circumstances must be the Government of India's ability to vindicate what they would regard as the appropriate frontier, since it would be idle to claim territory which could not be effectively protected or controlled."

Speaking about Nilang, the MoD continued: "The area under dispute is an extremely difficult country physically and climatically with hardly any communications. It, therefore, follows that operations in the area will have to be confined to short periods and undertaken by specially trained infantry organized on an ad hoc basis with very scanty artillery support and no support whatsoever from either tanks or aircraft. The administrative problems connected with an operation would be considerable. Even if the areas to be defended were narrowed down to the protection of the villages Nilang and Jadhang, with the present resources of the Army, it would be well nigh impossible to guarantee the integrity of the above villages. It will be equally difficult to afford hundred per cent protection to the small inhabited localities lying within the Indian frontier in this area."

The MoD conclusions were "Whatever solution the E.A.[21] Ministry adopt, it would be subject to the conditions set out above so far as the defence of the frontier will be concerned."

---

20 *Dzongpon* of Tsaparang.
21 External Affairs.

As for Nilang, it was decided to assert Indian customary rights in Barahoti; not doing so could have had serious consequences for the entire Himalayan frontier.

## The Take from the Ministry of External Affairs

A few months later, in September 1952, an official of the Ministry of External Affairs pointed out: "Last year there was some trouble over the opening of the market for trading with Western Tibet at Hoti instead of the established market known as Nabra in Tibet. The local Tibetan officials who used to collect certain dues from our traders suffered a loss and resented the functioning of the Hoti market. There is, however, no indication that the Tibetans wanted to establish a customs post at Hoti."

The issue was referred to G. Mukharji, the Home Secretary of the Uttar Pradesh Government who, on December 27, 1952, wrote back to the Foreign Secretary; the subject line of the letter read: "Border disputes and collection of taxes by Tibetans in Garhwal district."

Lucknow acknowledged the receipt of the Intelligence Bureau's note mentioned above and affirmed that the State Government had been keeping the Government of India in the loop as far as the developments along the Indo-Tibetan border were concerned.

The Home Secretary further asserted that no case of "encroachment has so far been reported though at one or two places tax collectors from Tibet did come in but were persuaded to go back."

He added that "it is rather embarrassing that tax collectors should come in at all and it is, therefore, requested that the matter may be settled finally with the Tibetan Government to not come in to India for purposes of tax collection."

Mukharji concluded: "Until this is done, it is feared that similar visits will be paid in future also creating unnecessary embarrassment for Government as well as for our people on the border."

The problem was that the Tibetan government was no more its own master and soon these borders areas were to become the Sino-Indian frontier. But Delhi was blissfully convinced that the border was a settled issue with China.

Mukharji also answered the question about the practicability for the State Government to station a small force of armed police on the border. Quoting from an earlier communication[22], the Home Secretary reiterated that "it would not be possible to stop any intruders from coming into our territory with the help of small police guards alone."

He further pointed out that it would be difficult for the State Government to make adequate police arrangements in such remote areas "on account of difficulties of climate and terrain."

He mentioned the creation of a Border Security Force which is "at present under examination with the Government of India" and stated "a force of that kind alone can be trained and equipped to function in those remote and difficult areas. Until that force is properly established, the State Government find it difficult to meet the situation by posting armed police in those areas."

It was only on October 24, 1962, four days after the Chinese massive attack, that the Indo-Tibetan Border Police (ITBP) was raised. But this has not stopped the Chinese from trespassing every year since then.

## The Panchsheel Negotiations

In December 1953, the talks for an agreement on trade and pilgrimage started in Beijing. As described in detail in Volume 2 of this study, it resulted in the infamous Panchsheel Agreement. Seeing at the way Indian diplomats were ready to bend backwards to accommodate any Chinese demands, Mao Zedong and his colleagues would find more and more outstanding issues to raise.

The Indian diplomats thought that by naming six passes for the traders and pilgrims, they had delineated a border.[23]

---

22 Dated December 29, 1951.

23 The six passes were (1) Shipki La pass, (2) Mana pass, (3) Niti pass, (4) Kungri Bingri pass, (5) Darma pass, and (6) Lipulekh pass.

Further they added "the customary route leading to Tashigong [Tashigang] along the valley of the Shangatsangpu [Senge Tsangpo or Indus] River may continue to be traversed in accordance with custom." Beijing refused to mention the other

India tried to include other passes: "Traders and pilgrims from India and Western Tibet may travel by the routes traversing the following localities and passes," but it was not accepted by China.[24]

But Delhi capitulated, China was then a friend, and ultimately only six passes were named.

The fact that India did not insist on its list resulted in a tragedy; China would soon claim the area south of Tunjun-la[25]; the negotiators had clearly not done their homework.

In a short note on the talks for the Tibet Agreement, written soon after the signature, the Secretary-General[26] of the Ministry noted: "It would also be desirable for us to establish check-posts at all disputed points as soon as possible so that there may be no opportunity for Chinese to take possession of such areas and face us with a fait accompli.

In this connection the opening remarks of Premier Zhou Enlai that "there are bound to be some problems between two great countries like India and China with a long common border… but we are prepared to settle all such problems as are ripe for settlement now" were significant.

In his note, Pillai further remarked: "We immediately countered this by saying that we had mentioned all outstanding questions in this region, and stressed this several times later the Chinese did not pursue the matter further. It is, however, likely that the Chinese may raise or create border problems if we are slow in advancing our administration right up to our frontiers, especially in the disputed areas which are fortunately not many. This is also a matter which requires further examination and consultations between the Ministries of External Affairs, Home Affairs and Defence."

---

passes and routes; China would soon claim Demchok as part of their territory.

24 The passes and routes mentioned by Delhi were: Tashigong, Gartok; Spanggur Tso to Rudok; Chiakang, Churkang, Ruksom; Tashigong, Churkang, Ruksom; Rudok, Ruksom, Rawang; Bodpo La; Shipki La; Keobarang; Shimdang; Gumrang (Khimokul); Tsang Chok La; Muling La; Mana Pass; Niti Pass; Tunjun-la; Marhi La; Shalshal Pass; Kungri Bingri Pass; Darma Pass; Lampiya Dhura (Lampiya Lekh); Mangshadhura and Lipulekh.

25 Tsangchok-la as well, claiming Nilang and Jadhang hamlets.

26 NR Pillai.

This would never really happen and the now Sino-Indian border would be forgotten in the process.

**The Ink was Hardly Dry**

It took only two months for India to discover that all problems had not been solved. The first Chinese incursion in the Barahoti area of Uttar Pradesh occurred in June 1954. This was the first of a series of incursions numbering into the hundreds which culminated in the attack on India in October 1962 ...and the incursions continue till date.

The ink had hardly dried on the famous Panchsheel Agreement, when the Chinese entered Barahoti. The irony of the story is that it was China which complained about the incursion of Indian troops... on India's territory!

Though Barahoti was well inside India's frontiers, the exchange of notes would continue during the following months ...and years. This exchange was the first of more than one thousand *Memoranda, Notes and Letters* exchanged by the Governments of India and China over the next ten years, published in the *White Papers* on China.[27]

TN Kaul who had negotiated the Agreement, before being sent back to Delhi for having an affair with a Chinese woman, philosophically explained later: "Territorial disputes have existed between near and distant neighbours through the ages. The question is whether they can and should be resolved by war, threat, use of force or through the more civilized and peaceful method of negotiation... Both sides still profess their faith in the Five Principles, and therein lies perhaps some hope for the future."[28]

The Five Principles had put Kaul and his colleagues to sleep.

Some officials soon realized the blunder. John Lall, who served as *Diwan* in Sikkim, commented: "Ten days short of three months after

---

27 The White Papers on China are available on the author's website; see: http://www.claudearpi.net/white-papers-on-china.

28 Kaul, TN, *Diplomacy in Peace and War* (New Delhi: Vikas Publishers, 1978), p. 98.

the Tibet Agreement was signed the Chinese sent the first signal that friendly co-existence was over… Significantly, Niti was one of the six passes specified in the Indo-Chinese Agreement by which traders and pilgrims were permitted to travel."[29]

Friendly co-existence had perhaps never existed.

## The 'Dispute' Starts

On July 17, 1954, a first note handed over by the Counsellor in the Chinese Embassy in Delhi to South Block briefly mentioned the issue for the first time. The Chinese asserted that "over thirty Indian troops armed with rifles crossed the Niti pass on 29 June 1954, and intruded into Wu-Je[30] of the Ali[31] Area of the Tibet Region of China. (Wu-Je is about one day's journey from the Niti Pass). The above happening is not in conformity with the principles of non-aggression and friendly co-existence between China and India, and the spirit of the Joint Communiqué issued recently by the Prime Ministers of China and India."

How Barahoti, located South of the Indian border, suddenly got a Chinese name is still a mystery today; the note continued: "It is hoped that the Government of India would promptly investigate the matter, and order the immediate withdrawal of the Indian troops."

As ardent followers of Sun Tzu's *Art of War*, the Chinese had probably decided on this aggressive posturing to justify their unsubstantiated claims. This was to be repeated often in the years leading to 1962!

On 13 August 1954, the Chinese Counsellor in Delhi delivered another note to South Block, providing more details on the so-called Indian intrusion: "Further investigations reveal that they were a unit of 33 persons attached to the local garrison in U.P., India. The unit was under the command of an officer called Nathauja[32] who was a deputy

---

29 Lall, John, *Aksai Chin and the Sino-Indian Conflict* (New Delhi: Allied Publishers, 1988), p. 238.

30 Chinese name for Barahoti.

31 Chinese name for Ngari.

32 According to Chinese pronunciation.

commander of the troops stationed at Kanman[33]. Together with the officer, there was a local official named Sopit Singh[34] of Chinal tribe in U.P., who was also a district magistrate of Walzanjapur[35] district. Besides, there was a doctor, radio-operators and soldiers. They were putting up in 17 tents." This was not in conformity with the Five Principles, the Chinese diplomat added.

Finally, on August 27, 1954, India woke from its stupor: "We have made thorough enquiries regarding the allegation ...our further investigations have confirmed that the allegation is entirely incorrect. A party of our Border Security Force is encamped in the Hoti Plain which is south-east of Niti pass and is in Indian territory."

The strange part of the story was that the Chinese were confused about the exact location of Wu-Je. The MEA stated: "none of our troops or personnel have crossed North of the Niti pass, as verbally mentioned by the Chinese Counsellor."

The Indian notes also pointed out that some "Tibetan officials tried to cross into our territory in Hoti plain without proper documents", which is not in conformity with the Agreement." The Ministry could only hope that Beijing would instruct the Tibetans "not to cross into Indian territory as we have instructed our authorities not to cross into Tibetan territory."

The correspondence was to continue for months and years in the same vein. It would soon become a regular yearly feature as the snows melted.

## Removal of the Sarji Post from Hoti

A report from the Indian Trade Agent (ITA) in Gartok, Lakshman Singh Jangpangi, provides another version of the happenings at Hoti and the intrusions.

Jangpangi first mentioned that the checkposts in UP normally recorded the dates when Indian nationals entered Western Tibet, but this information was not available with the ITA, who wanted the

---

33 Ibid.
34 Ibid.
35 Ibid.

governments of Punjab and Himachal Pradesh to supply the data to the Gartok Agency for pilgrims and traders separately on a monthly basis.

The ITA warned the UP authorities against even a slight harsh treatment of Tibetans which "will reflect on Indian nationals visiting Western Tibet, whose number exceeds to that of Tibetans coming down to India."

The ITA's report recorded that the *Dzongpon* of Daba had a *Sarji* post at Hoti for enumeration purposes for a few years.

After his return from Niti, the *Sarji* established his tent at Hoti in June 1954. A Provincial Armed Constabulary (PAC) contingent under Capt LM Tewari, the Company Commander and Chamoli Sub Divisional Officer was deputed to send back the *Sarji* to Tibetan territory in July; he was finally persuaded to shift his border post to Tibet.

But on hearing the news, the acting *Dzongpon* went himself to Hoti to reestablish the post. He argued that the Indian officers had taken possession of Tibetan territory by force and asked them to withdraw: "When he found that there was no effect of his argument on Indian officers, he hurried back and went straight to Gartok to report the matter to the *Garpons* and to the Chinese authorities," noted Jangpangi.

The PLA officer was asked by the Tibetans to send troops to Daba to help them drive away the Indian Police force from Hoti: "Eventually, a platoon of eleven under Yaun Wong, a Foreign Bureau official went to Daba, but stopped there and did not proceed towards Hoti." The PLA waited till mid-September, when the PAC picket usually withdraw, "thinking that he might get a chance to inspect the area," said the report.

But the Indian Police force remained at Hoti till late September, the PLA officer returned to Gartok; he, however, visited the Niti Pass, some 30 miles from Hoti.

Jangpangi commented: "If the Chinese really want to inspect the area, they can safely do in winter when it is inaccessible from India. Neither the Tibetan nor the Chinese officers whom I met during the course of our official business, made any reference to this matter."

The suggestion of the ITA was that to enforce India's right on the Hoti area, "it is desirable that *Sarji* post should not be allowed re-establish there. For this it will be necessary to move the Police contingent to Hoti as early as possible during 1955 trading season," in other words early June.

**New Intrusions in 1955**

A year later, on June 28, 1955, the MEA wrote: "Tibetan officials attempted to enter our territory in the Hoti plain. We have now received a report that a party of Chinese are camping at Hoti with 5 tents and 20 horses and that they have entered our territory without proper documents."

The note further requested that "instructions be issued immediately to these personnel to withdraw across the border over the Tunjun-la and to refrain from entering Indian territory unless they are in possession of proper documents."

Again it was repeated that it was not in conformity with the principles of non-aggression and friendly co-existence mentioned in the 1954 Agreement.

An Indian official, SK Roy, Special Officer Frontier Area[36], met the Chinese on June 28, 1955, in connection with the Chinese intrusions; the Chinese informed the MEA that their Government "has time and time again instructed the personnel of the frontier garrison not to move a single step beyond the Chinese border. Our investigations have confirmed that in the course of the last year and the current one there never has been any case of Chinese personnel crossing the border in the vicinity of the Niti Pass."

This was the best proof that the India-Tibet border had become the India-China border.

On July 11, 1955, the Chinese handed over a reply to TN Kaul, who was now posted in Delhi as Joint Secretary: "Another batch of more than 30 Indians soldiers crossed into Wu-Je of the Tibet Region of

---

36 Or SOFA. Later, the not-so-cosy job was re-designated as SOBA (Special Officer Border Area).

China on 25 June 1955 and engaged in constructing fortifications at places very close to our garrison forces stationed there."

A week later[37], India answered the Chinese note by saying this did not properly represent the factual position: "The troops mentioned were not in the Tibet region of China but at the Bara Hoti[38], on the Hoti plain in India which is South of the Tunjun-la."

The Chinese were told that the Indian troops withdrew in September 1954, as the outpost was a seasonal post; the MEA had some doubt if Barahoti and Wu-je were the same place; it admitted: "We are not aware of the exact location of Wu-Je, though the Counsellor of the Chinese Embassy mentioned that it was 12 kilometers North of the Tunjun-la, but we are quite confident that our troops have not, under any circumstances, crossed the border into Tibet Region of China."

Another note was given to the Chinese embassy in Delhi on August 18, 1955. It had received a report that the *Sarji*, who had come with the Chinese troops in the Hoti plain had tried to "realise grazing tax from Indian herdsmen grazing goats in the area. This is a new development which we would request the Chinese authorities to stop forthwith."

The exchanges continued during the following months.

**More Investigations**

On September 26, 1955, the Chinese embassy in Delhi mentioned[39] the informal note given by SK Roy on August 18: "Our repeated investigations made in Wu-Je area of the Tibet Region have proved that no Chinese personnel has ever crossed the border. On the contrary, it were the Indian troops that intruded into Wu-Je which had always belonged to Dabasting[40] of the Tibet Region within the Chinese boundary."

---

37 On July 18, 1955.

38 The orthography of Barahoti and Tunjun-la varies in the different reports.

39 The note was given by Kang, the Counsellor of the Chinese Embassy to TN Kaul, Joint Secretary in the MEA.

40 Daba Dzong?

The note added: "the Indian troops are still stationing at Wu-Je, and are incessantly carrying out reconnaissance activities on the Chinese garrison. Hence the situation is rather serious."

The Chinese conclusion was that "since no Chinese personnel has crossed the border, there could not have been such a situation as stated in your informal note."

On November 5, South Block sent another note to the Chinese embassy stating that there was clearly a misunderstanding on the location of Wu-Je: "We are quite definite that our personnel have at no time intruded into the Wu-Je area of the Tibet region of China but have throughout remained at Bara Hoti which is 2 miles South of the Tunjun-la."

It was emphasized that Chinese troops had come South of the Tunjun-la and camped at Bara Hoti alongside the Indian troops: "We would like to repeat that we are most anxious to avoid any possible incident and we, therefore, suggest that strict instructions should be issued that no personnel from the Tibet region of China should cross into India without due permission."

It repeated once more that the Indian troops "have not entered the Wu-Je area because they have never crossed the Tunjun-la, the border pass ...and Wu-Je was stated by Mr. Kang to be 12 kilometres North of this pass."

**The Chinese Crossed the Border Again**

On the same day, it was also pointed out to the Chinese that as the Indian detachment was approaching Damzan[41], which is 10 miles south of the Niti Pass (and therefore clearly in Indian territory), they were stopped by 20 Chinese soldiers.

The Chinese troops sent a message to the Indians that they would not be allowed to go via Damzan without the permission from the Chinese authorities at Gartok; the Indian troops continued to insist on going via Damzan as it was clearly Indian territory: "if the Chinese party used force to stop [them], they would be responsible for the consequences."

---

41  Probably near Gamshali.

Finally, Delhi asserted that "great restraint [had been] exercised by our detachment. The Chinese soldiers did not try to stop our detachment but wanted to remain on the Indian territory at Damzan without due and proper permission." The Indian note then gives the coordinates of Damzan, South of the Niti Pass, one of the passes named in the Panchsheel Agreement.

**The Tax System Between Tibet and India**

In the meantime, members of the Parliament started asking questions.

On December 2, 1954, the government was requested to inform the Lok Sabha about the number of Tibetan traders who had come down to India during the present season.

The answer was: "The number of Tibetan traders who bring wool and salt to Niti Ghati was about the same as during the past two years." The Government clarified further: "Owing to pushing back of *Sarji* post from Hoti, there had been some nervousness amongst Tibetan traders in the beginning, but later they visited Niti Ghati as usual. This [Indian] Agency[42] does not keep any data of these traders, but Bampa Police Check post records them."

The Parliament was also told that no fresh passport system had been introduced after the signature of the Tibet Agreement, though the Tibetans were now required to declare the number of their animals to the local official before proceeding down to India: "This is required for the purposes of official dues payable by them."

The Indian Trade Agent in Gartok explained to the Ministry that according to an old customary tax the Tibetans going down to Niti Ghati paid one *Tranka* (equal to Rs 9/6) per trader and Rs. 6 per hundred sheep taken with them to Dzongpon of Daba district; half of it (Rs 3) was paid by the Indian traders.

The Tibetans going down via other *ghatis*[43] had also to pay some dues to the Tibetan officer there, though it varied from place to place. The customary taxes were recovered from both the Indian and Tibetan

---

42  In Gartok.

43  Passes.

traders engaged in this border trade, they were, however, not uniform and changed from one district to other and were paid both in cash and kind.

Jangpangi noted: "As these taxes are old, [the] question of getting permission ...does not arise. These taxes being a private income to the *Dzongpon*." The Indian officer added: "So far there is no passport system for these traders coming down to India, they have in all cases to declare the number of their animals for purposes of realization of taxes. It is for this purpose the Tibetans have to report to the border district official before going down to India. The [Indian] Government have no proposal to approach the Chinese Government in this regard.

The note gave more details on the traditional dealings on the border: "The Tibet traders visit the adjoining villages in the districts of Almora, Garhwal, Tehri Garhwal in UP, Mahasu[44] in HP and Lahaul in Punjab[45] for barter trade of wool and salt with grain and *gur*[46]. Their visit to these places depends on the availability of grain there."

Importantly for the 'dispute', it clarified the role of the *Sarji*, a servant of *Dzongpon*. It was based on the visit of the *Sarji* that the Tibetans claimed Barahoti. Jangpangi wrote: [the *Sarji*] visits Indian villages first in order to ascertain whether there are any diseases amongst men or cattle. The routes are then declared opened after his report to the *Dzongpon*."

The Office of the Indian Trade Agent in Gartok did not keep track of the number and detail of Tibetan traders who came to India via Niti pass.

**A Note from the Historical Division**

On May 10, 1956, the Historical Division of the Ministry of External Affairs prepared a note on the border, part of it related to Barahoti: "In case a general discussion of the frontier is opened with China, we will have to bear in mind the possibility of their also reviving certain claims

---

44 Mahasu is located in Jubbal Kotkhai of Shimla District.

45 Now in Himachal Pradesh.

46 Jaggery.

## The First Incursions: the Case of Barahoti

now dormant. This is most likely regarding the Drokpo Karpo pastures in Ladakh."

The historical background was recalled: "In 1918, the Tibetans had kidnapped a Ladakhi in Drokpo Karpo and when releasing him asserted their right to the area; and since then they have never expressly renounced their claim. In 1929 the Surveyor General of India reported in favour of the Tibetan claim. Nor may the discussion be limited on their part to map claims."

Then Barahoti was mentioned: "The Tibetans assert their rights to establish an outpost at Bara Hoti, two miles South of the border pass of Tunjun La, and to graze their flocks around Lapthal ten miles southeast of Bara Hoti, and lay claim to territory even upto Badrinath, thirty miles south-west of Bara Hoti."

It noted that after the British had protested against the establishment of the Tibetan outpost at Barahoti in 1914, "the attempt does not seem to have been repeated after 1916."

It is only in June 1954, two months after the signature of the Agreement that "the effort of a Tibetan *Sarji* to set up a camp at Hoti had to be repulsed by our Border Security Force. The Chinese officially protested against this in 1955 and sent a detachment to Hoti; and throughout that trade season, Chinese and Indian detachments faced each other. It was also reported that Tibetan officials had collected grazing taxes around Lapthal. It was later decided to send a joint investigation team to determine whether Hoti plain is North or South of the Tunjun-la pass; but the Chinese Govt. has shown no anxiety to implement this proposal to solve a particular dispute."

With the Tibetans, the 'dispute' would have probably remained informal, but with the reinforcement of the Chinese presence in Western Tibet, the situation was bound to deteriorate. Regarding the 'joint investigation team', the discussion would continue during the following months …and years.

### Kaul Responds to the Note

The next day, TN Kaul suggested that the issue should be discussed by a larger meeting. He mentioned the note of the Historical Division received the previous day (along with a map showing the Indian line, the Chinese line and the 'Russian' line[47]): "It is suggested that Home and Defence Ministries may also be invited to the discussion that Prime Minister proposes to hold on the subject."

Kaul was of the view that if the Chinese raised the border issue: "we should tell them that our border is well defined and well understood and there is nothing to be discussed."

Regarding 'small specific areas' such as Bara Hoti or Nilang-Jadang area "where their troops have made incursions during recent years, we may discuss these on the basis of recognition of the passes at Tsang Chok-la and Tunjun-la as our boundary. "

Kaul noted that both passes were not mentioned in the Sino-Indian Agreement as a border pass; incidentally, he was the one who negotiated the Agreement with the results which had started showing.

The Joint Secretary brought again the Chinese suggestion for a joint Investigation Team to be sent to Barahoti to find if it was North or South of Tunjun-la: "If it was North, then it would be in Chinese territory; if South, then it would be in Indian territory. We may ask them to send an officer who can go there with our officer to verify this fact," and he added: "It is a ticklish matter which has to be carefully considered. Most of the disputed areas are not as easily accessible from India as from Tibet. The present time is perhaps more suitable for discussion …than later when China has consolidated her position in Tibet."

Strangely, the diplomat shifted the blame on some Western countries, "[which] are exploiting the possibilities of friction between India and China along the Indo-Tibetan frontier." He was keen to use this argument to "point out to the Chinese the desirability of settling this matter once and for all."

**The Nilang-Tsangchok-la Area**

Delhi was nervous not only about Hoti, but about other border posts too, particularly the Nilang area, south of the Tsangchok-la,

---

47  It is not clear what this 'Russian Line' is.

which marked the watershed in the region. TN Kaul asked the Indian ambassador in Beijing if he had lodged a protest with the Chinese government after some alarming information had been received from Nilang: "Chinese troops may try to come towards Gumgum Nela [nala] through Pullamsumda breaking border security force cordon or via other routes." The Ministry was told by the State Government: "We have set up seasonal checkpost at Pullamsumda and are sending reconnaissance parties regularly to Jelukhaze Pass[48] and other passes in the area."

The border security forces had been instructed "if Chinese troops come in small numbers our force should stop them and prevent their entry. If however, they come in larger numbers our officers should formally protest to them and put up physical resistance without resorting to fire. He should tell officer-in-charge Chinese troops if they come that matter is already under discussion between the two Governments and he will be responsible for consequences of any premature action."

The Ambassador was also informed that the Prime Minister desired that some pressure should be exercised on the Chinese Embassy in Delhi, while in Beijing, "you should press Chinese Government in Peking for a very early amicable settlement of the two disputes regarding Nilang area and Hoti Plain."

Again the old Panikkar view was repeated: "We do not wish to raise the general question of the Indo-Tibetan frontier which so far as we are concerned is well defined and well understood. We should confine ourselves to the discussion of the two disputes mentioned above where Chinese troops have crossed Indian territory."

The Joint Secretary further added: "In the case of Hoti Plain, even their own maps show this area in India," while in the Nilang area, Kaul noted that it seemed "the British had agreed to give some extra territorial rights to Tibet but the Tibetans wanted more. Since however, we have given up extra-territorial rights which the British enjoyed in Tibet it is only proper that the Chinese should give up any extra-territorial rights which British may have agreed to give."

---

48 Tsangchok-la.

Kaul referred to the surrender of all the rights India had in Tibet; this was a reasoning that China would certainly not understand, even less agree with. Finally, the Ambassador was instructed by South Block to keep the discussion informal, "but it is necessary to take up the matter urgently in order to avoid possibility of clash between Chinese troops and our security force."

The future would show that once China had claimed a place, the area would forever remain Chinese.

**The Ambassador Meets the Chinese Vice-Minister**

On May 23, 1956, the Indian embassy in Beijing informed South Block that the Ambassador had met Yuan, an official in the Ministry for Foreign Affairs. The Indian diplomat told his Chinese colleague about the details of the incident at Nilang on April 28. He also brought to the notice of the Chinese official; "the threatened movement of Chinese towards Gumgum Nala through Pullamsumda."

He reiterated that both Hoti Plain and Nilang were a part of Indian territory, pointing out that India had checkposts at Pullamsumda, "if the information received by us is correct there is a grave risk of incidents," Yuan was told.

The Indian diplomat suggested that instructions should be given to the local authorities in Tibet "to stop further incursions of Chinese into any part of Indian territory." He added that India believed that there should be an early amicable settlement, in line with that Agreement of 1954 and "that incursion of Chinese troops into Indian territory might lead to conflicts which will mar friendly relations which both Governments wish to strengthen."

Yuan was said to have listened gravely, before stating: "Situation of places is not clear and first thing is to check up actual situation. We believe Chinese troops will not cross Indian border".

When the ambassador reiterated that Nilang and Hoti Plain were on the Indian side of the border and movement of Chinese troops in these areas could 'lead to grave incident', Yuan just answered: "we shall inform local authorities in Tibet and ask them to avoid any possible friction," but he added "it is hard to say anything at present before situation is cleared but after the situation is cleared we are confident that an amicable settlement of this dispute will be arrived at."

Interestingly, later the Chinese Foreign Office telephoned to Paranjpe, the Indian translator, to ask him the names of the places mentioned by the Ambassador. A brief note was subsequently sent to the Chinese.

## The 'Dispute' Continues: Where is Wuje?

During the following months, the Chinese would insist on sending a joint investigating team to this spot. As the Ambassador was not aware of the details of the proposal, he asked Delhi: "I have no intention of raising this matter but I should like to know for my personal information what happened about this proposal."

The main reason for China to insist on sending a joint investigation team was that Beijing did not know that Barahoti was south of Tunjun-la.

On June 1, 1956, the Uttar Pradesh Home Secretary wrote to Kaul informing him that the Indian forces had reached Hoti before the Chinese; it was gratifying, he commented: "Detachment under command of Company Commander which left their camp at Timersain at 11:00 hours on 28th May reached Hoti safely at 21:00 hours on following day. Not finding Chinese there our forces have occupied both sites where I believe Chinese camped last year. One section posted at each site. Presume our forces should continue occupying both places. Detachment has really performed an excellent job in conditions of extreme severity and deserves all praise."

On June 8, 1956, Chen Chia-kang, a Chinese Assistant Foreign Minister, handed over to Bahadur Singh[49], the Counsellor in the Indian Embassy in China, a memorandum stating again that the Chinese Government was willing to undertake a joint investigation with the Indian Government "to settle the question of Wu-Je [Hoti] [but] in the meantime both Governments should refrain from sending troops into the Wu-Je area till the issue is solved."

---

49 Bahadur Singh later served as Political Officer in Sikkim between October 23, 1961 and December 1963.

Apparently a week later, RK Nehru, the Indian Ambassador to China told Ji Pengfei[50], the Vice-Foreign Minister, that Delhi had agreed to a joint investigation.

But nothing is simple, when one negotiates with China.

According to the Chinese note, RK Nehru was of the opinion that the joint investigation should be based on the contents of an informal talk in 1955 between Kang Mao-Chao, former Counsellor of the Chinese Embassy in India, and TN Kaul.

Kang and Kaul would have agreed that Tunjun-la was the border pass between China and India, and that therefore the aim of the joint investigation should be limited to finding out on the spot whether Wu-Je or Barahoti was to the North or to the South of Tunjun-la.

But the Chinese continued to insist that "Tunjun-la is proven to be within Chinese territory there is no historical record showing Tunjun-la to be a border pass between China and India."

Kaul had committed a huge blunder two years earlier in agreeing to not include Tunjun-la as a border pass. It was too late now.

**The Correspondence Continues**

On June 7, 1956, the Ministry of External Affairs told the Chinese Charge d'Affaires in Delhi: "We have throughout maintained that Chinese personnel have crossed the Tunjun-la from the Tibet region of China and entered the territory of the Indian Union, whereas the Chinese Embassy has maintained that our personnel have entered the Wu-Je area of the Tibet region of China."

---

50 Ji Pengfei was born in Linyi, Yuncheng, Shanxi in 1910. He joined the Chinese Red Army in 1931, and the Communist Party of China in 1933.

After the establishment of the People's Republic of China, Ji Pengfei worked with the Ministry of Foreign Affairs, and led diplomatic missions to the German Democratic Republic before being appointed as China's first ambassador to the GDR in 1953, being the youngest Chinese ambassador at 43. He was recalled to serve as vice-minister of Foreign Affairs in 1955.

India rightly contended that Barahoti was two miles south of the Tunjun-la whereas the Chinese Embassy has held that Wu-Je was 12 kms north of this pass.

The next day, the Chinese embassy answered: "Now that the Wu-Je area has already become passable, if the Government of China and India should again send their respective troops into that area as they did in 1955, a situation similar to that of 1955 will inevitably recur, in which the troops of the two countries confront each other. The Chinese Government cannot but be concerned about this, and it is presumed that the Indian Government shares the same feeling."

Not answering directly about the location of Tunjun-la, the Chinese embassy said the data available with them "proved that the Wu-Je area has always been under the jurisdiction of Daba Dzong of the Tibet Region of China. This area is within Chinese territory."

They further asserted that according to "historical records of this part of the Tibet Region of China adjacent to Indian territory, Tunjun-la is proven to be within Chinese territory. There is no historical record showing Tunjun-la to be a border pass between China and India."

It is interesting to point out that each and every area which had at any time been historically claimed by the Tibetans was automatically becoming part of the Chinese territory.

Beijing was, however, keen on a joint investigation by representatives of the Chinese and Indian Governments; it would be useful, they said: "The Chinese Government is willing to continue consultations with the Indian Government with regard to the method in such a joint investigation."

"The Chinese Government wishes further to suggest that, pending the settlement of the Wu-Je question by the two Governments through normal diplomatic channels, both Governments should refrain from sending troops into the Wu-Je area so as to avoid a situation in which the troops of the two countries confront each other, and to maintain the normal state of affairs along the Sino-Indian border."

The saga continued.

In the meantime, the Tibetans had taken Chinese officers to the 'disputed' borders and explained to them their own claim.

## One More Note

On October 3, 1956, an Indian note pointed out: "there seemed to have been an agreement between the Governments of India and China in regard to the location of the Indo-Tibetan border in this area at this Tunjun-La Pass."

It was on this basis that India agreed to a joint survey. The Ministry in Delhi had then "observed with surprise the appearance of what seems to be a change in the Chinese view of the position of this pass in relation to the border." To clarify further the Indian position, the note made the following points:

a)  The district of Garhwal, in which Barahoti is situated, is, and has always been, a part of India;

b)  The historical evidence to support this goes back many centuries;

c)  By possession and usage also Barahoti is, and has always been, part of India and Tunjun-la is, and has always been, the border Pass;

d)  The precise latitude/longitude of this pass is 30° 53' latitude north, 79° 59' longitude east. This may assist identification of the pass, and avoid the danger of confusion with any other pass.

Delhi felt that a "proper understanding of the actual situation is a basic preliminary to any joint investigation."

But the 'understanding' was not forthcoming.

## The Situation Continued Unchanged

During the following years, the stalemate continued.

Though the issue was not discussed during the visit of Zhou Enlai, the Chinese Premier, on January 14, 1957, Acharya, the Joint Secretary informed the Indian embassy in Beijing that "pending discussions we do not <u>repeat not</u> propose sending troops to Hoti area this year provided Chinese refrain likewise is confirmed. UP Government being instructed accordingly."

The embassy was requested to confirm that the Chinese had given similar orders. IJ Bahadur Singh, the Indian Charge d'Affaires answered a few days later that the Chinese Government had been informed, "[Chinese] Foreign Office state that discussions will now be held in the first half of March. Exact dates will be communicated to us as soon as they are fixed."

On February 9, 1957, Bahadur Singh reported that the matter was taken up with Foreign Office: "They said this was their own proposal but now that matter has been raised by us they would obtain confirmation from authorities concerned."

The bilateral negotiations would eventually take place in 1958; it would lead nowhere. Since then, every year Barahoti witnesses Chinese intrusions in an area which had never even been part of Tibet.

## 02

# The First Months after the Agreement and Zhou's Visit to India

### The Tibet Agreement and After

It is necessary to stop and look at the weeks following the 'Tibet' Agreement, in which Tibet was not even consulted.

On May 15, 1954, Nehru presented the Tibet Agreement to the Indian Parliament. After reading the preamble to the Agreement, Nehru spoke of the implications for Tibet; India had accepted that this peaceful nation could be brutally invaded and deprived of its autonomy, if not independence: "So far as Tibet is concerned, it is recognition of the existing situation there. In fact, that situation had been recognised by us two or three years ago."[1]

The fact that China claimed suzerainty over Tibet was not a proof that Tibet was a region of China. Similarly, the fact that China soon would claim large chunks of Indian territory (through newly printed maps) would not be a proof that these territories belonged to Beijing.

Nehru continued: "It is true that occasionally when China was weak, this sovereignty[2] was not exercised in any large measure. When China was strong, it was exercised. Always there was a large measure of autonomy of Tibet, so that there was no great change in the theoretical approach to the Tibetan problem from the Chinese side. It has been the same

---

1 *Selected Works of Jawaharlal Nehru* (thereafter SWJN), Series II, Vol. 25, *India and the International Situation*, May 15, 1954, p. 398.

2 It should be suzerainty.

throughout the last 200 or 300 years. The only country that had more intimate relations with Tibet was India, that is to say, British India in those days. Even then, when it was British policy to have some measure of influence over Tibet, even then they never denied the fact of Chinese sovereignty over Tibet, although in practice it was hardly exercised and they laid stress on Tibetan autonomy. Recent events made some other changes, factual changes, because a strong Chinese State gave practical evidence of exercising that sovereignty. So that what we have done in this agreement is not to recognise any new thing, but merely to repeat what we have said previously, and what, in fact, inevitably follows from the circumstances, both historical and practical, today."[3]

**The Biggest Thing**

While presenting the Agreement in the Parliament, he proclaimed: "Now we must realise that this revolution that came to China is the biggest thing that has taken place in the world at present, whether you like it or not."

In the same speech Nehru spoke about Agreement Panchsheel: "Live and let live, no one should invade the other, no one should fight the other... this is the basic principle which we have put in our treaty."

The historian S. Gopal described the Agreement in more realistic terms: "But this was clutching at straws after the main opportunity had been deliberately discarded. The only real gain India could show was a listing of six border passes in the middle sector, thereby defining, even indirectly, this stretch of the boundary. On the other hand, the Chinese had secured all they wanted and given away little; and that they regarded even this sanction of some Indian trade agencies and markets in Tibet as an interim concession was made clear by their objection to automatic renewal of treaty after the first term of eight years."[4]

In the course of the debate, JB Kripalani stated: "The plea is that China had the ancient right of suzerainty. That right was out of date, old and antiquated. It was theoretical; it was never exercised, it has lapsed

---

[3] Ibid.

[4] Gopal, Sarvepalli, *Jawaharlal Nehru: a Biography*, Vol. 2 (London: Oxford University Press, 1979), p. 180.

by the flux of time. Tibet is culturally more akin to India than it is to China, at least Communist China which has repudiated its old culture. The definition of colonialism is this that one nation by force of arms or fraud occupies the territory of another nation. In this age of democracy when we hold that all people should be free and equal, I say China's occupation of Tibet is a deliberate act of aggression."

**Ripe for Settlement**

We have seen that during the course of the negotiations in Beijing in 1953-54, both Panikkar and Kaul 'cleverly' avoided bringing the border issue to the table; this approach backfired and ended in a disaster for India.

In July 1962[5] the Indian Ministry of External Affairs said that in 1954, there was no difference of opinion between the two countries regarding the boundary alignment; there was "no reason to believe, during the negotiations leading upto the Agreement of 1954, that the Government of China were contemplating laying extensive claims to well-known Indian territory."

It was pure wishful thinking on the part of the Ministry to assume that Beijing would not lay extensive claims on India, as their maps, even then, already showed large parts of India as belonging to China.

In his biography of Nehru, Dr. Gopal put it very simply: "As suited the Chinese, the negotiations were carried on piecemeal on specific issues which were 'ripe for settlement' - an ominous masked phrase - and India weakly made no attempt to secure an overall settlement. By asserting that not only questions ripe for settlement but 'all outstanding questions' were being settled, the Indian side sought to score a debating point of no value. Semantics cannot guarantee an international frontier..."[6]

It was piecemeal diplomacy indeed.

---

5  By that time the Agreement had lapsed.
6  Note of TN Kaul, August 20, and Nehru's directive, 30 August 1953.

## Nehru's preoccupations

A letter addressed to GL Mehta,[7] the Indian Ambassador to the US, gives us a clear indication of the preoccupations of the Prime Minister at the end of June 1954. The exchange with Mehta discussed the Geneva Conference, where delegates were struggling to arrive at a solution acceptable by the big powers …and China.

Nehru remarked: "It has seemed to me that, broadly speaking, the British attitude of trying for a negotiated settlement was the only correct attitude. The US attitude is, I think, not only wrong, but wholly lacking in realism. The US may go on saying that they will not recognise China or agree to its inclusion in the UN. The fact remains that practically nobody agrees with them in this matter. Obviously, the UK does not. Casey of Australia[8] told me that he did not. So far as Eastern countries are concerned, such as India, Burma and Indonesia, they not only do not agree with the US policy in this respect, but will continue to follow their own policy even though the US may strongly disapprove of it."

The Prime Minster mentioned that the Korean question was 'completely deadlocked', though he was happy that the question of Indo-China had made some progress at Geneva: "It appears that an armistice is likely, unless the US comes down with a heavy hand to prevent it. If they prevent it, what then? What other course have they got?"

Nehru further commented: "The only thing they can try to do is to build up their South-East Asia Organisation [SEATO]. Such an organisation will not have the support of the principal South-East Asian countries, i.e., India, Burma and Indonesia. In these circumstances, it is doubtful if even the UK or Australia will support it. …SEATO, therefore, will be almost still-born."

---

7  Gaganvihari Lallubhai Mehta (1900-1974) was India's Ambassador to the USA between 1952 and 1958.

8  Richard Gavin Gardiner Casey (1890–1976). Engineer, diplomat, politician and governor, he served as the 16th Governor-General of Australia, in office from 1965 to 1969. He was also a distinguished army officer, long-serving cabinet minister, Ambassador to the United States, member of Churchill's War Cabinet, and Governor of Bengal. Casey was Minister of External Affairs of Australia between 1951 and 1960.

Tibet is briefly mentioned at the end of the Prime Minister's letter: "People talk vaguely and without understanding about this agreement and say that we have given up more than we have gained."

It was, unfortunately, a fact and soon the Indian Government would realize this, but at the end of June 1954, Nehru asserted: "What have we given up? We have only given up what in fact we could not hold and what in fact had in reality gone. We have given up certain rights that we exercised internally in Tibet. Obviously, we cannot do that. We have gained instead something that is very important, i.e., a friendly frontier and an implicit acceptance of that frontier."

But the border had not been secured, that was wishful thinking.

**A Letter from the PO: Sympathy for the Tibetans?**

To set the stage of Zhou Enlai's visit to India, less than three months after the signature of the Tibet Agreement, it is interesting to look at a note sent on June 18, 1954 by the Prime Minister to the Secretary-General of the Ministry; it provides a view of the happenings in Tibet soon after the signature of the Agreement. It is a pity that the questions raised by BK Kapur[9], the Political Officer in Sikkim, to which the Prime Minister answered, are not available. Nehru noted that Kapur's letter and his notes were important "not only in themselves, but because they are concerned with much larger issues. Indeed, they are concerned with our wider policy towards China and our general world policy."[10]

Nehru's first sentence resumed the Indian government's policy *vis-a-vis* Tibet: "Naturally, the Tibetans have our sympathy. But that sympathy does not take us far and cannot be allowed to interfere with a realistic understanding of the situation and of our policy."

---

9   BK Kapur (b.1910) joined Indian Political Service (IPS) in 1934; Liaison Officer in Lahore and Peshawar, 1947-48; Political Officer in Sikkim from March 1952 to March 1955; High Commissioner to Ghana, Nigeria and Sri Lanka between 1955 and 1964; Secretary, Ministry of External Affairs, 1965-66; Ambassador to Sweden and Finland, 1966-67.

10  All other documents in this chapter, except specifically mentioned, are from the Nehru Papers (JN Collection) held at the Nehru Memorial Museum and Library in Delhi. The 'papers' are not indexed.

Over the years, the 'sympathy' would not help the Tibetans; they would be left alone to deal with the Chinese.

Nehru came to the letter of the PO: "I have an impression that Mr Kapur has not fully appreciated this wider policy of ours. It is necessary, therefore, that he and others concerned should understand it and should realise that this policy is the only one which might be helpful to the Tibetans, not in the measure perhaps that they desire, but to some extent."

Nehru had earlier used the same words, to address the previous PO[11] as well as the officer-in-charge of the Indian Mission in Lhasa[12]. A Similar point was also made when Maj Bob Khathing took over the administration of Tawang in February 1951.

But let us come back to Nehru's analysis: "Any other policy of encouraging the Tibetans to oppose Chinese over lordship over Tibet would be raising false hopes in the Tibetans which we cannot fulfil and is likely to react unfavorably on the Tibetans. It would, of course, be opposed to the principles we have laid down in our recent Agreement with China."

This had been made clear several times to Sinha as we have seen in the first two volumes of our study.[13]

Nehru did not appreciate that Kapur had dared to say that the Chinese Government "is not likely to be influenced by considerations of non-interference," (which was a fact). This irritated the Prime Minister no end: "at the same time he [Kapur] hints that we should also not be influenced by any such considerations, except in so far as that we should not do anything which might create obvious difficulties for us."

Nehru observed: "That is neither a moral nor a practical proposition."

Let us remember that this note was written at a time when the Chinese walked into Indian territory in Barahoti for the first time.

---

11 Harishwar Dayal.
12 Sumul Sinha.
13 See Volume 1, Chapter 18 and Volume 2, Chapter 18.

Nehru, the Philosopher, could understand the impermanence of foreign relations: "No country can ultimately rely upon the permanent goodwill or bona fides of another country, even though they might be in close friendship with each other."

Taking the example of the Western Atlantic Alliance, he admitted that it may not function 'as it was intended'. He even wrote it was not inconceivable that China and the Soviet Union may not continue to remain friends. "Certainly it is conceivable that our relations with China might worsen", but quickly added, "there is no immediate likelihood of that." His conclusions were, "adequate precautions have to be taken."

He then came to Tibet: "If we come to an agreement with China in regard to Tibet, that is not a permanent guarantee, but that itself is one major step to help us in the present and in the foreseeable future in various ways."

He cited a possible agreement at Geneva about Indo-China and said that though there was no permanent guarantee, "it is certainly a big step forward to lessen tension which enables the countries concerned to think more objectively and peacefully and perhaps find a surer basis for peace."

He continued his lecture, "an objective and realistic understanding is made almost impossible by emotional responses."

It is what he had accused Dayal and Sinha of and now was accusing Kapur of been subjective too. He never linked the border issue to the occupation of the Tibetan plateau by China, but the officers on the spot did; Nehru continued: "I do not like Mr Kapur talking about Chinese communists, although they are communists. He should talk about the Chinese Government. In the same way, I do not like people talking about the Iron Curtain. The mere mention of these words confuses thought and shows that we are not considering a matter objectively." The Indian government would have to learn the hard way; this would take a few years.

Nehru in some ways was lucid, though he did not follow his arguments to their logical conclusion; he noted: "both the Soviet Union and China are expansive. They are expansive for evils other than communism, although communism may be made a tool for the purpose. Chinese expansionism has been evident during various periods of Asian history for a thousand years or so. We are perhaps facing a new period of such expansionism."

His views were to "fashion our policy to prevent it from coming in the way of our interests or other interests that we consider important."

He continued: "I can quite understand that many people in Tibet have been disappointed at the agreement between us in China over Tibet. This must be partly because of the colour put on it by the Chinese in Tibet."

In fact, what shocked many was that the Tibetans themselves were not consulted or involved, and were told only once the Agreement was signed.

The Prime Minister believed that the Tibet Agreement was quite inevitable: "It was recognition of a certain factual situation which we could not possibly change."

Nehru thought that India had got some advantages in many respects: "If we had not had that agreement, the position would have been no better for us in Tibet and a little worse for the Tibetans. It certainly would have been worse for us from a wider point of view."

What was this 'wider point of view' is not clear.

**The British Heritage?**

Nehru then came back to his old argument, that Indian rights in Tibet were largely derived from inheriting British interests "to which they succeeded in establishing in the days of British expansionism. We became the inheritors of British imperialism to a slight extent. We were popular with the ruling classes of Tibet at this stage because they thought we would come in the way of Chinese expansionism. We could not do so in Tibet and we could not possibly hang on to privileges which had no meaning in the present state of affairs."

This was only partially true, because the trade with Tibet predated by centuries the arrival of the British on the subcontinent. It was this trade which was in jeopardy, as we shall see.

It is difficult to fully analyse Nehru's comments in the absence of the PO's note, but according to the Prime Minister, Kapur would have said something "about [India] not throwing cold water on various movements in Tibet against the Chinese, though we should not associate ourselves [the Government] with them."

Nehru was 'clear' on this point: "Whatever happens in Tibet proper is beyond our reach. We can neither help nor hinder it. The question is what we do in our own territory. Do we encourage this or not? It is clear that we cannot encourage it. At best we can tolerate it, provided it is not too obvious or aggressive. A very delicate balance will have to be kept up. "

He had, of course, different policies when the question arose to defend the Algerians or Tunisians against 'French imperialism'.

The Prime Minister used the case of Kalimpong, a 'nest of intrigues and spies': "It is not only a centre of Tibetan émigrés, but also of Communists (Chinese). Also of Americans, White Russians and many others. "

The Prime Minister said that as India tolerated this: "we can tolerate also the Tibetans of various kinds and views. But if any of these indulge in aggressive activities which might lead to violence, then obviously we cannot tolerate them." He added an interesting point, which was absolutely true: "I am sure that the Tibetan émigrés in Kalimpong are in close touch with the Americans, White Russians and are being encouraged by them with money and in other ways." He added that he had heard that the Tibetans were also collecting arms: "All this seems to me childish and totally unrealistic."

Whether the last statement was correct or not is difficult to verify.

He found 'futile' the US efforts to bring down the People's Government of China using Formosa; he then asked a valid question, was it "the slightest degree conceivable that some petty violent effort organised by Tibetans and others on our border would produce results in Tibet?"

He strongly believed that even from the Tibetan point of view, "it can only prove harmful. There is not the least chance in the world of China leaving Tibet or being driven out of Tibet unless China is defeated in war. Of that, there appears to be no chance."

Nehru was strongly against 'adventurous' tactics beyond the borders of Tibet as they had "no meaning and can only embarrass".

If the Tibetans were peaceful and unobtrusive, they could stay in India, but "we should explain our policy and the world situation to the people from Tibet so that they may not misunderstand us."

However, in case they would indulge "in any aggressive action and the Chinese Government complains to us, we shall have no alternative left but to take some steps against them, at any rate to curb them."

The Prime Minister observed that the Tibetans should certainly not be handed over to the Chinese: "because they have a right of asylum in our country and we can give them the fullest assurance about this."

At the same time, Delhi was not ready to permit that its territory could be used "as a base of operations against the Chinese".

Nehru then developed an argument that he used in 1950 when the Chinese troops first entered Tibet, what he called 'the nature of the country': "It is most inhospitable, it cannot maintain large numbers of foreigners and the like. If the Tibetans are stout enough to keep up a spirit of freedom, they will maintain a large measure of autonomy and the Chinese will not interfere. If the Tibetans actively rebel, they will be ruthlessly put down by the Chinese and even their autonomy will go."

Interestingly, the Chinese were considered as foreigners.

A strange rationale then popped up; it was either the Soviet Union or China which had to be in Tibet: "one of these two Powers will have a dominating political influence there." But as for India, it cannot exercise any influence "for geographical as well as other reasons. As a friendly power to China, we can be helpful occasionally in the diplomatic field."

It is difficult to understand how Nehru was ready to accept a Russian influence in Tibet, while denying that of India, which had had centuries-old cultural and economic ties with the Roof of the World.

Then, came the case of Gyalo Thondup, the Dalai Lama's elder brother, "whom I met some years ago, [he] is obviously connected with various under-ground activities. Some time back we warned our officers not to get entangled in them. That warning should be given again. That does not mean that we should be unfriendly to him. It simply means that we should be friendly and frank and should explain the limitations of the position."

Gyalo Thondup has detailed in his poorly-written memoirs *The Noodle Maker of Kalimpong*[14], some of his dealings with the foreign intelligence agencies.

Nehru then reminded the Secretary-General of the Ministry that Tibet had been cut off from the world for a long time "socially speaking, [it] is very backward and feudal. Changes are bound to come there to the disadvantage of the small ruling class and the big monasteries."

He also developed one of his favourite theories: "Religion may continue to be a powerful force to hold the Tibetans together, but social forces are also powerful. Thus far the Chinese have been careful not to interfere with social customs, religion."

As we shall see, the 'reforms' would be slowly but surely introduced during the following years, bringing tensions between the Tibetans and the Chinese occupiers and in many cases violence, particularly in Kham province.

But in June 1954, Nehru pointed out, "the Chinese had not even interfered with the land system which is feudal," the Socialist Prime Minister, however, asserted: "I can very well understand these feudal chiefs being annoyed with the new order. We can hardly stand up as defenders of feudalism."

---

14  Gyalo Thondup and Anne F Thurston, *The Noodle Maker of Kalimpong: The Untold Story of My Struggle for Tibet* (2015).

Once again, he reiterated that the Tibetans living in India should not be handed over to the Chinese: "They have every right to live in India or to seek asylum in India and we shall respect that."

Discussing the Tibetan Trade Agency in Kalimpong, the Prime Minister agreed "it can continue for the present, but I rather doubt if it will be allowed to continue by the Chinese authorities. We must make sure, however, that the Tibetan Mission is not used as a cover for something else."

At the end of this long note, the Dalai Lama's treasure was mentioned; it was said to be kept in Gangtok, "I do not see the point of transferring it to Calcutta or elsewhere." The argument was that Delhi did not have a 'direct knowledge' of the Dalai Lama's wishes; as for India, "it does not much matter whether it is in Gangtok or in Calcutta. It is under our control. If adequate guards are not there, we should make arrangements for proper protection."

His conclusion for this matter was, it was far better to allow this matter to lie low: "If at any time the Chinese claim it, then we shall have to consider what we should do about it. For the present, our view should be that it is a private treasure of the Dalai Lama and it is for the Dalai Lama to dispose of it."

He reiterated Delhi's policy towards Tibet: "we continue our friendly feelings for Tibet and her people and make it clear that our traditional friendship with them continues."

However, this policy couldn't lead to "any course of action which is against our agreement with China. For the rest, we have to be vigilant and wide awake."

The Secretary-General was requested to explain this to the PO and BN Mullik[15], the Director of the Intelligence Bureau, before concluding: "We have to be very careful about our activities in Kalimpong because

---

15 Bhola Nath Mullik (b. 1903), joined the Indian Police in 1927 and served in various capacities in Bihar and Orissa; Director, Intelligence Bureau, Government of India 1950-1964, author of several books including, *My years with Nehru: The Chinese Betrayal,* 1971 and *My Years with Nehru: Kashmir,* 1971.

of the espionage and counterespionage that is continually going on there."

The issue of Kalimpong would come again and again during the following years; the argument would also often be used by Zhou En-lai.

## Zhou En-Lai's Visit

On June 21, 1954, Zhou En-lai the Chinese Premier, who represented his country at the Conference on Indo-China in Geneva, informed VK Krishna Menon, the Indian Representative at the Conference that on his way back to Beijing, he was ready to make a stopover in Delhi to meet Nehru.

The Indian Prime Mister immediately cabled his Chinese counterpart: "I am very happy to learn from your Ambassador[16] in Delhi that you have accepted the invitation to visit India which Mr. Krishna Menon conveyed to you on my behalf."

Krishna Menon had informed Nehru the same day, "I not only conveyed your invitation to Chou En-Lai, but mentioned it more than once and we talked it over. I believe I helped him to get over what he might have been regarding as prestige difficulties."

Nehru continued: "I am looking forward particularly to meeting you and of having the opportunity to exchange views. We are glad that your Excellency will be traveling by the Air India International. We are instructing our Consul General[17] at Geneva to place himself at your disposal for any help in regard to travelling or other arrangements that you might require."

Nehru expressed his deep appreciation for Zhou's efforts to terminate hostilities in Indo-China: "I earnestly hope that the direct negotiations now in progress will soon achieve this result and will thus lead to the next step of a peaceful settlement of the difficult problem which you have had to face at the Geneva Conference."

---

16 Yuan Zhongxian, also spelt Yuan Chung Hsien, Chinese Ambassador to India.
17 Samarendranath Sen.

Krishna Menon had described Zhou thus, "a fine and I believe, a great and able man; I do not believe that the Chinese have expansionist ideas. ...I think he is also somewhat happy that the British and they have got closer and that we broke down some barriers. I found little difficulty in getting near him. He was never evasive with me, even on difficult matters ...He is extremely shrewd and observant, very Chinese, but modern."

The dream that China was not expansionist would continue for eight years.

## A Letter to Chief Ministers

On June 24, as Zhou En-lai was landing in India, the Prime Minister wrote one of his bi-monthly letters to the Chief Ministers in which he mentioned the forthcoming visit of the Chinese Premier; it was a matter of considerable significance and historical importance: "It will be followed with close interest in other countries," he observed.

Nehru admitted that during the last two years he had been invited on more than one occasion by Chairman Mao Zedong to pay a visit to China: "On every occasion, when this invitation reached me, I expressed my appreciation of it and my desire to go to China."

But he did not want to make the visit "so long as the war was going on in Korea. ...Later, the Indo-China war flared up and became a world issue, and again it was not very suitable for me to go."

He repeated India's philosophy of 'live and let live and non-interference': "Our agreement with China in regard to Tibet laid down certain principles ...[which] are important not only as between us and China, but also in a wider field, whether that is Asia or even the world."

It is what he wanted to discuss with the Chinese Premier.

## The Talks with Zhou En-Lai

Surprisingly, during the encounter between Zhou En-lai and Nehru[18], Tibet would hardly be discussed; further, the border incident in

---

18 Five sessions of conversation between Jawaharlal Nehru and Zhou Enlai were held in New Delhi from 25 to 27 June 1954. The minutes of the talks were maintained by TN Kaul, Joint Secretary in the Ministry of External Affairs. The first session

Barahoti did not come on the table. The talks would run into five long sessions,[19] which concluded with a joint statement.

On June 25, 1954, the first session was consecrated to the talks in Geneva to decide the fate of Indo-China. During the second session on the same day, Zhou En-lai mentioned the preamble of India's 'Trade Agreement on Tibet': "If these principles are applied to all States of Asia, that would be very beneficial… In this way, we can prevent US attempts to organise military blocs in this area."

Nehru replied: "I agree with your line of thought—that these principles should be applied. They would be gladly accepted by these States. Certainly by Burma and Indonesia." Nehru further suggested that the best time to enlarge the Panchsheel to Asia would be after the settlement of the Indo-china conflict.

Zhou answered: "Yes… we should make efforts to facilitate its settlement and this should be settled first because there is a war on."

Later the conversation was broached on Burma.

During the rest of the meeting, only the Geneva Conference was discussed.

The next day, a third session took place, a lot of US bashing took place; while most of the discussion turned around West Asia and Egypt; later on the relations with Thailand and Japan were also discussed

In the afternoon of June 26, the fourth round of talks was held, during which Nehru spoke of a feeling of 'friendly confidence' in each other: "I am not talking of India and China only but speaking generally. Speaking of India, there is a slight fear—not much—whether in Ceylon or Pakistan or Burma—that India is a bigger country, perhaps stronger than these."

The Indian Prime Minister asserted: "China is also a powerful country, an integrated and powerful State. Therefore, there is a fear, not in India

---

on June 25, lasted from 3.30 pm to 6.15 pm. Zhou Enlai arrived in India on June 25 and left on June 28.

19  For full transcript, see http://www.claudearpi.net/wp-content/uploads/2016/12/SW-Vol-27.pdf..

but in other countries. It should be our effort to remove such fears regarding India and China. There is a big propaganda in Africa by Europeans—not by Africans—that India wants to expand, turn out Europeans and set up her empire in Africa."

A parallel was made about the position of India and China, though Nehru would always miss the big difference: China was a totalitarian State; India not.

During the fifth round, before the draft of the joint statement was discussed, Zhou mentioned that he had seen 'a good picture' in technicolour. It was *Jhansi Ki Rani*, based on the life of Rani Lakshmibai of Jhansi.

Nehru responded: "the story is not so good", to which the Chinese Premier retorted: "It is quite good and represents resistance against foreigners."

Nehru added: "It was a resistance by the feudal elements against foreigners."

Zhou agreed: "Yes. Resistance always starts from the upper classes."

On this, there was complete ideological agreement between the two statesmen.

At the end Zhou invited the Indian Prime Minister to visit China in 1954 itself. Nehru answered: "I should love to visit your country. But it is difficult to fix the time now…. Partly it would depend on our Parliament session, as I should like to be present during the session."

Zhou agreed to suit his counterpart's convenience: "Maybe we can fix the date later. But we hope Your Excellency's visit to our country will take place this year, as we have been expecting your visit for a long time—more than one and a half years."

Nehru's visit to China would take place in October.

**Trade and Frontier with China**

On July 1, two days after Zhou had left, Nehru wrote a note to the Secretary General of the Ministry of External Affairs about the trade with Tibet; it included the issue of the border with China, which was not discussed with Zhou. The Prime Minister had just read a report of Dr K. Gopalachari,[20] who participated in the Sino-Indian talks on Tibet in Beijing.

The Prime Minister first noted that an important event had just taken place "affecting the relations of India and China. This is the visit of Mr Chou En-lai[21] to Delhi, the talks he had with us and the joint statement issued at the end of those talks.[22] This visit and the joint statement undoubtedly mark an important step forward in our relations with China."

The Prime Minister at the outset observed: "I have previously written on several occasions about our general approach to China and Tibet. I need not say anything more about it here."

Nehru believed that the Agreement over Tibet marked "a new starting point for our relations with China and Tibet. The previous agreements have only a certain historical importance now. In any future consideration of this matter, the basis will be our Agreement of 1954."

It is a serious statement as it belittles the 1914 Convention and therefore the McMahon Line agreed upon by Tibet and British India during the Conference in Simla. The Prime Minister, however, asserted that India must work "with the full intention of giving effect to the Agreement."

He added: "We must work in a friendly way, friendly to China and Tibet."

He reiterated that all Indian officers and Trade Agents who dealt with Tibet "must understand our basic policy and must realise that they have to function in accordance with not only this Agreement but in keeping with that basic policy of ours vis-à-vis China."

---

20 Served in the Historical Division of the Ministry of External Affairs. Dr Gopalachari was adviser to N. Raghavan, the Indian Ambassador in Beijing, who led the Indian Delegation at the Beijing Conference.

21 Earlier written Zhou En-lai.

22 The Joint Statement was issued after talks in New Delhi on June 28, 1954. There is no mention of Tibet in it.

He repeated: "Our Consul-General in Lhasa, as well as our Trade Agent and officers at check-posts should be made to appreciate this fully."

Though he doubted the necessity of a special cadre of officers for the border region (which in fact already existed), he insisted that the Trade Agents should be carefully chosen. He later contradicted himself on the border cadre[23]: "while there is a certain advantage in having special cadres for specialised posts, there is also the disadvantage of having too many such special cadres. Specialisation is good, but there is always the danger of the specialists losing sight of the larger picture."

This 'larger picture' had been Nehru's leitmotiv since the Chinese entered into Tibet; as for the IFAS, it would continue to do good work during the following years.

**The Borders with Tibet, Now China**

Regarding the borders, the Prime Minister said that historical references should be given up, "except in some historical context, to the McMahon Line or to any other frontier line by date or otherwise." It is not clear what Nehru was trying to argue, probably that no reference should be made to Tibet and Sir Henry McMahon, a Britisher; he continued: "We should simply refer to our frontier. Indeed, the use of the name McMahon is unfortunate and takes us back to the British days of expansion."

But it was the days of Chinese expansionism which would have serious implications for India's security.

Referring to the maps, a matter also not discussed with Zhou En-lai, he noted: "All our old maps dealing with this frontier should be carefully examined and, where necessary, withdrawn. New maps should be printed showing our Northern and North Eastern frontier without any reference to any 'line'. These new maps should also not state there is any undemarcated territory. The new maps should be sent to our Embassies abroad and should be introduced to the public generally and be used in our schools, colleges."

---

23 The Indian Frontier Administrative Service (IFAS).

At that time, the survey of India was still circulating maps with large areas in Jammu and Kashmir shown as 'undefined'.

He told the Secretary-General that as a consequence of the Tibet Agreement with China, "this frontier should be considered a firm and definite one, which is not open to discussion with anybody."

It is not clear how the Agreement could prove a 'firm and definite frontier' as the Indian negotiators did not bring the issue to the table and no mention was made in the final text.

Nehru nevertheless wrote: "There may be very minor points of discussion. Even these should not be raised by us."

He, however, admitted that a system of check-posts "should be spread along this entire frontier. More especially, we should have check-posts in such places as might be considered disputed areas."

He further explained that the frontier "has been finalised not only by implication in this Agreement but the specific passes mentioned are direct recognitions of our frontier there."

This view was unfortunately wrong.

Barahoti was a case in point; as mentioned in the previous chapter, the pass of Tunjun-la, North of the small pasture ground of Barahoti, did not figure in the Agreement and the Chinese started moving south of the pass a mere couple of months after the ink had dried.

The Prime Minister rightly mentioned Demchok "considered by the Chinese as a disputed territory, as well as Tsang Chokla[24], "we should locate a check-post there," adding that along the UP-Tibet border and the passes leading to Joshimath and Badrinath, "we should have proper check-posts."

A Joint Secretary had mentioned the possibility of increasing the strength of the garrisons at some Indian 'border towns' such as Gangtok, Leh, Simla or Almora, Nehru commented: "I do not think this is necessary from the point of view of guarding this North Eastern frontier. In Leh, we have adequate forces. [In] Simla in Punjab, we have

---

24 Tsangchok-la, in today's Chamoli district of Uttarakhand.

also quite adequate forces. ...I do not consider it at all necessary to keep a large contingent of our forces near this border area."

Then came one of the hallmarks of Nehru's border policy, that the Army should not guard the borders: "we should have some kind of border militia. I like the idea that this Border Militia should be raised locally and used for the construction of roads. This will not only give a sensation of security to the people there but add to their self-respect. These people in the Border Militia would be the leaders in their villages and they could help greatly in organising construction work with voluntary labour."

Nehru further expanded his views on the militia; they did not need to have "a high standard of professional efficiency such as our border Scouts or the Assam Rifles have. ...one of their principal duties should be that of construction, cottage industries. ...This would be an innovation for us but it is a right and natural development."

The Defence Ministry was asked to study this alternative.

Then the Prime Minister dealt with cross-border trade, he felt that it should be encouraged: "There has been some hesitation on our part to do so and some items have been practically banned. I do not see why we should ban any item except arms and ammunition."

He rightly observed that Tibet was a natural market for India: "It is not a big market from the point of view of quantity. We should retain this market and supply them with various quantities of manufactured goods that they require."

Nehru noted that this would not help strengthening China's control over Tibet: "The small trade that will take place in this way will make little difference to the political or the military aspect. From the economic and psychological points of view, it will be advantageous to us."

Unfortunately, the Chinese would slowly take over the trade from the traditional players and install a monopoly in their favour on important items such as wool. They were unarguably the masters of the game.

Another topic had come up for discussion: should India allow trade on a large scale with Tibet in view of the transport difficulties: "That seems to me a wrong way to put it. We should allow as much trade as possible. If transport difficulties come in the way, they will limit the trade. ...we should agree to free and unrestricted transit of goods to Tibet through India subject only to our own demand and supply position."

It is not clear who had suggested a limitation of the trade with Tibet; it perhaps related to the rice supplied to the Chinese troops in Tibet.

Even here, the Prime Minister was against limitations.

When the issue of selling rice to China came up, on July 25, 1954, Nehru wrote to the Foreign Secretary: "I am clearly of [the] opinion that we should agree to sell rice to China almost in any quantity. We have got large stocks... If the Chinese want to send rice to Tibet we should not object to it... Our selling rice to China... will indicate our healthy food position and that of China in this respect."

The note continued on trade; it stated that the demand was so great "that these are smuggled across the Nepal-Tibet frontier, and they fetch fantastic prices in Tibet. Articles like bicycles, radios, textiles and any number of other things could easily be sent to Tibet through our normal channels."

However, he mentioned the reluctance to send goods to Tibet due to the apprehension that it would be used by the Chinese People's Liberation Army to consolidate their occupation: "We have sent small quantities of petrol. I think we should be prepared to increase these quantities. ...The petrol that is smuggled through Nepal to Tibet sells there, I am told, at Rs 50 a gallon!"

The Prime Minister's conclusion was that India "should develop a normal and healthy trade with Tibet. This will be advantageous also to our border people."

It was true, but as mentioned earlier, the Chinese would not see it this way.

The note ended on the question of the Indian frontier: "if we find that the Chinese maps continue to indicate that part of our territory is on their side, then we shall have to point this out to the Chinese Government. We need not do this immediately, but we should not put up with this for long and the matter will have to be taken up."

This was two days after Zhou En-lai's departure. Another opportunity had been missed, though it would not have changed the Chinese attitude in the matter.

One can think that these vital issues should have been discussed before the Chinese Premier arrived in Delhi, but they were not. The Secretary-General was nonetheless requested to send a copy of this note to the Ministries of Defence and Commerce and Industry.

**Another Letter to Chief Ministers**

The same day, the Prime Minister dictated another letter to the Chief Ministers.

Though nothing had been said on Tibet during the bilateral discussions with Zhou, Nehru mentioned Tibet at length in his missive: "It was clear that China would establish its sovereignty over Tibet. This had been China's policy for hundreds of years, and, now that a strong Chinese State had been formed, this policy would inevitably be given effect to. We could not stop it in any way, nor indeed had we any legal justification for trying to do so. All we could hope for was that a measure of autonomy would be left to Tibet under Chinese sovereignty."

The statement that it was China's policy for centuries shows how poorly Nehru was informed about the history of the Land of Snows, though several notes had been prepared for him by his officials during the five previous years.[25]

This misplaced sense of history would have disastrous consequences for the Tibetans and the Indian borders.

---

25 In 1950 alone, excellent notes had been prepared by Sir Girja Shankar Bajpai, the Secretary General of the Ministry of External Affairs and Commonwealth, KPS Menon, the Foreign Secretary, Harishwar Dayal, the Political Officer in Sikkim or Hugh Richardson or Sumul Sinha who headed the Indian Mission in Lhasa.

Then again, Nehru used the same argument; India had acquired certain special privileges from the British: "we were successors to certain expansionist policies of the old British Government. It was not possible for us to hold on to all these privileges because no independent country would accept that position."

He cited the Indian troops posted "in some towns of Tibet to guard our trade routes", and said: "we could not possibly keep these troops there."

After mentioning other privileges linked with trade and communications, he added: "The real influence of India, however, was something insubstantial but important. This was the reliance to some extent of the Tibetan Government on the advice of the Indian representative, whose position was also rather vague and not wholly justifiable by treaty."

He explained the Tibetan Government relied on the Indian Consul General "partly because this tendency was a relic from the old days of British dominance and partly because they were afraid of China coming more firmly into the picture."

Nehru believed that the only solution was to use "our diplomatic influence in favour of Tibetan autonomy. We did that as tactfully as we could, knowing that we could not make very much difference. I think, however, that our efforts had some influence and somewhat delayed the Chinese invasion of Tibet."

As we have seen in Volume 2 of this research, the Indian influence on China was nil and would continue to be negligible.

Once again, Nehru reiterated: "we could not help Tibet in any way to resist the growth of China's power in Tibet. This was wholly outside the range of practical politics and it would have been of very doubtful legality."

He told the Chief Ministers: "We explained this position to the Tibetan Government and assured them of our friendliness and of our wish to help within the obvious limitations."

He then described the sequence of events in Tibet.

- The Chinese established themselves at various strategic points in Tibet and were in a position to control the Tibetan Government and its activities.
- They have taken care not to interfere with the domestic set-up much.
- They have not interfered at all with their social conditions, although these are very feudal.
- They have built roads, established airfields because communications in Tibet were very bad.
- There has been much talk of Chinese troops' concentrations on our frontier with Tibet. There is not much truth in this except that some Chinese troops are present on the frontier and in various parts of Tibet.
- The total numbers are not great and are spread out. The chief defence of Tibet is its very difficult terrain and the inhospitable nature of the climate. It is no easy matter for very large numbers of people from outside to live there.
- We get news often from Kalimpong about these Chinese military preparations in Tibet. It must be remembered that Kalimpong is a nest of all kinds of spies and the information these people gather is utterly unreliable. It usually comes from some *émigrés* who leave Tibet.

The Prime Minister went on to tell the Chief Ministers that his government was clear "as to how far we could go into Tibet and how far we could not."

Delhi had decided to concentrate on important issues for India: "This was our frontier with Tibet." This intention was good, though it would not be followed by actions.

The Prime Minister then admitted the lack of infrastructure: "it took weeks and even months for our forces to reach that frontier;" but he reiterated that the frontier with Tibet (now with China) "including the McMahon line was a firm one and was not open to discussion." He added that from the defence point of view "we considered the Nepal frontier with Tibet also our defence line."

But the Panikkar doctrine still prevailed: "I did not think it necessary to address the Chinese Government on this question because that itself would have shown some doubt on our part."

Speaking about the behaviour of the Chinese Government in Tibet during the first years of occupation, "on the whole, [it was] good, though there were a number of petty instances which we found rather irritating."

Nehru explained the attitude of the Chinese, or at least what he perceived as the Chinese line of thought: "At the back of their minds they thought that we were tied up still with British policy. Gradually, however, the realization came that we were following an independent policy of our own and we took orders from nobody. This change may be dated from the date when we refused to sign the San Francisco Treaty[26]. Since then, the behaviour of the Chinese Government was much better."

He stated again that 'most people' recognized that the Tibet Agreement was definitely a good thing. His final conclusion was "We have recognized certain obvious facts of the situation and come to understandings about trade, pilgrimage routes between India and Tibet."

Defence and strategic issues were unfortunately omitted.

**Preventing the War**

An interview with William H. Attwood, Correspondent of *The Look* on August 31, 1954, gave some hints on Nehru's views of the often-mentioned 'larger picture'.

---

26 The Treaty of San Francisco is commonly known as the Treaty of Peace with Japan. It was officially signed by 48 nations in San Francisco on September 8, 1951; it came into force on April 28, 1952 and officially ended the American-led Allied Occupation of Japan. It served to officially end Japan's position as an imperial power, to allocate compensation to Allied civilians and former prisoners of war who had suffered Japanese war crimes during World War II, and to end the Allied post-war occupation of Japan and return sovereignty to Japan.

When Attwood asked the Prime Minister if communism was a major problem in India; Nehru replied: "I wouldn't call it a major problem. We [in India] have a hard core of dedicated party workers, but most people who call themselves Communists are just against the Government for one reason or another. A few trade unions are Communist controlled but on the whole their strength is declining. They have barely thirty seats out of 500 in Parliament and this participation in the business of Government has toned down their activities in the country."

Then, giving the example of Tibet, the reporter said that Delhi seemed more concerned about Western colonialism than about Soviet imperialism: "American arms shipments to Pakistan caused much more alarm in India than the building of Communist airfields in neighbouring Tibet."

Nehru agreed that he was right "to some extent. Asians are inclined to be suspicious of American policy." He then came to the airfields in Tibet: "they don't frighten us at all. Practically speaking, I cannot conceive of an attack on India across the Himalayas from Tibet. Those airfields are being built because there are hardly any other communications in the country. We do the same in the more inaccessible parts of India. I realise that communism is expansionist but they only go where they can go easily. Steps must be taken to prevent their creeping in elsewhere, but Tibet is not a problem."

The Prime Minister probably did not realize the extent of roads and infrastructure the Chinese had built in the first three years of the occupation of the plateau.

**Restraints and Firmness**

It is necessary to cite a debate on the international situation in the Lok Sabha on September 30, 1954 in order to fully grasp the Government's views on Tibet.

During the discussion, when a Member questioned Nehru about Tibet, he told the MP to forget the 'melancholy chapter of Tibet'.

Nehru asserted: "I really do not understand such a reaction. I have given the most earnest thought to this matter. What did any honourable

Member of this House expect us to do in regard to Tibet at any time? Did we fail or did we do a wrong thing?"

He requested the member who had doubts about the Agreement, "to just consider and try to find but what the background, the early history and the late history of Tibet and India and China have been, what the history of the British in Tibet has been and what the relationship of Tibet with China or India has been."

He stated that India did not want to assume an aggressive role of interfering in other countries and continued: "Many things happen in the world which we do not like and which we would wish were rather different but we do not go like Don Quixote with a lance in hand against everything that we dislike; we put up with these things because we would, without making any difference, merely get into trouble."

Once again is referred to the larger context: "Big things have happened in the world ever since the last War. And among the big things has been the rise of a united China. Forget for a moment the broad policies it pursues - Communist or near-Communist or whatever it may be. The fact is – and it is a major fact of the middle of the 20th century that China has become a Great Power-united, strong and great power."

He further argued: "Much is being done in China which is praiseworthy and we can learn from them and we hope to learn from them". After affirming that India was more industrially developed than China, he continued: "China no doubt, will go ahead fast. ...This is a country which inevitably becomes a Great Power. Leaving these three big countries, the United States of America, the Soviet Union and China, for the moment leaving them aside, look at the world."

Therefore, China had to be engaged, but in the process the Indian borders and Tibet were forgotten.

That was a tragedy.

# 03

# Nehru's Important visit to Beijing

**An Invitation**

During his visit to India in June, the Chinese Premier Zhou En-lai had mentioned that China was keen to welcome Nehru in Beijing sometime in 1954.

On August 27, 1954, N. Raghavan, the Indian Ambassador to China informed the Prime Minister that at 1:30 in the morning, he had 'a pressing call' from Zhou En-lai, who wanted to send a letter to his Indian counterpart.

It is said that after the Long March, several of the Communist leaders suffered from insomnia, explaining the early hour the Ambassador had to rush to Zhongnanhai.

The letter was an invitation for Nehru to visit China: "I have the greatest pleasure to invite your Excellency to visit China. ...I earnestly hope that you will permit my Government and people and myself to avail ourselves of this opportunity to reciprocate the warm reception accorded to me last June by the Government and people of India and by your Excellency. It is my deep conviction that your friendly visit to China will be of great significance to further developments of friendly cooperation between India and China and to further assurance of peace in Asia and all over the world."[1]

---

1 All documents in this chapter, except specifically mentioned, are from the Nehru Papers (JN Collection) held at the Nehru Memorial Museum and Library in Delhi. The 'papers' are not indexed.

The Chinese Premier gave some possible dates for the visit: between mid-October and the second week of November. Nehru was asked to decide a date accordingly: "My Government agrees that your plans to visit China will not be made public until final arrangements are made," wrote Zhou.

While visiting Rangoon, the Premier had invited "Premier [U] Nu who accepted, but expressed a desire to visit same time as you."

The Premier probably knew that it would complicate the trip, but he wanted Nehru's views on a joint visit: "I feel that since it was Nu who made request, it might be embarrassing to say 'no' especially as [there is] no suggestion to invite [the] Indonesian Premier also at same time."

Later in the meeting, Raghavan discussed Attlee's recent visit to China with Zhou, who was satisfied with its results.

Nehru must have been delighted by the warmth of the missive as he answered his ambassador immediately, 'gladly' accepting the invitation.

However, regarding U Nu, he saw a problem: "It is always a pleasure to me to be with Premier Nu of Burma. I feel however that the two of us coming together to Peking at this juncture would rather look like a conference and would take away from other aspects of this visit. It would be better if we visited Peking separately and had full talks there."

Nehru was ready to speak to U Nu and explain his views. Raghavan was asked to explain this to Zhou.

**A Program Prepared**

A quick program was chalked out: the Prime Minister would leave Kolkata on October 16; after one-night stopover in Hanoi, Vietnam, he would reach Canton[2] on October 18. The Prime Minister would stay 10 days in China, returning to Canton on October 29. The Ambassador was requested to accordingly draw a detailed program

---

2   Guangzhou or Canton is the capital and most populous city of the province of Guangdong.

   It is located in southern China on the Pearl River about 120 km north-northwest of Hong Kong and 145 km north of Macau.

after consulting Zhou; Nehru would use an Indian Air Force Dakota and would be accompanied by Indira Gandhi, his daughter.

Two days later, Zhou agreed to the program and to delink it with U Nu's visit. Raghavan wrote that Zhou would also inform the Burmese leader and suggest that he comes before or after Nehru. Ten days were fine for Zhou who looked forward to welcoming Indira Gandhi too.

Noting that it would be the first time that a foreign plane, other than a Soviet one, would fly over China, Raghavan told Nehru that he would make the arrangements for the same plane "to proceed from Canton to Peking also as it would be more convenient for you."

Things were moving fast.

Later that day, Nehru cabled the Indian embassy that he appreciated that Zhou had agreed with him regarding U Nu: "I do not mind if his visit slightly overlaps mine," he said.

He thought that an announcement could be made simultaneously from Delhi and Beijing, just stating that the Indian Prime Minister had received an invitation from the Chinese government to visit Beijing and that he had accepted.

Raghavan was asked to work on a more detailed program.

## The visit confirmed: a detailed program

The following day, another message detailed what was agreed so far: there would be no more than 10 or 11 persons accompanying the Prime Minister, who had suggested some names: Indira Gandhi, a personal attendant, a private secretary, a senior security officer, the Secretary-General of the Ministry[3], MO Mathai[4], a cameraman, a representative from PTI and a junior officer from the Ministry of External Affairs.

---

3  NR Pillai.

4  MO Mathai (1909–1981) was the Private Secretary to Prime Minister Jawaharlal Nehru. Mathai worked with the United States Army in India before becoming the Secretary to Nehru in 1946. He resigned in 1959 following Communist allegations of misuse of power and spying. Despite the allegations, Nehru maintained contact with him. He published his controversial memoirs in *Reminiscences of the Nehru Age* (1978) and *My Days with Nehru* (1979), when Indira Gandhi went out of power in 1977.

Nehru added: "The question of U Nu going to Peking has been definitely settled," as Zhou entirely agreed with his views.

On September 3, the announcement of the visit was confirmed by Zhou. Raghavan suggested three or four days in Beijing and then the Northeast "to see economic reconstruction and also one or two ancient cultural centers elsewhere connected with India."

There was also the possibility for Nehru to address the newly constituted People's Congress, which would be in session.

The next day, Nehru clarified that his visit to China was "chiefly to meet leaders there. I am not anxious to tour about much, but some touring probably desirable if convenient." Further, he was not eager to address the People's Congress.

On September 12, the Prime Minister reiterated that he attached "far greater importance to meeting people and talking to them than to touring," Nehru added: "Please inform Chinese authorities informally and politely that I hope much time will not be spent on elaborate feasts taking up a lot of time."

As the date of the visit was approaching, the Indian Prime Minister cabled his Chinese counterpart on September 21, officially confirming that he had received the invitation and his acceptance: "It was a great pleasure for all of us to meet Your Excellency in Delhi last June, and I shall be very happy to renew the contacts then made and to meet His Excellency the Chairman and other members of the Central People's Government in Peking."

Everything was set.

### Ready to Depart: the 'Friendship' Ideology

The day before his departure for China, the Prime Minister gave a press conference; he was grandiloquent about the new friendship between India and China: "these two great nations - India and China have lived for 10,000 years and want to do it another 10,000 years or more. The meeting, therefore, between the Prime Ministers of India and China is a very big thing itself and a world event."

He quoted his own speech in the Indian Parliament in which he had affirmed that India had the possibility of being the fourth great country of the world: "I was not thinking in terms of what was called 'great powers', nor had I any intention of comparing India with the great nations of Europe or elsewhere. I was merely pointing out the capacity and potentiality of India and not talking in terms of armed powers."

The Prime Minister continued in the same tone: "The whole idea of rivalry and competition between nations, big or small, has become out of date now and the idea of cooperation should take its place in order to solve the problems of the world."

He talked of the revolutionary changes that had overtaken the Asian continent: "The process is a continuing one. The fact that this is not liked elsewhere does not make it less significant, nor does it check it. Indeed, the obstruction placed by aggression in its way only made it more self-conscious and more determined to go ahead and for Asia to lead its own way."

He brought up the inescapable Panchsheel, while forgetting that Tibet, a small nation, though not in size, had lost its independence in the process.

He concluded, affirming that the Five Principles "are theoretically the perfect approach between two countries to rule out aggression or interference. If practically applied between countries, they rule out chances of conflict or even of friction. I, therefore, do not understand why some people in other countries do not appreciate these Five Principles except for the reason that they do not like any understanding or cooperation between India and China."

The *Hindi-Chini Bhai Bhai* season was in full bloom.

## The Meetings in Beijing

The titles attributed by the Editors of the *Selected Works of Jawaharlal Nehru* to these talks are telling. On October 19, Nehru met Chairman Mao and talked about 'Foreign Policy and Fear Complex'.[5]

---

[5] Apart from the Prime Minister, were present on the Indian side, the Indian Ambassador to China, N. Raghavan; for the Chinese side, Premier Zhou Enlai; Vice-Chairman Zhu De; Chairman of the Congress of Standing Committee;

The next day, Nehru met Zhou Enlai; the meeting dealt with 'Foreign Policies of America and China'.[6] The same day, Nehru and Zhou had an 'Exchange of Views on World Issues'.

On October 21, the talks with Zhou were centered on "Situation in South East Asia". Two days later, the Indian Prime Minister met Mao again and talked about 'War and Peace'. A press conference was organized in Beijing on October 26.

On October 20, Nehru and Zhou Enlai met for the first time in Beijing.

Tibet was hardly mentioned, except for KI Singh[7] about whom the Indian Prime Minister complained: "One man named KI Singh, who had created some trouble in Nepal sometime ago, fled to Tibet. He was then reported to be in China. Later on, news came that he was being openly entertained. When persons who are traitors to their countries are thus openly feted then people naturally get apprehensive."

Zhou refused to answer immediately. He wanted to talk about the US: "We very much approve of softening of tensions, but I must reiterate that the US is using the question of Taiwan to create tensions. And if we do not oppose she will expand. If we take counter-measures it will lessen what she is doing."

---

    Liu Shaoqi, Vice-Chairman of the Standing Committee; Sung Ching-ling, Vice-Premier; Chen Yun, Chinese Ambassador to India, Yuan Chung-hsien.

6  The talks were attended by NR Pillai, Secretary General and Raghavan, on the Indian side, while for the Chinese, Vice Foreign Minister, Zhang Hanfu, Yuan Chind Hsien, the Chinese Ambassador to India and the Director of Asian Department of the Chinese Foreign Office, Chen Chia-kang, accompanied the Premier.

7  Kunwar Indrajit Singh (1906 – 4 October 1982) known as Dr KI Singh was a Nepali Communist leader considered by some as the Robin Hood of the Himalayas after initiating an extensive land redistribution scheme in the early 1950s. In 1946, he joined the Nepali National Congress Party and actively participated in the 1950-51 revolution against the Ranas to establish democracy in Nepal. Because of his strong opposition to the 1950 agreement with India, he was arrested and jailed for 6 months. He escaped and fled to Tibet but returned after an amnesty by King Mahendra. He also served as the Prime Minister of Nepal for four months in 1957.

As regards the question of Communist infiltration, Zhou declared that it was "entirely a matter for the people of various countries. You referred to it in Delhi and you said that decisions were made by the people of each country and therefore, no interference was permissible from outside. As far as we are concerned, we will make greater efforts to implement the Five Principles. We can build greater confidence and show to the world an example that not only can we strictly abide by the principles. We can do it by specific examples and during your visit here we can talk more about some more specific questions."

Much later during the talks, the Premier came back to the Nepali Communist. He said that it was rather simple: "Singh came across the border to China from Nepal with thirty-seven persons armed with nineteen rifles and 500 bullets. We immediately disarmed them, gave them asylum according to international practice, because he is in favour of peace and cooperation. But if he engages in any activity for the overthrow of Nepal Government we would not allow him to do so. It will amount to interference in the internal affairs of another country."

Then Zhou Enlai cleverly brought up the case of the Dalai Lama to divert from KI Singh's case. The Tibetan leader, he said, "was not friendly to us and wanted to seek asylum in India." This refered to the first months of 1951, when the Dalai Lama took refuge in Yatung.[8]

In 1951, KM Panikkar, the then ambassador to China had raised the question with Zhou, stating that "if Dalai Lama came to India, India will have to give him asylum and all facilities as a religious leader." Zhou surprisingly told Nehru: "We agreed. Actually, however, he went only some distance from Lhasa[9] but came back. His brother and sister-in-law are still in India. And in fact, they have many contacts in Tibet. We do not mind it."

Incidentally, the Dalai Lama was in Beijing as this talk took place. Zhou knew fully-well that the Tibetan leader was not planning to take refuge in India, except if some dramatic events took place.

---

8   See Volume 1, Chapter 15.
9   Yatung in Chumbi Valley.

## The Tibetan Pilgrims

The next day, during his talks with Zhou, the question of the Tibetan pilgrims came up. After stating that India wanted to encourage intercourse between China and India, not only in the scientific and trade fields, but in the cultural one too, Nehru mentioned the Tibetan pilgrims: "There is a small matter which I may take this opportunity to mention to you. Some complaints have recently been received from pilgrims going to Tibet. Some of them are apparently being harassed by guards and I hope that Your Excellency will look into the matter. As you are aware, every summer there is large pilgrim traffic between India and Tibet. As an example of the sort of harassment to which these pilgrims are subjected, I would mention that one of my friends was stopped by the border guards who told him that he could not be regarded as a pilgrim because he was not wearing a monk's gown."

Zhou just answered that the pilgrims "will be treated according to the provisions of the agreement. We would like to check up on the matter and if there is something incorrect it will be corrected."

We shall look at the difficulties faced by the pilgrims in a separate chapter. The main issue would be the post and telegraph services on which India and China had a different interpretation of the Agreement.

That's was all about Tibet, though the first incursions had taken place in Barahoti and the three Indian Trade Agents in Tibet had started facing more and more difficulties on the plateau for the performance of their duties.

## Nehru and the Discovery of China

In his first public speech after his return, at the Brigade Parade Ground in Kolkata on November 2, Nehru went lyrical: "So I set out to discover India and the more I searched the more I understood. I began to realize that India is something so profound that it is very difficult even to understand her fully. You can see her myriad forms, in Calcutta, Bombay, Kashmir and Madras, or again at the borders of Burma and Tibet, which is a wholly different world altogether. So India has innumerable forms."

He continued to explain the importance of India's neighbourhood and Asia in general: "But once we became free, the barriers of the recent past were broken down and our thoughts turned once more to our neighbours, which was absolutely necessary. We began to search into our past to find the answers to our problems in the present. As a result, we have been drawing closer, day by day, to our neighbouring countries. In that sense, my visit to China and other regions of South East Asia was a voyage of discovery."

He elaborated on the importance of friendship with China: "Now that the obstacles to change have been removed and new forces are coming into play, Asia has become a revolutionary place where all kinds of upheavals are taking place. What does that imply? Years of stagnation and absence of change and progress have created tremendous problems for all Asian countries which need a solution. If they fail to solve them at the proper time, the problems will resolve themselves by revolutionary and chaotic methods."

His ten-day tour of China should be seen in the Prime Minister's idealistic perspectives as well as the day-to-day issues faced by the Indian officials on the plateau.

## Letter to Lady Mountbatten

Immediately after his return, Nehru sent a long report of his visit to Edwina Mountbatten. Was it proper for a Prime Minister to first report to a foreigner?

It worth quoting the Prime Minister's letter to his British friend: "This visit to China as well as the Indo-China countries has indeed been an event which has some historic significance. For me, it was a further discovery of Asia and it has left a powerful impression on my mind. China, of course is dominant in this impression - huge, massive country with an enormous population. But the point is that this enormous population, or much of it, is unified, organized and disciplined. It is a hardworking population with great capacity. One that has a tremendous sense of vitality and strength."

The letter went on in this vein.

Nehru was definitely enamoured of China. This had (and would continue to have) consequences for the Land of Snows.

## A Letter to the Chief Ministers and an Interview

Two weeks later, the Prime Minister wrote his usual bi-weekly letter to the Chief Ministers in which he mentioned his discussions with Mao and Zhou in Beijing; he cited the case of the maps: "So far as India was concerned, I [told Zhou], we were not much concerned about this matter because our boundaries were quite clear."

He also informed the Chief Ministers of his discussions regarding KI Singh and the Dalai Lama: "the Dalai Lama did not go to India but some of his relatives did go there and had been given asylum. The Chinese Government did not mind this."

On November 20, in an interview with Norman Cliff for the BBC, Nehru spoke about the warm welcome he received in China: "I had a very cordial welcome which, from the popular side, was very spontaneous and I was naturally very much impressed by it. Even the weather cooperated and we had lovely weather in Peking in October when Premier Chou En-lai told that they wanted to be very hospitable to the guests."

He wanted the world to know that China was hospitable.

## The Nitty-Gritty in Tibet

Interestingly, the day Nehru was leaving Beijing, TN Kaul cabled the Indian embassy in Beijing about the Chinese representative in Yatung refusing to acknowledge the existence of the Trade Agency which had been agreed to in the April Agreement: "Our Trade Agent Yatung called on Fu[10], officer-in-charge newly established Foreign Bureau at latter's request. Fu mentioned he had no information from higher authorities regarding formal establishment of Indian Trade Agency at Yatung."

Raghavan was asked to remind the Chinese about the terms of the Agreement and inform the Chinese that SL Chibber had been deputed as India's Trade Agent at Yatung, "he will also be looking after Gyantse

---

10 Fu Sheng.

agency until an agent is appointed there." The intimation would be on the same lines as the one given to the Chinese Government regarding the appointment of AK Sen as Consul General Lhasa in 1952.

Kaul pointed out the case of reciprocity with the Chinese Trade Agency in Kalimpong: "they should send us formal intimation regarding the establishment of trade agency at Kalimpong and names of officials appointed thereto."

On the ground, the Chinese were not interested to respect the Five Principles.

The Indian Prime Minister had still not realised that it was a one-way road; he was too engrossed in his future role not only as the 'neutral' chairperson of the cease-fire commission for Indochina, but also as the self-appointed leader of the newly independent nations of Asia and Africa.

**Two Small Incidents in Beijing**

Two small incidents indicated the future direction in which the relations between India, Tibet and China would go.

During the course of his visit, Nehru had the occasion to meet the young Dalai Lama for the first time. The nineteen-year old Dalai Lama had also been invited to spend a few months in China to 'see by himself' the miracles of the Communist revolution.[11]

As seen earlier, Tibet and the border issue had totally been ignored during the talks with the Chinese leaders. This encounter with the young Lama was for Nehru like a mirror reminding him that Tibet had been forgotten in the Treaty. During an interview, the Dalai Lama recalled: "We [in Tibet] had heard his name. India also was a country very close to our mind. I had personally heard about Nehru. When we heard that we will meet him, there was a bit of excitement. Pandit Nehru led by Zhou Enlai and many Chinese dignitaries were lining up when he reached the place where I was standing. Zhou Enlai said: 'This is the Dalai Lama.' Nehru remained motionless, no speech, not looking

---

11 During this period he had the occasion to have long discussions with Mao on the future of Tibet. Unfortunately, the Chinese leader's promises to him once again would not be kept.

in the eyes. He just stands in front of me, without speech, without moving, motionlessly he remained like that. I was a bit embarrassed. I told through the Chinese interpreter: 'I have heard a lot about you, and today I am very happy to meet you'. Nehru did not give a particular response, he seemed maybe happy, then he went to the next person. That was my first experience [with him]. [That day] I thought and felt that from Nehru's side, there will be no support for Tibet and no support for the Dalai Lama. During a short moment, many things that occurred from 1949 till 1954 [passed] in his mind, like lightning, that is my feeling."[12]

Was this strange silence of the Indian Prime Minister a sign of the days and years to come? When Nehru finally realized that he had been misled by China, it would be too late.

Another incident is worth relating. Sultan M. Khan, then an official[13] in the Pakistani Embassy in Beijing, mentioned it in his memoirs.

Khan remembered: "Sino-Indian relations continued to get closer, and Nehru received a very warm welcome on his visit in 1954. A few days after his visit, the Indian Embassy held a reception at which I overheard an Indian diplomat, who had acted as Nehru's interpreter, telling some of his colleagues that just before his departure for Shanghai, Nehru was in a very sombre mood, and had said to senior members of his delegation that after his talks with Mao, he was pessimistic about the relations with China, and foresaw a conflict in the future. The Sino-Indian conflict of 1962 was far away and seemed unlikely in 1954 in the hey-day of *Hindi-Chini Bhai Bhai*. I do not know on what basis Nehru foresaw this, but the 1962 war[14] was of India's making."[15]

Was it after listening to Mao's comment on the atomic bomb that Nehru was no longer sure of the success of his Five Principles?[16]

---

12 Interview of the Dalai Lama with the author.

13 He later became Foreign Secretary of Pakistan.

14 Khan quotes Neville Maxell to prove his assertion.

15 Khan, M. Sultan, *Memories & Reflections of a Pakistani Diplomat*, (London: Centre for Pakistani Studies, 1997), p.103.

16 During the 1950s, Mao's words on the atomic bomb may also be seen from a politically expedient point of view. A time when, without possessing persuasive

Though one cannot be certain of the veracity of Khan's comments, they appear to have some truth. It is certain that in June-July 1954, the Chinese leaders got the Indian support they needed at a very crucial moment of their history. It helped them to impose their views in Geneva. Six months later, their needs were not the same and this partly explains Mao's tough talk with Nehru.

Soon after the Prime Minister started preparing for the Bandung Conference. The story of Sultan Khan is somehow confirmed by Dr. Li Zhisui, Mao's physician, in his *Private Life of Chairman Mao*. As Mao recalled his meeting with Nehru, Dr Li realized the meaning of Mao's words about the atomic bomb: "…it was so hard to accept, how willing Mao was to sacrifice his own citizens in order to achieve his goals. I had known as early as October 1954, from a meeting with India's Prime Minister Jawaharlal Nehru, that Mao considered the atom bomb a 'paper tiger' and that he was willing that China lose millions of people in order to emerge victorious against so-called imperialists, 'the atom bomb is nothing to be afraid of'.

Mao had told Nehru, "China has many people. They cannot be bombed out of existence. If someone else can drop an atomic bomb, I can too. The death of ten or twenty million people is nothing to be afraid of."[17]

Nehru's second point was that though the US had won the war, they were still unhappy. He could therefore not accept Mao's argument; Mao had told him that though a war was bad and therefore should be avoided, still if it comes, one should welcome it.

---

weapons and faced with powerful enemies, some leaders played this game to maintain the morale of their people and the armed forces; though it is however also true that Communist regimes usually do not worry about casualties inflicted on their own people.

After the Second World War, Stalin sent Colonel General Dragonvysky, a great soldier hero of Jewish descent, to lecture in American universities about the Soviet contribution in the War. During one such lecture, when asked about the Soviet contribution, he wrote on the blackboard: 20,000,000 (20 million) soldiers.

Mao's response to Nehru on atomic weapons should be seen in this context.

17 Dr. Li also added: "In 1957, in a speech in Moscow, Mao said he was willing to lose 300 million people - half of China population. Even if China lost half its population, Mao said, the country would suffer no great loss. We could produce more people."

Nehru had some strong reservations. First of all, for him, "even without war, India would have attained freedom." He thought that in fact, India would have become free earlier without World War II.

Nehru believed that a third World War would be qualitatively different from the two earlier conflicts. Though the Americans thought that they could destroy the administrative, strategic and industrial centres of the USSR, in return, the Soviets would certainly not do nothing. American centres would be destroyed and it would trigger an uncontrollable chain reaction.

For Nehru, the hydrogen bomb would release energy which itself would create another energy which killed; no one would be able to control the chain reaction. The Indian Prime Minister believed that the industrialized countries would eventually be destroyed.

Mao agreed that there was a disagreement between them on this point.

He told Nehru that Mao's analysis about the US having benefited [by Hiroshima] and still having difficulties [being unhappy] was very good.

Mao also accepted Nehru's argument of the qualitative difference in weapons, though "victory or defeat hinges on the scope of destruction suffered".

Dr. S. Gopal, Nehru's biographer, said that after his meetings with Mao, Nehru minuted in a small note on the file; he said that the record of the encounter was not always accurate.

## The Bandung Conference

The period following the visit of Nehru to Beijing, was marked by a lull in the relations between the three nations. In Tibet, the Dalai Lama returned to Lhasa after receiving some assurances from Mao that the Communist reforms would not be immediately enforced on the Tibetan people. Upon his return Nehru became busy with the preparation of the Afro-Asian Conference in Bandung.

This Conference seemed the culmination of his personal ambitions. He had always wanted to be at the center of the stage amongst the newly decolonized nations. In Bandung, he was able to introduce Zhou Enlai to the other Asian and African leaders and could later declare (perhaps with false modesty): "It was not India's purpose to play any aggressive role or, indeed, to seek the limelight. Some newspapers, especially in India, naturally played up India's role. We felt, however, that it was better for us to work quietly. The fact, however, remained that the two most important countries present at the Bandung Conference were China and India."[18]

Though Nehru (and the Indian press) thought that the Conference was a great success, it was not everybody's opinion. It is worth quoting from the minutes of a meeting between Zhou, Nehru and U Nu: "In the course of my conversation with the Chinese Prime Minister and U Nu, the former asked me about the next session of the Asian-African Conference. There was talk of this being held in Egypt. What did I think about it? He also asked me about a proposal to have a liaison office. He thought that some such liaison office might be desirable."

The minutes continued: "U Nu said immediately that his mind was quite clear that there should be no kind of organisation or liaison office. Further that if another session of this Conference was held, he had decided not to send any representative of Burma to it. He was firm about it.[19]"

Nehru told U Nu that he considered the net result of this Conference very good, in spite of all difficulties and differences of opinion. He added that he was not referring to the resolutions passed but the effect produced by the Conference in Asia and the world. Though Zhou agreed, the Burmese Prime Minister refused to agree. He commented that the Conference only brought out differences of opinion and asked what was the good of repeating 'platitudes'. He was most probably referring to the Five Principles.

Though the purpose of the Conference was not to discuss 'small matters', Tibet was mentioned one day during a conversation between the Prime Ministers of Ceylon, Pakistan, Indonesia and Burma. Zhou

---

18 SWJN, Series II, Vol. 28, *Note to the Chief Ministers, 28 April 1955*. Also *Letters to Chief Ministers 1954-1967*, Vol. 4, pp. 159-171.

19 SWJN, Series II, Vol. 28, *Conversation with Chou En-lai and U Nu, Note to V.K. Krishna Menon, Bandung, 23 April 1955*, p. 124.

explained his views on the question. Nehru later reported: "When asked if he wanted to push communism into Tibet, Chou En-lai laughed and said that there could be no such question as Tibet was very far indeed from communism. It would be thoroughly impracticable to try to establish a communist regime in Tibet and the Chinese Government had no such wish. Indeed, they had appointed a committee, of which the Dalai Lama was the chairman, to consider what should be done in Tibet[20]. Tibet was an autonomous region of China and they had no desire whatever to interfere with its customs or ways of life. They had gone to Tibet because it was an integral part of the Chinese state and because it had been used for imperialist intrigues, meaning thereby the British recently and previously Czarist Russia.[21]"

Later, when someone questioned Zhou about Tibet, his answer was: "You cannot introduce socialism or communism into Tibet, you just cannot do it; maybe 50 years, 100 years later they may do it, I do not know."

Unfortunately for the Tibetans, Communism was already being introduced on a very large scale in Eastern Tibet and the Dalai Lama while returning to Lhasa in 1955 witnessed some of the dramatic consequences for the populations of the provinces of Amdo and Kham.

At Bandung, the Indian Prime Minister was again very impressed by his Chinese counterpart. On his return to India, he let everybody know: "The Prime Minister of China, Chou En-lai, attracted the most attention, both in public and in the Conference. This was natural as he was not only playing a great part in the crisis of the Far East but was rather a mysterious figure that people had not seen. He conducted himself with ability and moderation in the Conference and its committees. Whenever he spoke, he did so with authority."[22]

---

20 From 1955 to 1959, the Dalai Lama was the Chairman of the Preparatory Committee of the Tibet Autonomous Region.

21 SWJN, Series II, Vol. 28, *Note to the Chief Ministers, 28 April 1955*. Also *Letters to Chief Ministers 1954-1957*, Vol. 4, pp. 159-171.

22 Ibid.

Nehru was awed by Zhou, while completely blind to the danger for India of an emerging powerful China. He did not grasp the implications for India at that time.

During this period, the Chinese Liberation Army was busy consolidating its strategic occupation of Tibet, building several roads and one airstrip North of Lhasa. This was unquestionably Mao's main priority. No doubt that 'reforms' could be postponed till China could fully take control of the Roof of the World.

# 04

# Cartographical Aggression: the Implications for India

**First Mention during Nehru's Visit to Beijing**

It is during the just-related Nehru's trip to China that an important issue came up which would remain unresolved for several years with tragic consequences at the end.

On October 20, during an encounter between the Indian Prime Minister and his Chinese counterpart, the question of the Chinese cartographical aggression came up for discussion; for unknown reasons, it had not been brought to the table during the Tibet talks early that year.[1]

When Nehru brought to Zhou's notice that most of the Chinese maps showed large chunks of Indian territory as Chinese, Zhou answered: "It is a historical question and we have been mostly printing old maps. We have made no survey of the borders and not consulted with our neighbouring countries and we have no basis for fixing the boundary lines."[2]

The Premier continued: "We made our maps and revised them from the maps of other countries. At least we do not have any deliberate

---

1  Refer to Maps 2 and 3, pages 575 and 577.
2  All documents in this chapter, except specifically mentioned, are from the Nehru Papers (JN Collection) held at the Nehru Memorial Museum and Library in Delhi. The 'papers' are not indexed.

intentions of changing the boundaries as KMT had. The whole thing is ridiculous."

In fact, Nehru wanted to speak of the inaccurate maps …of Burma only.

Zhou pointed out to his Indian counterpart: "The question of boundaries between China and Burma was not settled even in Manchu regime and you will find differences even in our boundaries with the Soviet Union and Mongolia. We can further discuss the matter with U Nu, but we want time for preparation."

In other words, it was a question of time for new maps to be reprinted.

Nehru did not forcefully put the question of the maps to Zhou; he himself told Zhou: "I just casually mentioned to you some of the anxieties of our neighbours. We are not worried about this point. Our frontiers are clear but I mention it in the case of Burma because questions of this kind become a handle in the hands of the enemy. Supposing we publish a map showing Tibet as a part of India, how would China feel about it? But as I said, I am sure, the maps were old maps and you did not mean it."

The Prime Minister had readily agreed with Zhou's explanation about 'old maps'.

## The Burmese Maps

When Nehru told U Nu of his visit, he mentioned the maps published by China showing large chunks of Burmese (and Indian) territory as China's: "why China should have issued maps where parts of Burma and even of India are shown as parts of China. There is a very small thing to which also a reference was made [with U Nu]."

To call this a 'small thing' is rather surprising.

In the coming years, it would be the main issue between India and China, but at the end of 1954, it was only 'casually' mentioned.

It is amazing that very few in Delhi were worried about India's new neighbour …despite the ominous portend of the maps.

On December 12, at the end U Nu's stay in Beijing, a joint communiqué was issued: "In view of the incomplete delimitation of the boundary line between China and Burma, the two premiers held it necessary to settle this question in a friendly spirit at an appropriate time through normal diplomatic channels."

The erroneous maps still haunt the bilateral relations between Delhi and Beijing, more than 60 years later.

**A Note to the Foreign Secretary**

On November 14, 1954 after his return to India, the Prime Minister mentioned the maps again in a note to the Foreign Secretary: "I referred to Chinese maps which still showed portions of Burma and even of India as if they were within Chinese territory. So far as India was concerned, I added, we were not much concerned about this matter because our boundaries were quite clear and [it is] not a matter for argument. But many people took advantage of these old maps and argued that China had an aggressive intent, or else why to continue to use these maps. In Burma also this caused apprehension."

It would take hardly five years for Delhi to discover how aggressive China could be about her presumed borders. But at the end of 1954, India and China were still 'brothers'.

In the note to RK Nehru, the Foreign Secretary, the Prime Minister wrote, "China had not done any surveying to draw new maps. Their boundaries even with Mongolia and the Soviet Union were still not clearly demarcated and there were discrepancies."

As for India's boundaries, Nehru was not worried, he had "no doubt about our boundaries." Panikkar's influence was still present.

**The Chinese Maps**

The utterances of Zhou En-lai were not really convincing; Communist China had knowingly adopted the 'old maps' of the Kuomintang.

It is interesting to look at the history of these maps.

When the Japanese invaded China, many scholars of the Chinese universities moved from Eastern China to the relatively safer provinces of Sichuan and Yunnan to continue with their academic routines; particularly, a number of social sciences' professors, who had lost their research notes in the civil war, started looking for new fields of research; a surprisingly large number of scholars discovered that the two provinces were rich in 'ethnic' minority groups; a new field of research was born.

In 1950, Marshal He Long[3] gathered a handful of these scholars such as Li Anche whose specialty was Amdo, Yu Shiyu, Xie An and Ren Naiqiang for Kham to work on these minority areas.

## A Look at Ren Naiqiang

This well-known scholar (1894-1989) became an influential figure during the Republican era; today he is regarded as the founding father of Kham studies in China. He was born into a peasant family in Nanchong county in Sichuan province and graduated from the Beijing Advanced College of Agriculture in 1920; soon he discovered that studies of the borderlands were mostly copied from Western sources.

In 1926, long before the beginning of the Japanese war, Ren had started wandering through Kham. In 1929, with Liu Wenhui, the commander-in-chief of Sichuan Borderland Defense recruiting scholars to do fieldwork in Kham, Ren Naiqiang was appointed as the inspector of the Sichuan Borderland.

During his investigation trip, he married Lodro Chontso, the niece of Dorje Namgyel, the indigenous leader of Upper Nyarong; during that period, he wrote a large number of articles on Kham.

---

3 Marshal He Long (1896 – 1969) was a Chinese Communist revolutionary and one of the ten marshals of the People's Liberation Army. He was from a poor rural family in Hunan, and his family was not able to provide him with any formal education. He began his revolutionary career after avenging the death of his uncle, when he fled to become an outlaw and attracted a small personal army around him. He joined the Long March in 1935, over a year after forces associated with Mao Zedong and Zhu De were forced to do so.

After settling and establishing a headquarters in Shaanxi, He led guerrilla forces in Northwest China in both the Chinese Civil War and the Second Sino-Japanese War.

In 1936, when the Nationalist government formally established the new province Xikang in Western China, Ren Naiqiang found a new niche for his scholarship. After the Nationalists appointed Liu Wenhui as the Governor of the new province, Ren was encouraged by Liu to map the province and prepare a list of the main places.

Probably at the end of 1949, Ren Naiqiang met Marshal He Long who asked him if his map of Kham's borders was reliable. Ren Naiqiang explained in detail why the map was extremely dependable and how he had prepared it; later the map was copied and provided to all departments of the Communist administration.

He Long was then Third Party Secretary in the Southwest Military Administration and Military District under General Liu Bocheng (First Party Secretary) and Deng Xiaoping (Second Party Secretary)

On 10 January 1950, He Long sent his report to Mao Zedong, Deng Xiaoping and Liu Bocheng; he explained that he had found a scholar who had a good grasp on China and Tibetan affairs. He also strongly recommended that Ren's map should be circulated amongst the PLA officials.

He Long added that Beijing lacked such scholars and pleaded that if there were any such scholars in other places of China, they must be sent to the South-Western Bureau to continue the research on the frontiers.

The map which showed the borders of India in NEFA alerted Sir Olaf Caroe, Secretary in the External Affairs Department in Delhi, who started a long correspondence with London and Nanjing on the subject in 1942. The leaders of Independent India probably never cared to go through this file.

According to the reminiscences of Wang Gui,[4] in January 1951, Liu Bei, the head of the investigation team, went to Beijing for a meeting where he mentioned the situation on the border. During his stay, 'important' directions were given to him; as a result from January to April 1951, a detailed investigation was carried out about Xikang's geographical conditions, the Tibetan army, etc.

---

4   A member of investigation team that was first dispatched by the 18th Army when it entered Tibet.

Ren's map greatly impressed the Communist generals.

On November 8, 1951, Xu Danlu[5], head of the political division and the communication division of the Tibet Military Region, had a meeting with Surkhang Shape from the Tibetan Foreign Bureau to understand the treaties that had been signed by the Tibetan government with the foreign countries, i.e. British India and Nepal.

It is only after the PLA intelligence of the 18th Army started gathering information on Tibet that the Chinese government realized that India had 'occupied' Tawang.

It is said that it was only in January 1954 that Deng Xiaoping and Liu Bocheng informed the Central Military Commission regarding the political, military and geographical conditions of the Tibetan borderlands.

In 1954, the Communists had maps and they agreed with the Nationalists on the definition of China's borders; nothing needed to be reprinted.

**The Foreign Secretary Writes on Tibet**

A few months after his return from China[6], RK Nehru, the Indian Foreign Secretary wrote a note on the latest developments in Tibet; he mentioned the maps: "Our border has been clearly defined in our maps, but in the latest Chinese map, many parts of this area are still shown as part of Tibet."

He added that similar statements were made by General Zhang Jingwu in presenting his report on the Tibetan administration to the State Council: "Many speeches made on this occasion by Chinese and Tibetan representatives which are well worth reading. The broad conclusion to be drawn from these statements is that while direct pressure may have been used in the earlier stages, a new and subtler policy is now being followed."

---

5   Also Central Committee's liaison to the Dalai Lama on his trip to China in 1954-55.

6   On April 24, 1955.

The Foreign Secretary further analyzed: "Under the Constitution, regional autonomy has been conceded, in principle, to Tibet. Other concessions have also been made to Tibetan national sentiment. Sikang[7] or Eastern Tibet, which has always been a province of China, will now form part of Tibet. A Preparatory Committee representing all interests has been set up in Lhasa to prepare for regional autonomy."

The fact that Sikang would be a part of Tibet was erroneous. It would be realized by Delhi a few months later when the troubles erupted in Kham.

But early 1954, RK Nehru believed that "the national sentiment should be respected and that greater unity should be established both within the Tibetan national group and between the Tibetan and Han peoples;" he, however, pointed out: "A closer examination shows that the new policy might have other effects."

**The 'Mongolian' Fringe**

India had started worrying for her Himalayan Belt. Could Delhi match China in the welfare of the border populations?

RK Nehru wrote: "High priority has also been given to development plans, e.g., the setting up of agricultural farms, schools, hospitals, industrial units etc. A large number of experts have been sent from Tibet to China. This should also help to bring about closer integration at a later stage."

It was however felt that India should not be alarmed by these measures: "The Chinese have every right to secure their southwestern flank by developing the country and bringing about a closer integration of this area with China. We should not jump to the conclusion as some of us still do that all this is a prelude to aggression, or some form of penetration of our border area."

He nevertheless observed that some facts could not be ignored: "Our border has been clearly defined in our maps, but in the latest Chinese map, many parts of this area are still shown as part of Tibet."

---

7   Xikang or Sikang.

RK Nehru cited a speech of Liu Shaoqi, the Chinese President while introducing the Constitution, "[he] made a somewhat ambiguous statement about the territorial boundaries of China. He said that there was a proposal to define these boundaries in the Constitution, but this was rejected for two reasons. (a) It is not the proper task of the Constitution to describe the country's territorial boundaries, (b) In a federal state, all the federal units must necessarily be listed but ours is not a state of this kind… it is a unitary, multi-national state."

The Foreign Secretary remarked: "Technically, the position stated by Liu Shao Chi[8] is perhaps correct, but this is a reminder that parts of our 'Mongolian Fringe'[9] are claimed by China although the boundaries have not yet been defined." The problem was that the Chinese constitution recognized "the right of individuals or groups to take steps to preserve or perform their customs and habits and to take other measures in areas where people of their own nationality live."

In other words, if Monpas or other tribes lived south of the McMahon Line, the ones on the north could 'take measures'.

RK Nehru continued with his analysis: "if the changes envisaged by the Chinese actually take place in Tibet, some urge might develop on the other side to bring our border areas within the ambit of their influence. Even if there is no such deliberate urgency, Tibetan developments must inevitably have some repercussions on our side."

In fact, the most serious Chinese claims on the Indian borders today originated from Tibetan claims; whether it was Tawang, Barahoti, Nilang or north of Panggong tso in Ladakh.

RK Nehru wrote: "The answer to this is our present policy which has a two-fold aspect;" he suggested: "On the one hand, we have an agreement with China which is based on the principle of good neighbour relations. We should see to it that both sides adhere strictly to the provisions of this agreement. This means constant alertness to prevent interference from the other side, but it also means that there should be no semblance of interference from our side." This was a strange logic.

---

8   Liu Shaoqi.

9   The Indian Himalaya.

## Administration of the Borders

RK Nehru mentioned the Tibetan *émigrés*[10] living in India; the policy of the Indian Government was clear: "We are fully entitled to give them asylum and to let them function freely so long as they do not indulge in anti-Chinese activities. We have a special relationship with Tibet which is recognized by the agreement. One of the *émigrés* has, however, asked for our advice about the disposal of funds belonging to the Dalai Lama." He noted: "I think we should refrain from giving him advice about this."

But the second aspect was more worrying, it was about extending India's administration on the borders "as rapidly as possible and to develop this area by measures designed to improve the status of the people. Because of easier communications, we enjoy an advantage over China in this matter. We can bring about rapid changes which will keep our people many steps ahead of the Tibetans. Closer intercourse between Tibet and India is to be welcomed as this will give the Tibetans an opportunity to see something of the progress which is taking place on our side."

RK Nehru mentioned the development of these areas: "In Sikkim, progress is taking place, but conditions in Ladakh and in North UP are less satisfactory. Some schemes are held up there, but we are taking steps to expedite them. The weak spots in the chain are, of course, Nepal and Bhutan where a dangerous situation might arise if no steps are taken to improve internal conditions while progress is taking place in other areas, including Tibet."

For decades the border areas would continue to be neglected.

## RK Nehru's Report after his Visit to Tibet

On July 5, 1955, in the report of his visit to Tibet, though RK Nehru did not directly mention the maps, he wrote about Tibetan expansionism. Recalling the Northern and Northwestern Border Committee of 1951, the Foreign Secretary said that it was then suggested that this northern frontier was an area of 'potential danger'; the Himmatsinghji Report had pointed out that China was "at last united, militant and expansive

---

10 They are now 'refugees'.

and inevitably, in course of time, she would create trouble on our side. Twice before, when she was strong in Tibet, she asserted her claim to our border areas and the present government is not likely to give up an objective which has so consistently been pursued by its weaker predecessors."

In this context, the issue of inaccurate maps was important, acknowledged the Foreign Secretary, who observed that the Tibetans have a strong sense of nationality "which involves some risks for the Chinese. The new Chinese policy, however, is to bring about an integration of the two peoples and to build up a strong pro-Chinese party in Tibet. Tibetan nationalism directed and controlled by the Chinese as part of a larger movement embracing both the peoples, might, therefore, create some risks for us, while averting the traditional risks for the Chinese."

It was left at that.

## Another Note from the Prime Minister

On May 6, 1956, Nehru in a note to the Foreign Secretary admitted: "in Chinese maps, quite a good part of Assam is shown as if it belonged to Tibet. Also, a bit of the UP, bordering on Tibet. Some two or three years ago, we drew the attention of the Chinese Government to this."

In 1956, the Prime Minister pointed out again: "These maps were old maps from Chiang Kai Shek's time and that they had no time to revise them. They are exactly like the old ones except for a note that they are reproductions of the old maps." He kept parroting what Zhou Enlai had told him.

Jawaharlal Nehru reminded the Foreign Secretary that India had decided not to raise the question of the frontier with China, simply "because, so far as we were concerned, there was no dispute. The Tibet frontier ran along the MacMahon[11] Line and we consider it a firm frontier."

He recalled that Zhou had said, "we can settle frontier questions in a friendly way later." However, Nehru now realized that China had never clearly accepted India's frontier: "All that they have said is that the old

---

11 McMahon.

maps are not reliable," while for India "the frontier is as given in our maps."

While Zhou had explicitly said that only the questions 'ripe for settlements' had been solved, Nehru wrote: "At the time of the agreement with China about Tibetan questions, it was taken for granted by us that all pending questions between India and China had been settled."

He admitted that China had never "admitted this clearly, though they did not deny it either."

Nehru then raised another issue, the Russian maps also reproduced the Chinese maps in regard to the Indian border "and show a part of India as being in Tibet." The Prime Minister noted that every year, there were petty incidents on the UP Tibet border[12]: "Some Chinese soldiers come across up to ten or fifteen miles or even more. There has been no actual conflict but there has been some friction. They have ultimately withdrawn."

Nehru admitted that it was the Tibetans who started the Barahoti dispute: "long before the Chinese came to Tibet, there used to be such incidents. The local Tibetan Governor would send a group of persons to a village across the border and even collect some taxes. It took weeks and months for any of our people to reach there. By that time, the Tibetans had retired."

This was the worrying aspect of the wrong maps, because the Chinese were bound to take up the Tibetan claims with far more muscle than the local *Dzongpons*.

What should India do in these circumstances, asked RK Nehru: "we have, of course, protested in Peking[13]. But, should we take any other action? That is, should we definitely raise the question of the frontier with the Chinese Government? The frontier is not clearly demarcated and some doubt may arise about some point along it. The question is not, however, about some doubtful point but rather about a much wider territory which the Chinese maps show."

---

12  For Barahoti, see Chapter 1.

13  Beijing.

The Prime Minister's conclusions were that it did not necessarily mean a hostile or aggressive intention against India, "but taken together with occasional petty raids and the maps which continue as they were, does produce a sense of disquiet."

Then Nehru mentioned that the then Indian Ambassador[14] in Beijing thought that India "should bide our time and not take any active step."

It was starting to prove to be a serious misjudgment.

**A Note from the Historical Division**

Following the remarks of the Prime Minister, the Ministry of External Affairs' Historical Division produced a note on the India-China Frontier.

Again it reiterated that India's northern frontier was a traditional one and the respect for territorial integrity was written in the preamble of the 1954 Agreement: "[it] assumed the existence of a well defined frontier and this was confirmed by the mention in one of the articles of six border passes Lipulekh, Darma, Kungri Bingri, Nitti, Mana and Shipki."

But for a long time, the Tibetan border in the western sector had been shown as 'undefined' on the Indian maps; it was only in September 1954 that the Prime Minister instructed that "the entire boundary should be shown on maps as a continuous line and no reference should be made to undemarcated areas."

Incidentally, it was admitted that the Bhutan-Tibet frontier had not yet been surveyed and an officer[15] would soon be sent to carry out an on-the-spot survey and ascertain the views of the Bhutanese.

The note of the Historical Division said that on the other hand, China "has been bringing out maps of varying scales showing a frontier which cuts well into our territory. The most prominent of these are the maps of scale 1:4.2 million published in 1953, a map of the administrative division of China of scale 1:4 million early in April 1955 and a wall map of scale 1:8 million brought out early in 1956."

---

14  KM Panikkar.

15  TS Murty and one Maj Sinha.

The Historical Division examined the Chinese alignment in detail from Karakoram pass to Nepal: "In Ladakh, all Chinese maps show considerable Indian territory in China." It listed the main discrepancies.

While in Punjab and Himachal Pradesh, the boundary shown in Chinese maps corresponded to the Indian line, in Uttar Pradesh, Nilang and Jadhang areas were included in Tibet, while for the Sikkim-Tibet border: "Chinese maps seem to align this frontier correctly, though they are on too small a scale for us to be sure. But all Chinese maps show Sikkim and Bhutan outside India's international boundaries."

The Chinese maps showed the Bhutan Northern boundary correctly, but in the eastern region, near Tawang 'a New Map of Tibet' (March 1951) showed it as running north to south in an almost straight line, transferring some 1,800 sq. miles of Bhutanese territory to Tibet … and China. Other Chinese maps showed this frontier as a loop which annexed to Tibet a smaller area of about 1,000 sq. miles. As for NEFA, all Chinese maps showed the Kameng, Subansiri, Siang and Lohit divisions as part of China.

The Historical Division noted: "In three areas these claims to territory are not on maps alone. We have had reports that the Chinese are using the route from Western Tibet to Sinkiang that runs through Aksai Chin. A Nullah[16] runs through Demchok village and the local inhabitants regard it as the boundary between Tibet and Ladakh."

It further asserted: "The Kashmir Government is collecting revenue only from Nodozen to northern Damchok[17] and Indian checkpost personnel at Mayul and Damchok have confined their activities till now to this Northern half of the village. An Indian outpost was stationed on the Northern side in 1954 but was withdrawn in 1955. Chinese patrols from Tashigong[18] have visited southern Demchok over half a dozen times during the last three years."

---

16 Or nallah (in Punjabi) is an 'arm of the sea', stream, or watercourse, a steep narrow valley.

17 Demchok.

18 Or Tashigang.

The note observed that during the negotiations for the Tibet Agreement in Beijing "both sides claimed the whole village but left the matter to verification on the ground. In the Nilang-Jadhang area, no agreement had ever been reached between Tibet and India on the border."

It was pointed out that India claimed the Sutlej-Jadhang watershed as the frontier and in 1954 it was decided to establish Jadhang as a base checkpost with Pulamsumda further north as an advance post in the summer, while Nilang would serve as a checkpost for registration of traders."

It was admitted that these checkposts had not "adequately been established and on April 28, 1956, a party of twelve Chinese soldiers was seen about half a mile from Nilang village."

The note also mentioned some dormant claims like the Drokpo Karpo pastures in Ladakh, and of course Barahoti.

Interestingly, the Nepal-Tibet boundary was also included in the report. Regarding the Sikkim-China frontier, it was felt that China may claim in the future areas "which had been occupied by Tibet in 1886, and Giaogong, which lies North of the main Himalayan range, the traditional frontier in this region."

It was noted that in the *Russian Atlas Mira* (1954) the delineation of India's frontier was almost the same as on the Chinese maps, but unlike in the Chinese maps, Sikkim and Bhutan were shown within India's international boundary. In the NEFA, the Kameng, Siang and Subansiri Frontier Divisions (FD) and most of the Lohit FD were shown as part of China: "The Russian map does not follow the latest Chinese maps which include the whole of the Lohit Frontier Division in China. But the discrepancies between Russian and Chinese maps are minor and much significance need not be attached to them."

It is surprising that despite this knowledge of the 'discrepancies', Delhi decided to not react.

## Some Suggestions

The Historical Division suggested that because the maps showing India's boundary correctly had only been published three years earlier, "the Russian failure to demarcate the boundary as aligned by us is due to ignorance. But this argument cannot hold for the northeastern frontier which was defined by mutual consent as long ago as 1914 and has been shown in our maps during the last twenty years."

The Division made some suggestions:

(i) Maps showing India's frontier alignment be brought out as soon as possible, after taking a decision on the Kailash range, without waiting for the aerial survey of NEFA which is likely to take some time. We should have our officers on the Bhutan frontier by August.

(ii) Checkposts be established wherever possible and our administration pushed up to the frontier. Where checkposts are not possible, as in Aksai Chin, open and regular expeditions may be the answer. In cases of trans-border pastoral rights, India may adopt the British practice of explicitly informing Tibetan graziers that they are being permitted to enjoy their rights on what is clearly our territory, and they should seek this permission formally every year from our check posts.

Some of these recommendations would slowly be implemented.

## The Chinese Maps of the Border not to be Discussed

A few days earlier, when the issue of the Chinese maps of India's northern borders was to be discussed in the Parliament, Nehru did not want to raise the issue publically.

In a note written on September 6, 1956, he wrote: "I have only now seen these papers. I agree with the suggestion made in the office memorandum sent by the Ministry of External Affairs to the effect that it would not be desirable for this question to be raised in the Lok Sabha at the present stage. We have informally mentioned this matter to the Chinese Government previously and we have at the same time made it perfectly clear that, so far as we are concerned, there is no boundary question. We were assured then by the Chinese Government that the maps were old ones.[19] It is possible that we may raise this question in some other form in the near future."

He instructed the Lok Sabha Speaker: "I think that if this question is raised in our Parliament at this stage, this might prove embarrassing from the point of view of the negotiations between Burma and China. Also, it might rather come in the way of our taking this matter up more formally later with the Chinese Government."

He suggested to the Speaker that the question should not be admitted at this stage.

## The Visit of Bakula in Tibet

As we shall see in another chapter, DD Khosla, an Under Secretary to the Government of J&K, accompanied Kushok Bakula Rinpoche till Phari Dzong in Tibet in 1956. During his few days stay on the plateau, Khosla could gather a good amount of information. The most interesting was about the maps, he wrote: "the Chinese Government has secretly circulated a new map of Tibet among their official organizations and the pro-Chinese Institutions – in which they have shown the whole of Aksai Chin[20] (Soda Plains) hump as a part of Tibet. Kashmir's northern border as illustrated in this map shows some daring incursions into our Karakoram area of northern Ladakh and Baltistan. They have tried to bring out that the river Indus serves the purpose of delineating the frontiers of Tibet and Ladakh".

The interesting outcome of Khosla's report was that the bureaucrats in Delhi started realizing that something was wrong: parts of Kashmir were shown as a part of Tibet in new Chinese maps: "The Historical Division could not produce this map, the Indian Embassy in Peking was asked to secure a copy."

He further stated: "The most important point which I would humbly but emphatically stress is that we should take up the question of the 'New map of Tibet' referred to by me with the Government of India. According to history, Chinese have been creating false records and after

---

19 See SWJN (Second Series), Vol. 27, pp. 17, 19-20, 81-82; see also Vol. 33, pp. 475-479.

20 Aksai Chin in Ladakh, already occupied by China.

the lapse of sufficient time using it for their own advantage as if that were the correct record".

He then cited an example to corroborate his views: "Relations between China and Tibet have not been very cordial in the past. When the 13th Dalai Lama was enthroned, the Chinese Amban in Lhasa witnessed the ceremony as a spectator like the Nepalese representative and other guests. The Amban, however, sent a false report to his Government that he placed the Dalai Lama on the Throne and declared him as the God King of Tibet. After 30 or 40 years later this report of the Amban, which was totally false, was used by the Chinese to establish suzerainty over Tibet. I, therefore, apprehend that if we keep quiet, the Chinese might use this map against us after some time, specially when the boundary of Tibet and Ladakh has not been specifically defined."

On August 14, 1956, AB Bhadkamkar, the First Secretary of the Indian Embassy in China answered the Ministry about the wrong maps of the boundary distributed by China: "it is understood that there is nothing secret about this map as all Chinese maps seem to show this part of our border as part of Tibet. I understand, several copies of official Chinese maps were supplied to the Ministry last year by the Embassy. Since then, there have been only further reprints of maps for various purposes: some showing the political divisions, others the physical topography and others basic communications. If you need additional copies of these maps, we shall be glad to supply these on request."

Though the maps wrongly depicted the Indian boundary, the Indian embassy did not see it amiss; it even justified the Chinese claims: "Most of these maps are very small scale maps and it is difficult to say whether they are accurately drawn. The majority of the maps published so far are primarily meant for use in the middle schools. If better maps corresponding to our own 1":40 mile scale are published, these have certainly not been put on sale and are not available."

Bhadkamkar further admitted: "In fact, it is not only the Chinese maps which contain errors concerning our boundaries, but you might find it interesting to get hold of some Soviet Union printed maps also and it is possible that you might observe the same defects."

He then cited the example of a Russian documentary showing the visit of Bulganin and Khrushchev to India in 1955: "a map appears at one stage showing the route of the journeys undertaken by the visitors. Although we were able to have only a fleeting glimpse and the map could lay no claim to being an official scale map, the same defect was noticeable." The first secretary added: "This is merely by way of information."

'By way of information' meant that no action was required.

## Everything Goes on as Usual

A year later[21], the new Foreign Secretary Subimal Dutt answered GL Mehta, India's Ambassador in Washington, who had sent an article on 'China's-Expansionist Aims' published in the *Foreign Report* of July 18.

Dutt explained: "We are not at all concerned about the Sino-Indian border. China has for long been publishing maps showing parts of India, particularly a part of Kashmir and the whole North East Frontier Agency, within her borders. We have occasionally registered our protests. The reply given was that these maps were merely based on old maps. Our attitude has chiefly been that our frontier is traditional, well known and beyond dispute, whatever the Chinese maps may show. In accordance with this attitude, we have decided to show India's northern frontier on our maps as a defined and demarcated boundary."

The situation was fast deteriorating, but the Panikkar doctrine still prevailed in the corridors of South Block.

Subimal Dutt had to admit: "There have been occasions when a small number of Chinese troops have crossed into India. One of the more important occasions was at Bara Hoti in Uttar Pradesh a few years ago. The Chinese also came into Shipki La in Himachal Pradesh and into the Spiti valley in Punjab in 1956. The Chinese troops, however, withdrew from all these places. The two governments have agreed to settle these relatively minor disputes amicably by a joint survey and inspection on the spot."

---

21  September 21, 1957.

It has to be pointed out that two weeks later, the Aksai Chin road cutting across the Indian territory was officially opened.

On October 6, 1957, a Chinese newspaper *Kuang-ming Jih-pao* reported: "The Sinkiang-Tibet – the highest highway in the world – has been completed. During the past few days, a number of trucks running on the highway on a trial basis have arrived in Ko-ta-k'e[22] in Tibet from Yehch'eng[23] in Sinkiang. The Sinkiang-Tibet Highway... is 1179 km long, of which 915 km are more than 4,000 meters above sea level; 130 km of it over 5,000 meters above sea level, with the highest point being 5,500 meters.

Thirty ("liberation" model and Chissu 150) heavy-duty trucks, fully loaded with road builders, maintenance equipment and fuels, running on the highway on a trial basis, headed for Ko-ta-k'e from Yehch'eng. In addition, two trucks fully loaded with Hami melons, apples and pomegranates, all native products of Sinkiang, headed in the same direction. These fruits were gifts brought specially by the road builders of Sinkiang for the people of various nationalities."[24]

The circle was closed. It took nearly two more years for the news to be made public in India. In August 1959, Nehru dropped the bombshell in Parliament: what the Chinese called the 'Tibet-Sinkiang highway' was built through Indian territory.

To come back to Dutt's letter to the Ambassador in Washington, he wrote: "There is no evidence to support the charge that Chinese authorities have been subverting the ethnic minorities in Himachal Pradesh. There is a Mongoloid population of Buddhist faith on the border, but though they regard the Dalai Lama as their spiritual head, there is little contact with Tibet. One of our officers, who visited this area in May 1957, found no traces of Chinese subversion."

But it was too late to remedy; China had already built a road.

---

22 Gartok.

23 Yecheng.

24 Ling Nai-Min, *Tibetan Source book* (Hong Kong: Union Research Institute, 1964), p. 263.

# 05

# No Escort Anymore: the Earlier the Better

As mentioned in the previous volumes, Gyantse was the Headquarters of an Indian Trade Agency established under the 1904 treaty between the governments of Tibet and India. In 1950, a note from the Ministry of External provided details about the 'living conditions in Tibet for the officers to be posted on the plateau': "Accommodation of officers is in the Agency buildings which are built something like a military outpost," said the note.[1]

Indian Trade Agency in Yatung

---

1 *Living Conditions at Posts in Tibet, Gyantse & Lhasa,* To All Missions and Posts Abroad, Ministry of External Affairs; No. F. 7(4)Per/52, April 14, 1952. Available at the National Archives of India.

The 'agency' was the headquarters of the Indian Trade Agent and the Officer Commanding (OC) the military escort.

The accommodation of the escort was thus described: "Other rooms built around three sides of a square are occupied by Officers of the Trade Agent's Escort and the Civil Surgeon when in residence at Gyantse. The accommodation is not suitable for families."

The officer and troops, all messed together, using the same entertainment rooms: "There is usually a Major or Captain commanding the Escort, a Lieutenant as second-in-command, and a Captain in charge of the Indian Military Hospital." The note added: "The Escort is provided by the Indian Army and is purely ceremonial; it is not a garrison."

Following the 1954 Agreement and after more than 50 years of existence, the escort had to wind up. It was more a symbolic departure, India's presence in Tibet had to go; the Tibetans were not the masters anymore in their country.

Once Delhi had agreed that Tibet was part of China, other consequences were ineluctable. Along with the escort, another issue was the surrender of the wireless/telegraph (W/T) sets at the three agencies in Tibet "as the Chinese have adequate telegraph or W/T arrangements of their own."

A note from the ITA added: "We could not have pressed for the retention of our W/T sets without giving reciprocal rights to their agencies in India which was not considered desirable."

Once again, the government did not 'think' before 'getting rid of the colonial leftovers'.

## What was the Role of the Escort?

Though his role was rather informal, the OC sent regular reports to Delhi, while the ITA had a more formal function, recognized by the Tibetan government; he was regulating the trade between India and the Land of Snows. On February 2, 1952 the Indian Trade Agent in Gyantse wrote to the Political Officer in Sikkim: "I have seen today a secret correspondence from Army Headquarters, M.I.[2] Directorate,

---

2   Military Intelligence.

addressed directly to Officer Commanding, Escorts, Gyantse, in which the latter has been asked to submit to the former directly fortnightly reports containing intelligence about the Chinese troops in Tibet."

The ITA bitterly complained that a copy of the Army officer in charge of the Escort's report had not been sent to the Political Officer or even the Ministry of External Affairs in Delhi.

It was a typical case of *lèse-majesté*, as South Block was supposed to run the show in Tibet and even defence matters were supposed to go through Gangtok, the *plaque tournante* of the foreign affairs in the Himalaya.

The ITA continued: "As the Indian Army Escorts in Tibet are primarily a political affair, it is desirable that such reports are asked with the knowledge of the Political Department who should also be provided with copies of such reports."

Maj SM Krishnatry, the ITA, was probably right, though he himself came from an Army background and he had served as OC of the Escort for a few years after 1947; he told Gangtok: "I have informally advised the Officer Commanding, Escorts to do so and let the Army Headquarters know of the circumstances which render such a course advisable."

This incident demonstrates the relations between the civil and military authorities in Tibet and considering the promiscuity in which the two were living in the Fort of Gyantse, it was logical, one could say.

## What was the Escort doing in Gyantse and Yatung?

A series of dispatches sent through the Diplomatic Bag by the Officer Commanding the escort in 1952, gives an idea of its usefulness for India.

We shall quote from the fortnightly report for April 1952, addressed to Army Headquarters, General Staff Branch in Delhi.

Maj SL Chibber sent his report for the period ending April 5, 1952 in duplicate.[3] We quote:

---

3 *Fortnightly Report from Officer Commanding Gyantse Tibet*; Department Sikkim

1. **Disposition of Chinese Troops in Gyantse Area.**

    ➢ Sixty Chinese (60) soldiers left Gyantse on March 29, 1952 for Phari and after a stay of one or two days at Tuna left for Phari on 5th [April] morning.

    ➢ One hundred (100) Chinese soldiers already reported at Tuna left for Phari on April 3, 1952.

    ➢ No Chinese are reported to be on the way between Gyantse & Phari.

    ➢ There is no news about the activities of Chinese at Phari.

    ➢ There is no change in the garrison strength of Chinese in Gyantse area.

2. **Behaviour with Locals.** No change in the behavior of Chinese with locals as already reported.

3. **General**.

    (a) The Chinese are very busy these days in digging land for cultivation. According to locals even Chinese officers go and also work.

    (b) According to some of the locals one of the Chinese soldiers committed suicide – the cause is said to be continued ill health and according to some, charges & accusations alleged to have been made against him during recent anti-corruption drive.

    (c) It is also reported that Chinese Officers still hold their meetings – presume that these meetings are in continuation of anti-corruption drive

4. **Communications.** No Change.

5. **Economic.**

    (a) There has been no case of theft or robbery or dacoity during the period under review.

---

Agency, Branch Political, 1952; Ref: File No.rogs., Nos. 4(10)-P, 1952 (Secret). Available at the National Archives of India.

(b) It is reported that Tibetan Traders have approached the Chinese in Lhasa for sale of wool to them. Understand some of the traders have been called to Calcutta to discuss with Chinese Consul there.

(c) Chinese obtained their digging tools (picks, shovels) from India through Tibetan Traders.

(d) The prices of essential goods are rising day by day and economic conditions of the poor & the middle-class people continue to be bad.

There were three copies marked for the ITA in Gyantse: "For information and for favour of sending two copies to Political Officer after adding any remarks you may wish to add and to Ministry of External Affairs." Chibber had learnt his lesson; he himself would soon be promoted Trade Agent.

## The Case of Captain Macfarlane

It is worth mentioning another incident showing how the ITA, operating under the Ministry of External had been jealously preserving its leading role in Tibet.[4]

On September 4, 1953, the ITA sent a telegram to the PO and Delhi; the message was repeated to the brigade headquarters: "Captain Macfarlane Commanding escorts left early this morning to camp at about 25 miles beyond Yungla pass. I was neither consulted nor informed of this move. A few days ago when he casually asked for information about the route to Yamdrok Tso[5] I had told him we could NOT go beyond the trade Mart without Kashag's *Lamyik*[6] or Tibetan Trade Agent's permission. None, NOT even Captain Gupta knew of this move except his Subedar. Am informing you as I do NOT wish to be held responsible for any consequences or repercussions this may have

---

4 *Complaint of the Trade Agent Gyantse, that Capt Macfarlane, Commanding the Indian Military Escorts went to camp beyond Gyantse without his permission.* Department: External Affairs; Branch: F.E.F, 1953, File No. Progs., Nos. 13915(1201)-NEF, 1953. Available at the National Archives of India.

5 A lake on the way to Lhasa

6 Travel Permit.

under the present circumstances. Details of his plans are NOT known except that he is expected to return tomorrow evening. Presumably, your permission was obtained?"

It is the first time Nehru heard of the OC of the escort.

The same day, in a note to the Foreign Secretary, he wrote: "Who is Captain MacFarlane? Presumably, he commands our escorts. If he is an Englishman, his choice was unfortunate for this purpose."

When he got to know that the officer was Anglo-Indian, he was still unhappy with the 'colonial' connotation of his name.

On September 9, 1953, Brig AS Pathania, Director of Military Intelligence observed: "As the reasons of Capt Macfarlane's move outside the limits of the Trade mart are not known, action has been taken to call for his explanation. Instruction has also been issued to OC Escorts that in future he will not move outside the limits of the Trade Mart without consulting the Trade Agent."

The same day, HC Sarin of the Ministry of Defence said that Capt Macfarlane's explanation was called for: "When it is received, it will be examined what further action is necessary against him."

The ministry clarified the position of OC in Gyanste: "Captain Macfarlane is an Anglo-Indian with Indian domicile. ...my recollection is that Mr. [TN] Kaul told me that the decision in his Ministry was that in future persons with foreign sounding names should not be posted. I told him that we would bear this in mind. ...When the report from PO Sikkim is received by them, we would like to see it."

MacFarlane would remain in Tibet till the fateful floods in July 1954. He was to be relieved by Maj Nagal who perished in the disaster.

**The Importance of the Escort**

We have discussed the importance of the Indian military escort in the two first volumes of this study. Under the 1954 Agreement, it was decided to withdrawal the escort from Gyantse and Yatung.

On November 1953, a note, entitled "Main Points Which May Arise during Discussions at the Peking Conference", was prepared for the negotiations for the Tibet Agreement; it mentioned the escort: "We have already agreed to withdraw them, and the only matter for discussion is the phasing of the withdrawal. This is being worked out by the Political Officer in consultation with Defence Ministry. The only important point to be borne in mind is that the withdrawal should not take place all at once but in gradual stages. The Political Officer is also examining the question of what barracks to retain and which to hand over."[7]

The issue would not be discussed; the matter was closed from the start.

The view in Delhi was that it was part of India's colonial 'heritage'; India could not get rid of it fast enough.

**The Beginning of the Withdrawal**

The beginning of the withdrawal of the escort took place discreetly.

On October 6, 1953, the PO cabled Delhi about the 'Escorts in Tibet': "As the Trade Agent pointed out a good many matters will have to be settled with the Chinese and arrangements made for the future before a complete withdrawal of our escorts can be effected. This will necessarily take time. Our prestige in Tibet has received a complete jolt recently and it will help NO end if the Chinese can be persuaded to let the Mahrattas[8] relieve the Jats for the time being."

The ITA in Gyantse made some suggestions: "We need NOT send a 3rd Mahratta Platoon from India. Of the 2 Mahratta Platoons at Yatung one might relieve the 2 Jat Platoons at Gyantse and the other remains at Yatung in place of the Jat Platoon there. We will thus be withdrawing 3 Jat Platoons and in their place keeping only 2 Platoons in Tibet till their final withdrawal. I hope very much that this can be brought about."

His suggestion was to withdraw the Jat Platoon from Yatung as a first step, leaving the 2 Mahratta Platoons in Gyantse: "If the Chinese agree to one of these 2 Platoons moving up to Gyantse, the Jat Platoons at Gyantse can also come back."

---

7  All other documents in this chapter, except specifically mentioned, are from the Nehru Papers (JN Collection) held at the Nehru Memorial Museum and Library in Delhi. The 'papers' are not indexed.

8  Also spelt Maratha Regiment or the Marathas.

In the contingency that the Chinese disagree, the 2 Mahratta platoons would stay at Yatung: "The return of the Mahratta Platoons at this juncture will be regarded as a retreat, NOT only in Tibet, but also in these border states, and should be avoided if possible."

The 'border states' meant Sikkim and Bhutan.

In other word, Krishnatry was suggesting an honourable retreat.

On October 30, 1953, the ITA mentioned to the Political Officer in Sikkim the 'move of escorts': "I hear Jat Platoon from Yatung has since been withdrawn. Chinese reactions if any may be ascertained if possible. The prospects of our coming talks with China should have created favourable climate to ask them now to let us complete the escort relief in Gyantse also by Mahrattas. As pointed out by you this will help us NO end. The Chinese may be expected to agree to this in the present circumstances. If so earlier this is done the better without waiting for final decisions."

The Escort was seen by Delhi and Beijing as the symbol of imperialism; it had to be discontinued at the earliest.

**The Tibet Agreement**

Eventually, during the four-month negotiations in Beijing, it was agreed: "The Government of India will be pleased to withdraw completely within six (6) months from the date of exchange of the present notes the military escorts now stationed at Yatung and Gyantse in the Tibet region of China. The Government of China will render facilities and assistance in such withdrawal."

It was to follow the handing over "at a reasonable price of the postal, telegraph, and public telephone services together with their equipment and the 12 rest houses of the Government of India in the Tibet region of China."

India did not get anything in return.

On May 12, 1954, the Prime Minister, in a note to the Foreign Secretary wrote: "So far as the withdrawal of escorts is concerned, I do not know what negotiations are necessary. The sooner they are withdrawn, the

## No Escort Anymore: the Earlier the Better

better. We should remind Defence[9] about it so that they can make arrangements accordingly."

Two days earlier, the Political Officer in Sikkim was informed by Delhi that a senior army officer had arrived in Gangtok from Siliguri "en route to Gyantse to hold a board of survey preliminary to the withdrawal of Escorts. Please ask [AK] Sen in Lhasa to obtain clearance for his visit to Gyantse and request officer not to proceed until clearance is obtained."

The cable justified the move: "The things that we have agreed to give up, e.g., military escorts stationed at Gyantse and Yatung, posts, telegraphs and public telephone installations and the 12 rest houses had already been agreed, according to 1908 Trade Regulations, to be given up by the British to the Tibetans as soon as the latter was ready to take them over and make their own arrangements."

But there was a big difference with the past; the British were ready to hand over these assets to the Tibetan government, not to a 'foreign' power.

The same note rightly said: "The success of the present Agreement depends mainly on the spirit in which its provisions are implemented on both sides. The region of Tibet offers the prospect of improvement of relations with China as well as the danger of their deterioration. We have, therefore, to be friendly as well as firm, helpful as well as cautious in the implementation of the Agreement."

Unfortunately, as we shall see, the winding-up would not be smooth.

The note envisaged this: "It is, however, likely that the Chinese may raise or create border problems if we are slow in advancing our administration right up to our frontiers, especially in the disputed areas which are fortunately not many."

It did happen, and India would not be ready.

On May 20, the Ministry clarified that regarding the negotiations for handing over India's assets, only matters pertaining to the escort, the P&T and the rest houses had been discussed in Beijing: "We suggest that Chinese discuss matters relating to lands and Agency's compounds

---

9 Ministry of Defence.

in Yatung and Gyantse with our Trade Agents in Tibet or with us in New Delhi."

This would take one more year.

## The Consequences of the Withdrawal

On July 8, 1954, the ITA in Gyantse wrote to the PO about the need of guards for the Gyantse treasury: "As the gradual reduction of the strength of escort here has already begun, early order on the subject is requested. It is quite likely that in course of a few weeks the escort will be so small that according to military regulations it will not be possible for an escort to guard our treasury."

The next day, the Ministry cabled Gangtok, suggesting the withdrawal of escorts which would reduce "need for so much cash and possibly makes it unnecessary to keep treasury at Gyantse."

On July 22, the Indian Consulate in Lhasa brought up the issue of the Courier Service: "As pointed out by Trade Agent Gyantse, one pack animal will have to be taken by the couriers, as their journey will be delayed if they have to depend on hired transport. The exchange of bags at Pedi[10] will not be possible during the winter months, only as in the summer the ferry to take the animal across the river Tsangpo is suspended for five months."

It was further explained that during this period the courier from Lhasa would not be able to cross the river with the animal without risk: "We suggest that courier from Gyantse should come to Singma[11] to exchange bag with the Lhasa courier in the summer months."

The situation would soon change with the completion of the motor road.

## The End of the Escort

On December 9, 1954, Delhi informed the Consul General "As Gyantse installations completely destroyed by July floods no telegraph

---

10 Peldi or Baidi, 29°07'34" N 90°26'19" E

11 On the road to Shigatse, 29° 9'32.84" N 90°30'13.34"E.

office functioning there. Lines between Gyantse and Phari Zong[12] were also severely damaged by floods and have suffered considerably from pilferage by locals."

One of the consequences of the withdrawal of the escort was the poor maintenance of the telegraph lines by local Tibetans: "As Gyantse telegraph office is now dead it will be quite impossible to re-establish working between Pharizong and Gyantse. P&T Department state that not only new stores worth Rs. 20,000 would be required but repairs etc. may take up to 90 days. This will delay handing-over inordinately and we do not approve of it. …Chinese had agreed to repair installations at Gyantse. You might bring all this to the notice of the Foreign Office Assistant."

BK Kapur, the PO in Sikkim wrote to the Consulate in Lhasa on December 26, 1954: "As you are aware damage and pilferage has occurred only recently since the withdrawal of our escorts. We are quite prepared however to give Chinese reasonable assistance in putting lines in working order. We could provide all the material needed for repairs and also any technical assistance that they might require. We feel however that the execution of the work should be left to the Chinese. We would hand over all the material for repairs at Yatung though we would prefer to do so at Gangtok."

The Escort had been useful all these years for protecting India's assets in Tibet. Its discreet withdrawal marked the end of an era.

---

12 Sometimes written, Pharizong.

## 06

# Winding-up is Not Easy

**Background**

The outcome of the 1954 Agreement was the winding-up of the facilities owned by India in Tibet. It is one of the saddest chapters of the history of the relations between India and Tibet, primarily because India did not get anything in return, not even an agreed border.

After long and tortuous negotiations, India finally agreed to give away her postal and telegraph facilities as well as her *dak bungalows*[1] on the plateau; that was disappointing, to say the least.

**Postal and Telegraph Facilities**

On April 29, 1954, just after the Tibet Agreement was inked, N. Raghavan, the Indian Ambassador to China and Zhang Hanfu the Minister of Foreign Affairs exchanged Notes to supplement the main agreement.

One of the issues agreed upon was the Postal and Telegraph facilities run by India between India and Lhasa, via Sikkim and Chumbi Valley.

Point 2 of the Notes said: "The Government of India will be pleased to hand over to the Government of China at a reasonable price the postal, telegraph and public telephone services together with their equipment operated by the Government of India in the Tibet region of China. The concrete measures in this regard will be decided upon through further

---

1 Rest houses, originally for the postal services (*dak* in Hindi).

negotiations between the Indian Embassy in China and the Foreign Ministry of China, which shall start immediately after the exchange of the present notes."[2]

In the following pages, we shall look at the long tortuous negotiations to arrive at an agreement to finally wind-up the Indian postal and telegraph facilities.

Who could have imagined that it would take so long?

The next point mentioned in the Notes was the Indian Rest Houses in Tibet: "The Government of India will be pleased to hand over to the Government of China at a reasonable price the twelve (12) rest houses of the Government of India in the Tibet region of China. The concrete measures in this regard will be decided upon through further negotiations between the Indian Embassy in China and the Foreign Ministry of China, which shall start immediately after the exchange of the present notes. The Government of China agrees that they shall continue as rest houses."

On paper, this looked easy; it would be rather painful.

**The Negotiations Start**

It is only on July 1, 1954, three months after the signature of the above agreement that the correspondence for the surrender of the Indian facilities, started. The Indian embassy in Beijing sent a cable to TN Kaul, who had negotiated the accord. Though he had fallen into a honey trap as we have seen in Volume II, on return to the Indian capital, Kaul was given, as Joint Secretary, the charge of China and Tibetan affairs in the Ministry of External Affairs.

The Kashmiri Pandit was informed that an Indian Government official, Ram Chundur Goburdhun[3], had met a Chinese official called Ho, a

---

2   All documents in this chapter, except specifically mentioned, are from the Nehru Papers (JN Collection) held at the Nehru Memorial Museum and Library in Delhi. The 'papers' are not indexed.

3   Ram Chundur Goburdhun was an Indian diplomat. He attended Royal College Port-Louis and the *Institut français du Royaume-Uni* and studied law at the University of Lille II in France. As a barrister, he became a member of the Middle Temple in London; later he joined the Indian Foreign Service. From January to

couple of days earlier. Ho gave him a short questionnaire regarding the telegraph system and the Indian installations in Tibet. Beijing was waking up to the fact that they had to take-over the facilities.

Answers to some of these questions were suggested by the embassy to South Block, but the Chinese had decided to send a representative "to take over only after getting full inventories and clarifications."

The Chinese had apparently no clue of what had been offered to them; they told the Indian embassy that they "would appreciate [the] Indian personnel continuing in their service for about two to three months. They have made various suggestions regarding continuing both postal and telegraph service without interruption."

Two days later, a message to the Consulate in Lhasa mentioned a first incident which had just taken place. A Tibetan mail runner had been attacked at Tsepaning, some six miles from Chusul[4] on the way to Lhasa: "He was held firmly by the neck and deprived of the mail bag carried by him. The attackers were definitely identified to be Tibetans."

After the mail runner had filed a complaint with the postmaster in Lhasa, enquiries were started by the Dzongpon of Chusul. However, the investigations in the vicinity of the place where the attack took place, were unsuccessful. Later, the Consulate was informed, who took immediate action: "Matter has been reported to the Foreign Bureau for immediate action," wrote PN Menon, the Indian Consul General, in one of his reports.

The situation had begun to deteriorate for those working in Tibet for the Indian government.

---

February 1953 he was Deputy Secretary at the Ministry of Foreign Affairs in New Delhi; from 1953 to 1955 he served in the Indian Legation Council in Beijing and from 1955 to 1958 in the Legation Council in Paris. From 1967 to 1969, he was Ambassador to Ankara (Turkey); from 1970 to 1985 he became legal advisor to the Supreme Court in New Delhi.

4   Chusul or Chushul was a village located 48 kilometres southwest of Lhasa. It lies on a river which soon joins the Yarlung Tsangpo river. Today, the Lhasa Gonggar Airport lies to the southeast of the town.

## Chinese Proposal

On July 12, Delhi cabled its embassy in Beijing, answering the month-old query; the Chinese had communicated the way they wanted to conduct the postal transactions in Tibet: "Chinese will use their own stamps for letters and telegraphs after taking over. Our proposal for the continuance of the existing rates for one year applies only to terminal traffic between India and Tibet, while international traffic will be governed by international regulations in force. Existing rates will apply not only to existing stations but also new ones in Tibet region."

Further, there would be only two types of telegrams, 'Express' and 'Ordinary'. The language for Morse will be English and the telegraph line, up to the Indian border frontier[5] would be maintained by India; while in Tibet, it would be looked after by China.

On August 3, the Ambassador to China was informed by the Ministry that "for administrative and other reasons, we feel that our permanent India-based postal staff should not be asked to serve under Chinese in Tibet after the handing over of P&T installations."

It was also suggested that locally employed extra-departmental and part-time staff, as well as the permanent and temporary staff of Tibetan origin, should be transferred and serve thereafter the Chinese authorities (provided this was agreeable to China and the staff).

The cable further suggested to fix the handing-over date of these installations in such a way "as to allow the new Chinese staff who would take over from our permanent staff sufficient time to get acquainted with the procedure of working of the existing communication system."

Yatung was proposed to be the terminal for the exchange of Indo - Tibetan mail.

## A Question in the Parliament

A month later, BK Kapur[6] camping in Saugang, near Gyantse, had to provide an answer to an interesting question about the implementation

---

5  Jelep-La pass.
6  BK Kapur (b.1910), Political Officer posted in Sikkim from March 1952 to March 1955.

of the 1954 Agreement, filed in the Lok Sabha. The answer was that the Chinese Government "have taken no substantial steps to implement the agreement after its ratification by both governments, but past practices in matters of trade and pilgrimage continue. It appears the contents of the agreement have not yet been fully explained to local Chinese and Tibetan officials though implications of the agreement have been explained from time to time by the former to the latter."

As a consequence, wrote the PO, the "intercourse between our officials on the one side and Chinese [and] Tibetan officials on the other in regard to trade matters is easier now than it used to be in the past."

This was not to last.

**An Encounter in Yatung**

On October 23, the ITA in Yatung informed Delhi that he had met Fu[7], the Officer-in-Charge of the newly established Foreign Bureau at Yatung. Fu wanted to discuss the occupation of the *dak bungalows* by the Chinese personnel. He told Chibber that he had no information from the central authorities "regarding the formal establishment of Indian Trade Agency at Yatung", though this was part of the April 29 Agreement.

The ITA requested Delhi to inform the Chinese authorities about "Article I (2) of the recent Sino-Indian Agreement and also my appointment as Trade Agent."[8]

---

7   Fu Sheng and Dyinka Dorje Gyaltsen were the top negotiators for the Chinese side. The person who assisted in the commercial negotiations and then later was appointed head of the group supervising all trade through Yatung was Guo Shulin.

    Tan Shuiyuan was appointed head of the Yatung Post & Communications Bureau while Li Jishan and a Tibetan Norjye, another fourth ranked official, were in charge of the Yatung Courier Post Administration.

8   Article I (2) says: "The Government of China agrees that the Government of India may establish Trade Agencies at Yatung, Gyantse and Gartok. The Trade Agencies of both parties shall be accorded the same status and same treatment. The Trade Agents of both Parties shall enjoy freedom from arrest while exercising their functions, and shall enjoy in respect of themselves, their wives and children who are dependent on them for livelihood freedom for search."

It has to be pointed out that the Chinese appointed a representative very late. A group of officials left Lhasa on horseback for Yatung in September 1954 only. It took them 12 days to reach their destination. On October 1, 1954, the Yatung Foreign Affairs Office was officially inaugurated by Fu Sheng, as its head. He came from a military background and spoke some English. Fu's Deputy Office Head was an old Tibetan named Dyinka Dorje Gyaltsen. He had stayed in India for a time and briefly worked for the Tibet Government; he also spoke English. Tremon Sonam Banjur, a 4th rank civilian official, was another Tibetan working in the Bureau; he was handling Tibetans returning home via Yatung. He was 30 years old and had previously served the Tibet Government in Gartok

Regarding the *dak bungalow,* Fu was told that pending the transfer of the *dak bungalow* to the Chinese, "the Indian personnel should be in possession of passes issued from this office.

Fu refused to commit himself for the passes. AK Sen, who was returning to India at the end of his tenure as Consul General, accompanied Chibber for the discussions as he knew Fu from Lhasa.

On October 30, TN Kaul wrote to N. Raghavan, the Indian Ambassador in Beijing and all the India posts in Tibet, mentioning the encounter between the ITA and Fu: "You will recall there was long discussion during negotiations of Tibet agreement regarding inclusion of word 'maintain' in article I (2) of Agreement. You may, however, inform Chinese Government that Mr. SL Chhibar [sic] is deputed as our Trade Agent at Yatung and will also be looking after Gyantse Agency until an agent is appointed there."

Kaul also cited the intimation given to Chinese Government regarding the appointment of AK Sen as Consul General Lhasa in 1952.

In the meantime, the Consulate in Lhasa had granted official visas stamped 'On Government Duty' to Lee Chih-ken, Vice Trade Agent and Hsieh Lang-tao, Secretary of the Chinese Trade Agency in Kalimpong. This was done before the Chinese Government officially intimated India "of establishment of Trade Agency at Kalimpong and names of officials appointed thereto."

But reciprocity was not a concern for the Chinese.

## The Views of the Chinese Ministry

A month later, Goburdhun wrote to Kaul to inform South Block that the *Waichiaopu*[9] had finally given its opinion regarding the transfer of the rest houses and posts and telegraphs installations in Tibet; there was no hurry from the Chinese side even if six months had passed since the Agreement had been inked. The Indian official cabled: "Posts and telegraphs services at Yatung, Phari and Gyantse; Chinese suggest handing-over work be completed in two steps:

(i) Chinese to depute personnel to these offices on November 25 to familiarize with work and also check equipment

(ii) Second step will be formal taking over exact date for which will depend on completion of first step which Chinese expect will not take long."

The Chinese proposed a few concrete steps regarding the date of formal take-over; it could be decided by two local officers, i.e. the Indian Consul General[10] in Lhasa and the Chinese Foreign Office Assistant in Tibet who could work out the details of the hand-over. The Indian personnel would only withdraw after the hand-over: "Chinese will take over local employees and will pay bonus pension; Gyantse installations will be repaired by Chinese."

Regarding the Rest Houses, it could also happen the same way:

1. Take-over in two steps. First step to start on November 25 and specific measures to be discussed by appointees of both sides locally.

---

9   China's Ministry of Foreign Affairs.
10  PN Menon was in the process of taking over from AK Sen.

   Menon, born in 1920, joined the Indian Foreign Service as a War Service Officer, 1947; Consul-General of India, Lhasa, October 1954-November 1956; First Secretary, Indian Embassy, Rome, April 1957-May 1958; Consul-General of India, Damascus, June 1958-February 1959; Director (External Publicity), MEA, 1959-62; Consul-General, San Francisco, 1962-65; Ambassador to Cambodia, 1965-68; Joint Secretary, Additional Secretary and Secretary, MEA, 1968-72.

2. Chinese agree to the price for the rest houses, though since the Gyantse rest houses were damaged, it was suggested to have a revaluation locally made by both sides.

For the price of equipment, a local estimation was proposed.

A week later, Delhi reacted and informed its agencies in Tibet that the Chinese may depute some personnel to the Indian P&T offices by November 25 "to familiarize themselves with work and with equipment."

Any repairs would be carried out by the Chinese after the hand-over.

Delhi wanted both the Rest Houses and P&T installations to be handed over on same day: "Until formal handing-over Rest houses will remain fully under our control and any use of them by the Chinese will be subject to our permission and convenience."

**Going into the Details**

The ITA in Gyantse was informed that the price of equipments such as crockery and furniture had already been prepared; it was separate from the cost of the *dak bungalows*. Regarding the equipment, it was stated that the prices, "have been arrived at after a checking by two executive engineers and we do not see why any further estimates should be necessary especially as we are handing over P&T installations absolutely free."

The ITA was instructed that if the Chinese started bargaining "you may as well compromise accept a minimum reduction of 25% in the prices of equipment."

It was hoped that the formal hand over of P&T installations and the Rest Houses could be finalised by January 1, 1955: "Must impress on you the fact of low morale of our P&T employees who wish to return home as soon as possible," said the cable adding "Consul General Lhasa may await final instructions before initiating discussions in Lhasa."

It would take a few months more.

## The First Meeting

Soon after his arrival in Lhasa, Yang formed three teams to tackle with India the local issues in Gyantse, Yatung and Gartok. The team members were mainly selected from the 18th Army and local Tibetan officials were co-opted as assistants.

On November 25, Menon (Counsel [sic] General) informed Delhi that he had met his counterpart Yang Gongsu[11], in charge of the Foreign Bureau in Lhasa.

Yang mentioned that the *Waichiapou* had instructed him to meet Menon; he already knew about the two-phase hand-over. About the first one, he suggested to postpone the date of starting the process to December 1:

"Since installation and *dak bungalows* lie over the trade route from Gyantse to Yatung, Chinese have deputed one of their officers Yin Fa[12], a Foreign Office man to be in direct charge of the takeover duties. Yin will have two separate teams for dealing with Posts and Telegraphs installations and the Dak Bungalows."

The Chinese negotiators in Yatung for the dak bungalows were officials from the Gyantse Party Work Committee named Li Jishan and Zhou Keren.[13] Yang, however, stated that the final decisions would be taken

---

11 Also written Yang Gongsu. Yang was the Waichiaopu's representative in Lhasa. Yang was a career diplomat who would later hold the post of China's Ambassador to Nepal in the 1960s.

12 Yin Fatang later became Tibetan Autonomous Region's Party Secretary (March 1980 – June 1985). In 1954, he was the senior Chinese PLA officer and Communist Party official in Gyantse. During the floods, Yin had been Second Deputy Director of the Flood Relief Committee to assist flood victim (the Director and First Deputy Director were Tibetans).

13 The post and communication negotiations were handled by several officials especially dispatched to Yatung from Beijing, Chen Yang, Tan Shuiyuan and Na Qihui. With regard to the transfer of responsibility and the management of trade along the Yatung-Gyantse road, Fu Sheng and Dyinka Dorje Gyaltsen were the main negotiators from the Chinese side. The official who assisted in the commercial negotiations and then later was appointed head of the group supervising all trade through Yatung was Guo Shulin.

with Menon in Lhasa. Menon said he would report to Delhi and did not commit for any date for starting the first phase.

Yang said that the first phase would only be to ascertain the 'actual position' of the installations, *dak bungalow*, properties, equipment and local staff employed.

The local staff would be transferred during the second phase: "He hinted at formal handing over ceremony to be held at Lhasa once final date for transfer is fixed," wrote Menon.

During the first phase, India would retain the full responsibility for all installations and *dak bungalow* properties; the Chinese would assume responsibility only from the date of final take-over.

Menon noted that he had not so far received any list of the Posts and Telegraphs installations, equipment and details regarding evaluation of the *dak bungalows* and their furniture and crockery, the staff and their pay and allowances."

Though the length of the first phase could not be anticipated, Yang said that he wanted to complete the work expeditiously as it would strengthen the practical implementation of Sino-Indian Agreement and the close friendship between two countries.

## Another Meeting

On December 2, the Consulate in Lhasa informed Delhi that Chen Yang, an officer of Ministry of Posts and Telegraphs in Beijing and a Tibetan, Theiji Dingja, in charge of the Rest Houses, would be part of the supervising team.

Yin Fatang would have a general supervisory role over the two teams at Gyantse and Yatung and interact with Maj SL Chibber, the ITA in Yatung.[14]

Chibber was asked to go to Gyantse and immediately get in touch with Yin Fatang to start to work on the first phase.

Yang was concerned that the Posts and Telegraphs equipment could deteriorate due to the uncertain date of transfer.

---

14 He was acting ITA in Gyantse.

Menon had to request Delhi: "Grateful if Posts and Telegraphs authorities are requested to ensure that installations and lines are maintained and handed over in efficient working condition."

The Consul noted that the Chinese were aware of the extent of losses due to the floods in July 1954 in Gyantse and also the subsequent pilfering by local Tibetans: "We should ensure that transfer is carried out in a way which will set at rest Chinese apprehensions," wrote the ITA.

Maj Chibber was moreover instructed to go ahead and start the work of estimating the Indian assets.

The next day, Delhi approved Menon's points: "P&T Department being requested to inform [the] Engineering Supervisor Radhakrishnan to report to ITA Yatung." Radhakrishnan's role was to help checking and estimating the telegraph equipment.

The Indian ITA was asked to tell Chen Yang that "his apprehensions are unfounded and damage to lines is now being caused through pilferage by locals. …We also understand from the P&T Department that linesmen are often under move from one place to another under the orders of EST[15] Gangtok. Accordingly, absence of linesmen from their posts, need not always be interpreted as dereliction of duty."

Finally, the ITA was told, "bear in mind that handing-over would be better the sooner it is."

The late arrival of the Chinese officials had delayed the process for several months.

**The Negotiations Progress**

On December 7, Maj Chibber communicated to Delhi that he had met Hou Chi[16], Theiji Dingja, Chen Yang, Hsi Chao Hai and Lee Chi Sang were also present. They had seen the minutes of the meeting between Yang and Menon in Lhasa.

---

15 Engineering Supervisor, Telegraph.

16 Hou Jie was Gyantse Party Secretary, while Sha Ke was his Deputy Party Secretary.

Hou asked about the animals attached to the *dak bungalows*. The ITA said he would check with his Government.

Hou Chi asked Chibber two questions:

(1) When the actual checking of rest houses and its equipment should start?

(2) Who is the Posts and Telegraphs Officer to hand over Posts and Telegraphs installation and when will he be arriving.

After Chibber said that the work of checking of rest houses could start as soon as the teams were ready, it was decided to start on December 10 from Saugang.

The Chinese were informed of the arrival of a P&T[17] officer who would contact Chen Yang. It was agreed that after checking each rest house, a list of equipment would be signed by both parties, later the list would be sent to Gyantse for Yin Fatang's endorsement.

Two days later, Menon wrote to Bhadkamkar, an officer in the Ministry in Delhi in order to get some clarification: "Gyantse installations completely destroyed by July floods, no telegraph office functioning there. Lines between Gyantse and Pharizong were also severely damaged by floods and have suffered considerably from pilferage by locals. Understand that 5 miles of line simply does not exist now."

The telegraph office in Gyantse was dead and it was impossible to re-establish the line between Phari Dzong and Gyantse.

The P&T Department estimated that stores worth Rs. 20,000 would be required and it would take 90 days to complete the repair work: "This will delay handing-over inordinately and we do not approve of it," asserted Menon.

The Chinese had earlier agreed to repair the installations at Gyantse.

Only the installations from the Indian border up to Phari Dzong[18] could be maintained in working order: "The responsibility for preventing further pilferage and damage through thefts rests with the Chinese

---

17 Radhakrishnan.

18 Sometimes written, Pharizong.

who are now in control of law and order in that region," observed the Consul General.

There was more, the construction of the road between Phari Dzong and Yatung had caused great damages to the lines, mainly because of the blasting.

## The ITA Meets the Chinese and Tibetan Officials

On December 9, Chibber cabled Delhi that he met Theiji Dingja and Chen Yang again. Dingja raised a minor point regarding the Gyantse *dak bungalow* where the main building had been completely destroyed during the floods: "Most of its timber has been removed. Arrangements are being made to remove the remaining timber."

The real issue was that some out-houses and stables had been temporarily repaired for the 'menial servants'. The Tibetan official wanted a valuation, but insisted that alternative accommodation for the servants would have to be found.

When Chen Yang asked who would be responsible for the installations during the first phase, Chibber explained that in view of "the recent pilferage by locals it is essential the headman of respective areas are asked to (look after them)."

But the Chinese now wanted the Posts & Telegraphs installations to be in working order before the checking started; it was a change from their earlier stance, which was bound to delay further the transfer.

## Meeting in Lhasa

The talks were going on in parallel in Lhasa.

The next day[19], Menon reported his discussion with Yang Gongsu. The animals attached to the *dak bungalows* were not mentioned: "This is an obvious try-on to secure our animals also in the bargain," wrote Menon who suggested that India should argue that the animals were not part of the Posts and Telegraphs installation and equipment.

Things were, however, progressing slowly.

---

19  On December 10, 1954.

On December 13, Delhi was informed that the details of *dak bungalows* and equipment, cutlery, crockery and personnel would be handed over to Yang Gongsu the next day and Menon would ask "whether [or not] Chinese require out-houses and the stable in Gyantse."

If they wanted them, the value should be estimated on the same principle as for the *dak bungalows*, viz. Rupees 10 per square foot of plinth area less depreciation of 1% per annum.

The report asked instructions from Gangtok, "since Chinese are great sticklers for details, would be grateful if you could indicate immediately the exact amount of out-houses, stable accommodations required at each place and your own conception of reasonable rent."

In the meantime, the Political Officer questioned the suitability of the Indian couriers continuing to use *dak bungalows* after the transfer to China. In case it was transferred, it would mean that alternative accommodations would have to be found.

The Consul wrote to the PO: "Presume we are not getting permanent halting accommodation for couriers operating on the Lhasa-Gyantse stretch."

The next day, the Consulate cabled Maj Chibber in Yatung, about the Chinese desire to take-over out-houses and stables in Gyantse.

The ITA was also informed that the Chinese had accepted that the *dak* animals were not part of the Posts and Telegraphs equipment. They could remain with the Indian Agency.

## New Questions about the Equipment

Though Yang Gongsu had accepted the valuation of *dak bungalow* buildings, he raised questions about the equipment; but Menon noted: "I gathered the impression that such an appraisal may not lead to substantial variations in prices and that Chinese want to finalize these transactions with minimum of discussion between handing over teams."

The Indian Consul however accepted to start a bargain as he had been authorized by Delhi: "on understanding that it would lead only to minor variations in prices."

The list of the *dak bungalows*, their prices, equipment, including cutlery and crockery and the Tibetan personnel serving was then handed-over to the Chinese officials.

## Repairing the Lines

On December 30, Lhasa asked the PO to arrange to send some stores to repair the lines near Yatung: "the cost of stores and their transportation charges will be borne by us."

The cable added: "when working conditions are better in Tibet we hope to be able to spare technical personnel to help Chinese repair and restore P&T lines," but the first phase of P&T installations handover "should be completed as soon as possible. Radhakrishnan, who is at Yatung should assist Chibber as much as he can and may thereafter return to Gangtok."

The talks about the details continued.

Four days later, the Foreign Affairs Assistant orally indicated that China was prepared to provide "sufficient accommodation at every *dak bungalows* for couriers and their animals without payment of rent on a reciprocal basis." But the Chinese couriers going to Kalimpong "would in return expect similar facilities in our *dak bungalows* in Sikkim."

As for the Lhasa-Gyantse route, identity cards would be issued to the Indian couriers. The Chinese demonstrated "their willingness to observe both the letter and spirit of the Sino - Indian Agreement on Tibet," thought Menon.

## Two Remaining Issues

On the next day, it was agreed that two issues remain to be solved:

(1) The evaluation of India's houses and stables at Gyantse

(2) The evaluation and transfer of the stable at Gautsa and the *dakwallas* quarters at Champithang.

The Indian officials were keen to complete the transfer as soon as possible. However, the repair of P&T lines between Phari and Saugang would still have to be pending.

Champithang Dakbungalow

Nearly two months later, on March 2, the Consulate in Lhasa told Maj Chibber that the Chinese had proposed 'as a provisional measure' pending formal agreement "with a view to avoid interruption in postal communications after the handing over of our posts and telegraphs system in Tibet, we [India] may agree to make Yatung the terminal point for handing over Indian mail for Tibet and also for receiving mail from Tibet for India."

It was further suggested that during the interim period, each side would collect postal dues "in accordance with their existing rates and retain such revenue themselves."

Similar arrangements were to be done for the wireless communication: "If we agree to this they would let us know the call signs etc. of their wireless station in Lhasa in exchange for ours."

It was expected that the volume of mail and wireless traffic would be greater from India to Tibet, than in the opposite direction; in which case, India would be the beneficiary. Yang Gongsu made this proposal simply because China did not have trained personnel to take-over the installations at that time.

## The Final Agreement

A solution was getting closer …at least an agreement could now be signed.

On March 31, the Foreign Secretary spoke to Apa Pant, the PO; the former agreed to the proposal of the Indian Consul in Lhasa: "Formal handing over and taking over ceremony finally fixed for 13:30 hours local time on 1st April 1955." The Chinese had agreed to insertion of the phrase 'as a gesture of friendship' after word 'compensating'.

They had also accepted the continuation of present posts and telegraphs arrangements up to April 11. But to the great regret of the Indian officials, there was no time to prepare a Hindi version of the agreement.

Finally, the protocol for transferring the Indian posts and telegraphs installations and *dak-bungalows* in Tibet, to China was signed on April 1, 1955. Menon reported that: "suitable speeches were made by me [Menon] and the Foreign Affairs Assistant [Yang] on the occasion."

General Zhang Guohua[20] and the Tibetan Kalons[21] were present, though once again the Tibetans did not participate in the negotiations, except for the presence of Theiji Dingja.

General Zhang later offered a banquet to celebrate the occasion.

## An Uneasy Interim

During the following weeks, interim arrangements were put in place, the ITA in Yatung wrote on April 6: "The Chinese posts and

---

20 Lt Gen Zhang Guohua, born in October 1914 in Yongxin County of Jiangxi Province, was the first CCP's Party Secretary of Tibet from January 24, 1950 to February 1952. He had been commander of the Southwest Eighteenth Army Corps of the People's Liberation Army (PLA) and as such, he led the main attack force in the 1950 Chamdo campaign against Tibetan forces, in the summer of 1950. It is said that Zhang was chosen for his special knowledge of Tibetan culture as Mao Zedong did not want to alienate the Tibetans.

As Party Secretary, he was succeeded by Gen Zhang Jingwu.

Zhang Guohua later became Commander of Chengdu Military Region between 1952 and 1965; during this period, he played an important role in the War with India. He died on February 21, 1972 at the age of 57.

21 Cabinet Ministers.

telegraphs office shifted in our post office building today and started booking telegrams for India both at Phari and Yatung. They want to use our post office building at Yatung temporarily till they could fix up lines at Tischee."

They also started collecting telegraph revenue: "it is likely they [Chinese] will do same as regards to postal side booking and registration of parcels, money orders from next mail day."

The next day, the Consulate in Lhasa suggested "as far as language of telegrams was concerned we might also provide facilities for sending and accepting messages in Tibetan since the majority using the W/T station at Darjeeling may turn out to be Tibetans."

Nothing was simple.

## A New Complication: the Eviction of the *Dakwallahs*

On May 29, a message from Menon informed Gangtok and Delhi that "the Chinese officer had few days previously visited the [*dak baunglows*] primarily to stick pictures of Mao Tse-tung and propaganda posters in the rooms of these bungalows and secondly to secure eviction of *dakwallahs* from the quarters they used to occupy in them."

Only three to four days notice was given to them.

Though most of them could find alternative accommodation, the Indian Consul noted: "Chinese action clearly contrary to understanding reached with them in Lhasa in December last by which our *dak* couriers were to continue using these bungalows in exchange for similar facilities extended to their couriers in our d*ak bungalow* on the Jelep-la Kalimpong route."

Menon reasoned that the fact that the "newly instituted Chinese mail service from Gyantse to Yatung required similar facilities in these *dak bungalows* may be the cause for precipitate Chinese action."

Reading Menon's report the PO suggested the matter should immediately be taken up with the Foreign Bureau in Lhasa to ask them "to revert to past practice till proper alternative arrangements can be made for accommodation of our *dakwallahs*."

**Indian Dakbungalow in Phari with fort and Chomolhari in background**

Why this was not discussed during the previous month is difficult to understand?

Pant asserted that in view of the new situation created by the Chinese, "suggest someone from our Trade Agencies at Yatung and Gyantse visit their respective sectors soonest possible and examine present work of our *dak* services."

It was not the first time that the Chinese had gone back on their words.

## Discussions with the Chinese Start Again

On June 3, Maj Chibber informed Delhi that he had discussed the issue with Fu Sheng who replied that he had referred the matter to Yang Gongsu in Lhasa, but the *dakwallas* could not be allowed to stay permanently.

A week later, Menon was informed by the Foreign Bureau that they had received a report from Yatung complaining about the Indian ITA: "Mr. Chibber[22] has been distorting Mr. Yang promise to Mr. Menon."

---

22  One of the different spellings of Maj Chibber's name.

As the new issue came up, the Foreign Bureau drew a sharp distinction between our *dakwallas* and 'couriers'; they argued that the Indian *dakwallas* were 'messengers' and not couriers: "the question should not be mixed up. …Mr. Chibber's exertion on this point is far from satisfactory".

Further, the Foreign Bureau insisted that the Indian 'couriers' should have passports duly visaed by their authorities and since the Chinese Posts and Telegraphs service was now functioning in Tibet, the Indian *dakwallas* were "no longer necessary and request that they be withdrawn, since continuance of this messenger service runs against the understanding between India and China regarding handing over of Posts and Telegraphs service in Tibet."

On June 10, Menon received further complaints about Chibber, "when Fu Sen[23] requested Mr. Chibber to withdraw the enumeration post, Fu was told that the post was a part of the trade agency office and that Chinese should not mind his internal business."

Foreign Bureau added that this post involved "a violation of their sovereignty and runs against the spirit of mutual respect of each other's territorial integrity and sovereignty and request that the 'Counting Post' be immediately withdrawn and its functions stopped forthwith."

A year after the signature of the Tibet Agreement, the situation was becoming complicated.

The controversy about the *dakwallahs* was nevertheless not over.

On June 15, Delhi instructed to inform the Chinese that present Tibetan *dakwallas* were "couriers and that their names and the frequencies of their visits to various stages between Yatung and Gyantse [would] be communicated to them [the Chinese]."

In fact, said Delhi, they had always been treated as couriers although before the transfer of P&T services they used to function, in addition, as *dakwallahs*: "There is no truth whatsoever in the suggestion that we are at present running a messenger service in Tibet."

---

23  Fu Sheng.

**Dakbungalow in Tuna**

The Chinese had been told in December that these personnel as well as the animals used by them, were not part of the P&T system operated by India. South Block added: "We do not, therefore, understand statement that these couriers are no longer necessary and should be withdrawn with the functioning of Chinese P&T services in Tibet."

It was also pointed out by Delhi that to replace "partially or wholly existing Tibetan couriers by Indian nationals will inevitably take some time."

## Another Meeting

On June 19, Maj Chibber reported his meeting with Fu Sheng on the previous day; he suggested that the former should discuss the matter with the Indian Consul. The Indian official suggested that Gyatso, the Vice Consul should immediately take up the matter with the Foreign Bureau in Lhasa.

A complete list of the *dakwallas* serving between Chameschang and Gyantse and later to Lhasa, was provided to the Foreign Bureau.

The present frequency of the service was then twice a week.

The Indian embassy in Beijing interfered the next day in the correspondence; it commented: "[Chinese] action without prior consultation high handed. Shall take up with *Waichiaopu,* if so instructed …shall informally ask *Waichiaopu* to instruct the Bureau to deal more politely."

It was not only a question of dealing politely, but also of changing the agreed goal posts.

On August 2, Kaul wrote to Pant that until the formal appointment of Indian couriers "it is absolutely essential that present Tibetan *dakwallhas* continue carrying our official mail. …We take serious view of Chinese attempt to make position of our Tibetan employees untenable."

Kaul agreed that the appointment of Indian couriers may take a few months; therefore, the present arrangements had to continue.

## A Final Solution?

Two weeks later, Menon sent a long cable to the Ministry in Delhi, to report a meeting in Lhasa about the *dakwallas.*

Yang Gongsu, Dzasa Luishar, the Tibetan Vice Foreign Affairs Assistant and Fu Sheng were present. Menon mentioned the Indian authorities' concerns about the *dakwallahs*; they were keen to keep the same arrangement until a final settlement was reached.

Yang argued again that this service was contrary to the spirit of the Sino-Indian Agreement. He again mentioned that "until we get couriers from India [Indian nationals] we may continue to employ the present Tibetans as employees of Trade Agency as messengers. But these messengers had to run between Yatung and Gyantse without changing."

The discussions continued on the same tone: "It appears that they feel loss of their prestige in the eyes of Tibetans if they allow our courier service on the present lines," commented Menon.

Yang insisted that in the Sino - Indian Agreement, the extension of courier service from Gyantse to Lhasa was not stipulated: "However he has no objection to our having messengers between these places."

As the road between Gyantse and Lhasa was to be completed in three months, Menon was keen to ask Chinese to allow jeep courier instead of the present service: "We can have Indian couriers for this [jeapable] section," he wrote.

The Consul further suggested a bi-weekly service should continue: "But in view of difficulties being put up by Chinese, it is suggested that we have once a week service from Yatung to Gyantse for classified correspondence."

Ordinary mail in sealed bags could use the Chinese postal service.

**The Issue is not yet Solved**

The saga continued.

On August 22, Pant told Kaul "I cannot understand how Chinese in Lhasa consider that our present mail service is contrary to the spirit of the Sino-Indian Agreement."

There was a special clause saying that the Trade Agencies would continue to enjoy "the privileges and amenities of courier mail bags and communication in code." Pant suggested employing the *dakwallas* for some other work: "It would not be appropriate to dismiss or discharge any of them because Chinese object to their employment by us."

Pant believed that the Chinese were only objecting for the 'prestige'.

The next day, Kaul replied from Delhi: "the present mail service is not contrary to Sino - Indian Agreement; Raghavan, the Indian Ambassador in his note signed by the Chinese Vice Foreign Minister had mentioned: 'Trade Agents and traders of both countries may hire employees in the locality.

Kaul added that due to the difficult terrain and travel conditions "we cannot agree to change in mode of operation of Tibetan *dakwalas*. They must, therefore, continue functioning as at present."

The Joint Secretary rightly pointed out: "Even after introduction of Indian couriers, present Tibetan employees will be required to live at various stages for providing animals, carrying mail bags and assisting our couriers."

Further, there was no way that couriers could travel from Yatung to Gyantse or Gyantse to Lhasa without halting at intermediate stations and the Indian Consulate General at Lhasa was entitled to the customary diplomatic bag.

A month later, Delhi was informed that the *Waichiaopu* was agreeable to our Tibetan *dakwalas* being designated 'Messengers of Trade Agencies' and "being given facilities of accommodation at Rest houses during the performance of their duties upon presentation of certificates given to them by the local Bureau of Foreign Affairs."

The authorities in Tibet were supposed to have been informed; Delhi nevertheless observed: "We shall have to reconsider the whole question next year by which time Chinese expected to complete road Gyantse and Yatung."

On September 26, the Chinese Embassy in Delhi informed South Block that the issue had again been discussed with the *Waichiaopu* which contended that neither the system of post station nor relay messengers has yet been stopped.

Beijing felt that India should institute a 'through' messenger system "from post station to destination without changeover at intermediary stage and if this was done it would be unnecessary for us to establish a parallel set of rest houses."

The India representatives had earlier objected to have to set up "parallel rest houses" and pointed out that the families of messengers "were merely staying in such accommodation as they themselves had found."

It was again pointed out that due to the difficult terrain; it was not physically possible to have a 'through system' (without stop).

The Indian report observed that it appeared that the Chinese wanted the Indian messengers to "actually use rest houses and there should be no impression that Indian Government continues to have 'posts' along the route."

The embassy tried to explain that while the families of Tibetan messengers would be living in the vicinity of rest houses, the messengers themselves, while on duty, would stay "at rest house and not with their families at so-called post stations."

On October 29 a message was received from the Consulate in Lhasa, Menon wrote: "I agree with Chibber that we will need two jeeps for running courier service from Yatung to Lhasa when motor road between these two points opens early next year. Road up to Phari can be expected to be motorable by beginning December."

The Consul General was of the opinion that with the eight couriers envisaged by the Ministry and the retention of existing *dakwalla* establishment between Gangtok and Yatung "it should be possible to run weekly service between Yatung and Lhasa and twice weekly from Gangtok to Yatung."

Regarding the number of Tibetan *dakwallas* to be retained after introduction of motor courier services; Menon suggested that it would be unwise "to terminate services of all these loyal Tibetan personnel who have been in our service for very many years."

His suggestion was a maximum seven out of eleven existing *dakwallas* between Yatung and Gyantse could be absorbed, the remaining four could transferred in the Trade Agencies at Yatung and Gyantse: "If Government approves couriers scheme on these lines essential to plan for immediate provision of two jeeps so that new courier scheme may come into force simultaneous with opening of Lhasa-Phari-Yatung road."

Menon added that the jeeps should resemble the Indian postal mail vans.

## The Conclusion

On November 3, the Consulate sent a telegram to Gangtok mentioning that India had "not accepted the position that this consulate is not entitled to the services of the same couriers who will serve our trade agencies of Yatung, Gyantse."

The Consul said that that he did not envisage "insuperable difficulties in extending our courier service from Gyantse to Lhasa," and since a motorable road had been opened "I feel it would be more appropriate for us to start with jeep courier service on this sector employing personnel."

Menon noted the rapidity with which Chinese introduced motor traffic on the Lhasa to Gyantse road "without even giving a second thought to its repercussions on local muleteers;" he believed that they would the same way introduce "motor traffic over Gyantse-Phari-Yatung road once it is opened. It would, therefore, be unwise for us to attempt to perpetuate an outmoded courier system running on *dak* animals."

He further pointed out that all evidence showed "the Tibetans themselves welcoming such nationalization of transportation. For instance, [the] Kundeling Monastery and a number of others have already acquired vehicles for use on these roads."

Menon's conclusions were that the proposal "for motor courier service between Gyantse and Yatung was suggested ahead of the completion of the road because we anticipated that sanctioning of vehicles, their supply and the redeployment of existing *dakwallas*, will take some time. It is understood that the existing system should continue until it can be replaced by new arrangement."

A comprehensive jeep courier scheme showing the cost compared to the old system was dispatched to the Political Officer. It would solve the problems of 'posts' on the way. The Tibetan landscape would never be the same.

# 07

# Tibet's Slow Incorporation Starts

## The View from Gangtok (January – June 1955)

It is interesting to take a look at the report sent by the Political Officer in Sikkim; he represented the Ministry of External Affairs in Gangtok and was responsible for Tibet, Bhutan and Sikkim.

First, BK Kapur and later Apa Pant occupied the seat at the Residency in Gangtok; every month they sent a detailed report on the evolution of the situation in the Himalayan States. In this chapter, we shall go through the first six months of 1955.

## Apa Pant Takes Over

On February 7, 1955, Apa B. Pant[1] took over from BK Kapur as Political Officer in Sikkim. Two days later, Pant called on 'His Highness'[2]

---

1. Born on September 11, 1912, Apa Saheb Bala Saheb Pant was the second son of the tenth ruler of the Aundh State located near Pune in Maharashtra. After doing his schooling in local institutions, he graduated (BA) from the University of Mumbai and secured his master's degree (MA) from Oxford University. He passed his Barrister at Law from Lincoln's Inn and returned to India in 1937 at a time the Indian freedom movement was gaining pace.

   He started his career as the Minister of Education of the Aundh State in 1944 under his father. After India's Independence, he joined the Indian Foreign Service.

   During his long and prestigious career, he served as the Indian Commissioner in various African countries and later, in Indonesia, Norway, Egypt, United Kingdom and Italy.

2. Sir Tashi Namgyal (26 October 1893 – 2 December 1963) was the ruling Chogyal of Sikkim from 1914 to 1963. He was the son of Thutob Namgyal. He was the

and the next day, the Maharaja returned his visit: "He gave me the impression of being a very large-hearted, generous person of a highly artistic temperament but frustrated and very unhappy." The PO added that the Maharaja had "submerged himself in his religious practices not perhaps because he is interested in religion but because he wants to protect himself from the outside world and from shame and horror."[3]

Pant found Sir Tashi Namgyal a lonely man, feeling that he had been wronged and neglected by his children who gave him neither love nor respect: "I felt really drawn to this pathetic figure," wrote Pant.

Pant explains to Kaul[4] that apart from his monthly official reports: "I would continue to send to you either weekly or fortnightly letters about various problems." He admitted that there was "a great deal of work around and whoever said that Gangtok was an easy place from the point of view of work did not just know what he was talking about."

Pant remained posted in Gangtok till 1961.

## Last Report from BK Kapur

At the beginning of 1955, BK Kapur, who left Gangtok on January 17 and relinquished his charge February 5,[5] sent his last report in which he mentioned the completion of the two vital roads connecting Lhasa

---

11th ruler of the Namgyal dynasty, succeeding his half brother Sidkeong Tulku Namgyal, who had ruled from February to December in 1914, till his untimely death. Tashi Namgyal was a strong advocate for closer links with India.

He was married in October 1918 to Kunzang Dechen, and they had 3 sons and 3 daughters. The eldest son died in a plane crash during World War Two. On his death Sir Tashi was succeeded as Chogyal by his second son Palden Thondup Namgyal.

During his reign, he introduced land reform and free elections.

3 *Political situation reports on Sikkim from the Political Officer in Sikkim Gangtok. Department: External Affairs, Branch: NEF, 1955, File No. File No. 30(3)-NEF/55.* Available in the National Archives of India.

4 PN Kaul, the Joint Secretary in the Ministry of External Affairs.

5 Apa B. Pant took over charge at Gangtok on February 7.

with Sikang[6] and Chinghai[7] provinces of China: "Bridging the Kyichu river outside Lhasa, the Chinese were able to hold the formal opening ceremonies of these roads on the 25th December. The celebrations were held in style and amidst much rejoicing."

The PO mentioned the usual laudatory speeches made by Chinese and Tibetan officials and the scarves which were presented to a portrait of Mao Zedong. The Nepalese and Bhutanese Agents joined in the rejoicing, though a significant issue was the absence of the photographs of the Dalai Lama and Panchen Lama: "in the past their photographs, of a somewhat smaller size, were invariably displayed alongside those of Chinese leaders."

Tibet had already drastically changed.

PN Menon, the Indian Consul General reported that truck loads of rice and flour had been brought to Lhasa and the vehicles were being utilized on the return journey for sending Tibetan wool to China: "The transportation of Chinese and Tibetan goods on these roads has thus already begun, and may be expected to increase steadily."

Suddenly, China no longer depended on India to survive on the plateau.

Kapur rightly noted the export of Tibetan wool to China would inevitably have repercussions on Tibet's trade with India: "Hitherto Tibetan imports from India have been largely financed by the sale or barter of Tibetan wool in Indian markets."

The report said that 'among foreign visitors in Tibet [are] some members of the Chinese Youth League"; it meant that Chinese were still considered 'foreigners' in Tibet by Gangtok?

---

6   Tibet-Sichuan Highway.

   Sikang or Xikang is a province of the Republic of China and later of the People's Republic of China. It comprised most of the Kham region of traditional Tibet. The eastern part of the province was inhabited by a number of different ethnic groups, such as Han Chinese, Yi, Qiang and Tibetan, while the western part of the province was only inhabited by Tibetans. Xikang was a special administrative region of the Republic of China until 1939, when it became an official province. The provincial capital was Kangding from 1939 to 1951 and Ya'an from 1951 to 1955.

7   Tibet-Qinghai Highway.

Other 'foreigners' were some Czechoslovakian photographers who were busy filming the celebrations for the opening of the two roads.

Some progress was made for the transfer of the P&T installations and rest houses, he observed. The Indian Trade Agent in Yatung sent to the Chinese representatives a large quantity of telegraph poles and wires for the repair of the telegraph line between Phari and Saugang: "Due to pilferage and other causes the line between Phari and Saugang has been out of use for several months." Delhi also offered to provide technical advice for undertaking the repairs.

**Report for the Month of February 1955.**

Pant had told Kaul that his monthly reports would be more matter-of-fact. But in fact, they continued to be longish and flowery.

About the situation in Tibet, the Report stated: "The process of integration of Tibet into the political and economic pattern of life that is developing in China proceeds apace."

Let us remember that the Dalai Lama was at that time visiting China.

Pant noted that the Tibetan leader and General Zhang Jingwu had been made "permanent members of the Central People's Government in Peking and that the Panchen Lama has been made the Vice-President of the Central Government." Pant had it slightly wrong. The Dalai Lama was just made a deputy chairman of the Standing Committee of the National People's Congress, while the Panchen Lama would be elected deputy chairman of the Political Consultative Conference in December.

Pant continued: "On the Dalai Lama's becoming a permanent member of the Chinese Government, it is reported that some of the Tibetans fear that he could not perhaps return back to Lhasa."

The PO mentioned that many Tibetan nobles were worried about this development and some were seriously thinking to leave the country and migrate to India. The procedure for such matters was for the Kashag to get the previous sanction from the Chinese before any leave was granted." [8]

---

8   According to Melvyn Goldstein, on October 1, 1954, "Mao had actually raised

Pant mentioned also the Chinese Goodwill Missions visiting Tibet were becoming a common feature of the Tibetan life. One of these missions which was called 'the Comforting Mission' arrived in Lhasa in the beginning of January and left after a month; it was given receptions at different places. There was also a Cultural Mission which had visited Chumbi Valley. They used to show films produced in the Soviet Union and dubbed in Chinese.

Regarding the question of granting autonomy to Tibet, Pant was rather vague. He said that it would not be considered in the near future: "Naturally a good many of the Tibetan leaders would like Tibet to become at least an autonomous State." Retrospectively, we know that 'autonomy' meant nothing for the Communist regime.

More importantly, Delhi was informed about the two highways which had just reached Lhasa; the traffic conditions in Lhasa had created new problems: "The local police are being trained to handle vehicular traffic where they were only capable of directing muleteers and pedestrians. The Chinese in their enthusiasm to improve traffic conditions thought of pulling down one of the ancient Chortens situated at the gateway to a village near Lhasa. This met with very strong protests from all parties concerned and it appears that this project is abandoned."

The Chorten would be demolished a few years later.

**The New Highways**

The inauguration of the new highways was celebrated with great éclat: "During these celebrations, the Chinese indicated in their speeches that trade with India would also increase and not decrease. The opening of

the issue of the Military-Administrative Committee at his first meeting with the Dalai Lama. He surprised the Dalai Lama by telling him both that it was still too early to implement all of the clauses of the Seventeen-Point Agreement and that it was no longer necessary to create a military-administrative committee."

"These committees, Mao said, were meant to be transitional until people's governments could be started and had already been terminated in all large regions. He proposed, therefore, that Tibet skip this stage and go directly to creating the Tibet Autonomous Region, with the Dalai Lama as its chairman and the Panchen Lama as the deputy chairman. An autonomous region, Mao said, would be better for Tibetans, because it would be in accord with the new constitution, which specified that minority regions will exercise autonomous rule."

the two roads and the arrival of many trucks loaded with goods from China resulted in the fall of prices of the local goods from China and traders who held stocks of these goods were worried." It was clear that the Chinese were going to start, "as many road projects as possible." It was also mentioned that a meeting of the Foreign Bureau Sub-Office was held at Gyantse to consider the construction of the Lhasa-Gyantse road.

Some prominent Tibetan residents were invited to attend the deliberations, while the Tibetan labourers, previously engaged on the Lhasa-Chamdo road had been diverted to the new project.

The Monthly Report cited the price of Indian petrol which had registered a fall of price of almost 50%: "Chinese petrol, pumped from some of the western Provinces of China, has made its appearance in Lhasa. This petrol is of reddish colour and it is reported to be not as good as the petrol exported from India."

The fare for travelling on the new highways was given: about Rs. 180 for a passage between Lhasa and Chamdo and a load of one maund was charged Rs. 84.

Another development was the apparition of Chinese paper currency first used by Chinese: "The notes thus circulated were printed in 1949 and 1950 and resemble the dollar notes of KMT[9] days."

Delhi was informed that a Chinese Officer Lieu Thou-trang[10], 'in charge of the Southwest Army, was on a 'welfare mission to Tibet'; he visited the Chumbi Valley, Yatung and Gyantse. He addressed several meetings in the Chumbi Valley and "expostulated on the achievements of the People's Liberation Army since their entry into Tibet."

Lieu cited the developments in cottage industries and agriculture, he asked the Tibetans to co-operate and make the Chinese plans successful: "The Chinese seem to be keen to develop agricultural activities on

---

9   Kuomintang.

10  The reference maybe to Marshall Liu Bocheng, the 'One-Eyed Dragon' who was commander of the Southwest Military Region of China. Deng Xiaoping was his Political Commissar in 1950 during the Battle of Chamdo.

modern lines in Tibet and have instituted the use of tractors for the cultivation of lands at Medu Kongkar[11] near Lhasa," added Pant.

The return of the Dalai Lama to Lhasa was announced for April 1955: "Arrangements for the welcome of the Dalai Lama on his return to Lhasa are under way. Three groups of parties consisting of Tibetan officials and the abbots of various monasteries are likely to leave Lhasa soon to participate in the grand reception."

A rumour was circulating in Lhasa that representatives from Russia, Mongolia and Chinese Turkistan would be stationed at Lhasa, but it is doubtful that the Communists wanted Xinjiang representatives.

In the meantime, surveys in the Kham area were completed. The Communists were planning to introduce the famous 'reforms' and impose land rent and also acquired all the fallow land. A census of the population was also taken. One example of the new changes: before the occupation of Chamdo, there were few Chinese traders in the region, now they outnumbered the Tibetans. Many Khampas from Chamdo and the neighbouring areas had already left their homes for Lhasa, as a result, the Chinese had to impose restrictions on the merchants and pilgrims travelling to Lhasa: "there has been great influx of pilgrims to Lhasa from these areas as people fear that with the arrival of the Chinese the Tibetan religion would disappear."

It was also reported that many Chinese Army officers had been seen moving along the Khampha Chu valley[12]. The Trade Agent in Yatung believed that they were reconnoitering routes leading to northern Sikkim from Yatung.

In the meantime, Delhi was informed that Maj SL Chibber, the Indian Trade Agent in Yatung, had left for Gyantse and Lhasa "to attend the celebrations connected with the formal handing over of the P&T installations and the rest houses in Tibet to the Chinese."

This has already been mentioned.

---

11   Meldro Gungkar Dzong.
12   Near the North Sikkim border.

## Report for the Month of March 1955

Pant's second Report spoke of a new area of economic and social change being ushered in Tibet; he wrote that some of the Tibetan officials "are coming forward to co-operate wholeheartedly with these new programmes but most of them await the arrival of the Dalai Lama from his tour in China before they make up their minds about these revolutionary changes."

The PO informed Delhi that some sections of the younger generations felt that these changes would ultimately benefit Tibet: "In the Chumbi Valley the people have expressed greater enthusiasm and co-operative spirit …than is visible in other parts of Tibet."

In the meantime, rumours continued to fly high in Lhasa, the latest was that the Dalai Lama's status had changed in the roll of precedence in China and there were 15 or 16 persons above him; further some of his administrative powers in Tibet would be curtailed.

During a ceremony at the Potala Palace in Lhasa, it was noticed that the seats meant for the Regent and the Prime Minister were now occupied by two Chinese generals. On the second day, the Chinese were conspicuous by their absence. At the same time, the Bhutan Agent had received extremely low precedence while the Nepalese Officer was not even invited; he later told the Indian Consul General that he had made a verbal representation to the authorities.

A message from the Dalai Lama, still in Beijing was broadcast through loud speakers in Lhasa: "He urged maintenance of law and order and referred to the need for banning the use of Atom Bomb and other nuclear weapons," wrote Pant.

China had started to use the Tibetans for their own propaganda purpose; they also tried to enlist the support of Tibetans for protesting against the use of the atom bomb: "At Yatung also the Chinese held meetings where the Chinese and headmen spoke and stated that Russia had more powerful bombs than the Americans. After the meeting votes were cast against the use of atom bombs."

Interesting information was provided by the PO: over 10,000 persons (read Tibetans) were employed by the Chinese in Poyul region in

Southern Tibet for cutting timbers for construction work. Poyul was located north of the NEFA.

At the same time, 500 Chinese troops had left for Gyantse to assist in the road construction work. The Lhasa–Gyantse–Shigatse road was now expected to be completed within the next eight months. The Tibetan Government had to depute officials to assist the Chinese in the recruitment of Tibetan labourers; the alignment proposed followed the Tsangpo river for a considerable length; the road link to Gyantse was to be a diversion from the main route to Shigatse.

While the energy of the PLA seemed to be concentrated in the construction of new roads, it was announced that the Tibet-Qinghai highway had been completed "in such a haste that during the summer, owing to slush and swamp, it is considered that this highway would not be fit for vehicular traffic."

Some eye witnesses said that the road was still in a very temporary condition, but the Tibet-Sikang highway was well constructed and would be the main artery of communication between Lhasa and China.

The Chinese propaganda continued unabated; a party of 50 Chinese artists visited Gyantse and Yatung, performed and projected movies; Pant admitted that while these events were for Chinese propaganda, in Gyantse "some miscreants threw stones at the projector. Attempt to catch the culprits amidst the big crowd was however not successful."

Another amazing information, the Chinese distributed rice to the flood victims in Gyantse, but the Trade Agent thought that it was "the same rice which was handed over by BK Kapur on behalf of the Government of India at Saugang."

A rather strange incident, a marriage ceremony took place in Yatung, where two Chinese officials married Tibetan women. A Senior Chinese official spoke in favour of such inter-marriage; China, he said, had no objection to Tibetans marrying Chinese girls. A PLA circular stated that the Chinese were allowed to marry Tibetan girls provided both sides agreed.

In March, some troops left the Chumbi Valley; between 300 to 400 Chinese PLA soldiers moved at night in direction of Lhasa, via Nyero, avoiding Gyantse. The Chumbi Valley headmen were told by the Chinese that the soldiers were going on leave to China; it was very doubtful.

Pant said that a report from Kalimpong confirmed that it may be due "to the tension in international relations over the Formosa question and that some of these troops may be going over to participate in the fight for the offshore islands."

The PO had received the information that some wool produced in Nagchuka[13] region was being diverted towards Xining in Qinghai province. The reason is the low price of grain in Xining which "attracts better barter deals in Kokonor[14] markets." The Report mentioned that the Tibet-Qinghai highway (through which the wool trade passed) was threatened "by Kazaks living in this area, but the Chinese appear to have come to an understanding with the Kazaks and the route is now reported to be safer."

On the lighter side, the monks were restricted the use of motor-cycles and bikes around the Jokhang Cathedral in Lhasa "but this does not seem to be rigidly enforced against the Chinese personnel."

Finally, Phu Rapga Pangda Tshang[15] who had been deported from India in 1946 had returned to Sikkim from Tibet; Rapga wanted to stay permanently in India, but his demand for asylum was pending. In the meanwhile, he was allowed to proceed to Kalimpong where some members of his family had been residing since 1939.

**Report for the Month of April 1955**

The work of the Preparatory Committee of the Tibetan Autonomous Region "for an evolving form of local autonomy for Tibet" was attracting very great attention, said the Report, which affirmed that Ngapho Shape[16], "the personal representative of the Dalai Lama who has been the chief instrument in bringing about of the Sino-Tibetan Agreement, had been appointed to Secretary-General."

13 Today's Nagchu.

14 Famous lake near Xining in Qinghai province.

15 Pangdatshang.

16 Ngabo Ngawang Jigme.

This is a very partial view on the history.

Pant was probably too new in Gangtok to appreciate the role played by Ngabo since the Battle of Chamdo and after.[17] The PO however added: "The part that Ngapho[18] Shape is playing in all these developments has puzzled quite a few Tibetans." Later in the Report he remarked that although the reaction of the general public to the Chinese proposal was generally favourable "as they hope that this will usher in a new era of prosperity and progress", many officials were not pleased.

The PO also noted that the Chinese were showing great energy and organizational skill to reform certain aspects of the administration, "Starting of schools and welfare centres, organizing of social events such as cinemas, is attracting at least some of the inhabitants of Tibet."

The PO believed that the people in the Chumbi Valley were taken in by the Chinese efforts to win over the Tibetan people. Once again, the inter-marriages were mentioned: "One of the aspects of the policy of establishing closer bond between Tibet and China is the great encouragement, even at times through a great deal of propaganda, that is being given to Sino-Tibetan marriages."

However, many Tibetans feared that the Chinese would marry the most eligible Tibetan girls "and produce a new generation of Sino-Tibetans who would have deeper emotional feelings towards China."

This intermarriage phase would not last. It would practically stop after the Dalai Lama took Exile. Pant however prudently added that "this aspect of Chinese activities in Tibet requires careful watching."

As already mentioned, on April 1, 1955, China took over the Postal, Telegraph and Telephone services with their equipment and the Rest Houses with their equipment, which had previously been operated by the Government of India. It was the end of an era.

Yarphel Pangdatshang, Rapga's elder brother who was nominated Joint Leader of the Tibetan Trade Mission in Kalimpong, was said to have submitted a leave application to the Chinese Government; he did "not

---

17 See Volume 1, Chapter 15.
18 Written Ngapho in some files.

intend to serve any more and would like to return to Tibet to spend a quiet life there." The real reasons for this resignation were unknown. Pant just submitted that after the establishment of the China Trade Agency in Kalimpong, the Communist Party renewed its activities "not only in the town itself but also in the interior."

Further, the number of Chinese shops had increased in Kalimpong and the Bank of China in Calcutta had decided to re-open the branch which had earlier existed, but was closed down owing to lack of business.

During the month of April, the Chinese propaganda continued full swing; anti-American meetings were organized in Gyantse: "the speakers condemned the action of Americans in helping the illegal occupation of Formosa by KMT," said the report.

The Tibetans were exhorted to come forward and co-operate with the PLA to drive the 'war mongers' from their motherland; leaflets condemning the use of atom bombs were distributed. Driving the US out of Tibet was a strange proposition as there was no American on the Roof of the World, but this did not disturb the Chinese leaders.

Delhi was informed that the Dalai Lama was now expected to arrive in Lhasa by the end of June via Chamdo, while the Panchen Lama would use the old traditional route via Nagchuka. He was expected in Shigatse by the middle of July.

Interestingly, the road work on The Gyantse-Shigatse sector had to stop for want of sufficient number of labourers who were paid 10 dollars and 50 seers[19] of grain per month.

In Shigatse, the strength of Chinese troops had been cut by half. Only 500 soldiers remained, the other half had been sent to Western Tibet. It was not easy to discern a pattern behind the Chinese strategy of changing the garrisons, though it was mainly limited to road construction.

---

19 A *seer* is a traditional unit of mass and volume used in large parts of Asia till the middle of the 20th century. It remains in use only in a few countries such as Afghanistan and Iran. In India, the seer (Government seer) was defined by the Standards of Weights and Measures Act as being exactly equal to 1.25 kg (1.792 lb). However, there were many local variants of the seer in India.

In Chumbi Valley, the PLA presence was estimated at 150 troops and 35 at Phari: "Further movements of Chinese troops from the Chumbi Valley towards Lhasa has taken place. This sudden departure of Chinese troops from the Chumbi Valley has given cause to many speculations amongst the locals." Was something brewing in the Mainland?

These were just speculations, though the Indian Trade Agent in Yatung believed that the Chinese had "so well established themselves in the Chumbi Valley that the absence of troops in large numbers would not make much difference to their gaining the political aims."

Let us remember that the ITA, Maj Chibber had served in the Jat Regiment before being sent on deputation for the Ministry of Foreign Affairs.

As they had done in Western Tibet, the Chinese were keen on a census of the adult population in Gyantse and Khampa dzong; the headmen were requested to submit a list of persons residing in their respective areas: "The headmen, however, view this with suspicion and are reluctant to comply with the Chinese demands."

During a cinema show at Gyantse, the attendance was usually poor; the Tibetans were getting tired of Chinese propaganda. It was said that they preferred to cultivate their fields.

In the bazaars in Yatung, a few miles lower south of Chumbi, the Chinese had installed loud speakers: "Peking news is relayed and local announcements and instructions are continuously given." The takeover of the P&T installations by the Chinese was thus announced as well as the damages on the telegraph line on the Chumbi-Jelep-la section. The Chinese propaganda assumed that there were some 'foreign agents' working against them who did not like their taking over of the Indian facilities. Later the announcement was amended, 'foreign' became 'imperialist'; it was however clarified that 'foreign' did not include India, a friendly nation.

The PO was informed by the ITA in Yatung that the villagers on the trade route had been extending their cooperation to the Chinese "by charging very low rates of transport. The reason for this was the promises made by the Chinese to open schools, hospitals for the benefit of the villagers."

Another strange story: Muja Depon was one of the heroes of the Battle of Chamdo[20]; he had fought exceedingly well against the invading Chinese troops. After being posted as Tibetan Trade Agent in Yatung, he got into trouble over some unsettled accounts with the Chumbi Valley headmen. Though the Chinese did not like the Depon, they offered to work on the compromise. The April Report said: "The dispute has been settled. Under the agreement Muja Depon will repay all the money due from him to the headmen of the Chumbi Valley; the Chinese Officer standing surety for him."

The strange part of the deal was that the Depon, was now working very closely with the Chinese; he had a red Communist flag flying over his residence instead of the usual Tibetan flag.

**Report for the Month of May 1955**

The main event in May was the return of the Dalai Lama to Lhasa: "the political, social and economic developments would be speeded up considerably," said the Report.

The PO reported about the Dalai Lama's visit to Xining, capital of Kokonor province[21], where he received a huge welcome. He also visited the Kumbum monastery where his brother Taktser Rinpoche, an incarnate Lama of the famous monastery, served as the abbot before escaping to Lhasa in 1951. Pant wrote: "The Dalai Lama granted a public audience at the monastery when about 10,000 people from various places from the Kokonor province and from Sinkiang, Kansu, Inner Mongolia were present."

The Tibetan leader also went to his birthplace where he met his relatives; he had not seen them for the past 16 years. At a farewell banquet before leaving the region, he said that "Tibet and Kokonor could not develop closer relations until the liberation on account of the Imperialist policy of the KMT regime."

This was obviously a propaganda strategy from the part of China to use his visit to denounce the 'imperialists'.

---

20  See Volume 1, Chapter 15.
21  In fact Qinghai.

The Tibetan leader also went to Labrang Tashi Kyil monastery,[22] where Han Chinese, 'Kansu Mussulmans' and a Tibetan majority, cohabited: "The Dalai Lama and party stayed in Labrang for five days during which period many functions were held in their honour. The Dalai Lama is reported to have expressed his gratification at the opportunity afforded to him by his visit to Peking and also to perform pilgrimage at the important monasteries of Labrang Tashi Khil and Jye Kumbum," said Pant.

The young Lama was happy to see the prosperity of the people of the region "as a result of the protection of the Government of China". He insisted on the importance of good relations between the people and the monk officials. Pant stated that he had no information about the outcome of the conference held in Bejing on March 9, but "there are strong indications of vital changes taking place in the internal administrative structure of Tibet."

The Report continued: "As usual the Chinese propaganda machinery has started its work in spreading report of the wide spread welcome accorded by the people of Tibet to the forthcoming changes."

Several officials were named as having welcomed decisions that nobody knew: "These persons are also said to have stated that these new changes will surely improve Tibet's administration, its economy and education to an extent never seen before."

It was a great opportunity for Tibet to be able to secure such "facilities made possible through the guidance of the Chinese Communist party and a generous Mao Zedong."

The PO, however, noted that "the proposed changes do not seem to have evoked great enthusiasm or universal approval from all Tibetan quarters. There is considerable anxiety amongst certain sections of officials about the exact implications of the administrative reorganization and the set-up of the new departments proposed in place of the old." The monks have been greatly influenced "by this anxiety and nervousness due to the fear of all these changes lest they affect religion."

---

22  Labrang Tashi Kyil is in today's Gansu province.

At the same time, the common man was "supremely oblivious of the implications of the mooted changes." As we shall see, this would not last long, it would soon be the 'common men' who would spearhead the revolt against the Chinese 'reforms'.

In May, 1955, it was believed that the new 'regional autonomy' for Tibet would be introduced as early as July or August after the return of the Dalai Lama to Lhasa. It is what the Communists considered as "the real and complete liberation of Tibet;" at the same time, many understood that the new administrative set-up "will mark the subjugation of Tibet, making the Dalai Lama powerless and a puppet of Peking."

The subjugation was slowly taking shape and the three big Monasteries around Lhasa were "dead against the proposed reforms setting up regional autonomy in Tibet". They rightly alleged that it would diminish the authority of the Dalai Lama: "Although there is considerable opposition to the changes contemplated by the Chinese, it is doubtful if there will be any overt opposition to the proposed reforms," noted Pant who added that the people lacked leadership: "They also do not demonstrate any definite ideological approach to the situation. Faced with the fervour and faith of the communists, the Tibetans seem at the moment lost."

It was absolutely true; further, there was no sense of national unity, or even simply of a Tibetan nation to be defended. The next two years saw, for the first time, the emergence of a 'national' concept taking birth on the Roof of the World. By the time it fully matured into a political emancipation movement, it would be too late.

Pant observed that the Tibetans in Shigatse were getting fed up with the Chinese; he quoted a propaganda meeting held by the Chinese, "when people were asked to express their reactions to the speeches of the Chinese in the meeting, they left the place one by one. The Shigatse people also appear to be becoming more and more critical of Che Jigmey[23] and others who are collaborating with the Chinese."

---

23 Also spelt Jigme.

Chantung Che Jigme (1910-1978). In 1926 Che Jigme travelled from Shigatse to Beijing where he studied Chinese for several years before joining the administration of the 9th Panchen Lama who was in exile in China. He quickly

The PO was informed that a survey party consisting of experts had come to Lhasa to look into the prospects of economic development for 'New Tibet': "This party which [consists] of 41 members will publish a report on the results of their survey. The Chinese do not seem to be losing any time in implementing decisions which they consider important from the point of view of bringing about changes in Tibet."

At the same time as, surveyors were busy selecting a site for a hydro-electric station on the Lhasa river; another 15-member team was on its way to Shigatse for the same purpose: "the decision to build these two power stations together with permanent flood-prevention dike systems on the Lhasa and Nyangchu Rivers, a tannery and an iron works in Lhasa and a steam power plant in Shigatse is reported to have been approved by the State Council in March 1955."

The Chinese had decided to move fast, principally with the infrastructure. The preliminary road survey and alignment of the proposed Lhasa-Shigatse-Gyantse highway had been completed and road building materials were collected at various points in order to speed up work: "Lhasa and Yangpachen[24] are two such centres at this end and reports speak of construction work as having started in the direction of Shigatse from Yangpachen."

---

rose in the Panchen Lama's Administration. He was eventually rewarded and nominated as the Panchen Lama's Representative in Chungking, Sichuan.

In 1937 when the 9th Panchen Lama died in Jyekundo, Qinghai, Che Jigme was involved in all the behind-the-scenes political maneuvering to choose the 10th Panchen Lama.

In 1951, Che Jigme brought the 10th Panchen Lama to Beijing to meet Mao Zedong and then, thanks to a last minute Chinese intercession, personally participated in the 17 Point Agreement negotiations as the only non-Lhasa Tibetan delegate. When the PLA 18th Army marched into Tibet, Che Jigme joined General Fan Ming and the Independent Brigade sent by General Peng Dehuai's Northwest Field Army in support of the 18th Army. After the 10th Panchen Lama penned his famous 70,000 character criticism of Chinese policies in Tibet in 1962, Che Jigme's fate followed his master's and he was removed from all his posts and sent to prison in 1964.

24 Yangpachen Monastery is a Tibetan Buddhist monastery in today's Lhasa City. It is historically the seat of the Shamarpas of Karma Kagyud school. It is about 85 km southeast of Lhasa on the northern side of the Lhorong Chu valley above the Lhasa-Shigatse highway.

Some 2,500 workers who had worked on the Tibet–Sichuan highway, had been sent to construct the Lhasa-Shigatse section. The first stage was to be 90 kilometers long; the first batch of workers started the road construction from Gyantse on March 14: "The Chinese have an ambitious scheme to absorb about 10,000 people affected by last year's floods on this road construction. In addition to their own resources the Chinese are expecting aid from both the Lhasa Tibetan Government and the Panchen Lama's administration in Shigatse."

Though it was said earlier that the new Tibet–Sikang highway was far better than the northern road, the Report indicated that it was in a state of 'tolerable repair' and it needed strengthening against the ravages of the rainy season: "As a preliminary step the paving of the Lhasa–Chamdo road with a layer of chipped stones is being undertaken. The work from the Lhasa end has progressed up to about 50 kilometers. The middle section of the same road (the portion between what is mentioned as Pao He bridge in Kongbo at a distance of 300 kilometers on the road is undergoing improvement and widening."

Further, a great deal of work such as clearing the marshy lands adjacent to the road, widening of its surface or making drainage channels to clear away rain water, strengthening of temporary bridges were the task given to the Tibetan workers: "It looks doubtful whether all this can be done during this summer before the rains break out," the Report noted.

Delhi was informed that the economic situation in Tibet had improved after the two highways became functional: "consumer goods are reported to have flooded the markets of Lhasa."

As a result, great hardship was experienced by the local traders: the goods imported from India could not compete with the ones from China, which were selling at comparatively lower prices.

The discontent in Kham area had not stopped, noted Pant; one of the many reasons was that the local population was compelled to sell their food grains to the Chinese Procurement Board at low prices.

In the field of education, or more correctly propaganda, some 200 men and women (Tibetan and Chinese) were said to be trained at the Chi

Tso Lapta[25]. They studied languages such as Chinese, Tibetan, Hindi, Urdu or Nepali: "It can be safely assumed that all young Tibetans studying at this school would automatically be expected to join the ranks of the Youth and Women's Leagues in Tibet," said the Report.

And the promising ones "would be given chances to join the departments of the Government which under the proposed administrative reorganisation." Pant added: "The emphasis on Hindi, Urdu and Nepali being taught in this school shows a desire to have well-trained people who could be utilized for various types of work in Nepal, India and even Pakistan."

And obviously, the most devoted students were the Chinese: "Judging from the fluency of one Chinese official in Lhasa, Chang Chi Fing in the Nepali language which he learnt in that school, the outgoing students of this school can well be expected to have a good working knowledge of these languages."

Also, in the field of propaganda, the Youth League[26] had a meeting in Gyantse; songs in Tibetan and Chinese were played through the loudspeakers for the public; it was followed by short speeches in Tibetan and Chinese announcing that an electric power station at Shigatse would soon be installed and the whole of Shigatse town would be electrified. The Chinese planned to import the entire plant[27].

Meanwhile, on April 21, leaflets containing anti-Chinese material, strongly condemning the Chinese rule in Tibet and the proposed administrative reorganisation were thrown into the Lhasa Cathedral and in the Barkhor area: "Generally people were interested in the leaflets and suspect the work of some monk officials who are said to be bitterly opposed to the forthcoming changes."

The Chinese reaction was that the leaflets had been printed and imported from a foreign country. "India!!!" said the PO.

---

25  General School – previously known as the language school.

26  Shonu Tsongdu.

27  Probably from the Mainland?

Continuing on the propaganda side, some Chinese women had been touring Shika[28] to 'educate' Tibetan women on domestic science; telling them that women were equal to men.

At the same time, a rumour circulated that the Chinese would bring some 500 Chinese girls trained in Communism to Lhasa and they would be encouraged to marry monks: once the monks are married "they will be given loans to carry on trade." The PO noted that the Chinese were experiencing a serious resistance to the new changes from the monasteries: "Perhaps this is the subtle means of overcoming this resistance and hastening the process of sinification of Tibet," wrote Pant, referring to the marriage of monks attempt.

As for the cultural exchanges, a team of Tibetan dancers and musicians had been sent to Beijing, while the Tibetan Government in Lhasa had instructed the authorities of Gyantse to recruit the dancers from the interior villages: "Many a dancer on learning what was coming have fled from their homes!!" noted the PO.

Despite the new roads reaching Lhasa, there was "a distinct threat of famine in Gyantse area …largely to last year's floods[29] and scarcity of water at the time of sowing of crops."

The aftermath of the floods was still looming over the region as only half of the total cultivable area could be sown in 1955; the remaining area was left uncultivated due to the scarcity of water. Further, famine conditions were reported in Pemako area, North of NEFA, while deaths due to starvation had been reported from Tsona.[30]

Delhi was informed that Gyalo Dhondup, the elder brother of the Dalai Lama, had visited Kalimpong in the third week of May; he stayed at Reting[31] Labrang, near the Pangdatsang House. The Tibetan leader's elder sister[32] was accompanying him; during their short stay, they met the Chinese Trade Agent: "The Chinese appear to be doing their best

---

28  Zayul area, north of the Lohit Valley.
29  Of July 1954. See Volume 2, Chapter 23.
30  North of Tawang in NEFA.
31  A former Regent of Tibet.
32  Tsering Dolma.

in winning over the confidence of these Tibetans officials who are more or less settled down in Kalimpong."

The Chinese were also trying to woo Tsipon Shakabpa[33], "[the] uncalled for visits are usually paid to him [Shakabpa] by high Chinese officials such as the Consul General, Calcutta, and the Embassy officials when they visit Kalimpong. The subject matter of the talk [is about] his return to Tibet for the betterment of the country and the people."

But Shakabpa and Gyalo Thondup would soon be the strongest proponents of Tibetan independence. Apparently, the Chinese felt that "the continued stay of important Tibetans in India may make it difficult for them to win over completely the Tibetan people. They seem therefore to give special attention to the persuasion of the Tibetans residing in India to return to Tibet."

This did not work.

**Monthly Report for June 1955**

The Dalai Lama and the Panchen Lama were back in Tibet; this event would trigger important changes on the Roof of the World. According to the PO's Report, "The arrival of these great dignitaries was celebrated with the usual traditional pomp and splendor. The return of the Dalai Lama is of special significance at this juncture as it is only on his return and perhaps only after he has given some indication of his mind that the reaction of the Tibetan people to the scheme of the Preparatory Committee that is being instituted as the new form of government in Tibet is going to be clear."

People from all over Tibet were "disgruntled and angry that a new form of government is being fostered on them without their consent or cooperation," noted Pant who believed that the reaction of the masses, and particularly the monasteries, would soon take place: "It is not

---

33 Tsipon Wangchuk Deden Shakabpa (January 11, 1907 – February 23, 1989) was a Tibetan nobleman, scholar and former Finance Secretary of the government of Tibet. Shakabpa joined the Government at the age of 23, in 1930, as an official of the Treasury, and was appointed Minister of Finance in 1939, a position he held until 1950. Later, he shifted to Kalimpong where he became one of the main proponents of an Independent Tibet.

unlikely that some protests and demonstrations take place in Lhasa and other towns against the establishment of the Preparatory Committee."

But the Tibetans started also to be resentful about the integration of the Tibetan Army into the PLA; they were upset with the new currency reforms too.

But it looked as though nothing could stop the Chinese who had started settling in Tibet, while making arrangements to send Tibetan youths over to China for 'education': "Some of the high officials whose children have been in China for a couple of years are, however, expressing dissatisfaction at the kind of education that is being given to them in China. Their main complaint is that there is a serious attempt made to turn the Tibetan children into Chinese [nationals]."

The PO further commented: "From the point of view of culture, tradition and their religion, these young boys taken to China would be the losers". It was at least what their parents felt.

The Youth Leagues was also used to spread Communism to "win over the population to their views and ways of life." The conclusion of the Report: "the condition of affairs in Tibet at the moment is very fluid."

It was clear that the Tibetans would not accept "the suzerainty of the Chinese, both emotionally and physically. If the Chinese with the help of some of the Tibetan officials whom they have won over try to go too fast in Tibet there is likelihood of their being faced with strong and even well organised and pre-planned opposition."

This was exactly what happened during the following years; the situation in Kham was moreover worrying, said the Report: "[The] Chinese have not so far introduced any social or economic reforms in Kham. Khampas who had been subjected to illegal exactions by the Tibetan officials all along have been given three years exemption from payment of taxes. The period of exemption ends by the end of this year."

It was not factually correct that the 'reforms' had not started in Kham, but it was true that it was not easy to get fresh news from the Eastern province.

In the Chumbi valley, closer to India, the Chinese were trying to persuade the Tibetans to send their children to join the Youth League: "Eight children in all, four from the Lower Chumbi Valley and four from the Upper Chumbi valley are reported to have volunteered." In general, the parents were unhappy to send their children to China.

It is around this time an earthquake affected Sichuan and Sikang; it caused a lot of devastation and destroyed a third of Tachienlu.[34] The road between Chamdo and Lhasa had been seriously damaged; a bridge was said to have been completely destroyed, forcing the Dalai Lama to cancel his visit to Tachienlu.

Pant also informed Delhi that the Changlo bridge over the Nyang river near Gyantse had just been opened to traffic. The Chinese immediately posted guards on both sides; it was also reported that the headmen in Gyantse area were ordered that every house should send a male member for construction of roads.

All this was adding to the resentment.

**Movement of Troops**

Like in the previous month, movement of troops was reported in Yatung. One night, some 100 soldiers arrived at Chorten Karpo, North of the Sikkim border and Galinka[35]; after a couple of days' stay, they left. About 135 troops were stationed in Chumbi at that time; out of which about 50 were in the valley while the others were in Chumbi (30), Yatung Bazar (10), Chorten Karpo (15) and Galinkha(30).

That was not much, considering that it was the main border with India.

The permanent membership of the Youth League in the Chumbi valley was estimated to be eight. The members received Rs 150 per month for broadcasting the Chinese social welfare's schemes: "The nature of the 'welfare' work done by these Youth League members is not known," commented the Report.

---

34 Tachienlu or Kangding or Dartsedo is today a county-level city and the seat of Garzê Tibetan Autonomous Prefecture in Sichuan. Kangding's urban center is called Lucheng, which has around 100,000 inhabitants.

35 In Upper Dromo, the northern part of the Chumbi valley.

A body of leading men in the Chumbi valley, was to advise the Chinese on local as well as other policy matters; they were usually lavishly entertained wherever there was a meeting, it was "the only important work this body does", said Pant who added: "The members of this body after such feasting are informed of the decisions arrived at by the government at Peking or Lhasa and asked to cooperate."

The summary of world news was distributed during these meetings 'in which China figures very prominently.'

But there was a price to pay to be looked after so lavishly, the Chinese warned the headmen that "they should not call on any foreigners without the specific permission of the Chinese nor should they send any of their representatives to receive any foreigners at the border or the checkpost."

It was obviously targeting the Indian diplomats posted in Yatung.

Pant reminded Delhi that during his visit to Yatung some headmen of the valley had called on him: "They were keenly desirous to receive the Foreign Secretary at the Chema checkpost together with the Indian traders but were stopped from doing so."

The Chinese told the headmen who had been approached to supply the transport for the Foreign Secretary's return trip that they could not do so directly: "All such requests must come through the Chinese and the transport should be supplied only when they instructed them." The Chinese did not agree when a senior headman proposed to inform the Foreign Bureau after they had supplied the transport.

The situation was fast deteriorating for the Indian presence in the valley; little could be done, with India having agreed to whatever the Chinese wanted during the talks in 1954.

It was reported that a Tibetan girl from Yatung had to marry a Chinese army person; it was the fourth such marriage since the arrival of the Chinese in the Chumbi valley: "The marriage was celebrated by having a big feast at the Chinese Supply Post in Yatung Bazar and all the Chinese officers attended this feast." In the meantime, two girls and one boy from Phari had 'volunteered' to join the group of youngsters being sent to China, they were imparted lessons in Communism prior to their departure for China.

Another example, the son of a peon working in the Indian Consulate at Lhasa 'volunteered' from Yatung bazaar. He had appeared for his matriculation at Gangtok and was getting a stipend from the Government of India for his studies. A total of 25 such boys and girls were supposed to have signed in from the Chumbi valley, all between 17 and 25 years old. While the girls would have to stay one year in China, the boys' studies would last three years. In Yatung, they were 'encouraged' to mix and eat with the Chinese soldiers and officers and take part in variety shows and later speak about it in laudatory terms.

The Chinese were making efforts to have informal contacts with the Indian and Nepali traders in the Yatung bazaar; two officers – one knowing Hindi and the other Nepali – visited the traders to try to converse with them: "One of them even paid a visit to our Medical Officer attached to our Trade Agency and said that he had just dropped in, so that he could have an opportunity to converse in Hindi and thus improve himself in that language," wrote Pant who however felt that they belonged to the Chinese Intelligence.

Coinciding with the celebrations for the Dalai Lama's return to Lhasa, on June 30, the Chinese summoned all headmen of the valley to discuss plans for the construction of a school in Yatung, but the rumour was that it was only organized to inaugurate the arrival of Communism in the valley.

In the meantime, news was received about the Lhasa-Qinghai highway, the road would not be usable for motor vehicles during summer on account of countless marshy areas; it is what Tibetan travelers coming from Xining via Nagchuka had reported earlier; even for animals, the services of 'expert' nomad guides was necessary during the summer. Other reports also said the Lhasa-Sikang motor road may be in unusable condition this summer: "They feel that due to numerous landslides last year between Giamda and Pome the mountain slopes have become too soft and there may be many more landslides this year."

After India had handed over the Posts and Telegraphs to the Chinese, the latter had established an office at Goshampa House in Lhasa.

Telegrams and mails for India were accepted, though the Tibetans and Nepalese traders complained that mails from Lhasa to Kalimpong and vice versa were taking some 18 days to reach their destinations: "It is suspected that the Chinese accumulate mails until it is equal to one full mule load and then dispatch them."

A more worrying incident was a fight between Tibetan soldiers and five Khampa muleteers in Chumbi. One of the muleteers was stopped by the Tibetan soldiers and asked to pay a grazing toll and when he refused to obey, he was pulled from his mule and beaten with stones. The Khampa muleteer then stabbed three of the soldiers with his dagger. Soon armed Tibetan and Chinese soldiers arrived on the spot and the muleteers fled. The Khampa who had killed the soldiers was however arrested and put in a cell at Chumbi after having been given 200 lashes.

The Chinese also started recruiting young boys; twenty of them were imparted military training in the Chinese Military camp at Shigatse.

As soon as the new Chinese primary school was opened at Yatung, many children and adults were admitted; at the same time, the Tibetan school run by some local people was closed.

In Lhasa, another public school was opened in the heart of Lhasa city; Tibetans have been requested to send their children to the new school: "The present strength of the school is 2,000 and only Tibetan is being taught at present. Chinese propose to introduce teaching Chinese also in due course."

The salary of a teacher was 150 dollars per month and it was said that many Tibetan teachers were appointed. Under Chinese advice, the Tibetan Cabinet decided to pass a Bill making education compulsory in Tibet.

Interestingly, some of the goods imported from India were now sent by trucks to China as these vehicles on their return journey to China were generally empty: "The Tibetans do not seem to be very happy at this and greatly resent this. They feel that the Chinese assurances that the Lhasa market would be flooded with food grains and goods once the road from Lhasa to China was opened was only a false propaganda."

The Chinese have started publishing a two-page newspaper on a small litho press at Gyantse. It mostly contained propaganda material and was distributed to a few selected Tibetans only.

The circulation of paper currency had started in Lhasa "but great care is being taken by the Chinese to do so only [when] the Chinese are sure that [these Tibetans] are their supporters. ...the Chinese are trying this method to test public opinion."

**The Dalai Lama Returns**

Finally, after a several-months visit to China, where he had attended the first Chinese National People's Congress, the Dalai Lama returned to Lhasa on June 27. He was accompanied by Gen Li Chuah[36], Deputy Commander of the PLA's headquarters. The Dalai Lama gave a speech recalling his journey to the "capital of our Motherland" and his meeting with Mao Zedong "the great leader of all the nationalities," he had "received intimate instructions from Mao," he asserted.

Speaking of the Chinese Constitution, the young Tibetan leader declared that it was an "achievement unheard of in China's history. The Constitution consolidated the interests of the entire Chinese people. Strengthened the great unity of amity, love and cooperation among the various nationalities and defined the rights and duties of the people. In particular it gave recognition to the rights of various national minorities to equality. All of us must study the Constitution well and support it. We Tibetans feel it a great honour and are proud of ourselves in being a member of the great family of our motherland."

Did he say that? It is very difficult to verify, but it is what the Indian Consul reported to Gangtok.

About the Preparatory Committee, the Dalai Lama said that it was a "great achievement for the Tibetan nationality and Tibetan people on the road to happiness." He would have added that considering the fact that the Tibetans were "comparatively backward in the economic

---

36 Maj Gen Li Jue (1914-2010). Gen Li very briefly was head of the 18th Army's General Logistics Department, before being transferred in Tibet as Deputy Commander of the Tibet Military Command in the mid-1950s. He was responsible for the Military Intelligence in Tibet.

and cultural fields it is all the more necessary to rely on the selfless and comparatively long-term assistance of the Central Government, the advanced Han people and Han cadres."

Pant said that the Dalai Lama was reported to be full of praise for the Chinese people and the Chinese government. He even spoke of Communism: "the unparalleled achievements attained in various fields in the short space of a few years under the correct leadership of the Chinese Communist Party and the great policy of Chairman Mao Zedong enables the fraternal nationalists of the whole country to unite into a great family of love and cooperation."

Once again, these were his reported words. He would have concluded by praising the great achievements "both political and religious and the construction of Sinkiang-Tibet and Chinghai-Tibet highways during my absence in China has not only laid a good foundation for national defence, but will contribute to greater unity among the fraternal nationalities and pave the way for various constructions in Tibet."

'National defence' against whom?

It could only be against India. It was true that the construction of the two roads was a great engineering achievement.

## 08

# Tibet's Assimilation Continues
# July - December 1955

**The Report for the Month of July 1955**

In this chapter, we will continue to look at the happenings in 1955 on the Tibetan plateau. Life was slowly changing. The Indian officers started realizing that Tibet would never be the same.

In his July Report[1], Pant first mentioned the People's Association, the *Mimang* and its activities: "The Peoples' Party seems to be on the increase within Tibet. There is a general feeling that this popular movement which desires progress for Tibet, change in the administrative setup and a fully independent Tibet is getting better organized."

Though it could not be formally called a political party, it was nonetheless a popular movement: "Some of the more powerful officials and most of the leaders of the monasteries from all parts of Tibet are seriously examining the issues and discussing how to solve various problems that confront them."

One could say that it was the first time in the history of Tibet that the masses decided to take the future into their own hands and at least debate the Chinese presence in their country. The PO's report continued: "There are some who still put their faith in the capacity

---

1 *Political situation reports on Sikkim from the political officer in Sikkim Gangtok. Department: External Affairs, Branch: NEF, 1955, File No. File No. 30(3)-NEF/55.* Available in the National Archives of India.

of the Chinese to institute progressive reforms and yet not to interfere with the internal autonomy of Tibet."

This popular movement was not well-known outside Tibet, mainly due to the lack of communication with the outside world; it should, however, be noticed that in his Last Testament the Thirteenth Dalai Lama had mentioned the danger that Communism could bring to the nation.

Pant observed: "There are others who though in the beginning believed that the Chinese would help them to throw out reactionary, corrupt official cliques in Lhasa and other places of Tibet, are now disillusioned and feel that unless the Chinese are thrown out of Tibet there can be no real progress for that country."

For the poorer sections of the Tibetan population, the arrival of the Chinese in Lhasa was like the arrival of extra-terrestrials; it is only after the first years of occupation that they realized that their country would never be the same.

The Report from Gangtok said: "It appears that immediately the desire of most of these 'nationalists' is to postpone the implementation of the new scheme of government, the Preparatory Committee."

How could this be done? Always practical, some Tibetans thought that if the Dalai Lama himself could be persuaded to undertake some large religious ceremonies, which would last for a few months, "during this period no political, economic or military changes would be instituted."

The *Mimang* movement also thought of reviving an old Committee, the *Lekcho Lekung*, "appointed to examine the present administrative and economic setup and suggest improvements."

However, Pant believed that some officials "may insist that this Committee should examine the proposals under the Preparatory Committee scheme before these are put into practice." In other words, the Chinese would have to vet the 'reforms'.

The situation was not simple; many Tibetans were influenced by the Chinese while others were ready to start a non-cooperation movement; according to Pant: "There is also a possibility that some of the officials who are disgruntled and disappointed may refuse to execute the orders that may be issued under the Preparatory Committee scheme. They would, in fact, non-cooperate with the working of this scheme."

## The Panchen Lama's Monastery

Another complication was that there were serious disagreements between the advisers and officials of Tashi Lhunpo[2] and the Government at Lhasa. The rivalry between the 'officials' of the Dalai Lama and the Panchen Lama had been an issue for decades. Now there was another player, the *Mimang* who "also have been greatly agitated and there was some question of 'direct action' against Tashi Lhunpo. Wiser counsels prevailed and the possibility of a minor, or even a major, civil war has been averted. The cooperative attitude of Tashi Lhunpo officials with the Chinese has brought about this general feeling against them."

It, however, appeared that the *Mimang* and the monks had been discussing the problems facing Tibet and "there is general agreement on the necessity of instituting a different kind of administrative set up in Tibet, it appears that only a federal constitution for Tibet would satisfy the Khampas and the people of Tsang."

It was an interesting though late development: if Tibet had been united, or a 'confederation' formed in 1950, the Chinese would have not been able to occupy so easily the Roof of the World.

We shall come back to the *Mimang* movement later.

## The Situation in Western Tibet

News from Western Tibet was also sent to Delhi: the general conditions remained the same though the pressure on the local populations from the Tibetan officials, especially the tax collectors was decreasing; they did not want to be seen as the villains: "The Chinese are also trying to create a better impression on the people by paying one *dayang*[3] or Rs.3 per day as wages and selling consumer goods at cost price to the needy people."

---

2  Written 'Tashi Lhempo' in the Report. The Tashi Lhunpo was the seat of the Panchen Lama.

3  Silver dollar.

The PO commented that the population in this region "seems to be shedding away their more acute suspicions of the Chinese though they cannot be fully reconciled to the Chinese. Some of them have started approaching the Chinese to seek redress against certain Tibetan officials."

At the same time, the Chinese were taking Tibetan youth for 'training' them in China; five of them were selected from Purang and others from Rudok and Tsaparang: "Originally they intended sending only one person from each district. The exact number of these youngsters to be sent to China is not yet known."

The Chinese were openly talking of building a motorable road from Western Tibet to Lhasa and to complete it before the next trading season, i.e. the summer of 1956: "But so far there have appeared no signs of any activity in that direction," noted Pant, though it was a fact that the Aksai Chin road was well underway at that time and the ITA would inform Delhi about it in Gartok during the summer.

A law and order incident took place near a new bridge constructed by the Chinese over Kyi chu river in Lhasa when some boatmen tried to set fire to the bridge. Earlier people were ferried across the river by Tibetans who thus earned their living, but the Report explained: "The Chinese sentries at the bridge apprehended them in time and their remaining accomplices have been rounded up."

The Lhasa population greatly resented what happened to the boatmen: "There was even a rumour that they were being skinned alive by the Chinese on a certain date near the bridge. A big crowd went to witness the event but it all proved to be a hoax."

## Road Construction

At the same time, the development of the infrastructure, particularly the roads was going on full steam: "A regular stream of Peoples' Liberation Army is said to have been sent to speed up the construction of Lhasa–Shigatse road." There was even a rumour saying that a bridge over the Brahmaputra[4] was nearing completion.

---

4 Pant probably means the Yarlung Tsangpo.

Pant also informed the Ministry that as Gen Zhang Guohua left for China to attend 'some important meetings', senior Tibetan officials and members of Youth League went to wish him goodbye.

Interestingly, the Chinese were not invited to the celebrations held in Gyantse to welcome the Dalai Lama back in Tibet.

Due to the problems between the Lhasa Government and the Tashi Lhunpo; when Lhasa approached the Panchen Lama's monastery for the construction of a portion of Shigatse-Gyantse road[5]; the monastery refused to supply any labour: "consequently the Chinese have stopped giving any help to this area."

According to Pant, some Chinese officers with the help of the Panchen Lama were preparing "a list of Tibetan officers and others suspected to be anti-China." Some 45 persons were already reported to have been blacklisted; the Report said: "In a public speech at Lhasa Sherab Geshey[6] (Khempo) a great supporter of the Chinese is reported to have praised the Chinese for the improvements but said that they have yet not been able to solve the problem of the poor masses."

His words were apparently resented by the Chinese "but it has been an eye-opener to the Tibetans in general."

More amusing, appeared that the Chinese stationed spies in an adjacent room where a meeting was held between the officers of the Dalai Lama and the Panchen Lama in Beijing to discuss the future administrative set up of Tibet; the spies could overhear the discussion: "Both the Panchen Lama and the Dalai Lama however came to know of this later on." It was probably true.

The Chinese authorities in Lhasa were said to allow "free and frank political discussions among the members of the Youth League," but when one member who had gone to school in Darjeeling asked about the freedom of expression and press in China, stating that in India

---

5   Lhasa was to undertake the construction of Phari-Gyantse portion and the Tashi Lhunpo was to construct the rest.

6   Geshe Sherab Gyatso, a native from Amdo province, who collaborated with the Chinese in the early years.

anybody could criticize a leader, and if it was the same in China, the answer "was somewhat evasive."

A Chinese official explained that the Chinese leaders were elected "by the members of the public in pursuance of free franchise."

Some other Youth League members said that it was desirable to maintain cordial and friendly relations with India: "India had been supplying to Tibet various essential commodities and was also very liberal in all her dealings with Tibet." To this, a Chinese officer replied that India was a true friend of China and "never failed to lend her support to China on any international issue," adding that it was the earnest desire of the Peoples' Government to strengthen the existing friendly ties with India.

In Yatung a new Tibetan Trade Agent was appointed in place of Depon Muja, Rimshi Dingja was to be assisted by Chatu-Tshang[7], Choktey, Shap-to Kusho and the youngest son of Kusho Chanya.

A new telegraph line between Gyantse and Phari was installed after necessary material was sent to Saugang from Gyantse to repair the old one.

The Panchen Lama finally arrived at Shigatse on July 8, on his way to Lhasa where he met the Dalai Lama.

Some 18 boys and 9 girls were sent from Yatung to Beijing for education and training. On July 13, they were given a send-off at the football ground where tents were pitched by the Tibetans; *chang*[8] and tea was served.

Waiting for the final decision regarding the new administrative set up, the expansion of the Chinese Trade Agency in Kalimpong remained pending; the Report mentioned that Yarphel Pangdatsang "is often seen visiting his younger brother, Phu Ragpa who is known for his anti-Chinese feelings. Mr. Ragpa is generally said to be keeping aloof from the Chinese."

---

7 Chatushang.
8 Tibetan beer.

Regarding the Indian border in NEFA, the Dzongpons of Pemako, North of Siang Frontier Division told the Tibet Government that a Dzongpon in Pemako was unnecessary and only a burden on the public.

Also North of NEFA, a school had been opened at Tsona by the Tibet Government in collaboration with Lobsang Shoda, the brother of a senior official; a person called Ugen Chewang of Gyanggar was nominated as a teacher: "People of Tsona are reported to have refused the Chinese sponsoring the school."

The authorities at the Lhasa Primary School were busy enrolling fresh students. While some 500 children came for admission, only 300 could be admitted due to shortage of seats. Six class rooms had been added to the existing school accommodation.

It was now rumored that October 1 was the date for the introduction of the new form of Government in Tibet.

According to the PO, the number of industrial workers in Tibet would have gone up to 3,000; they were mostly engaged in workshops and factories run by the PLA such as printing presses, iron and carpentry shops.

But all was not well on the plateau; thirty Tibetan labourers had been arrested by the Chinese at Gyamda[9]; they would have set fire to a Chinese military ration store seeking revenge for the non-payment by the Chinese of their wages; the PO commented: "Situation still appears to be tense."

During August 1955, some 260 Chinese troops had arrived at Galinka and Chorten Karpo in the Chumbi valley in place of the troops that left on leave or were transferred from December 1954 to March 1955. It was said that some 500 more were expected: "Distribution of these troops in the Chumbi valley is not yet known. Arms and ammunition left by the troops earlier is being collected by them."

Further information of military value was the scarcity of foodgrains in Tsona area "attributed largely due to ban on export of foodgrains from Tawang and Bhutan. The Chinese, however, seem to have given

---

9   In Kongpo region.

priority to the import of foodgrains from China along the Lhasa-Chamdo[10] road where trucks have been kept in reserve for quick and easy transshipment in the event of landslides."

Delhi was told that the period of service for the Army, Navy and Air Force personnel (not officers) in the Chinese army is three, four and five years. From 1956, it was announced that the officers would wear their rank badges: "The question of ranks to be allotted to various personnel is still under consideration by the Chinese.[11]"

It is not clear what the Chinese Navy was doing in Tibet; it is, however, possible that the PO got the information from a general notification.

In Yatung and Chumbi valley, Chinese soldiers were reported to be helping the local people in harvesting potatoes. Of the 160 Chinese soldiers said to be staying in Yatung bazaar, some 130 soldiers were seen every morning on parade in the football ground.

In Western Tibet, the main concentration of the Chinese troops was at Garkunsa, Gartok, Rudok, Barkha, Khojarnath, Taklakot and Tashigang. The troops were generally engaged in the construction of houses and barracks for the troops.

## The Monthly Report for the Month of August 1955

The Tibetans could not really understand what was happening to them.

Pant commented at the outset of his August Report: "During the absence of the Dalai Lama in China the people of Tibet were in a more or less bewildered state regarding the recent political and economic developments in Tibet and were unable to make up their minds as to whether they should cooperate or disassociate themselves from these changes."

This situation would continue to deteriorate during the following years. When the Dalai Lama arrived in Lhasa, some 50,000 people came from all parts of Tibet to welcome him and offer prayers; they were keen to present "a petition expressing their reactions to the new economic administrative and political changes envisaged." The

---

10 Sichuan-Tibet Highway.

11 Earlier, they had no badge or insignia showing their ranks.

program was discussed with the entourage of the Tibetan leader and the representatives of the *Mimang*. Tibetans found a way: the Dalai Lama would give sermons "in which he would indicate his own advice to the people of Tibet"

But after he spoke, the impression created was "of great happiness and of even elation because of his forthright advice. Some had feared that the Dalai Lama would perhaps be won over by the Chinese and would not take any strong action."

What had the Dalai Lama said?

He spoke harshly about 'past mistakes' of the Tibetan people; he mentioned "corruption, nepotism, idleness and the attraction of the Tibetan officials to pursuits of leisure, luxury and near enjoyments."

He urged the people of Tibet to take a united stand for the betterment of the country and asked everyone to work hard to make Tibet "an independent progressive, peaceful, spiritual country."

The Dalai Lama also categorically declared that the Chinese had come to Tibet only to help the Tibetans and that they would 'return back to their country' after the Tibetans were fully instructed in the art of running a modern government.

One wonders how the Tibetan leadership were so naïve at that time, though they were not the only ones, many in India thought that a dose of socialism would be good for Tibet. The Dalai Lama was reported to have told his countrymen "no guest could remain in the house if the host did not want him to be there".

The references to the Chinese leaving Tibet and the 'independence of Tibet' satisfied the people; they now knew that the Dalai Lama stood for a free and progressive Tibet, especially after the Tibetan leader urged his people not to wear Chinese dress, adopt Chinese customs and food "[you] should not leave our own way of life."

The Dalai Lama told the huge crowd, estimated at 60,000, who had come to listen to him that if they worked in a united manner and give up all their vices, they would be able to improve Tibet: "In that case the help of the Chinese people will not be necessary.

He said that the '*Rang Kyong Sishang*', the new autonomous status of Tibet "would be beneficial to all".

The PO in Sikkim concluded: "It remains to be seen how the scheme of the Preparatory Committee drafted in China would now be put into effect or as to whether some new machinery would be created to bring about change and progress in Tibet." Pant noticed that the Chinese were more and more aware of the Tibetan growing feeling for 'independence'.

He believed that the Chinese would try "to accommodate themselves with this new spirit." This was a misreading on the part of the Political Officer!

Pant also analyzed that despite the rising tide of Tibetan nationalism, the Chinese were able to bring many new developments: roads, hospitals and schools: "The Chinese army is also participating in various schemes of agricultural and other developments. Troops in the Chumbi valley, in Tsang and other areas, have been instructed to actively help the people in their farm work and it has been reported that in Yatung a few of the army personnel are deputed to serve water to the bazaar people!"

He concluded that all these acts of cooperation and kindness were "bound to have some effect upon the Tibetan mind."

Due to the Chinese pressure, many Tibetans started to feel themselves closer to India: "the number of patients taking advantage of the Indian Consulate Hospital at Lhasa is reported to be increasing. Mostly monks and Tibetan soldiers who are said to be 'fanatically loyal' to the Dalai Lama, seek the medical aid. The same people call the Indian officials in the Consulate General, 'our officials' and 'Dikyi Lingka', 'our office'.

**Will the Chinese Leave, Once Tibet is Ready?**

In the meantime, the Chinese continued with the same propaganda argument; once the Tibetans would be ready, they would leave. Some Tibetan members of the Youth League were told that "Tibetans should work hard to become capable of shouldering the responsibility of the administration of their country." They were given the example of Inner Mongolia where the Chinese personnel withdrew when the local people were able to run the administration in an efficient way. They promised the same for Tibet.

The road construction work was continuing apace, the Chinese were concentrating on one portion of the Shigatse–Lhasa road said to be the most difficult portion of the entire project: "Nearly 4,000 Chinese labourers of the Peoples Liberation Army are said to be working on this portion. Due to the very high altitude of this pass, about 17,000 ft., a good number of Chinese are reported to have fallen ill," observed Pant, but the progress was slow, though officials believed that once this portion was completed the remaining portion of the road would be easier.

The Report noted that some "ten thousand arms of different kinds and large quantities of ammunition belonging to the Tibetan Government, which has been lying in the Potala compound have now been removed to a strong room inside Potala in order to keep them safe from the Chinese."

This could not have escaped the notice of the Chinese intelligence.

In a small way, India too had started engaging in propaganda, the Dalai Lama was shown a film about the Indian Republic Day celebrations in 1954 and Nehru's visit to China: "These films were recently loaned out by our Consulate at the request of the Dalai Lama" The young leader 'liked' them very much.

It was reported that the differences between Lhasa and the Tashi Lhunpo administration had been amicably settled in China; Ngabo apparently stood up against the demand of an independent province of Tsang. Mao Zedong and Zhu De too did not favour Tsang as independent province.

When the Dalai Lama expressed the desire to use his own car for the last stage of his return before reaching Lhasa, the Chinese did not permit him to do so as they "feared lest a time bomb was placed in the car." At the same time, they presented him with six cars built on the jeep Soviet model: "These cars are garaged in Norbu Lingka. The drivers for these cars are reported to be Chinese and paid by Chinese Government."

The Tibetan boys and girls from Chumbi valley and Shigatse passed through Lhasa: "These children although at present still wearing their own Tibetan dresses will have to discard these after Chamdo and wear the Chinese school uniforms." They were provided with free boarding and lodging and 10 silver dollars as pocket money per month.

Some Tibetan traders and officials who returned from China reported the existence of huge dumps of petrol on the road between Chamdo and the Tibetan capital, while a Chinese colony of some "100 neatly constructed houses has come up in the Pome region. An extensive area around here has been brought under cultivation."

An interesting development narrated by the PO is that after their return from China, most of the servants of Tibetan officials had a completely different outlook: "They no longer believe in utter submissiveness to their masters." The masters just 'ignored' this new attitude.

The headmen of the Chumbi valley and people of Yatung were called by the Chinese for a meeting. They were lectured by a Tibetan, Theiji Dingja, serving as Vice-Head in-charge Foreign Bureau. He urged the people to improve the cleanliness of the Yatung bazaar. He mentioned the general improvement in cleanliness in Lhasa since the liberation; it was previously a very filthy town, he said. Diseases are now gradually vanishing in the Tibetan capital. He also admonished the headman for calling on "visiting foreigners (meaning particularly Indian officials)". It was highly improper and undignified, he asserted: "The people must first seek permission from the Foreign Bureau if ever they want to call on any foreign visitor to the valley." The rationale behind this new ban was that Yatung was "an important trading centre it was likely that there are agents of the imperialist powers and the people should be on the lookout for such people and report them to the Foreign Bureau."

News from Western Tibet said that small parties of Chinese were seen constantly moving between Gartok and Taklakot in Western Tibet: "plenty of stores, wireless equipment and furniture is reported to be arriving in Gartok from Lhasa. In this area Chinese are reported to be making best use of the medium of cinema for their propaganda. Even in out of the way places like Barkha, the Chinese Army Welfare officers are showing films to the people in the open."

A census was also conducted in the area by two Chinese officers who received help from the Tibetan Garpons.

While Minsar, the Indian enclave in Western Tibet was not mentioned, the Report spoke of the Bhutanese 'pockets'. They were still under the control of the Bhutanese officials "who exercise all judicial powers on their subjects. Chinese are reported to be trying to find out as to how these pockets in Tibet came to be in the possession of Bhutan. The Bhutan Government's official there has been approached many a time with such questions from the Chinese but he is reported to have evaded any direct answer." It was also reported that according to an old agreement the Bhutanese subjects in Tibet were only liable to contribute towards free transport to the Tibetan Government, but were not subject to any other taxes.

The PO informed Delhi that there was a rumor that the Chinese had signed an agreement with Russia, for the latter to explore minerals in Tibet: "They will also operate the mines when they are discovered for a period of 30 years. Some Tibetans, who have come to know of this, allege that the Chinese communists are now selling Tibet to Russia."

The economic scene was fast changing. The Chinese authorities decided to relax some of the restrictions for the issue of Bank drafts to Tibetan traders: "The traders will, however, be required to sign an agreement to import such goods from India only as ordered by the Chinese authorities."

In Lhasa the authorities had to obtain the permission to allow more wool to be exported to India; Beijing was keen to keep a balance of trade between imports and exports between India and Tibet.

But as for the wool trade, Beijing permission was now required for what had been usual practices for decades. The people of Amdo engaged in business to trade with India required also an advance permission "before proceeding to India and furnish sureties who would guarantee their return to Tibet within a specified time." They were not permitted to bring any American and British goods. The PO suggested that these restrictions were the result of the Chinese living under constant fear of the pro-KMT or other anti-communists establishing contacts with Tibetans.

A section of the report was entitled 'Information of Military value'.

Some 3,000 troops had arrived in Lhasa from China; they had come to replace the troops already stationed in Tibet who would return to China, Delhi was informed, while the number of troops in Western Tibet were much less than in 1954: "Such troops as were considered to be old and not fully indoctrinated with communist doctrines were transferred to China and replaced by younger blood."

A new command, called the Sikang-Tibet Army Group was in the offing and would have under its command the 16<sup>th</sup>, 17<sup>th</sup> and 18<sup>th</sup> Armies.

**Report for the Month of September 1955.**

It was now announced that the work of the Preparatory Committee would start soon. In one speech, the Dalai Lama asked the Tibetans to 'cooperate' in the new developments in Tibet for the betterment of the conditions of the people: "He urged them to leave aside lassitude and ignorance and to work unitedly and hard for the upliftment of the country."

Ngago was the most active of the Tibetan officials in support of the Chinese. He had been "working full speed to usher in the new form of the governmental machinery", asserting that Chairman Mao himself had assured the Dalai Lama in Beijing that "the Chinese were in Tibet only to help the Tibetans to gain 'real independence' and that after their task of giving assistance in the economic, social and political transformation of the country was done they would return back to China."

The Dalai Lama several times specifically said that "the Chinese were in Tibet only as long as the Tibetans wanted them there in order to assist them in their task of the development of their country."

But the Chinese, on the contrary, were settling in every day in a more concrete manner. For example, the road to Gyantse was now completed and trucks from Lhasa had arrived on October 7: "The speed with which this work has been done and the organizational efficiency of the Chinese army are really remarkable. It is obvious that all this is making a deep impression on the minds of the Tibetan people. Even persons outside Tibet in these border areas have been impressed by the efficiency and speed with which these road works have been accomplished."

This was indeed a remarkable feat.

At the same time, a new drive for improvement of roads to Lhasa was taking place: "The actual work, it is said, would be conducted by the Depons[12] (COs of the three Tibetan regiments) under the guidance and supervision of the Chinese personnel."

As for the Xining-Lhasa highway, many had feared that it would not be fit for traffic during the monsoons, but the Chinese had laid "big boulders at the marshy area and the alignment of the road has been at the foot of the mountains. …Passengers, merchandise goods and building material are now being freely carried on this road."

The Chinese were regularly informing the general public of Lhasa via loudspeakers of their achievement: some 40 miles of the Shigatse-Lhasa road had been completed. It was also announced that within 28 days they would make the road between Phari and Gyantse motorable once they had completed the Gyantse-Lhasa road.

By now, the PO knew the prowess of the PLA; he commented: "There seems every possibility of the Chinese achieving this aim within 28 days as the trade route between Gyantse and Phari is quite wide, if large labour forces are put on the job at certain places."

Some 10,000 Chinese were working on the Lhasa-Yangpachen[13] road: "Majority of those Chinese are reported to be ex-KMT soldiers who are undergoing sentences of hard labour."

Though the propoganda announced that the Chinese would return to China once the 'reforms' were implemented, the PLA planned to extend the road up to the Indian border. Another road connecting Western Tibet to the Nepal border was planned to Nyalam[14].

---

12 Commanding Officers.

13 Yangpachen is the seat of the Shamar-pas, on the way to Shigatse.

14 Nyalam is a small Tibetan town near the Nepal border. It is today the county seat of Nyalam County in Shigatse Prefecture. It is located 35 km from Dram (or Zhangmu town), which is one of the landports between Nepal and Tibet. Nyalam is situated at 3,750 metres above sea level.

The Sending of students to China continued; some 90 boys, including 30 from the language school, 30 from the primary school and 30 from the Muslim school were selected to go: "The Selection Board is reported to have rejected about 20 students who are feeling much disappointed and feel that they have been rejected as they came from poor families."

At the same time, several Tibetans were sponsored for a sightseeing tour to China; out of 120, some 40 were Tibetans officials; it included Kapshopa Theiji, Lhalu Dzasa, Samdup Photrang Se and Thongpa Khonchung, all high officials.

A meeting was held in camera in Lhasa to discuss the new forms of government. There was a hot discussion between those who had visited China and those who had never been out. The latter argued that nothing substantial had been achieved for Tibet by those who went to China, but Ngabo defended those who had visited China. The main points discussed were:

(a) one thousand Tibetan officers would be required for administrative setup

(b) The Tibetan army's strength would be reduced to merely 1,000 strong – 500 would be the Dalai Lama's body guard regiment and 500 would be used as police force.

(c) Ways and means of making a compromise between the Dalai Lama and the Panchen Lama.

(d) Currency reforms.

It was stated that Ngabo had stopped attending the Kashag meeting ... in view of his work connected with the new administrative setup.

Changes had started taking place at all levels; a report mentioned that the Dalai Lama had called on all the heads of departments to submit their accounts: "Quite a few of the officials who have been guilty of neglect and have not kept their accounts properly and upto date are reported to be much worried."

More importantly, rumors circulated that the Chinese had decided to divide the province of Sikang into two different regions – area East of Yangtze river has been included in the province of Sichuan and the western part would remain with Tibet. This would officially happen in 1965.

However, it was clear from the start that the Preparatory Committee of the Tibetan Autonomous Region [PCTAR] was only to deal with the Tibetan areas west of "the natural boundary along the Yangtze river", in other words, Kham and Amdo province were excluded.

Tibet itself was proposed to be divided into three administrative zones – Central, Western and Eastern.

The Political Officer noted that a multi-racial cultural delegation visited Lhasa; it consisted of ten members from Russia, Poland, Czechoslovakia, France, England and Italy; a Russian was the leader, who stated that the West did not know much about Tibet and her literature.

The Report mentioned that the leader expressed his gratitude to China for giving the opportunity to the delegation "to study things on the spot and promised to give full publicity to Tibet and its culture on their return to their countries." They had an audience with the Dalai Lama.[15]

The Dalai Lama continued with his religious duties. On September 16 and 17, he blessed some 5,000 monks from Drepung and 2,000 from the Sera monastery who had come to Norbulingka

---

15 According to the Tibetan News Summary dated September 15, 1956, the names of the members of the delegation were:

1. Maneen - Editor of *Rhen Tao Pao* (People's Paper) of France.
2. Foo Chingneekaoff- Editor, *Tran Lee Pao* of Russia.
3. Kha Shesi-Editor, Youth League publication called *Tran Lee Pao* of Russia.
4. Dolin – Editor, *Taitay Thung-shun-rhi* from Germany.
5. Paopa – Editor, Check *Thang Shun* of Switzerland.
6. Wee Nin Ton – Editor, *Koong Rhen Pao* of Great Britain.
7. Ngaphuston – Editor, *Go-Ming and Chen We-Pao* from America.
8. Belly Saychi-Editor, *Zewszaypin Pao* of Poland.
9. Malemantalee – Editor, *Thonchee Pao* from Italy.
10. Mrs. Leekhatay Editor, *Shinyeesay Pao* from Italy.

The Newar traders celebrated the Nepal-China agreement[16]; on the occasion, the Nepalese officer invited Chinese officials and the staff from the Indian Consulate General for lunch. General Fan Ming, Yang Gongsu, and the Tibetan ministers attended. Photographs of King Tribhuvan, the Dalai Lama and Mao were displayed.

The Chinese propaganda continued. Gen Zhang Jingwu broadcasted a message on Radio Peking describing the progress in the fields of educational and economic reconstruction in Tibet under the National Economic Plan, "Tibet had just started to march along the glorious path of happiness." He called for support from all Tibetans for the Preparatory Committee. He even criticized the misconduct or lapses of some Chinese in Tibet who "had brought disgrace to the great Chinese nation by violating Tibetans' religious customs, sentiments." He emphasized the united efforts by the Chinese "to defend the natural boundaries of their great Motherland."

Was he pointing a finger at India? Who else had a natural border?

Delhi was informed that a few trucks had arrived in Lhasa with Chinese silver dollars; it was to be given to the Tibetan Government "as first installment towards gradual replacement of their currency."

Interestingly, it appeared that some Chinese dollars were already in circulation in villages along the Assam-Tibet border (NEFA).

The Communist reforms were gradually introduced, the Chinese started imposing heavy taxes on merchants involved in private trade in Kham on both luxury goods and essential commodities; the idea was to do away with private trade. Yarphel Pangdatshang in Lhasa at that time was planning to call for a meeting of Lhasa merchants to protest.

A dozen cars were imported from India by the Chinese; these were assembled by some Nepali mechanics. Further some 6,000 bicycles and 100 motor cycles were also expected.

Regarding the 'military information', the PO told Delhi that a wireless station had been set up by 15 Chinese PLA at Metok Dzong in the

---

16 For the Treaty, see http://www.claudearpi.net/wp-content/uploads/2019/01/1956-Nepal-Communist-Chinese-Treaty-on-Tibet.pdf

Pemako area[17]: "Public messages are not accepted by this station. It appears the station has been set up to collect border intelligence and transmit to Lhasa and Peking," wrote Pant.

It is clear that by 1955, the Chinese had come closer to explore the NEFA border with India. Their presence would increase during the coming months and years. At the same time, more military barracks were under construction in Lhasa as well as a hall for holding important meetings, a rest house and a hospital.

Chinese engineers were working on an old hydro-electric plant at Dote in Lhasa area to increase its output to ten times more than its present capacity.

**The October and November Reports**

The Chinese were working full swing on the construction of roads, but also on the establishment of small industries in Lhasa. They envisaged building up a 'healthy' industrial setup in Tibet, though a working class with revolutionary ideas "does not seem to get hold of the imagination of the Tibetan people," wrote Pant.

Rumours were that bands of 'robbers' were wandering around in the Tsang, Kham, U and Nagchuka areas: "Some consider that these 'robbers' are actually underground nationalists; a truck carrying some gold bullion from Lhasa to Chamdo was attacked and robbed by these thieves."

A ceremony was organized at Gyantse for the opening of the new Gyantse-Lhasa motor road: a big gate had been constructed to welcome the 37 trucks and two jeeps which arrived at Gyantse on October 22 early morning: "From this gate the caravan proceeded slowly in a procession, the first truck was carrying the photograph of Mao Tse Tung on its bonnet with scarves hanging on both sides. Officer in Charge of the Foreign Bureau Hou-Chi-Tang who is also the Director of Road Construction at Gyantse was seated on a high seat in the luggage carrier with his Deputy, Depon Den-Chung."

---

17  North of the Siang Frontier Division of the NEFA.

Caravan leaving Indian Agency in Gangtok

Tibetan and Chinese officials in Gyantse, c. mid-1950s

Further a Chinese band and Kusho Rimshi Dode, a Tibetan official deputed from Lhasa, led the procession. Some 5,000 people including the ITA and the Nepalese Officer were invited for the function. On the occasion, Beijing sent a message translated by the Political Officer: "What was believed to be impracticable by the people of Tibet has now made possible by the ungrudging cooperation of the people themselves and a motorable road between Shigatse and Gyantse has this day been opened for vehicular traffic. This great task was achieved through the good guidance of our Chairman, Mao-Tse-Tung and also through the close cooperation of the people of Tibet. We have received ungrudging help and cooperation from all local administrative authorities at various places on the road, the Namagang Lekhung of Tashi Lhumpo, the Oyen Lekhung[18] of Shigatse and the Oyen Lekhung of Gyantse, to achieve this objective. By our combined effort the difficult problem of transportation of goods by means of vehicular traffic has now been completely solved for the time to come."

The Communist Party boasted of connecting the three big cities, Lhasa, Shigatse and Gyantse by motorable road. The Party said that with the new roads, food commodities could now be speedily transported at low cost: "This would no doubt contribute greatly towards the welfare and prosperity of the people of Tibet."

The construction work also greatly helped to create employment for the people affected by the floods and relieve their hardships: "The road between Gyantse and Phari would also be constructed shortly and we would expect similar cooperation from all of you to help us in construction of this road".

After the opening function the guests were taken round an exhibition of handicrafts exhibiting items like cloth, shoes, books, sweets, tea pots as well as locally grown vegetables.

During the same month, reports mentioned that the road between Gyantse and Phari had been completed in 28 days. The Report noted: "Military and other government vehicles have started plying on these roads although no public carriers are yet permitted. The road has not been officially opened as yet.

---

18 Youth Department.

Politically, the situation was getting tighter for the Tibetans, for example, members of 'Oyen' (Youth League) in the Chumbi Valley were directed to provide to the authorities their speeches in advance for the Oyen's meetings.

The Chinese often changed or altered the speeches of the Tibetans who were then allowed only to read their papers.

During one of these meetings, one of the ex-headmen proposed that the Yatung bazaar be handed over to the headmen of Lower Chumbi valley to whom it originally belonged. The Chinese did not like the suggestion, but promised to look into the matter as the administration of the bazaar was run by Trimon Se Kusho, a Tibetan employed by the Chinese along with three Chinese officials.

The Chinese had started using disgruntled Tibetans or those having a problem with the Lhasa government; Tendup Kapshopa was one of them. After attending the World Youth Conference at Warsaw, Poland, Kapshopa returned to Lhasa and gradually became popular with the Chinese: "They have found him useful in finding out the past histories of the Tibetan officials. Tendup's father was imprisoned by the Tibetan officials and he bears a deep grudge against them."

A report mentioned that Dorji Nima,[19] the sister of Dalai Lama was trying to persuade Gyalo Thondup, Dalai Lama's elder brother, to return to Lhasa.

In the meantime, Muja Depon, the Tibetan Trade Agent at Yatung was told by the Chinese authorities that his post "was no longer necessary and was abolished." He had to return to Lhasa.

In Lhasa, the Chinese started constructing barracks on the Lhasa-Shigatse road opposite the Drepung monastery. People believe that the Chinese intended quartering soldiers in these barracks to keep an eye on the Drepung monastery monks numbering over 7,000, although the exact purpose of constructing these barracks was not known.

During the month, fresh Chinese troops, not in large numbers, reached Lhasa. Most of these newcomers had not been posted earlier in Tibet

---

19  Probably Tsering Dolma.

and they found it difficult to cope with the high altitude of the plateau, said Pant.

**Report for the Month of December 1955.**

The main talk on the Roof of the World was the possibility of the Dalai Lama visiting India for the Buddha Jayanti celebrations: the population, whether lay or monks would be delighted if the trip could materialize: "Most feel that on this great and auspicious occasion it is the 'duty' of the Dalai Lama to be present in India and take part personally in the celebrations."

The Political Officer believed that the Dalai Lama himself has been enquiring about the weather conditions in India during October and November: "unless some ulterior pressure is brought to bear upon him, it is not unlikely that he visits India during the winter of 1956."

Like the previous month, additional troops arrived on the plateau and were posted between Gyantse and Shigatse. Delhi was informed that machine guns with a few pieces of field artillery and ammunition arrived at Shigatse in covered trucks: "All this material has been kept at the Chinese Military headquarters. It is reported that more consignments may be arriving soon." In addition, the Panchen Lama's special bodyguard regiment received an additional 1,400 fully equipped Sichuanese troops.

However, there was no immediate plan to establish an airfield at Shigatse though amphibian aircrafts had landed on a lake; this probably refers to Namtso lake and perhaps Damchung airport nearby.

The Chinese were suspecting some Tibetans to have contacts 'with the outside world' via secret wireless sets. The PLA was checking the information with 'imported detectors'.

Three representatives of the *Mimang*, the Peoples' Party, Alo Chodze, Bhoomdhang Drunyee and Lhabchu were said to have been called to the Norbulinka, the summer palace of the Dalai Lama to meet the Kashag. They were told that they must stop having meetings of the *Mimang* and not discuss political matters. The PO added: "These three representatives are not by any means the head of the now well organized *Mimang*."

The Kashag would have told them: "so long as the prestige and power of the Dalai Lama and of the Tibetan Government and its people remained intact, there would be no need for the people to meet."

The *Mimang* representatives said that they had sworn "before all the persons present here and by Lord Buddha that we would continue to meet and to work for the country".

They 'flatly' refused to stop the *Mimang* movement.

The situation was steadily worsening; it was reported that a number of Tibetans had been arrested in Lhasa, as well as in Kham for anti-Chinese activities and seven had been executed in the Tibetan capital only for speeches they delivered at a public meeting.

All sorts of rumors had started circulating, some Tibetans predicted war, famine and disease, "water was seen flowing out of the two gargoyles (dragons) in Lhasa[20] which is considered a bad omen."

From the Chinese side too, the situation was deteriorating; they were greatly upset of the opposition shown by the Tibetans to the formation of the Preparatory Committee "which was made very clear to them by the Tibetans in the form of a representation."

To stop the opposition gaining further strength, the Chinese asked the *Mepon*[21] of Lhasa to issue an order banning private or public meetings.

Another sign that everything was not smooth for the Chinese, Ragashar Shape left suddenly for Beijing "on account of the representation made by the Tibetans suggesting certain changes in the constitution and terms of reference of the Preparatory Committee."

Tibetan complaints were responsible for the postponement of the meetings of the Preparatory Committee. Ragashar Shape, accompanied by his wife, wanted also to extend some personal invitations for the Chinese officials to attend the meetings of the Committee.

A copy of the representation submitted by the *Mimang* to the Government about the Preparatory Committee was sent the Dzongpons

---

20  Probably in the Jokhang Cathedral.
21  City Magistrate.

in Gyantse for briefing the people and "explaining to the illiterates the contents", however the Dzongpons did not openly take any action.

An incarnate Lama of Drepung Monastery, Chunzeeling Tulku was reported to have revealed that the total number of monks in Drepung although exceeding 7,700 monks, had been reduced to 6,000. The reason was that monks were not arriving anymore from either Outer or Inner Mongolia, probably on account of high cost of living in Lhasa.

Rumours were floating that the Panchen Lama had been indulging "in some kinds of vices which an Incarnate Lama should not do."

His very position as an incarnate Lama was reported to be open to many controversies. The people of the Tsang area themselves were not fully reconciled with him being accepted as the true incarnation of the Panchen Lama. People seemed to have greater faith in the other person, who was a monk in the Sera monastery and who is the son of Chandzo[22] Nangse, an official of the Tibetan Government, as the incarnate of the Panchen Lama. There was a general wish that the Panchen Lama should demonstrate religious convictions more prominently in his acts and in his bearing.

Depon Muja, who served as Tibetan Trade Agent in Yatung, had left for Lhasa; he was reported to have joined his new post as Sho[23] Magistrate. The PO noted that as he often opposed the Chinese, he was finally removed from his post in Yatung; the Chinese "created the feeling that as Depon Muja's main job was to deal with foreigners, his appointment or existence in the valley became unnecessary with the establishment of the Chinese sub-office in the Chumbi Valley."

The fact that Muja had gone on pilgrimage (and business) to India in 1954, leaving his son as acting TTA helped the Chinese to get rid of him. They used the headmen to agree about the establishment of the sub-office of the Foreign Bureau, in which case a Trade Agent had become unnecessary. When on his return from India, the Depon found the attitude of the local headmen changed, he went to the Chinese who asked him to fly the Chinese flag over his house. The Depon first

---

22  Estate Manager.
23  Village below the Potala Palace.

resisted as he wanted to fly his own Regimental flag only; but finally he had to abdicate: "It cannot, however, be said for definite whether the abolition of the post of Trade Agent was on the recommendation made by the local headmen or in accordance with the policy of the Tibetan Government of integration of various posts," said the Report.

After Muja's departure, only one Tibetan Government official remained in the Chumbi valley, now under the administrative control of the Dzongpon of Phari: "The people in general however feel that there should be an official from the Tibetan Government stationed in the valley. The headmen seem to be happy with the prospect of not having a senior official supervising them," reported Apa Pant.

While the struggle for the post of Tibetan Trade Agency was taking place at Kalimpong, Dzasa Yuthok had been trying hard to get the job, "but the Chinese are not likely to post him there as it is reported that in 1952, he had secretly carried American arms and ammunition into Tibet and also some letters from the Americans for the Dalai Lama."

Some reports said that the Dalai Lama was "making brisk preparations for visiting India. Considerable amount of publicity has been given by the Dalai Lama's Court officials that His Holiness would visit India on an invitation from the Government of India".

It was also rumoured that the Tibetan leader would be carrying fifteen complete sets of Kangyur[24] for presentation in different places in India.

But what really worried the Chinese were the plans of the Dalai Lama to visit several places in Southern Tibet, especially one place called Chhonkke Gyel, near the Tibet-Bhutan border. After the Tibetan leader declined any Chinese escort, the Chinese suspected that he may escape to Bhutan and …"if the Dalai Lama goes to India he may not return back."

Another rumour circulated, Beijing would have declared Sikang[25] as an Autonomous State, headquartered at Tatsienlu[26]: "There is a likelihood

---

24 Scriptures consisting of 108 volumes.

25 Eastern Tibet.

26 Also known as Dartsedo or Kangding in Chinese. Today, the seat of Garze Tibetan Autonomous prefecture.

of the eastern Tibet being declared as an autonomous region also. As soon as it is finalized the Liberation Committee formed for eastern Tibet at Chamdo would be dissolved. Sikang is reported to have been split up into two provinces, or zones, north and south zones and different methods of administration are employed in both these provinces."

A few months later this would trigger the Khampa rebellion.

Pant then noted in his Report: "A stricter control is reported to be exercised over the people of the northern zone as this area is becoming the centre of economic and industrial activity. The Chinese have a plan of shifting a large number of their population to this sparsely inhabited area for permanent settlement."

While the resistance to Chinese advance in the North had been ruthlessly eliminated, in the East, the Khampas continued to fight. Experts had started carrying out extensive geological surveys on the plateau. It was said that the advancing PLA had discovered iron ore deposits, while coal found near Medu Gongkar was not worth an economic exploitation, but oil deposits in the Tsaidam area were "plentiful and large Chinese settlement are developing very rapidly in this area."

In the meantime, the Chinese were able to control the wool trade; the Pangdatsangs were active in purchasing wool from the traders in Tibet; they were supported by Chinese authorities "who are making every effort to prevent the export of wool to India." The Report mentioned that the Tashi Lhumpo monastery was used for this purpose: "One of the methods used by the Chinese is said to be offering of higher prices than those prevailing at Kalimpong. Traders are being dissuaded from selling wool to Marwaris."

The swift construction of roads was welcomed by most Tibetans, though some sections of the society thought that "the free flow of vehicular traffic would naturally mean their losing their daily bread."

Apa Pant probably referred to the muleteers; a petition had been sent from Phari to Lhasa requesting the government not to permit the Chinese to transport merchandise goods by motors from Phari to Lhasa and vice-versa; there was no objection to the Chinese carrying goods for their own use only by motors.

The Chinese were certainly in no mood to entertain complaints or petitions when their interests were at stake.

Year 1955 witnessed a rapid consolidation of the Chinese presence on the Tibetan plateau. It concretized with new infrastructure, mainly roads linking the strategic centers, including one to the Chumbi Valley and the Indian border.

The Tibetans and the Indian officials could feel that things would never be the same, though the Chinese tried to put a break on the reforms, waiting for the 'reforms' to be introduced under the aegis the Preparatory Committee of the Tibetan Autonomous Region. We shall see this in the following chapters.

# 09

# Developments in Tibet: Implications for Sikkim

**A Note from the Political Officer BK Kapur**

To understand the implication for India of happenings in Tibet, it is necessary to look at the border areas, particularly Sikkim and Bhutan.

The note on Sikkim, Bhutan and Tibet written by BK Kapur, Pant's predecessor, on the occasion a Regional Conference of Heads of Mission South-East Asia, helps to understand the situation on the ground. It goes into the nitty-gritty of the concrete issues faced by the people of Bhutan and Sikkim.

Kapur first provided a description of his office in Gangtok: "The Political Officer in Sikkim deals with three countries: Sikkim, Bhutan and Tibet. Sikkim and Bhutan are closely tied to India by treaties and may be termed as her protectorates."

The PO then connected the happenings in Tibet with the Himalayan States: "Tibet until recently laid claims to independence. The Chinese occupation of Tibet, their increasingly tightening grip over her affairs, and their concerted efforts to convert this intensely religious and feudalistic country into a Communist State cannot but help creating a deep impression on the border States of Sikkim and Bhutan."

This aspect had certainly not been taken into account when Delhi (read Nehru) decided its Tibet policy in November 1950[1]; whatever would happen to Tibet, would have serious implications for India's borders, including Sikkim and Bhutan, simply because the people are "tied to the Tibetans by common bonds of race and religion."

Kapur rightly observed: "These two small States on our borders have thus assumed an importance which they did not possess in the past, and their integrity and welfare have become matters of real concern to us. It is with this in mind that their internal affairs and foreign policies should be examined."

One could add that it was also true for the populations in other areas of the Himalaya, in the NEFA, Uttar Pradesh[2] and Ladakh in particular.

The PO then described the relations with Sikkim: "Under a treaty concluded with Sikkim, [the State's] defence, communications and external relations become India's responsibility, leaving Sikkim autonomy in regard to its internal affairs. Earlier, as a result of breakdown in the administration, the Maharaja had asked for and obtained the loan of the services of an Indian *dewan*[3]. The administration of the country has been in the hands of the *dewan* ever since."

Kapur elaborated on the steps already taken: "The revenues of the State have increased; respect for law and order has been restored; a High Court has been set up; State Council with a majority of elected members has been formed; and two Executive Councilors have lately been associated with the *dewan* in the administration of the State."

This was a down-to-earth description of Sikkim's relations with India.

Then followed remarks on Sikkim Foreign Policy; under the 1950 treaty "the external relations of Sikkim, whether political or economic or financial, shall be conducted and regulated solely by the Government of India: and the Government of Sikkim shall have no dealings with any foreign power," wrote the PO, who also noted that the State of

---

1 See Volume 1, Chapter 14.
2 Today's Uttarakhand.
3 At that time, Nari Rustomji.

Sikkim had no representative at Lhasa, though the Maharaja, his eldest son, and two daughters were married to Tibetans: "Recently the Maharajkumar has been to Tibet on a visit to his in-laws, and during his sojourn at Lhasa had several opportunities of meeting top ranking Chinese officials."

Kapur then elaborated on Tibet's internal affairs: "The Sino-Tibetan Agreement of 1951[4] determines the present relations between Tibet and China. Although Tibet was assured autonomy in regard to its internal affairs and although the country continues to be administered by the Kashag (Tibetan Cabinet) in the name of the Dalai Lama, there is an increasing tendency on the part of the Chinese to exercise strict supervision and control over the administration."

As we have seen in Volume 2 of this study, between 1951 and 1954, the Chinese consolidated their position by building roads, opening hospitals and schools, starting The Youth League and setting up small scale industries; Kapur mentioned the two major roads connecting Lhasa to Xining in Qinghai province and Chamdo with Sichuan province which "have given the Chinese a firm hold over the country."

The PO further remarked: "Reports show that the process of road building is to continue with equal vigour towards the direction of India and Nepal to the South, and towards Sinkiang to the north."

Tibet had become an integral part of China and had "no foreign policy of its own," though Kapur mentioned the 'Foreign Bureau' at Lhasa and its sub-offices in Gyantse, Yatung and Gartok: "Indian and Nepali representatives in Tibet have been told to approach these offices and not Tibetan officials directly."

The Indian representative in Gangtok remarked that for the people of Sikkim and Bhutan, the Chinese occupation of Tibet and the expected advance of Communism to their borders was a cause of great concern as the relations between India and China were affecting them directly.

---

4  The Seventeen-Point Agreement.

## The Political Parties in Sikkim

Then the PO dealt with Sikkim's internal affairs; he provided a description of the three main political parties, the Sikkim State Congress, the National Party and the Praja Sammelan Party.

The Sikkim State Congress comprised mainly of Nepalese 'with a sprinkling of Bhutias and Lepchas', he noted: "This party seeks to secure a more liberal administrator for the State and does not like the weightage given to the two minority communities – Bhutias and Lepchas."

At the same time the Sikkim Congress was keen to be affiliated to the Indian National Congress. It strove for the support of his Indian counterpart, hoping "to secure the abolition of communal reservations and thereby ensure the rule of the majority community in Sikkim – the Nepalese. It does not favour a merger with India."

As for the National Party, it was essentially a party of the Bhutia-Lepcha communities: "It has a natural sympathy and affection for Tibet and the Tibetans. Towards India, it is fairly well disposed; it is all for receiving aid and assistance from India without in any way limiting Sikkim's autonomy or constitutional position," said Kapur, who added that it placed Sikkim first and last.

The Praja Sammelan Party, it was explained, was a Nepali party and its main plank was a merger with India: "It would like Sikkim to be made into a Chief Commissioner's province and, meanwhile, would like the *Dewan's* regime to continue."

The Praja Sammelan did not have much support as the overwhelming majority of the Nepalese supported the Sikkim State Congress and the Bhutias and Lepchas were behind the National Party.

Delhi was informed that no inroads by the Communists had been noted: "There are no Communist parties as such working in Sikkim or Bhutan, nor have any concerted efforts been made so far from outside to introduce Communism."

The PO added a word of caution: "The activities of individual Communists cannot however be ruled out particularly in Sikkim where there are no restrictions on the movement of Indian nationals."

He cited the case of KI Singh, the Nepali Communist who escaped to Tibet; Kapur remarked that some his followers in eastern Nepal may have tried to influence a Sikkim tribe – the Limbus. Kapur admitted that in terms of influence, it was not necessary to mention the foreign tourists and the missionaries occasionally visiting Sikkim.

As far as the fashionable 'Asian consciousness' was concerned, it was non-existent: "the problem is not so much the promotion of Asian consciousness and solidarity, as the strengthening still further of their ties with India," noted the PO, who remarked that some efforts needed to be done "at weaning them away from Tibetan influence."

Because Sikkim's and Bhutan's bonds through race and religion were with Tibet, Kapur suggested a two-pronged approach:

(a) Inculcating taste for the democratic way of life in the populations.

(b) Making the Sikkimese more dependent on India for material things.

He cited the steps already taken by the State: "An experiment has been made with countrywide elections to a State Council and the appointment of two elected members as Executive Councilors."

Moreover, a seven year development plan had been worked out between the Government of India and the *Durbar*[5]; it envisaged to provide better communications, building schools, hospitals, and improving agricultural and horticultural farms as well as setting up of small scale industries.

The Indian official also mentioned literacy and education which could "tie them still further to India and her way of life."

The same policy was suggested for Bhutan, though Kapur admitted that many in the Government of Bhutan "will not look ahead and

---

5   Court of the ruler.

seem bent, for personal reasons, on letting the existing state of things continue."

We shall look at this in the next chapter.

**Publicity Policy and Commercial Relations**

The PO noted that the Sikkimese people were not cut off from India; they read the newspapers and many had attended schools and colleges in India: "For remoter regions of Sikkim however it would be desirable to distribute publicity material. Steps to this end are being taken," he stressed.

As far as publicity in Tibet was concerned, it was more difficult: "the Indian officer at Lhasa used to distribute periodicals and magazines to Tibetan officials and others; it is becoming difficult to do so now."

Only Indian films were still popular.

About the commercial relations, Kapur explained that for import and export of goods, Sikkim and Bhutan were treated as parts of India: "They are placed on the same footing as the Constituent States of India and do not suffer from any special disabilities. Both countries are dependent for all type of goods from India. No special steps are needed therefore to bring these countries into closer commercial relations with India."

As mentioned earlier, the commercial relations with Tibet continued during the first years of Chinese occupation and the volume of Indo-Tibetan trade even increased for some time, mainly due to the larger demand for Indian goods by the Chinese troops stationed on the plateau: "There is the possibility of this trade decreasing now that Tibet has been linked with China by roads fit for lorry traffic," observed Kapur. It is what would happen at the end of the 1950s.

The PO proposed that scholarships should be regularly offered to Sikkimese and Bhutanese students for studying in India: "The difficulty is in getting a sufficient number of educated young men for higher studies in India. The two high schools in Sikkim are already affiliated to the Calcutta University."

It was proposed to invite the members of the ruling family of Sikkim from time to time to visit India. The PO cited the example of the previous Republic Day[6] celebrations when the Maharaja and Maharani of Bhutan, with a large party of officials, had come to Delhi and toured different historical and developmental sites: "Efforts in this direction can be increased," said the PO who noted that even the Tibetan masses are more informed about India than about China, but "how long this partiality for India and things Indian will last is a matter for speculation. The Chinese are making serious efforts to indoctrinate the people and assimilate them in their fold." It was going to increase in the coming years, but with little success for the Communists.

**Administrative and Security Collaboration with Sikkim**

The collaboration between Sikkim and India was already assured, noted the PO, citing a number of Indian officials and experts who visited Sikkim for the implementation of the Development Plan, though for Bhutan, the position was unsatisfactory: "The difficulty is that the Government of Bhutan are unwilling to receive any advice or assistance for the improvement or development of their country."

Kapur affirmed that even in the field of security, the Bhutanese were opposed to obtaining advice from India's military experts and "take comfort in the belief that should an emergency ever arise vis-à-vis her northern neighbor, India will always be ready to support Bhutan."

This state of affairs would change during the following years; soon the Bhutan Government would start to send officers and soldiers for training in Indian military establishments.

**Indian Traders in Sikkim**

In Sikkim, most of the trade was in the hands of Indian merchants, even in the villages: "These Indians have been in Sikkim for generations, but they have not acquired Sikkimese domicile. Their main grievances are that although they are eligible to vote, they cannot stand for election to the State Council, and cannot acquire land outside the bazaar areas," stated Kapur.

---

6   On January 26, 1954.

In Bhutan, the problem did not exist as there was hardly any Indian trader permitted to reside in the Land of the Dragon, though in the borders of southern Bhutan, a large number of Indian merchants, headquartered on the border, traded with the Bhutanese.

At the end of his note, the PO mentioned the Indian traders having shops in Sikkim and Kalimpong, as some had branches at Yatung: "A beginning has been made by a few merchants to open shops further inland at Phari. They are entitled to do so both at Phari and at Gyantse under the recent Sino-Indian Agreement."

As we shall see, this would not last long, and the Indian traders would face more and more difficulties with the Chinese: "Fairplay and sound business dealings will earn them and their country respect in these lands," thought Kapur; the Chinese however would not see it this way.

## Apa Pant arrives in Gangtok

Beginning of February 1955, the new PO Apa Pant took over from BK Kapur; he was more a philosopher than a diplomat.[7] As soon as he arrived, he wrote a personal letter to TN Kaul, his direct boss in the Ministry of External Affairs, who despite having been caught in a honey trap a year earlier, was now Joint Secretary in the Ministry.

Having just reached Gangtok, Pant told Kaul: "I feel as if I have been here for quite a while. This may be due to the fact that I have had the opportunity of reading some material about Sikkim and Bhutan before and also because I could meet members of the Royal family in Delhi."

He noted the special "atmosphere of this beautiful part of the world."

On the way, in Calcutta, he had the occasion to acquaint himself with the situation in Gangtok. He met S. Majumdar of the Intelligence Bureau.

He also noted the journey from Calcutta to Gangtok "in a crowded plane full of American tourists travelling to Darjeeling".

Pant described the drive from Bagdogra to Rangpo; it was a first introduction to the foothills. At Rangpo, Pant was met by Tseten Tashi,

---

7    BK Kapur was from the Indian Political Service.

the Private Secretary to the Maharaja; he had organized a lunch to welcome the new PO: "The local gentry with flowers and flags greeted us at almost every village and it was interesting to see how all these people were reacting to the arrival of a new PO."

There were places where the road was damaged and the party had no alternative but "to make your own road before you can proceed any further." Pant was told by the Executive Engineer that all the road repairs would be completed before the coming of the monsoon.

This sounds familiar, even more than 60 years later.

**The First Reception**

In Gangtok, Pant was received by all officers working in the Political Office, as well as the Commander of the Military Detachment; an imposing array of officials indeed; he noted "the air of officialdom that one finds around the dark corridors of the Central Secretariat."

The next day, the new PO started receiving 'uninvited and unannounced' delegations, particularly Sonam Tsering, the Executive Councillor, with members of the National Party.

Pant described the scene to Kaul: "Though ostensibly they had come to greet me it was obvious that they also wanted to discuss some 'ideas' with me."

The Tibetans spoke first; despite the fact that they had been living in this part of the world for the last 25, 30 or even 50 years, they were not allowed to purchase land and settle down permanently in Sikkim. Their leader was Sardar Pema; he bitterly complained that the Tibetans were discriminated against: "every time they go or come from Tibet they have to get passes and permits as if they were 'foreigners'."

The PO could only tell them that he would have to discuss the issue with the *Darbar* and Sonam Tsering, the Executive Councilor.

Pant, the philosopher gave them a lecture: "They were fortunate in residing in such a magnificent part of the Himalayas wherein wealth abounded all around them. The rivers, the mountains, the forests, the minerals were all crying out for exploitation and proper utilization for the benefit of all who reside here. …the real problem of areas such as Sikkim was the problem of being able to make use of the wealth that existed."

Pant was fast initiated to the 'peaceful' and disparate political culture of the Himalaya. When the turn of Sonam Tsering came, the Councilor was chiefly concerned about 'Nepali friends'.

After the National Party had left, the State Congress led by its General Secretary Kaisar Bahadur Thapa met the PO, and informed him that the Congress was organizing *Seva Dals*[8] in Western Sikkim: "Instructors should be available to all the political parties who required their services to organize volunteer corps."

Pant also lectured them; he told the Congress that they should actively participate in the development of the area and should organize their activities in such a way that they could work for all the people of the State and not only for a certain section.

The General Secretary then hinted that Sikkim was a part of India and not a separate State; diplomatically, Pant answered that "India would always be ready to give all help for the development of this area but that the real work shall have to be done by the people of Sikkim State themselves."

The PO noted that at this stage, the difference in attitude between the National Party and the Congress was obvious; the National Party wanted to keep contact with the past, while the Congress was keen to let the 'flood waters' rush in and was anxious to see a rapid transformation: "to the Nepalis a rapid change is attractive because that would assure them better prospects of security and an honourable place in the society."

One realizes how this border State was unsettled due to the sharp differences of opinion between the different ethnic groups and political parties.

---

8  The *Seva Dal* is the grassroots front organization of the Indian National Congress, with a chapter in all the states of the Indian Union. The members of the organization are known for wearing the Gandhi *topi* (hat).

### Calling on the Maharaja

On February 9, Pant called on 'His Highness'[9] and the next day, the Maharaja returned his visit: "He gave me the impression of being a very large-hearted, generous person of a highly artistic temperament but frustrated and very unhappy." The PO added that the Maharaja had "sub-merged himself in his religious practices not perhaps because he is interested in religion but because he wants to protect himself from the outside world and from shame and horror."

Pant saw Sir Tashi as a lonely man, feeling that he had been wronged; the Choegyal felt that his children were neglecting him and giving him neither love nor respect: "I felt really drawn to this pathetic figure," wrote Pant.

Pant informed Kaul that apart from his monthly official reports: "I would continue to send to you either weekly or fortnightly letters about various problems." He admitted that there was "a great deal of work around and whoever said that Gangtok was an easy place from the point of view of work did just not know what he was talking about."

We shall go through some of these reports, after studying a second letter sent to Kaul.

### Five Weeks Later

Pant wrote again to Kaul; by that time, he had settled down and already started touring Sikkim, 'an exquisite experience'.

He told the Joint Secretary that he was convinced that unless the Political Officer travels for eight months in the year, he would not be in a position to understand the way things were developing in the Himalayan State.

---

9   Sir Tashi Namgyal (26 October 1893 – 2 December 1963) was the Chogyal of Sikkim from 1914 to 1963. He was the 11th ruler of the Namgyal dynasty, succeeding his half brother Sidkeong Tulku Namgyal, who had ruled from February to December in 1914, till his untimely death. Tashi Namgyal was a strong advocate for closer links with India. He was married in October 1918 to Kunzang Dechen, and they had 3 sons and 3 daughters. The eldest son died in a plane crash during World War Two. On his death he was succeeded as Chogyal by his second son Palden Thondup Namgyal. During his reign, Sir Tashi introduced land reform and free elections.

It was necessary to adapt his tempo of life "down to the level of the tempo of the life of the people of this territory." He spoke of the necessity to travel on a pony or just walk "to have enough time to adjust yourself to the emotional and the physical way of life of these people."

During his first visit, he was often driven around by the Maharajkumar.

He took his "hat off to the cultivators in this region who cleared the forest and have made such excellent terraced fields that agriculture has proved to be, in this region at least, a form of engineering."

The description of his trip is captivating: "you are received by these dignitaries [and escorted] by the local band for nearly a couple of miles!! Though the tone, of the rhythm of this band varies but little from place to place, in these mountains and valleys the reception by the local band, whether it belongs to a monastery or the local *Kazis*[10] is most appropriate."

He described the *dak bungalows* as usually well furnished, clean; everywhere, he was preceded by bearers and cooks who, "with admirable efficiency laid out your clothes and prepared hot water for your bath, you are again confronted by the local gentry with presents."

In another word, a raja's life for the Political Officer!

Pant continued to report: "I was pleased that at almost every place the Maharajkumar gave considerable time to the local gentry and explained to them the purpose and the way the Seven Year Plan was going to be put into practice. He also invoked from them their co-operation in this great task."

He observed that in western Sikkim most of the inhabitants were Nepalese: "There were also a certain number of Lepchas and Bhutias as well as Limbus and Rais. As you know, the Limbus and the Rais are the first arrivals in this part of the world from Tibet and with the Lepchas could be termed as the original inhabitants, indigenes. ... The Nepalese of course being the most recent arrivals are the most de-tribalized, active, and as it were overflow into this part of Sikkim by the sheer force of their numbers."

---

10 Kazi, an honorific title used historically in Sikkim.

Pant had the occasion to often talk to the Maharajkumar about the problems confronting his State: "One of the major problems is of course the creating of a feeling of loyalty, a sort of regional patriotism, for Sikkim."

Pant commented: "As you know the Nepalese have a desire to look over the shoulders either towards Nepal or towards India and hanker often for a greater Nepal or merging with India."

The PO told the Crown Prince that unless the people "feel that they belong to Sikkim and have a good and prosperous future in Sikkim, they can never give their best in the service of Sikkim."

When they visited Pemayangtse, the oldest monastery in Sikkim, there was a dispute "about who is to become the head of this monastery and there is a Rimpoche[11] who has come all the way from Tibet to stake his claim."

Further there was another quarrel between the tenants of the monastery's lands and the monks: "In the ancient times, the tenants did service to the monastery and to the monks for the use of their lands. Now apparently they refuse to do the service."

The Maharajkumar told Pant that the fault lay with the monks "who demanded more service from their tenants than was due and also because as the monks were not either pious nor learned the tenants did not spontaneously feel that they should serve the monastery."

Coming down from Pemayangtse, the party visited a few schools and monasteries, the PO observed: "After seeing the monasteries which in many ways have lost contact with the people, it was refreshing to hear a prayer song from these schools in praise of Lord Buddha. I think the emotional dynamism and spiritual inspiration for the people of Sikkim can and should come from refined aspects of Buddhism. The intellectual and theological aspects of Buddhism are and can be acceptable to almost all of Sikkim including the Nepalese."

Pant concluded his letter: "I am sorry to have made this tour note such a long one but I think that there should be some account of these places on record for future Political Officers to go by."

---

11  Rimpoche is a reincarnated Lama. Now written Rinpoche.

But Pant was known in the Ministry for his 'longish' notes. It could become a problem, as very few did take time to read them.

For our purpose, it gives an idea of the forces at play on the edge of the Tibetan plateau during these tumultuous years.

**The Seismic Changes**

It is crucial to understand the internal situation in Sikkim and Bhutan following the seismic changes brought by the Chinese arrival in Tibet; it had indeed serious implications for the Himalayan States as well as for India.

Another note from the Political Officer is relevant as it gives the background of several issues faced by the Sikkim State.[12]

The PO reported to the Ministry of External Affairs in Delhi about the recent developments in Tibet which "have their effect not only on the security of India and her border States, not only on the flow of free trade between India and Tibet, but also will have its effect on the lives of the people residing along these border areas of India."

In the years and decades to come, with the degrading relations with China, this would become more and more apparent.

The PO pointed out the people affected by these changes: "the Indo-Mongoloids who inhabit the region from Outer Mongolia, to areas well beyond Sikkim and even to the very plains of India and from Szechwan[13] to Ladakh, spreading over large tracts of Nepal, Himachal Pradesh and UP, have settlements on both sides of our frontier."

All these regions have in common a religion, often called 'Tibetan Buddhism'. Pant mentioned the Mongoloid populations, "linguistically and ethnologically distinctly from the Chinese and with affinities with the Shan people of Burma, Siam and Indo-China," which have been affected by the Chinese occupation.

The last contention about Burma and Indo-China may not be scientifically correct, but "it is assumed that in this vast area people

---

12 It probably dates from the end of 1955.
13 Sichuan.

of this stock numbered about eight million. It would not be an exaggeration to say that nearly forty per cent of these people either reside directly within the frontiers of India (Nepal is included for convenience as being within the frontiers of India) or have direct social, religious and emotional contacts with their brethren across the border," wrote Pant.

For any watcher of what was happening in Tibet, it was obvious the Indian populations from Ladakh in the West to the NEFA in the East would be affected.

The Himalayan belt had for centuries been directly connected with Tibet: "What happens in Tibet therefore is of, immense psychological and emotional importance to the people inside our very frontier," commented the PO.

His analysis started with a brief outline of "the recent historical ties between China and Tibet and Tibet and Russia over the past few hundred years." Pant mentioned the invitation of the Fifth Dalai Lama by the Manchu Emperor to Beijing: "[the latter] showered full honours on him [the Dalai Lama] as a fully independent sovereign. With the devoted backing of the Mongolian chieftains, the Dalai Lama was so powerful at that time that the Chinese Government sought security, through the blessings of this high potentate." The PO rightly noted that the Mongol chieftains were the most powerful challenge 'to the very existence of China'.

Always fond of giving history lessons to his colleagues, Pant continued: "Till the beginning of the 18th century, in fact till 1720 the Chinese recognised and treated Tibet as a completely independent country. It was, however, with the increased interest of Russia and other outside powers in Tibet that China felt insecure and attempted several invasions of Tibet."

Pant further explained to South Block: "since 1720 the Chinese have interfered in the internal affairs of Tibet time and again and had attempted to establish their influence firmly there. The Tibetans however didn't recognise the overlordship of the Chinese till the beginning of the 20th century, when the 13th Dalai Lama fled to Mongolia and later on to Peking from the invading forces of the Younghusband expedition."

We shall not reproduce the rest of the 'lesson' which is historically doubtful. In any case, Pant rightly concluded: "That is of course past history".

The PO however mentioned the visit of the Thirteenth Dalai Lama to Beijing in 1908; since then, he said, China has gone through two revolutions: "The Kuomintang regime was so weak and the 13th Dalai Lama such an astute and powerful ruler that for nearly 35 years, Tibet was left free to function as an independent country."

He noted that the Tibetan Government more or less ignored the Chinese *Ambans*[14] and even disregarded their military escort stationed, further stating that both the British and the Russians encouraged the Tibetans to seek her independence.

After Independence in 1947 some Indian diplomats and politicians, often great fans of China, found it strange that Tibet would try to get its independence acknowledged. It was probably more convenient this way. Nobody questioned India's freedom struggle? Can this not be called double standards?

Pant made another strange comment: the British would have continued to take more active interest in Tibet and support her 'independent' status, if they had not been busy in "more lucrative concessions in Shanghai and Hong Kong."

At the same time, according to Pant, the Chinese found it profitable to settle large numbers of their population in "the sparsely populated areas of Inner Mongolia and around the Tsaidam[15] marshes and the Kokonor Lake[16] as well as Jyekundo[17] regions rich in oil and minerals where they find admirable opportunity for colonising their populations."

---

14 The Emperor's representatives in Lhasa.

15 Tsaidam or Qaidam is a hyper-arid basin that occupies a large part of today's Haixi Mongol and Tibetan Autonomous Prefecture in Qinghai Province.

16 In today's Qinghai Province.

17 Jyekundo or Gyegumdo in Tibetan, is today a part of the Gyêgu township in Yushu Tibetan Autonomous Prefecture in Qinghai Province. Gyêgu is also referred to as Yushu, synonymous with the prefecture of Yushu and the city of Yushu.

Pant's conclusions were rather odd: "This necessitated [China's] effective occupation and control of Tibet. ...In case of war the vulnerable coast line of China can be abandoned for a safer and more secure central Asia region."

All this shows a poor understanding of China.[18]

The Political Officer's lesson was not over: "The Tibetans themselves are yet only vaguely aware of all the implications of the Chinese policy of occupation and expansion over their country," adding that "historically they have always opposed the Chinese domination and emotionally most of the Tibetans not only feel apart and different from the Chinese, but have often been strongly antagonistic to them."

This was absolutely true; he then admitted that with the advent of Communism in China "the whole picture assumes a new perspective. As long as both in Tibet and China there were corrupt inefficient feudalistic regimes the rivalries of the ruling cliques or the animosities, of two different types of people held general sway over the political scene."

More interesting are the following remarks: "Now a new religion, Communism, faces the Tibetan people and this new religion would certainly try to compete with Buddhism for the conquest and the control of the souls of the Tibetans."

The Political Officer added a factor to the new 'religious' dogma: "the Chinese revolution with a new dynamism and a new social philosophy taking shape under their very eyes some of the Tibetan intelligentsia disgruntled and disappointed with inefficiency and corruption in Tibet did feel attracted towards this new China and felt that for reforms nearer to home especially when no other country was capable of rendering it the help of the Chinese revolutionaries would be advantageous."

This is a fact that many Tibetans were dreaming of a societal change; it resulted in many collaborating with the new regime during the first years: "knowing the temper of the new regime in China, [they]

---

18 We have analyzed in Volume 1, Chapter 3 of this study the reasons which triggered the so-called 'Liberation' of Tibet.

acquiesced in the advent of the rule of new China over Tibet and sought to co-operate with it as best as they could."

Pant further pointed out: "We have thus in Tibet a very interesting spectacle. The Chinese are determined to occupy Tibet and colonise parts of it for their own material and security reasons. China has never recognised any treaties made between Tibet and the outside countries such as Russia or Great Britain. ...In the great game of international politics the fate of Tibet was bartered for a few concessions in Shanghai or Hong Kong!"

Unfortunately for the Tibetans, it was not a mere spectacle and the fact China did not recognize the treaties signed by the British, meant that India had no 'agreed' border with China, now occupying Tibet. Did Pant realize this?

About Russia, Pant commented that though greatly interested in Tibet: "[it] was never in a position to seriously challenge either the Chinese or the British interests in Tibet. She has however never been very happy over the Chinese supremacy over Tibet."

He said that recent 'direct contacts' between Tibetans and Russia were not discouraged [by Lhasa?]: "The Tibetans also on their part have been greatly attracted by the fact that Russia gave some kind of 'independence' to Outer Mongolia whilst the Chinese 'absorbed' Inner Mongolia."

There was no doubt that the Tibetans would have liked to be recognised as an independent nation by China, Russia and India: "Nothing would please them more than to be the cause of an international agreement."

Pant recalled the Simla Agreement in 1914 "when China walked out of it and disclaimed any agreement or concurrence about the status of Tibet."

He even remarked that China had advised Tibet to claim parts of Nepal and also Bhutan and Sikkim. There is no record of this.

Though there are a number of inexactitudes in the 'lesson', this letter gave a background of how history was seen from Gangtok.

## The Mongoloid fringe

Though the term used by the PO, the 'Mongoloid fringe' may not be exactly correct, the PO however made noteworthy remarks, "The Chinese have never bound themselves by treaties such as those that were arrived at in the Simla Conference nor have they directly or indirectly recognised treaties made with Bhutan or Sikkim."

He cited the temptation to attract the border peoples situated within India's boundary from Ladakh to the East: "Their road making activities near our borders may be legitimately undertaken to improve the life of the Tibetans within their own border areas; these roads however may make it more easy for some people of North Sikkim, Bhutan or NEFA, Ladakh and Nepal to have better access to Tibet and at a later date the peoples of these areas might come to depend more on Tibet than India for their trade, commerce, education, cultural contacts and general livelihood."

Pant rightly assumed that the Chinese were preoccupied about "the effective occupation of their side of all our border areas, especially in the North Sikkim and the Towang[19] and Siang sectors of NEFA. Not only road building but the establishment of checkposts, removal of more pro-Dalai Lama officials and their replacement by more 'obedient' ones has been undertaken."

This is what Sumul Sinha, the head of the Indian Mission in Lhasa till 1952 and later posted in South Block, had time and again warned the government; Pant added: "Some detachments of the Chinese military as well as surveyors have been 'exploring' along our frontiers."

His conclusions however probably pleased Delhi: "In spite of all this, any serious military or other threat to our security from such actions is not, at the moment, seriously visualised."

As we shall see, TN Kaul in the Ministry would repeat the same refrain.

---

19 The proper spelling is 'Tawang'.

## The Border States

However, the report asserted that States such as Bhutan and Sikkim had little attraction towards the Chinese after Tibet's occupation: "The sympathies of the Bhutanese or Sikkimese and certain sections of the Nepalese do certainly go out in full measure towards their Tibetan brethren across the border. They feel that their religion, their culture, their way of life is in danger."

The two small Himalayan States were however watching carefully the happenings in the North; Pant noted that the efficiency and vigour "with which the Chinese have acted in respect of road building, building of schools, hospitals has certainly created a deep impression on the minds of our own people."

Pant remarked that the Chinese activities would one day lead to the loss of a separate culture of the Tibetans as a people and "would mean also their absorption into China."

Sikkim and Bhutan clearly realized that Tibet was in the process of losing its identity, though the Communist slogans spoke of equality, social justice, development of industrial wealth, it had "not yet attracted the common masses of the people in Tibet."

It was a fact that road building as well as increased trade had temporarily brought employment and some wealth to a large section of the border population "but [it] has also threatened all those living on providing transport with unemployment. Bad government, unjust taxes, nepotism and social snobbery had created desperation amongst many in Tibet, but most hoped and felt that all this can be remedied and improved conditions established without having to pay the price of being absorbed into China."

Philosophically, Pant argued that, if with China's help, Tibet could succeed "in preserving at least some form of her own way of life and also succeed in 'progressing', then the peoples within our own frontiers may look upon the life of the people across our borders with less fear and greater appreciation." It was not to be the case.

He concluded that for the next fifteen to twenty years, Communism would not attract the Tibetans, though he added that some of the

Tibetan students studying in China "may on [their] return turn more catholic than the Pope and preach the New Doctrine, but few would listen and fewer get converted."

This turned out to be true; it was something which was certainly not expected by Communist China.

But Pant believed that if the Chinese managed "in actuating the people without the use of too much of force and without establishing the dictatorship of the proletariat," in other words, without denying the Tibetans their own way of life "they have a certain chance of winning the real friendship of the mass of the people." It showed a poor understanding of Communism, particularly the Maoist version.

The questions raised by the PO would be answered four years later; In March 1959, the Tibetan uprising would take place in Lhasa and the Dalai Lama would have no other alternative but to take refuge in India.

**The Situation in the Mid-Fifties**

The danger of Communism was obvious for the Himalayan population. But in 1955, the PO could still ask: "One wonders whether the Chinese are conscious and whether they can function that way situated as they are and whether they will have the real good will and the patience to use the right means over a long period of time in spite of the resistance, frustration and anger now discernible in Tibet." The postponement of the reforms announced by Zhou Enlai during his visit to India in 1956/57 demonstrated that the Chinese were somehow conscious of the need to 'go slow'.

In 1955, the PO saw two possibilities, Tibet could get "more or less resigned and reconciled to her position as one of the Autonomous Regions of China" or the second alternative, some kind of a conflict could take place within Tibet.

As mentioned, the revolt erupted in Eastern Tibet a few months later and spread three years later to Central Tibet. But at the end of 1955, Pant was still dreaming that if the Tibetans were able to "evolve a more prosperous and more satisfactory pattern of life without losing their traditions and their religion in cooperation with the Chinese the peoples of these border regions would certainly look towards Tibet with admiration and sympathy."

The PO admitted that India had to do something to revitalize her own borders: "In view of all these changes in Tibet, we have also to see how we have to proceed in bringing about the emergence of a new and more satisfying life to the peoples residing in this border region."

In the second alternative, in case of a revolt in Tibet, if the process of 'absorption' triggered violence and misery, "the people of this region would judge China who professes democratic and humanitarian standards of behaviour according to their actions. ...In Bhutan, in Sikkim, in the West Bengal districts of Darjeeling and Kalimpong people do express their hope that friends from outside, especially India would at least try to understand sympathetically the condition of affairs inside Tibet."

The border populations hoped that the contacts Tibet had had with India for thousands of years "will not now be broken and that India would at least continue to satisfy the thirst for cultural and spiritual life that the Tibetans know and feel only India can satisfy."

Pant then made an interesting and quite profound remark.

**The Tibetans also Friends of India**

India's smaller neighbours felt that India's being very friendly to China would not help the Tibetans to safeguard their identity: "People in this region however ask whether Tibetans are not also friends of India and perhaps closer friends than the Chinese."

Pant believed that the amount of friendship that "grows between all these people of the Indo-Mongoloid stock and us would by and large help to stabilise the position in this border area. ...A feeling amongst them that they have someone who has a faith in this better destiny and who appreciates their cultural and spiritual attainments would by itself be of help to them."

Unfortunately, India did not want to 'offend' China, especially after Nehru's trip to Beijing in October 1954; the time of the great *Hindi-Chini* honeymoon had come.

For the PO, the other factor was that the people of Tibet felt deeply attracted towards India "and have often looked to her for moral and spiritual guidance."

He concluded his note in philosophical terms: "All peoples treasure an independent existence and the Tibetans are certainly no exception who are, as it is, a very proud people conscious of their history, their traditions and their culture. The process of history is never really predictable."

He thought that 'a compromise formula' could be worked out "for living together under new relationships; at times a synthesis takes place which includes the two cultures and produces a more satisfying life."

It was a myth in the mind of someone unable to understand Communist China; he wrote strange words: "From darkest Africa to the highest Himalayas such communities are dragged out to contribute to the ever evolving, ever growing pattern of world culture. Tibet and these border areas of Bhutan, Sikkim, and Nepal are an episode in this great process of world history."

World history had turned sour for the Tibetans.

## The Tension between Nepalese, Lepchas and Bhutias

A few months later[20], another report from Apa Pant provides us some information on the ethnic and social situation in this strategic region. It is important to understand how these issues were impacted by the events taking place across the Himalaya.

Pant described Sikkim as a geographically and demographically small country: "It is barely 3,000 sq. miles in area and nearly one third of it is uninhabitable because of high mountains and low malarious valleys."

In 1955, it had a population of about 1,50,000 people, out of which 90,000 were Nepalese, while 45,000 were Bhutias and the rest Lepchas. Amongst the Bhutias and Lepchas were included the Rais, Limbus, Tamangs and some of the tribes of Gurungs; the Lepchas with the Tamangs and the Rais were the original inhabitants, explained the PO:

---

20  Early 1956.

"Both the Nepalese and the Bhutias are immigrants - one from the West and the other from the East."

Again Pant gave some explanations which may not be historically correct; the Nepalese and the Bhutias originally came from the same Indo-Mongoloid stock, while most of the Nepali tribes such as the Newars, the Gurungs and even the Pradhans migrated from Tibet.

According to the PO, the ruling family of Sikkim traced its origin to Kham ...but before they settled down in Eastern Tibet, they inhabited what is today Himachal Pradesh.

The report continued in the same rather unscientific vein: "The Indo-Mongoloids have in the past couple of thousand years travelled from the foot hills of Himalayas to the highlands of eastern Tibet and back again at least half a dozen times."

His conclusion was that the Nepali populations residing in Nepal, Sikkim and Bhutan migrated into these areas earlier than the Bhutias, who arrived 'only' between 800 to 600 years ago: "The latest invasion of Bhutias of course occurred with the present ruling family, the Namgyals, about 350 years ago," Pant wrote.

With the arrival of the Namgyal ruling family from the Chumbi valley, which was then part of Sikkim, "the real process of 'colonisation' of this territory by Bhutias started."

At that time, parts of Western Bhutan were also under the Namgyal family, i.e. the Bhutias; Pant added: "Bhot is also a word for Tibet."

He further explained that as the Namgyals arrived in Sikkim, the ruling family made a pact of 'blood brotherhood' with the Lepcha, Tamang and the Rai tribes already residents of Sikkim: "The Lepchas and Bhutias thus feel themselves to be particularly close to each other since that time."

Bhutias had already adopted Mahayana Buddhism as a religion and "kept their contacts with the Buddhist seats of learning in India."

At the same time, the Lepchas, the Rais and the Tamangs followed their original animistic faith and never converted to Buddhism; the Bhutias and Lepchas however intermarried quite extensively: "There is a process of acculturation going on between the Bhutias and Lepchas over the last three centuries but [it is] not [a] complete integration."

The description continued asserting that most of the Nepalese in Sikkim were Hindus: "They are more industrious, better farmers and generally more rich because of their hard work. They have also gone ahead in education and occupy many important posts in the administration. They are numerically in a very strong position."

However, the ruling tribe of Sikkim are the Bhutias and the Lepchas, who considered the Nepalese as 'invaders': "They feel that the Nepalese really do not belong to Sikkim."

For Pant, this explained why for religious and social functions in Sikkim, the ruling family and the rich Bhutia families never invited the Nepalese: "For all purposes the Nepalese do not at all exist for them. Till the establishment of the democratic constitution, it will be safe to say that Nepalese were hardly in the picture even in Sikkim's political life."

But economically they were the dominant force, the major producers of wealth in Sikkim.

The analysis continued: "With the arrival of the Nepalese in Sikkim, the Bhutias and the Lepchas started to feel physically as well as emotionally insecure." One of the reasons of insecurity was the rapidly growing number of the 'ever prolific Nepalese'; "the Nepalese not only profess a different religion but most of them feel greater attraction towards Indian districts of Darjeeling and Kalimpong than towards Sikkim," added Pant.

The struggle for India's independence had an effect on the minds of the Nepali populations in Sikkim, quite a number of them had even suffered jail sentences during the Movement and they now could not understand why this small protectorate State of Sikkim had been allowed to remain 'independent', while the other large states of India had merged in the Union: "One has to face the persistent demand of the Nepalese for merger of Sikkim with India," Pant asserted.

The PO believed that the demand for merger with India had recently accentuated the fears in the Bhutias' and Lepchas' mind, "[they] feel that in the big sea of multifarious communities in India [they] would be like a drop in the huge ocean and would lose their identity and separate existence."

According to Apa Pant, this would explain why they keep "apart and create a myth somewhat unrealistic about their traditions, their culture, their language, their own way of life."

He then made another comment: "Sikkim is really a group of communities living side by side but not really a nation, a politically cohesive unit."

He cited the fact that the Nepalese had to pay higher taxes than the Lepchas, the Bhutias and also the residents of Kalimpong and Darjeeling districts; he pointed out that their representation was not in proportion to their numbers and "emotionally as well as physically they are not accepted as 'first class citizens' of Sikkim [which] makes them long for union with India."

This lack of loyalty towards Sikkim made the Nepalese suspect, for the PO: "The more the Nepalese feel attracted towards India and start slogans for integration with India the more Bhutia-Lepchas feel insecure and desire some formula which will 'protect' them from liquidation."

These alarmist views, even if seen through an Indian official's eye, were rather disturbing in view of the strategic position of the Himalayan State.

**India Walks In**

One of the objectives of the seven-year development plan was to create "a new basis for cooperation and understanding between the various tribes inhabiting Sikkim."

The plan was supposed to tackle "the psychological, physical, economical and social necessities by creating a synthesis of the various elements that inhabit Sikkim, [so that] these fears, the suspicions would gradually diminish."

Practical cooperation between the different sections of the society would weld Sikkim together, thought the bureaucrats in Delhi. It was rather utopist to believe that "common economic ventures such as cooperative farms, small industries, dairy farms, fruit gardens, village handicrafts would weld these small groups into one community," while common residential schools with a common language would create a common cultural and social patterns of life." Then Sikkim would become a really stable and a prosperous unit, believed the Indian government representative.

Delhi's (and Gangtok's) idea was to remove the discriminations against the Nepali populations. Eventually, the democratization of the society would happen differently twenty years later, but that is another story.

## A Note by TN Kaul

On April 17, 1955, TN Kaul in the Ministry of External Affairs answered some question raised by the Political Officer about the doubts and suspicions of people of the Tibetan origin on the policy India should follow towards the borders.

Kaul remarked that the Maharajkumar as well as his sisters and some Tibetan officials in Kalimpong had been talking in a reserved manner towards India. The diplomat said that Khen Chung,[21] a former Tibetan monk and some members of the Tibetan Trade Agency in Kalimpong called on him in Kolkata when he was returning from Shillong.

Kaul wrote: "He is a loyal and patriotic Tibetan, but very anti-Chinese. He feels very strongly that Tibetans are being coerced by the Chinese to adopt the Chinese system, but they will never accept this new system and give up their ancient heritage willingly."

Khenjung told Kaul how the Chinese used to coerce him and that he had refused to obey the orders of the Chinese, when he was in Shigatse area. The Indian official noted: "I rather think that he was exaggerating but there is no doubt that he is a trusted man of the Dalai Lama" who sent him to India to look after the Tibetan Trade Agency in 1953.

It was only recently that the official had handed over the charge of the Tibetan Trade Agent to one of the Pangdatsang brothers. Kaul reported

---

21 Probably, Khenjung Lobsang Gyaltsen. Khenjung along with Gyalo Thondup, the Dalai Lama's elder brother and Tsipon Shakabpa, the former Finance Secretary living in Kalimpong, would form a trio known as 'Jenkhentsisum'; in the coming years they would fight hard for Tibetan independence.

that Khenjun wanted his advice about the personal treasure of the Dalai Lama, now lying at the palace in Gangtok. Should it be given to the new Trade Agent?

The former monk argued that the treasure had been sent by the Dalai Lama "when he was the sovereign ruler of Tibetan and even if the Dalai Lama wrote to him to hand over the treasure he would be doing so only under Chinese pressure." Kaul had no answer to this; he just told Khenjun that he would have to study the files: "This matter may be examined separately," said the report.

More importantly for India, Khenjun mentioned the situation of Tibetans in Kalimpong; he said that they were unduly harassed by the police and by …the Chinese communists. The Tibetans wanted a yearly residential permit instead of having to register every two months with the local police. Some were even keen to take Indian nationality. When Kaul was asked his views on this, the diplomat reiterated that the Government's policy towards the Tibetans: "was one of special friendship and we would examine whether their inconveniences in Kalimpong could be removed."

For Indian citizenship, Kaul gave a bureaucratic reply: "if they fulfill the rules on the subject and were otherwise not undesirable they could apply for it." It meant nothing.

When Khenjung asked if he should go back to Tibet or stay in India, he was told that "if he wished to stay on in India he could do so, provided he did not indulge in any subversive political or anti Chinese activities."

The former ITA was told that he could meet Apa Pant and discuss these issues with him.

The most positive aspect of the encounter was that Kaul realized the strong resentment felt by the Tibetans against China's occupation of Tibet: "The Tibetans are a proud and nationalistic people and would naturally like to retain their identity and autonomy."

He however commented that "they did very little to consolidate their position and improve their internal conditions in the past."

Kaul gave Khenjung the often-mentioned argument, "India could not have given military aid to the Tibetans …if we had done so it would only have led to greater destruction in Tibet."

The diplomat's conclusion was that India's relations with China were friendly: "China will think twice before implementing any expansionist plans southwards for some time to come." The old rationale was brought forward again. "The [Chinese] have plenty of problems on hand and they have to consolidate their strength inside their country."

The following months and years would see serious incursions in Barahoti and Nilang (then Uttar Pradesh) and Shipkila (Himachal Pradesh).

Kaul once again reiterated that while there was no immediate threat from China vis-a-vis India "at present or for the next few years, we cannot take this as an absolute guarantee for the future."

It was clear that Nehru's government had accepted the invasion of Tibet as a fait accompli: "It is likely that the Chinese will absorb the Tibetan people and colonise Tibet, as they did Manchuria," noted Kaul.

Coming to the Indian borders, Kaul foresaw a reaction against the Chinese in the border areas of India, "particularly in Sikkim and Bhutan where the people of Tibetan stock have greater chance of maintaining their autonomy and identity in alliance with India than with China."

He asserted that the Tibetans were more and more looking to India for support and encouragement for maintaining their identity and culture. He suggested doing everything possible to help the Tibetans "on our borders and even those coming from Tibet in this direction."

The Indian diplomat commented: "[We should] not raise any false hopes among Tibetans coming from Tibet about giving them any military or other aid to oppose the Chinese in Tibet. That is an internal matter for China and it is for the Tibetans to tackle it with the Chinese to the best of their ability."

That would be the policy of the Government during the following years …it remains so today, more than 60 years later.

Kaul did not elaborate on the implications for the Indian borders.

Interestingly, he mentioned the vested interests in Tibet who entertain "lurking hopes of a future war in which China may be involved when it will be their opportunity to strike back and regain their independence. We should do nothing to encourage these hopes."

A war with China would take place seven years later; it would not help the Tibetans, though, believed Kaul: "we should show special friendship towards Tibetans coming from Tibet in general and our own Tibetans in particular to at least make them feel that India entertains special regard for them."

However, the Tibetans were not to abuse India's hospitality or "indulge in political and subversive activities or do any propaganda against China with whom we have friendly relations," said the Kashmiri Pandit.

He welcomed the fact that Sikkim and Bhutan "have begun to realize that their future lies in friendship with India rather than with a Tibet under Chinese occupation."

Delhi awaited a request from Bhutan before offering the Land of the Dragon help or advice: "with Bhutan we would be particularly careful in handling them gently and slowly as they are apt to be touchy and suspicious."

To conclude, he strongly suggested improving "the lot of Tibetan population along our borders in India. The extent to which we succeed in improving the lot of these people will determine in the mind of common man whether the Chinese system or the Indian system is better."

The situation in the Tibetan plateau periphery was indeed worrisome.

What the true remedy was, now that India had left Tibet to her fate, was not obvious.

## 10

# The Foreign Secretary in Tibet

**RK Nehru in the Chumbi Valley**

In a first occurrence, the Indian Foreign Secretary RK Nehru, passed through Tibet on his way to Bhutan in June 1955.

His report gives us a good idea of the situation in the Chumbi Valley and southern Tibet at a time the areas witnessed tremendous changes.

Nehru[1] crossed over the Nathu-la pass[2] and entered the Chumbi Valley on June 11; he immediately wrote: "Travel conditions became less comfortable after the frontier was crossed."

Though China worked hard to complete new roads upto the Indian border, the mule path on the Indian side was far better, remarked the Foreign Secretary, "[it was] kept in good repair by the Central PWD. On the Tibetan side, the path is rocky and muddy and no attempt has been made to improve it."

In a few months, the situation would drastically change with the improvement of the road network on the Tibetan plateau. At the time of Nehru's visit, the PLA was concentrating on the Gyantse-Phari section of the road.

Nehru visited one of the guest houses which had recently been handed over to the Chinese, he recalled: "Our first night was spent in the

---

1 In this chapter, except if otherwise specified, 'Nehru' refers to RK Nehru, the Foreign Secretary and not to Jawaharlal Nehru, the Prime Minister.

2 'La' in Tibetan means 'pass', therefore more correctly, it should be written 'Nathu-la' though sometimes written Nathula or Nathu La.

Champithang rest house. ...Unlike the rest houses on our side which are clean and comfortable, we found this rest house in a deplorable condition, many propagandist pictures adorned the wall, but the furniture and fittings were filthy."

*The Tibet Album* of the Pitts River Museum described thus these guest houses: "[They] have been put up every ten or fifteen miles along the way from Gangtok to Gyantse. They were originally built soon after the Younghusband expedition of 1904, but most of them have been enlarged or rebuilt since. They are intended for the use of Government officials but are also at the disposal of tourists, a limited number of whom are each year allowed up the trade route. ...This bungalow has three rooms - a small dining-room and two bedrooms..."

The narration of the Foreign Secretary continued: "All these minor discomforts were, however, overshadowed by the beauty of the landscape. The mountain side was carpeted with flowers which are much more profuse on the Tibetan side than ours. From the top of the Nathula, we had a view of Chomolhari and other high peaks which we shall not easily forget."

McDonald, the British Trade Agent in Gyantse in the 1920s, did the short journey between Yatung and Champithang: "Seven miles above this place is the bungalow of Champithang, where a halt will be made. On the road from the monastery to the bungalow, wonderful views of the path from the Jelap [pass] to Rinchengong are obtained, as well as of the pass itself. From Champithang to the top of the Nathu La takes about an hour. At every turn of this part of the road, fresh snow views are seen, including the wonderful mass of Chomolhari. It is six miles from the Nathu-la to Changu[3] bungalow, through Sherathang[4], an old camping ground, and past several dark and gloomy tarns. The

---

3 Tsomgo Lake, also known as Changu Lake, is a glacial lake in the East Sikkim district located 40 kms from Gangtok at an elevation of 3,753 m. The lake remains frozen during the winter season. The lake surface reflects different colours with the change of seasons and is held in great reverence by the local Sikkimese people.

4 Sherathang was a village in Sikkim near Nathu-la in India. Today, it is the site for excise, customs and checking for trade between India and China. Rinchengang is the corresponding location in the Chumbi Valley. It is located 8 km below the Nathu-la.

scenery is wild in the extreme, and of surpassing grandeur. Changu Bungalow is situated at the end of the lake of the same name, in a basin surrounded by mountains. The Changu lake is beautiful, especially in the sun. There was at one time a scheme to harness the waters falling from the lake, [running] a big hydro-electric plant, to supply northern Bengal with power. At present, the plan has been dropped."

The next day, Nehru visited the Kargyud[5] monastery on his way to Yatung: "The head Lama and monks gave us a warm reception, including an excellent Chinese style lunch."

The Foreign Secretary recalled that the monks of the monastery visited him in Yatung the next day as well as when he returned from Bhutan: "The Head Lama gave some indication that they would welcome a gift from the Government of India for carrying out repairs in the monastery. I do not know whether the Chinese will allow this, but Shri Apa Pant is examining this matter."

It was clear that any such donation or support needed first to be cleared by the local branch of the Foreign Bureau. The times had changed; Indian officials had now to work through the Chinese institutions.

Nehru stayed at Yatung for two more days and June 14, his party left for Bhutan: "The border was crossed at a point, 8 miles south of Yatung."

Twelve days later, the Indian diplomat returned to Yatung and remained two more days in the Chumbi Valley. Finally, on their way back to Gangtok, he spent again a night in Champithang and crossed Nathula the next day.

**General Impressions**

In his report, the Foreign Secretary offered his 'general impressions'; the Chumbi valley is thus described: "[it] is a relatively small area with an estimated population of about 6,000. Its importance lies in the fact that it is the only area south of the great Himalayan range which is under foreign control. Until 1792, the valley was part of Sikkim, but it was lost to Tibet and is now part of China."

---

5   The Kagyud or Kargyud is one of the four main schools of Tibetan Buddhism.

One should remember that Harishwar Dayal had suggested the possibility of India occupying the Valley in case of Chinese invasion of Tibet. In December 1950, this was vehemently rejected by the Prime Minister.[6]

RK Nehru then explained that it was an important area for other reasons too: "The main trade route from India to Tibet lies through the valley. There are several passes leading from the valley into Sikkim. The only convenient all-weather route from India to Western Bhutan lies through Sikkim and the Chumbi Valley. The various invasions of Sikkim by the Tibetans and the Bhutanese have also taken place through this valley."

Incidentally, Nehru's homonym, the Prime Minister, would travel the same route and spend two nights in Yatung on his way to (and back from) Bhutan two years later.

RK Nehru observed that the local administration was under the responsibility of an official known as the Tibetan Trade Agent (TTA): "This official is appointed by the Lhasa authorities and has a fairly high rank. He has some executive and magisterial powers and there are two headmen under him who are nominated by the leading residents of groups of villages."

Till 1951, before the arrival of the Chinese in the Valley, the TTA had close dealings with his Indian counterpart, the ITA in Yatung; it was with him that the Indian official coordinated most of his needs.

Nehru explained that the Chinese had now their own representatives comprising the PLA officers, but also a civil administration working under the Assistant of the Foreign Bureau in Lhasa. At the time of Nehru's visit, the Chinese staff consisted of a passport officer, check-post officials, a supply officer and some postal and telegraph staff. Some Chinese teachers had just come to man the only school in the valley; it was located at Pipithang on the track leading to India.

Nehru mentioned the presence of the PLA: "There is a military force numbering at present about 150 under a commander for the whole valley. The size of the force has recently been reduced. This may be due

---

6   See Volume 1, Chapter 16.

to the fact that Chinese military personnel are employed mainly on road building which has been stopped for the present in the Valley."

The building of roads was the first priority though the Chinese should have been aware that there was no danger coming from India.

As we have seen, the report of the Officer Commanding the detachment of the Indian military escort in Tibet showed this constant change in the strength of the Chinese PLA's presence in the Chumbi Valley; it mainly fluctuated with the needs for the road constructions. India on her part, had detachments of the Maratha Light Infantry posted in Siliguri and Gangtok; however, the escort was recalled from early 1954.

**All Facilities, No Courtesy**

After the Foreign Secretary's visit to Bhutan via Yatung had been notified to the Chinese, South Block was told that Nehru would receive all facilities and courtesies: "I received all the facilities needed, but no special courtesies were shown," commented Nehru.

He explained the new situation: "Apparently the practice in the past was for the Tibetan officials to call on a visiting representative of the Government of India. This practice has been discontinued under instructions from the Chinese. The Tibetan Trade Agent sent word to our trade agent[7] that he wanted to call on me, but had not found it possible to do so."

It was a diplomatic way to say that the Chinese did not allow the Tibetan official to call on the Indian diplomat. The reason was simple: "It is part of Chinese policy to prevent direct intercourse between Tibetans and Indian officials. They want the Tibetan people to treat us as foreigners and they are jealous of the special relations which existed in the past between our officials and Tibetans." Nehru further observed: "Similar steps were taken by them in 1906-11 when they were in effective control of Tibet."

Nehru would have been more correct if he had said "when a Chinese warlord invaded the Land of Snows in 1910-11."

In 1954, no Chinese official called on Nehru while he was camping in Yatung. Philosophically, the Foreign Secretary noted: "It was not

---

7   Maj SL Chhiber.

necessary for them to do so and I do not think that they meant any discourtesy."

However, Chinese officials accepted the ITA's invitation to a lunch party in Nehru's honour; they came in full force.

Nehru came back to the issue, which showed that despite the Agreement signed fifteen months earlier, all was not rosy on the Tibetan plateau under the new dispensation: "Some of us in Delhi, however, expected that the Chinese would show some special courtesies on this occasion. I did not expect them to do so as by informing them that I was on an official visit to Bhutan we had placed them in a difficult position."

The Foreign Secretary thought that the right thing to do was to notify China about his visit to Paro, though South Block was aware that China claimed "Bhutan as their vassal state. This claim was last made in 1910, but it has never been given up. As recently as 1948, the claim was repeated by the Tibetan Kashag."

It is important to understand the attitude of the Chinese vis-à-vis Bhutan, because more than 60 years later, it might not be very different: "in the past [the Chinese position] has been that we cannot have special relations with Bhutan without their concurrence. I presume this is still their position, though it is not being asserted openly," wrote Nehru.

His conclusion was that the Chinese could have refused to give his party transit visas, "but this would have led to a conflict. The alternative was to give visas, but to take no special notice of the visit. This is what they actually did. They were very friendly at the party, but not one word was spoken about our visit to Bhutan."

It appeared as if the Spirit of Panchsheel was evaporating fast.

**The Situation in the Chumbi Valley**

The Foreign Secretary enquired about the latest developments in the Valley: "Yatung itself is a shanty town and is dominated by our trade agent's lovely house on the hill side.[8] The Chinese officials are living in hired houses in some of the villages. Our superior accommodation

---

8   The Indian Residency was destroyed by the Chinese at an undetermined date, possibly during the Cultural Revolution, or later.

gives us a special status which must be a source of irritation to the Chinese."

There is no doubt that it created a sentiment of jealousy among the Chinese officials who often lived in rented houses, while the ITA possessed a 'palace' dominating the bazaar. The beautiful and spacious India House no longer exists today. We have been unable to find out when it was destroyed. For the Chinese, it was undoubtedly the symbol of British (and Indian) colonialism. As mentioned earlier, the Indian Prime Minister would spend two nights at the residence of ITA in September 1958.

RK Nehru described another 'irritating' souvenir for the new colonizers: "On the high cliffs overlooking the town, the various Indian regiments which have served in Yatung have engraved their names and emblems. Beneath them floats the Chinese flag in a small house occupied by one of the Chinese offices. I cannot believe that the Chinese like this, but they have made no attempt to remove the emblems."

The ITA had been asked by the Chinese to close down our enumeration post in Yatung; he admitted: "We have done so as we are not entitled to keep this under the Agreement."

At the time of Nehru's visit, discussions were taking place about the demarcation of the area of the Indian Trade Agency: "We should take a firm stand on our rights under the agreement but should not insist on keeping any non essential area. I have given instructions to our Trade Agent about this," Nehru noted.

**The Position of the Tibetans**

The Tibetans were in a difficult position as the Chinese were openly trying to win over the younger generation of Tibetans, though according to Nehru: "They are not openly interfering with the administrative setup. Nor are they interfering with the monasteries and other institutions. They are expanding educational facilities and are trying to create a pro-Chinese outlook among that younger generation." However, the brightest among the young Tibetans would soon be sent to China for education.

Nehru mentioned the two Leagues which had been set up: one for older people and another for the youth: "These leagues are controlled by Chinese official and I understand that meetings take place frequently. I presume that pro-Chinese propaganda is carried on through these leagues."

He described the situation in the Chumbi Valley: "Loud speakers have been installed in some of the villages and there are many pro-Chinese broadcasts."

A large number of children had started wearing Chinese dress: "In the school at Pipithang[9], both Chinese and Tibetan are taught and there are some Chinese soldiers who are learning Tibetan. A group of young people both boys and girls, is being sent to the school of National Minorities in Peking."

According to the Foreign Secretary's information, the Chinese intention was to build a new generation of cadres and later "officials of the old school should be replaced by Tibetan communists who have been trained in China."

This is what the Chinese hoped, though, during the coming years, it would not really materialize.

## The Indian Borders

Nehru then touched upon a serious subject (for India at least), "the possible effect of these developments on our own border peoples."

He noted that the Indian population south of the Himalaya were mainly of Tibetan stock "and in many cases, they have close religious and other links with the Tibetans. The frontier shown on our maps has also not been accepted by the Chinese and there are many dormant claims which conflict with our established rights."

It is interesting to note that the Foreign Secretary admitted that the border was not fixed; India had definitely missed a chance to solve the border issue during the talks of the 1954 Tibet agreement. The consequences are still being felt more than 60 years later.

---

9 Some of the villages of Lower-Dromo (Lower Chumbi) area were Lingmathang, Pipithang, Chumpithang, Galinggang, Dhongchengang and, Rinchengang.

RK Nehru commented that when the question was examined four years earlier[10], it was suggested that "this northern frontier is an area of potential danger. It was pointed out that China is 'at last united, militant and expansive' and inevitably, in course of time, she would create trouble on our side."

He may also have had in mind the report of Sumul Sinha mentioned in Volume 2 of this study.[11] The diplomat commented: "Twice before, when she [China] was strong in Tibet, she asserted her claim to our border areas and the present government is not likely to give up an objective which has so consistently been pursued by its weaker predecessors."

This reminds us of the words of the historian RC Majumdar: "There is one aspect of Chinese culture that is little known outside the circle of professional historians. It is the aggressive imperialism that characterized the politics of China throughout the course of her history, at least during the part of which is well known to us. Thanks to the systematic recording of historical facts by Chinese themselves, an almost unique achievement in oriental countries.... we are in a position to follow the imperial and aggressive policy of China from the third century BC to the present day, a period of more than twenty-two hundred years ...It is characteristic of China that if a region once acknowledged her nominal suzerainty even for a short period, she should regard it as a part of her empire forever and would automatically revive her claim over it even after a thousand years whenever there was a chance of enforcing it.[12]"

It is doubtful whether the Indian Prime Minister pondered on this view.

## Another difficulty

But the Foreign Secretary pointed to another issue, the Tibetan irredentism: "[they] have a strong sense of nationality which involves some risks for the Chinese. The new Chinese policy, however, is to bring about an integration of the two peoples and to build up a strong pro-

---

10 He probably referred to the report of the Himmatsinghji Committee of the North and North-Eastern borders of India.

11 See Volume 2, Chapter 18.

12 RC Majundar, *The Organiser* (New Delhi: Special Dewali Issue, 1965).

Chinese party in Tibet. Tibetan nationalism directed and controlled by the Chinese as part of a larger movement embracing both the peoples, might, therefore, create some risks for us, while averting the traditional risks for the Chinese."

It was certainly a real problem which needed to be considered; RK Nehru noted: "We should, of course, be on our guard, but I do not think that we should exaggerate the risks. We have an agreement with China which is based on good neighbourly relations. This, of course, is not enough. There is always some danger of infiltration, both of ideas and of undesirable elements."

In many ways, the head of the Indian diplomacy had sharper views than the Prime Minister (who was also Foreign Minister). Unfortunately, his warnings would not be heard in the corridors of South Block, though he affirmed: "Later, other dangers might arise if some weakness develops on our side. On the whole, however, at present, we are in a stronger position in our border areas than the Chinese seem to be in Tibet."

Despite all the efforts of the Chinese Communist Party to woo the local population on the northern side of the Himalaya, the Himalayan population remained truly nationalistic and faithful to India.

## Tibet's Relation with China

The diplomat's analysis of the Chinese relations with Tibet is fascinating. He observed that they were "based on conquest and domination and …there is an innate dislike of the Chinese among the Tibetans. The Dalai Lama's support of the Chinese is an important factor but I think his difficulties are generally appreciated."

It has to be noted that the young Tibetan leader was just back in Tibet after spending several months in China: "Fraternal relations are being built up between the two peoples, but it may not be easy to overcome the psychological resistance to this policy," noted Nehru.

In Gangtok, Nehru had met Pangda Tshang[13], a leading Tibetan *émigré* in Kalimpong who had recently come from Kham where he held an

---

13 It is not mentioned which of the Pangdathang brothers the Foreign Secretary met; it was probably Yarphel.

important post under the Chinese: "Unlike other emigres, e.g., Gyalo Thondup, he seems to have some contacts with the people. He spoke to me about the sense of frustration of the Tibetan people and their desire to throw off the Chinese yoke. He also showed his appreciation of India's policy."

Nehru, however, commented: "We should not, of course, accept everything that comes from emigre sources. Nevertheless, my general impression is that there is a strong undercurrent of resistance to the Chinese in Tibet which is perhaps confined at present to certain classes, but might assume larger proportions in the future."

The first signs would appear a year later when the monastery of Lithang would be bombed by Chinese airplanes. In June 1955, the Foreign Secretary's conclusions were clear: "We should not, in any case, become complacent, but should continue to take adequate measures to safeguard our interests."

Nehru believed that India was still in a strong position for two reasons: "First, we have a long record of friendship with the Tibetan people. We may have failed to help them in their hour of need, but unlike the Chinese, we have never tried to impose our domination on them." The second reason that he cited was the Buddhist religion which came from India; saints and preachers such as Padma Sambhava and Atisha[14] "occupy a high place in their spiritual hierarchy," he asserted.

His conclusion was that the old religious and cultural link "gives us an opportunity to develop closer relations with the people of Tibetan stock on our side. We cannot take a direct part in religious movements, but there are proposals for the opening of an Indo-Tibetan cultural centre which deserve our sympathy and support."

He probably referred to the Institute of Tibetology in Sikkim; he added that proposals would be coming soon from the Maharajkumar

---

14 Atisa Dipa kara Srijnana (982 - 1054 CE), a Buddhist Bengali religious leader and master. One of the major figures in the spread of 11th-century Mahayana and Vajrayana Buddhism in Asia, who inspired Buddhist thought from Tibet to Sumatra. Atisa is recognised as one of the greatest figures of classical Buddhism, and Atisa's chief disciple Dromtön was the founder of the Kadam School or New Translation schools of Tibetan Buddhism.

of Sikkim: "Closer cultural and other links with our border people will help to strengthen our ties with the people of Tibet."

Nehru pointed out another issue in 'India's favour', the active development policy of the Government to "strengthen our position in these areas." He asserted that Sikkim occupied a key position in this scheme: "Every Tibetan who passes through Sikkim can see the effort that is being made, with the Government of India's help, to promote the welfare of the people. Healthy influences will radiate from Sikkim in the direction both of Bhutan and of Tibet as a whole." His experience was that in comparison, no such improvement could be seen in the Chumbi valley.

He then referred to an article of Sulzburger[15] in *The New York Times* which mentioned "the struggle in the high mountains between the Indian and Chinese systems." RK Nehru commented: "I did not see much evidence of a struggle. The Chinese are at present on the defensive and their main concern is to overcome Tibetan opposition and to break the nexus between India and Tibet."

His suggestion was to remain active and continue to look after the welfare of the border peoples "and develop closer relations with them". The Foreign Secretary added: "These measures should, of course, be combined with effective occupation of territory up to the border and necessary measures for defence. The only part of the border area where the situation is dangerous from our point of view is Nepal. China is already probing in this direction."

Unfortunately, it was not just the Nepal border which was 'dangerous'.

---

15 Arthur Ochs 'Punch' Sulzberger Sr. (February 5, 1926 – September 29, 2012) belonged to a prominent media and publishing family. Sulzberger became Publisher of *The New York Times* in 1963 and Chairman of the Board of *The New York Times* Company in 1973. Sulzberger had written a 'colourful' article on the situation in Tibet and the developments on the Indian borders. In a note RK Nehru, remarked: "Some of the reports which we have received about these developments are conflicting. Tibetan emigres have complained of coercion by the Chinese and of attempts to bring about Tibet's integration with China by force. Sulzberger has presented a different picture which is probably more correct."

## The Trade Between India and Tibet

The Chumbi Valley was traditionally the main artery for the trade between Tibet and India. Nehru noted that the Agreement with China was working satisfactorily: "Imports from India have increased enormously while exports to India are more or less stationary. The main import which is taking place at present is rice."

As we have seen in Volume 2[16] of this study, it was mainly due to the shortage of food after the arrival of some 20,000 soldiers on the plateau.

Nehru noted that there were eight or ten Indian nationals living in the Valley: "They are mostly agents of Indian firms who are supplying goods to Tibet. These firms have made large profits." There were also a number of Indian shops in the bazaar in Yatung. In 1958, Nehru would walk down the Agency to meet a large delegation of traders.

The Foreign Secretary rightly remarked that the increase in imports from India was mainly due to the Chinese requirements: "It might almost be said that it is we who are sustaining the Chinese army in Tibet," a fact that many refused to see in Delhi.

Nehru added: "The Chinese have built two new roads, but the bulk of their requirements are still met from India. Perhaps one of the reasons why they have stopped road-building for the present in the Chumbi Valley is that they would like to divert trade as far as possible from India to China."

The entire report is an excellent analysis of the situation in Yatung and the Chumbi Valley in 1955. Coming from the Foreign Secretary it gave more weight to this rare insight from an Indian senior official in Tibet.

The fact that the Chinese officials did not call on Nehru should have rung warning bells for the Indian government.

---

16  See Volume 2, Chapter 5.

# 11

# India's Relations with Bhutan

## The Nepali Factor in Bhutan

Before we look into the relations between India and Bhutan, it is necessary to stop for a moment at the border between India and Bhutan, where troubles between Nepal and Bhutan were brewing. These incidents did not help to establish a relation of trust between the Himalayan Kingdoms; further, it could create a crisis between India and the Land of the Dragon. It was indeed a tricky issue.

In March 1954, the Druk Gyalpo, the Maharaja of Bhutan informed the Indian Government that some people of Nepali origin, who had gathered on Indian territory had intruded into Bhutan "to create disturbances ...and since [the] Indian territory was being used, it was the responsibility of the Government of India to control the situation."[1]

Two months later, on May 9, the Indian Prime Minister finally replied to the Maharaja of Bhutan; Nehru had taken a long time to answer as he wanted to enquire about the matter, though "information had reached us at an early stage about these troubles on your border territory," he said.

On receiving the Bhutanese king's complaint, the Indian government had contacted the Governments of Assam and West Bengal as well as the Political Officer in Sikkim.[2]

---

1  All documents in this chapter, except specifically mentioned, are from the Nehru Papers (JN Collection) held at the Nehru *Memorial* Museum and Library in Delhi. The 'papers' are not indexed.
2  BK Kapur.

On April 3, Delhi had received more information from Bishnuram Medhi[3], the Chief Minister of Assam that the Bhutan State Congress wanted to send a delegation to Nehru and it had been decided that "no *satyagraha*[4] would take place before their return".

The Prime Minister had also been told that the office of the Bhutan State Congress at Senalpara, near the Bhutan border, had been closed and that the Nepal Congress leaders had left the area.

Nehru indicated that the Nepalis had been informed that Indian territory would not be allowed to be used for any aggressive movement against Bhutan: "Our officers carried out our instructions in this matter Your Government must know this fully. ...The agitation subsided then, chiefly, because of the action we had taken," the Maharaja was told by the Indian Prime Minister.

Nehru explained that India had to function within her Constitution and the Fundamental Rights guaranteed by it; he spoke of "a large liberty even for agitations against our own Government. Opposition parties can function and are represented in Parliament. They can arrange demonstrations against the Government. They write in condemnation of our Government in newspapers and deliver strong speeches." Nehru added that it is only if there is violence that the government intervenes.

It is not sure if the Maharaja was convinced, though it was explained "our Supreme Court is anxious to protect the freedom of action of our people and judges governmental action strictly," continued the Indian Prime Minister who added that it was just to indicate the limits "within which we can function, ...[we are] in some difficulty in dealing with agitations, if they continue to be peaceful."

Nehru then cited a letter from Jigme Dorji, the Bhutanese Prime Minister, received through the PO in which he suggested that 'security proceedings' might be instituted against some of the office bearers of the Bhutan State Congress.

---

3   Bishnuram Medhi (24 April 1888 – 21 January 1981) was an Indian politician and freedom-fighter who served as the Chief Minister of Assam from 1950 to 1957 and Governor of Madras State from January 1958 till May 1964.

4   Satyagraha, in Sanskrit 'insistence on the Truth'. It is a form of nonviolent resistance or civil disobedience. Someone who practices satyagraha is a satyagrahi.

The Prime Minister continued to lecture the Maharaja: "We have to find out the causes of discontent as well as legitimate grievances and seek to remove them so that all sections of the population might feel that they were being treated equally and with justice by the authorities."

He quoted the 'trend of world affairs' and how major changes have taken place in various parts of the world, as well as in Asia: "No one can put a stop to these ideas and the desire of people everywhere to have a larger measure of freedom as well as an advance on the path to democracy."

It appeared more a threat to the Bhutanese monarchy, believed the Prime Minister: "These ideas will no doubt reach Bhutan and it is a wise policy not to wait for pressure from outside in order to remove any legitimate grievance," concluded Nehru, who told the Maharaja: "The real remedy rests with Your Highness' Government and not with the Government of India."

There is no doubt that the Bhutanese could only resent such a letter. Nehru probably did not realize this.

## A Report from BK Kapur

To better understand the situation and before going into the views of Apa Pant, it is necessary to listen to his predecessor in Gangtok, BK Kapur[5].

In a note to Delhi, the PO had described Bhutan as "essentially a one-man rule, a benevolent despotism, not so benevolent towards the Nepalese settled in southern Bhutan who are about one-third of a total population of some 6 lakhs. The Maharaja maintains a firm grip on the administration, keeping a strict watch on his northern as well as his southern borders. He keeps an Agent in Kalimpong who was until a few years ago also the Assistant for Bhutan to the Political Officer."

Kapur continued to describe the political scene: "The people are backward and live in a state of the primitive agricultural economy. There are hardly any educational or medical facilities. The country is quite fertile for a mountainous area, with plenty of water and numerous

---

5  See Chapter 2, Footnote 9.

valleys. It can well support its existing population and more. The people in central and northern Bhutan who are Bhutanese (of Tibetan stock) seem to be content with their lot, partly because they know nothing better and partly because of loyalty to the ruler who metes even-handed justice and takes care to see that there is no oppression or undue exactions by his officials."

The issue of the Nepalese population settled in southern Bhutan was explained to Delhi, Kapur asserted that the Maharaja's position was weak: "[the Nepalis] differ in race and religion from the Bhutanese, are a hard working community, are sensitive to discriminatory treatment accorded to them by the administration, and are susceptible to influences from the towns of neighbouring North Bengal and Assam."

Regarding Bhutan's foreign policy, the officer of the Political Service noted: "Bhutan has hitherto kept her doors closed to her northern and southern neighbours though she does a certain amount of trade with both. With the encouragement of the British, she has kept her south frontiers closed to India and her people."

Kapur cited the previous Maharaja who would have told a British officer that "if an Indian were ever to be appointed as Political Officer in Sikkim, he would never be allowed to set foot in Bhutan."

The PO admitted that since the British had left the subcontinent, the Maharajas of Bhutan "have climbed down from this high and mighty attitude, have extended hospitality and shown the necessary respect to two Indian Political Officers who have visited Bhutan during the last few years, but they have not deviated from the policy of keeping their doors tightly shut again India."

The PO explained that the restrictions on the entry of Tibetans from the North were also strict, though Bhutan had an Agent at Lhasa for many years: "His functions are not clearly defined; he engages in trade, primarily for his own benefit, and maintains a link between the Tibetan Government and the Maharaja's." But with the recent appearance of the Chinese on the stage, the Agent was "exposed to their attention and influence which seem to have increased of late. Efforts made to persuade the Maharaja to withdraw the Agent have proved unavailing."

On the other hand, it was an indication that he was deliberately trying to maintain contacts with the Tibetans and their rulers.

The political setup was also described, the only political party was the Bhutan Rashtriya Congress, set up in north Bengal and Assam "by a few Nepalese who had come away or been turned out from southern Bhutan. This party is in opposition to the Maharaja's regime and, from time to time, creates difficulties for the Government. The latest incident was a demonstration of some satyagrahis who went in March last from Patgaon in Assam to Sarbhang in southern Bhutan, where in the alteration that ensued, three satyagrahis were killed and two injured."

It was what the Maharaja had objected to, leading to Nehru explaining India's position.

## The State of Bhutan in the Mid-1950s

As we have looked at India's relations with Sikkim, let us now look at Bhutan's relation with India (and Tibet) during the period under study as the State was also seriously affected by the Chinese take-over of Land of Snows.

India's relations with Bhutan were regulated by the Treaty of Friendship between India and Bhutan signed in 1949 in Darjeeling.[6]

Under the 1949 Treaty, India undertook not to interfere in the internal administration of the Country; the text mentioned that Bhutan would be guided by India's advice in regard to external relations.

The Bhutanese version of the Treaty was slightly different; the wording said that Bhutan agrees to be guided by the advice of India in regard to external relations, whenever such advice was beneficial to Bhutan.

---

6 See: *Treaty of Friendship between India and Bhutan*, National Legislative Bodies/National Authorities 8 August 1949, available at: http://www.refworld.org/docid/3ae6b4d620.html.

For present Treaty, see: https://mea.gov.in/Images/pdf/india-bhutan-treaty-07.pdf.

In one of his reports to the Ministry of External Affairs, Apa Pant, the PO gave an excellent description of the 'Hermit Kingdom'. Though written in 1956, we shall quote from it.

Pant wrote: "Bhutan has always been very chary of her Independence. She concluded her first treaty with the Indian Government in 1906 when the Manchu Emperor organised the invasion of Tibet. When there is a threat from the North she seems to take protection from her neighbour to the South. The dominant factor however in Bhutan's relations with the outside world is her nationalism and suspicion."

In the mid-fifties, Bhutan had a stable government.

**The Role of the Shabdrung**

Pant loved to give history classes to his colleagues in South Block (who did not always have the time to read his long notes): "About 350 years ago Bhutan was just a geographical area inhabited by warring chieftains, robbers and marauders. There was no security of life or property. Though vaguely Buddhist the people followed devil worship and animism. Then came the great Sharbdun[7] the first Dharma Raja."

'Shabdrung' used to be a title to address high lamas from Tibet. In the Dragon Kingdom, it referred to Ngawang Namgyal (1594–1651), the founder of the Bhutanese State and his successive reincarnations.

Ngawang Namgyal, who had come from Tibet, belonged to the Drukpa lineage of the Kagyu school of Tibetan Buddhism. For the first time, the Shabdrung managed to unify the warring valleys under a single rule; today he is still revered as the third most important religious figure after Gautama Buddha and Guru Padmasambhava.

The Shabdrung reformed not only the religious life of the Bhutanese but also the administration of the Country by creating four *Penlops* or Governors in Paro, Thaga, Thimbu and Trongsa; he nominated a *Dev Raja* from amongst these *Penlops* as the senior head of the Kingdom's administration.

Ngawang Namgyal established the dual system of government under the Great Tsa Yig legal code, vesting the political power in the *Druk*

---

7   The Shabdrung.

*Desi*, assisted by local *penlops*. A religious leader, the Je Khenpo, held power over monastic affairs, even though the successive incarnations of the Shabdrung had the ultimate authority over both spiritual and temporal matters.

The most powerful *Penlop* was recognised as the hereditary *Dev Raja*, or Maharaja of Bhutan.

Apa Pant explained that something happened when the grandfather of the present Maharaja was installed on the throne: "The last of the powerful *Penlops*, the Paro *Penlop* was however actively taking part in the struggle for power till 1946 when he died. With the internal fights between the *Penlops* and other Chiefs for power in the political field the attempt to get rid of the influence of the *Dharma Raja* also continued."

The PO noted that none of Shabdrung's successors "were as capable, saintly or powerful as the first Shabdrung. So often the battle was very unequal. There is a rumour that in the recent past an incarnation of the Shabdrung was liquidated."

In 1956, the PO observed that there was no Shabdrung; moreover, "it is said that, as the incarnation of the Shabdrung would mean trouble and even civil war in Bhutan, such an incarnation will not be allowed to take place."

It would probably make too much shade for the Maharaja.

Apparently, the British had already encouraged the reduction of the Shabdrung's power; for them, it was easier to deal with a single authority, the Maharaja. Another issue was that the recognition of a reincarnation of the Shabdrung was done by powerful monasteries of Tibet and it meant constant interference from the northern neighbour in the affairs of Bhutan; it was not welcome.

## Bhutan Post-Indian Independence

During India's struggle for Independence, Bhutan, like Tibet remained unperturbed, Pant wrote: "She [Bhutan] was left more or less alone by the British administration in India and felt in no mood therefore to enter the field of battle for Indian Independence. Bhutan though watchful of all that was happening in India, felt more concerned about happenings in Tibet and China;" if not China, certainly about Tibet.

During the first decades of the 20th century, Bhutan was fiercely trying to keep her singularity as well as her differences with Tibet. In this, she was supported by the British who created a "myth of the 'Hermit Kingdom' and encouraged her in her mood of isolation," said the PO, and added: "Even the mention of better road connections between India and Bhutan was considered a sacrilege by many a Political Officer."

Though it was not yet fashionable to speak about 'happiness', the Bhutanese people remained 'happy'.

Pant continued his description of Bhutan; looking at the South of the Country, he remarked that it was "ethnologically as well as sociologically and religiously a people of a different way of life. …the dominant factor amongst the Bhutanese certainly is a feeling of intense nationalism. They feel that their status as an independent country should be recognised by the outside world."

This was written in 1956.

Something more worrisome for Delhi was the fact the Bhutanese had a tendency to look at Europe for assistance: "They have at times expressed some kind of a fear of Indian expansionist tendencies," noted the PO.

But for their development needs, observed Pant: "Bhutan is in a way afraid of approaching India, because she feels that Indian help may mean one day Indian domination and the denial of her 'independent' status. This feeling of shyness or fear has been so acute that even in very small matters the Bhutanese are still afraid of 'giving in' or losing face."

The PO cited the case of hydrological stations, an issue still existing 60 years later; in the 1950s, she 'hummed and hawed' for three years before accepting these stations to be established.

Similarly, for funds for educational and economic developments; Bhutan remained 'careful' in the way she approached India.

The PO admitted however that the mood was changing: "The fear of the possibility of domination by India and the denial of her independent status is getting diminished."

Bhutan was ready to accept help under certain conditions; the Maharaja's government expected India to be 'a good friend and an elder brother' who could advise on what was really needed by the Country, while respecting the Country's Independence: "She would not be averse to accepting help that is given spontaneously by us without expecting any return from Bhutan. She has thus accepted gratefully the donation by India of scholarship to about 35 of her students to study in Indian institutions where Hindi is the medium of instruction."

## The Changing Mindset

At the same time, though Bhutan did not mind India's help to construct roads inside her frontiers, the Dragon Kingdom remained afraid of opening up her frontiers on the Indian side.

Interestingly, the PO noted that the change of mood was probably due to the happenings within Tibet: "Once Bhutan is certain that India is not interested in 'creating troubles' inside her frontiers and sponsor 'democratic' movements or encourage any other checks to the present authority such as the emergence of the Shabdrung in order to replace the rule of the Maharaja and also once she is convinced that her 'independent status' in one form or another is acceptable to India, there is no doubt that she would rely more and more on the help, assistance and guidance that India can give her."

As we have seen, the Indian Prime Minister was not averse to a dose of democracy and he had told this to the Maharaja in no uncertain terms. For the Bhutanese, this probably did not help in building trust with the 'big brother'.

## The Chinese Pressure Mounts

There is also no doubt that the Chinese pressure had started to be felt in the Hermit Kingdom. The Maharaja certainly did not want to go the 'Tibetan way'. Bhutan probably realized that unless a minimum material progress took place and some contact with the outside was made, there was very little chance to survive between two giant neighbours, i.e. China and India: "She now vaguely understands that history does not tolerate a vacuum and that if ideologically, socially, politically or economically she remains backward she will become a vacuum and would stand in the danger of being absorbed."

Pant remarked that the stirrings of popular movements was not yet obvious; further the popularity of the young, intelligent, extremely well-meaning and shrewd Maharaja helped a great deal: "The people of Bhutan strangely enough though more or less happy and prosperous and though they indeed are under a feudalistic system have started to bestir and ask questions."

It is the Fourth King, the son of Maharaja Jigme Dorji Wangchuck, who in the 1970s on his own, introduced democracy. In 1956, when this note was written: "Though their demands are yet inaudible to the outside world, the necessity to satisfy these urges is becoming more and more apparent to those who guide the destinies of Bhutan," wrote the Indian diplomat.

For Pant, the Maharaja was extremely intelligent and a hard worker and some of his advisers realized the urgent necessity of marching with times: "Their usual desire that they should receive help from some 'outside' sources besides India is generally now being replaced by a feeling that they should go to India for advice and assistance."

It was certainly a positive sign for Delhi which had messed up the Tibetan case a few years earlier; officers like Pant knew this well, though according to him: "This process of awakening and re-adjustments to the modern life in Bhutan need not and should not be unduly hastened."

The PO believed that it was only through 'education of the present ruling clique' that a proper rate of balanced developments could be achieved.

The first step was to have an educational system with Hindi as one of the mediums of instruction; further the curricula needed to be modeled on the lines of some Indian universities: "This process of getting the youth of Bhutan trained and taught in Hindi would certainly create bonds between us and Bhutan that would be permanent and lasting."

Pant advocated 'spontaneous and unhurried' contacts between the two nations: "There should be no imposition or forcing of views or even cultural, emotional or other attitudes."

The conclusion of the PO's report was that Bhutan should be encouraged to develop her own cultural, political and economic patterns of life, as well as her own national status which "in the ultimate analysis bind that Country more to India than to anyone else. Already we are so near to each other and already there is such a great desire visible to come even nearer."

This would be India's Bhutan policy during the coming decades.

## Another Note from Apa Pant

On February 24, 1955, Apa Pant, recently posted in Gangtok, penned down a note addressed to the Joint Secretary and the Foreign Secretary, to share his thoughts on Bhutan and her present and future relations with India. Pant had just met some Indian officials dealing with Bhutan. He mentioned RN Banerjee, the administrator of the Maurakshi project, who earlier was posted as District Commissioner in Jalpaiguri, who knew the Bhutan Duars[8] well: "I also had a session with S. Majumdar from the Intelligence Bureau and met several times Rustomjee[9], the *diwan* of Sikkim and Jigmee Dorjee."

He was also in contact with the C.I.D.[10] and I.B. officers stationed in Kalimpong and in Gangtok. Pant also admitted that he had done

---

8  The Dooars or Duars are the alluvial floodplains in northeastern India that lie south of the outer foothills of the Himalayas and North of the Brahmaputra River basin. This region is about 30 km wide and stretches over about 350 km from the Teesta River in West Bengal to the Dhanshiri River in Assam. This forms the gateway to Bhutan.

Dooars means 'doors' in Assamese, Bengali, Maithili, Bhojpuri, and Magahi languages. There are 18 passages or gateways between the hills in Bhutan and the plains in India.

9  Nari Kaikhosru Rustomji (b. 1919); joined [CS, 1941; Adviser to Governor of Assam for Tribal areas and states of Manipur, Tripura and Cooch-Behar, 1948-54; Dewan of Sikkim, 1954-59; Adviser to Governor of Assam for NEFA and Nagaland, 1959-63; Adviser to Bhutan Government, 1963-66; Chief Secretary to Assam Government, 1966- 1971; Chief Secretary to Meghalaya, 1971-77; Publications: *Enchanted Frontiers: Sikkim, Bhutan and India's North-Eastern Borderlands* (1971); *Bhutan: The Dragon Kingdom in Crisis* (1978).

Often written 'Rustomjee'.

10 Criminal Investigation Department

his homework and gone through all the files in the PO's office and "compared notes with the reliable veteran of this mission Rai Bahadur Sonam Topden."

His first comment is that Bhutan was 'afraid' of India: "her advisers have taken great pains to proclaim it time and again," wrote Pant.

Bhutan felt that what happened to Hyderabad may happen to her or it could be 'Sikkimised'. The PO's reaction was that the fear was exaggerated and those who came in contact with India were putting on a 'bit of an act'.

Pant believed that these officials were not really afraid of India: "That is just an excuse to delay certain things such as the appointment of a Political Officer,[11] or the survey of the Manas River."

The analysis of the diplomat was that "Bhutan hoped that by delaying the development of positive contacts with India they may be able to build up their position in some respects like Nepal."

Pant cited some of Bhutan's 'advisers' such as Tashi Dorjee "[who] hopes that outside help, especially from America can be had to 'build up' Bhutan."

It was a fact that Bhutan was busy making a plan with the help of Dr. Craig[12] and Abers for her all-round development; according to the PO: "Tashi Dorjee, Jigmee Dorjee[13], Rani Chuni Dorjee and others

---

11 Posted in Bhutan, he would have been a Deputy PO under Gangtok.

12 Dr Albert Craig was the superintendent of the Charterish Scottish Mission Hospital in Kalimpong and was invited by Ashi Kesang Choeden Wangchuck, the Maharani to treat Bhutanese suffering from leprosy, goiter and other venereal diseases. He is remembered as the doctor who contributed immensely in the country's medical field and also as the doctor who saved the third King's life when he had a heart attack in 1962.

13 Dasho Jigme Palden Dorji (14 December 1919 – 6 April 1964) was a Bhutanese politician and member of the Dorji family. By marriage, Dorji was also a member of the Wangchuck family. Appointed Chief Minister (Gongzim) in 1952, he became the first man to hold the title Prime Minister of Bhutan (Lyonchen).

As brother-in-law of the Maharaja, Dorji helped to drive the king's modernisation policies. However, his reforms antagonised both the military and the religious institutions leading to a corporal in the army assassinating him in April 1964.

like them, are intensely 'patriotic' for Bhutan and feel 'superior' to the 'dhotiwallas' i.e. the Indians. They have not yet accepted the Indians as the successors to the British. They still feel that culture, power, help can be got from the West alone."

In order to maintain their independence and show their separate identity, they raised a national militia and made the arrangements for minting Bhutanese rupees. The PO lamented that only when it was inevitable, the 'Hermit Kingdom' would ask India's help: "They will be happy if they could do without it."

Pant raised the question: what could India do about it: "How can we really make the Bhutanese believe in our bonafides?"

According to the PO, the Bhutanese do not think as yet that theirs and India's' destiny was the same. It was not really necessary for them to come to India's fold, but "gradually they could be convinced that their interests and those of India's are not antagonistic."

In that context, some preliminary talks were useful, the PO thought; he suggested that he should visit Bhutan and meet the Maharaja; he also wanted the latter to come over for a tour of India.

He stressed the importance of regular and continuous contacts.

Pant was keen to sorts out smaller 'organizational matters' such as various permits, concessions or courtesies afforded to the Bhutanese.

Rightly or wrongly, many Bhutanese felt that "they are made to 'stand and wait at the door' before their requests are considered."

His suggestion was to decide policies which could help to avoid unnecessary delays. The PO's Office had already taken some decisions in this direction for issues such as cloth control or foreign exchange for the purchase of wireless equipment. He wanted to remove as soon as possible small 'pin-pricks' which caused "incalculable harm to the betterment of friendly relationship."

Regarding the survey of the Manas River, he suggested not to include non-technical personnel for 'ulterior purposes' in the party that will go into Bhutan. He accordingly told Jigme Dorjee "to be perfectly easy on that score …with the team of surveyors we may send a 'Liaison Officer' but this matter also should be made perfectly clear to the other party."

The most serious problem for the Bhutanese was the possibility of the appointment of a Deputy Political Officer, to 'stir-up trouble' in the Kingdom: "I told Jigmee indirectly that surely Bhutan is not like a house of pack-of-cards that it will crumble at the slightest suspicion of a puff!!"

The Agent was also asked if he believed that India's objective was to "disturb a really peaceful state of affairs."

However, the PO thought that gradually Bhutan would realize India's sincerity; he also discussed this issue with Rustomjee, the *diwan* of Sikkim.

It appeared that when TN Kaul visited Gantgtok, he told Rustomjee and Jigmee Dorjee that the former could be the first Indian representative "if that was acceptable to Bhutan."

Pant did not agree; he saw 'distinct disadvantages' in making Rustomjee the first official Indian representative in Bhutan; the reasoning was that he was presently working as an 'honest broker'; a friend of both the parties. Rustomjee saw the point and agreed with Pant, who also thought that the diwan's presence was indispensable in Sikkim for the next two years at least: "He cannot and should not act as both the Diwan of Sikkim and an Agent in Bhutan."

This dual position was physically impossible as it would take twelve days to go to Bhutan and if he was to stay for three months in the Kingdom, it would mean four months absence from Sikkim.

His conclusion was that someone else should be found as permanent representative; someone with the rank of a Deputy Secretary or Consul General rank. Pant admitted that he had a few suggestions.

The first priority for him was a visit to Bhutan "to tackle this matter personally on the spot."

He gave to the ministry his order of priorities:

    1) Periodic contacts with Jigmee Dorjee and others.

2) finalising the matters that are pending with us e.g. cloth control, wireless equipment, *Kheda* operations[14], forest roads etc.

3) Organizing a tour to Bhutan.

4) Getting through the Manas project.

5) Appointment of the Deputy Political Officer for Bhutan.

Some actions were to be taken by India, others by the Bhutanese.

Coming back on the appointment of an Indian representative, he mentioned that Bhutan would like the officer to work independently and not under Gangtok's control, but Pant was of the opinion that it would be "unwise and unnecessary to have a separate establishment away from the control and advice of Gangtok. The person appointed should work under the general direction and guidance of Gangtok."

Another idea was to appoint a Bhutan Agent in Delhi, though Pant believed that it would not be presently advisable: "I think if we go step by step and clear the ground as we go along there should be no difficulty. We must not allow ourselves to be rushed into things."

Such were the plans to deal with Bhutan, what was happening in Tibet had to be taken into consideration too.

## A Letter to the Joint Secretary

On March 8, 1955, the Political officer wrote to TN Kaul, who as Joint Secretary was looking after Tibet, Sikkim and Bhutan in the Ministry of External Affairs. Pant quoted a long talk with Jigme Dorji.

A news item had circulated in some news papers that Jawaharlal Nehru would be visiting Bhutan for the inauguration of the new Bhutanese Constitution. Jigme Dorji told the PO that DK Sen, the Legal Adviser

---

14 *Kheda* (or *khedda*) was a stockade trap for the capture of a full herd of elephants that was used in India. The elephants were driven into the stockade by skilled mahouts mounted on domesticated elephants. This system was practiced widely in North-east India, particularly in the state of Assam. The khedda practice and other methods of trapping or capturing elephants have been discontinued since 1973 following the enactment of a law under Schedule I of the Wildlife Protection Act, 1972.

to the Government of Bhutan was working on a Constitution. Dorji admitted that it would take some time before it was completed and he was not aware of any invitation sent to the Prime Minister to visit Bhutan, though the 'general invitation' given earlier by the Maharaja when he was in Delhi stood.

There was no other invitation for the Prime Minister, though the monarch had specifically told Indira Gandhi and RK Nehru, the Foreign Secretary that he was keen to have them in Bhutan. The Agent had also been authorised by the Maharaja to invite the PO to visit Bhutan.

Pant told Kaul that he thought: "it would be a very good idea if all those persons, who have been thus invited, go to Bhutan," though he remarked that it would be 'more convenient and advantageous' if all these invitees do not travel at the same time. He wondered if the Foreign Secretary (accompanied by his wife) would like to visit Bhutan in the near future: "June and July would be good months perhaps and as there are some celebrations during this period it would be possible for us to fix up a programme for their visit."

Apa Pant suggested to Kaul that he could himself go to Bhutan in September or October; he observed: "I do not know when Mrs. Indira Gandhi would like to visit Bhutan but a visit for her could certainly be organised at her own convenience."

The PO asked Kaul to talk to the Foreign Secretary and let him know so that he could again talk to Jigme Dorji: "It appears that the Maharaja of Bhutan, as well as Jigme Dorji, are very keen that these visits should take place in the near future."

**Kaul's Views**

Regarding the Constitution, Pant said that he had received a letter from the President of the Bhutan State Congress in Siliguri, asking him to convey an invitation to the Prime Minister, but "this matter is not yet even under consideration." No such visit was planned.

A few days later, Kaul, who requested the Foreign Secretary to show Pant's letter to the Prime Minister, commented on the PO's suggestions.

About Bhutan's 'fear', the Joint Secretary felt that they are not just a bit of an act, but they were probably genuine; he added that it, however, existed "mostly in the minds of vested interests" like the Dorji family and DK Sen: "The Maharaja would, perhaps, be more willing to have closer contacts with India although Jigme Dorji makes out that it is the Maharaja who is hesitant."

About the vested interests trying to get help from the West, the Kashmiri Pandit said: "this tendency is on the decline. Even Jigme Dorji realises that Bhutan cannot do without aid from India. Getting aid from the West is probably 'a bit of an act' so that we should offer aid to them."

He noted that India should not make any offer unless specifically approached by Bhutan.

Kaul agreed that the Maharaja should be invited for a tour of India, but after The PO had met the monarch: "If he then feels satisfied with the Maharaja's attitude, he could perhaps extend the invitation while he is still there." Again, the Joint Secretary suggested not to be too over-anxious to build the bridge.

Regarding the invitation to Indira Gandhi, the Foreign Secretary and his wife and to Kaul himself, he admitted that PO was right; the visits should be staggered; further, Indira Gandhi could go with the Prime Minister; this would happen three years later, in September 1958.

Kaul felt that the Foreign Secretary could first go …to make contacts with the Maharaja: "I should like to postpone my visit till September or October."

He made another suggestion, Delhi could invite the Maharaja of Bhutan to visit India on the next Republic Day and he fully agreed with Pant that India should not unnecessarily delay the grant of permits, concessions, etc. to Bhutan: "They are rather touchy and these small pin-pricks do create suspicion in their minds."

Regarding the survey of the Manas river, as the Maharaja was probably going to agree to it, no Intelligence or other agents could accompany them.

About the appointment of an Indian Agent in Bhutan, he concurred that Rustomjee could not perform two jobs at the same time: "Perhaps a younger and more junior officer should be sent." The Agent would work under the Political Officer, who was Political Officer for Tibet, Sikkim and Bhutan.

Regarding a Bhutanese Agent in Delhi, Kaul observed that it did not mean that he would be the Agent of a foreign power, "as even Kashmir has a Trade Commissioner in Delhi."

Kaul said that he discussed the issue with Balraj Kapur[15], the previous PO who said that if "this is the only hitch in sending an Indian Agent to Bhutan, we may agree in stationing a Bhutanese Agent in Delhi."

And this, of course, without a diplomatic status.

**The Prime Minister Intervenes**

On March 17, the Prime Minister sent a note to the Foreign Secretary, agreeing to India's general approach; relations should continue as before: "There is no question of our trying to rush or push things there. This will not help and, in a sense, there is no need for hurry." Nehru advised to remain alert and develop good relations with Bhutan.

He clarified that there was no question for him to go to Bhutan for the inauguration of the new Constitution. He justified his decision by the time involved: "If airfields, etc. are made, then it would be a different matter. Indira Gandhi also is not likely to go. She has not been keeping well and this long journey might be too much for her."

However, he said Apa Pant should certainly go there: "it would be a good thing to have occasional visits of our people to Bhutan."

---

15  BK Kapur.

Nehru remarked that so long the Dorji family[16] and DK Sen[17] were occupying "positions of importance in Bhutan, we are likely to have to deal with a hostile atmosphere. They are bound to think, and rightly, that any change in Bhutan will affect their personal and vested interests."

The Prime Minister agreed that the Maharaja[18] and his wife[19] should be invited to India "but we must not overdo this kind of thing."

The Maharaja and Maharani had come to India in January 1954. They toured many cities and participated in the Republic Day celebrations.

Regarding the question of appointing an Indian Agent in Bhutan, Nehru decided that it should be kept open: "It may be mentioned whenever a suitable time for this arises." And he also agreed that it would not be right for Rustomjee to be appointed an Indian Agent; while regarding a Bhutanese Agent in Delhi, he noted that the issue has not come up: "If it is raised, we can consider it. I have no particular objection.":

That was the final word.

**Report of Apa Pant's Visit to Bhutan**

The PO finally visited Bhutan. On his return, he sent a long letter to Kaul: "I have been trying to absorb the general atmosphere and learn as far as possible about the history, the social conditions, the religious life, etc., of these enchanting and charming people."[20]

---

16 The Dorji family was in close familial collaboration with the Wangchuk dynasty, extending over a 75-year period. This alliance had provided the foundation for the creation of a stable and centralised monarchical polity after 1907.

17 DK Sen (b. 1897), an international lawyer responsible for helping *Bhutan* draw up its treaty with India and the Bhutanese Constitution as an Adviser to the Bhutan Government.

18 Jigme Dorji Wangchuk (1928-1972); ascended the throne of Bhutan on 27 October 1952 as the third King in line of the Wangchuk dynasty and ruled till his death in 1972.

19 Ashi Kesang Wangchuk.

20 Apa Pant, *India's Relations With Sikkim And Bhutan*, 1956, Nehru Collection.

He thought that his views would help the Foreign Secretary who was due to visit the Dragon Kingdom a few months later.

Bhutan has had a most fascinating history wrote Pant: "About a thousand years ago this part of the Himalayas was inhabited by some aboriginal tribes who have the same racial strain as the Lepchas in Sikkim. I do not think anyone knows how long these Lepchas have been living in this part of the world in secluded isolation and tranquil happiness. About a thousand years ago due to certain internal strife and fights between themselves, some tribes from the Markham area of Tibet came down South and invaded what is today Bhutan."

He admitted that there were no historical records showing if a single or half a dozen of tribes came to settle down in Bhutan, but "within a period of about 150 years they absorbed the aborigines and themselves became Bhutanese."

The history lesson continued: "After this a couple of hundred years later there were one or two invasions by people from Central Tibet who came and tried to establish their suzerainty in Bhutan. Today the linguistic and racial differences between western and eastern Bhutan is reasonably marked."

Pant explained that in Bhutan the eastern people were called "the half-tongue people" due to the fact that aborigines from eastern Bhutan could not speak any language properly; the Maharaja himself proudly told Pant that he was "a half-tongue person".

The note mentioned that people from Markham in Tibet who settled in Bhutan were Buddhists from the Kargyud school, disciples of Marpa the Translator and Milarepa, the great yogi. The story of the Shabdrung[21] was then recounted: "with the arrival of the British on the scene the four *Penlops* yielded place to one ruling family and the survival in some form of the Shabdung hierarchy. By this time however the power of the Shabdung had diminished considerably and in the field, there was only the Penlop of Paro and the hereditary Maharaja who could fight with each other for secular authority."

---

21  Written Shabdung by Apa Pant.

He later mentioned the revival of the authority of the Shabdung which brought again chaos to Bhutan: "People like Jigme Dorji and others feel that if Bhutan is to progress in the modern way she cannot afford to have two authorities ruling in the field at one and the same time."

It was clear that the ruling family was not keen to share the power, but there was also another aspect pointed out by Pant: "The authority of the Shabdung means also the greater contact and perhaps the authority of the persons from the Karmapa and other important monasteries from Tibet. The fight between the Shabdung and the ruling family here can also be represented as a fight between the local people of Bhutan and those who would look to revive their contacts with Tibet and seek their help."

However, it was not really a serious danger, noted the PO, who brought another issue: "When I talked to the Maharaja about the religious system in Bhutan, he said that apart from some of their monks going for pilgrimages to Tibet and to India the church in Bhutan was completely self-sufficient and they required nobody's guidance and help for the carrying out of their religious duties."

The main monasteries in the State were maintained through the State revenues, while smaller village monasteries were looked after by village folks. There are two chief monasteries, one at Punakha and the other one at Thimbu. The administration was run by a group of abbots, called the Khempos and the Chief Abbot is the Jekhempo[22], the head of the Bhutanese Church; Pant commented: "the Jekhempo is usually the senior-most and the most learned abbot". He is appointed with the approval of the Maharaja: "No person could be appointed to the post of the Jekhempo without his explicit sanction." Thus it ended the spiritual authority of the Shabdung "in the complete victory of the secular forces."

The system continues more than 60 years later.

## The Centralization of the Secular Authority

The Political Officer's narrative continued.

---

22 Also written Jekhenpo.

The centralization of power was systematically undertaken and with some thoroughness, noted Pant: when the old *Penlops* died, their places were not filled and when the last one, the Paro Penlop died in 1947, he was succeeded by the Maharaja who became the Paro Penlop: "Though the centralization of the secular and temporal authorities has been completed, it cannot yet be said that Bhutan has set her foot on the way to modern progress."

After his visit, Pant realized that many advisers of the Maharaja thought that "modernization and opening up of the country to the outside world would bring in ruin and unhappiness to Bhutan."

However, others like Jigme Dorji, were keen to build up "the foundation for modernization of Bhutan systematically but gradually and usher in an era of progress with caution."

For the PO, the Maharaja was a very shrewd and capable ruler "who does not want to displease other advisers as well and is always trying to strike the middle course. I find that he is very popular with the common mass of people. He also has sound ideas for the progress of his State."

The main problem for developing Bhutan was to find the necessary revenues: "the Government of Bhutan are reasonably anxious to develop their mineral and industrial resources."

This was in the mid-1950s, but interestingly, it is still valid today, Bhutan is keen on the development of their country, "without upsetting the present pattern of life too much," remarked Pant.

At the same time, many thought that the industrial and mining developments could help develop better educational facilities, better hospitals and build roads.

This was a serious dilemma.

## The National Militia

In Paro, the PO was given a salute by the Maharaja's troops: "I was impressed by their smart turn out and efficient drill. At the present moment, there are about 3,000 to 4,000 persons under training and

2,000 to 3,000 who are called in regularly each year for one month's service."

The Government of Bhutan was keen to provide the National Militia with boots, patties[23] and uniforms. The creation of the Militia was Jigme Dorji's idea; he told Pant that it created "a great sense of unity amongst the people of Bhutan." While the Maharaja was the head of the National Militia, Jigme Dorji was its chief organizer: "The usefulness of this Militia for the securing of the power of the Maharaja can be understood."

In Pant's opinion, the process of centralization would be hastened by the creation of this Bhutanese National Force; he, however, pointed to a possible problem: "The question whether this force can be utilized to subdue some of the minority elements in the State such as the Nepalese is to be considered."

Pant broached the fact that there was no Nepalese in the National Militia; Jigme Dorji explained that "once the Nepalese declare themselves to be the permanent citizens of Bhutan there would be no difficulty in getting them into the National Militia."

The comment of the PO was that when this happens, "it may not become necessary for us to fear the use of such Militia against the minority groups in Bhutan."

At the end of his note Apa Pant, observed that many interesting things could happen in Bhutan in the near future; one of the most significant was that "the Maharaja and his advisers are now seriously thinking of establishing better bonds of friendship with India."

He did not find any animosity or fear in the minds of his interlocutors, though the PO agreed that India had not yet properly established her bonafides: "if we are genuine and really desirous of friendship the Bhutanese would not withdraw their hand."

---

23 Puttees or *Patties* in Hindi are long woolen bandages about four inches wide and about six-eight feet long which is worn around the lower part of the legs starting from boots upwards ending just below the knee. It prevents the legs getting bruised by rubbing against sides of the horse. Patties are generally worn by rank and file officers who wear long leather riding boots, serving dual purpose of boots and the patties.

He believed that it was important to remember that the Bhutanese had a strong nationalistic mind: "They value their independence and the fact that they have been secluded and concealed from India and outside world for so many centuries has created in their minds a 'devotedness' to their separate existence."

India should not minimize Bhutan's desire to remain independent, as it also wanted to be friendly with India, commented the PO.

The Maharaja was keen to link Bhutan's destiny with India: "In foreign relations and in other matters they would indeed be very willing to be guided by India."

Pant added that especially when India's foreign policy was "laid down by such an enlightened leader as Pandit Nehru." The PO probably knew that the Prime Minister would read his report and would be pleased.

Bhutan was also keen to take India as a model for her educational system: "they want to make Hindi as their language after Bhutanese. They are not keen to develop English or foreign languages except in higher standards."

Pant saw the possibility that "the Bhutanese would be drawn to us as real and lasting friends," if India refrained from interfering in the internal affairs of her neighbour.

Again, the PO's conclusion was that there was no hurry, there was no need to "unduly hasten the process and be impatient if it takes some time for the Bhutanese to accept our bonafides."

The next day, the PO had another discussion with the Maharaja, on industrialization, and also again on education: "I will not be surprised if he visits India for this purpose in November and December." commented Pant on the Maharaja's interest in education.

About forestry, it was decided to invite Arjun Singh, the Chief Conservator of Forests of Sikkim to Bhutan. The Maharaja also mentioned that Bhutan was thinking of increasing the country's revenue as "hospitals and schools cost money".

Further, he was keen to have a geological and mineral survey of Bhutan, for which India could help. The conclusions of the PO were: "The Maharaja is really a remarkable character. He told me of his plans for the reorganization of the monasteries. He has got all the monks now to pass an examination before they are formally and permanently taken in. Those who fail are turned out of the monasteries. Formerly all those who were too lazy used to flock to the monasteries. He has also started to give the monks instructions in painting, weaving, carving, etc."

Pant said that he has been able to do so due to his popularity with the common people.

This paved the way for the crucial visit of the Foreign Secretary to the Dragon Kingdom.

# 12

# The Foreign Secretary's Visit to Bhutan

## The Foreign Secretary's Tour

RK Nehru, the Foreign Secretary, accompanied by his wife and some officials, visited Sikkim, Tibet and Bhutan from June 6 to July 2, 1955. His stopover in the Chumbi Valley has already been discussed.[1]

It took the party four days to walk from Tibet to Bhutan's border; later Nehru reached Paro, where he was received by the Maharaja. The party stayed for four and a half days till June 23 in Paro and returned to Tibet and India. The Foreign Secretary submitted his tour report to the Prime Minister on July 5, 1955.

## The Visit

On June 14, 1955, RK Nehru left Tibet for Bhutan, it was the first time that an Indian Foreign Secretary would visit the reclusive Kingdom.

'As a gesture of courtesy', the Maharaja of Bhutan sent several horses to Yatung; the Maharaja's special representatives, Prime Minister Jigmi Dorji and the Dzongpen of Dukye[2], came to the border, in the midst

---

[1] This document is available in the National Archives of India. *Report by Shri R. K. Nehru, Foreign Secretary on his visit to Bhutan*. Department: Ministry of External Affairs, Sikkim Agency; Branch: Political; 1955; Ref: File No. Progs., Nos. 4(29), 1955 (Secret).

[2] Probably Drukgyal Dzong.

of a pine forest, some 40 kilometers from the nearest inhabited village; they received RK Nehru, who was provided a guard by the Bhutan militia.

The first few kilometers to Charithang, where the party first halted were strenuous; the climb was extremely steep. The next day, they reached Damthang; the journey was even more exhausting. The Indian diplomat had to cross two high passes in pouring rain. On the third day, they reached Haa where they were lodged in a picturesque guest house. Nehru noted in his report: "The whole journey from Charithang to Ha[3] is through some lovely mountain country."

On their way from Haa to Channana[4], the party crossed another pass and after camping one night on the road, they proceeded the next day to Paro.

They were received two miles away from town: "We came down into the valley in a procession, led by high Bhutanese officials, groups of dancers and musicians and the Maharaja's bodyguard," observed Nehru.

At the Paro guest house, the Maharaja, the Maharani Rani Dorji and senior Bhutanese officials were waiting for them; the India party witnessed an impressive parade by the Bhutan Militia and though the Maharani was expecting, she had come especially from Thimbu to meet them.

The journey had taken four days from the Tibetan frontier. The following five days were spent in Paro; the Indian officials were busy with different functions: "Apart from the usual entertainment, there was an archery contest and some folk dances. We showed some Indian films which attracted quite a crowd."

Finally, on June 23, Nehru and his party were seen off at Paro by the Maharaja and the Maharani: "The Maharaja rode with us to the original reception point where a picturesque farewell ceremony was held."

---

3  Written 'Ha' in the report.
4  Probably Chelela.

On their return journey, they walked (or rode) double stage, they stayed two days in Haa and one at Charithang; on June 26, they were back in the Chumbi Valley, from where they proceeded to Yatung.

Nehru noted: "our visit took place on the invitation of the Maharaja. This was the first time that Bhutan was visited by a senior officer from Delhi."

During Nehru's discussions with the Maharaja, the latter expressed the wish that the Indian Prime Minister should visit Bhutan as soon as possible: "This shows some change in the traditional Bhutanese attitude of keeping the door shut against Indians. The door will not be thrown open, but I think the Maharaja is groping his way towards closer relations with India," remarked the Foreign Secretary.

**Some General Observations**

Nehru's first observation was that there was still fear and suspicion in the Bhutanese mind, "but there is also a growing sense of the need for India's protection and help. The Maharaja hinted to me that the subsidy which Bhutan is getting is not adequate." For the Indian official, there was no doubt that the monarch felt "that these friendly visits might help him in obtaining some financial assistance. Perhaps he also feels that we have been misinformed of the situation in Bhutan and he would like us to see things for ourselves."

The Foreign Secretary however admitted that he did not see much of Bhutan during his brief visit, he only visited the two western valleys; however: "I had some useful talks with the Maharaja and Jigmi Dorji. There were other officials present, but I could not talk to them because of the language difficulty." He realized during these encounters that the Maharaja and Jigmi Dorji represented "the more progressive element in the State. I was also impressed by the young Maharani whose influence is likely to increase if she can produce a son."

RK Nehru also noted that he now doubted "whether our approach to the Bhutanese problem does not need some change of emphasis. There has been too much emphasis in the past on political matters and not enough understanding of the Bhutanese point of view."

In a way, the visit was an eye-opener for the head of the Indian diplomacy, who soon would be transferred to Beijing as Indian ambassador to China. Nehru wrote: "The social and economic approach has been largely neglected. I have read some earlier reports and I find that the British approach was somewhat different. They were giving constant advice about social and economic matters. No attempt was made by them to bring Bhutan more closely under their direct control."

Delhi had been trying to keep a delicate balance between political intervention and laissez-faire: "Bhutan, along with other border states, has come into prominence since the Chinese occupation of Tibet."

Delhi could not afford to have another Tibet situation at its gate.

## Some Difficult Choices

Already in his note written in Yatung, Nehru had mentioned a difficult choice. The relations with Bhutan were governed by the 1949 Treaty; RK Nehru spoke of two important provisions: "We cannot interfere in Bhutan's internal affairs, but the Bhutanese have to accept our guidance in their external relations."

The Foreign Secretary elaborated his views after returning to India: "The ruling elements in Bhutan are zealous of their rights under the treaty. We have assured them time and again that we have no intention of interfering, but in view of the developments that are taking place across the border, Bhutan's stability and independence are a matter of concern to us. We are entitled to know whether adequate steps are being taken to maintain Bhutan's stability and independence."

Delhi clearly realized that the political environment had changed after Tibet's occupation by the Chinese forces and it was in the interests of both Bhutan and India to take into account the other's susceptibilities and concerns: "we have been making some demands which may have caused some irritation to the Bhutanese;" wrote RK Nehru, who cited the case of 1948, when it was suggested that Bhutan should accede to India, which 'alarmed and shocked' them: "Since then we have asked them several times to accept a resident Political Officer and to withdraw their agent from Lhasa."

The Foreign Secretary explained India's point of view; could Delhi exercise "effective control over Bhutan's external relations and watch internal developments more closely?" the Bhutanese had not accepted these demands as yet.

Nehru realized that Delhi should try to understand the Bhutanese point of view; for example for the appointment of an Indian Political Officer in Paro, "we are making a demand which the British never made under more or less similar circumstances." He cited the time when the Chinese entered Tibet in 1910, "their troops moved into the Chumbi Valley and they claimed Bhutan as their vassal state. The British rejected the claim, but in spite of these aggressive moves, they made no attempt to station a Political Officer in Bhutan."

Since the time of India's Independence, several Indian officers had suggested this move; it prompted Nehru to ask: "Are we more distrustful of the Bhutanese, or do we fear the Chinese more?"

He admitted that the posting of a Political Officer was an old British tactic for "bringing a country under their control." The Bhutanese concern was to keep the existing status, "higher than that of Sikkim. Our demand must have appeared to them as the thin end of a wedge which would ultimately lead to a reduction in their status."

The Foreign Secretary mentioned some other practical issues which had not been properly considered in Delhi: "Bhutan has no fixed capital and the entire governmental machinery is centered on the Maharaja who has to move about from valley to valley to maintain his hold on the administration. Is it our intention to build houses for the Political Officer in all the Bhutan valleys?" Nehru said that there was no place for a PO to live except as the Maharaja's guest.

**A Bhutanese Agent in Lhasa**

Regarding the issue of a Bhutanese Agent in Lhasa: as few Tibetan traders visited Bhutan, while many Bhutanese traders were established in Lhasa, they needed the help of an agent; by asking the Bhutanese traders "to entrust this work to our [India's] Consul-General, or to attach the agent to him, we are asking them to accept a voluntary reduction in their status."

The Bhutanese Prime Minister Jigmi Dorji told Nehru that Bhutan was ready to withdraw the Bhutanese Agent "if there was no work for him, or if the Chinese ask for the appointment of their own Agent in Bhutan."

This was out of question for the Bhutanese.

As for an Indian PO (or Deputy PO) in Bhutan, Dorji said that it might be possible sometime later, when Bhutan has a fixed capital. Nehru believed that the Bhutanese could eventually agree, with the condition that they would have their own representative in Delhi.

The Foreign Secretary had the feeling that DK Sen, the International lawyer advising Bhutan may have had a say in this: "He may have suggested that they should hold out as long as possible and then make this demand on a basis of reciprocity." By appointing a representative in Delhi, Bhutan would gain some international status: "I think we should drop this approach for the time being and concentrate on other matters. We already have a Political Officer, though he is not resident in Bhutan. We can exercise all the control we need by letting him visit Bhutan frequently," commented the diplomat.

**Closer Relations with Bhutan**

Nehru suggested a change of approach aiming "at the building up of closer relations through social and economic channels." The idea was to bring India and Bhutan closer: "Closer political relations will follow and in due course the Bhutanese might accept our demands without trying to drive a bargain."

The fact that Apa Pant, the PO accompanied Nehru gave both the Foreign Secretary and Pant, a clearer picture of the situation on the ground: "the trend of development in Bhutan is generally sound. There are many matters, however, in which our help is needed and will probably be accepted as a result of the new contacts which are being developed." The relation should become less political and more pragmatic was the conclusion.

## Administrative Structures

In his note, Nehru observed that he was struck by the virile qualities of the Bhutanese people: "They are soft-spoken and have a quiet manner, but they seem to possess a strong sense of discipline, an independent outlook and great powers of endurance."

He saw this in the militia, in schools or with ordinary peasants: "The school children showed a high order of intelligence and keenness on learning."

What struck the Foreign Secretary was the anti-Tibetan attitude of the Bhutanese; while for most Tibetans, Bhutanese were savages: "the Bhutanese have some contempt for the Tibetans," he wrote. The Bhutanese Government realized this danger and "has taken effective steps to meet" the possibility of infiltration taking place from Tibet.

Nehru noted that there were few Tibetan settlers in Bhutan, but no one was allowed to enter Bhutan without a permit: "The permit system is administered by the men of the militia who have check-posts at all important points. In addition, groups of militia men carry out patrols on all important routes. Finally, the village headmen and others have instructions to report the arrival of every stranger. It is difficult for any stranger to escape this net and I think these arrangements are working satisfactorily."

Infiltration from the North was definitely an issue which had started to make India nervous.

According to Nehru, the Bhutanese militia comprised of 5,000 men, but only 2,000 were armed; all able men in the kingdom received compulsory training. The Foreign Secretary was deeply impressed by "the discipline and soldierly bearing of these men. I was informed that some of them had expressed a desire to fight for India in Kashmir. Their attitude on the whole appeared to be pro-Indian, but anti-Nepalese and anti-Tibetan."

An interesting comment, the Foreign Secretary noted that the militia was aware of the issue of Kashmir, despite their reclusiveness and lack of means of information.

Nehru realized that the old conflict between the Dharma Raja, the Dev Raja and the *penlops* had been resolved and the trend was for centralization of power: "The *penlops* or provincial governors who were more or less independent have been eliminated. The Dharma Raja was the supreme religious authority and he shared some power with the Dev Raja. The last Dharma Raja died 30 years ago and no new Dharma Raja has been appointed."

Dharma Raja referred to the Shabdrung; we have discussed the issue in the previous chapter.[5]

According to Nehru, the administrative structure was primitive, but it answered the needs of the people; he cited the nine provinces or *dzongs*; nine *tahsils* in the Nepalese area with a senior official[6] for each *Dzong* or *Tashil*, directly responsible to the Maharaja. At the level of the villages, headmen were nominated by the community for a group of villages.

## Constitution and Reforms

Some work had been done to frame a constitution and codify the criminal and civil laws. The Maharaja told Nehru that it was prepared by Bhutanese officials under the former's personal direction.

Another important development was related to land reform; as Bhutan's economy was based on agriculture, the first priority was land reforms: "He has given up his own land to the peasants and is trying to persuade his step-mother and uncle to follow his example," wrote Nehru.

The State's main revenues were first land tax and then cattle tax, grazing fees, but also sales of timber. While some taxes were in kind, the land tax accounted for 75% of Bhutan's total revenue, a rather

---

5   Nehru wrote: "A hereditary monarchy has been set up and the Maharaja has absolute powers. He is assisted by a council consisting of some high officials and a leading abbot and also by an assembly consisting of some nominated headmen and others. Both the council and the assembly are advisory bodies. The council advises the Maharaja on external and important internal questions, while the assembly advises him on less important internal questions. These bodies are summoned at the Maharaja's discretion."

6   *Dzongpen*: Chief Magistrate of province; *Drung*: Chief Magistrate of isolated part of Province; *Nyerchen*: Chief Revenue Officer; *Zimpon*: Maharaja's representative in province.

modest Rs. 50 lakhs. Nehru said that half of the total proceeds went to the monasteries.

Nehru further remarked: "Payment to the monasteries will, of course, continue, but this payment will be made in cash unless the monasteries insist on payment in kind." The Foreign Secretary was told by the Maharaja that he knew that contribution to the monasteries constitute "a drain on the resources of the state. The monasteries are, however, a powerful factor in the state and it is not possible for the Maharaja to stop or to reduce these payments." Like in Tibet, the monasteries were an important political factor.

**Bhutan's 'Problems'**

The report also discussed some of the problems faced by the Dragon Kingdom. The first difficulty was the geography of the land: "high mountain ranges which run at right angles to the great Himalayan range. These ranges separate the various valleys in which the bulk of the population lives."

All this made communications difficult: "it takes nearly two weeks for the whole length of the country to be traversed. Development of communication is a vital problem."

The problem was that Bhutan did not have the financial resources to take care of this, though the country's economy was more or less self-sufficient; some rice was exported to Tibet and timber to India, while Bhutan imported textiles and consumer goods from India. The trade with Tibet was steadily declining, while the exchanges with India had been increasing.

RK Nehru noted: "There can be no real progress in Bhutan unless the resources of the State are more fully exploited. There are vast soft-wood forests in the north and in the central parts of the country. There is also some hope of finding some mineral deposits."

More than 60 years later, Bhutan is still facing similar issues, and is often in a dilemma whether to let India exploit its natural resources.

India suggested an economic survey: "but there is some hesitation to invite experts from India or to ask for development aid. This is probably due to some fear that this might lead to loss of independence or Indian intervention in Bhutan's internal affairs."

Nehru's opinion was that India should not offer aid, or even assistance in carrying out a survey[7], at that time: "We should confine ourselves for the present to giving the Bhutanese an opportunity to see the developments that are taking place in India." The idea was to reduce the 'fear', though it was clear that without India's assistance "they cannot make much progress."

## Health and Education

In the domain of health, there was a prevalence of venereal diseases decimating the population: "There are a few dispensaries in some of the valleys, but there is an extreme shortage of medical personnel."

The Maharaja planned to open a small hospital in Punakha. One Dr Craig of the Scottish Mission in Kalimpong had already given some penicillin injections to V.D.[8] patients, but it was clearly not enough.

During the Foreign Secretary's visit, an Indian Medical Officer, assisted by Nehru's wife opened a dispensary in Paro; during their four-day stay some 300 patients were treated; the team left a large quantity of medicines on their departure.

Nehru's suggestion was to provide training to Bhutanese medical personnel: "If medicines are needed or asked for, they should be liberally supplied, subject to arrangements being made for their proper use."

He believed that Bhutan needed a Chief Medical Officer, who could organize an effective drive for the control of disease.

Another issue was education; at the time of RK Nehru's' visit, the main centres of learning were the monasteries, "but this learning is not of a high order." The Maharaja wanted to use the monasteries for ordinary educational purposes and have open schools: "This is a sound move in view of the lack of teachers and other educational facilities in the State."

---

7 Survey would be carried out in the summer of 1956.
8 Venereal Disease.

The few elementary schools taught both Hindi and Dzongkha[9]; it was noted that nobody was interested to learn Bengali, Assamese, or Nepali; in case Hindi teachers were not available, English was taught.

One problem had been due to the fact that the Hindi school in Kalimpong where the Bhutanese teachers were trained had closed down; the Foreign Secretary remarked: "All possible help should be given to Bhutan for the training of Hindi teachers. Across the border, the Chinese are making a determined effort to teach Chinese and to give a pro-Chinese outlook to Tibetan children."

One of the motivations of the Indian diplomat was to balance China's influence on the other side of the Himalayan range.

Nehru also looked into the role of the monasteries, 'a powerful factor in the State'. Like as in Tibet, religion had a strong hold on the people; at the time of the visit, there was no *Dharma Raja*[10], "but I understand that there is some demand in certain quarters that this gap should be filled."

A Tibetan nominee as Shabdrung always frightened the Bhutanese who did not want to be influenced by their northern neighbour; according to the Foreign Secretary: though the Maharaja respected the religious sentiment of his people, "he is naturally not anxious to revive an institution which will clash with his own authority. His aim is to build up a national church which will be directly under his control."

This explained the predominance of the Je Khenpo, the Chief Abbot of Dratshang Lhentshog[11], the senior religious hierarchy of Bhutan. His primary duty was to lead the Dratshang Lhentshog, and arbitrate on matters of doctrine, assisted by Five Lopon Rinpoches.[12]

---

9   Bhutanese language.

10  The Shabdrung.

11  Central Monastic Body.

12  The present Je Khenpo is the leader of the southern branch of the Drukpa Kagyu sect, which is part of the Kagyu tradition of Himalayan Buddhism.

   In 2008, the office of the Je Khenpo was codified as part of the new Constitution of Bhutan; under Article 3 Section 4, the King appoints the Je Khenpo as the spiritual leader of Bhutan on the recommendation of the Five Lopons.

The sitting Je Khenpo was also formally the leader of the southern branch of the Drukpa Kagyu sect, which is part of the Kagyu tradition of 'Himalayan' Buddhism.

The Foreign Secretary however commented: "a national church if it is to command respect, has to produce a high order of religious leadership. In Bhutan, this leadership is lacking and the Maharaja will be well-advised to send some of the principal monks for training to India."

It is not clear where the Indian diplomat wanted to train senior monks in India, though he commented: "If the national church fails to command respect, the people might turn for guidance to the great monasteries in Tibet, or develop an interest in other ideologies."

Nehru's conclusions were: "The Bhutanese need our advice, help and guidance and if this is given in such a way as not to make them feel that they are losing their independence, or control over their affairs, I have no doubt that the two countries will draw closer to one another."

Nehru was however aware that vested interests were always ready to criticize India though: "as a whole [the people] will welcome our assistance and will be on our side."

In one way the presence of Apa Pant was reassuring for the Bhutanese as well as for Delhi: "Pant has made a good impression on the Maharaja and on the other people whom he met."

He would continue to deal with Bhutan till 1961.

## Another Worry for Delhi

India was worried about the treatment of the Nepalese minority in Bhutan: "This minority is confined to the southern *terai* and is regarded as a foreign element," wrote Nehru. But how could India interfere in this purely internal issue? The Foreign Secretary asserted: "Bhutanese fears are understandable as the Nepalese have a much higher birth rate than their own."

He cited the case of Sikkim where the Nepalese had outnumbered the local population; Bhutan feared a similar situation in their own country. He noted the many restrictions imposed on the Nepalese. For example, they were not represented in the council or in the assembly; not even in the militia which was purely Bhutanese. Nehru was told that a new citizenship law was being framed which would give citizenship rights to the Nepalese wishing to make Bhutan their home.

Interestingly, on his return in Yatung, Nehru received a representation from a Nepalese organization in Bhutan. They demanded representative institutions and reforms, "I doubt whether the time is ripe for setting up a representative government in Bhutan. The example of Nepal is not very encouraging," commented Nehru.

## The Bhutan-Tibet Border

Another serious issue was the Bhutan-Tibet frontier which had not been demarcated: "In the west, on the Chumbi Valley side and in the north-east, the frontier is uncertain. Elsewhere the great Himalayan range constitutes a natural barrier, but no part of the frontier has been fully surveyed."

The Maharaja told the Foreign Secretary about the constant disputes between Tibetan and Bhutanese graziers on the north-eastern frontier, near Tawang: "the Tibetans had suggested that direct negotiations should take place between the two Governments for a frontier settlement."

The Maharaja's suggestion was a tripartite conference between India, China and Bhutan to finalize the frontier and demarcate the areas.

Nehru commented: "I showed the Maharaja our maps and pointed out that the frontier question has been studied by us carefully. I explained to him that it is desirable that Bhutan and India should compare notes and reach some firm conclusions, after which Bhutan should take such steps as are possible to make her possession effective up to the frontier."

But for India, a tripartite conference was unnecessary and even undesirable.

The Maharaja was told that India's expert[13] on frontier questions was presently in Gangtok; he could visit Bhutan if the Maharaja agreed "to receive him and to give him necessary facilities for studying the Bhutanese records."

---

13  Probably TS Murty of the Indian Frontier Administrative Service.

It is what he did; in the process, following the watershed principle, the trijunction between Sikkim, Tibet and Bhutan was fixed at Batang-la. This would become the object of a conflict in June 2017 between China and India.[14]

## Flood Control

Finally, there was the issue of flood control; after several rounds of talks an agreement had been reached; some Indian experts would help to establish the necessary warning equipment on the trans-boundary rivers.

The general conclusion of the Foreign Secretary was that his visit marked a new phase in the bilateral relations. It was indeed important in view of the distressing situation prevailing in Tibet.

The stability of Bhutan and the 'happiness' of its monarch and people was a crucial factor and certainly the best protection for the security of India's northern border.

## The Prime Minister's Comments

On July 15[15], the Prime Minister made some comments on the note of the Foreign Secretary; he found the report 'interesting and instructive' and he agreed with the main conclusions: "our approach to the Bhutanese problems should be somewhat varied in emphasis." India should give up the idea of pressing for a Political Agent in Bhutan, he thought.

RK Nehru had commented that Bhutan would not accept India's demand for a resident Political Agent in Bhutan, due to her concern about her status as higher than that of Sikkim.

After RK Nehru had suggested closer social and economic relations with Bhutan, the Indian Prime Minister wrote: "We should concentrate more on the social and economic approach."

Jawaharlal Nehru observed that the advice of DK Sen, Bhutan's main adviser "is seldom likely to be in favour of India," and India should

---

14 The Doklam incident in June-August 2017.

15 RK Nehru's note was sent on July 5.

lay greater emphasis on the social and economic side: "help should be given when asked for and not thrust upon Bhutan."

The Prime Minister thought of some opportunities to be offered the Bhutanese for training in India; he suggested:

(1) Survey work;

(2) Medical and health;

(3) Hindi language and general education;

(4) Engineering;

(5) Any other that is suggested might be considered.

The Prime Minister's note asserted that India could provide help for these activities: "we should try to send to them such persons. But the initiative should come from them."

He also affirmed that a study of the floods which should be undertaken as it was important to India. Again, it was mentioned that it was desirable to invite the Maharaja and the Maharani to visit India.

Regarding his own trip to Bhutan, he wrote: "at the moment I do not know when I can do so. Presumably, it will have to be in summer time. This summer is out of the question."

Being keen to write to the Maharaja, the Foreign Secretary was requested to prepare a draft with important points.

## A Letter to the Maharaja of Bhutan

The next day, the letter was ready.

The Prime Minister first mentioned RK Nehru's trip to Bhutan; expressing India's gratitude 'for the courtesy and hospitality' given to the Foreign Secretary, Jawaharlal Nehru noted: "I was naturally interested in his report."[16]

Let us remember that Jigme Dorji Wangchuk, the Maharaja, today referred to as the Third King, had visited India in January 1954 and had participated in the Republic Day celebrations.

---

16 SWJN, Series II, Volume 29, op. cit.

Nehru reiterated that he would like to visit Bhutan: "My difficulty is how to find the time for it. But the attraction of visiting Bhutan and meeting Your Highness again is great and perhaps sometimes or other I shall manage to reach there." It would not be in 1955, he wrote.

In the meantime, Jawaharlal Nehru hoped that the Maharaja and the Maharani could visit India again: "we would welcome your visiting many of our projects which I am sure will be of interest to you." As in most of his letters, Nehru praised the Five Year Plans: "we are now preparing the Second Five Year Plan which is likely to be much more ambitious."

He mentioned the emphasis on heavy industry and 'village or household industries' and the Community Project Scheme and the National Extension Service for rural areas, which "have brought about a remarkable change".

Nehru praised the monarch for the land reforms he had started.

The Foreign Secretary had reported that the Maharaja had put a ceiling of thirty acres on large landholdings, distributed his own lands to his subjects, made the land revenue equitable and abolished it altogether in case of poor farmers with smaller holdings." Nehru also remarked that "land reforms form an essential foundation for progress in other directions."

He expressed his happiness about the agreement on flood control which had just been signed between the two Governments as an initial step: "Accordingly flood control stations were opened at various places and the Bhutanese staff trained." At the end, the Prime Minister reassured the Maharaja that India would cooperate in the joint task.

He also noted that Delhi would always be happy to send technicians or experts to Bhutan whenever they were needed and to train some Bhutanese young men and women in India.

**Policy Towards Bhutan**

On the same day, a note was sent by the Prime Minister to the Foreign Secretary, in which the former commented on some remarks made the previous day by KM Panikkar, former Ambassador to China and now a Member of States Reorganisation Commission.

We shall mention Panikkar's note because his observations were related to the report on Bhutan written by RK Nehru on his return from Paro.

The Foreign Secretary spoke of the Chinese claims over Bhutan made in 1910 and repeated in 1948. Panikkar's view was that though the situation required careful handling there was no serious danger of the Chinese putting forward any claim to suzerainty over Bhutan.

The Prime Minister answered: "I think we need not worry at all about Chinese or Tibetan claims on Bhutan or Nepal. Whatever might have happened in the past, and there is hardly anything that has happened to support these claims, I cannot imagine any such claims being advanced now."

He clarified India's "positive policy of friendship …we must give no impression to the Bhutan Government that we have any desire to have political or other control over it. We should not push our men there and it is only when they want any help that we should send it."

It was a repetition of what the PO and the Foreign Secretary had suggested.

About financial help: "I would not rule this out. But if this question is raised, it would be better, I think, to give them some financial credit here for purchases in India." In any case, Bhutan had not asked for anything so far.

RK Nehru had said that Hindi was "a source of strength to us and we must treat it as an instrument for projecting the Centre's influence in our border areas."

Panikkar suggested the opening of a high level Hindi school in Kalimpong, to which the Prime Minister agreed: "This should cater especially for the Sikkimese and the Bhutanese. But it should also invite tribal folk from the surrounding areas. This school should, I think, also encourage the teaching of Tibetan and Bhutanese languages for our people."

Panikkar, Nehru's 'chief' advisor for Tibet and Bhutan, also said that a small polytechnic might be attached: "The school should be directly under the Central Government who should finance it," wrote Nehru.

It is a pity that the strategic issues were not raised by India, but it is however certain that the Foreign Secretary's visit to the Dragon Kingdom, was a first positive step towards a better understanding of the mutual perceptions.

# 13

# Pressure is Mounting on the Borders

## Development and Security of India's Borders

Scanning through the documents available for the period under study, one does not find many notes, reports or correspondence dealing with the border issue apart from the first border incidents in Barahoti, Shipki-la and Nilang/Jadhang area.

This can be explained by the fact that the Indian Government was in the process of building a fraternal relation with its Chinese counterpart.

There was no 'border' between friends or brothers.

However, on September 14, 1954, the Prime Minister wrote a note to the Foreign Secretary in which he mentioned the frontiers: "It seems to me obvious that we should have some kind of a Border Security Force for such areas. This Border Security Force should consist partly if not largely of men recruited from those very areas, officered by the Army. This may even be some kind of a territorial militia."[1]

From the early years, Nehru did not want the Army to man the borders; he thought that a police force or a militia would be enough.

In the note, probably copied to the UP government, the Prime Minister said: "I do not like the idea of our regular Army being stationed there. I think that, till such time as the Border Security Force or Militia is not organized, the UP Government should place their Police there. I am

---

1  All documents in this chapter, except specifically mentioned, are from the Nehru Papers (JN Collection) held at the Nehru Memorial Museum and Library in Delhi. The 'papers' are not indexed.

inclined to agree with the UP Government that this is not a normal activity of the State Government. So far as finances of it are concerned, the Central Government should make itself responsible. But otherwise, the UP Government should take charge."

This note followed the first Chinese intrusions in Barahoti in June 1954; Nehru pointed to the Chinese inroads: "The difficulty of keeping anybody in winter at a height of 16,000 ft. is obvious, whether it is the Army, the Police or Border Security Force. The only possibility appears to be to keep some of our forces, whatever they are, for the non-winter months there and to leave a small local guard there for the winter months. After all, there cannot be much danger of anybody trying to come there during the winter. If it is difficult for us, it is at least equally difficult for the others."

Till today, the patrols have never stayed during winter in Barahoti or other adjacent areas; the intrusions every year would start in May/June when Tujun-la pass opened.

Nehru continued: "The Defence Ministry can certainly be asked to consider this matter from various points of view and advise us. I suppose we have to allow the next winter to pass without adequate arrangements. But we should be prepared to have our men there by spring time."

Having ruled out the Army, it was not easy for the latter to give an opinion though Nehru concluded: "The question of some kind of a Security Force for the border should be fully examined."

The matter would be examined again and again during the following years.

## Countering Chinese Moves on the Frontier

Two years later, on May 12, 1956, another note was sent to Subimal Dutt, the Foreign Secretary, in which Nehru observed: "These are rather old reports which I had not seen previously. Since these reports were received, there have been rumours about fairly widespread uprisings in Tibet against the Chinese, which were bombed and crushed by the Chinese authorities. It is difficult to say how far these reports are correct. Probably, there is some exaggeration in them but, at the same time, there is also some measure of truth."

The editor of the *Selected Works of Jawaharlal Nehru* added in a footnote, that according to some reports published in the Indian press in the first week of May 1954, "a serious uprising had occurred two months earlier among the Golok tribesmen of eastern Tibet. The tribesmen were stated to have massacred an entire Chinese garrison of 800-900 men, leading to retaliatory Chinese military action in which a number of Golok villages were reported to have been bombed with heavy civilian casualties."

As always, the press was far better informed than the Government, though the reasons given for the uprising were the high taxation imposed by Chinese authorities and resentment at inroads made on the Dalai Lama's authority. Though the reports spoke of compulsory indoctrination of youth and requisitioning of grain for the Chinese Army, the famous 'reforms' were not mentioned.

For the Indian Government, the building of roads and airstrips by the Chinese in Tibet appeared to be a natural development from the Chinese point of view: "In order to hold and develop Tibet, they must have these communications," remarked Nehru. It was true, but at the same time, it had serious implications for India's borders.

The Prime Minister admitted: "roads right up to our border and airstrips near our border create a new situation for us, which we must bear in mind. I rule out any kind of physical or aerial attack on India for a considerable time to come at least. So far as infiltrations are concerned, they have to be met by other means."

This was written in 1956; hardly six years later, India suffered from a massive attack by the PLA, the consequences of which are still felt more than 60 years later.

In a language similar to all successive governments in Delhi, Nehru asserted what was required: "Proper check posts on the border and a certain vigilance right along the border, development of communications on our side and general economic and like development of our areas which, of course, is rather a long term programme."

He further mentioned his 'little' worry about the persistence of the Chinese maps "indicating parts of our territory as being in the Chinese State. I think that we shall have to take up this matter some time or other."

It was decided to take up the issue with the Communist Government 'separately', Nehru nonetheless added: "we should take up with the Soviet Government, their maps of this border area, which appear to be a copy of the Chinese maps."

He affirmed that from a military point of view, India could 'do little' except:

(1) Setting up check posts at all suitable points on the border;

(2) Giving efficient training to border personnel in mountain warfare; and

(3) Developing roads and other communications.

Nehru could not accept the suggestion that India should have long-range bombers: "This is against our basic approach to the problem of defence. They are too costly and, if we get them, it means that we do not equip ourselves with more useful aircraft and delay, to some extent, our industrial development. The basic strength that India should aim at will only come through rapid industrial development. For the moment, this means fulfilling the Second Five Year Plan."

The Prime Minister said that he was 'astonished' that a few weeks earlier, the PO estimated "Chinese troops in various areas of Tibet as one hundred twenty thousand. Apart from this figure being much too big to be easily accepted, the difference between this figure and Menon's figure of forty-five thousand is very great," wrote Nehru.

He requested the Foreign Secretary to check the source of his figures.

**New Developments on the Borders**

In his Report for the month of March 1956, the Indian Consul General in Lhasa, PN Menon informed Delhi that a new road had just been opened in Tibet: "It is the 200 kilometres highway between Gyantse and Yatung which was opened to traffic on March 29. The new highway links Southern Tibet with the rest of China via Lhasa. It was reported that at Yatung crowds of peoples turned out to greet the arrival of the first convoy of over thirty trucks loaded with cargo."

The 'crowds' had probably no other choice but to attend.

A Chinese report published in Beijing mentioned the construction of the highway divided into two sections: "The first section totaling over 150 kilometres between Gyantse and Phari was opened to traffic last November. Work on the second section from Phari to Yatung started in the latter part of December and was completed 20 days earlier than scheduled."

The infrastructure was fast progressing towards the Indian border.

**Survey the Bhutan-Tibet Borders**

Around that time, alarm bells had started ringing in Lhasa and Gangtok.

On April 13, 1956, PN Menon mentioned to Apa Pant about some rumours heard in the Tibetan capital; it spoke of widespread discontentment in the Po region bordering on Lohit and Siang Frontier Divisions of the NEFA.

Two weeks earlier in his weekly letter, the Consul General had already reported "considerable troop movements (up to 60,000 Chinese troops) into these areas including the Tsona Dzong areas facing Tawang on our side." That was just North of Tawang.

On April 30, Menon cabled Delhi that while scores of officials, including Defence Minister Marshal Chen Yi[2], had assembled in Lhasa to inaugurate the Preparatory Committee for the Tibet Autonomous

---

2 Chen Yi (August 26, 1901 – January 6, 1972) was born in Lezhi County near Chengdu, Sichuan, into a moderately-wealthy magistrate's family. He became a Communist military commander and politician. He served as Mayor of Shanghai from 1949 to 1958 and then as Foreign Minister of China from 1958 to 1972. A comrade of Lin Biao from their guerrilla days, Chen was a commander of the New Fourth Army during the Sino-Japanese War (1937-1945), spearheaded the Shandong counter-offensive during the Chinese Civil War, and later commanded the Communist armies that defeated the KMT forces during the Huaihai Campaign and conquered the lower Yangtze region in 1948–49. He was made a Marshal of the PLA in 1955.

Region: "A conspicuous absentee from Lhasa at the moment is General Li[3] (who apart from being the Director of Road Construction it is now understood is also at present Head of the entire Chinese Intelligence in Tibet)," according to the Indian report.

**Who was Maj Gen Li Jue?**

We have briefly met Maj Gen Li Jue, when he accompanied the Dalai Lama on his way back from Beijing in 1955.

Let us remember that the construction of the Sichuan-Tibet highway[4] and the Qinghai-Tibet highway had been carried out under the 18th Army's General Logistics Department of the PLA with the support of civilian construction engineers from Sichuan and the First Army's General Logistics Department from Lanzhou.

Gen Li Jue had been the head of the 18th Army's General Logistics Department before handing over to Maj Gen Chen Mingy;[5] he was deeply involved in the infrastructure construction on the plateau.

What was Gen Li doing in Southern Tibet was the question raised by Menon?[6]

Menon told Pant: "Li may well have been the high ranking Chinese military officer who carried out an inspection of the Tibet-Bhutan Frontier as mentioned by Chibber[7]."

The Indian officials in Tibet could realize that pressure was mounting on the Indian borders …as well as the Bhutanese northern frontiers, which had not been demarcated.

Delhi was keen to help Bhutan to survey her borders with Tibet; it included Northern Bhutan, the Western borders with the Chumbi

---

3  See Chapter 7, Footnote 36.

4  The northern and southern branches.

5  Maj Gen Chen Mingyi (1917-2002).

6  After leaving the 18th Army logistics post (in 1953), Li Jue became Chief of Staff for the Tibet Military Region and then in 1956 was promoted to one of the Deputy Commanders' positions of the Tibet Military Region.

7  Maj SL Chibber.

Valley and the trijunction between Sikkim, Bhutan and Tibet, which attained fame during the Doklam incident in June 2017.

Pant informed Delhi that TS Murty, an officer of the Indian Frontier Administrative Service, extremely knowledgeable in the frontier issues was already in Thimbu: "Impossible for him reach Delhi before 28th [May] and even then as rivers in Southern Bhutan are in spate."

One Maj Sinha, who belonged to the Survey of India, had just arrived in Gangtok and was waiting to leave for Bhutan; he was to meet Murty at Paro on May 29 to help Bhutan for the survey of her borders.

Pant observed: "I am a little vague about Major Sinha's mission to Bhutan at this juncture. At best he could only make preliminary reconnaissance and appreciation of the work that shall have to be undertaken and preparation of detailed maps and chalking out boundary line later with the help of trained personnel."

The PO explained the rationale: "The main work shall have to be undertaken by half a dozen triangulators working for at least six months. Major Sinha can only explain to the Bhutan Government and get their concurrence to such a party working in Bhutan at a later date. For this purpose, he should proceed as soon as possible to meet Murty at Paro."

It was clear that Maj Sinha's visit was for preliminary work only: "[he] need not spend more than a month at the most within Bhutan," noted the PO who added he would explain the position to Jigme Dorji "to obviate any likely misunderstanding."

In the meantime, in view of the urgency, Pant had to postpone TS Murty's interview[8] for the Indian Frontier Administrative Service. On May 16, SK Roy wrote to Pant from South Block regarding Maj Sinha's visit to Bhutan; the latter had to accompany TS Murty.

Roy explained that Maj Sinha: "should function as Survey Officer accompanying Murty to assist him. Discussions with Bhutan Government would better be done by you or by the Ministry. Sinha should not <u>repeat not</u> undertake any policy discussions with either

---

8   Incidentally, it was TS Murty who received the Dalai Lama at Chuthangmu on March 31, 1959 when the latter arrived in India.

Jigme Dorji or His Highness of Bhutan. Please make this clear to both Sinha and Murty."

As we have seen the Royal Government was very touchy about the Indians surveying their border; at the same time they needed the Indian know-how.

**Another Note about the Chinese Intrusion**

In a previous chapter, we have looked at the genesis of the first Chinese incursions inside India's northern border, in Barahoti in June 1954; it was hardly two months after the signature of the Agreement on Tibet.

In a way, Barahoti could be explained by the fact that Indian negotiators omitted to insist on Tunjun-la as a pass notified in the Agreement. This gave an opportunity to the Chinese to claim an area south of the border pass.

But what happened two years later, cannot be justified under the same principle. It was a gross violation of the Indian territory.

On September 8, 1956, India had to deliver a *note verbale* to the Chinese Charge d'Affaires in India; one week earlier, some Chinese troops had trespassed in an area south of a pass notified in Article IV of the 1954 Agreement.

The *note verbale* read thus: "The Government of India have received a report that on the 1st September 1956, a party of about 10 Chinese Army personnel entered and took up a position about 2 *furlongs*[9] from Hupsang Khad[10] on the Indian side of Shipki-la pass. The Party withdrew after the Officer-in-Charge of the Indian Border Police pointed out to the captain-in-command of the Chinese military personnel that the Indian territory extends up to the Shipki-la pass."

This is one of the first notes published by the Ministry of External Affairs in Volume 1 of the *Notes, Memoranda and letters Exchanged and Agreements signed between The Governments of India and China 1954 –1959*[11], the first ones being about Barahoti.

---

9   An eighth of a mile or 220 yards.

10  A *Khad* or *Khud* is a deep ravine or a chasm.

11  Also known as White Paper 1. See, http://www.claudearpi.net/white-papers-on-china

It was observed: "The crossing of the Shipki-la pass by the Chinese Army personnel without visas and passports violates the Sino-Indian Agreement of April 29, 1954, in which the Shipki-la pass has been recognised as the border between India and Tibet region of China at that place."

There was, of course, no question of 'visas' as the Chinese had deliberately crossed into Indian territory, though Delhi still hoped for a mistake: "[we] presume that the Chinese Army personnel crossed into Indian territory by mistake and not deliberately."

The note concluded by requesting Beijing "to issue strict instructions to the authorities concerned that no unauthorised persons should cross into Indian territory in this manner in future, as otherwise there is a danger of breach of peace."

Delhi was still living in a dream world; it wanted action be taken against the offenders and to be 'informed of the action taken'.

**A New Report of the Border Incident**

Two weeks later[12], this time it was an *aide-mémoire* which was given to the Chinese embassy in Delhi. It stated that since the handing over of the note to Fu Hao, the Chinese Chargéd' Affaires, Delhi had received two more reports about the serious situation that had developed "between the Chinese and Indian border patrols in the region of Shipki-la Pass on the Indo-Tibetan border."

The first incident occurred on September 10, "a party of Indian border Police on its way to the Shipki-la pass sighted a party of Chinese military personnel on the Indian side of the frontier," the report stated before continuing: "The Chinese Party was commanded by a captain and consisted of at least ten persons. The Indian Patrol signalled the Chinese Party to withdraw, but the latter did not do so. Thereupon, on the Indian patrol trying to advance, the Chinese personnel threw stones at it and threatened to use their grenades."

In the evening, the Indian Party approached the Chinese and discussed with them. According to the *aide-mémoire*, during the encounter, the

---

12  On September 24, 1956.

Chinese commander said that he had "received instructions from the Tibetan Government that the border extended up to Hupsang Khad and that Indian personnel should accordingly not advance beyond Hupsang Khad."

The Indian Commander argued that the border was at the Shipki-la pass; he further suggested that the Chinese should accordingly withdraw.

However, the Chinese troops refused to listen, "as the following morning, they were again soon on the ridge above the roadway on the Indian side of the pass." The standoff continued the next day[13].

The Ministry's *aide-mémoire* told the Chinese Government "[you] will no doubt agree that in throwing stones and threatening to use hand grenades, the Chinese patrol offered such provocation as could easily have resulted in serious and regrettable incidents."

An even more serious development "likely to cause an ugly situation" soon followed, said the *mémoire*.

It described the facts thus: "on September 20 at 4:45 am, a party of 27 Indians Border Security Force came face to face with a party of 20 Chinese soldiers and officers two miles on the Indian side of the Shipki-la pass. The Indian Commanding Officer asked the Chinese Officer to withdraw his troops."

The Chinese captain said that he had received no communication from his Government, but he added that his instructions were clear, "namely to patrol right up to Hupsang Khad, and in carrying these out he was prepared to face the consequences. He concluded that if the Indian Party went beyond Hupsang Khad he would oppose it with arms."

The Indian Ministry stated that it was pained and surprised at the conduct of the Chinese Commanding Officer, adding: "It is not difficult to visualise that the natural and direct result of such attitudes, if continued in, may be one of clash of arms."

Delhi reiterated that the pass was clearly the border, as acknowledged in the Sino-Indian Agreement of April 1954: "the Government of

---

13 September 12.

India consider any crossing of this border pass by armed personnel as aggression which they will resist."

Beijing was told that India had ordered the Border Security Police Force "not to take any action for the present in repulsing this aggression and to await instructions which they hope the Central People's Government will issue immediately."

The State Force was however instructed that on no account they should withdraw from their position or permit Chinese personnel to go "beyond where they are even if this involves a clash".

Delhi requested immediate action from China: "Otherwise there might be an unfortunate clash on our border which will have undesirable results."

The situation had become hot.

**The Prime Minister on the Chinese Incursions**

Once Nehru realized that the Chinese had entered Indian territory, his attitude changed. On September 21, the Prime Minister wrote to the Foreign Secretary: "This is a serious matter and we cannot accept this position."

The Prime Minister instructed his officials: "We should, of course, protest in emphatic language both to the Chinese Embassy here and to the Chinese Government through our Ambassador in Peking."

Moreover, he thought that was not quite enough: "The question arises as to what directions we should give to the Himachal Pradesh Government which they can pass on to their police force at the border. From the telephone account, it appears that our party consists of 27 persons of the Border Security Police and the Chinese party consists of 20 officers and men. Thus, the numbers on both sides are small and there is a slight advantage on our side."

He ordered the Indian troops that: "on no account [they should] withdraw from their present position, which appears to be between the Shipki-la pass and Hupsang Khad."

The Prime Minister's position was rather firm: "They must remain there even at the cost of conflict. For the present, they should not force their way beyond this place, as this would presumably mean a conflict with the Chinese. But it must be made clear that they must remain where they are and if the Chinese advance further, they should be checked."

He made clear that India considered the crossing of the Shipki-la without permission as improper and an aggression. He asserted that the Chinese should go back: "We would not permit them to go any further and if they did not go back, we would have to take further steps in the matter. We are not doing so immediately because the matter has been referred to Delhi and Peking and because of our friendly relations we should like to avoid a clash. But if there is any further aggression, a clash is inevitable."

The Prime Minister suggested that Himachal Pradesh Government should immediately send more troops or the Border Security Police to the pass.

He also mentioned that in the Indian protest to the Chinese Embassy, it should be stated that "in view of the fact that Shipki-la is clearly the border and is acknowledged as such even in our agreement with China, we consider any crossing of armed forces without our permission as aggression and we have to resist it."

He added: "…we attach great importance to this matter and request immediate action by the Chinese Government. Otherwise there might be an unfortunate clash on our border which will have undesirable results."

The orders were "on no account to retire from their position or to permit the Chinese forces to go beyond where they are, even if this involves a clash".

Delhi had started realizing that the good days of eternal friendship with China were over; darker clouds were gathering.

## A Meeting at the Ministry of External Affairs

On October 3, a meeting of representatives of Ministries of External Affairs, Defence and Home, and the Himachal Pradesh Government[14], was held in Delhi to consider the Chinese activities on the Indo-Tibetan border (mainly in Himachal Pradesh).

TN Kaul, who chaired, gave an account of the recent events in the Shipki-la area; he pointed out that during previous weeks the Chinese had transgressed into Indian territory on three occasions. He informed the participants about the notes handed over to the Chinese Embassy in Delhi on September 8 and 22, while the matter had also been taken up by the Indian embassy with the Chinese Foreign Office in Beijing.

Kaul reiterated the Prime Minister's concerns; it was a serious issue and it was not enough to lodge a protest with the Chinese: "He had instructed that specific directions should be given to the Government of Himachal Pradesh to be passed on to the border checkposts and that these checkpost personnel should on no account withdraw from their present position."

The meeting was told that Nehru had decided to let the Chinese know that "any further aggression into Indian territory would lead to unhappy results."

Kaul noted that this meeting was called "to make specific recommendations to meet the present situation and future eventualities."

---

14  The External Affairs Ministry was represented by TN Kaul, Joint Secretary; Col PN Luthra, Special Officer, Frontier Areas (SOFA); Dr. Gopalachari, Deputy Director, Historical Division; KV Rajagopalan, Under Secretary and MS Nair, Under Secretary.

The Defence Ministry's representatives were HC Sarin, Joint Secretary; Maj Gen MS Wadalia, Chief of General Staff; Brig KH Katoch, Director of Military Operations; N. Sahgal, Joint Secretary and Rajkumar, Deputy Secretary, Home Ministry were present for the Home Ministry while the Himachal Pradesh Government was represented by KN Channa, the Chief Secretary and A. Gupta, the Inspector General of Police.

## The Discussion

According to the representatives from the Himachal Pradesh government, the Chinese had already withdrawn from the posts and they were not likely to return to this area during the present season.

The information was confirmed by SK Roy, the SOFA; Roy had been touring in Western Tibet and he had just crossed back into India via Shipki-la. For the State government, the issue was not immediate, but it was necessary to formulate "a definite line of action to meet eventualities in the spring."

The following points were on the agenda for the meeting:

(i) The desirability of sending some troops in adequate strength to Namgia[15] and if possible to Shipki-la pass before it closes;

(ii) The question of making arrangements for the next spring so that our border security police are in position in Shipki-la Pass before the Chinese come, and

(iii) The building of aluminum huts, cave shelters and other allied matters

The Himachal representatives' suggestion was that it was not necessary to send more troops to the area presently; it had already been done before the withdrawal of the Chinese troops: "Since the Chinese troops had now withdrawn and were not likely to return during this season, the purpose would be served if a permanent police outpost was opened at Namgia [village] and some cave shelters and aluminum huts were constructed as near Shipki-la as possible before the next spring."

The Home Ministry's representative agreed that sending troops now might have the opposite effect of what India desired; it could trigger the return of the Chinese. North Block was against sending troops as they did not wish to divide them into 'penny packets', particularly if there was the possibility of a clash. Kaul read out two telegrams sent by SK Roy who was against sending any troops at that time.

---

15 The last Indian village before the pass.

## The Recommendations

The meeting made four recommendations:

(1) Since the Chinese troops had withdrawn it was not necessary at present to send our troops to this area, but a few Army officers may be sent to make a reconnaissance right up to Shipki-la and suggest ways and means of meeting a possible threat from Chinese troops next spring and draw up plans accordingly.

(2) A permanent police outpost should be established at Namgia village with an increased strength.

(3) India's border personnel should be in physical possession of Shipki-la pass before the April 1 next and earlier, if possible. For this purpose, a permanent party, even though of a very small size, should be posted at the pass itself, or, if not possible, as close to the pass as possible. Construction of cave shelters and aluminum huts should be taken up immediately and these should be ready before March 1957.

(4) Constant patrolling from Namgia up to the pass should be done from now on as often as possible, weather permitting.

It was also felt that since Chinese were likely to trespass into the Indian territory in other areas, therefore reconnaissance "should be made of all the disputed areas by Army personnel who should make specific recommendation about the places, as close to the frontier as possible, where border police posts could be established."

These resolutions had little chance to be implemented in view of the apathy of the Indian bureaucracy.

## Where else could the Chinese Trespass?

An interesting list of places where the Chinese may trespass was mentioned: "The reconnaissance should in particular cover the following places, and their recommendations should be sent as soon after spring 1957 as possible."

The passes and areas mentioned were Lanak-la, Dokpo Karpo and Spanggur Tso in Ladakh, Shipki-la in Himachal Pradesh and Tsang Chok-la, Mana Pass, Niti Pass, Tunjun-la, Hoti Plain, Darma Pass, Kungi Bingri Pass, Lipu Lekh Pass all in Uttarakhand.

At the end of the meeting, the Himachal representatives raised the question of an increase in the strength of the border police and also the issue of their rations. This demand was agreed by all the participants. The Himachal Government was to furnish the details "indicating the financial commitments involved for further consideration."

This was approved in principle.

**Another Note from the Prime Minister**

On October 8, 1956, the Prime Minister sent another note to the Foreign Secretary: "There is no question of sending any troops to the Shipki-la now," Nehru wrote "even in the spring next year, I do not envisage the necessity of sending troops. The fate of Shipki-la is not going to be decided by fighting or by a large show of force."

He, however, agreed that it was desirable, "for some Army officers to reconnoitre and see the place at a suitable time now or early next year."

He concluded: "The main thing to do is to have a Police outpost there and that our personnel should be in physical possession of the Shipki-la when the snows melt. Also, it is desirable for us to investigate the other passes."

One problem faced by India from the first years of Independence was, who should be responsible for the border areas. It was eventually delegated to the Ministry of Home Affairs, which unfortunately had neither the capacity nor the training to defend the borders ...and lacked the strategic vision to do so.

**The 1960 Border Talks: the Historical Background**

To really understand the issue of this new border 'dispute', it is necessary to jump forward in time and quote from the Report of the Officials published in 1961, after several rounds of talks on the boundary issues held between officials of India and China in the course of 1960.

India's described the alignment in the Middle sector thus: "The Middle Sector of the boundary between India and China lies from the junction of the Indian States of Jammu and Kashmir and the Punjab and the Tibet Region of China, to the tri-junction of the boundaries of India, Nepal and China. The boundary throughout lies along the main watershed in the region between the Spiti River and the Pare Chu, between the tributaries of the Sutlej and between the Ganges and the Sutlej basins."[16]

The report noted that in this sector, the Chinese alignment conformed for most part to the traditional Indian alignment except for four areas where the Chinese position did not follow the watershed to include pockets of Indian territory. It was Chuva and Chuje in the Spiti area, the Shipki pass, the Nilang-Jadhang area (called Sang and Tsungsha by the Chinese) and Barahoti (Wu-je), Sangchamalla and Lapthal.

The Indian traditional and customary alignment at the Shipki pass was described in detail; first it was stated that Shipki pass is on the Zanskar range, which itself formed a well-defined watershed frontier.

Further, the Shipki pass had been the traditional and customary boundary between the States of Bashahr[17] and the Kingdom of Guge which was incorporated in Tibet in 1720.

The fact that the Shipki Pass was always a part of Bashahr was attested by many travelers. India quoted some.

In his memoirs *Account of Koonawar*[18] *in the Himalaya*[19], Alexander Gerard wrote: "October 12, Marched to Shipki, nine miles. The road ascended a little, and then there was a steep descent into the bed of the Oopsung. Here the rocks were more rugged than any we had yet seen: they were rent in every direction, piled upon one another in wild disorder, in a most extraordinary manner not to be described,

---

16 For *Report of the Officials of the Governments of India and the Peoples' Republic of China on the Boundary Question*, Ministry of External Affairs, Government of India; see http://www.archieve.claudearpi.net/maintenance/uploaded_pics/OR_Part_1.pdf

17 Now part of the Himachal Pradesh State of India.

18 Kinnaur.

19 Published in London in 1841.

overhanging the path and threatening destruction to the traveller. From the Oopsung the road was a tiresome and rocky ascent, to the pass which separates Koonawur from the Chinese dominions, 13,518 feet above the level of the sea."

The Indian officials explained to their Chinese counterpart that Oopsung was Hupsang and Gerard had clearly mentioned that the boundary was located at Shipki pass.

EB Wakefield visited the area in 1929. In the report of his journey published in *The Himalayan Journal*[20], he stated: "Having crossed the Shipki pass into British territory on the 11th October he halted for a week at Pooh whence he reached Simla on 2nd November."

In 1960, India produced a large number of maps proving this point: "All this evidence showed that the traditional and customary alignment in this area lay where Indian maps were now showing it."

Somewhere else in the Report, it was mentioned that "the Chinese side failed to appreciate the significance of the contemporary accounts of travellers and the unofficial maps cited by the Indian side, even though they had not hesitated to quote such evidence when it suited them."

There was no doubt that historically the pass had been the border.

## Other Arguments in Favour of Shipki Pass as the Border

In their argument, the Chinese merely asserted that they could not agree that these maps showed the traditional Indian alignment. However, said the Report: "they brought forward no evidence to support their contention. Instead, they again drew a comparison between official and unofficial maps. …The map published in China as recently as 1957 and cited by the Indian side proved that even Chinese maps had been showing the correct alignment in this area till about three years ago. However small the scale of the map, it showed very precisely the boundary along the Shipki Pass."

The report further stated that the Chinese claim to the Shipki Pass area was sustained by only evidential argument: "the people of Shipki

---

20  Vol. II, April 1930, page 103.

village had constantly used the pastures west of the Shipki Pass and that these areas belonged to them."

India said that no proof of ownership could be brought forward with this argument: "Even proof of use of these pastures had not been provided, although mere use of pastures, even if the assertion be true, could prove nothing."

It is a fact that pasture rights were often used in the Himalayan to define the borders; further, the pasture rights were subject to frequent changes and depended on leases between border villagers.

In 1960, the course of the negotiations between the 'officials' of India and China, a series of questions was asked to the Chinese representatives. It became clear that the Chinese did not have an in-depth knowledge of the border in this area.

**The Shipki-la Route and the 1954 Agreement**

The main Indian argument was that the route to Tibet was passing through Shipki-la Pass; it was the major artery in this area. India argued: "as sheep were used in this part as pack animals, people of both countries used the pastures besides the route." Indian shepherds used the pastures lying "between Shipki-la and Shipki village, and even beyond."

The Chinese stated that the inhabitants of Shipki village had claimed the territory south of the pass in 1930; to which India answered that a unilateral claim to Indian territory put forward as recently as 1930 by Tibetan villagers "could not be regarded as scientific proof of the traditional and customary basis of the boundary."

The Indian negotiators explained that traditional definition of a border was "something of long and ancient standing. It could not be created in 1930."

The boundary alignment in this sector was marked by the watershed, and the border passes were clearly named.

But more serious was the fact that China brought forward the argument questioning the relevance of the 1954 Agreement.

The Government of India could not agree to this; for Delhi, the Agreement had "a bearing on the boundary between the two countries and that normal relations between India and Tibet could not have been established if the Chinese Government had at any time made, or even had in mind claims to large areas of Indian territory contiguous to the Tibet Region."

It was also argued that Article 4, enumerating the border passes, made it clear that they delineated the border and that "China had reserved no claim to the territories West of Shipki Pass and South of the other five passes."[21]

Article 5 (2) of the Agreement further provided for inhabitants of 'border districts' travelling to and fro across the border.

It was undoubtedly a blunder of the Indian negotiators to have not insisted on a proper delineation of the border during the 1954 negotiations. If a proper boundary had been agreed to, the question of Barahoti, located south of the Tunjun La or Shipki-la would have never occurred.

In 1960, India argued again and again that the limits of its territory and the precise alignment of their international boundaries "had been well-known for years and had been repeatedly and authoritatively confirmed in public."

In 1954, a good occasion to define the border had been missed; hardly two years later, consequences started to appear. The lapse would be fully used by the Chinese Government to their advantage during the following years.

In 1960, the Indian officials asked their Chinese counterparts why Beijing had not disputed the statements of the Indian Government in 1954; the Chinese had in fact never raised any claims to the traditional Indian territory until Zhou Enlai's communication of September 8, 1959.

---

21 Article 4 stated that "traders and pilgrims of both countries may travel" by the passes: "If these passes, however, had been within China, there was no reason why the agreement of the Indian Government should have been necessary for Chinese travellers using what would have been Chinese passes."

It was however undoubtedly wrong on the part of India to have not included the border in the talks for the Agreement in early 1954.

In 1960, India repeated that "despite frequent occasions and opportunities, the Chinese side had not till September 1959 disputed the traditional Indian alignment, they were estopped[22] from doing so. The Chinese side, being unable to refute this, described this principle of estopped as absurd;" this did not change the situation on the ground. China had outmaneuvered India.

India pointed out that 'estopped' is an elementary principle of international law whose importance required no elaboration or emphasis; and it was no serious refutation merely to set it aside as 'absurd' without giving any reasons at all for showing why it could not be regarded as valid or applicable."

The Chinese kept cleverly arguing that they had signed a Five Principles Agreement with Burma and Nepal "but yet had since held negotiations with them on the boundary," India repeating that "in the 1954 Agreement the two Governments could only have confirmed the territorial integrity of each other's country if they had had clear and precise knowledge as to the alignment of their common boundary."

It was a fallacious agreement, but the 'clever' Panikkar doctrine that the boundary issue was not to be raised by India first, had turned into a trap.

---

22  Estoppel is a judicial device in common law legal systems whereby a court may prevent, or 'estop' a person from making assertions or from going back on his word.

# 14

# The Advance in the Subansiri Sector of NEFA

## Two Reports

It is not easy to find documents on the advance of the Indian Administration in the North East Frontier Agency (NEFA) in the 1950s; however, two remarkable documents detailing the difficulties faced by the brave officers of the Indian Frontier Administrative Service (IFAS), were found.

The first is the memoirs of the wife of Maj Surendra Mohan Krishnatry,[1] Assistant Political Officer (APO) in Taliha[2] in the Subansiri Frontier Division whom we have already encountered in Tibet in the first two volumes of this study. Geeta Krishnatry meticulously recorded their adventures on the way to the border during this difficult posting. This will provide some glimpses of the situation on India's border in the remote Subansiri Frontier Division (FD) of NEFA in 1958.

The second one is the *Report on an Exploratory Tour Undertaken in The Upper Subansiri Area and the Tsari Chu Valley* by Capt LR Sailo, who succeeded Krishnatry as APO in Taliha. This covers the period between January 21 and March 28, 1957, at the time the Dalai Lama and his party were returning to Lhasa after their visit to India.

---

1. SM and Geeta Krishnatry, *The Border Tagins of Arunachal Pradesh – Unarmed Expedition of 1956,* (New Delhi, National Book Trust, 2005).

2. Taliha is a village in today's Upper Subansiri of Arunachal Pradesh. It is located 32 km North of Daporijo, the District headquarters. It is today one of the 60 constituencies of Legislative Assembly of Arunachal Pradesh.

In a preface to Geeta Krishnatry's book, BG Verghese[3] rightly remarked: "Prior to Independence, India's eastern marches were scarcely known, unlike the North West Frontier Province bordering on Afghanistan and adjacent lands where the Great Game was played out. The Northeast, a huge swathe of densely forested cis-Himalayan territory was a land of mystery - wild, unexplored and constitutionally 'excluded'. These Frontier Tracts lay secluded behind a so-called Inner Line along the foothills edging the Assam Valley, rising in serried ranges to the Himalayan rampart and the Forbidden Land of Tibet beyond."

It was the frontier with Tibet (now with China); India could not 'exclude' or even ignore these areas anymore.

Though a couple of chapters in the previous two volumes of this study have dealt in some detail with these unexplored border areas of India, the Subansiri Frontier Division where Krishnatry was sent after his six-year stint in Tibet, was far more remote and unknown than Tawang area of Kameng Frontier Division.

Verghese explained the background of Krishnatry's posting: "Little was known of the vast mosaic of tribal communities inhabiting this region. In October 1953 an Assam Rifles Major and his unsuspecting column of 42 men[4] and supporting staff were massacred at Achingmori in Tagin country on account of what later transpired was an inter-tribal dispute over a woman. The country was shocked."

Hardly a year after the massacre, the former major of the Maratha Light Infantry walked in these inhospitable areas inhabited by the Tagin tribe, who were considered quite warlike.

The area was not an ordinary frontier track, as every twelve years, it witnessed the Pure Crystal Mountain pilgrimage of Tsari, one of the most sacred pilgrimages in Tibet.

One of the characteristics of this pilgrimage was that it was running across the McMahon Line; half was in Tibet, half in India.

Tsari had always been synonymous of 'sacred place' in the Tibetan psyche. With the Mount Kailash and the Amye Machen in eastern Tibet,

---

3   Who was associated with The Centre for Policy Research in New Delhi.

4   Some records say 46 people died in the ambush.

the pilgrimage around the Dakpa Shelri or Pure Crystal Mountain had, for centuries, been one of the holiest of the Roof of the World.

The Pure Crystal Mountain lies at 5,735 meter above the sea in the Tsari district of southeastern Tibet. Toni Huber has been one of the foremost scholars who has written a great deal about this region from which the Subansiri and the Tsari rivers flow. "The area of the two rivers into which Tsarong[5] ventured for military and commercial reasons had for centuries defined a very significant territory for both Tibetans and neighbouring non-Tibetans" wrote Huber, who described thus the region: "[these] rivers encompassed the southern slopes of the famous Tibetan holy mountain of Dakpa Shelri at Tsari. The large-scale, 12-yearly circumambulation of Tibetan Buddhist pilgrims around the mountain known as the *Rongkor Chenmo*, had the character of a state ritual for the Ganden Phodrang[6]. Pilgrims in this huge procession crossed the McMahon Line below the frontier village of Migyitun in Tsari district and followed the Tsari Chu southwards. They then turned back up the Subansiri westwards, crossing the McMahon Line once again to reach the first Tibetan frontier settlements in Chame district. In doing so, they traversed non-Tibetan lands during this entire southern leg of the procession. This was the territory of the Mra[7] (Tibetan: Morang Loba) clan, which ran downstream along the Tsari Chu valley and around its junction with the Subansiri at Geling Sinyik[8], and also of the neighbouring Na (Tibetan: Khalo, Lungtu Lopa) community of Takshing, which extended upstream along the Subansiri heading westwards towards Tibet."

The terrain made the area almost inaccessible.

**The Preparations for the Expedition**

To come back to Krishnatry's book and the massacre of the Assam Rifles column, the preface observed: "Under the Raj, the answer would have been a punitive expedition. However, the new Indian Government stopped short with apprehending the ringleaders of the incident. The

---

5   Tsarong, the Commander-in-Chief of the Tibetan Army.
6   The Tibetan Government.
7   Or Mara.
8   Gelensiniak.

task of establishing friendly contact with the people and bringing the region under settled administration awaited volunteers."

The holy *parikrama* around the Takpa Shelri[9], which took place every twelve years was due in 1956, the season prior to the arrival of Maj Krishnatry. The Major's terms of reference according to Verghese "were to ensure a peaceful pilgrimage, prevent trespass into Indian territory and establish an administrative centre as near the international boundary as possible. In order to demonstrate his friendly intentions, Krishnatry took two bold and imaginative decisions." This made the expedition even more interesting.

**What were these Decisions?**

First, Krishnatry convinced the authorities to take his wife Geeta along; further his party would not be carrying weapons. On January 24, 1955, they left from Daporijo, where the NEFA administration's stores were kept; thereafter, everything would need to be airlifted (and airdropped).

A journey full of wonder and adventure started with "cobras, leeches and mites, dense jungle and precipitous gorges, some traversed perilously on rope ladders clinging to the face of the mountain."

"The Tagins were childlike in their curiosity and full of fun," said Geeta Krishnatry; they valued safety pins, needles and thread, and payment in eight anna coins - not the smaller four anna variety - as these were good for making trinkets and garlands. They were amazed by Geeta's hand mirror "as viewers doubled up with laughter on seeing their own grimacing faces," commented the major.

While his wife distributed needles, 'Krish', as the APO was known, gave away hoes, axes and spades to the villagers. It was the best way to convince them of the benevolence of the Indian State.

Verghese conclusions were right to the point: "The peaceful opening up and integration of Arunachal[10] is a little told story and sadly even less appreciated. It ranks among the greatest achievement of Indian

---

9 Also written Dakpa Shiri.
10 NEFA then.

nation-building. The further development and political growth of this sequestered corner of India have been unique and merit tribute to the sagacity and foresight of those that made it happen. Geeta and SM Krishnatry are among that band of unsung heroes." It is a pity that the adventures of these intrepid explorers and civil servants are not better known.

## The Expedition

In his introduction, Maj Krishnatry explained his decision to go unarmed: "Most exploratory expeditions in the tribal frontiers have been armed or armoured with heavy escorts much to the cost and suppression of human rights, occupation of their lands, burning of villages, molestation of women, looting of livestock, crops and banning of trade. This was the trend in Abor, Mishmi and Miri expeditions led by the British armed forces during the 19th and early 20th centuries. The tribes of Arunachal Pradesh, thus fought back with stockades and their native resources. Peace was elusive due to revengeful bloodshed."

The former Indian Trade Agent in Gyantse described this tiny corner of the Subansiri FD which remained "the last to be explored for want of takers earlier for fear of warlike Tagins. It was for this that my wife and I volunteered and planned an unarmed friendship expedition. She became the soul of this expedition."

It was indeed the last unexplored region of the Country. Nobody had ever walked to the McMahon Line in this area. Krishnatry and his wife would themselves have to stop several days march from Migyitun, the border village in Tibet and the starting point of the pilgrimage.

Krishnatry explained his decision to ask Geeta to accompany him: "I felt that a woman was a more secure safeguard against tribal onslaught, while Geeta was firm she would rather trust peace with tribals than with armed escort in our company. This unarmed and unescorted expedition has served to be a watershed in the administrative history of Arunachal Pradesh and has, if it is to be believed by the cynic, set the pace for lasting peace between the tribals and the administration unlike the other tribal communities of the north-east region of India."

The Achingmori massacre had taken place less than two years earlier on the itinerary that Krishnatry proposed to take. The objectives of his journey were described thus: "This fairy tale is all about the multi-dimension expedition reaching out to the last line of our administrative control with benefits to the last villages Limeking, Ging and Na enclaves in order to evaluate their living conditions on the borderline, cooling off of the Tagin trauma caused by arrest of the ring leader of Achingmori massacre."

The Assistant Political Officer wrote: "When I took this expedition, Tibet was on my mind." The comparison with the feudal society in Tibet would remain present during his two-month tour.

**The Tagin Tribe**

As he departed, the APO received a briefing on the Subansiri region.

Mara Tabe, the *Gam*[11] of Limeking, Krishnatri's destination, explained to the Indian official that the place from where the Tagins migrated far in the North centuries ago, away from Tsari area in Tibet, which later became their habitat; little was known about the life and customs of the Tagins; Tabe, for example, explained: "It was not correct that Tagin houses were as large as those of Daflas (Nishis) whose largest house seen by me was an elongated housing structure containing as many as 15 hearths (family units or dormitories)." The Tagins were more individualistic and the largest Tagin house contained four hearths only.

Two days after their departure, the couple celebrated the Republic Day. They had an important visitor, Baki Tadi, the *Gam* of Chete, a leader of Balu clan, "whose dignified bearing and charming smile won over Krish. It was love at first sight. He gave him lots of firsthand information about our tour. He was rather a good intelligent speaker," Geeta wrote.

Baki told Krishnatri that Tabe was scared of coming to Taliha because of the Chinese and Tibetans: "People en route were not unfriendly but they did not know how to treat a *migom* (officer) as they had not met any."

---

11  The headman.

Capt Thukral of the Survey of India, who had reached only up to Chekhe in 1952, about 5 days' march away, had then been victim of a serious incident. Baki provided his own eyewitness version of the sad episode; he explained that the captain was shot at with a poisoned arrow which, in fact, was not targeting him but Bini Dachak, the Political Interpreter[12] accompanying him.

It was a reprisal to kill Bini Dachak of Miri tribe, who had stabbed a villager because the latter, while lighting his pipe, inadvertently scattered hot embers on the coat of the interpreter. The villager swore to take his revenge. The villagers were later genuinely regretful for Thukral's injury.

**Independence Day's Celebrations**

On that day, Krish spoke to about 2,000 Tagins at a community lunch: "not too bad a gathering," commented his wife. The APO praised the Tagin people who had the blessings of Ab Tani and Nyido, their first ancestors. He urged them to forget the bad episode of Achingmori massacre; he was here only to talk about their future prosperity, he affirmed.

Krishnatry said that he had come with his wife not to fight but to convince them to trust India; the Government had no evil intentions. The APO said that he would be going up to Limeking and Taksing and also to Migyitun[13] if the people desired so and "would make friends with the last brothers and sisters of this Country who had lost contact with the others."

The APO also said that Jawaharlal Nehru, the Prime Minster, wanted the hill people to progress and prosper, to have plenty to eat and buy and peace should prevail without any fear of each other: "He appealed to provide porters to help the programme with the blessings of our common ancestor, Ab Tani."

---

12  Known as PI.
13  In Tibet.

Krishnatry reiterated that he wanted to assure everybody that he had not come to catch them, punish them, burn their houses or loot their property; not even to settle cases among themselves.

His mission, on behalf of the Government of India, was different; he had come to find out what they needed or to hear what they had to say; he added that it just so happened to be a pilgrimage year; if possible, he would attend it. Geeta said that her husband did not make any false promises, he merely listened and agreed to help according to the Government's capacity. "Why should we not help you, if you help us?" was the answer of the villagers who attended.

**A Meeting Before their Departure**

Later, Krishnatry asked all the *Gams* to stay for a day as he wanted to "intimately talk to them to chalk out the details of the tour, thus briefing [them] as frankly and openly as possible."

Early morning on January 27, 1956, they sat around a fire "engulfed in the thick fog and started the meeting." Krishnatry wanted to put the thrust of the expedition on the *Gams*; he explained: "The Chinese professed friendship with India so far, but we shall have to be ready to thwart any evil design on their part." Geeta said that Krish was cautious not to inject an overdose of fear to avoid panic.

The features of the APO's exploration were then explained:

- a) It was exploratory in nature; to study their problems, to help them out unless they did not want it and not to burden them with administrative demands; therefore, no Assam Rifles force had come.

- b) No cases were to be settled and none should come for cases.

- c) Political presents to both poor and rich will be given as a token of friendship and goodwill.

- d) Peace must be maintained by all villagers and as we were not to harm them, they should also not try to harm or hinder the party.

- e) People must not run away but come to meet the APO.

f) Payment will be made even for a blade of grass if taken from anyone. We were coming only to give them, not to ask anything from them except porters.

g) Camps should be prepared and tracks improved on immediate payment.

h) Mem Saheb[14] was coming to meet and talk to the women and know their problems.

i) We are all sons of the common ancestor Ab Tani. We are, therefore, not Americans, nor *Kundens*[15], but the same as the Tagins.

j) We want to fight none and are friendly both with *Nime*[16] and *Kundens* but if anyone harmed Tagins in future, we will take up the cause of our brother Tagins. Yet we shall not interfere with customs, traditions, dress and religion but on the contrary promote this.

k) We will not interfere with trade with Tibet or contacts with the Tibetans.

The purpose of the APO's tour had thus been made clear.

## The Tsari Pilgrimage

One headman Baki Tadi, gave Krishnatry some information about the *Helu*, the Tsari pilgrimage. He said the Tibetan Government paid a heavy price to the Mara and other Tagins so that they did not obstruct the passage of the pilgrimage and harass them; on the occasion, the Mara Tagins were trading with the Tibetans using a barter system. Dyes, skins, cane and rice were exchanged for swords, salt, beads and woolen blankets.

Mara Tagins purchased rice from Mayu (lower) Tagins to sell it off. On their side, Tibetans alone reserved the right to sell to Tibetan

---

14 Geeta Krishnatry.

15 The Chinese communists.

16 The Tibetans.

Government or in others Tibetan areas[17]. Tabe had been called to the *Helu* for preparing tracks and also to negotiate for gifts.

Nime Deba[18] had sent a word to Tabe that this year Krishnatry's party should not go to Migyitun as the Chinese were also not coming. Apparently, the tribal population thought that the APO and his group were Americans and would fight with *kundens;* Tabe said that he was anxious to remain neutral.

**Limeking, the Base Camp**

We have to cut a memorable and arduous journey short, but four weeks later, the couple reached Limeking. On 21 February 1956, Geeta Krishnatry wrote: "The morning broke fresh and clear with a beautiful view of the snow mountains - perhaps more assuredly Takpashiri[19] and Palden Lhamo, the consort. We leisurely breakfasted waiting for Tabe who had first come at 7.30 am and found us asleep. He came again later slowly with his wife and sat down a few yards away from our table. His wife watched each and every action of ours."

The local Tagins had never seen the plains men[20] before; they thought that they were 'Amergans': "They were irked but impressed by the use of knife and fork combination and commented boldly about it. As we finished breakfast, Bishan Thapa[21] came running to announce a sortie was coming."

The author wrote that "this caught us pants down as we had told them we would clear the DZ[22] by 12 noon. But meteorological report of 'All Clear' did not come by too often and when they came they would come to off-load their quantified commitments for season."

---

17  Counties or dzongs.
18  A Tibetan official.
19  Dakpa Shelri.
20  The *Nipaks*.
21  The wireless operator.
22  Dropping Zone.

The narration continued: "We left Tabe and villagers bewildered as we jumped out to lay on DZ signals on the ground and to light smoke fire."

Geeta recounted that Dr. Bannerji, the doctor of the expedition, did a wonderful job in 'getting up' both in record time, while Krish took the mike to welcome the pilot and to inform him not to drop at Naba due to porterage non availability.

'Roger' said the pilot and Krish returned to the DZ to cross-check the preparation: "Thapa now took over the set nervously and foolishly asked the pilot to wait for 5 minutes for clear report. The zone was ready which fact was not visible to Thapa from his position. The pilot said 'okay', turned and dipped over us and made a beeline for Naba. We returned vainly hoping it would come back and knew the pilot would empty out the aircraft belly at Naba rather than wait. Naba was unprepared and unexpecting and so some loads spilled over to the Subansiri gorge. There was nothing one could do."

This was a regular story of air dropping in remote places of the border regions.

**Life in the Camp**

Geeta recalled the face of the villagers when they saw her coming out of her tent with a silk sari: "They of course had never seen fine silk, much less a sari in their remote lives. *Nime* [Tibetans] also put on silks but not so fine and were very impressed when I told them it was handwoven. Tabe and his wives came in and touched it and shook their heads at its finesse. I told Tabe that in India cloth even finer than that was handwoven."

Later, the villagers ceremoniously sat in a circle around Krish: "In the middle lay an array of sumptuous presents of blankets, rice, covered with cloth. Tabe sat quietly trying not to look at the presents, deep in his thoughts. Nguri Tern had told us previously that Tabe was very influential equally with the Tibetans and the people of the Khru valley and the Kamla valley."

Tabe then explained that all the routes converged at Limeking "which was a centre of power and all the tribes including the Tibetans looked at him as a key man to be cultivated and followed. He blamed Mayu Tagins for bringing in *Nipak*[23] Government in his domain. He was very unhappy at this as he would no longer remain influential and enjoy the monopolistic power in his sphere."

Geeta Krishnatry commented: "Nguri Tern's[24] diplomacy had worked to collect all intelligence and gauge his mind. Mara Tabe also did not want to accept the shot gun Krish had brought to present him as our frontline man. He pretended to be too old to use it."

Mara Tabe said: "Moreover, your Saheb will not be able to give me as much as *Chue*[25] did. What benefit will I have with *Nipaks*?"

How very true was his appreciation of the situation. Tabe wanted Tern to advise Krishnatry to keep Mara people out of administrative fold so as to leave his options open, but Tern had said he could not possibly say such things to a big officer like Krish."

Krish apologized for visiting them at an inconvenient time and causing Mara Tabe worry about his Tibet connection, but he added: "the foreigners whom they had referred to as 'Amergan' had neglected the welfare and development of frontier hill people and left them to their fate. Those hills and mountains had remained cut off and a feeling of alienation had grown between brothers and brothers. But once the foreign rule had ended, it was like a meeting between two brothers after centuries of parting."

Krishnatry said that he knew of Tabe's fame and the presents to be given to him were in full recognition of his status.

Tabe answered, "Abu, I must tell you frankly: we Mara people had heard of *Nipaks* but never seen them. On the other hand, we had

---

23 The Indian Government.

24 Political Interpreter Nguri Tem belonged to the category who were already well versed with the rules of the game laid down by the Indian Government. Nguri Tern had translated to the tribal people Krish's speeches so often on long tours that he used to be dubbed as 'His Master's Voice'.

25 The Tibetans.

known *Nime* people for many generations. And we have learnt to look upon them like we do to our own parents. Now that Sarkar[26] has come or rather has been brought here by the Mayu Tagins whose black deeds are well known. I am happy to hear what you have just now told me. But I would like to be left out as I am now too ill and may die soon. …I will be useless for Government work. Please do not appoint me a *Gaon Bura*,[27] nor give me these presents."

Krish told the headman that he should not fear death, the Indian doctor would remain to treat him when he returned safe from the *Helu*; he would be completely cured of his illness.

Krish added that he knew what was there in Tabe's mind including his attachment for *Nime* people and fear of *Kungens*[28] "Tabe must have known what would be the fate of *Nime* people after *Kungens* had conquered their country by force and it was time to think of safeguarding their present habitat from occupation by them and their being driven further to Mayu Tagin area."

Had Cha Dzong Chue[29] not told Tabe that *Gyagars*[30] were their friends, and now he wanted to tell him that *Kungens* also were *Gyagars*' friends and have never fought each other.

Tabe should, therefore, not fear, but also not depend on *Nime* alone for succour in times of need: "He could ask the Chue, if required. Tabe who had kept smiling all the time replied to this by saying that Saheb seemed to read his mind correctly," wrote Geeta.

"My doubts and misgivings are cleared," said Tabe.

Krish assured Tabe that there was no likelihood of fighting between *Nipaks* and *Kungens* and "even if it came, it would be peace again between big countries."

---

26 The Government.

27 Headman.

28 Chinese Communists.

29 The *Dzongpon* of Chayul.

30 The Indians or *Nipaks*.

Four years later, Longju a few days march away would see the first clash between the *Nipaks* and the *Kungens*. The Longju incident remains in India's collective memory as the first serious clash with the Chinese.[31]

Tabe said that he was very happy now and he accepted a brand new single barrel shot gun which was in one of just-dropped wooden crates.

That year, Krishnatry did not go further than Limeking.

We shall leave Krishnatry here and jump to the next 'cold' season.

## The Sailo Tour in 1957

In November 1956, Capt LR Sailo, Krishanatry's successor as APO in Taliha of Subansiri Frontier Division was instructed by the NEFA administration to proceed to explore "the hitherto unvisited areas of the upper Subansiri and the Tsari Chu[32] valleys upto the international borders on the West and North respectively of Limeking[33] during the cold season of 1956."

Sailo explained the rationale of his tour: "Being unvisited neither from Tibetan nor from the Indian side of the border, our knowledge of these areas is very limited in spite of the accounts gathered from the people of Limeking area who have frequent contact with the border people of both the valleys in courses of their barter trades and on the occasions

---

31 The Chinese considered that Longju was part of their territory; this resulted in the first serious clash between India and China in August 1959. On September 1, 1959, the Ministry of Foreign Affairs of China gave a note to the Indian Ambassador in China stating: "According to verified investigation conducted by the Chinese Government it is confirmed without any doubt that the armed clash between Chinese and Indian troops which occurred on August 25 1959 in the southern part of Migyitun in the Tibet Region of China was solely caused by Indian troops unlawful intrusion into the Migyitun area and their unwarranted provocative attack on Chinese troops. The facts pointed out in the Note of the Ministry of Foreign Affairs handed over to the Embassy on August 27 were true and established. The Indian troops must bear full responsibility for this serious border incident." (White Paper II, op. cit.).

This was, of course, not India's version.

32 Chu means river in Tibetan.

33 India's last outpost in the Subansiri valley.

of the Dolo[34] pilgrimage, the route of which passes through the Tsari Chu and the upper Subansiri valleys."

He pointed out that neither Captains Bailey and Morshead in the 1910s nor the explorer-cum-Botanist Kingdon Ward and his colleague, Frederik Ludlow in the 1940s, visited the Tibetan Frontier villages of Migyitun; it was terra incognita.

During the cold season of 1952-53, Capt Thukral had visited the Subansiri valley and two of the Survey Assistants reached up to Limeking and returned. It is on this journey that Thukral was accidentally shot by a Tagin with poisoned arrow near Kodak village, a few miles from Taliha, as mentioned earlier.

In October 1953, a group from Lower Tagin village in Taliha area ambushed and massacred officials with Assam Rifles escort at Achingmori on the left bank of the Subansiri, about 8 miles from Taliha: "As a result of this incident, a strong expedition was sent to the Tagin country and the ring-leaders were arrested and sentenced to various terms of imprisonment. The expedition was immediately followed by establishment of outposts at Dinekoli and Taliha with a view to tightening up control over the Tagin country."

As we saw, in the first months of 1956, Maj SM Krishnatry established an outpost at Limeking but did not go further.

In January 1957, a month before Sailo's expedition, one Kumar, Superintendent in Limeking was instructed to reconnoiter the route up to the confluence of the Subansiri and the Tsari *chus*. He reached his objective and proceeded as far as Lower Na settlement and "returned leaving the task of exploration up to the international border for the main party."

Sailo's two-month exploratory tour party left Taliha on January 21, 1957 and returned on March 29, "after successful exploration of the borders with Na and Migyiyun settlements".

## Objectives of the Tour

According to Capt Sailo's report, the main aims of the exploratory tour were:

---

34  Also called Tsari pilgrimage.

1. To attempt to solve by aerial reconnaissance the detailed problem posed by Maj SM Krishnatry regarding the exact location of Limeking and the courses of the western branch of the Subansiri river and of the Tsari chu which originates from Migyitun.

2. To prepare a sketch map showing the locations of villages or settlement and the courses of rivers.

3. To establish population figures of the various villages and settlements.

4. To explore up to the international borders with Migyitun and Na settlements by way of friendly relations with the Chinese and Tibetans across the border and not to be involved in any definite commitment in the event of any border dispute and to avoid armed clash at all costs.

5. To do everything possible to develop friendly relationships with the settlements of lower Na and make them look towards our Administrative Center at Limeking.

6. To submit recommendations about the correct administrative setup required including about an APO's Headquarters in the Tagin area; some sort of administrative center in the general area of Limeking and suitable places for establishment of Police Check Posts to safeguard the integrity of India's border along the Subansiri and the Tsari *chus,* or any other passes which might be found.

7. To handle tactfully during the tour, various problems such as, slavery, inter-village raids particularly in the case of inter-village feuds, South of Limeking on the watershed with the Ramla valley and to collect as much information as possible about the villages and passes in this area to help the Political Officers, Ziro and the Additional Political Officer, Aporijo to assess the administrative requirements for the Kamla valley and whether the area should be administered under the Political Officer in Ziro or under the Additional Political Officer in Aporijo.

8. To collect and send as much intelligence as possible regarding the Chinese activities across the border including international border matters, on the law and order situation, on geographical discoveries and any important matters which could be obtained during the tour.

These were the instructions given to the APO, who had the advantage of having an Army background.

## What did Sailo Achieve?

In his report to the Advisor to the Governor of Assam, the young Captain first mentioned that he could locate Limeking vis a vis the international border. A great achievement in itself considering that no Government officer had ever walked to the McMahon Line; though Captains Bailey and Moorshead had delineated the famous frontier from the other side of the 'Snow Line'.[35]

Sailo informed his bosses in Shillong: "The exploration of the Subansiri westwards of Limeking upto the international border beyond Lower Na settlements has been completed and the confluence of the Subansiri and the Yume chu has also been ascertained to locate at MO 4691 and not at MO 6593 as shown on the existing quarter inch map."

For the first time, the Indian administration in the NEFA could print proper maps of the area[36], Sailo wrote: "Having determined the precise location of the confluence of the Subansiri and the Tsari *chus* which locates at MO 6892 and not at MP 1097, the Tsari Chu valley has been explored up to the international border with Migyitun settlements."

A sketch map of the area was prepared with the locations of the villages and smaller settlements as well as the rivers, mountains, and main routes linking the villages; it included the population figures of these settlements.

Like his predecessor, Sailo could write: "The exploratory tour has been carried out with the policy friendly border relations with the people

---

35 The McMahon Line.

36 Maps of the area are still not available in the public domain today.

across the border and friendly relationship has been developed with the people of Lower Na and Migyitun settlements."

Let us remember that Migyitun was on the Tibetan side of the border and the departing point of the Tsari Pilgrimage.

With his Army background, the young Captain could collect some intelligence: "Reliable and confirmed information regarding the Chinese activities across the border has been obtained during the course of the exploratory tour."

We shall come back to this.

**Strategic Information Collected**

India could for the first time think of opening posts near the Tibet (now China) border: "The exploration of the upper Subansiri and the Tsari Chu Valleys up to the international borders has enabled proper assessment of the administrative setup required for the Tagin area and checkpost for the integrity of our international border on the Subansiri sector," noted Sailo.

This would have implications two years later, at the time of the Longju incident, for the preparedness to defend the McMahon Line.

Sailo gave a geography lesson to his colleagues of the IFAS as well as the bureaucrats in Shillong and Delhi; he explained: "The whole area is drained by the Subansiri and its tributaries which flow through narrow precipitous gorges. A belt of dense jungle thinly inhabited on both banks of the Subansiri from its confluence with the Sipi River continues until the border area is reached, when, the tangled jungles give place to pine and rhododendron covered slopes."

Reading Geeta Krishnatry's and Sailo's accounts one realizes the unbelievable difficulty to man the Indian frontiers in these areas. It has to be noted that the village of Takshing, the last village before the border on the Subansiri river, finally got a road only in 2018, as these lines were being written.

The description continued: "The general physical feature of the country is mountainous, greatly cut up by water courses and difficult of access. The mountain valleys are mostly covered with jungle and the crests of the ranges are hidden in snow. The steepness of the slopes and the density of the jungle render it extremely difficult country both from the point of view of the movement of troops and road-making, particularly from Naba and upwards. The movement along the valleys is confined almost entirely to the track which follows partly the river banks and steep slopes above the river bank and it is almost impossible to climb out of the valley except up the large streams. Unlike some other big hill rivers, the Subansiri has practically no flat ledges, probably due to the steepness of the country through which it flows with swift speed."

This would indeed make the deployment of troops difficult, two years later.

**Origin and Language**

An ethnological study was also conducted by the APO. They got to know that "The people of the area under report call themselves Tagins but they normally prefer to describe themselves as men of a certain village or settlement. The Tagins undoubtedly belong to Tibeto-Burman origin."

Cosmology of the tribes was also touched upon: "The Tagins claim their origin from one ancestor named *Tani*. In the matter of genealogies the Tagins have good memories and almost all sensible grown up persons can trace their accounts from Tani. While accepting their origin from Tani, the upper Tagins in Limeking, Na and Migyitun settlements claim their descent from *Nido* (rain). Unlike other Tagins, those who claim their descent from *Nido* (Rain) do not eat chickens. Tagin as a tribe is one without any broad divisions but the tribe is made up of several clans. They speak one dialect known as Tagin dialect. There are slight variations in the dialect of the Lower and the Upper Tagins but the Lower Tagins can easily understand the Upper Tagin and vice versa. The dialects of the Gallongs of the Siang Frontier Division, the Miris and the Bansnis of the Kamla and the Khru Valleys also seem to be very similar to Tagin dialect."

A genealogical chart was given as an Appendix to the report by the diligent officer.

The history of the Tagin tribe was also described. At one time, they were warlike savages, but in the 1950s, they were said to be peaceful and law-abiding people, "but they are thriftless, litigious and lazy."

It was said that men usually do not like to work leaving the greater share to women, in the fields or at home: "Inter-tribal or inter-village feuds were formerly of frequent occurrence and the spirit of revenge is usually passed down from generation to generation."

An interesting aspect was that the wealth of a Tagin was calculated in wives, slaves and cattle; Sailo commented: "The laziness of the average Tagins will undoubtedly stand in the way of their future economic development. In spite of freedom upheld in the Tagin society, the moral standard of men and women is not low."

When it came to some suggestions to the Indian Government, the APO stated that "expansion and consolidation of administration in the Tagin country being of recent occurrence, the line of communication is still at an infant stage. We have a fair-weather Dakota landing ground at Daporijo, which situates at the southern extremity of the Tagin area on the right bank of the Subansiri."

One of the main difficulties was that there were no proper porter tracks connecting these areas to Daporijo: "beyond Taliha right up to the international border the track is practically non-existent although it is possible to pass through during the cold season by following river-bank routes, a considerable portion of which submerge under water during the monsoon.

Unfortunately, the tracks were so steep and dangerous in several places, that it was difficult to reach the border: "There are no navigable rivers in the area. Porters are the only and indispensible form of transport whereas Wireless Telegraphy is the only means of inter-communication with the outside world," wrote Sailo.

Further, due to its extreme hilly nature, there was no suitable flat open ground for a landing ground in the entire Tagin country; even to find usable DZ's was a problem: "The local people normally use rope bridge which consists of 4 to 5 strands of stout canes attached at the extremities only, and lying loosely side by side. A cane ring lubricated with wild plantain supports the small of the back of the traveler who lies with his head towards the sky and employs his hands and feet in crossing the bridge. River crossing by this means is slow and very uncomfortable," observed the APO, who however remarked that raft ferries could be used in the Subansiri River only in the lower reaches: "where level waters are available at odd places."

He had also noted that the Tagins were skilful at constructing cane suspension bridges over the rivers and "in fixing ladders, foot-holds and hand-holds on cliff-faces by using jungle materials which are always available on the spot."

It would take several decades to make these areas accessible.

**Tribal Organisation of the Tagins**

Surprisingly, according to Sailo, there was little or no tribal, clan organisation among the Tagins, though in some cases, they would join forces to combat a common enemy "within certain narrow limits. It is improbable however that such combination would result in any form of combined organisation as each village is the unit and completely independent of its neighbor."

Only a few headmen had influence outside their villages, the APO thought it was unlikely that villagers could combine into a fighting force from more than a few groups of settlements.

The report admitted that the Tagins were more warlike than most of their neighbouring tribes, "but they have fully realized the authority and power of the Indian government since the operation as a result of Achingmori incident. Villages are small and are very seldom put in a state of defence." It was explained that their main defence was the difficult nature of the terrain.

They were usually armed with long spears, small knives, bows and arrows poisoned with aconite. Only a few people possessed Tibetan flintlock muskets and the effective range of the arrows was 80 to 100 yards. Sometimes, they would wear a cane helmet which could protect against sword-cuts. They generally used ambuscade or surprise attack. Sailo also said that it was unlikely that they would put up a strong defensive stockade against better-armed troops or stand against a well-armed Rifle Company.

## The Limits of Transportation

The main problem faced by the Indian administration was the transportation: "In view of limited porters being available in the Subansiri valley, all supplies such as rations, equipments, ammunitions etc of the troops must be airdropped for any operation in the area."

That was a huge problem; it still continues to be so more than 60 years later as the road between Limeking and Takshing is only partially opened.

For Sailo, the best season for military operations in the Tagin country was from November to March. Incidentally, two years later, the Chinese would attack the Assam Rifles in August.

## Sites for Posts and Defensive Positions

The Army background of Captain Sailo was extremely useful; he provided to the authorities in Shillong, a list of different sites to open or later to maintain posts. He gave a detailed description of different places as reported by the APO:

- a. Daporijo had a Landing Ground[37], the most suitable for Base Operation.
- b. Taliha and Dinekoli, about 30 miles from Daporijo, at an elevation of about 2,300 ft on the right and left bank of the Subansiri, respectively. Their DZs could be good defensive positions for the Subansiri Valley. At present, a porter track connected these two places; it would however not be a problem to convert them into muleable tracks.
- c. Nalo (on right bank) and Mochu (on left bank), located a few miles below the confluence of the Sebar and the Subansiri. It commanded the routes leading to Tibet along the Sebar and Kobu Rivers. They were suitable places with the possibilities of DZs in both places. The two places are

---

37 Or LG.

located at an elevation of about 3,000 ft. and were connected by porter tracks. The distance from Taliha and Dinekoli was approximately 20 miles. Mule tracks could be constructed to Nalo and Mochu without much difficulty.

d. Nacho (on right bank) commands two routes leading to Tibet along the Meni and the Koduk rivers was connected with the left bank by cane suspension bridge just below the confluence of the Subansiri and the Koduk. Nacho was a good camping ground with good water supply and possibility of DZ. Nacho was situated at about 3,000 ft and located some 42 miles from Tahila. Nacho was connected by porter track which could be converted into a mule track.

e. Naba (on right bank), about 59 miles from Tahila also provided a good camping ground with an emergency DZ. There was the possibility of constructing a mule track up to Naba.

f. Ging, about 3 miles from Limeking towards the border. The present DZ at Limeking could be improved by making a new DZ above the station. There was possibility of fairly good DZ above Ging village but water point was rather far. Ging and Limeking were connected by porter track with Tahila. The entire track required improvement for movement of troops but from Naba and onwards, the nature of the country seemed difficult for constructing buildings.

g. Takshing (on right bank of Subansiri) and Longju (on left bank of the Tsari Chu) one of Lower Na and Migyitun settlements respectively were suitable sites for opening Border Check Posts. Takshing was about 46 miles and Longju about 48 miles, Limeking and Ging (on right bank), about 7 miles from Tahila commanded the main routes to Tibet along the Subansiri and the Tsari Chu from Limeking. Longju was at an elevation of 9,200 ft, whereas the elevation of Takshing was estimated to be about 7,000 ft. The international boundary was roughly 1 mile from Longju and about 4 miles from Takshing.

h. Takshing and Longju had good DZ while at Longju, there was a possibility of constructing an Otter LG.

i. There was neither regular track nor traffic from Limeking to Takshing (Lower Na) and Longju (Migyitun). The contacts with the two places were confined to winter season only. There was, however, possibility of constructing porter track to Takshing along the right bank of the Subansiri by crossing the Subansiri somewhere near Gelensiniak (the confluence of the Tsari Chu and the Subansiri) along the Tsari Chu valley to Longju.

The APO explained that the nature of the Indian side of the border, along the Subansiri sector, was extremely difficult whereas the Tibetan side of the border was comparatively easier and more open, at least for air and road communications: "The difficulty has been greatly increased by absence of human habitations between Limeking and the Lower Na and Migytun settlements," concluded Sailo.

**Relation between the Tagins and the Tibetans**

An interesting part of the report dealt with the relations between the Tagins and the Tibetans; it was generally good, said Sailo: "This good relation seems to have been established as a result of annual barter trade between the Tagins and the Tibetans and also a diplomatic relation which Tibet has to maintain with the Tagins on the occasions of the *Dolo*[38] pilgrimage, the route of which passes through the Tagin country."

The relations had not always been good as Toni Huber[39] recounted in his master work on the subject; however, Sailo commented: "In spite of contact since long time past, the Tibetan influence on the social, economic, cultural and religious life of the Tagins on the whole is very poor."

This was a fact in 1957.

---

38 Referred to also as the Tsari pilgrimage; see Map 5, page 581.

39 *The Cult of Pure Crystal Mountain: Popular Pilgrimage and Visionary Landscape in Southeast Tibet*, (New York, Oxford University Press,1999)

## Chinese Activities

Even more interesting, the young Captain reported about the Chinese activities in the Tibet area across the Subansiri sector. According to information gathered from the locals by the APO: "the development had increased both in tempo and importance since the later part of 1954."

Sailo observed that the PLA activities are "reported to have confined to reconnaissance of the border regions by following the valleys of the Nye Chu, the Char Chu and the Tsari Chu with temporary post at Lhuntse Dzong, Chayul Dzong, Sanga Choling, Konam Dzong, Chikchar and Kyimdung Dzong."

Sailo estimated that the strength of Chinese in these areas varied from 100 to 400: "Only a few Chinese were reported to have actually visited the frontier settlements of Migyitun and Lower Na."

It is only after the flight of the Dalai Lama in March 1959, that the number of Chinese troops would greatly increase. The report mentioned: "During the later part of 1954, four Chinese soldiers visited Migyitun and returned to Chikchar after staying only for a few days."

But in the early part of 1956, another four Chinese, apparently from a medical unit, came to Migyitun and returned to Chikchar after halting for a few days, as the previous party did: "The Chinese were also reported to have carried on their propaganda in various areas and as far as the frontier villages. They distributed propaganda picture magazines on the development of the people of Communist China."

Sailo had seen copies of these magazines which had been kept by villagers of Lower Na and Migyitun settlements: "They looked the same as what we have seen in India except that they are printed in Tibetan character," noted the APO.

The two parties had apparently distributed the magazines to each house of Migyitun border settlement. More serious, the soldiers had carried out anti-Indian propaganda and said that the Chinese[40] and Migyitun

---

40 Called 'Kunden' by the Tagins.

people, being of the same stock were one whereas the Indians[41] were quite different with deep black eyes with long hair on their bodies and even on their faces."

The Chinese would repeatedly use this argument, even in the prisoner of war (PoW) camps in Tibet after the 1962 War to bring about a split between the Gurkhas and the North and South Indians.

When Sailo's party visited the area, the locals realized that there were also Indians with 'slanting' eyes. He said that the people of Migyitun stared at them when they landed in the Tibetan village. Kele, the Tibetan Headman of Pampte told them when the party visited his house that "the Chinese description of the Indians was all wrong and that all the members of my party looked exactly like Tibetans and not as hairy as the Chinese described Indians to them!"

The APO reported that according to his information, the villagers had requested the Chinese not to establish a post at Migyitun and in case the *Jagars* come, they would make the same request. The Chinese warned people in Migyitun "to immediately report news of Indian party's arrival or visit to Migyitun failing which they would be cut to pieces."

Though no Chinese visited Migyitun again till Sailo's visit to Migyitun on March 5 and 6, 1957, in winter 1954, two Chinese soldiers had come from Lung[42] and visited Lower Na settlements; they stayed four days in the house of one Taluk; they distributed material to the villagers and during their stay they looked around in the surrounding villages: "As the two Chinese did not have interpreter with them, their means of conversation with Na people was limited and mostly confined to gestures. After staying four days they returned towards Lung (upper Na)."

In early 1955, a Chinese visited Lower Na and asked the villagers to show him the way to Mara (Limeking). He pretended with the people of Lower Na that he was Indian and wished to go to India via Limeking; he was told that the track was too bad and that he would not be able

---

41 Called '*Jagars*'.
42 MR MO 3091.

to go to India via Limeking. Sailo said that he proceeded up to a cliff known as Pebebada[43] and later returned to Lower Na without boots and his equipments: "Unlike the parties who visited Migyitun, the Chinese who visited Lower Na were without arms and for want of knowledge of the local dialect; their means of conversation was very limited."

According to the APO's information, no Chinese visited Lower Na again after 1955 till Sailo arrived on February 18, 1957: "It is not a fact that the Chinese who visited Pebebada put a boundary mark by peeling the bark of a tree near Pebebada cliff. Neither the parties who visited Lower Na nor the parties who visited Migyitun claimed a particular area or put any boundary marks during their visits."

This would certainly push the Indian authorities to fix the border at Longju without referring the issue to the Chinese.

The latest information was that most of the Chinese troops had been withdrawn from these forward posts during the later part of 1956 leaving only 4 or 5 persons at Lhuntse Dzong. The APO added: "Unconfirmed report said that the Chinese withdrawal was due to fighting between the Chinese and the Tibetans in the Kham area."

Rumours of the uprising in Kham had spread "as far as the border villages of Lower Na and Migyitun settlements, that one old and influential monk told the people of Kham area, just before his death, that those who would eat a piece of his flesh after his death would not die in the hands of the Chinese and their bodies would become proof against any Chinese bullets!"

The APO said many Tibetans believed the dying monk and they were reported to have eaten the flesh "and actually fought the Chinese in the Kham area and killed several Chinese," but, subsequently the Tibetans were out-numbered.

An unconfirmed report had reached the border that the Dalai Lama advised the Tibetans to lay down their arms and to stop fighting the Chinese till the period of the five-year agreement with the Chinese Government would expire.[44]

---

43 Approximate MR MO 5593.

44 This probably refers to Zhou Enlai's promise to report the reforms.

Further, some reports said that 100 Chinese with one officer reinforced Lhuntse Dzong and summoned Tibetan Officials of Chayul Dzong and Sanga Choling for consultation in connection with construction of road between Lhuntse Dzong and Chedang[45]: "No report on the Chinese intention of returning to their forward posts along the Subansiri sector has so far been received," noted Sailo.

However, the Chinese had started lavishly distributing presents including cash, whenever they visited a place. The Tibetan Officials of Chayul Dzong and Sanga Choling had received Chinese rifles, radios and gramophones.

Though the roads in Central Tibet and towards Chumbi Valley were progressing fast, there was no move as yet to build roads towards the Indian border: "substantial progress has been made in the construction of motorable roads and air-fields in Lhasa areas, no confirmed report of actual making of motorable roads and airfields in the Tibetan region across the Subansiri frontier has been received. The Chinese troops stationed at Lhuntse Dzong are reported to have received their supplies by air-dropping," stated Sailo.

The Chinese authorities were clearly concentrating on the main road-links to the Mainland and the road towards Sikkim: "Neither Chinese colonization of the areas nor intention of replacement of Tibetan officials by direct Chinese administration across the region along the Subansiri sector has been reported."

But here, like in Yatung or Gyantse, several Tibetan boys and girls were chosen and "sent to unknown destinations without obtaining the consent of the individuals nor their parents, presumably for indoctrination."

They were probably sent to China for 'study' like we have seen in other places in Central Tibet: "This rumour seems to have increased the fear of Chinese in the minds of the Tibetans. If these rumours were true, the Chinese might try to establish schools in Tibetan region after completion of indoctrination of the boys and girls."

This had also started in areas like Yatung or Lhasa.

---

45  Probably Tsetang.

## Attitude of Tibetans

Generally speaking the Tibetans across the McMahon Line were 'not very happy' with the Chinese: "They hate the Chinese in general and pay a high regard to Indians."

Some recommendations were given by Sailo:

   a. Border checkposts: Along the main Subansiri Valley, Takshing, one of the Lower Na settlements, approximately 4 miles from the international border was suitable for establishing a border checkpost. Takshing was the last village of Lower Na settlements towards the border and had a good water supply and DZ; the site was also tactically sound. Takshing commanded routes leading to Tibet through the main Subansiri Valley, the Yume Chu and the Sagamal.

   b. Along the Tsari Chu Valley, Longju (a Tagin village) which was one of Migyitun settlements was suitable for establishing border checkpost. Longju was situated approximately half a mile from the international boundary but the actual post may be sited some distance south of Longju settlement where there is DZ and a possibility of Otter LG[46] which required hard labour and considerable expenditure. Longju was located at an elevation of 9300 ft and was covered with snow till March.

   c. At present, the routes to Takshing and Longju were opened only during winter months (normally from December to March). Lower Na and Migyitun settlements had no contact with Mara settlements (Limeking) during summer for want of tracks. There were no human habitations on the routes to these settlements from Mara. Hence, the necessity of constructing road communication from Mara linking the two settlements could not be overemphasized if India was to establish check posts at Takshing and Longju.

   d. The only available building materials at Takshing and Longju would be pinewood. Canes and bamboos were not available

---

46 Landing Ground.

in these localities[47]. The only solution would be to use planks for roofing, walling and flooring. Adequate number of sawyers, carpenters, nails would have to be arranged.

e. Due to absence of human habitations on both the routes to Takshing and Longju, which at present 8 days' march each from Limeking, porterage would be a great problem and air-dropping would be the only solution.

f. The question of opening check posts on the less important routes along the Meni, the Koduk and the Kobu rivers needed to be examined only after actual reconnaissance of the routes by land. During the aerial reconnaissance of these routes, not a single place was found suitable for DZ as the valleys were extremely narrow with high mountains mostly covered with snow.

This was an accurate description of the situation on the ground; unfortunately, Longju would witness the first serious clash with the Chinese PLA in August 1959; that was after the Dalai Lama took refuge in India.

It is clear that in 1957, the Chinese were not in a position to undertake a military expedition against India.

---

47  Probably due to high altitude.

## 15

# The Uprising in Eastern Tibet

In 1955, some events not directly linked to the relations between India and Tibet started to unfold in Kham.

The Tibetan activist Jamyang Norbu has put it in perspective from the Tibetan point of view: "The people of Kham, or Eastern Tibet, rose up against Chinese occupation when Communist authorities began to implement 'democratic reform', the program to eliminate monastic and tribal leadership and eradicate the traditional social system. The program involved *thamzing*[1] struggles, public humiliation, beating, torture, forced confessions, imprisonment and often executions. Suicides were widespread in areas where democratic reforms were announced."[2]

These events had serious consequences for the Chinese occupation of the plateau and the outcome would regularly be reported by the Consul General in Lhasa as well as by the ITAs.

Jamyang Norbu recounted the origin of the uprising in Lithang in Kham: "In exile folklore, an archetypal origin of sorts has been ascribed to the events of 1956 in the Lithang Uprising. The paramount resistance chief of Lithang, Yunru Pon was not only a very young and an enigmatic personality, but he also died under the most dramatic of

---

1 *Thamzing* was a struggle session during which those deemed class enemies were publicly humiliated and tortured in the Mao era, particularly during the Cultural Revolution.

2 Jamyang Norbu, *The Forgotten Anniversary - Remembering the Great Khampa Uprising of 1956*, see https://www.phayul.com/mobile/?page=view&id=14993&t=1&c=4

circumstances. He and other Lithangwa chiefs and warriors defended the great monastery of Lithang (founded by the 3rd Dalai Lama) against numerous Chinese infantry assaults, artillery bombardment, and bombing by Chinese aircraft based at Chengdu. When his ammunition ran out Yunru Pon faked a surrender and approaching the Chinese commander shot him dead with a concealed pistol, before being gunned down by Chinese soldiers in a most spectacular manner. One eyewitness, Loto Phuntsok, testified to the International Commission of Jurists in 1959, that 500 Chinese soldiers fired on Yunru Pon."[3]

The Tibetan author has an interesting take on the happenings in Lithang; he believes that the uprising "should be considered the beginning of our great national revolution because these were not isolated events but involved many districts, regions and tribes. The uprisings were, surprisingly, coordinated to quite an extent. According to one source twenty-three major chiefs of Lithang, Chatreng, Batang, Lingkashi, Nyarong, Gyathang, Gyalrong, Horko, Gaba and other areas, communicated with each other and arranged a common day to launch the uprising. This was the eighteenth day of the Tibetan New Year of 1956."

The uprising in Kham was important for several reasons; first it was the first rebellion again the Chinese presence in Tibet; it was also a clear message that the 'reforms' could not be forced on the masses in Eastern Tibet. The movement later spread to Central Tibet, eventually forcing the Dalai Lama to leave the country in March 1959.

**Discontent in Tibet**

Delhi was aware that something was brewing in Tibet.

On July 25, 1955, the Prime Minister wrote a note to the Secretary General of the Ministry, that in the course of a talk with the Maharajkumar of Sikkim, the future Choegyal told Nehru: "There was a good deal of discontent in Tibet. At present the question agitating the people there was the formation of the Committee, of which the Dalai Lama was the Chairman, to frame Tibet's Constitution or whatever it

---

3   For Jamyang Norbu. op cit.

was.[4] The Chinese Government would appoint this Committee. It was not clear to me how this Committee would be constituted, but the Maharajkumar seems to indicate that some people were going to be elected or nominated by Tibetan groups to it."[5]

The Consul General[6] in Lhasa had reported a fear that during the Preliminary Committee's nomination process, 'the extremist anti-Chinese wing' would be gathering in Lhasa to try to take the control of the Committee: "Having done so, they would probably take up a strong attitude against China and possibly even demand independence. If they did so, there was again the possibility of the leaders of this movement being arrested. If this happened, there would be trouble in Tibet," wrote Nehru.

According to the same note, the Maharajkumar hinted at trouble spreading outside Tibet into some border regions of China, like parts of Yunnan Province.

Nehru commented: "I am passing this on for record in the Ministry for what it is worth. I am inclined to think that the Maharajkumar tends to give a one-sided picture of the situation, because his own contacts are with a particular type of person who comes out of Tibet. We should not, therefore, accept his appraisal as necessarily correct. But it does indicate that things are not well in Tibet."

Unfortunately, the situation was extremely serious and it would continue to deteriorate during the following months.

---

4  As a result of adoption of the Chinese Constitution, the State Council passed a resolution for the establishment of the 'Preparatory Committee for the Autonomous Region of Tibet' (PCART) to further integrate the administration of Tibet with that of PRC. With the Dalai Lama as Chairman, Panchen Lama and Zhang Guohua as Vice Chairmen and Ngapo Ngawang Jigme as Secretary General, the fifty-one-member PCART was to function as the central administration of Tibet.

5  All other documents in this chapter, except specifically mentioned, are from the Nehru Papers (JN Collection) held at the Nehru *Memorial* Museum and Library in Delhi. The 'papers' are not indexed.

6  PN Menon.

## Popular Revolt in Eastern Tibet

In his report for the months of November and December, 1955, Menon had mentioned that the Chinese did not rely on common Tibetans.

This had been a fact from the time the first Chinese troops arrived on the plateau till the March 1959 uprising which forced the Dalai Lama to flee to India; the so-called masses never accepted the Chinese presence and the Communist leadership in turn never relied on the common folks.

The report of the Consulate informed the Ministry that during early December some rumours had started circulating in Lhasa that a large number of Khampas had arrived in the Tibetan capital: "[they] were conspiring with the monks of three big monasteries for an open revolt against the Chinese." Menon explained that this created panic amongst the Chinese: "They barricaded their camps, dug trenches, reinforced guards, tightened their security measures which included carrying of arms at all times by their personnel (civilian as well as Army). Even those Tibetans who normally had free access to some of the camps and the residences of Chinese had to possess a permit which was carefully checked by the sentries before they allowed entry."

The rumour mill was turning faster than the prayer wheels in Lhasa. One day three hundred Chinese labourers camping in one of the parks in Lhasa disappeared one night: "They left most of their belongings behind. We understand that as these people were unarmed, the Chinese removed them into a safer place."

It just showed the deteriorating atmosphere in the Tibetan capital. A telling comment from Menon: "The benefits which the Chinese are bestowing on Tibetans by opening schools, hospitals, construction of roads at enormous cost has not in the real sense attracted the common Tibetans. It is only the armed strength of the People's Liberation Army in Tibet that is keeping the Chinese flag aloft in Tibet."

One can imagine the situation in Eastern Tibet where the reforms had systematically been introduced (forced) by the Communists; however, the reports reaching Lhasa from Kham were still conflicting: "Some said that the trouble was in full swing and spreading and Chamdo was in insurgents' hands while according to some the trouble had been checked effectively by Chinese and it was now only limited to sporadic cases of 'hit and run'."

The news was mainly conveyed by people arriving from Kham, despite the ferocious repression "there are still some dissatisfied Khambas[7] who ambush Chinese motor convoys and raid Chinese supply points on Lhasa-Sikang highway.[8] Most of these insurgents have taken to hills and are in small parties. And it has not been possible for the Chinese to round them up."

In Lhasa, not everyone was enamoured of the Khampas, but "the general hatred of Tibetans especially Tibetan monks, the severe cold and other difficulties and hardships on account of lack of proper means of communications are not deterring Chinese from carrying out their development programmes in Tibet," observed the Consul.

The 'development' work continued relentlessly. Menon cited: "[the] Nagchukha - Gartok[9] road is under construction; the road between Lhasa and Tsethang is nearing completion; a fully air conditioned hospital is coming up steadily East of Potala at Lhasa; construction programmes at Shigatse, Gyantse, Yatung and other important places in Tibet are in full swing. The hydro-electric power station at Dote, near Lhasa, which the Chinese took over from the Tibetan Government has been provided with new engines and is now providing more power for lighting in Lhasa. Some of the streets in Lhasa have now street lights."

---

7   Normally spelt Khampas.

8   Lhasa Sichuan.

9   Wikipedia says: "The 301 Provincial Road (S301) is a very scenic trip in the middle of nowhere. This asphalted road passes through remote areas, so you need to be prepared. It's 1,374 km (853 miles) long and stays for a long time very high (over 4,500m above the sea level) over a long high plateau. Even in summer, the temperature might drop from 20°C at daytime to -10°C at night. In July and August, it may rain continually for several days and you even can confront with snowy days. …The bigger problem than the condition of the road is extremely low oxygen for engine combustion. It has a well-deserved reputation for being dangerous because of unpredictable snowstorms and blizzards, and driving under these conditions, can be extremely challenging. The road links the cities of Ngari and Nagqu."

The Chinese were banking on these 'gifts' to the masses to convince them of their benevolence. But sometimes a small incident would aggravate the Tibetan resentment. One day, the Chinese dropped six of their parachutists just outside Lhasa: "The exact purpose for which they were dropped is not known. But people in general felt that the Chinese wanted to show to Tibetans that in case of trouble they can get reinforcements by air also," noted Menon. Anxiety was mounting on the plateau.

**A Letter from Mao**

Already by the end of 1955, Mao knew that it would not be easy to impose reforms on the recalcitrant Tibetans. At that time, the Communists made a differentiation between the populations of Eastern and Central Tibet. While Mao was ready to wait for the implementations of the 'reforms' in Lhasa and around, the same 'reforms' were ruthlessly implemented in the Kham region.

On November 25, 1955, the Great Helmsman wrote to the Dalai Lama: "you should not be in hurry," to undertake reforms as if it was the Tibetan leader who wanted to force unwanted reforms on his own people; this 'advice' would not translate into improved conditions on the ground.

It is worth quoting the Great Helmsman's letter: "Thank you for your letter of 6 July 1955. I miss you a lot. I miss those happy moments when you were in Beijing and we were together. When can I see you again? Maybe in another three years when the second National People's Congress starts its meeting, you will come. Many things happened after you left Beijing, and I feel pretty good about these things. The PCTAR is going to be established soon. People of all ethnic groups are all very happy about it. Tibet is moving forward, but certainly you should not be in a hurry. It will be enough if there is some progress each year. I hope you take good care of your health. Things are generally good here, despite some mistakes we made. We are trying to correct our mistakes. China is a big country that is not rich and strong at the moment. We hope to make China a rich and strong country through the efforts of people of all ethnic groups, and through a few five-year plans. Tibet is full of hope, and I hope you do a good job in Tibet. I am very glad to see the Tibetan flowers you sent me with your letter. I now send a flower to you. I hope to get your letters often. Just drop a few words. You don't have to be formal. Please ask Comrade Zhang Guohua about other things. I have told Zhang Guohua to consult with you fully. Wishing you happiness and good health."[10]

This would not stop the growing resentment against the Chinese occupation.

After a few years of reforms and the increasing resentment of the local populations against the Chinese occupation, the people started to revolt. We talked about it in a previous chapter.

The April Report noted: "A very serious armed uprising has broken out in the Dzako area[11] against the Chinese authorities." The revolt was apparently triggered by the introduction of land reforms and attempts to disarm the Khampas: "At a place near Darjye Gompa near Kantze, over 500 Chinese troops were killed in bitter fighting. The difficult terrain is helping the people to resist the Chinese, who are adopting ruthless measures, including aerial bombing," said the Consulate.

Delhi was informed that the trouble had also spread in a south-easterly direction and had reached the Lithang area: "The monks and landed classes have joined together and are said to be determined to inflict the maximum damage on Chinese."

In Lhasa, the population had heard of the troubles and "there is considerable nervousness of its spread to other areas of Tibet," noted the Report.

For the first time in May, the serious armed uprising in Eastern Tibet was confirmed: "the trouble has spread to the adjoining Amdo and Kham areas and shows no signs of disappearing. All reports speak of wide-spread guerilla attacks by the rebels against the Chinese Forces and their communication lines, including the Tibet-Sikang highway."

---

10 Melvyn C. Goldstein, *A History of Modern Tibet, Volume 3: The Storm Clouds Descend, 1955–1957*, (Berkeley, University of California Press, 2014), page 288.

11 Lying between 32 and 32.5 degrees North and 99 and 100 degrees East.

Some information received in Lhasa tended to confirm that both sides had suffered heavy casualties (the Chinese casualties were estimated at a few thousands).

One report, probably untrue, spoke of large numbers of freed KMT prisoners and even PLA deserters joining the Tibetan rebels.

Another report mentioned the capture of truck loads of Chinese ammunition and arms by the 'insurgents' including some anti-aircraft guns. It was not easy for the Consulate to check all the rumors, though there was strong evidence showing attacks on bridges, road workers on the Tibet-Sikang highway which had brought communications on this route to a standstill. The Report added that there was ample evidence of large scale movement of Chinese troops into the troubled areas from Central Tibet.

In June, Delhi was informed that the revolt in the border areas of Tibet and China continued; it was assuming more and more the shape of guerilla resistance on the part of organised bands in these areas. Menon commented: "The earlier report about the complete destruction of the Lithang monastery by bombing by Chinese planes has not proved to be entirely correct. While some damage was done by bombing to the town the monastery sustained only slight damage."

However some reports mentioned that a number of Chinese soldiers and officers had been captured by the 'rebels', the trouble was affecting the areas of Chok-chung, Chatin, Dragor, Tongkor, Chokrong, Nyaktong; all in Kham province of Eastern Tibet; this was in addition to the Dzako and Golok areas already mentioned. Menon, who had sent a special report separately added: "There are also reports of local clashes between the people and Chinese soldiers in the Derge and the Poyul areas."

The following month, the Consul had to admit that there were conflicting reports about the revolt in the border areas of Tibet and China: while some reports spoke of it as dying down, others said it was becoming a widespread guerilla resistance: "The truth seems to be somewhere in between and there are some indications that a team of Chinese officials has been sent from China to enquire into the causes of the trouble and also to effect a settlement with the partisans," noted the Report.

In August, a Mission was sent by the Tibetan Government to the troubled spots 'under the instructions of the Central Government in Beijing'. The Mission consisted of Ngapho Shape (Leader), Gyawa Karma-pa, Topgye Pangdatshang, Mento-pa and a 5th rank official named Dencha who had some experience of Eastern Tibet and his 'reliability from the Chinese point of view.'

The Consulate believed that the Mission demonstrated 'in a conclusive fashion' the lie of Chinese propaganda which said that there was never a revolt in Tibet or in Tibetan speaking areas of Eastern Tibet; the reports spoke of an intensification of the trouble and the Sikang highway being impracticable due to the constant rebel attacks.

The Report specifically mentioned the considerable re-deployment of Chinese troops "in such a way as to surround the whole troubled belt so that the Chinese can undertake a big campaign if the present peace Mission fails in its objective."

Delhi was informed in September of the return of the Tibetan Government Mission: "From most reliable sources it is understood that the Mission failed in its purpose. The party led by Ngapho Shape had proceeded to Chamdo and tried to contact the main leaders of the present revolt. The leaders refused to turn up and conveyed their feelings through some minor intermediaries."

Unfortunately we don't have the full report from the Indian Mission Lhasa as it was sent in a Weekly Letter, Menon, however, noted: "One thing is clear that the pacification of the troubles through negotiations backed by the moral authority of the Dalai Lama has received a serious set-back and that the Chinese will now be forced to deploy all their military resources in that area and its neighbourhood in order to suppress the revolt."

It was a great setback for the Chinese themselves. The Consulate now believed that "this will be a long drawn out affair as the populations revolting have taken to hills and jungles which are perfect sanctuaries and bases for carrying out guerilla warfare."

It was now confirmed that the troubles had virtually severed the Sikang highway for normal traffic. Menon had been informed by the Czechoslovak trade representative in Beijing who had brought to Tibet some diesel trucks manufactured in the Tatra factory: "He admitted that they had come by the Tsinghai[12] route and were returning by the same road as the Sikang highway could not be used for obvious reasons."

He further told the Indian diplomat that the temper of the people revolting is one of "extreme bitterness and fatalism and therefore the prospects of their giving up the struggle in return for vague Chinese promises to return to the status quo are very slim."

It was indeed.

## The Visit to India

Though we shall deal with the Dalai Lama's and Panchen's Lama visit to India at the end of this volume, a small incident related to the Khamba revolt in worth relating here.

It happened in January 1957, while the Dalai Lama was visiting the place where the Buddha had been enlightened.

In his report of the visit, Apa Pant, the PO noted: "Gaya was also a rush because that very next day arrived news that fresh fighting had broken out in the eastern Kham areas and that the people with their newly formed Buddha Battalions *Tensung Sangye* were anxious to take up arms at the word of command from the Dalai Lama in Tibet itself against the Chinese."

In Lhasa too, the situation was tense: "News arrived that fighting had taken place in a Lhasa cinema where four persons were killed and that the Chinese had put up sand-bag barricades around all houses where Chinese were staying and that a contingent of 500 Khambas had arrived to incite the Lhasa people to 'fight' it out now when the Dalai Lama was in India, safe," wrote Pant.

At that time, many in the Lama's entourage wanted the Tibetan leader not to return or at least, to stay as long as possible in India: "Gaya was a

---

12  Qinghai.

rush because there was pressure from the pilgrims who had come from Tibet recently for the Dalai Lama to delay his departure for Tibet so that 'they could fight it out with the Chinese."

The oracle had to be consulted and a quick decision taken about the 'hurry-up-the-pilgrimage' message from the Chinese Embassy in Delhi. Two messages from Zhou Enlai were received and discussed: "Gaya at the same time was also the place of quiet and peace and of the scholarly dignity of a sermon held under the Bodhi tree in the ancient traditional way, a sermon lasting for nearly four hours explaining the Four [Noble] Truths and the Eight-Fold Path, a sermon which was listened to in pin-drop silence, a sermon where not even a baby cried," wrote Pant.

The alarming messages were probably one of the reasons which decided the Dalai Lama to return to his homeland.

**Situation as the Dalai Lama Returns to Tibet**

In his report to the Ministry in February 1957, the PO detailed the happenings in Kham: "Anti-Chinese uprisings in Eastern Tibet appeared to be continuing. In November [1956], to coincide with the visit of the Dalai Lama to India and in order to bring pressure on the Chinese authorities, about 20,000 Khampa rebels are said to have assembled at Kamdok Thuga and the Chinese garrison there was wiped out. The Khampa leaders of Sikang and the Amdo rebel leaders of Chaukar, Thuchu etc. in the North appeared to be operating in collaboration. There are reports, of the Chinese, on the one hand, attempting to conciliate the people of the troubled areas by saying that there would be no 'liberation' except with the 'consent of the people', and on the other of their having destroyed some monasteries in Kham by bombardment and machine-gunning from the air."

But that was not all, the Tibetan Government in Lhasa and the Chinese authorities became more and more nervous; Pant mentioned greatly strengthening precautionary measures "against possible uprisings in Central Tibet and augmenting the military force in the Lhasa area. There was an increased display of equipment by large bodies of their troops who were frequently staging route-marches in the city and its neighbourhood."

The presence of the Dalai Lama could play an important role to cool down the possibilities of an open conflict. It was one of the reasons why the Tibetan leader was keen to return to Lhasa; the report said: "There was some apprehension that following the absence of the Dalai Lama from Tibet there would be a serious outbreak of anti-Chinese agitation, but the fear has not, by and large, materialized, perhaps due to appreciation of the strength of the Chinese military force, and probably also due to the Dalai Lama's own appeal to the people, on the day of his departure for India, to maintain order and peace in the country."

According to another report from Lhasa, the Khampa rebels had planned to stage an armed revolt on December 15, 1955 in the Tibetan capital with the help of the several thousands of Khampa monks studying in the three big monasteries. The monks ultimately refused to participate to the uprising: "The monks are reported to have pointed out that a revolt against the Chinese would be most unfortunate specially when the Dalai Lama was in India as the Government of India's guest," remarked the PO.

In his next report in March 1957, Pant said that Kham did not seem to be normal as yet: "There are reports that Chinese military convoys carrying arms and ammunition and supplies are still being attacked and looted by the rebels in that region, and this is believed to be the chief means by which the rebels replenish their fighting power."

It was also said that they were assisted by KMT military officers who had been released from captivity in various parts of Kham: "In Chamdo, the number of Chinese troops is reported to be some 10,000. They seem to be somewhat nervous and fearful of attacks from the Khampa Tibetans. Elsewhere, however, the law and order situation was generally quiet."

The situation was overall quite worrisome, but there was nothing that India could do, except to analyze the unfolding events.

## Some Conclusions

The developments in Eastern Tibet would have several consequences:

- ➢ They would trigger an uprising in Kham whose consequences poured over into Central and Western Tibet.
- ➢ It would force the Communist leadership to go slow on the reforms. Even though the PCTAR was officially set up in March 1956, many of its features would not be implemented before April 1959, once the Dalai Lama left Tibet for India.
- ➢ The Chinese would accelerate the rhythm of development, in particular the construction of roads.
- ➢ To show their bonafide intentions about the 'reforms', the Chinese would risk allowing the Dalai Lama to attend the Buddha Jayanti celebrations in India. We shall come back to this in the next chapters.
- ➢ The Indian Prime Minister would often dismiss the happenings in Eastern Tibet, as rumours. It would probably be one of the factors which stopped him to support the idea of the Dalai Lama staying on in India after the Buddha Jayanti celebrations.

After their visit to India, as we shall see in the last chapters, the two highest Lamas of Tibet would return to the Roof of the World to try to retrieve the situation, but the conditions in Tibet looked already beyond salvation.

# 16

# The Changes in Western Tibet

On January 4, 1955, Lakshman Singh Jangpangi, the Indian Trade Agent in Gartok submitted the Annual Report of his tour of Western Tibet, to Apa Pant, the Political Officer in Sikkim.[1]

Like every year, Jangpangi started from Almora and proceeded via Lipulekh Pass to return through Niti Pass and the Garhwal route.

Before starting the journey, the ITA spent time in Kolkata to purchase the required stores for the following months on the Tibetan plateau; Delhi too was on his itinerary for a briefing and consultation with officials of the Ministry of External Affairs.

Necessary cash was withdrawn from the Treasury at Almora for the entire tour, this included the cost of transportation: "I received all possible help from the district authorities of Almora and Garhwal and my appreciation of their kind help," he wrote.

The ITA's party consisted of a doctor, an accountant, an enumeration clerk, a *jemadar*[2], a ward orderly and six *chaprasis*.[3] Most of the 'seasonal' staff joined the team at Almora.

---

1 Annual Report of the Indian Trade Agent, Gartok; Department: Ministry of External Affairs, Indian Trade Agency Gangtok; Branch: Western Tibet; Year: 1955; File No. Progs., Nos. 9(5)-WT, 1955. Available at the National Archives of India, New Delhi.

2 A junior official. Originally, a *jemadar* was an armed official working for a zamindar (feudal lord). He was in charge of fighting and conducting warfare, mostly against the peasants and common people who lived on the lord's land.

3 Usually, a junior office worker carrying messages or files.

## The Communication

The Almora-Lipulekh and Niti-Garhwal routes were recognized trade routes linking India with Western Tibet under the 1954 Tibet Agreement: "These routes, therefore, require to be maintained properly up to the Indian border, so that the authorities on the other side can be asked to keep their side of border clear for traffic as long as possible. The condition of some of these roads is deplorable and there is practically no road other than beaten track on the Tibetan side of the border," observed Jangpangi. Was this because the Chinese had not started implementing the Agreement on the ground?

Jangpangi gave more details on the state of the infrastructure on the Indian side of the border.

The ITA first described the route from Almora to Lipulukh Pass: "The bridle path from Almora to Askote[4] was in good repairs, except one or two damaged bridges. The next stage from Askote to Garbyang which was still under the control of the Almora District Board was in a very bad condition for want of proper maintenance and improvements. The Board [of the UP government] with a limited fund at its disposal cannot attend to proper repairs of this neglected road which became very dangerous during the rainy season when some portion of it washed away dislocating whole traffic for a considerable time."

Today, more than sixty years later, the access to the border passes and the Tibetan plateau remains difficult, but in 1954, the ITA stated: "Even in normal time this road is not safe for animal transport, so coolies are employed from Dharchula to Garbyang, 35 miles. The last lap from Garbyang to Lipulekh is not maintained at all. The whole stretch of this last portion is a beaten track and goes over to Nepal for about 6 miles."

Jangpangi reiterated the political and commercial importance of the route, as it was also the main route for pilgrims on their way to Kailash.

---

4  Askot or Askote is a small Himalayan town in today's Pithoragarh district of Uttarakhand in India. It is a part of Kanalichhina development Block and Didihat Tehsil.

Jangpangi could only suggest that the Uttar Pradesh Government should give top priority "to this neglected and important road. There is also necessity of Rest Houses from Dharchula to Garbyang and at Kalapani, 6 miles below the pass."

His return route via Garhwal was also described: "There is a motorable road from Kotdwara[5] rail-head to Pipalkoti, 157 miles and the bridle path thereafter to Niti village is good for pack animals except for the suspension bridges which are shaky and dangerous. The road from Joshimath to Niti, 44 miles, suffers from inadequate repairs, which is not due to lack of funds but lack of supervision. When I came down through this road early November, [the] whole population of Niti Bhotias were on downward migration and they were experiencing lots of trouble over diversion on damaged portions of the road, which could have been repaired properly, if the Department took a little care," reported Jangpangi.

The last 19 miles from Niti village to the Pass, there was no road; though rumours were circulating that the Government planned to construct a road up to the border; the ITA wrote: "If this last portion is completed, this road will be the easiest of all the roads and the pass is very low, about 14,000 [feet]."

Jangpangi also noted the improvement of the last portion had already been sanctioned by the Central Government; the need of Rest Houses on the route from Joshimath to Gialdung, one stage beyond Niti village was also mentioned.

### The Almora-Kungri Bingri Route

The third route mentioned by the ITA was from Almora to Milam and Kungri Bingri pass; though he did not use it in 1954, he had been informed that "the repair work there was not satisfactory. This is another route mostly frequented by the pilgrims and bulk of the trade with Western Tibet passes through it."

Jangpangi noted that the road was under the Public Works Department up to Milam though last portion to the Kungri Bingri pass was not

---

5   Kotdwar is a tehsil in Pauri Garhwal district. Its old name was Khohdwar, meaning the gateway of the river Khoh; Kotdwar is located on the bank of river Khoh.

maintained: "It is essential that this last portion may also be improved. This route also lacks from the absence of Rest Houses for the tourists," he observed.

## The Knela to Darma Pass and Joshimath to Mana Pass Routes

The report mentioned that there were good roads up to the last villages of Bidang to the Darma Pass and to Mana Pass, though the last portion before the border was not maintained: "There is need for improvements of these portions. These two routes are also recognized links with Western Tibet," he informed the PO.

## The Simla-Shipki Pass route

Known as Hindusthan-Tibet road, it was one of the best routes to reach Tibet. There were Rest Houses all the way from Simla to Namgia village, the last stage on the Indian side: "I do not know now what the present condition of this road is, but Bashahri traders complained that the last portion from Chini to Shipke[6] is being neglected by the Department."

Jangpangi suggested that the issue should be taken up with the concerned authorities.

His conclusions on this important issue of the trade routes to the plateau, were that if the proper improvements of all these trade routes and other minor tracks were properly made "there is every likelihood of increased trade with Western Tibet. The Sino-Indian Agreement and subsequent Trade Agreement of 1954 have cleared the way for smooth trade with Tibet."

Unfortunately, not much effort would be done by India during the following years, and even less on the Tibetan (now Chinese) side, despite the trade agreement.

## The Border Trade

After briefly describing the routes, crucial for the trade but also for pilgrimage and for strategic reasons, Jangpangi gave an idea of the trade with Western Tibet.

6   Shipki-la.

His first remark was: "The volume of Indian export trade was far in excess of the past average. This was mainly due to the conclusion of Agreements with China on Tibet and partly to the Tibetan Kumbh year falling in 1954." He, however, admitted that even if Indian traders were confident "of continuance of their trade dealing with Western Tibet and were hopeful of [a] good year, but their expectation did not materialize fully."

They could not dispose of all the goods that they had taken to the plateau, and the margin of profit was too small considering all the trouble and expenses they had incurred while taking merchandise to Tibet: "The cloth business showed an exceptional depression and it proved profitless to the merchants," the ITA commented.

Jangpangi provided the main reason: many Tibetan traders got scared of the Chinese activities during 1953 and they stayed away from Trade Marts: "The Chinese had then also told all the Tibetans of their intention of extending trade to the Tibetan villages themselves."

Jangpangi explained that contrary to the expectation, "the Chinese suddenly withdrew from the competitive market and purchased goods for their requirements only."

Unfortunately, the Tibetans had no knowledge of this change. The ITA affirmed that the Chinese changed attitude had "a bearing on the fruitful discussion of our delegation at Peking. The Tibetans got news of Sino-Indian Agreement and Chinese withdrawal from official trading when they actually came to the Marts, it is therefore expected, unless anything untoward happens, to have a hopeful effect on next year's trade, which is likely to be beneficial to both Indian and Tibetan merchants."

With very few Tibetan merchants coming to the Marts, the local goods and even the Chinese brick tea became scarce and expensive; the wool import to India became affected by this: "The Indian traders in their zeal to have larger quantity of wool paid competitive price up to Rs.120

per *maund* [7] and price of *pasnam* [8] (goat fur) also rose to Rs.12/8 per *seer* [9], nearly double to that of last year."

While the barter of grain was favourable to Indian traders, the transaction had lost some market, due to the fact that cheap Indian salt was now easily available in remote hill areas which had formerly depended on Tibetan salt: "As this barter deal brings in wool as well, it will continue so long wool is available for Indians."

The Chinese did interfere with the Indian and Tibetan trade. They did not enter into wool, salt or borax market in 1954; they, however, allowed the Tibetan officials [10] at Purang to continue their activities as middle-men, thereby earning a good profit. Jangpangi also noted that that year, the Chinese took very little interest in Indian goods; in fact, they were getting a regular supply from their agents [11] at Taklakot.

Rather unfortunately, the *Shungtshonga* [12] interfered in the Indian trade at Chakra: "In his official capacity, [he] corners whole stock of *gur* [13] at the Mart and does not allow other Tibetan merchants to buy it unless his own requirements are fulfilled," wrote Jangpangi. At the same time, other Tibetans did not dare to compete with him and the Indian traders were thus left with no alternative but to sell their *gur* to him at the price he decided: "He bought 7,000 *bhelis* [14] at Rs. 1/12 per

---

7   The maund is the anglicized name for a traditional unit of mass used in British India which was first standardized in the Bengal Presidency in 1833, when it was set equal to 100 Troy pounds (82.28 lbs. av.). This standard spread throughout the British Raj. After the independence of India the definition formed the basis for metrication, one maund becoming exactly 37.3242 kilograms. A similar metric definition was used in Nepal and Bhutan.

8   Pashmina.

9   One seer is equal to 0.93 kilogram on average. One maund is 40 seers or 100 troys. One seer is equal to 80 tolas (one tola being equal to 11.6 grams).

10  The *Dzongpon* and the monastic traders.

11  The Biansi and Chandasi traders.

12  The Tibetan Government Trader.

13  Jaggery.

14  One *bheli* was equal to 1 *seer* (in India, the *seer* was defined by the Standards of Weights and Measures Act as being exactly equal to 1.25 kg (1.792 lb).

*bheli* where as market price was Rs. 2: "Thus it was an evident loss to Indians," reported the ITA.

As we shall see, the Tibetan *Dzongpons* were small emperors in their own districts and most of the time, conducted private businesses for their own profit.

## The Trade Marts

During 1955 Jangpangi's tour of Western Tibet, out of ten Trade Marts recognized by the 1954 Agreement, only six – Taklakot, Gyanima, Khargo, Chakra, Nabra and Gartok – functioned. Two other Marts at Ramura and Puling as well as other former trading centres, did not operate. The reason was either excessive taxation or political reasons.

The fairs at two new Trade Marts[15] at Tashigang[16] and Shangtse did not take place though the traders were allowed to visit the Tibetan villages in Rudok county as before and the Chinese did not place any hindrance on their entry: "It is just possible this question may be raised during next season."

A detailed description of the Marts was provided by the ITA in Gartok.

## Taklakot Mart

This Mart was located near the Indian border at Lipulekh, 8 miles down from the Pass. The traders from Bians and Chaudas in Almora district of UP, as well as Nepalis from adjoining villages, visited the Mart for usual barter trade. However, Jangpangi noted that the number of Tibetans who came for trade was less than in previous years.

Like in Rutok, there was no interference from the Chinese, but the *Dzongpon* conducted his private barter trade to the detriment of Indian interests. The Chinese did not object to these private dealings, "[the *Dzongpon*] had a free hand and did more trade than in the past years."

The ITA also noted that the Indian traders were handicapped in their contact with Tibetan nomads: "the *Dzongpon* was, therefore [the]

---

15 See Map 6, Page 583.

16 Near Demchok in Ladakh.

master of the Mart and exploited both Indian and Tibetan traders to his own benefit."

At the Taklakot Mart, Indian traders were able to get enough salt and borax but very little wool; they, however, managed to purchase wool at Thokar, on the Southern shore of Lake Mansarovar. The barter of grain and salt was favourable for the traders "as the *Dzongpon* being an interested party did not let the rates go higher, but the price of wool purchased in open market or from the *Dzongpon* was very high,' wrote Jangpangi.

Interestingly, the Chinese, who had shown great interest in Indian goods during the previous year, were "quite indifferent and bought only a few selected goods. They have either accumulated a considerable store or they were depending on the supplies from their agents."

The traders did not have any difficulty in getting cloth for export to Western Tibet as they could buy cloth from any firm and anywhere in U.P. on a license fee of Rs. 20. The quantity of cotton and woolen cloth exported to this mart was much greater than in the previous season.

The Chinese tea bricks and the Tibetan woolen cloth bought in barter by Indian merchants were resold to Tibetan peasants, who supplied wool in exchange.

The cash transaction was minimal, though it had increased after the arrival of the Chinese; however, the Indian traders mostly still depended on barter trade. The ITA observed that the Tibetan goods were very costly, nearly five to six times the prices of the previous season.

The ITA pointed out that his extra-territorial judicial powers had lapsed after signature of the Tibet Agreement: "The traders, however, settled their minor differences between themselves. The Chinese did not interfere in such mutual settlement, but whenever they were approached by any person they simply passed on to the *Dzongpon* for necessary action."

Jangpangi only settled a few minor cases between Indian traders: "The Chinese officer at Taklakot did not take any interest in such cases."

The cases in which Indian and Tibetan traders were involved had to be dealt by the *Dzongpon* who had "his own way when I was away from the Mart" said the ITA, who explained that the Tibetan official exerted his influence in getting grain from Indians at a favourable rate: "On hearing this complaint I wrote to him to desist from such actions. He informed me that he did not do it."

Another issue cropped up, the Indian and Nepalese traders had been allotted different places to trade; the Tibetans and Nepalese had their business at Gutkon, while Indian traders went to Belhithanka, three quarters of a mile away: "The traders intending to go to either of the markets have to carry their goods to and back. Neither of them are allowed to halt for the night away from their allotted markets." This made their life extremely difficult; further, a custom post had been introduced by a former *Dzongpon* for the benefit of his private trade.

The successive *Dzongpons* had never agreed to the proposal to have one market for all the traders: "As the Mart has now been recognized, this disability should be resolved."

When he arrived in Gartok, Jangpangi discussed the issue with Yang Jen-San, the Vice-Chief of the Sub Office of Foreign Bureau in Gartok, who agreed that the matter needed to be examined on the spot and a suitable site for the Mart could be selected for the 1955 trading season.

Earlier the Chinese Officer at Taklakot, when asked to remove this irritant, had informed the ITA that he was only concerned with the border security and could not take up matters regarding the trade mart.

It was noted that the Chinese had now a hospital at Taklakot, which was only for the use of their own personnel. Finally, it appeared that they were short of modern medicines, reported Jangpangi: "They came to us for penicillin which they required for a dying soldier. So naturally all the Tibetans and even the acting *Dzongpon* himself came to our dispensary for medical propaganda (treatment?) as in the past," wrote the ITA who added: "The Indian traders and pilgrims were given all possible medical aid during my stay at Taklakot."

This too was not going to last.

## The Tharchen Trade Mart

Tharchen, a Bhutanese enclave was the main base-camp for the pilgrims walking around Mt. Kailash; it was also a trade market.

The pilgrims usually purchased their surplus articles and arranged transport from this village.

The Indian traders who used to purchase wool from nomads, had started opening shops for the *yatris*; in 1955, it was a consequent trade market with some 40 shops manned by Johari, Biansi, Chaudasi and Darma traders from Almora, Niti traders from Garhwal and Ladakhis.

Tharchen had not been recognized as an official Trade Mart; probably because it was Bhutanese territory, the Chinese did not object to its continuance.

The ITA mentioned in his report that the enclave was administered by the Bhutanese Government's representative in Western Tibet, who had his headquarters in Tharchen and "enjoys full control over all Bhutanese possessions in Western Tibet and Tibetans are also subject to his jurisdiction when visiting these places which the Tibetan authorities have not challenged so far," wrote Jangpangi.

The Bhutanese representative called Dodo told the ITA that he would give all possible help to Indian pilgrims to Kailash. He confided that some Chinese from Amdo who interpreted for the PLA also did the *yatra*: "They told Dodo that Mao Zedong had given religious freedom to all members of PLA. It was the first time when Amdowas[17] employed in PLA did the pilgrimage of Kailash." The ITA added: "It may just be possible that they were spying for the Chinese."

In 1954, Dodo had not yet been prevented from collecting the usual revenue for the Bhutanese government, though he was made to contribute grain and transport it for the Chinese and Tibetan officials. According to Jangpangi, "the Chinese also made enquiries from him about the past history of these villages." Dodo said that he was ignorant "for fear that he might endanger the interests of his country." He added

---

17  Inhabitants of Amdo Province.

that it can only be seen "whether the same policy as in the case of Minsar will be applied for these Bhutanese villages.[18]"

We shall come back to Minsar later.

### Bongdu Trade Market

Another small market called Bongdu lay five miles from Tharchen; some 15 Indian traders were established in the village; trade had started a few years earlier when the former Bhutanese representative "put certain obstacles in their direct transport and other arrangements with Tibetans. The present Bhutanese officer was trying to bring them back to Tharchen as Bongdu falls under the jurisdiction of Tibetan authorities," said Jangpangi.

### Thokar Trade Market

It was another pilgrim centre near Lake Manasarovar. The pilgrims who were unable to go to Kailash, used to visit Thokar situated on the southern shore of Lake Manasarovar "otherwise pilgrims go to Mansarovar after going round of Kailash."

Biansi and Chaudasi traders from Taklakot were trading in Thokar and also purchased wool. The trade transaction was as usual. The Chinese did not visit the place in 1954, but the representatives of *Dzongpon* of Purang and *Tshasyo*[19] imposed on the Tibetans a levy of 2% to 5% on the wool.

### Gyanima Khargo Trade Mart

It was another recognized Trade Mart and the largest Mart in Western Tibet, though there was no permanent settlement and traders had to live in tents. It was mainly visited by Johari traders from Almora; the traders from other Marts also visited the place to get goods not available in their own marts.

---

18  For the Bhutanese enclaves, see Volume 2, Chapter 12.
19  Tibetan Salt Collector.

Jangpangi stayed 13 days in the Mart: "The Indian merchants came there as usual, but a remarkably small number of Tibetan traders visited it during the present season."

The Indian merchants, who had hoped for a good market on account of the Kumbh Mela year, had brought a greater quantity of goods than the previous years, but there "was a general depression in the demand for Indian goods and for cotton cloth being the lowest."

The sale of Indian goods depended more on barter than cash sale and the Chinese bought only certain varieties of cloth and did not take interest in others as they were getting their supplies through Indian traders at Taklakot." Unfortunately, most of the Tibetan traders stayed away for fear of Chinese interference in wool trade.

Along with cotton cloth, there was a fair demand for woolen goods, broadcloth, serge, gabardine, suiting pieces and flannels, but they did not fetch attractive prices "due to the overflow of these varieties. The Tibetan peasant traders showed interest in them because Tibetan woolen cloth was either very costly or not available at all."

Some cases of theft and dacoity were reported at the beginning of the fair; ultimately the Indian traders had to engage their own *choukidars*[20] for doing night patrol: "The Chinese made no effort in this regard and the Daba *Dzongpon*, administrator of the Mart was represented by a petty servant."

One day a party of seven PLA visited the Mart, but they were only interested in border inspection.

As the extra territorial jurisdiction of the Trade Agent had lapsed, the traders had to settle their mutual cases amongst themselves; there was an incident during which an Amdo nomad drew his sword after a quarrel with an Indian trader. It was settled between the ITA and Dzongpon's servant: "Amdo did approach the Chinese official, but he directed the Dzongpon's servant to settle the case in consultation with me. The Indian traders again approached me in their mutual cases for settlement and there was no objection from the Chinese."

It was clearly a year of transition.

---

20 Watchmen.

## Chakra Trade Mart

Chakra was another recognized Mart frequented by traders from Darma and Almora. They used to barter grain with salt and wool and sell *gur,* nothing else. On August 1, Jangpangi visited Silti, one stage below the Mart where the traders did most of their barter business.

He wanted to find out whether the *Barkha Tasam,* the administrative officer of the Mart had kept his promise of 1953 of remitting grain supply from nine villagers of Darma: "I was satisfied that he did not recover this grain from Darma people concerned. The latter were also happy to see that their trade with Tibet resumed, which was the mainstay of their livelihood," said Jangpangi who also reported that the traders got enough wool and salt and also had good bargain for the *gur* that they sold to Tibetan *dokpas*: "After finishing their barter trade at Silti, they came to Chakra for sale of *gur* and got good price for it." There was an unusual demand for it: "The traders would have got still better price, if the Tibetan Government trader[21] had not cornered this commodity for his own benefit."

Jangpangi noted that the Chinese visited Silti in August on their way to Darma pass, but they did not halt at the market more than one night.

## Nabra Trade Mart

Nabra was also recognized as a Trade Mart; here, the trade was confined to the traders of Niti[22].

The traders got a good bargain in their barter trade of grain with salt: "As they were not very keen about salt which was selling cheap in Garhwal due to extension of cart road to Pipalkoti[23] in the interior of the district, they sold surplus grain to local Tibetans and to the PLA contingent at Daba."

---

21 The *Shungtshonga*.

22 In Garhwal.

23 Pipalkoti is a small and scenic town situated at an elevation of 1,260 mts above sea level. It is located 17 kms after Chamoli on NH58. Today, Pipalkoti acts as a relaxation point for people traveling to Badrinath, Auli, Hemkund Sahib and Valley of Flowers.

It was also reported that in addition to grain, cloth and *gur*, the traders exported potatoes and onions which were sold at a good price to the Chinese: "As this trade proved quite attractive it is just possible they may export these vegetables in larger quantities next year."

However the traders complained that the number of *Dokpas*[24] visiting the Mart was less every year "owing to the various exactions from them by the *Dzongpon* of Daba and his subjects." They preferred to go down to Niti valley instead of staying back at the Mart, even if they had to pay an extra tax.

The ITA made an interesting remark: "Unless the Chinese intervene, this collection of alleged unjust dues will continue. The *Dzongpon* himself is interested in sending *dokpas* down to Niti for the sake of his income."

A servant of Dosur Se, the acting *Dzongpon* called on the ITA: "He was careful not to mention about the Chinese contingent at Daba which was brought down from Gartok by him in order to drive out the Provincial Armed Constabulary men from Hoti,[25] but the Chinese did not go beyond Daba[26]."

Some mud huts had been built by four traders at Nabra; they had not yet been assessed but, "the Chinese have now authorized the *Garpons* to assess revenue on land occupied by such huts at Gartok, built also by the Niti traders," noted Jangpangi.

**Shangtse Trade Mart**

The town was a recognized Trade Mart for the Bashahri traders, but the Tibetans were caught unaware of the new changes, though the Bashahris were allowed to travel to Rudok and areas northeast of Gartok: "The Chinese did not object to this trading in the villages. With exception of a few Garhwali and Bashahri traders who did a little trade there, a regular fair was not held during the season of 1954." The Tibetans were absent.

---

24  Tibetan peasant traders.
25  Barahoti.
26  This has been studied in Chapter 1.

The ITA explained that like in the case of Tashigang Mart, the traders – Lahauli, Ladakhi and Bashahri – for whom this Mart has been recognized in place of Rudok and Ralang, visited Rudok and adjoining villages without any obstruction from the Chinese.

Jangpangi reported that he had met some Foreign Bureau officials at Gartok, but they did not mention anything about the Indians trading in Rudok district: "The traders will thus get time to settle their debts as far as possible because they are fully aware that Rudok will be closed to them sooner or later." He noted that a small contingent of PLA was seen around: "The *Dzongpon* informed me that they had come for the inspection of the boundary with India. Some member of the party with officer-in-charge had gone to Daba and Tholing. It may be that they were watching the movements of the *Dzongpons*."

The ITA suggested to the *Dzongpon* the reduction of the high rate of taxation on the Mana-Garhwal traders, so that the trade at Ramura could be resumed; later it was considerably reduced once the ITA reached Gartok and took up the matter officially.

**The Gartok Trade Mart**

Before the signing of the Tibet Agreement, Gartok used to be the only Trade Mart in Western Tibet, though the bulk of trade "was being carried out in other now recognized Marts and all over in Western Tibet."

The ITA reached Gartok on September 22. He did not visit Tashigang Mart as no fair took place with the village bordering Ladakh.

Both the Indian and Tibetan merchants used to assemble during the time of the *Gar Tsharchen*[27] at the end of September, but in 1954, the trade transactions were dull: "The Indian traders although were able to clear their stock but the margin of profit was a bare minimum. Owing to storage difficulties merchants tried to dispose of their goods at any price. The past experience showed that whenever unsold goods were left behind, they were misappropriated by the people with whom the goods were left behind."

---

27  *Gartok Annual Fair.*

The ITA noted that the Bashahri traders passed through Gartok on their way back from the north-eastern villages, but they had brought less wool due to the high prices of wool and sheep; some Ladakhi traders also came to Gartok, but very late. They brought dry apricot and apples and got good prices for them; there was practically no fruit in Tibet despite the great demand.

Jangpangi met many Tibetan officials, including *Garpon* Lobzang Chhewang, Kyarisipa Bhu (son of Garpon Kyarisipa), Thubten Sangye, the Tsaparang Dzongpon, *Shungtshonga*, the *Serpon*[28], stewards of the ex-Garpons; Sangye was then acting as *Chanda Tshasyo*[29] for the Daba and Tsaparang districts. The ITA said that the Garpons were a bit hesitant in the beginning, "the Chinese had cautioned them that they should henceforth discontinue intercourse with Trade Agent as they (the Chinese) were responsible for the External Relation of Tibet and all the formalities would, therefore, be observed by them alone."

All these officers were for the first time paid a salary …in grain.

Jangpangi had a good contact Garpon Chhewang who was grateful to the Political Officer in Sikkim for all the help that he got in his journey to Gartok via India. The ITA remarked that *Chhongjo*[30] of ex-*Garpon* Marlampa still had great influence amongst officials, though the Chinese authorities did not like him: "My relation with all these Tibetan officials was very friendly and cordial as before," noted the ITA.

Jangpangi also met the officials of sub-office of the Chinese Foreign Bureau, particularly Sun-The-Fu[31]: "He was holding dual charge of the Military Commander and the Chief of Sub Office of the Foreign Bureau in Western Tibet. He had come to Gartok for the Chinese Republic Day celebration on October 1. The ITA also had encounters with Yang Jen San, Vice Chief of Sub-Office of Foreign Bureau to discuss matters pertaining to improvement of trade and the removal of

---

28 Gold Tax Collector.

29 Salt Tax Collector. Thupten Sangye, a monk official, later took over as Dzongpon of Tsaprang.

30 The Chongzoe or Stewart.

31 Also known as Sung Si-ling.

unjust taxation; they also spoke of the housing for the Gartok Agency, the wireless facilities and the protection of pilgrims and traders in Tibet.

Jangpangi also reported that he "exchanged hospitalities and in all these meetings we had free and frank dealings and our relation was most cordial and friendly. They had often expressed their readiness to help us in every way possible."

The Gar Tsharchen took place on September 29 and 30; apart from the trade, the annual event comprised of horse racing, display of riding, shooting and dancing: "The prize ponies always belonged to the Garpons or Dzongpons although commoners are also asked to take part. The Chinese did not take part in any of the events as they did in 1953 fair."

During Jangpangi's stay at Gartok, Bakula Rinpoche passed on October 6, 1954, on his way back from the Kailash pilgrimage. During a tea party in the Lama's honour, local Tibetans came to receive his blessings. Bakula told the ITA that he was being shadowed by the Chinese.

**Some other Trade Marts**

The fairs at Ramura, Puling and Tashigang Trade Marts did not take place in 1954. The Ramura Mart had been deserted since 1951 due to the high rate of local taxation, but after the Dzongpon of Tsaparang agreed to reduce the taxes "it is hoped trade will be resumed there from next season."

The problem with Puling was that it depended on the situation in Nilang, which was now a 'disputed' place: "possibility of resumption of trade there seems doubtful," wrote the ITA.

**The Dongbra Mart**

Jangpangi did not visit the Dongbra Mart, four stages south of Shangtse on the Gartok-Shipki pass route, as when he was nearby, the fair was already over. He was however told that the Bashahri traders got enough wool and salt though price of wool was high there as well.

Some of these posts collected useful statistical data of Indian trade with Western Tibet. Jangpangi was keen that they "should continue so long as trade with Tibet continued." He was hopeful that after the signature of the Trade Agreement, "the volume of trade will increase considerably."

It was not to be.

### The Taxation of the Traders

The ITA reported that on Chinese instructions, the *Garpons* started to levy a tax of Rs 1 per tent per month on Indian traders at Gartok. As there were no houses, the Indian or Tibetan traders lived in tents throughout the entire season: "The Garpons were not keen on levying this tax, but they were asked by the Chinese to recover this tax on land occupied by Indian traders' tents."

As mentioned earlier, a reduction of tax for the Mana-Garhwal traders from 20 percent to 10 percent on the grain exported by these traders to Ramura Mart was implemented in consultation with the Tsaparang *Dzongpon*.

### The Law and Order Situation

According to Jangpangi, law and order had considerably improved; except for a few minor cases of looting of foodstuffs from traders and pilgrims, no dacoity occurred in Western Tibet in 1954, "though the Chinese have not yet made policing arrangements in the Trade Marts".

Further, the ITA was promised by the Foreign Bureau officials who had not yet taken over the administration of Trade Marts from the Tibetans, that they would make better arrangements the next season.

After the Indian traders engaged *chowkidars* for night patrol, the cases of theft were controlled better: "The Chinese were dealing with the criminal cases themselves and asked for such help as they needed from local Tibetan officials. There was no serious case in which Indians [were] involved," noted Jangpangi.

### The Chinese Activities in Western Tibet

Most importantly, the ITA noticed that the Chinese were slowly consolidating their position, both politically and economically: "Their supply position of foodgrain and other essential goods is much more stable than in the past years. They did not show any eagerness to amass all possible essential goods, although they purchased these in all the markets."

Jangpangi continued: "Besides local purchases they are getting a regular supply of goods from Sinkiang[32] and Lhasa, though the method of transportation is still slow and expensive on animals. Vehicular transport has not started to come to Western Tibet and horse or bullock carts have not been seen."

As seen earlier, the Chinese established a sub-office of the Foreign Bureau for Western Tibet at Gartok. Interestingly, they did not appoint any Tibetan officer as in Gyantse and Yatung; in fact, the Garpons were not connected with the Bureau: "They are not in the confidence of the Chinese authorities. They have constructed a 12 roomed one storey house at Gartok in which Bureau office and personnel and wireless station are housed."

It was pointed out time and again that the Chinese officials devoted more time to construction work than any other business, including administration. During his encounters with the Chinese officials, Jangpangi noted that the former had not yet studied the trade situation in the area: "They were otherwise friendly with me and maintained a cordial relation and they frankly acknowledged their ignorance in many matters pertaining to Trade Marts and other allied subjects."

They told the ITA that during the coming season, they would go in detail into the arrangements and would implement the Agreements in letter and spirit.

In 1954, they did not interfere with the Indian trade except by "creating a sort of depression in the markets they had tried to buy goods as cheap as possible." In 1954, they did not enter into the wool trade as in 1952 and 1953 and the Indian business was not restricted in the recognized Trade Marts and when the traders travelled to Tibetan villages beyond the Marts to purchase wool: "They were friendly with Indian traders."

---

32  Now Xinjiang.

The ITA observed that they were "still trying to win over Tibetans in general who have not yet allayed their suspicious."

In fact, the Chinese had started to engage local people to collect items such as firewood grass and were paying them good wages and handsome prices: "They are still telling Tibetans that their assurance of relieving Tibetan subjects from high and unjust dues of their officials have not been fulfilled."

Jangpangi remarked that once the unjust dues and *pujjar*[33] of Tibetan Government would be abolished, "public will certainly be drawn closer to them. The main problem with Tibetans in general is poverty and unjust dues to the officials." The ITA also noted that these officials were "either apprehensive of them [the Chinese] or have become their 'yes' men."

The four Tibetan officials in Western Tibet were often represented by their servants who were 'all yes-men'.

Security measures in the area had not yet been tightened, though the Chinese had three military stations at Rudok, Gargunsa and Taklakot. It was observed that men kept moving from one post to other. Jangpangi added that they were also keeping a small contingent at Gartok during summer.

The ITA asserted that there was no remarkable increase in the total number of military personnel. It was ascertained from local officials and people: "Their supply position being more stable, they may increase the number of troops for the purpose of patrolling all the routes leading from Western Tibet to India and Nepal which was evident from their keen interest in border areas in 1954."

More importantly, Jangpangi informed Gangtok and Delhi: "They may also want them for road construction work which may be taken in hand from the next summer."

That was the Aksai Chin road which, though it had earlier been surveyed, started to be built sometime in 1954.

---

33 Goods compulsorily sold by the Tibetan officials to their 'subjects' at a much higher price.

The approximate number of Chinese troops in Western Tibet was about 1,300 officers and men in October 1954.

It was pointed out that house building activities were brisk, though the timber shortage 'slackened the pace': "They have added some rooms to the barracks at Gargunsa, Rudok and Taklakot" and as mentioned, a 12-room house at Gartok of timber, they depended on irregular supply from villages on the Himachal border where some willows and white poplars had been planted from grafts coming from the adjoining Indian villages: "The houses built for military personnel at above headquarter have enough open space inside the enclosure. All the houses they have built are one storeyed."

It was also noted that no effort had started to improve the roads to the Indian border: "The reported motorable roads between Sinkiang and Rudok and Gartok and Lhasa have not yet been constructed."

Again, the Aksai Chin road, we shall come to it in a separate chapter.

The camel caravans were still used for the transport of goods from Rudok to Sinkiang, "whereas yaks and mules are being employed on Gartok-Lhasa route."

It was also reported that no airfields had been built so far: "The present means of transport are animals – camels, yaks, donkeys, mules and ponies. The PLA have their own animal corps and also depend on local supply especially on Gartok-Lhasa route."

1954 was clearly a year of transition for the PLA in Western Tibet.

**The Chinese attitude**

In the months following the signature of the Tibet Agreement, the Chinese maintained a friendly and cordial attitude towards the Indian Agency: "It has been enhanced through our constant contact and frank discussions. They have shown their eagerness to lend a helping hand to the Indian nationals as far as possible," noted the ITA, who added that however, they did not provide any effective protection to the pilgrims and traders during the season.

A Chinese checkpost was located at Pala, near Taklakot on Almora-Taklakot Mart route; Jangpangi commented: "The scrutiny and check was a bit severe in the beginning, but on my representation, they relaxed it to some extent and also abandoned the double passport system introduced in the beginning of season which required Indian nationals to take out permits at Pala and again at Taklakot and issued them at Taklakot."

It was the only checkpost on the routes to India in 1954.

## The Pilgrims to Kailash

In 1954, the number of pilgrims to Mt Kailash and Lake Manasarovar increased considerably. The ITA says that the approximate figure was 1,300, excluding the Indian traders; the majority traveled via Lipulekh Pass: "If the amenities for journey in the upper reaches of passes are improved, there is every likelihood of more pilgrims being attracted to these places."

There were no rest houses on the routes, which were often dangerous: "the pilgrims are at present perforce taking shelter in the shops and villages, which are most inconvenient to them," wrote Jangpangi who noted that the transport arrangements were also unsatisfactory.

In his report, the ITA made some suggestions:

(a) The transport agencies could be opened in the upper *pattis*[34] of districts bordering on Western Tibet.

(b) Some temporary huts could be built at each stage on Almora-Lipulekh and Almora-Milam routes, the two mostly frequented routes

(c) Some sanitary arrangements to be made by the district authorities at least during pilgrim season from May to August.

## Mail and Telegraphic Arrangements

In 1954, the ITA's arrangement was that the mail was dispatched through the Indian postal service to the last Post Office before the border and from this place, a contractor was engaged to carry the mail to Gartok. Two mail-runners were seasonally employed for taking mail

---

34 A Patti is a part of a village inhabited by a clan. In Chamoli district, a '*patti*' also means the area around the village, i.e. the village lands.

from Gartok to wherever the ITA camped: "This is a very slow system, as mail reaches from Gangtok headquarter and [then] New Delhi in about 20 days and vice-versa, but in abnormal conditions Agency remains cut off for months together."

No mail arrangement existed for the Indian traders and pilgrims.

Jangpangi reminded Delhi that till 1953, the Agency was provided with a W/T station, making it possible for him to contact the headquarters on a daily basis.[35]

In 1954, the ITA pointed out that the Gartok Agency was cut off from the rest of the world for one and a half month due to heavy snowfall in September and October: "In order to watch the movements of Trade Agent it is necessary to provide him with a wireless station, which will also help Indian nationals in time of distress in a far off place. We requested the Chinese for such facilities, they only agreed in the second week of October and then I found their rates exorbitant (Rs.8 per word). I, therefore, did not avail this expensive means of communication without prior sanction of the Government of India."

The following year, the pilgrims would face more difficulties to visit the Holy Mountain.

## The Agency Medical Activities

The medical services were restricted to the Agency personnel and Indian nationals, however, many Tibetan officials and local folks visited the Indian doctor who gave free consultation and medicines.

The Chinese had opened dispensaries at Gargunsa, Gartok and Taklakot for the PLA personnel; they did not look after the general public as yet.

The conclusion was that it was necessary that a Medical Officer should accompany the ITA to Western Tibet to look after the needs of Indian nationals, pilgrims and traders.

---

35 See Volume 2, Chapter 13.

## An Agency in Western Tibet

In the Sino-Indian Agreement on Tibet, it was agreed that the Gartok Trade Agency would function throughout the year and Gartok was to be its headquarters. The ITA noted that Taklakot was better suited for a permanent headquarters than Gartok for various reasons:

- ➢ It had a permanent population whereas Gartok was only a seasonal Mart.
- ➢ The heights of Gartok and Taklakot were 15,100 and 13,000 feet respectively.
- ➢ Taklakot was near the Indian border.

Delhi was informed that the Chinese were unable to provide houses for the Agency, though they promised that they would lease the land for the purpose: "As the Chinese have started giving lease of land to Indian traders at Gartok, we may also ask them to lease land for the traders' shops in all the Marts where there are no houses at the present moment." Jangpangi's argument was that if the Indian traders were given housing facilities, "there is every likelihood of permanent business establishment of Indian merchants in Western Tibet."

As we shall see, it was not to be.

## The Indian Village of Minsar

Bad news for India was reported from Minsar, the Indian village in the vicinity of Mt. Kailash. "Because of loose hold of the Kashmir Government," Minsar was slowly passing into Tibetan control, wrote the ITA, adding: "After a lapse of 3 years, a petty Leh Tehsil official visited the village with Shri Bakula, Deputy Minister of Kashmir, but he was not allowed to collect the annual revenue of Rs.264/13/ which was in arrears since 1951."

Because Bakula Rinpoche was 'on leave' for his Kailash pilgrimage, he apparently did not look into the issue, though he authorized a remission of revenue for two years after being approached by the villagers.

Jangpangi, however, remarked that the *Garpons* told a Ladakh official that the issue "had been referred to the Tibetan Government for orders, and until then they could not allow him to collect revenue from the village. As this official had taken up the matter himself with the Tibetan officials, I did not interfere."

The ITA added that the matter had to be settled one way or other: "If it is decided to surrender the control over this village, the inhabitants may be given free option to migrate into Ladakh and be rehabilitated there."

It is regrettable that this topic was not discussed during the negotiations for the Tibet agreement; an opportunity was missed.

In conclusion, the trading season had been a year of transition, as the Chinese had not had 'time' to look into the trade issues, trying first to consolidate the infrastructure on the plateau. Hence, during the first year after the Tibet Agreement by and large the trade had continued on the earlier pattern, except some local variations.

# 17

# On the Indian Side of the Himalaya: The Situation in Tawang

It is necessary to spend some time on India's frontier with Tibet in the North-East. Though the area was not yet disputed, it would soon become central to the relations between India and China. Here too the occupation of Tibet was slowly bringing strategic changes on the ground, though the Indian government was still living in the clouds of the Philosophy of NEFA.

On April 13, 1956, the Indian Consul General in Lhasa sent a communication to Delhi about the latest developments in Eastern Tibet: "the present regime in China is determined to bring these wild turbulent and armed tribesman[1] under effective control as well as to tap the area for its wool furs, deers horns, musk and other similar products."

NP Menon, the Consul added something which should have worried India; he wrote about "rumours recently of wide spread discontentment in the Po region[2] bordering on our Lohit and Tsiang[3] Frontier Divisions [FD]."

---

1   The Khampas.
2   Bome County (or Po-yul) is a county in today's Nyingchi City in the Tibet Autonomous Region. It was the seat of a quasi-independent kingdom until the early 20th century when troops of the Dalai Lama's Lhasa government integrated it forcefully into the central Tibetan realm. The kingdom of Po-yul was an offshoot of the ancient dynasty of the first Tibetan kings of the Yarlung Valley. Its inhabitants had a reputation as fearsome savages which meant most travellers kept clear of it and so it was one of the least known areas in the Tibetan traditional feudal establishment.
3   Siang Frontier Division.

In a previous Weekly Letter,[4] Menon had reported: "considerable troop movements (up to 60,000 Chinese troops) into these areas including the Tsona Dzong areas facing Tawang on our side."

Two days later, Menon wrote to Apa Pant in Gangtok. He said that General Zhang Jingwu[5], General Wang Qimei[6] and Wang Feng[7] were in Lhasa taking part in the work of The Preparatory Committee; they were part of the Central Delegation led by Marshal Chen Yi with Wang Feng as vice leader.

Menon noticed that an important official was absent: "A conspicuous absentee from Lhasa at the moment is General Li[8]," wrote the Consul; he had left the Tibetan capital to carry out an inspection of the Tibet-Bhutan Frontier.

## Visit of the Advisor for Tribal Affairs for the NEFA in Tawang

It is in these circumstances that Verrier Elwin, NEFA's Advisor for Tribal Affairs visited Tawang, though his trip was, unfortunately, more an anthropological trip than linked to strategic issues.[9]

---

4   Of March 27, 1956.

5   Director Chairman Mao's Office in Beijing and concurrently Central Government's Representative in Tibet.

6   General Wang took Ngabo Ngawang Jigme prisoner during Chinese invasion of Tibet in October 1950.

7   Wang Feng was Vice Chairman of The Commission of Nationalities Affairs in China.

   The Northwest University for Nationalities was established in August 1950, directly under the leadership of the State Ethnic Affairs Commission. It was the first minorities' university after the PRC's founding. Wang Feng, who was a revolutionary of the older generation, was appointed the first chief. The predecessor of the school was the Lanzhou branch of the Northwest People's Revolution University. From February 1950, Northwest University for Nationalities became established on its current foundations.

8   Maj Gen Li Jue (1914-2010). Gen Li Jue was very briefly head of the 18th Army's General Logistics Department before handing over to Maj Gen Chen Mingyi (1917-2002). Chen was given the credit for overseeing the successful completion of the Sichuan-Tibet highway.

9   *Notes on A Pilgrimage To Tawang by The Adviser For Tribal Affairs, NEFA in May-June 1956*; available in the Nehru Papers (JN Collection) held at the Nehru *Memorial* Museum and Library in Delhi. The 'papers' are not indexed.

We shall extensively quote from Elwin's report.

On May 8, 1956, he left Shillong, the headquarters of the Governor of Assam under whom the British-born anthropologist was working, "on a pilgrimage to the great Lamasery at Tawang."

The fact that he called his tour a 'pilgrimage' showed that his motivations were more spiritual than strategic.

He arrived in Tawang on May 23; he wrote that he "was thus privileged to be present for the Buddha Purnima celebrations, which were conducted with fervour, dignity and splendour."

It was a long journey of 180 miles "of peaceful walking and pony-riding from the point at which one leaves the dust and tumult of mechanised transport." The entire trip lasted a month, this included three double marches of 18 to 20 miles daily, but the party halted five days at Bomdila and three at Tawang.

Elwin was accompanied by his wife and Sachin Roy, the Cultural Research Officer attached to his office and the Political Officer in Charduar, the latter's headquarter, who joined them; the party walked till Dirang Dzong. This trip, remarked Elwin, was "one of the most memorable adventures that NEFA has to offer."

He spoke of the beauty of the landscapes: "the distant mountains white with snow, the nearer hills dressed in pine, oak and fir; the smell of the pines; the water-falls and streams; the banks carpeted with wild strawberries; the great displays of rhododendrons and a score of other multi-colored flowers."

He recounted that the journey over the Sela Pass from Senge Dzong to Jang is "unforgettable; haunted, mysterious, remote, the great Pass gives the authentic thrill - distance and height are forgotten in wonder. And as you descend, there are the flowers." He even got poetic: "If there is a Paradise in NEFA, this is it, this is it, this is it."

As for the people, they were described thus: "Quiet, gentle, friendly, polite to a fault, industrious, good to animals, good to children, you see in them the influence of the compassionate Lord Buddha on the ordinary man."

The anthropologist noted that though they may have little theology, they were very religious: "They are artistic too, even if their art is sometimes restricted by poverty to the love and decoration of flowers. But they nearly all have pretty things, generally made by themselves - a coloured sash, a decorated hat, a silver sword, and little cups exquisitely painted of wood or china."

The advisor further described the populations that he came across: "They have a real dignity; they are people who like to do things properly. They believe in protocol. Precedence, a certain gravity and order, courtesy, the ceremonial of daily life mean a lot to them."

And perhaps, more importantly, they were happy to be under the Indian Government: "Although many economic and spiritual links with Tibet remain in every village I heard expressions of sincere loyalty and appreciation of what the [Indian] Administration had done and was doing for them."

Elwin cited three things that had made a great difference to their lives since Maj Bob Khathing marched into Tawang in February 1951.[10] He cited the lifting of the burden of taxation, the payment of fair porterage rates and the ending of the Drekhang's[11] monopoly on salt and rice.

Then followed the description of the Monpa villages "as attractive as their inhabitants." As no Monpa would dream of living at ground level, the houses are usually two or three-storeyed: "They are on the whole fairly clean, and the people love to be near water."

In Dirang Dzong the river ran through the village while in other places streams helped turning the prayer wheels or even "ingenious grindstones which save the women many hours of labour."

---

10 See Volume 1, Chapter 20.

11 The official responsible for the supply of rice. In Tibet, the control of the supply of rice was, like in most posts, shared between a lay and a monk official.

Elwin noted that nearly every village has its *gompa* (temple[12]), its *kakaling*[13] and several *manes*[14] with their fluttering prayer-flags, "these mute witnesses to an ideal life create an atmosphere of serenity."

Probably a discipline of Jean-Jacques Rousseau, the French philosopher, the Advisor saw a high degree of civilization, and "only the most insensitive can make this journey without returning a humbler and a better man. …our staff must go first to learn, and only then to teach, with diffidence."

Many other contemporary authors had only seen misery and poverty in these areas, but it was this type of report that immensely pleased the Prime Minister.

**The Officers**

In Kameng[15], Elwin said that the Indian officers posted there "seemed to enjoy unusually happy and intimate relations with the people. Many of our institutions are going well. There is a fine spirit in the staff, a spirit of self-help …and a spirit of enterprise."

He found the place had 'less de-tribalisation' than any place that he visited earlier: "The interpreters are smart, intelligent, loyal."

In Tawang, he was impressed by the 'unity of the staff' with the Assam Rifles, SIB[16] and the civil staff working together well. Most of these officers spoke Monpa or Tibetan fluently. It is difficult to say if the picture was not painted too rosy.

---

12 Or Monastery.

13 Ceremonial Gate; Wikipedia says: "At the entrance to the monastery there is a colourful gate structure, known as the Kakaling, which is built in the shape of a hut-like structure, with side walls built of stone masonry. The roof of the Kakaling features mandalas, while the interior walls have murals of divinities and saints painted on them."

14 Elwin writes 'shrines', in fact, prayer wheels.

15 It is not clear what Elwin calls Kameng, because the entire area was the Kameng Frontier Division.

16 Subsidiary Intelligence Bureau.

Elwin gave credit to RS Nag, the Political Officer. The name of Nag's predecessor, Maj Khathing was also mentioned: "the Abbot of Tawang told me that he regarded him as one of his dearest friends and remembered him daily in his prayers."

The name of Maj PN Kaul, who would serve as Consul General in Lhasa a few years later was also cited: "the present PO has brought imagination and enterprise to bear on an already favourable situation with the most encouraging success."

He spoke of his strong practical common sense, his sympathetic and friendly approach to the tribal people, intelligent imagination …and the creative enthusiasm for beautiful things that has already revived the local industries."

The British-born advisor then gave a few words of criticism.

## The Fundamental Problem

He first noted that in most places in NEFA, there was a vexatious situation due to "the impact of the atomic age on a Stone Age people." In Tawang, it was different, there was a conflict between two civilizations, "one of which is indeed immensely superior in technological achievement while the other is equally distinguished by spiritual faith, by simple dignity, by compassionate goodness."

He said the Monpa culture was in many ways "above the kind of culture that we are able to introduce within its boundaries."

The romantic assessment continued in the same vein; of people, many of whom were great gentlemen, "whose way of life is higher than that of the majority of our staff, who live better than all but the most senior of our officers - better housed, better and more appropriately clad - who are more reflective, more sensitive to aesthetic values, of more elevated manners."

In Elwin's views, the Indian establishment looked "alien and a little shabby compared to theirs." He said that the Indian staff, "in their rather poor European dress, with short coats, …in the dreadful hovels considered suitable for Government officials at high altitudes, riding on hired or borrowed ponies, are not impressive."

At the same time, the Tibetan *Dzongpen*[17] who lived at Dirang, stayed in a house whose walls were eight feet thick while the Indian Base Superintendent had a hut of open bamboo matting of perhaps two inches.

While the Tibetans could talk directly to the people, the majority of the Indian staff required interpreters. However in Tawang, some Indian officers had adapted themselves: "They wear the fine fur hats that are popular locally; in winter they wear the warm Monpa dress; they eat with chopsticks; they can swallow cup after cup of butter tea. …they enjoy yak's meat; they can talk freely in Tibetan and Monpa."

The Advisor went on with this strange suggestion; he said that the Indian officials were all very anxious that "their acclimatization should be made complete by the provision of double-storyed stone houses in the Monpa style."

Elwin mentioned that in Dirang Dzong and Rupa, the contrast between the people and the officers was startling: "On one side is the old dignified colourful life, good houses, good clothes, good manners; on the other side is the rather brash, jejune, conventional existence of a low-grade staff trained neither in aesthetics nor manners: bad houses, bad clothes."

His advice to the government was the Indian officers should at least wear the local dress, warm, durable, dignified, appropriate. He added that it might be expensive at first, "but in the long run is probably economical. It eliminates an entire apparatus of pullovers, scarves and mufflers." His argument was that the Monpa's income was far less and they could afford it. He thought that all low-paid staff, especially schoolmasters should be given this type of outfit: "it is of political importance that our men should not look strange and alien; they must fit into the picture."

Retrospectively, it was rather childish. One should, however, note that on the other side of the McMahon Line, the Chinese wanted to dress the entire population in their grey suits.

---

17 Also written *Dzongpon*.

But the remarks which follow have serious implications for the defence of the borders considering how close Elwin was to the Prime Minister. Elwin noted: "When we consider the vast sums of money spent on safeguarding frontiers with check-posts, police and guns, the Indian way of fortifying by culture and sympathy is very inexpensive."

Would providing local attires to the Indian staff help in protecting the Indian borders? India would have to pay dearly six years later for following such romantic philosophy.

The Tribal Advisor continued, he said that the Political Officer had set the example by wearing a Monpa dress. He even mentioned Nari Rustomji, the former NEFA Advisor, "was not ashamed to go about in Sikkimese attire when he last visited Shillong and Delhi."

Elwin saw it as a way to counteract "the influence of the type of material civilization that China is spreading across the border."

He cited the import of jeeps and electric generators: "Both these things are good, but even more important is the strengthening of the spiritual bonds, which can only be done by the right people behaving rightly. The Monpas must come to feel that they belong to India and that India belongs to them. If they are to feel that, it is essential that the Indians they meet should not look or behave like strangers."

He certainly had a point, but this could not counterbalance the strategic infrastructure being built by Gen Li Jue and his colleagues on the other side of the watershed.

The Advisor's conclusion was, "Let us help our low-paid staff to dress appropriately. ...Let us approve entirely new methods of house construction and give our officers good, double or treble storyed homes of stone with CIG[18] sheets for roofs. Let us help the people to put up *kakalings*, repair their broken shrines, show a keen interest in their religion."

He believed that it would be good and in the end "cheaper and more effective than trying to impress them with examples of India's might."

---

18  Corrugated galvanised iron.

He further suggested that the Indian officials should all make a careful study of Buddhism.

He also complained that all the notice-boards, even in Tawang and Dirang Dzong, were in English. The names of the places should be changed into local language, he advised: "There was a suggestion that a place where I was thrown from my horse might be named Elwin's Fall, but I rejected the well-meant proposal for fear that the expression might be misconstrued."

His main objection was that many signposts that he had come across, were for the benefit of the official staff rather than for the people.

His suggestion was to use local language transcribed into Devanagari script, "perhaps in both Monpa and Hindi".

He thought of banishing names such as 'Dialect Teacher', "as if there was something extraordinary about a teacher who knows the local language" or 'Hindi Teacher', which suggests the imposition of an alien language, or even 'Colony' - Medical Colony, Agricultural Colony.

**Schools**

For Elwin, the schools illustrated the problem. The Tawang Monastery was described as a combination of an old-fashioned cathedral school and a 'basic education centre'. He explained that though many boys join the monastery to be trained, many marry and leave the *gompa*: "These boys are attached in groups to different senior Lamas who act as tutors. Some of the boys study in the library, others look after the ponies, cook in the kitchen, practise agriculture, care for the cattle, while yet others are trained in dancing, art-work and even printing."

He added that the boys work in an atmosphere of art, religion and learning sitting on the floor on cushions covered with decorated mats: "The atmosphere is almost that of one of the elder European Universities or of a Cathedral school." The Advisor observed that the young monk thus gets trained "in hygiene, the dignity of manual work and learn fundamental lessons of discipline, obedience and religious faith which remain with them all their lives."

While eulogizing the religion education, he criticized the government school for looking like a parody: "It is housed in a small hut of open cane-work which admits the cold and damp. The boys sit perched on inconvenient benches at silly little desks. The walls of the school are decorated with a few rather bad charts and maps." He pointed out at the time of his visit that often the teacher did not know a word of the local language "and was laboriously trying to impart the elements of Hindi to his pupils. There was nothing of beauty, of art or of their own tradition to inspire the children."

Elwin went on to criticize the government set-up at Rupa, Shergaon and Dirang Dzong "the buildings, the atmosphere, the games, the entire set-up is as foreign as could possibly be imagined to the rich traditional culture of the people. Our schools will either destroy this culture or will themselves be destroyed by it."

The Advisor had apparently already suggested that some pictures of Buddhist themes should be provided to the schools and "a simple manual of fundamental Buddhist teaching might be used."

He advised tolerance and not to be strictly secular "in an area where the entire population follows a particular religion, in giving some support to that religion."

The Advisor suggested that as the Ministry of Transport had produced some 'attractive' posters of Sanchi, Bodh Gaya and other Buddhist themes and it would be good to obtain five dozen of each of those that might be suitable and distribute them to our schools and other institutions.

He was delighted that in the schools he visited, children were wearing their own tribal dress: "The Sherdukpen boys at Rupa look charming in their decorative hats and the few girl students were equally delightful in their colourful traditional garments."

But the schools' attendance was 'disappointing'. Only a few teachers spoke the local language: "At Dirang Dzong, the teacher gave a little speech of welcome to us, but he had to do it in Assamese and get it translated by an interpreter. At Tawang, the [school] master, who is new, does not know the language at all."

One of the reasons was the frequent transfer of the school-masters. A teacher in Lish[19] told Elwin that he had passed in Abor language, later learnt Chang, but he was transferred into a third language area.

Regarding the curriculum, the anthropologist wrote: "the ideal would be for us not to have a separate school at all, but to make a grant to the monastic school, just as Government makes grants to mission schools all over India. We should persuade the Lamas to allow us to help them by giving them two or three additional teachers who should themselves, if possible but not necessarily, be Buddhist."

And they should wear the local dress: "They could improve the practical training given, introduce better methods of agriculture and the care of animals, make better sanitary arrangements and introduce Hindi, geography, arithmetic and other subjects."

He wanted the Political Officer to speak to the Abbot of the Tawang monastery; "it would make all the difference to the progress of education in Tawang."

In Dirang Dzong, he believed that the Dzong[20], a splendid building should be repaired and modernized: "It could be made into a really beautiful Hostel and Middle School. Local artists could paint the walls and ceilings and there would be plenty of room for hostel, kitchen, and class-rooms."

In Rupa and Shergaon, the local *gompas* could be used "just as is done in Siam and Ceylon. It would help to make the education programme a success and the revival of the local art and culture."

All these were fine and valid suggestions, but the strategic location of the place was not considered.

## Training Centers

Verrier Elwin was impressed by the training center in Bomcila: "It is being conducted with imagination, enthusiasm, fidelity to our directives and a keen business enterprise. Its emporium should be a model throughout NEFA."

---

19  In today's Dirang Circle of West Kameng district.

20  Administrative building in a district headquarter.

He found some progress being made in reviving the various arts and crafts of the locality. The wood work too was good, though the Advisor objected to the design of wooden ashtrays: "An ashtray might certainly be made for export, but it should be designed on some local model."

He was less satisfied by the work in Tawang; he noted that it was the only place in NEFA where painting was practiced: "Artists paint the ceilings of the *kakalings*, decorate the large and small prayer-wheels which are to be found everywhere, paint scrolls and pictures of the Buddha and famous Rinpoches."

His conclusions and suggestions were that art should be encouraged. He noted that most of the temple painting was at that time done by artists from Tibet: "Some arrangements should be made for training boys in painting both at Tawang and Bomdila," he added.

## The Hospital at Tawang

He inspected the hospitals at Rupa and Dirang Dzong; in Rupa the doctor was keen and efficient, though the hospital was not attracting as many patients as it had the previous year, while in Dirang Dzong, there was no doctor; it was manned by a compounder: "He seemed to be doing his best under very difficult circumstances."

The Advisor said that he was impressed with the work of Dr Kar at Tawang: "His hospital is in as good condition as sanctions and our engineering policy permit, [as] the walls admit the wind and the rain, and the roofs leak. But everything is very clean and Dr Kar himself, who speaks the language fluently, is clearly devoted to his profession and to the people in his charge." Further, he was popular.

However the hospital staff "appears to be larger than the number of patients." Again, Elwin noted the dress for the patient: "Dr Kar informed me that the patients dislike wearing the sort of clothes provided by the Administration and he urged that he should be allowed to purchase suitable clothes of local manufacture for them."

This was in line with the policy: "it should certainly be done if we wish to attract more patients to the hospital." The problem of local blankets was also raised: "the horrid cotton blankets usually provided should be banned forever both in Tawang and in all our hospitals."

He objected to a nice-looking girl who was treated for syphilis sitting on a bed in the same ward as a young man in another bed, though the local patients were not bothered with the segregation of the sexes: "In every part of the world treatment for venereal disease is regarded as given under conditions of complete secrecy and I feel strongly that precisely the same professional respect should be paid to a poor tribal as to a patient in a modern city."

The tour went on.

**Leprosy Home at Tawang**

The Advisor also reported about the health services, the Leprosy Home at Tawang was disappointing. He said that it was due "to the curious lay-out of the buildings and partly to inadequate supply arrangements."

He compared them with Leprosy Homes in Siang built in Abor villages with each patient and his family in a separate house built in Abor style: "the people of this area dislike sharing rooms with other people but the wards consist of small rooms in long buildings and some of these are occupied by two or even three patients."

He found that the Tawang 'arrangements' imposed a very great strain on the patients when it rained or snowed: "The result moreover is that the patients' wards are as cold, official and unlike a Home, as could be imagined."

Here again, Elwin thought that the leprosy home should be in the style of a Monpa village, "as the Leprosy Home at Along has been built in the style of an Abor[21] village, many more patients would be willing to come. …Every house should be built solidly of stone and be double-storeyed and in exactly the Monpa style except for the addition of CIG sheets on the roof. I would suggest that a small *gompa* might be built for the consolation of the patients and at the entrance we should have

---

21 Abors are the inhabitants of the Abor Hills, which are bordered by the Mishmi Hills and Miri Hills, and drained by the Dibang River, a tributary of the Brahmaputra. During the British Raj, the Hills had a reputation as a troublesome area, and military expeditions were sent from time to time. The region was named Abor Hills District from 1948, with headquarters at Pasighat, but later bifurcated into the Lower Dibang Valley and Lohit districts.

a *kakaling* which might be suitably painted with scenes depicting the Buddha showing compassion to the sick."

He added that he was depressed when he saw the patients at Tawang: "They were lined up to greet me standing in a drizzling rain with heads bowed and hands held before them as if they were criminals. This should never be done in any Leprosy Home."

He quoted from a note written by Maj Khathing in October 1953: "In future, I would like to suggest that all the dresses are locally arranged by the MO[22]. After all the patients will be going back to their villages when they are completely cured and there is no sense in making them accustomed to coats, pants and shoes."

Retrospectively, this insistence of local dresses did not make much difference. More than sixty years later, the local population in Tawang is proud of their local attire which they use at the time of festivals, but during normal times, they use the same dresses than anywhere else in India.

Elwin wrote that he hoped that the Medical Department "will take this matter up and arrange for the purchase of appropriate local clothes for the patients without any further delay. This should also include the purchase of local shoes, even if these are more expensive."

He even suggested that a similar policy should apply to the blankets provided for the patients: "Why could we not purchase local blankets for these unfortunate people even if they will be more expensive?"

Though with good intentions, it was clearly excessive, but the report was bound to please the romantic tendencies of the Prime Minister.

When the anthropologist was told that the patient could not weave because of some problems in the supply of wool, he found it 'disgraceful': "They do not need instructors: all they need are implements and raw materials," was his reaction.

---

22 Medical Officer.

## Political Presents

Elwin praised RS Nag, the Political Officer for establishing a tradition of 'political presents'. When another Advisor visited the area, he had given silver-headed walking sticks as presents to the local Chiefs: "this created a very good impression," he wrote.

Elwin himself distributed presents for the local leaders in Dirang Dzong, the Senge Dzong and the Tawang Gompa: "it might be a good thing that in certain exceptional cases such as the visit of the Advisor or of other very senior officers to the interior and on the tours of the Political Officer himself, we should arrange for political presents of some value to be given to the Chiefs."

Elwin said that he was not in favour of cutting political presents: "I doubt if that will be a practicable thing before the end of the Second Five Year Plan …The visit of a senior official is still an important event in such places and some kind of present should continue to be given for a few years to come."

He wanted fewer offerings and better gifts. The PO needed to be consulted in the matter; for example, instead of "cheap enamel cups and saucers and aluminum pots, he suggests excellent wooden cups and saucers, plates and dishes, locally manufactured, this would stimulate the industry in Kameng."

## The Abbot and the Gompa

Then, the report came to the *gompa*, the centre of the life in Tawang. The Khempo[23] or Abbot of the Monastery at Tawang was Gelong[24] Kesang Phuntsog: "[he] is a man who reflects in his own person the beauty of holiness. He is one of those rare and precious beings who can occupy a high position with humility; he is entirely free of pretentiousness, simple and joyous as a child, winning his way by love rather than by a display of authority or pomp."

---

23  Written Khempu.

24  Gelong means monk.

The description continued: "Among the Lamas of the monastery he is outstanding and I hope that he will continue to guide its destinies for many years to come."

He shared the views of the Political Officer, "on the establishment of the present Abbot in a strong position both in the discipline of the monastery and in the affection and respect of the lay people of the villages, much of our future progress in this area will depend. In this, a good start has already been made."

He rightly noted the importance of the Tawang Monastery, "[it] should prosper and develop. For generations, it has been a centre of light and inspiration to the people round. That light must now shine more clearly and with a better-directed aim."

Again, Elwin mentioned that "if we are to have a school at all in Tawang, it should be in the monastic premises." Even the training center should be associated with the monastery, he believed: "To train the young Lamas in improved methods of agriculture will be the surest way of introducing such methods to the laity in the villages."

What was worrying for the Advisor was that the numbers of boys seeking instruction from the Lamas was decreasing: "In twenty years this famous establishment may decline. I suggest that we should not let this happen. Let us revive this ancient institution, inspire it with wider ideas, bind it with unbreakable bonds to the India that gave it its great exemplar work through it, and I am sure that as time goes on we will not only see the people really progressing along the lines of their own genius, but we need have no apprehensions concerning the political situation, which might so easily become difficult, in the area."

Sixty years later, the *gompa* still commands respect and political influence in the region.

## Self-Help and Village Institutions

The report mentioned the remarkable progress made in persuading the tribal people to make roads and put up buildings on a self-help basis: "In so far as this promotes and preserves the self-reliance of the people, this is an excellent thing." He, however, noted a paradox: "Although the villagers are often willing, under the inspiration and persuasion of our officers, to give free labour for roads and schools, they are becoming less and less willing to maintain their own institutions."

In several places, he found people working on the roads and erecting schools and guest-houses, "but failing to repair the water-mills which are so great a boon to their womenfolk."

He remarked that one of the ten great *dharmas* of a Bodhisattva is to rebuild a decayed shrine; he, therefore, suggested that the government "should regard all the broken-down *kakalings, gompas*, water-mills, *manes* as historical monuments, and partly with official monetary assistance and partly on a self-help basis persuade the people to rebuild and repair them." It would have a good political effect, he said.

He added that the remarkable pantomimes that the Monpas and Sherdukpens were doing so well, should be supported, recalled that an artist at Dirang Dzong prepared for him a set of nine masks: "We are not to keep our people as museum specimens; we should equally avoid the danger of turning their finest products into museum specimens." He recommended that the PO should present each village a set of masks or a pair of trumpets "…schools too should have sets of dancing-dress, masks and so on."

While reading this report, one should keep in mind that the area had been under Tibetan jurisdiction till 1951. The progress achieved in five years was quite remarkable.

**Hindi and the Tribal Languages**

About the language, the Advisor noted that Hindi was making rapid and encouraging progress; most of the interpreters spoke fluently: "school children are taking to it with enthusiasm; and some people are learning it of their own accord."

Elwin's idea was to persuade some monks in the *gompa* to also learn Hindi: "it would be well worth while going to the expense of appointing a special teacher, who should himself be a Lama or at least a local Buddhist." The anthropologist added: "the idea of Hindi as the instrument of unity with India is gaining ground."

His main worry was the tribal languages; India had to provide "the apparatus for study but also for arranging for the employment of local tribesmen who would teach their language to members of the staff."

He recommended that financial provision should be made "and made quickly, for the ad hoc employment of tribal tutors in every outpost and headquarters ...Unless we do this, I doubt if we will make much progress."

**The Importance of Kameng**

Before concluding, he observed that Kameng Frontier Division had been the Cinderella of NEFA: "there is no missionary problem, no vexation about Law and Order; it can tick over; it is all right."

Elwin believed that the Western half of Kameng FD was of great importance, politically, religiously and culturally. He explained why it was politically important, "Lhasa still exercises a strong religious influence - I received, for example, several deputations asking that a certain Rinpoche in Tibet might be allowed to come and perform various religious functions in Tawang, Dirang Dzong and other places."

As a annexure to the report, Elwin mentioned: "This raised an interesting problem about citizenship. The Rinpoche had been born and had lived in India during his last incarnation and had been reborn in Tibet for this. This was seriously suggested as a reason for permitting him to come to India now. The Ministry for Home Affairs might well consider how far residence in India during a previous incarnation qualifies for Indian citizenship after rebirth!"

For Elwin, a well-administered Kameng FD "will not only mean a loyal and contented people looking to Delhi for help and leadership, but it might also set an example and help allied tribesmen in Bhutan and Tibet."

He asserted that Kameng was the place where the Prime Minister's policy had the greatest chance of success: "We are to build a new house on old foundations - and our difficulty in some areas is that the foundations are not very secure. Here at least there is something strong and fine on which to build. But it is essential that such building should be done with intelligence and imagination. It is equally essential that we should be prepared to spend a little money."

The Advisor wanted money to be invested for promoting art, religion and culture. His final conclusion was: "Much will depend on the ability [of the director] to inspire the members of his staff with his own unswerving loyalty to the Prime Minister's ideals, the Philosophy of NEFA."

Unfortunately, this remarkable anthropological approach only marginally aided with the defence of the borders.

## An answer from Delhi

On August 6, 1956, TN Kaul, the Joint Secretary in the Ministry replied in detail to Verrier Elwin's point.

He asked KL Mehta, the Advisor to the Governor of Assam the steps that Shillong intended to take to implement the recommendations made by Elwin. Kaul wrote: "We should like to know in particular about the following":

1. Has any order been issued for school masters to learn the local language?

2. Why do the majority of our staff require interpreters? Has the order regarding learning of local languages been translated into action?

3. As for the study of religion by our officers we do not think it is enough to make a list of books when those books will not be available in sufficient numbers.

4. We are shocked to hear about such vulgar notice boards as "Boom Town Bomdila". We hope these would be removed without delay. We also agree with Elwin that all notices should be in the local language put into Devanagari script and the local script.

5. We also agree that expressions like 'dialect teacher', colony etc. should be replaced.

6. Would you kindly let us know what has been done and what is being done about distribution of photos of Buddhists and other themes and of our leaders in NEFA.

7. Would you kindly explain why there has been no doctor at the large medical set-up at Dirang Dzong for over six months?

8. We should like to know the state of radio sets and gramophones. We hope they are not in the same state of bad repairs

9. In the case of IFS officers we give them certain inducements to pass exams in foreign languages. Perhaps something in this line might be recommended, as the provision of teachers by itself will not necessarily ensure success in this matter.

How this could be implemented, nobody knew.

**The Chinese views on Tawang**

Though there was nothing wrong in the Tribal Advisor's report, it showed the bent of mind and preoccupations in Delhi at a point in time when China was said to be amassing 60,000 troops north of Tawang.[25]

To order the local civil servants to wear Monpa dress was inconsequential in view of the serious threat coming from the north. But it appeared that the entire government machinery, from South Block to Bomdila via Shillong, was living in an imaginary world as regards to Chinese intentions.

It is true that China was yet to start officially claiming the entire NEFA as theirs; in fact, there was a surprising silence about the border from the Chinese government's side during the first years of their occupation of the Roof of the World; but by the mid-fifties, the PLA began to bring thousands of troops to the Indian borders.

It is where General Li Jue, mentioned earlier in this chapter, played an important role. Ultimately it would take a few more years for China to officially express some objection to the McMahon Line.

Why didn't China object to India occupying the territory south of the McMahon line earlier? This is an important question.

---

25 This figure was probably highly exaggerated.

According to Chinese sources, during the first years after their arrival on the plateau, China had adopted a policy of temporarily overlooking some issues which they intended to solve later. This would explain the remark 'ripe for settlement' mentioned by Zhou Enlai[26].

A Chinese report explained that the Communist regime had "first to take care of peace within the country and liberate Tibet. [Beijing] did not have time to spare for dealing with the border issues with India. Also, they were not very alert about the Indian incursions and not enough research had been carried out on this issue. India made full use of this opportunity and captured Tawang."

On April 12, 1952, the Communication Department of the Central Military Commission (CMC) presented a report on the topic "A report on the military, political and economic situation of present day Tibet".

The top-secret report was given to Mao Zedong, Zhou Enlai and the United Front Work Department; it was the most detailed report on Tibet till date. The report categorised the situation of Tibet into four areas:

> ➤ The conspiracy of the ruling class of Tibet of destroying peace through agreement.
> ➤ The destructive activities of the imperialist powers in Tibet,
> ➤ The military situation in Tibet and
> ➤ A few Tibet and economic issues that demand attention.

There were also three attached documents to the report:

> ➤ The religio-political organisation of Dalai Lama's administration
> ➤ The deployment of the Tibetan Army on the plateau
> ➤ The 'foreign army' (i.e. Indian) outside the boundary of Tibet and a map of Tibetan monasteries and the different production units.

---

26  See Volume 2, Chapter 20.

Among these papers, was attached a second report which detailed the state of the Indian Army stationed at Tibet (i.e. the Escort). It mentioned the presence of Indian Army

- ➤ At Gyantse with the presence of 60-70 Indian troops as well as 10 Nepali army men[27]
- ➤ In Walong region of Xikang,[28] 60 Indian troops
- ➤ At a place called Wa Zha,[29] located 15 km south west of Zayul *Dzong*, India had 22 Indian soldiers
- ➤ In Chu shu le,[30] in the Western sector of the Indo-Tibet border – 50 Indian Army personnel
- ➤ In Mon Tawang, 12-day travel from Lhasa on the boundary with Bhutan south of Tsona *Dzong*); 500 Indian troops.

The investigation made it clear that the Central Committee of the Party knew about the Indian 'occupation' of Tawang.

Finally, the Tibet Work Committee got an understanding of the situation about the McMahon line; and on October 21, 1953, a telegram was sent by Gen Zhang Jingwu to inform accordingly the Ministry of Foreign Affairs.

The TWC's and the ministry's understanding of the situation on the border was a result of India telling the Chinese authorities that Indian would like to continue to exercise its rights and enjoy benefits in Tibet as in the past. The Central Party instructed the TWC to carry out a research on the special rights enjoyed by India and Nepal in Tibet.

It was clear that the preoccupations of the Chinese authorities were not the same as their Indian counterparts; there was no 'Philosophy of Tibet' for the Communists.

---

27 Protecting the Nepali Agent?
28 The historical province of Kham region and West Sichuan.
29 Rima, North of Kibithu?
30 Chushul in Ladakh?

# 18

# Kushok Bakula's Tour in Tibet

An interesting event during the period under study was the visit of Kushok Bakula Rinpoche in Tibet. We shall follow his encounters with the main actors on the Roof of the world and the implications for the relations between Tibet and India …and China.

### A Life devoted to Ladakh

The 19th Kushok Bakula Rinpoche was born in 1918 in the Royal Palace of Matho.[1]

In the course of his life, Bakula had a most distinguished political and diplomatic career; ending with serving as India's ambassador to Mongolia where he was instrumental in reviving Buddhism.

He was also a member of the Fourth and Fifth Lok Sabha.

In the early 1950s, Bakula was part of the J&K Constituent Assembly representing the Ladakh region. He would often speak in favour of the integration of J&K; he was proud that J&K was an integral part of India, "that great country of high ideals and glorious traditions to

---

[1] The 19th Kushok Bakula Rinpoche (19 May 1918 – 4 November 2003) was a Buddhist lama, who also served as India's ambassador to Mongolia. He is known for his efforts in reviving Buddhism in Ladakh, Mongolia and Russia.

He was the youngest child of his father, Nangwa Thayas, the titular King of Matho, his wife, Princess Yeshes Wangmo of the Royal House of Zangla. He was recognised by the Thirteenth Dalai Lama as a reincarnation of Bakula Arhat, one of the Sixteen Arhats who were direct disciples of Gautama Buddha.

which the nations of the world look for guidance and which is one of the potent factors for the maintenance of world peace."[2]

Bakula's visit to Tibet in 1955/1956 is a not-well known episode of his life. It is particularly interesting because India faced a difficult situation after the Chinese take-over of the country, at a time Delhi was dreaming of an eternal *Hindi-Chini* brotherhood.

The Deputy Minister for Ladakh Affairs in the J&K Government would soon understand the political implications of his visit.

**The Lapchak Mission**

On May 29, 1955, TN Kaul in the Ministry wrote to the Indian Embassy in Beijing to inform N. Raghavan, the Ambassador, that the Kashmir Government wanted to send a Trade Mission from Ladakh to Tibet as it had been done for centuries[3]; another mission had been customarily traveling from Tibet to Ladakh every year: "Kashmir has not sent one since 1948. We see no objection to exchanging Trade Missions between Ladakh and Tibet, but we do not wish to relate them to old treaty of 1684 or 1842 between Kashmir and Tibet, nor do we wish to observe old custom of our Mission carrying official presents for Tibetan authorities as Tibetan Mission does not carry similar presents for our authorities."[4]

The Joint Secretary asked the Ambassador to check with Beijing: "You may sound Chinese Government informally that in view of our friendly relations and 1954 Agreement between India and China in regard to Tibet we would like to encourage friendly contacts between Ladakh and Tibet and sending a trade mission."

---

2   Today, the airport at Leh is named after Kushok Bakula Rinpoche.

3   An interesting reading on the subject is Abdul Wahid Radhu, *Tibetan Caravans: Journeys from Leh to Lhasa* (Tiger Publishing, New Delhi, 2017) or Claude Arpi, *The Life and Time of Abdul Wahid Radhu, the last Caravaneer*; see: http://claudearpi.blogspot.com/2011/02/life-and-time-of-abdul-wahid-radhu-last.html.

4   All other documents in this chapter, except specifically mentioned, are from the Nehru Papers (JN Collection) held at the Nehru Memorial Museum and Library in Delhi. The 'papers' are not indexed.

Why this was not discussed during the negotiations for the 1954 Agreement is a mystery? It should have been part of the package deal.

A day later, Kaul wrote: "You should make it clear that mission would only be a Trade Mission for sale and purchase of goods. Kindly telegraph Chinese reaction. We have sounded Chinese embassy here informally but not give any written note."

Raghavan immediately answered: "Feel Chinese Government may welcome any kind of Ladakhi Mission which will suggest or further special relations with Ladakh. But should we officially encourage such special regional relations?"

Raghavan brought an interesting point to the discussion, China had never admitted officially that Ladakh was part of India: "Considering non committal attitude of Chinese regarding Ladakh and possibility of Tibet claiming Ladakh as their own or vice versa and further possibility of the exploitation of delegates as often done at Peking in case of similar missions, should we encourage any special mission from Ladakh to Tibet even for trade?"

As mentioned in Volume 2 of this study, a serious difference had erupted between the Indian and Chinese negotiators regarding Demchok, which the Chinese claimed as theirs.[5]

The Ambassador gave his point of view: "Mission for sale and purchase of goods need not necessarily be confined to Ladakh or even Kashmir but can well include all interested in Indo-Tibetan trade. I feel that if Ladakhis want to send special trade mission to Lhasa it must be without the official blessing or sponsoring. After hearing from you further shall take up matter if necessary."

On June 3, the Ministry clarified: "we have considered the matter carefully and discussed it with [PN] Menon our Consul General Lhasa, who is here. We feel that it would be better to sponsor the trade mission officially and send it under the leadership of a reliable official. This would ensure that our traders will not show any subservience to Chinese authorities and would develop Indo-Tibetan trade. If Chinese (are) agreeable it would give an opportunity for our traders and officials

---

5   See Volume 2, Chapter 22.

to go right up to Lhasa from Tashigang[6] via Shigatse which the Chinese had not agreed to previously."

The Ministry[7] told the embassy that Delhi was ready to consider a proposal "to include other people from border areas who are interested in Indo-Tibetan trade, if possible. The main thing to emphasize is that it is an officially sponsored trade mission in pursuance of the 1954 Agreement on Tibet."

One can only repeat that it is regrettable that the issue was not discussed in 1954.

On September 8, Kaul again cabled Raghavan in Beijing about the Trade Mission from Leh to Lhasa. The issue had been discussed with the Chinese Embassy in Delhi in May: "It is out of desire to foster and increase volume of trade between India and Tibet that we are suggesting official trade Mission which will proceed from Leh to Lhasa along overland route via Demchok, Tashigang, Gargunsa, Gartok, Barkha, Tharchen, Shamsang, Sakya, Raga, Gyatru, Lhotse Dzong, Shigatse and Gyantse.[8]"

It was further clarified that the Trade Mission would not sign any agreements or contracts in Tibet: "Trade Mission will consist of traders from our border areas with an official as leader."

The Ministry was keen that the Trade Mission should be given all facilities "for trading along route as well as at destination namely Lhasa."

The embassy was requested to cable back the Chinese reactions "so that appointment of trade Mission and collection of goods may be completed in time."

The age-old traditional caravan from Ladakh to Tibet would soon be dropped.

---

6    The village on the Tibetan side of Demchok.

7    Probably TN Kaul.

8    Spelling of some of these places is approximate.

## The Lapchak and Choba Missions

On December 27, 1955, South Block communicated to the Chief Secretary of the Jammu and Kashmir Government about the Choba Mission, the annual counterpart of the Lapchak Mission. The Chinese Government had apparently never been informed of any such mission earlier: "As you may know, they have refused our request to send a mission from Leh to Lhasa to foster Indo-Tibetan trade, on the ground that the proposed mission would be beyond the scope of the 1954 Agreement."

It was therefore decided to refuse "to treat the Choba Lhasa Mission officially and therefore not <u>repeat not</u> give them any cash or other presents."

The Ministry had however no objection to provide to the members of the Mission normal facilities allowed to ordinary traders: "Any gift to monasteries [in Ladakh] made by the Mission may be accepted."

The Consulate in Lhasa was asked to tell the Mission informally that "since the Chinese Government have declined to accept an official mission from Leh …regret your inability to accept similar mission from Lhasa and to give the mission any special facilities not provided by the 1954 Agreement."

The principle of reciprocity had to work both ways.

## A Letter from KM Panikkar

At that time, KM Panikkar, the former ambassador to China was a member of the States' Reorganisation Commission.

On October 8, he wrote to the Prime Minister about a suggestion that Himachal Pradesh should be merged in the Punjab: "The Chini and Pangi areas of Himachal Pradesh and the Lahul and Spiti areas of the Punjab seem to us, however, to stand on a different footing from the rest of the proposed state. The people there are mainly Indo-Tibetans, mostly nomadic, and not ethnically, socially or politically integrated with the life in India. We did not visit this area, but during our stay in Rampur Bushair[9], we came across large numbers of them from the Chinese side."

These populations were mainly in contact with Tibet, Panikkar noted: "With the developments now taking place in Tibet this population is likely to come more and more under Lhasa with which their contacts are already close. Though there is no trouble at the present time, we cannot overlook the fact that with the economic and political changes now taking place in Tibet, a change may come in the not too distant future in the attitude of these people."

His conclusion was that India should "hasten the cultural and economic development of this area. They should also be gradually brought into closer relations with India. Such a policy could not be followed effectively, if this border is attached to any State administration."

His recommendation was for the rapid assimilation of the border populations "into the broad frame work of Indian life, the Government should urgently examine the question of constituting an Agency area of these regions and administering them directly along the lines developed in the NEFA."

This was never done, but Himachal was not merged into Punjab.

It is probably in these circumstances that it was decided to send a representative of the border area, namely Bakula Rinpoche, to Tibet.

## Kushok Bakula to Visit Tibet

Also on October 8, 1955, Apa Pant informed Delhi of the receipt of a telegram from the Consulate General in Lhasa regarding the visit of Kushok Bakula Rinpoche: "Foreign Bureau was approached on the subject today (wanted to talk to Foreign Bureau Assistant personally but he is outstation hence sent Vice Consul to see his Secretary). They wanted to know if Kushak[10] Bakula ever visited Tibet before or not."[11]

---

9 In today's Kinnaur.

10 Most of the cables spelt Kushok as 'Kushak'.

11 *Shri Kushak Bakula's visit to Tibet*; Department: External Affairs; Branch: NEBA; 1955; File No. Progs., Nos. 1(7)-SOBA, 1955. Available at the National Archives of India, New Delhi.

The Chinese wanted to know the number of personal attendants accompanying the Rinpoche: "Is he visiting for pilgrimage or also in connection with anything else (they have been informed that the visit is purely for pilgrimage)."

The Foreign Bureau Secretary had promised Menon to take up the issue with the 'Local Government', in other words, the Tibetan Kashag.

On October 31, the Political Officer in Sikkim answered the Ministry: the Rinpoche had studied at Drepung Monastery for 15 years 1927 to 1942 and visited Kailash-Mansarovar on pilgrimage in 1954[12]: "The visit to Shigatse and Lhasa will be mainly one of pilgrimage, but since he holds the responsible position of Deputy Minister in one of the Indian states, this visit will also result in strengthening cultural and religious links between India and the Tibet region of China."

Menon also requested the Foreign Bureau "to provide guards and other facilities for party from border to Lhasa and also if possible motor transport from Gyantse to Lhasa on new road." For several reasons, Delhi felt that it was an important visit which should be organized on official level.

On November 11, 1955, Kaul came back on the details of Bakula's visit to Tibet: "We do not wish to exaggerate importance of Kushak Bakula's proposed visit. He is really going on pilgrimage but we are giving it official colour to emphasise our relationship with Ladakh."

It was proposed that Bakula could arrive in Gangtok by the end of November; he would be accompanied by a J&K official, as well as Nirmal Sinha, the Cultural Attaché in the PO's Office who spoke Tibetan: "Sanction for Sinha's special equipment being applied for. No sanction for additional saddlery necessary as ordinary transport should be engaged," read a cable. The visit was slowly getting formalized.

## On Which Visa will Bakula Travel?

Two days later, the Ministry informed the Indian embassy in Beijing that Bakula's visit was 'officially' sponsored: "It is in our discretion to issue passports and get them duly visaed for officials even when they

---

12  See Chapter 19 of this Volume.

travel on pilgrimage. Chinese cannot object to this procedure. Kushak Bakula occupies an important official position in one of our states and we wish him to be given not only ordinary facilities as a pilgrim but also courtesies due to a Deputy Minister in one of our states."

Kaul cleverly wrote, "This would ensure Chinese acceptance of our relationship with Kashmir and Ladakh."

On November 18, Menon cabled Delhi from Lhasa: "Chinese insistence on treating Kushak Bakula as private pilgrim during his forthcoming visit does not appear to be inspired by desire to treat him like other pilgrims under Sino-Indian Agreement on Tibet. Foreign Bureau here had approached me only two days ago for issue of visas on Chinese passports of a Tibetan official and his family who they state are proceeding on pilgrimage to India. I have deliberately held up issue of visas to this party pending the resolution of Kushak Bakula's case."

The Consul General continued on the issue raising the question of China recognizing J&K as part of India.

Kaul had been suspecting that Beijing was ambivalent about J&K...and Ladakh: "The Chinese authorities are unwilling to accord any kind of tacit recognition to Ladakh's status as an integral part of India. Further, they seem to be nervous about the contacts which Kushak Bakula may establish here with important monasteries and their religious heads."

Menon pointed that the Chinese were keen to win the support of the monastic order for their presence in Tibet; in these circumstances, it was difficult for Beijing to refuse the visit of the Ladakhi leader and this explained why it would eventually be allowed.

Menon, therefore, suggested that: "in addition to visa some kind of letter of introduction from the Chinese Embassy which would clearly state Kushak Bakula's official position and instruct their local authorities in Tibet to grant him all facilities."

The Consul mentioned some sort of *'laissez passer'* sometimes given to holders of diplomatic passports "may perhaps be advanced in support of this request. You may also like to consider giving some publicity to the effect that Kushak Bakula's visit to Tibet is being officially sponsored and that he would receive courtesies in Tibet, as soon as all formalities for his visit are completed."

Acting on the principle of reciprocity, Menon remarked that if the Chinese Embassy agreed to affix visa on Bakula's passport: "I also propose to grant visas to the Tibetan official and [his] family. I am presuming that the Chinese will not be making any special endorsement in Kushak Bakula's passport while granting visa to the effect that he is proceeding as a private pilgrim."

A tentative program was forwarded: "Please confirm that authorities in Tibet are providing escorts etc., and will supply transportation for party and baggage consisting of thirty to forty maunds and that journey by road will be possible from Phari to Lhasa."

**The Preparations of the Visit**

A note of TN Kaul, the Joint Secretary in the Ministry pointed out some of the difficulties mentioned earlier.

On November 16, 1955, Fu, the Councilor in the Chinese Embassy in Delhi paid a visit to South Block regarding the tour of Kushok Bakula to Tibet. China welcomed the visit, he said, but as 'a private pilgrim'; the Lama did not need to carry a passport or have a visa. Fu even quoted the 1954 Sino-Indian agreement "pilgrims need not carry such documents." He also said that Beijing would provide "whatever facilities were available in Tibet." Fu just requested the dates and the places that Kushok Bakula and his party intended to see.

TN Kaul immediately saw the trick, China was not keen to acknowledge that a 'Kashmiri' carried an Indian passport. Kaul pointed out that the trip was officially sponsored by the Governments of India and Jammu and Kashmir (J&K): "[Bakula] was not an ordinary pilgrim, but occupied an important official position in one of our States. He was visiting not only Lhasa, which was covered under the Sino-Indian Agreement, but also Shigatse and certain monasteries from Lhasa, which were not covered by the Sino-Indian Agreement."

Kaul further argued that though under the Agreement, passports and visas were not necessary for pilgrims, this did not forbid the use of passports and visas. He explained that India regularly issued "diplomatic passports to all important officials in India visiting foreign countries and to get them duly visaed by the countries concerned."

The Joint Secretary pressed not only for the visa, but also for a letter of introduction: "Bakula should be given not only the ordinary facilities due to a private pilgrim, but also facilities and courtesies due to an important official of a friendly government."

It was crucial, as Kaul did not want to accept the Chinese argument that J&K (and Ladakh) were disputed territories, therefore it would be better for Bakula to go as an ordinary Indian citizen. Fu finally said: "We shall welcome Kushok Bakula as a private pilgrim, but if the Government of India wants, the Chinese Embassy could give him a visa."

The Counselor added that he was not aware that the Lama planned to visit Shigatse and other monasteries around Lhasa; Kaul reminded him that he had mentioned this to him earlier; Fu nevertheless agreed to give Bakula "all possible facilities regarding guards, escorts."

Kaul commented that his impression was that the Chinese were reluctant to recognize an Indian passport for the Kushok: "but on our insistence agreed to issue visa on such passport. They were, however, particular in emphasizing that they would treat him as a 'private pilgrim'."

After the Chinese agreed to stamp Bakula's diplomatic passport, Kaul decided not to press further "since giving visa on our passport would amount to indirect recognition of the official position of Kushak Bakula."

SK Roy, the Special Officer for Border Areas[13] (SOBA) was requested to follow up with the embassy; the next day, he confirmed that he was arranging to get the passports of the delegation visaed.

The other details such as special equipment allowance for the winter season and other allowances were swiftly passed by the Ministry and the Defence Ministry was requested to lend whatever items were required for the journey. The J&K Government appointed DD Khosla to be the liaison officer for Bakula. During the following weeks, Khosla would

---

13  Formerly, SOFA (Special Officer, Frontier Areas).

regularly inform Jammu about the whereabouts and fitness of the party through wireless.

## The Report of DD Khosla

Durga Das (DD) Khosla, an under Secretary of the Political Department of the Jammu & Kashmir Government, was to accompany Kushak Bakula to Tibet, but had soon to return from Phari due to health problems.

On his return, he wrote a 'Tour Note to Tibet' which is worth studying.

The party headed by Kushok Bakula, consisted of DD Khosla[14], Dr Nirmal C. Sinha and the four Ladakhi officials, S. Stobdan, Deputy Project Officer, Ladakh Development Block, Leh; Geshe Ishe Tundup, Bodhi Teacher, Government High School, Leh; Gelong[15] Nikdel, attendant; Tundup Phunchok, a cook and two orderlies.

They left Jammu on November 18, 1955 and reached Delhi the next day; they stayed for three days in the capital, before leaving for Varanasi on November 23. While in Delhi, the party received a briefing from officers of the External Affairs Ministry and Kushok Bakula took the opportunity to call on Dr Radhakrishna, the Vice President of India who was Chairman of the Buddha Jayanti Committee. He probably discussed the Dalai Lama's participation in the celebrations, to be held the following year in India.

The party stopped two nights in Sarnath before proceeding to Siliguri by rail. They continued their journey to Kalimpong, Darjeeling and finally Gangtok. Khosla noted that Kalimpong was "a very important town on the border of Tibet and centre of lot of espionage and political intrigue. People working for China, Tibet, Bhutan, Russia and other nations can be found here."

---

14 Author of the report.
15 Monk.

### The Press reported the visit

On December 2, a correspondent of a newspaper based in Kalimpong wrote about "Kashmere's Lama Deputy Minister on Pilgrimage to Tibet."

The article elaborated on the Ladakhi Mission: "The incarnate lama had gone out for his morning exercise when I called at the hotel to see him ...Winter morning sun was bathing us with pleasant warmth and while we sat and talked the incarnate lama Sri Kushak Bakula who has been the Deputy Minister for Ladakh affairs in Kashmere Government since January of last year arrived. Had it not been for the officials present who rose and bowed, I could not have recognized the great personality who stood before me stripped of all Governmental and priestly grandeur wishing me good morning with a broad smile of childlike innocence. Thin and rather tall for his race the Lama accepted my greetings with repeated bows and offered me a seat with the characteristic humbleness that marks all great lamas."

Apparently, the Rinpoche told the reporter that he proposed to visit all principal monasteries in Tibet and he would be out of India for about three months: "He was glad that he was carrying with him the good wishes of our people and Government to the people and Government of Tibet and that his endeavor was to see the long-existing ties of co-operation and friendship between the two countries grow stronger day by day."

Bakula explained that his mission was "to foster better cultural relations between India and Tibet." A short biography was then given by the reporter: "At the young age of ten he was sent to Tibet where he studied theosophy, philosophy and culture for fifteen years at the famous Drepung Monastery – one of the three pillars of Tibet – fifteen years of continuous study at this seat of learning and his great subsequent studies have equipped him for a prominent position and he is considered today as one of the greatest saint-scholars of Buddhist philosophy and culture."

The article cited the spread of Buddhism in the Himalaya: "Throughout centuries, scholars, saints, thinkers have travelled from Tibet to India for study and pilgrimage. From India also scholars and seekers after truth made pilgrimage to Lhasa, Shigatse, Kang Rimpoche (Holy Kailas) and Mapam-Tso (Manasarovara)."

It was interesting that the visit of the Ladakhi party could trigger such an article, as at that time, very few were aware of Ladakh. Incidentally, the Chinese occupation of Tibet was not mentioned.

**Towards Sikkim**

Their stay in Kalimpong was short, after two days the group proceeded to Gangtok where they had to make the necessary arrangements for the visit to the Land of Snows. In Sikkim, Bakula stayed with the PO, Apa Pant at the Indian Residency.

Khosla explained the political background: "The Trade Agents at Yatung, Gyantse, Gartok and the Consul General at Lhasa are administratively under the control of the Political Officer at Sikkim, though in political and policy matters the Consul General in Lhasa is directly under our Ambassador in Peking."

The party left for their tour of Tibet on December 6, 1955; after passing a day in Sherathang and Changu[16], where they slept in well-equipped *dak bungalows,* on the way they could admire the beautiful lake, they crossed over Nathu-la on January 8.

Once on the Tibetan side, the first *dak bungalow* was in Chumpithang, some seven miles from the pass; let us not forget that the bungalows between Nathu-la, Yatung, Phari and Gyantse had been handed over to the Chinese a few months earlier.

The report mentioned that after Chumpithang, they saw their first *gompa*[17]; later in Chumbi valley, they encountered the Chinese Police and Army who checked their passports. The J&K official recalled: "I had a very surprising experience at this place. Shri Kaushak[18] Bakula had gone a little ahead and I was all alone with one servant when I

---

16 Tsongmo Lake is located 18 km fromm Nathu-la, the border pass with Tibet at an elevation of 3,753 m (12,313 ft). The lake surface is said to reflect different colours with the change of seasons and is held in great reverence by the local Sikkimese people.

17 Written 'Gumpa'.

18 Another spelling for Kushok.

reached this Check Post. When I presented my passport to the Chinese officer in-charge, an interpreter who was also a Chinese and who knew a little Hindustani enquired from me why I was going to Lhasa. I told him that I was on duty with Shri Kaushak Bakula who was a Minister. He was surprised to hear this and at once retorted that Shri Kaushak Bakula was a Ladakhi and that Ladakh being a part of Tibet, an Indian officer could not be connected with him."

Poor Khosla had to explain at length that Ladakh was a part of Jammu and Kashmir State and that Kushok Bakula was a Deputy Minister in the Kashmir Government. He told the Chinese border guard: "I belonged to the Kashmir Secretariat service and had been deputed to accompany Shri Kaushak Bakula. I was then cleared from this Check Post and reached Yathung[19] in the evening."

In Yatung, the Party stayed in the Indian Trade Agency located in 'our own spacious building', Khosla said: "At present Maj Chhiber[20] is our Trade Agent at this place. The Chinese have concentrated some of their forces here also. They are also building a school at a cost of about a lakh and a half[21] of rupees. The building is under construction."

The Rinpoche's discussions with Maj Chibber were unfortunately not recorded in the report.

On December 9, the Ladakhi party reached Gautsa where Bakula spent the night at a monastery called Thinker *Gompa*[22]: "Next day we left Gautsa and reached Phari. Unfortunately, Khosla felt sick; he developed a pneumonia and he had "a very restless time." Khosla later mentioned in his report that Phari, located at an altitude of 16,000 ft, was the highest inhabited place in the world and was famous for its fierce winds, freezing cold and lack of oxygen: "We stayed there for two days and as I was incapable of undertaking onward journey, I was sent back by Shri Kaushak Bakula."

---

19  Yatung.

20  Maj SL Chibber

21  1,500,000 rupees.

22  Probbaly Dungkar Gompa, the monastery of the famous Lama, Dromo Geshe Rinpoche (Dromo is the Tibetan name for Chumbi).

Though Khosla's trip was cut short, he could gather a good amount of information. We shall go through it. Khosla first raised the issue of maps, already mentioned in Chapter 4.

The report continued on the new roads built by China.

(i) Lhasa-Shigatse-Gyantse-Phari road.

> This road is roughly 380 miles in length. 275 miles viz. from Lhasa-Gyantse via Shigatse is roughly 275 miles and was built in about 8 months. The journey in a jeep from Lhasa to Gyantse takes about two days. Another 103 miles of road from Gyantse to Phari was completed in 60 days. The quality of hill road is striking and displays enormous physical effort put into the construction. The work has been completed with the most primitive kind of instruments like, pick axes, shovels large sized scales for carrying earth (metal containers balanced on either side of a bamboo pole) and small blocks of trees trunks for leveling the top surface of the road. The road is of a standard type consisting of large size granite rocks filled up and strengthened with earth, all by manual labour. A number of small streams were not bridged, the vehicle merely driving through. Though an iron bridge has been constructed near Shigatse, the Tsangpo[23] river is crossed on wooden ferry capable of transporting 2 large sized vehicles. The road passes through mountainous area crossing a pass over 17,390 ft. which descends into a wide open plain. The Chinese have made no attempt to build a road over the firm grassy soil; its contours being marked out by running heavy trucks. Throughout the route a number of small primitive bridges have been built with logs, the inference being that it was intended to erect permanent bridges shortly.

(ii) According to the old established trade route there was a direct line from Gyantse to Lhasa (about 150 miles), Shigatse being on another side. The Chinese have, however, aligned the new road via Shigatse (275 miles).

---

23  Yarlung Tsangpo, which will become the Siang and the Brahmaputra in India.

Khosla was a fine observer; it is regrettable that he could not continue his journey to Lhasa. He gave the reasons which might have prompted the Chinese to build this road between Yatung and Shigatse:

(a) To include Shigatse which is the second largest city in Tibet and headquarter of Panchen Lama on the route.

(b) Its proximity to the area famous for high quality wood.

(c) To have full military control over Central Tibet so that there is little likelihood of an armed revolt against the present Chinese regime.

(d) To flatter Panchen Lama and to use him for political ends in favour of the Chinese.

Khosla further noted: "(c) and (d) above are, however, my own inferences. These are however based on some knowledge which I acquired by reading certain literature on the History of Tibet."

He explained his interesting point of view: "History reveals that the previous Panchen Lama was a stooge of the Chinese and had fled from Shigatse – his headquarters – to China, as a result of some differences between him and the previous Dalai Lama.[24] During that period also the Chinese had been exploiting the presence of the Panchen Lama in China against the Dalai Lama in Tibet. It may be also of interest to note here that although some efforts were made by the previous Dalai Lama to reconcile with the previous Panchen Lama, the Panchen Lama never came back to Tibet and actually died while in China. The present Panchen Lama was also discovered in the Chinese territory."

He continued his remarkable analysis:

(e) It is a matter of vital important for us to note that the Chinese are rather fast in building roads on all sides touching the Indian border. As I have already stated, a road from Lhasa to Phari has been completed and is open to vehicular traffic. Phari and Chumbi are also connected by road except for a stretch of about 4 miles between Phari-Gautsa. This stretch has already been surveyed and construction of a road on this portion was expected to be completed within a couple

---

24  In 1923.

of months. After this is done Lhasa will be connected with Chumbi by a motorable road. The road from Chumbi to Gautsa is a double track *pucca*[25] road. Thus on the Tibetan side the road will touch our border at Nathu-la, being only 12 or 13 miles away from the Pass.

It is one of the most remarkable reports written about the prevailing situation in Tibet in the mid-fifties. Khosla also explained: "On the Ladakh side, the Chinese propose to build during the next year a road from Taklakot (Purang) to Rudok via Kailash, Gartok[26], Gargousa[27] and Tashigang. Tashigang is only 12 miles from our last border village of Damchok[28] in Ladakh. Rudok is another important place in Tibet at a distance of about 30 to 40 miles from Damchok. From Gartok to Rudok (180 miles) the road survey has already been completed. At Gargousa the Chinese have built a hospital in 1953. This hospital is being extended. Gargousa is also the Military Headquarters of the Chinese. A Wireless Station has also been set up here. At Gartok where we have also a Trade Agency, the Chinese have constructed some buildings and established a branch of their foreign office. Again at Taklakot they have established a Military Headquarters and a Wireless Station. Between Taklakot and Kailash construction of Rest Houses is under consideration and it was learnt that these will be completed during the next year."

One can imagine the amount of information Khosla would have been able to gather if his health had permitted him to continue his journey to the Tibetan Capital.

Once again, it is regrettable that his astute observations were not even noticed in Delhi; though on the question of Chinese maps, it triggered a discussion as we have seen.

## Kushok Bakula's Report

The Report of Bakula Rinpoche addressed to the Chief Secretary of the J&K Government in Srinagar was sent on June 6, 1956, after his return

---

25 'Proper permanent' road in Hindi.
26 The last two in Western Tibet.
27 Gargusa.
28 Demchok.

to Ladakh. It is entitled: "Report from Deputy Minister for Ladakh Affairs on His Tour of Tibet in November 1955 to March 1956".

Bakula clarified that he led a Cultural Mission to Tibet sponsored by the Government of India and J&K: "This Mission provided me an opportunity to visit Lhasa once again after 15 years." On his previous trip, the Rinpoche had been in Lhasa "carrying on my studies there at Drepung, the biggest Buddhist Monastery of Tibet."

We shall not repeat Khosla's report, but the Rinpoche said that he met not only Dr. Radhakrishnan, but also Yuvraj Karan Singh in Delhi in connection with the Buddha Jayanti. After Sarnath (Varanasi), the party stayed for a week in Kalimpong during which they met Gyalo Thundup, elder brother of Dalai Lama, Dr. Roerich, the Russian scholar and Tsipon Shakappa, 'a fugitive noble of Lhasa'. Shakbapa and Thundup were the main protagonists of an Independent Tibet.

As mentioned, in Gangtok, Apa B. Pant hosted them at the Residency in Gangtok; Bakula cited the five important stages from Gangtok to the border: "Das-mile[29], Pandra-mile[30], Chhangu[31] and Sera Thang[32] and Nathu-la."

He said that the crossing of the Nathu-La pass over to Tibet "was negotiable, with no snow". They were received by one Phunchok Wangtak of the Tibetan Foreign Office who had been deputed by the Chinese authorities: "Next day we reached Yatung. While I stayed for the night at Tungkar *Gompa*[33] of Yatung valley to perform certain pujas there, some of my companions stayed at the residence[34] of Major Chibber, Indian Trade Agent at Yatung."

In Phari, two stages away, they were received by a Chinese officer named Ko, also attached to Foreign Bureau; from then onwards, an interpreter and five guards accompanied the Mission. After halting for a day and visiting small temples, Bakula and his party proceeded to Gyantse on

---

29  Ten miles.
30  Fifteen miles.
31  Tsongmo Lakem or Changu.
32  Sherakthang.
33  Dungkar Gompa in Upper Dromo (Chumbi) Valley.
34  India House in Yatung has been destroyed by China.

December 12; he recounted: "Before the Chinese constructed jeepable road in Tibet, it used to take 5 days to reach Gyantse from Phari instead of one day now."

At Gyantse, the Ladakhi party stayed at the residence of the Indian Trade Agent[35] where they spent two nights. Bakula said when they went to the monastery in Gyantse, there were some 500 resident monks.

He noted an unpleasant incident which took place during the party's stay: "While I was just going to take a snap of the lamas in the principal Prayer Hall of the *Gompa*, a Chinese *sepoy* came forward and pushing me backward prevented me from doing so. This was a clear act of impertinence as I had been allowed to take two cameras in India to Tibet. The Indian Trade Agent, Gyantse reported this incident personally to the Chinese authorities at Gyantse but they pleaded ignorance about the same."

This type of incident showing the arrogance of the new masters of Tibet would happen more and more in the following months and years, the senior Chinese officers pleading ignorance each time.

A report of the Indian Trade Agent complemented Bakula's own report. On December 12, Bakula and Nirmal Sinha arrived at Gyantse from Phari in a jeep provided by the Chinese. The baggage and rest of the party arrived in a truck later on in the evening: "All of them were accommodated in the Agency. It is regretted that Shri Khosla had to return back to India from Phari due to reason of health. On arrival here the Deputy Minister expressed his desire to extend one day of his stay at Gyantse. He wanted to visit the monastery and local Foreign Bureau was informed accordingly."

The next day, Bakula visited the monastery at Gyantse: "I accompanied the party to the monastery. The Abbot of the Gyantse monastery was kind enough to make very satisfactory arrangement in the monastery. All the sacred alters and shrines were thrown open for the party and I should like to add here that the authorities of the monastery have shown the greatest courtesy to Kushak Bakula," wrote the ITA.

They also called on the local officials at the Foreign Bureau.

---

35 Tempo, the acting ITA.

## On the Way to Tashilhunpo

Let us return to Bakula's report.

On December 14, they moved to Shigatse, famous for the Tashilhunpo monastery, the seat of Panchen Lamas. Their stay was arranged by the Chinese authorities in a newly-built quarter. During their 15-day sojourn at Shigatse, the Panchen Lama gave them three audiences at his residence: "He invited the members of the Mission to lunch also. On all the three occasions we invariably found Mr. Ko of the Chinese Foreign Bureau attending to the Panchen Lama. The monastery of Tashilhunpo[36] was visited several times. I met the Ladakhi lamas (approx. 300) reading there and strongly exhorted them to work hard. I further performed pujas in the monastery a number of times."

The Rinpoche admitted that besides the Panchen Lama, he could not meet any important persons while at Shigatse, though Nirmal Sinha and Stobdan met with two of the Panchen Lama's non-ecclesiastical ministers "who were found highly speaking of our Prime Minister and India's foreign policy."

Though the residential quarters provided by the Chinese were not bad, Bakula requested to be shifted in the monastery "to be more accessible to pujas". The Chinese authorities refused.

According to a report of the Intelligence Bureau (IB), the Chinese Foreign Bureau at Gyantse "was believed to have made special arrangements at the request of Shri Kushak Bakula to arrange for his stay and that of his Ladakhi followers at the Tashilhunpo monastery while the other government officials accompanying him were accommodated at Government Guest House, Shigatse."

Originally the two groups were to be accommodated at one place. The IB asked the Ministry (through the ITA) to look into the issue.

Another report from the Consulate in Lhasa informed Delhi that Bakula Rinpoche had an audience with Panchen Lama at Shigatse on December 17; Kushok Bakula asked the Panchen Lama for a special sermon on December 27 and the next morning the party was invited for breakfast by the Panchen Lama: "Kushak Bakula desired that these

---

36 Written Tashi Lunpu.

details be communicated to Bakshi Ghulam Mohammad[37] and to National Conference of Leh." He wanted the Kashmir Prime Minister to be aware of his whereabouts.

## The Visit to Lhasa

Bakula's continued his trip using a new road; the journey from Shigatse to Lhasa just took 1 ½ day by jeep, while, "in olden times the same took 10 days." They crossed the Yarlung Tsangpo with a big ferry at a place called Staktukha (?)[38].

The party finally reached Lhasa on December 29; they stayed at Dekyi Lingka with PN Menon, the Indian Consul General.

As there was no arrangement from the Chinese authorities for their stay at Lhasa, Ko and the guards left them "free to move about wherever we liked," noted Bakula.

However, the Tibet Government had organized their stay in 'a well-known building at Lhasa'; Bakula continued his report: "I did not move to the building immediately as I first wanted to visit Drepung, the Gompa where I had spent so many years in the past. I therefore moved to Drepung Gompa. A huge number of lamas gave me a good reception at the monastery."

At that time, the Dalai Lama was in retreat and nobody was allowed to see him; they had a few days free before having an audience, as a result a 15-day programme was made for the Ladakhis to visit some of the famous monasteries, such as Trak Yarva[39] and Drigung Thil[40], not far

---

37  Prime Minister of Kashmir.

38  Chaksam or Chushul?

39  Trak Yerpa is located on a hillside in Taktse County. The entrance to the Yerpa Valley is about 16 kms northeast of Lhasa on the northern bank of the Kyichu. From there, it is another 10 kms to the famous ancient meditation caves in the spectacular limestone cliffs of the Yerpa Valley. The famous legendary hero Gesar of Ling is said to have visited the valley. The holes his arrows left in the cliffs are believed to be evidence of his presence.

40  Drikung Thil monastery is located on the south slope of a long mountain ridge about 120 km north-east of Lhasa. It looks over the Shorong valley at an elevation of 4,465 metres and commands a panoramic view of the valley. The monastery belongs to the Drikung Kagyu sect of Tibetan Buddhism. Three other monasteries of this sect are located nearby, Yangrigar, Drikung Dzong, and Drikung Tse.

from Lhasa: "All these Gompas lie in a track where mules and ponies alone form the means of transport," wrote Bakula, who added that as it was the winter, it was 'considerably' cold.

**Going to China?**

Bakula seemed to have been keen to continue his pilgrimage …to China; around New Year 1956, he asked Delhi if the Chinese Ambassador had formally extended an invitation to him to visit Buddhist places in China such as Dunhuang or the White Horse Monastery in Beijing.

Menon told Delhi that the Ladakhi Lama wanted to know the Government of India views on this, "since question of financing onward trip to China either overland from here or by air via Calcutta has to be settled in consultation with relevant authorities."

Interestingly, the Lama was not keen to attend the opening session of Kashmir Assembly mid-February 1956: "He would be happy if he can complete China tour and return to India by the end of February 1956."

The Indian Consul General in Lhasa commented: "If China trip materializes, [Nirmal] Sinha hopes to persuade Bakula to shorten present Tibetan tour and thus avoid meeting with second Ladakhi tour group now reported to be between Phari and Shigatse and eventually expected to reach Lhasa soon."

On January 3, the PO wrote back to Menon about the request from Bakula to visit China, it would be "more or less a waste of time," said the PO who added: "He [Bakula] should be encouraged to visit important monasteries in Eastern Tibet such as Derge and also other monasteries in Nagchuka, Chamdo and Jeykundo areas. It would be most advisable if Sinha accompanies him on these tours. If Bakula approves help should be given to him to organize these trips."

The Consul was more categorical: "He should be persuaded to abandon his ideas of visiting Buddhist shrines in China."

The same day, Pant got an answer from Delhi, which had not sanctioned any proposal for Bakula to visit Buddhist spots "outside Tibet nor have Chinese mentioned it to us."

Delhi was also direct: "We do not consider it proper to fish for the invitation and suggest that if Kushak Bakula is approached he should decline it."

South Block continued: "We think it necessary for Kushak Bakula to return as soon as he has finished his visit to places of pilgrimage in Tibet. For your information, we are not in favour of his extending his visit outside Tibet and suggest you put it up to him tactfully that development and other work in Ladakh is likely to suffer by his prolonged absence."

On January 12, South Block reiterated that "Bakula should be allowed to extend his present tour in Tibet if he so desires. We should not appear to be restricting his activities too much otherwise effect likely to be opposite to what we desire. However, while communicating with him please inform him that Kashmir Prime Minister would like him to return for next Assembly Session."

Two days later, the PO cabled Delhi a request from the Ladakhi Rinpoche to at least stay in Tibet for some more time as the Tibetan New Year and the Great Prayer Festival (Monlan) were coming up; Kaul wrote: "Unless there are special reasons and serious objection I feel Kushak Bakula should be allowed to extend his stay in Tibet till 21st March. He is visiting Tibet after many years and this will probably be his last visit there. He is genuinely interested in religion. He is also highly respected in Tibet. His participation in various religious functions and also in alms distribution during Tibetan New Year has definite value for us." The visit to Beijing was out.

**Now Staying in Tibet**

A few days later, the issue of the alms to be distributed during the Monlam was discussed "over 15,000 monks from all parts of Tibet and Mongolia gather together. Usually, Consul General Lhasa also distributes alms on this occasion. Rupees 7,500 for this purpose is therefore really a small amount. Our donating only Rs. 1,000 will not be appropriate. Alms distribution on this occasion by a high official from India has certain definite propaganda value. You should consider this matter on its merits."

On January 18, in a telegram addressed to Delhi and Lhasa, Pant said: "As it has now been decided that Kushak Bakula should stay on in Tibet till end March no doubt you would afford him all help in the organisation of tour and give him help in his religious functions etc. If adequate amounts for alms etc. not provided in your budget it would be advisable to ask for additional financial help."

Delhi was requested to provide all assistance to Sinha in the organization of Bakula's tour, Pant added: "Sinha has discussed fully with me implications of Kushak Bakula's visit to Tibet."

On January 31, Sinha wrote to SK Roy from Lhasa regarding a loan of Rs 15, 000 to Bakula "for purchase of manuscripts and printed books. …Bakula wants to book orders for printing to be started in Tibetan next year early. Orders for priority to be placed by end Tibetan current year i.e. February first week. If the loan is sanctioned advise Menon accordingly and arrange promptly dispatch of funds via Gangtok."

It is not clear if the loan was finally sanctioned.

**The Return in Lhasa**

A report of the Indian Consul General in Lhasa mentioned that after a few days in Drepung, the Ladakhis left January 11 "on a pilgrimage to various monasteries lying East of Lhasa and returned to Lhasa on January 22. After another brief stay in Drepung, the party shifted to Lhasa on January 25."

Kushok Bakula had a meeting with General Zhang Guohua on January 25 and a private audience with the Dalai Lama on January 30: "Subsequently Kushak Bakula took part in the ceremonies connected with the Monlam (Great Prayer), during the course of which he distributed alms to the monks. The presence of the Bakula party has enabled us to assess the extent of Ladakhi connections with the Tibetan monasteries in Central Tibet."

The Rinpoche's nephew, Shas Rinpoche was the Head Lama of Rezong Gompa in Ladakh; he was then receiving his religious education in Drepung and as he had to perform some important *pujas*, "he was eagerly waiting for me." Bakula, therefore, went to Drepung to participate in his nephew's celebration.

Later that day, Bakula paid a courtesy call to Gen Zhang Guchua, the Commander of the Chinese forces in Tibet at his residence in Lhasa: "He is the highest Chinese Officer present in Lhasa these days," noted Bakula. We don't know what transpired during the encounter.

**Republic Day Celebrations**

On January 26, the Ladakhi party participated in the Republic Day celebrations at the Indian Consulate General: "I hoisted the National Flag and spoke a few words about the significances of the day. The Maharajkumar of Sikkim, who was present on the occasion, also spoke a few words."

Again on January 27, the Dalai Lama granted a public audience to the entire Bakula's party in the Central Cathedral in Lhasa and finally, a private audience was given by the Dalai Lama at the Potala Palace on January 30.

Later that day, Bakula and Sinha were invited for lunch at the residence of Gen Zhang Jingwu: "At the end of the lunch I thanked the General for his lunch as also for the very good transport arrangements made for the Mission. Further, I expressed the hope that the age-long cultural ties between India and China will be closer and closer in the times to come." Zhang answered that he had similar hopes and expectations.

From January 31 to February 2, Bakula, along with his nephew, attended sermons given by the Dalai Lama.

After a few other visits around Lhasa, they proceeded on pilgrimage to Ganden and Samye monasteries on February 7: "This time it took us 14 days to cover the pilgrimage."

He explained that these two *gompas* are famous throughout Tibet because Ganden, which counted 3,300 lamas at that time, was founded by Je Tsongkapa, the reformer and founder of the Yellow Sect while Samye "is said to have been built by Guru Padmasambhava, the great Mahayana saint."

While they were in pilgrimage in Samye, Losar, the Tibetan New Year took place. The day was celebrated with great merriment, recounted the Lama: "I was now keen to return to Lhasa soon to attend the famous annual Prayer Congregation[41]," which started on the 2nd day of the Tibetan 1st month and lasted for the whole month.

They reached Lhasa on February 2, 1956[42]. Their place of residence was shifted to a beautiful building lying just below the Potala. During the following weeks, Bakula attended the Monlam. He took the opportunity to meet some important personalities who are listed in his report.

1. The Dalai Lama.[43]

2. General Zhang Jingwu: "He is said to be the counterpart of Dalai Lama as appointed in Tibet by the Chinese People's Republic," wrote the Ladakhi lama.

3. The Mother of Dalai Lama.

4. The Ven'ble Ganden Tripa, who represented the best brain of the Lamas of Tibet (and the head of the Yellow Hat sect).

5. *Chikiap Khempo*[44], the elder lama brother of Dalai Lama (Lobsang Samten).

6. Lt Gen Liushar: "one of the signatories to the last [1951] China-Tibet Agreement".

We shall come back to the latter.

**Time to Return to India**

The visas granted to the Mission were valid till the end of February 1956 only: "But since the Mission was not likely to finish its pujas and pilgrimage before the month of March, the Government of India was moved to sanction extension of the visas by one month which was

---

41 Great Prayer Congregation or Monlam Chenmo.

42 The 6th day of the first Tibetan month.

43 Interestingly, Bakula does not write the customary His Holiness before the name of the Tibetan leader.

44 Or *Jigyab Khenpo* the highest monk official in the government. His responsibilities included oversight of the Dalai Lama's personal attendants and private treasury. Between 1952 and 1956, the Dalai Lama's brother Lobsang Samten was Jigyab Khenpo.

duly granted," wrote Bakula. It is not clear how the Indian Consulate could grant a visa extension to stay in Tibet to the Ladakhi Mission. Bakula Rinpoche probably meant that the Consulate recommended the extension to the Chinese authority.

On February 22, the Chinese sponsored a first meeting of a Council of Tibetan high-ranking Head Lamas at Lhasa: "I was invited by the concerned Chinese authority to participate in the meeting. I accepted the invitation. As per agenda of the meeting the invitees were requested to express their grievance if any against the development works of the Chinese in Tibet."

Bakula, who was known to be a strict disciplinarian gave the other lamas a lecture: "I commended their development works but it was pointed out that it was not proper from the standpoint of the Buddhists to destroy *mani* walls[45] falling on roads which the Chinese troops were doing in the course of their building new roads in the length and breadth of Tibet."

It was probably easier for him to speak than for the other lamas residing in Tibet.

As the Monlam Festival was coming to an end, the time had come to return to India and Ladakh: "I sought my last audience with the Dalai Lama which was granted without delay."

The party left Lhasa on March 3, shortly after attending the last Prayer Congregation: "The concerned Chinese authorities placed as on our former journey, a jeep and a truck at our disposal. Another Chinese officer in place of Mr. Ko, one interpreter Lonxang[46] and 5 guards reported to us again and they saw us off at the last end of their border."

In just two days, they were back in Shigatse, where they met the Panchen Lama; they stayed for a week at the Tashilhunpu and left for India on March 19. The return journey was uneventful, except the road having been improved, the journey was slightly faster.

---

45 Prayer wheels containing the mantra *Om Mani Padme Hung*.
46 Probably Lobsang.

## The Rinpoche Meets the Prime Minister

At New Delhi, Bakula was received by the Prime Minister for some 90 minutes during which he reported about his tour to Tibet which had taken place at such a crucial time; China still needed India's goodwill while asserting more every day their presence on the Tibetan plateau.

To complete his report, the Ladakhi Lama wrote a few lines about the political situation in Tibet and the resistance of the people of Tibet against the Chinese occupation.

Bakula concluded his report: "There are about 20,000 Chinese troops at present working all over the country. They build roads and buildings. A few schools for teaching Chinese and Tibetan languages have been opened at Lhasa and Shigatse. One Hospital equipped with an X-Ray plant is said to have been opened at Lhasa. The Chinese at present do not interfere with the normal activities of the *Gompas* (monasteries)."

According to the Rinpoche, the Chinese were going around "declaring that they will not be interested with [in] the religious affairs of the Tibetans for times to come." But Bakula continued: "Yet the deep-seated suspicion of the Tibetans – both lamas and laymen – against the bonafides of the Chinese people is all common and contagious. They argue that confirmed unbelievers like the Chinese cannot be expected to remain unconcerned with the Tibetan religion for long. Yet the Chinese are sparing no pains to popularize themselves among the public through press and platform."

It is probably what the Rinpoche told the Prime Minister during their encounter; he added in his report: "There is a big fund of good-will available among the Tibetans for India and her great Prime Minister. This, I think, has its principal cause in the existence of the freedom of religion in India as also the cause that the Tibetans had received huge quantity of rations in their troublesome times a few years ago."[47] In fact, the Dalai Lama and his countrymen are looking forward to receive India's helping hand in their hour of need."

The Chinese did not keep their words and Delhi did not pay heed to Bakula's warnings about the Chinese troops.

---

47 See Volume 2, Chapter 5.

## Nirmal Sinha's Report

As mentioned earlier, Dr Nirmal Sinha was attached to the PO's Office in Gangtok.

On April 11, 1956, he also filed a report with the Ministry; his report was mostly a complaint about the treatment meted to him by the Ladakhi attendants of Bakula. In his report addressed to the SOBA[48], Sinha narrated at length his difficulties with his J&K colleagues: "I understood from the very beginning that I was as much a member of the pilgrim party as the three other lay, that is, non-clerical persons (Khosla, Stobden and Marchen) and that I would be entitled to the same facilities out of governmental funds as these three."

The problems for Sinha started in Lhasa: "In the first week of our stay at Lhasa, Bakula party, that is, disciple Rigdol, the Controller of Funds and Provisions, evinced great reluctance to provide food to my peon Dorje. Dorje was naturally not willing to fend for himself when he found other non-clerical elements (now being slowly but steadily strengthened by members of the private Ladakhi pilgrim party) being fed from our provisions and funds."

Nirmal Sinha needed Dorje who was "a loyal and trusted hand and of immense use both as my waiter and informant (unconscious) – I volunteered to pay for his food without any arguments."

This would cost him some Rs.120 for Dorje's food in Lhasa alone; however: "My acceptance of this situation encouraged Bakula party to go further. Without giving me any previous warning, in Drikungzong[49] (60/70 miles from Lhasa) from about 15th January supply of food was stopped. I was then cut off from my base in Lhasa, my own provisions (mainly tinned stuff) were almost consumed thanks to liberal participation of Ladakhis both in our own party as well as the private party, and I was left with two alternatives' either to take only *tsampa* (barley) or to undergo fasting."

---

48  SK Roy.
49  Drikung Thil.

He finally returned to Lhasa after the party's second round of pilgrimage but "I could not any longer carry out Apa Saheb's[50] instructions to be with Bakula party almost all the time. I stayed with Menon for 27 days at a stretch that I was in for a serious breakdown. The dust of Shigatse on the top of the malnutrition brought an attack of allergic asthma. Thanks to Chibber and his good doctor I got rid of the allergy at Yatung but discovered that I was suffering from a general breakdown and that my fasting experiments had, among other things, enabled me to get rid of 16 lbs of perhaps unwanted flesh!!!"

The Cultural Attaché explained that as he did not want "to strain in any way my good relations with Kushak Bakula, I avoided discussions about my difficulties with him. I know for certain that disciple Rigdol and some very greedy and crafty Ladakhi monks in Drikungzong were responsible for this course of action. I desisted from the natural temptation to know whether Kushak Bakula willingly accepted their advice or was quite helpless!!"

He wanted nevertheless to be refunded for his expenses. On May 5, SK Roy replied to Sinha's letter: "I am sorry indeed to hear that you have had such a difficult time. In the party and in fact much of these difficulties could have been sorted out and possibly prevented if everything had not had to be done in such a rush. Actually, the question of your being supplied provisions out of Govt. funds would naturally never arise. As an Officer appointed to accompany the party you would draw your T.A.[51] and D.A.[52] according to whatever rates are applicable."

Roy suggested that Sinha should request the Finance authorities: "to draw your daily allowance as usual because you have paid for your food yourself and such portion of the transport charges as you paid for yourself in addition to any other elements which are allowed to you locally."

---

50  Apa Pant, the Political Officer.

51  Travel allowance.

52  Daily allowance.

On May 20, the Political Officer stepped in regarding some donations that Nirmal Sinha, had been authorized to do to the Tibetan monasteries while in Tibet.

Sinha was entitled to make cash offerings up to Rs. 1,000 "to various monasteries and institutions in Tibet that Kushak Bakula and party visited and offered cash and other offerings. If Sinha, the only Government of India official attached to the party, had not made the customary cash offerings, it would have been interpreted otherwise by the monastic authorities and it was in our interest that he did so."

Pant continued corresponding with BK Acharya, the Joint Secretary in the Ministry: "Sinha happened to be the first Indian officer to visit some of the remote monasteries. A total sum of Rs. 731/- details of which are enclosed, was given as cash offerings. Sinha had kept me informed of these offerings in his correspondence and had my authority to do so. You will find reference to some of these offerings in his reports."

The PO recommended Sinha should be reimbursed "he would request for issue of necessary sanctions for 1957-58 for the Information Service of India, Gangtok, if no special grant is made available."

It had not been easy for the representative of the Political Officer.

**A Funny Incident**

With the arrival of the Chinese on the Tibetan plateau, they started changing the spellings of the names of the persons and places on a regular basis.

PN Menon, the Indian Consul in Lhasa once wrote to JN Sircar, the Under Secretary (NEF)[53] in the Ministry of External Affairs: "I cannot quite make out the Lt. General Liuyu Shah at all [in Bakula's report]. There are only two Tibetans who have military ranks corresponding to Lt. Generals viz. Ragashar Shape and Ngapho[54] Shape. There is one Dzasa Liushar[55] who is a monk official who is the Vice Director of the

---

53 North-East Frontier.

54 Ngabo Ngawang Jigme.

55 Loling Thupten Tharpa. A monk official. Born in 1913. Also known as Liushar. Made a La-chag (Treasurer) in May, 1938. Promoted to Dzasa and appointed as

Foreign Bureau and was previously the Foreign Secretary of Nepal for a number of years. But this Liushar has no pretensions of either military rank or potentialities."

The Consul asked South Block to clarify.

On October 10, the Under Secretary in the MEA asked Khosla to check: "We are not able to place this gentleman."

Five months later, on March 31, 1957, Khosla finally answered: "the full name of the gentleman is reported to Neshar Thupstan Tharpa and is known to the outsiders by the short name of Napa Ahapa. He is said to have visited China several times and has written a booklet in Bodhi about these visits."

Though we have seen it in the case of Barahoti/Wuje, it was only the beginning of the name-changing tactics used by the Chinese.

---

Monk Secretary of the Foreign Bureau in February, 1948. Appointed Joint Chief of Guides to Chinese officers in Lhasa in August, 1951, in addition to the duties as monk Secretary of the Foreign Bureau.

# 19

# The Life of the Consul General of India in Lhasa

In 1956, PN Menon, the Indian Consul General in Lhasa was completing the third year of his tenure in Tibet. Through his monthly reports, we shall try to reconstitute the main issues that the Indian diplomat had to face at the end of his time in Tibet.

First and foremost was the organization of the Buddha Jayanti, the 2500th anniversary of the birth of Gautam Buddha, but he also had to deal with the uprising in Eastern Tibet and the outcome of the consolidation of the Chinese presence on the plateau.

The Monthly Reports sent to the Ministry give a fairly good idea of the situation of the plateau. We shall quote Menon extensively, though we have re-arranged the content of his reports by topics to make it clearer.[1]

It must be noted that Menon had a defence background, having been in the Indian Navy before joining the Foreign Service.

At the beginning of each report, the main events of the month(s) are summarized. The 'monthly' reports relate events of one or in a few cases, two months.

During January and February 1956, the Consulate had the visits of Bakula Rinpoche and the Maharajkumar of Sikkim. At that time, India's intention was to invite the Dalai Lama and Panchen Lama to

---

1 *Monthly report of Consulate Lhasa*; Department: External Affairs, Sikkim Agency; Branch: Political; 1957; File No. Progs. Nos. 4(10)-P. Available at the National Archives of India.

India later in 1956, "considerable interest was attached to these visits [and] on the acceptance of the invitations by the Tibetan leaders."

This issue will be dealt with separately in subsequent chapters.

The report usually started with a few paras on the relations between Tibet and the new occupying power.

**Road Construction**

As we have seen in a previous volume[2], the construction of roads was the priority for Communist China. During the two first months of 1956, we are told that the construction of the motor road linking Phari with Gautsa[3], "upto which the road from Yatung had been completed by 1954-55, was taken up in earnest."

It was expected that by the end of March 1956, the road would be completed up to Yatung: "The entire road from Lhasa to Phari and beyond is very much of a fair-weather road and it would require considerable efforts during the next summer and winter seasons on the part of the Chinese road builders before it can equal the standards of the Tibet–Sikang highway," mentioned the Report.

The construction of the road network was crucial for the Chinese to complete and consolidate the occupation of the plateau.

Already considerable damage had been done to the Gyantse – Shigatse section, despite its limited use: "no vehicle can do more than 20 miles an hour on that stretch."

Menon noted that the rapid construction of motor roads on the Tibetan plateau was bound to have some repercussions on the existing mule transports on "which the people of these areas had depended for their livelihood so considerably in the past."

The Consul General also stated that "a certain amount of grumbling among these circles is beginning to be heard."

As for India, which had surrendered all its right in Tibet, "the strategic and political consequences of these improvements in communications

---

2   See Volume 2, Chapter 10.

3   Gautsa is located between Phari and Yatung in the Chumbi Valley. See Map 4 page 579.

on the border States like Bhutan and Sikkim should also not escape our attention" Menon rightly remarked, before adding: "For the first time in history it has become possible for China to transport by modern vehicles large bodies of men from their peripheral provinces like Tsinghai[4] and Szechuan[5] to our frontiers in the Chumbi valley, etc."

The Indian diplomat continued to argue: "While we should not underestimate this achievement of China's planners, [but] we should not forget that it will still take a number of years before the Chinese are able to make these roads *pucca* ones."

The future would prove him wrong.

Six years later, a war would take place on the slopes of the Himalaya. The roads and communication in general in Tibet would make the difference.

Interestingly, the Chinese announced the introduction of a proper bus service between Chamdo and Lhasa with occasional trips up to Shigatse.

Tibet was changing fast.

In March, Delhi was informed that the Chinese had taken a convoy of trucks from Nagchukha to Gartok in Western Tibet over the Changthang plateau. The Consulate remarked that the road "whose contours have been marked out on this trip is very much like the Tibet-Tsinghai road running between Sining[6] and Lhasa."

Delhi was also told that great stretches of the new route to Gartok did not require any construction 'except just levelling up': "Gartok in Western Tibet is now linked with China via Nagchukha and through the Tibet-Tsinghai highway."

Further, the motor road from Phari to Yatung was completed on March 29, 1956 and during a special function held in Yatung, it was formally opened.

---

4   Qinghai.

5   Sichuan.

6   Xining.

We have already seen that the Maharajkumar of Sikkim and Kushak Bakula were able to return to India using a motor vehicle up to Yatung.

**Air Strips in Tibet**

The January-February Report spoke of some kind of construction work, including levelling of land at Zangra Dung[7]: "One version is that an air strip for landing of planes is being constructed at Zangra Dung. It is clear that the Chinese activities on the Tibet-Nepal frontier are on the increase," noted the Consul general who further commented, "there is considerable speculation about Chinese intentions in the aviation field in Tibet in the near future. Most of the talk is about the construction of landing grounds."

Delhi was informed that the decision to build an aerodrome in Lhasa had been taken: "The site mentioned lies approximately a mile east of the Sera monastery. It would be recalled that Aufschnaiter[8], while he was here with Harrer, had marked out an area in front of Sera monastery as suitable for a landing strip."

Menon said that the newly selected site was 'well east': "There are reports of the possibility of Chinese planes flying over Tibet in the near future possibly as part of aerial reconnaissance of the approach route to Lhasa."

In the April Report, he mentioned for the first time, the construction of an airport: "Aviation has come to Tibet. On 3rd April a four-engined (Piston engines) plane which had taken off from Lanchow flew over Lhasa and its valley. The plane which resembled a Liberator[9] flew for 15 to 20 minutes before flying back in the same direction from which it came."

The Report continued to describe the historic event: "On April 22 morning, a similar four-engined plane flew over Lhasa and dropped

---

7   North East of Dzongka Dzong, north of the Nepal border with Tibet.

8   Peter Aufschnaiter was a Tyrolean mountaineer, agricultural scientist, geographer, and cartographer. His experiences with fellow climber Heinrich Harrer during World War II were depicted in the film *Seven Years in Tibet*.

9   The Consolidated B-24 Liberator is a four-engined bomber used by the Royal Air Force.

leaflets containing congratulatory slogans for the opening of the Preparatory Committee."

The Indian Consulate was now aware that the Chinese authorities were constructing a large airfield at a place called Umathang[10] in the Damarea[11] located northwest of Reting Gompa[12].

According to Menon, two Russian experts, "whom we have seen in Lhasa, are now at the airfield site supervising work." Kapshopa Theiji has been appointed as the Tibetan official in charge of the project and a few thousand Tibetan labourers were recruited for the purpose. The work was expected to be completed "within the next two months. Thus, an aerial link between Central Tibet and China proper will be established within the next few months."

The April Report mentioned again the construction of the Umathang aerodrome; it had just been completed and the first Chinese planes landed on the aerodrome on May 26: "I gather from the Chinese authorities themselves that the aerodrome has only been completed in a preliminary way and that it will take a few months more before it can support regular air services," wrote Menon.

During the inaugural flights, only two-engine planes were used, the Consul General concluded: "[it] lends considerable evidence to the existence of an aerodrome half way between Lanchow aerodrome and Umathang. This could well be the Jyekundo airfield. ...There is

---

10  Umathang is in Damshung County (Dzong).

11  Damshung or Damxung is a county North of Lhasa. Its administrative town is Damshuka. The terrain is rugged, including the western Nyenchen Tanglha Mountains, with their highest peak rising to 7,111 metres.

In fact, the first flight to Lhasa took place in 1955 at Damshung Airport, North of Lhasa near the Nam tso lake. Damshung was then the world's highest airport.

According to *China Tibet Online*: "There was even no telephone in the Damshung Airport. The civil aviation flight team of Beijing Administration used Ilyushin Il-18s. The plane flew from Beijing to Chengdu, and must arrive at Damshung in the forenoon of the next day and leave as soon as possible, because the strong wind in Damshung will blow after the midday, making the airport filled with stones."

12  Located approximately 70 miles north of Lhasa.

no doubt that aviation has come to Tibet and that we may expect its extension to all parts of Tibet in the not too distant future."

Something rather surprising was also mentioned, India and China were ready to collaborate to have flights from Tibet to India. Menon wrote: "flights by Chinese and Indian planes took place successfully."

It cited a Chinese plane which completed the flight from Tangshung aerodrome[13] to Bagdogra and back on 21st October. The Indian Air Force Ilyushin aircraft with its crew led by Group Captain Ranjan Dutt flew from Jorhat to Tangshung on the morning of 24th October flying over Lhasa in the process."

Then the Indian aircraft flew back on October 26, flying over Gyantse and Yatung: "The most pleasing thing was the great co-operation extended by the Chinese authorities for our flight and the great reception they gave to our flyers on landing," wrote Menon, who told Delhi that at this 'out of the way aerodrome' the Chinese held a banquet involving "transportation of food from Lhasa itself. The Chinese appear extremely keen to have an Indo-Tibetan air link if possible. Since the time taken by the Chinese plane from Tangshung to Bagdogra was only a little over an hour the speeding up in travel that would come about by the establishment of an air link between India and Tibet can be well imagined."

It would never materialize though the Panchen Lama would return from India by air a few months later.

In December, the Chinese dropped six parachutists just outside Lhasa: "The exact purpose for which they were dropped is not known. But people, in general, felt that the Chinese wanted to show the Tibetans that in case of trouble they can get reinforcements by air."

This was probably part of the Communist Party's propaganda work.

## More Roads

In his June Report, the Consul came back to the building of roads on the plateau; he informed Delhi: "There is more and more talk of Chinese plans to construct a direct road running from Gyantse area to

---

13  About 109 miles North of Lhasa in Damshung area; in fact in Uma Thang.

a point or two on the Sikang[14]-Tibet highway which will incidentally open up the Lhoka and Thakpo[15] areas lying South of Lhasa."

One of the rationales would be to facilitate the exploitation of the natural resources of these two areas, "the plan, if fulfilled, in the next year or so would mean the strengthening of Chinese hold over South and South Eastern Tibet."

It is what eventually happened.

Menon could see the danger for the Indian frontiers: "The nearness of the two areas proposed to be developed to our North East Frontier Agency and Bhutan lends considerable significance to these moves. In fact, there is some reason to believe that the Chinese are beginning to take serious note of the developmental activities in our North East Frontier Agency and its possible repercussions on the Tibetan people living in Tibet across our border."

By the mid-1950s, the Chinese leadership in Lhasa realized the historical importance of Tawang and other areas North of the McMahon Line, the Report concluded: "The communication and other developments on the Tibetan side of the North East Frontier Agency and the frontiers of Bhutan will, therefore, require our close and detailed attention in the future."

The first serious intrusion into the Indian territory in this area[16] took place less than three years after these words were written.

In his September Report, the Consul General noted: "As part of their recent efforts to open up the Southern Tibetan areas adjoining Bhutan and North East Frontier Agency the taking up of the construction of the Lhasa-Tsethang road via Chusul assumes some significance."

Tsethang was located in the Yarlung Valley in Lhoka area.

It was not only the roads which were developing fast, the airstrips too; according to Menon: "Chinese authorities have now claimed the completion of the aerodrome in Umathang in Dam. No regular

---

14  Kham province.

15  Dakpo.

16  Longju.

air services have so far been started between this aerodrome and Lanchow.[17]"

In the month of October, the news about the construction of the Lhasa-Tsethang motor road was confirmed: "Chinese authorities have now announced that they hope to complete the Lhasa-Tsethang motor road by the middle of December this year."

Delhi was informed that the road had reached some 30 miles from Lhasa and was already motorable, "the completion of the rest on time is a certainty", concluded the Report.

In December, the Nagchukha-Gartok road was under construction while the road between Lhasa and Tsethang was nearing completion.

**Defence Issues**

The Monthly Reports seldom provided information on defence.

However, the March Report said: "It was understood from a reliable source that the Chinese have moved about four to five thousand fresh Chinese troops from the Sining[18] area to the Nepal Tibet border. Most of the troops passed through Shigatse while a small number passed through Lhasa."

Menon gave a brief description of the troops' equipment, "they have slightly heavier weapons than those issued to troops in Central Tibet. One of the reasons given for this move is Chinese nervousness over foreign mountaineering activities inside Nepal."

It is doubtful if it was really the reason; the movement of troops was probably linked to the construction of landing grounds in Zangra Dung as well as the landing of amphibian boats on the Pekhu tso[19]: "[it] may turn out to be part of preparations for receiving the troops."

---

17 Lanzhou.

18 Xining in Qinghai.

19 Lake Paiku is a lake at 4,591 meters elevation in the Kyirong county of Shigatse City. It is 18 kms south of the Yarlung Tsangpo. The lake is 27 kms long and 6 kms wide at its narrowest. It is surrounded by mountains reaching 5,700 to 6,000 meters.

In April, Delhi was told that the Tibetan Army Regiments had been issued Chinese uniforms: "While the entire Kusung Regiment[20] has been kitted up in this fashion, in the case of the other three Regiments the new uniforms have been issued only upto the non-commissioned officer levels." The Consul remarked that it was one of the decisions taken by the Chinese State Council in March 1955 for the Tibetan Army: "and it may well turn out to be the first step in the full integration of the Tibetan Regiments in the PLA."

It would not be so.

## Miscellaneous Consular Work

The report brought to the notice of the Ministry that some Welsh mountaineers had been arrested by the Chinese in Tibet and were being sent back via Gangtok: "The Nepalese Officer has no information apart from a letter received from the wife of one of the mountaineers to intercede on her husband's behalf."

Apparently, the negotiation for the release of the mountaineers and their Nepalese Liaison Officer was conducted between the Nepalese and the Chinese in Delhi: "It seemed likely that the mountaineers would be released on the Nepal frontier itself," wrote Menon.

In March, Menon visited the three big monasteries (Drepung, Sera and Ganden) and distributed the annual cash presents on behalf of the Government of India: "At all these monasteries, I was received in a mostly friendly fashion and the senior Abbots expressed their appreciation of the efforts of our Government in reviving Buddhism in India."

They took the opportunity to speak of the dependence of Tibet on Indian goods and urged the Consul to continue sending monks from Ladakh, Kulu, Himachal Pradesh and other Himalayan areas for study in the Tibetan monasteries.

## The Trade with India

The January/February Report informed that "The Chinese Bank in Lhasa has now started issuing rupee drafts to traders here but only on

---

20 The Kusung Regiment is the Bodyguard Regiment attached to the Dalai Lama.

a quarterly basis." Unfortunately for the traders, the total quantity of exchange which could be given in one year had not been specified, "therefore [there are] some doubts about exchange prospects."

At the same time, there was some talk of setting up exchange banks in various towns of Tibet. This would help the Chinese to hasten the 'currency reforms', in other words, the Tibetan currency would be withdrawn and replaced by Chinese paper currency.

Menon commented: "It is however unlikely that this would happen before the end of the year …by which time the new administrative changes[21] would have come about."

The pattern of trade was changing, not even two years after the signature of the Agreement on trade and pilgrimage.

The negotiators during the 1954 talks did not realize that they were burying the traditional Tibetan trade with India. A first indication showing the new State control of the trade became apparent when the Chinese authorities set up a special procedure for the sale of certain Chinese goods and the mode of payment to be made by shopkeepers who sold these items; the Consul General wrote: "The traders who receive articles like Chinese brick tea, cigarettes, fountain pens, sweets and tinned stuff are required to get them in bulk and to issue certain coupons on sale to the buyers as well as to the Chinese Bank in order that the Bank may make recoveries for the goods from the account of the purchasers of the goods and reimburse the traders account."

It was clear that China wanted to progressively take control of the entire trade on the plateau; the Communist authorities "are trying to encourage deposits in their bank by this method as well as Indian traders to utilise their savings in purchasing goods from China."

The goods were then sold for prices prominently listed in the shops.

A month later, the Report noted that ever since India had started to allow (under a permit system) import into India of Chinese silver dollars "there has been a regular flight of this currency from Tibet to India. Large quantities of Chinese silver dollars are being sent from Central Tibet to Phari for sale to Marwari traders."

---

21 The setup of the PCTAR.

The Report added that the Chinese authorities have so far not shown any concern about these developments: "part of this indifference may be due to a willingness to part with their hoards of these coins as helping their currency reform here [in Lhasa], it could also indicate their desperate need to get goods from India which are no longer financed by this rupee drafts on a big scale," added the Report.

By May, 1956, the situation had changed, "There are unmistakable indications of Chinese intentions" to restrict the free export of silver dollars from Tibet.

With effect from July 1, a rigid control was to be instituted at Yatung for the export of silver dollars; the Chinese planned to setting up a Customs Post: "As the Chinese authorities are not in favour of allowing much freedom to Tibetan traders about the kind of goods they order from India, it is likely that as in the case of rupee drafts issued by them the export of dollars would be restricted to purchase goods which they specify to be imported."

It marked the end of the 'good days' for the Indian traders; further the Chinese feared "that the Tibetans may try to transfer their assets to India if they are given too much freedom to export silver dollars to India."

When a senior member of a delegation from Beijing addressed a meeting with the Tibetan traders in Lhasa, he advocated "the need to concentrate on internal trade and to gradually lessen the dependence on foreign trade [read India]"

The traders, aware that India was still dependent on trade with Tibet, mentioned their desire for the links with Tibet to continue as before.

The Report, however, observed: "Evidence was also forthcoming of certain subtle Chinese attempts to split the local traders on the basis of their rival interests. Thus the local Muslim traders, who are not so well to do, were promised financial assistance in return for trying to take over the unduly large volume of trade which the Nepali traders, who were described as foreigners, were monopolizing." It was the old colonial trick to favour one against the other, to win influence.

In July, it was confirmed that the Chinese authorities were going to set up an office at Phari to control the export of silver dollars from Tibet to India.

There was some opposition from the Tibetan traders against a total ban on the exports "and the Chinese are now getting reconciled to these exports so long as the traders will bring back goods of which they are in short supply like cement, petrol and structural steel," wrote the Consul General.

According to Menon, there was a delay in setting up the new Commerce Department under Rimshi Pangdatshang.

Delhi was also told that there was a theory in Lhasa that the Chinese were planning "to get rid of as many silver dollars as possible before they introduce paper currency."

He cited the fact that some Chinese personnel had started making payments to shopkeepers in currency notes in a small way: "The shopkeepers accept them at a much lower rate (while the silver dollar is equal to 15 sangs 5 Shokangs, they have fixed only 10 sangs for the paper note) and then sell the notes to Khampa traders who make payments of taxes on goods coming from China in such notes."

During the following months, the situation continued to deteriorate.

The October Report mentioned 'indications' that traders with Indian connections in Lhasa were on the point of gradually withdrawing from Tibet and transferring their assets to India. One of them was a firm called Abdul Aziz Ladakhache.

According to the Consulate: "Usually these Muslim traders have a shrewd idea of the shape of things to come and their precautions give some clue to the possibility of greater Chinese control over trade in the near future."

In the meantime, the restrictions on the export of dollars from Tibet were introduced on September 1; it immediately resulted in pushing up the prices of commodities and transportation rates. Menon told the Ministry: "We have taken up this question with the Chinese Foreign Bureau in the light of specific difficulties of the Indian traders at

Yatung, Phari and Gyantse. The Chinese have assured us that as far as pilgrims are concerned they will not impose any restrictions on export of dollars and that the other issues will be examined in consultation with the department concerned."

The situation would continue to deteriorate in the months to come.

## Relations with Nepal

In the April report, the Ministry was informed that one or two Tibetan representatives would be included in the Chinese delegation which was to attend the King of Nepal's coronation. They would represent the Dalai and Panchen Lamas; however, remarked the Consul, the Nepalese Officer in Lhasa was totally ignorant about it.

On May 2, the King's coronation was celebrated by the Nepalese Officer in Lhasa. Strangely, apart from the Foreign Bureau officials, no high ranking Chinese or Tibetan officials attended the party; the excuse was that everybody was busy with the final day celebrations of the Preparatory Committee, which might have been true.

Due to the shortage of accommodation, the Nepali nationals too had started suffering in Lhasa. In two or three cases, the house owners of Nepalese traders tried to secure their eviction: "The Nepalese Officer has not been able to secure much assistance from the Foreign Bureau in settling these matters and it looks as though the Chinese are indulging in a policy of pinpricks and masterly inactivity on the eve of the Sino-Nepal talks."

It was certainly a tactic to get concessions later.

In August, the Sino-Nepal talks were to commence in Kathmandu. The talks centered around Nepal's position in Tibet and the association of Tibetan delegates with the Chinese delegation; for the first time in talks with another State, the Chinese associated a representative from Tibet in their delegation: "They never ventured on this step when we had our negotiations in Peking for the Sino-Indian Treaty on Tibet in 1953-54," rightly noted Menon.

Ragashar Shape[22] was sent to Nepal; he was accompanied by five others[23] who joined the rest of the Chinese delegation, who had assembled in Delhi.

The report mentioned that the Chinese authorities took extraordinary security precautions to hide Ragashar's movement on his way from Lhasa to Gangtok; they had cleverly disguised his identity by giving his name out as Pintso Rapje[24]. Another incident typically Chinese: "At Yatung when applying for our *dak bungalow* passes they curiously made the Baba Interpreter, the leader of the party instead of Ragashar."

Menon said: "I find from reports from Nepal that the Chinese are closely guarding Ragashar from newspaper correspondents although publicity is at the same time being given about his important role in these talks as a member of the Preparatory Committee of the Tibetan Autonomous Region [and] ex-commander-in-Chief of Tibetan Army."

The Report also mentioned the Chinese efforts to camouflage Ragashar's physical identity; for example, it was noticed on a photograph of the Kalon's arrival in Kathmandu that he had been given a hair cut in Calcutta and he wore Chinese clothes; Menon advised: "It would be in our interest to keep a close watch on these talks at Kathmandu itself."

In September, the new Sino-Nepal Treaty on Tibet and Friendship was signed. As there was delay in publishing its terms, not many comments appeared, finally the Tibetan News Summary published the text which appeared in the press in India on September 24. In Lhasa, the Nepalese Officer posted in the Tibetan capital was still in the dark; he had not received any information from his Government. The Indian Consulate was unable to assess the local Chinese and Tibetan officials' reactions as the Tibetan delegation to the talks was not back. Menon however noted that there were "increasing indications that China's approach to Nepal corresponds to that of her approach to the small Indo-China States like Laos and Cambodia."

---

22 Maharani of Sikkim's eldest brother.

23 'One Chinese, one 'Baba' (Tibetan from Batang) interpreter and three Tibetans officials' said the Report.

24 The Chinese pronunciation of Phuntso Rabgye – the personal name of Ragashar Shape.

The Consul added "we can expect China to plan a programme of skilful economic assistance to Nepal and thus gradually strengthen her trans-Himalayan objectives to the extent possible." At the time, the feeling among the Nepali trading community in Lhasa was that they were bound "to suffer adversely by any new treaty which involves the abrogation of Nepal's extra-territorial rights in Tibet guaranteed by the treaty of 1856."

A month later, Delhi was informed that the relation between the Nepalese Officer[25] at Lhasa and the Nepali community in Lhasa continued to be strained. Further, the half-caste Nepalis[26] were unhappy with the rest of the Nepali Community as they were not consulted during Sino-Nepal negotiations for the new treaty. They had however been given the choice to decide their future: "From present trends it appears that the most of them will take Chinese nationality when the Sino-Tibet agreement is fully implemented."

It was only in October that all the details of the new Sino-Nepal treaty on Tibet were fully known. The reaction of the Nepali trading community was "an unmitigated gloom while the Tibetan officialdom and traders are naturally overjoyed by the disappearance of Nepalese extra-territorial rights etc."

In the meantime, the 'divorce' between the Nepalese Officer and his community was complete, "judging by the way they have completely boycotted his Dushera function and refused to indulge in the customary street procession dancing." Apparently, the Nepali traders had forced the Nepalese *Vakil* to send his *Subba*[27] to Kathmandu to plead their case in the negotiations; false information had earlier circulated that he was visiting an ailing mother.

The first outcome of the treaty was that the Nepalese *Khacharas* informed the Nepal Officer that they would stop paying the customary nominal poll tax, thus indicating that they would take en masse the Chinese nationality.

---

25  Known as the *Vakil*.
26  Known as *Khacharas*.
27  His assistant.

Menon told the Ministry in Delhi: "The ineptitude of the Nepal Foreign Office is illustrated by their failure to supply till now a copy of the latest treaty to their *Vakil*. He has only seen the local Tibetan version published in the Chinese Tibetan News Summary and also a cutting from the *Gurkha Patra*[28] sent to him by a friend in Kathmandu."

Menon's logical conclusion was that if Nepal was interested in protecting the interests of its nationals in Tibet in the future "under the terms of the new treaty she would be well advised to depute better-trained officials."

Or at least keep them posted of the important developments: "Otherwise the decline and disappearance of Nepalese nationals from Tibet by harsh application of local laws would only be a question of time. If we can discreetly advise the Nepalese in Kathmandu on this we would be doing a great service to her and her hapless nationals in Tibet."

Ironically, sixty years later, Nepal is well represented in Tibet, through a Consul General, while India has lost all her rights and advantages.

## The Panchen Lama is Back

In April, the Panchen Lama came back to Lhasa with a large entourage for attending the Preparatory Committee meeting. As he arrived in the capital, he was given a grand welcome; he later called on the Dalai Lama at the Potala.

During his stay in the Tibetan capital, the Panchen Lama stayed in the Lhasa Cathedral. He returned to Shigatse on May 7, after taking part in the meetings of the Preparatory Committee. They had to leave before the Central Delegation proceeded to Shigatse to make arrangements to welcome him.

In Lhasa, the Chinese authorities widely distributed Mao badges and peace-dove brooches. The case of many Khampas, who had arrived from Eastern Tibet, beating up persons wearing badges, were reported.

In June, as a result of serious difference of opinion between the monks of Tashilhunpo monastery and the Panchen Lama and his officials, 'an

---

28 Nepali newspaper.

ugly situation' developed in Shigatse. The Report stated: "The cause of the trouble was the insistence on immediate land reforms by the Panchen Lama and the stout opposition to it by the leading monks of the Tashilhunpo monastery."

The Indian Consul gave some details; one of the versions was dramatic: "the Panchen Lama sent for one of the senior Abbots in Shigatse to discuss the implementation of land reforms. The Abbot expressed his strong opposition to such ideas and in the heated argument that followed, the Panchen Lama is reported to have lost his temper and shot dead the Abbot with his own revolver."

Though it was undoubtedly 'fake news', it created a great deal of resentment among the monks and triggered 'a certain amount of violence'; the Panchen Lama's officials were threatened. The resentment was mainly against Dzasa Che Jigme[29], "who is considered as the right-hand man and evil counsellor of the Panchen Lama." As a result, partly to save his life and partly to divert the resentment against the Panchen Lama, Che Jigme decided to immediately leave Shigatse: "He let out before his departure that he had shot dead the Abbot, [it was] not the Panchen Lama. Che Jigme fled to Lhasa and is credited with having proceeded to China along with the members of the Central Delegation in the plane in which they left," wrote Menon.

But the story was not that simple, Che Jigme was soon back in Lhasa, staying in a house belonging to the Panchen Lama: "The presence of the Panchen Lama's car in Lhasa during these troubles led to rumours that even the Panchen had fled to Lhasa for safety."

In the end, Menon told Delhi that after thorough enquiries: "I am convinced that there is no basis for this rumour and that the car may well have brought Che Jigme to Lhasa and stayed on for a few days before being returned to Shigatse."

The Chinese authorities in Shigatse apparently adopted a neutral attitude, "although they can be expected to safeguard the Panchen Lama's position if it becomes necessary."

---

29  See Chapter 7, Footnote 23.

The conclusion of the Report was that "it is clear that the Panchen Lama's position in Tibet is none too secure as yet."

We shall study, in the next chapters, his difficult relation with the Dalai Lama.

### The Foreign Bureau in Lhasa

In the meantime, Yang Gongsu became the Director of the Foreign Bureau. On June 23, he left for consultations with the Chinese Foreign Office in Beijing. Ya Hanzhang, a member of the CCP's Tibet Work Committee in Tibet, remained behind as acting director in Yang's place. Menon said that according to a reliable source, Yang Gongsu would be away from Lhasa for some months: "While it is possible that Yang's present visit to China is in connection with [the] briefing by the Chinese Foreign Office, now that the Foreign Bureau in Lhasa has been separated from the Central Government's Representative's Office[30] in Tibet and has become purely an organ of the Foreign Office."

The Consul General believed that Yang, who was a key Communist official in Tibet, "may have been entrusted with some special mission connected with recent developments in Eastern Tibet [and in] Shigatse."

It was also suggested, though it is doubtful as Yang had been posted for 'a fairly long spell' in Lhasa, that he could avail a vacation in China before returning to Tibet. This was not usually how it worked for the Party cadres. In the meantime, it was noted that the Sub Offices of the Foreign Bureau in Gyantse and Yatung had been strengthened by the deputing of trained officials of the Foreign Bureau from Beijing.

A month later, it was confirmed that the sudden departure of Yang Gongsu was linked with the negotiations with Nepal; he was to be a member of the Chinese delegation to negotiate the treaty between China and Nepal on Tibet. As we have seen, some Tibetan officials later joined the delegation in Delhi.

### Sending Children to China for Education

In July, Delhi was informed of a new scheme: a few hundred boys and girls from various parts of Tibet had been sent to China for admission to

---

30  Gen Zhang Jingwu.

The National Minority Institute. At the same time, a group of Tibetan women belonging to the Women's Leagues, was sent on a sightseeing tour of China. This was another indication how the Chinese planned to bring the Tibetans on their side.

The report also mentioned "the organisation of the school children in the various Chinese Schools in Tibet into the well known Communist Young Pioneer Movement."

The Indian diplomat commented: "the picture that emerges is one of sustained efforts on the part of the Chinese authorities to mould the young people from school children to youth and Women Leaguers into the ideological pattern prevailing in China proper. There is no doubt that the present regime is convinced of the long term advantages accruing to it from such a policy."

In November, the campaign took a new spin; the Chinese started recruiting Tibetan youth of both sexes aged between 15 and 25 for their Administrative School. They put up posters in different parts of Lhasa: "Besides assuring career after successful training, they offered food, clothing and 15 Chinese silver dollars[31] as out of pocket expenses. The response was not very encouraging in the beginning, but later probably due to relaxation in age limits and also for economic reasons, a number of young Tibetans came forward and joined the ranks of the would be administrators of New Tibet."

The Consulate informed that the school, running from two different places had already 2,000 trainees: "besides the Tibetan youths we learn that there are a number of Chinese Muslims boys and girls (commonly known as Ho Ho) and Bhabas[32] (residents of border districts of China and Tibet)."

For the first time, in August, a Young Pioneer's Camp was organised in Lhasa. The children were drawn from various parts of Tibet: "It was a great success and during its fortnight's existence a number of parents of the children in the camp visited them and saw them at work and play."

---

31  Rs. 45 as per Chinese exchange rate.
32  From Batang in Eastern Tibet. Also written 'Babas'.

Apparently, the organisers had worked for two months to complete the preparations for the holding of the camp; they were happy with the results: "The camp is a pointer to the way the Chinese authorities are preparing to take charge of the younger generation of Tibetans and mould them into the type that would make them ideal citizens under a Communist State," noted the Report.

The camp coincided with school vacations in Tibet, and was followed by intense activity connected with the training of these children for the ceremonies and festivities for the October 1 celebrations.

It was clear that there was a strong ideological underlining in each and every Chinese action.

The Consul, however, remarked: "we might bear in mind that the percentage of such children who are caught up in such Chinese activities is still insignificant on account of the present regime's inadequate resources in Tibet. But this is a deficiency which time and the fresh injection of trained Han cadres into Tibet can be expected to overcome in a few years time."

In the meantime, the debate on the rapid introduction of land reforms continued; the Consulate remarked: "Apart from younger Tibetan officials influenced by the ideology of Socialism and therefore advocating these changes, there has been the strange spectacle of some old land holding aristocrats expressing support for land reform."

The report cited Dzasa Samdup Photrang, a senior official, who was the latest convert to the land reforms; usually, it was to please the Chinese or for economic reasons: "Apparently these Tibetan officials have very little conception of the implications of such social changes and their impact on the feudal society of Tibet. The Chinese authorities have been trying to lull them into a sense of security by promising them compensation in cash."

Menon also quoted one monk official saying that the question of compensation was all right, if it was paid before the lands were taken, but in any case, a too rapid change of the present social order could have disastrous consequences for the monasteries and the clergy in general; as they fully depended on their estates. One question remained: had the Chinese made up their minds: "but judging by the propaganda being made in support of land reform the time cannot be delayed by more than four or five months."

In the meanwhile, energy had started to turn towards the important event which was to take place, i.e. the visit of the Dalai Lama and the Panchen Lama to India …as well as that of Zhou Enlai.

## The Indian Boundary

More serious for India, the Report mentioned that a Tibetan official of the Foreign Bureau accompanied by a Chinese and a Tashilhunpo official had left for Western Tibet in July "for looking at the boundary." Menon guessed that it could relate to the unsettled Tehri-Tibet boundary "it might also have some relation to the Nepal boundary in case it should come up at the Sino-Nepal talks."

A month later, the news was confirmed: "the Foreign Bureau official who has been deputed to Western Tibet rather suddenly for looking into the border is Trakpa Yargye[33], a monk official with previous service experience in Western Tibet."

More details were given, the monk official Trakpa Yargye served as Bongba Chikyap[34] in Western Tibet from 1940 to 1942 and could, therefore, be expected to know all the previous Tibetan claims on Tehri Garhwal borders. Menon pointed out: "His departure for Western Tibet with some Chinese officials assumes considerable significance in the light of some border trespassing by Chinese patrols recently into our territory in these areas."

In September, it was reported that the Chinese were devoting considerable attention to the development of the Lhoka region lying to the South of Lhasa and the Tsangpo river.

---

33 The report referred to page 134 of the *Who's Who in Tibet*, not available with us.

34 Bongba is a village in Gegye Dzong, today in Ngari Prefecture of the Tibet Autonomous Region. It is situated at an altitude of 4,542 metres (14,904 feet).

## Geological Parties

In Lhasa, it was reported[35] that several Chinese geological parties had started survey work in Tibet; the minerals discovered or their commercial potentialities were not mentioned. However, due to the regular announcements about the need to develop factories and the systematic attempts to recruit Tibetan labourers for training: "it can be assumed that some industrial development is being envisaged for Tibet on the basis of these mineral finds."

Particularly mentioned was the presence of coal in the Dam area, North of Lhasa[36] as well as near Medu Gongkar. The Consul General's conclusions were: "developments in the industrial sector can, therefore, be expected to take the form of coal mining and perhaps some small scale iron industry for turning out agricultural implements."

It was also said that some 50 Soviet technical experts would come to Tibet in 1957. We do not know if they ever came.

## Buddhist Association of China

Interesting news was reported in October; the formation of the Tibet branch of the Buddhist Association of China. It came at a time when the Chinese authorities announced their decision to put off by three years their plans to bring land reform in Tibet.

On October 6, the Tibet branch of the Buddhist Association of China was inaugurated at Lhasa. Menon believed that it had great significance because it was "the first attempt to bring to Tibet the pattern of State intervention in religion already perfected in China proper through bodies like this."

Beijing had realized that religion in Tibet was a vital factor and "without ultimately capturing the minds of the followers of Tibetan Lamaism it would be impossible to make any impress of a fundamental nature on Tibetan society."

The Consul General suggested watching the activities of the Tibet Branch of the Buddhist Association of China as "the Chinese seem to

---

35   By the Tibet News Summaries.

36   Where the airport was located.

be quite perturbed by the psychological impression we have created all over Tibet by our Buddha Jayanti celebrations and its attendant cultural propaganda offensive," he added: "I was highly amused to be told by a Chinese official of the Foreign Bureau that India and China were both Buddhist countries, an emphasis on Buddhism which is rather recent and obviously part of a new propaganda line."

It was probably what decided China to participate in the festivities in India and allow the visit of the Dalai Lama and Panchen Lama to the Buddha Jayanti.

**The Reforms**

In October 1956, the Chinese authorities announced that they did not intend to rush into land reform in Tibet; the question could be considered during the next three years, if the conditions were ripe for it. The Report noted: "there is no doubt that this announcement has been precipitated by the strong opposition of the three big monasteries of Drepung, Sera and Ganden which was conveyed to the Tibetan Government as well as the Chinese authorities in writing."

Further, the continuous troubles in Eastern Tibet, as well as the rising tension in Central Tibet had probably contributed to the Chinese decision: "The general reaction among the propertied classes is one of obvious relief although there is some tendency not to put complete faith in Chinese promises," commented Menon.

The fact that the propaganda campaign for land reforms continued despite the assurances of their deferment, made many people wonder whether it was not out of sheer expediency that the Chinese authorities have given their present policy decision, noted Menon.

The Chinese National Day was celebrated in Lhasa in the usual colourful fashion. Apart from a rally, the main function consisted of a banquet, an evening theatrical performance staged by the school children of Lhasa.

The Chinese authorities were intensifying their efforts to recruit young people of both sexes in Lhasa, partly to man many jobs under the new departments of the Preparatory Committee and partly with a view to keep under employment all those elements who may cause troubles during a period of disturbances.

**Miscellaneous News**

The report of September 1956 mentioned the steady flow of East European visitors to Tibet during the summer, there were some 20 of them hailing from East Germany, Czechoslovakia and Hungary; they all lived in a building near the new Lhasa Auditorium. They had to stay at least till October 1, to participate in the functions for China's National Day: "I have been able to find out that the three East European countries representatives here have brought diesel trucks made in their countries with the specific view of finding out their suitability for Tibet and their subsequent sale to China," observed Menon who added that it was a good pointer to the present difficulties of transportation of petrol fuel to Tibet or even to the shortage of petrol throughout China.

In another report, the Consul wrote: "I was particularly impressed by their pluck in driving up all the way from Peking in their diesel trucks. Although they have been allowed to meet select Tibetan groups, I got the impression that they were rather isolated and were all the time fully chaperoned by their Chinese guides escorts," affirmed the Consul.

He further commented that despite all propagandist stories about the productivity of the oil wells, the potentiality of the Tsaidam basin and the newly discovered oil region of Xinjiang: "I get the impression that without the development or a much greater network of railways than at present contemplated in China, it would be many years before the entire North West, Sinkiang and Tibet would be capable of supporting a modern oil based economy. Thus considerable interest focusses on the steady drift of Russian and East European technical personnel to these vast undeveloped regions of China including Tibet."

It was probably one of the reasons why the Chinese were in a hurry to start the survey of the new railway between Lanzhou and Lhasa; it was scheduled for early 1957: "The picture that emerges is one of long term planning which will provide China an integrated North and South West region which can absorb some of the teeming millions of the over populated neighbouring Chinese provinces in the process. We can be sure that the Chinese will try to profit by the experience of the Soviet

Union when faced with similar problems in their Central Asian and Far Eastern Provinces after the revolution. It is altogether a fascinating development which will merit close study on our part."

It was without counting on the Sino-Soviet split.[37]

An important event for India-Tibet relations was the introduction of Tibetan Broadcast by All India Radio. Menon said that all the Tibetans, including acting Shapes[38] expressed their gratitude to the Government of India for introducing the Tibetan programme. They appreciated the easily understandable language and the news items that gave international news which they were unable to get before with Peking Radio, also broadcasting in Tibetan, but giving mostly news about development in China.

They all requested the Indian Consul to convey to his government that the broadcast time should be increased (at least by another five minutes.

**Change of Guard**

On November 12, 1956, PN Menon left for India on transfer. Before his departure, he called on the Dalai Lama and General Zhang Jingwu, the Central Government's representative in Tibet. He was also entertained by the Preparatory Committee during a farewell party.

Maj SL Chibber took charge of the Consulate General from Menon in the afternoon of November 17, 1956 at Yatung. He arrived in Lhasa on December 30, 1956.

---

37 In 1956, the Sino-Soviet relations began to deteriorate when Khrushchev initiated the de–Stalinization of the USSR in a secret speech, *On the Cult of Personality and Its Consequences (25 February 1956)*. He criticized Stalin's policies — especially the purges of the Communist Party of the Soviet Union and the killing of Stalin's personal and political rivals. From Khrushchev's de–Stalinization of the Soviet Union arose a serious domestic problem for Mao who had emulated Stalin and Stalinism, in the development of Chinese communism. The Hungarian Revolution of 1956 aggravated the situation. The Chinese Communist Party formally denounced Khrushchev's de–Stalinization policies as ideological revisionism of Marx.

38 Cabinet Ministers. He also mentioned Mary Taring (who was very much pro-Chinese those days).

Maj SL Chibber, Indian Trade Agent in Gyatse, c. mid-1950s

PN Menon, Indian Consul General in Lhasa (1954-1956)

## 20

# The Preparatory Committee of the Tibetan Autonomous Region

The preparations for the Preparatory Committee of the Tibetan Autonomous Region (PCTAR) started in March 1956. The Report of the Consul General[1] noted that the tempo of activity of the Chinese and Tibetan officials had gone up substantially. The first meeting of the Preparatory Committee was scheduled to be held during the last week of April in Lhasa: "The Youth and Women's Leagues have been pressed into service for all kinds of activities like making flags, new uniforms and teaching their members local folk dance," Delhi was informed.

It was announced that delegates would come from other parts of China; they would represent other Autonomous Regions and National Minorities. A large building 'with a fine hall and auditorium', expected to be the venue of the meetings of the Preparatory Committee, was already nearing completion: "The pressure on housing accommodation has increased considerably in Lhasa on account of the influx of fresh Chinese civilian and military personnel. Quite a number of these civilian personnel are being billeted in the houses of rich Tibetan officials," reported PN Menon.

The preparations for the function did not help the already-existing housing scarcity, "even the house in which the Dalai Lama's mother lived [was taken], necessitating her move to another small building near Norbu Lingka estate."

---

1 See previous Chapter 19, Footnote 1.

Menon observed that the Chinese population had increased and "now there are more Chinese women in Lhasa than before."

On April 28, the Indian Consul in Lhasa cabled the Political officer in Gangtok to inform Pant that Gen Zhang Jingwu, the Central Committee's representative in Tibet, Gen Wang Chingming[2] and Wang Feng[3] would come to Lhasa to take part in the Preparatory Committee's deliberations.

With Marshal Chen Yi, they would form the CCP's delegation; Wang Feng was to be the deputy leader. As we have seen, General Li Jue, who apart from being the Director of Road Construction was also the Head of the entire Chinese Intelligence set up in Tibet, was on an inspection of the Tibet-Bhutan Frontier.

Interestingly, the Indian Embassy in Beijing was requested to send a booklet entitled *A Guide to New China* published by Foreign Languages Press Peking; it contained the names of all most important Chinese personalities and their functions. It probably corresponded to the *Who's Who* prepared by the British officials posted in Tibet.

India had started getting interested in the Chinese leadership.

**The Formal Inauguration**

The formal function for the establishment of the PCTAR took place on April 22, 1956. Five days earlier, a Central Delegation arrived in the Tibetan capital, with representatives of various Autonomous Regions of China; it was led by Marshal Chen Yi, the Vice Premier: "They were given a great welcome and the Dalai and Panchen Lamas were present at the place of reception two miles outside the city."

This was an unbelievable gesture in conservative Tibet, where in the past, important visitors had to wait for weeks to call on the Dalai Lama in the Potala or the Norbulingka palaces.

---

2   Wang Qimei was a senior commander and official from the Southwest Bureau. He led the advance troops of the Eighteenth Army to Lhasa in September 1951. Gen Wang had taken Ngabo Ngawang Jigme prisoner during the military operations in Chamdo in October 1950.

3   Vice Chairman of Commission of Nationalities Affairs in China.

It took ten days for the Preparatory Committee to adopt some rules of procedure and listen to reports on recent developments on the plateau[4] ...and to decide on the membership of its Committees. Prominent Chinese and Tibetans, including the Dalai Lama and Panchen Lama were said to have given 'important' speeches.

A large theatrical and acrobatic group, which had come from Beijing with the Central delegation, entertained the audience.

The Indian Consul General recounted, "Marshal Chen Yi told me when I met him on May 1 that they will link Lhasa by rail with China by 1961," Menon added: "The rail link I understand will most likely follow the Lanchow[5]-Lhasa route over the present Tibet-Tsinghai[6] road. The choice of Lanchow as the terminal in China is significant."

According to the Consul's information, the Lanzhou-Urumchi[7]-Alma Ata[8] railway would be nearing completion by 1961, while Lanzhou was bound to become a most important transportation hub in China: "The choice of a route via the Tsaidam marshes and Chang Tang[9] and Ko Ko Nor[10] areas may also indicate possibilities of development of mineral resources in these areas like petrol, coal, iron."

According to Menon, China was keen to establish a firm link with Central Tibet through the construction of a railway whatever be the cost of its construction in terms of human labour and capital resources.

He also commented that members of a 'Tibetan sightseeing party', who had gone to China, were now back in Tibet and were taking part in the meetings of the Preparatory Committee.

---

4  'Since the Chinese absorption of Tibet,' said the Report.
5  Lanzhou.
6  Qinghai.
7  Xinjiang.
8  Kazakhstan.
9  Chantang, the Northern Plains.
10 Kokonor or the Qinghai Lake.

Marshal Chen Yi, between the Dalai Lama (left) an the Panchen Lama (right) in 1956 in Lhasa, on the occasion of the inauguration of the Preparatory Committee for the Tibet Autonomous Region

## The First Meeting

For the first meeting of the Preparatory Committee, representatives from all parts of Tibet came to Lhasa for the occasion: "Among them, I noticed a Mishmi type of individual wearing clothes like our tribesmen in NEFA. On being asked by a member of my staff, he said that he had come from Sanga Choling area,[11]" wrote Menon.

In 1956, like today, the 'tribal' representative from the border areas wore 'local' ornaments. In the case of the Mishmi delegate, he had an ornament across his chest and back with a row of Indian rupees minted in the 1930's or early 1940's with King George's portrait: "He wore a silver eight-anna bit in both ears also. At the welcoming ceremony for Marshal Chen Yi, he was also present and gave a scarf to the Marshal."

Until today, meetings of the National People's Congress in Beijing or the TAR's Regional People's Congress in Lhasa every year are attended by 'border' minorities in full regalia.

---

11  93 degree East and 28.5 North degree approximately.

The preliminary sessions of the Preparatory Committee ended on May 2 with a public meeting in Lhasa; it was addressed by the tutors of the Dalai Lama and Panchen Lama on behalf of their respective leaders; Generals Tan Guansan and Zhang Jingwu, as well as Ngabo Shape, were in attendance.

A new administration for U-Tsang and Kham areas was set up and the Dalai Lama was nominated Chairman of the Committee with the Panchen Lama and General Zhhang Guohua as the first and second Vice-Chairman respectively.

Ngabo Shape, Dzasa Lhamon from Shigatse and Topgay Pangdatsang from Kham as well as Chen Ching-po, a leading member of the Central Committee were nominated Secretaries of the Preparatory Committee.

Several new departments, i.e. Administration, Finance, Ecclesiastical, Industries, Education, Development, Agricultural, Transport, Trade and Commerce, Security, Law were set up. It was said that the new fifteen departments would need two thousand Tibetan officials to man them.

Each department would have four heads, one each from U, Tsang, Kham and one Chinese: "It can be safely assumed that the Chinese head of departments will pull all the strings and ensure that the Departments would function according to Chinese desires," rightly noted Menon.

What seemed to bother the Consul was the future of the existing Departments of the Tibetan Government like the Kashag[12], Yiktshang[13], Tsikhang[14] once the new Departments would be established and start working. "There is considerable speculation," said the Report which added: "The Preparatory Committee also established its Standing Committee for its further meetings in the future."

It included the Dalai Lama and Panchen Lama, General Zhang Guohua and 52 other members, once again representing U, Tsang and Kham areas and China.

---

12  Cabinet.

13  Ecclesiastic Department.

14  Finance Department.

Marshal Chen Yi and the Central Government's delegation took part in the Preparatory Committee's deliberations and later left for Shigatse, Gyantse and Yatung. Marshal Chen Yi only visited Shigatse, while Wang Feng, his deputy continued to Gyantse and Yatung. They were given 'a great welcome' at Shigatse and in the Chumbi Valley, but the reception "of the people of Gyantse was rather lukewarm."

Wang Feng in his speech at Gyantse praised the Tibetan resistance against the Younghusband Expedition in 1904. The drama and acrobatic troupe accompanied the delegation and performed in all the three cities.

The June 1956 report mentioned that the Standing Committee of the Preparatory Committee held some more meetings in Lhasa. Important issues were discussed, like the question of a ban on the export of Chinese silver dollars to India or sending of a large sightseeing party consisting of senior Tibetan monks to China.

Beijing was keen to showcase to the Tibetans the land reforms and other development projects undertaken in China; according to Menon, the Chinese authorities in Tibet, "chastened by the recent troubles in Eastern Tibet and Shigatse, are now anxious to create the right kind of popular support before actually embarking on land reforms in Tibet."

The issue of 'reforms' and their postponement would be the main topic of political discussion during the visit of the Dalai Lama and Zhou Enlai to India at the end of the year.

The Report spoke of 'loose talks' in Lhasa about the Chinese land reforms; their Tibetan supporters had particularly "created a general feeling of insecurity among the propertied classes including the monasteries of Central Tibet."

The Consul noted that the feeling that the Chinese might go slow on land reforms for a year or two, was mainly due to the "rebuff they have met with from the common people of Kham".

A month later,[15] the Preparatory Committee started holding regular meetings every Friday in the house which earlier belonged to the Dalai Lama's family: "These meetings are being attended regularly by the

---

15  In July 1956.

Dalai Lama and it looks as though that the 15 new departments set up under the aegis of the Preparatory Committee will start getting into their stride much sooner than most people expected when they were set up."

An interesting remark by the Consul General was that the Chinese had been able to take along most of the Tibetans so far: "the dynamism and thoroughness of the present [Chinese] regime in Tibet has been demonstrated by the remarkable way they have succeeded in roping in almost all the Tibetan officials here without consideration of age in connection with the manning of these departments."

The Consul, however, observed some dissatisfaction among the younger Tibetan officials "who have been more or less arbitrarily allotted to various departments without consulting them."

The Chinese apparently tried to reassure the younger staff; they said it was only "a first step for familiarising them with proper systems of work and that later on they could be assigned to work to which they are really suited."

The ad-hoc allotment of work, however, created serious problems; for example, the very senior Dzasa Tsarong had been put in charge of the construction department. As such he had to look after the road construction: "The old man who is past 68 has to personally supervise the road construction projects along with other members of his department who are much younger to him in age."

The Chinese tried also to persuade the women of 'well-to-do' families to get involved and take up some work in the Women's League or the Language School. They were told that they should follow the noble example of Madam Soong Ching Ling[16] who still worked despite her age. The Chinese leadership, according to Menon, believed that "by drawing into its multifarious activities all the official class including their wives and children, it would be possible to effect a radical change in their outlook." For Communist China, it was the best way to reform a 'backward' Tibetan society.

---

16  Madam Sun Yat Sen.

The news about an early introduction of land reforms continued to float around during the coming weeks. The Report of the Consulate said that "one active and voluble exponent of such reform in recent weeks has been a junior monk official, Shokhang Jetrung, who holds a paid job in the Youth League."

Shokhang went around Lhasa and the neighbouring areas, to give speeches strongly advocating the immediate adoption of land reform measures. In his lectures (compulsorily) attended by all officials in Lhasa, Shokhang would compare the position of the land owning class to those "on a horse and who if not prepared to come down voluntarily would have to be pulled down forcibly." Menon commented: "The audience was apparently shocked to silence but curiously enough have not raised any protests at such proposals."

He further observed that the Chinese have "hit upon a good propagandist in selecting Shokhang Jetrung. ...As a young man he is most popular here and has a push and unconventionality most unusual for Tibetans. Although a monk he is far too gay to be really celibate or orthodox. There is also evidence increasingly becoming apparent of some youthful Tibetan aristocrats giving up their properties and joining the Communist order and living like the Chinese."

The Monthly Report concluded: 'It is too early to say whether this trend will catch on but there is no doubt of its existence and of its encouragement from the Chinese side."

The situation was evolving fast on the Roof of the World.

A month later, the new departments of the Preparatory Committee got their final shape; the establishment of the Secretariat[17] was a further step while the speeding up of the construction of the new Headquarters building helped the main departments of the Preparatory Committee to become truly functional.

Dzasa Samdup Photrang[18] was nominated the head of the Secretariat "a step which is indicative of the extent of Chinese trust in him as well as a recognition of the value of associating leading members of Tibetan

---

17  *Tho-cho Lekhung* in Tibetan.
18  Maharajkumar of Sikkim's father-in-law.

aristocracy with the new changes contemplated under the proposed Tibetan Autonomous Region."

In the meantime, the Chinese authorities continued to buy houses in Lhasa to accommodate some of the new departments and the Chinese personnel sent from China to look after them: "The influx of Chinese cadres to Lhasa has been quite noticeable in recent months and it would be no exaggeration to say that the Chinese population of Lhasa has more than doubled itself during the last eight months or so."

At the same time, the Chinese slowly but steadily increased their participation in the internal Tibetan departments, "the gradual replacement of the older institutions by the sheer presence and example of the work done by the Chinese cadres." It was the end of the old administration; the end of a world in many ways.

The November/December Report noted a steady progression of the various departments of the Preparatory Committee: "The absence of the Dalai Lama, the Panchen Lama and other important Tibetan officials from Tibet has not affected its normal functions," wrote SL Chibber who had replaced Menon in November.

Another noticeable appointment was Liushar Dzasa[19] nominated as Acting Secretary General in place of Ngapho Shape, who was in India with the Dalai Lama.

Even in the absence of the heavy weights, the Committee continued to take decisions on several matters: "The only difference which the absence of above dignitaries has probably made, is that the Committee has not been able to hold its General Meeting," noted the Consulate.

**The Beginning of the Tibetan Resentment**

On February 25, 1956 as the Monlam[20] was taking place, a large number of anti-Chinese leaflets were distributed in Lhasa. Menon said that it was a repetition of last year's incident in similar circumstances:

---

19 See Chapter 18, Footnote 55. Loling Thupten Tharpa. The report noted that Liushar Dzasa (now Shape) was Vice Director of Foreign Bureau and also Chief of Law and Order organization which was still in its elementary stage: "From this it appears that he comes next to Ngapho Shape on Chinese list of confidants."

20 Great Prayer Festival.

"The Chinese authorities re-acted sharply on this occasion and are expected to take more drastic measures this time and try and prevent a recurrence of the incident in future."

The first step was the arrest of Alo Chantzo, a trader and leader of the Mimang Peoples' Party; Menon remarked: "The Chinese have made known their interpretation of this incident as having been inspired by Imperialist powers."

Who was the 'Imperialist power'?

It could be only India, as it was the lone power to be represented in Lhasa. Nepal did not really classify under this label.

In the Tibetan capital, the Monlam Festival, which used to take place every year around Losar, the Tibetan New Year, always attracted a large influx of monks and pilgrims, mainly due to the Dalai Lama's presence. The Consulate regularly reported the full details for such functions in its Weekly Report which are unfortunately not available to us.

In the March Report, the arrest of Alo Chantzo was again mentioned; it had been followed by the arrest of two more leaders of the same party, Bumthang Trungyik and one Shigatse Lhayap; interestingly: "The Tibetan authorities have retained these individuals in their own custody and so refused to hand them over to Chinese authorities," wrote Menon who admitted that both the Chinese and the Tibetans showed "considerable caution in handling these cases."

In August, the Consul General mentioned again the arrest of Alo Chantzo and Bumthang Trungyik. They had been released on August 27 due to the three powerful monasteries (Drepung, Sera and Ganden) standing as surety "for their future good conduct."

As for the third leader, Shigatse Lhayap, he had apparently died in custody; Delhi was told: "It is significant that the Chinese did not press either for the trial or punishment of these leaders despite all the threats of severe measures held out by them at the time of the distribution of anti-Chinese leaflets in Lhasa city."

Menon noted the caution of the Communist regime "which provides the best indication of its consciousness of its still uncertain hold on the allegiance of the Tibetan people."

The Chinese were still hoping to win the hearts of the Tibetans.

During this period the Indian Consulate in Lhasa often showed films to select audiences, including Chinese cadres; it was the case for three Indian films dubbed in Chinese.[21] The general reaction of Tibetans who saw these films was good, said the Report: "they have been heard remarking about the higher technical standards and aesthetic qualities of our films as compared with Chinese films which are mostly of a propagandist nature."

But India would remain far behind in terms of propaganda compared to Communist China.

**Some Conclusions**

Though the setting-up of the PCTAR was not directly related to the relations between India and Tibet, it was a turning point in the history of the Land of Snows. It is worth mentioning some of the implications for India envisioned by Menon:

a) By including divergent interests in Preparatory Committee, the Central Government has reduced the power of the Dalai Lama. If, as Sulzberger[22] says, the Dalai Lama is still "recognized as the Supreme temporal and ecclesiastical power", I am not sure that in future he will be able to exercise this power effectively.

b) The various organs of the autonomous administration will be controlled by the Central Government, i.e. Beijing. Important appointments will be subject to the Central Government's approval. Residuary power will vest in the Central Government which will also be directly responsible for many important matters.

c) There will be no interference with existing institutions, but urgent measures are being taken to build up Tibetan cadres

---

21 The films were *Do Bigha Zamin*, *Awara* and *Toofan*.
22 See Chapter 9, Footnote 14.

and a Tibetan Communist party. An organizing committee has been set up for this purpose. It is through this agency that larger changes, including closer integration, will be brought about at a later stage.

It was the end of the autonomy enjoyed by Tibet for centuries … all in the name of 'autonomy' for the 'masses'.

# 21

# Will the Dalai Lama Visit India?

The preparation of the Buddha Jayanti was a symptomatic event which demonstrated the new role of the Chinese in Tibet and their absolute control over the lives of the Tibetans, particularly the Dalai Lama and the Panchen Lama.

It would take more than one year for them to agree to a visit of the two leaders to India for the 2500$^{th}$ anniversary of the Buddha.

We shall go into the details of the preparations for the celebrations and the last minute 'permission' given to the Lamas to visit India, who two years earlier had been in China on the invitation of the Chinese Communist Party.

### A Meeting with the Maharajkumar of Sikkim

On July 28, 1955, the Indian Prime Minister met the Maharajkumar of Sikkim in Delhi. In the course of the conversation, the possibility of inviting the Dalai Lama for the Buddha Jayanti celebrations was discussed for the first time. Nehru observed that his Government wanted to invite the Tibetan leader, though it was too early to take any concrete step. Delhi thought to first sound the Chinese Government, "the invitation itself would probably have to go through them, even though it might also be sent separately and directly."[1]

---

1  All other documents in this chapter, except specifically mentioned, are from the Nehru Papers (JN Collection) held at the Nehru Memorial Museum and Library in Delhi. The 'papers' are not indexed.

Nehru's plan was that when the new Indian Ambassador[2] would go to Beijing, "he might informally sound the Chinese Government." Then only would the next step be taken: "It was obvious that the Dalai Lama would not be able to come here unless the Chinese Government approved of it," said the Prime Minister to his guest.

The Maharajkumar explained to Nehru that someone would have to go to Tibet to deliver the invitation; he suggested that he could do it before the next winter. The Prime Minister explained that it would also depend on the developments in Tibet "…which would probably govern the Chinese Government decision."

The Prince of Sikkim had met the young Dalai Lama before the latter went to China in 1954; the Dalai Lama was not at all happy, said the Maharajkumar who had it from reliable sources: "the Dalai Lama had not changed his opinion because of his visit to China and was still dissatisfied with things as they were."

The Prince remarked that the Panchen Lama was exceedingly unpopular with the Tibetans and was considered more or less a stooge. He also spoke of a great deal of discontent in Tibet in general; he mentioned the formation of the Preparatory Committee (PCTAR) to frame Tibet's new constitution.

Nehru commented: "the Maharajkumar seems to indicate that some people were going to be elected or nominated by Tibetan groups to [the Committee]. It was this process of election or nomination that was going to take place and for this purpose, many important persons were gathering in Lhasa more particularly the extremist anti-Chinese wing was gathering there and they wanted to control this committee."

The Maharajkumar then hinted that this could trigger trouble which might spread outside Central Tibet into some border regions[3] of China.

For Nehru, the prince gave a one-sided picture of the situation, "because his own contacts are with a particular type of person."

---

2   RK Nehru was Indian Ambassador to China from November 6, 1955 to July 27, 1958. He replaced N. Raghavan (September 13, 1952 to November 5, 1955).

3   Kham and Amdo in particular.

## The Decision about the Dalai Lama's Visit

On September 1, 1955, TN Kaul wrote to the PO in Gangtok to inform him that the decision about the Dalai Lama's visit to India "will be made in Peking and not in Lhasa. Our new Ambassador to China[4] will broach this subject with Chinese Government on arrival there."

It was only after the Chinese Government had agreed that other steps could be taken, "kindly explain this suitably to Maharajkumar," wrote Kaul.

Tibet had clearly lost the autonomy that the 17-Point Agreement had promised in May 1951.

In November 1955, the Maharajakumar nevertheless decided to visit Lhasa to 'officially' invite to the Dalai Lama to participate in the Buddha Jayanti celebrations: "as the Dalai Lama is head of [the] Monastic order as well as the head of Tibetan Government, it would be[quite] appropriate to send him [the] main invitation and ask him to convey the invitation to [the] Panchen Lama and other important Tibetan dignitaries," said a note from the Indian Government, which was not sure about the procedure to follow for the Panchen Lama.

The situation was confused, to say the least.

The Prince of Sikkim was to extend the invitation on behalf of the Mahabodhi Society of India: "Mahabodhi invitation should not mix up with the official invitation from the Government of India," but there should be no feeling that the Government of India was "hesitant about extending a straight-forward invitation" to the Dalai Lama.

But once the invitation of the Mahabodhi Society was sent, nothing moved for several months.

## The Date is Approaching

The celebrations in India were to start in November 1956.

---

4   RK Nehru. At the time of Kaul's cable, N. Raghavan was still in China.

**Maj SL Chhiber, the Panchen Lama, PO Apa Pant, the Dalai Lama crossing over Nathu-la on their way to India (November 1956)**

On March 24, 1956, PN Menon, the Consul General of India in Lhasa wrote to the PO in Gangtok; he had some information on the latest position regarding Dalai Lama's participation in Buddha Jayanti: "Chinese authorities in Lhasa had sent a telegram to Peking advising that Dalai Lama was [at the] political and religious points of view extremely immature and should not <u>repeat not</u>, therefore, be allowed to proceed to India. This was done without consulting anyone here."

The Chinese proposed two alternatives to the Dalai Lama: Trijang Rinpoche[5] and Shasur Shape to represent the religious and lay set-up in Tibet respectively; he added: "The Peking authorities have accepted this suggestion."

Menon commented: "Trijang Rimpoche while no doubt a highly respected religious dignitary is author of astonishing statements when in China with Dalai Lama that Mao Tse-Tung like old Manchu

---

5   The Dalai Lama's Junior Tutor.

Emperors is an incarnation of Jamyang [6](Manjusri Buddhist Apollo). He has come in for considerable criticism here for this statement."

The Consul also said that Shasur Shape had the reputation of being the dullest Shape in the Tibetan Kashag and according to Menon: "[the] Dalai Lama's family I am told are intensely unhappy at turn of events and are most skeptical now of his being allowed to come to India."

The Consul's suggestion to the Government of India was: "unless we are prepared to take up question at highest level in China, we can rule out Dalai Lama's participation in our Buddha Jayanti celebrations."

That was it.

**The First Invitations**

On April 28, 1956, Delhi informed Gangtok and Lhasa that during a discussion in Beijing, the *Waichiaopu*[7] had mentioned that of the eight names previously suggested by India to attend the celebrations, the Buddhist Association of China had 'consulted all the invitees', but only three of them had expressed their willingness to attend. This would imply that Dalai and Panchen Lamas were informed, though we doubt this statement."

In May, an invitation was sent to Rani Chuni Dorji of Bhutan[8]. Delhi was informed that the Bhutan Government wanted to participate in the exhibition by sending about 150 exhibits, including rare manuscripts, thankas and other objects of Buddhist art.

Two days later, the PO clarified that a Lamay Namgye was the second Bhutanese person to be invited to the Buddha Jayanti, he would be

---

6   Jampeyang or Manjusri, the Bodhisattva of Wisdom.

7   Ministry of Foreign Affairs.

8   In 1916, the British offered Sonam Tobgye Dorji, the post of Bhutan Agent. In 1918, he married Rani Chuni Wangmo, the sister of the king of Sikkim. They had five children. His eldest son Jigme Palden became Prime Minister of Bhutan; the second eldest, a daughter Tashi, helped in the affairs of the Bhutan House; Kesang Choden, married the third King of Bhutan; Ugyen was the reincarnation of a high priest in Tibet and Lhendup. They were all born and brought up in Bhutan House and educated in the elite schools set up by the British within Darjeeling and Kalimpong.

accompanied by an interpreter. Rani Chuni was first on the Bhutanese list; about the exhibit, the Bhutan Government wanted to know "when these objects should be sent to Delhi and also when invitees are expected to reach India."

The event had started to take shape.

## A Visit by the Indian Ambassador to Lhasa?

On August 30, Menon enquired about a possible visit to Lhasa of RK Nehru, the Indian Ambassador to China.

Addressing Bahadur Singh, the Charge d'Affaire in the Indian Embassy[9] in Beijing, PN Menon requested more information on the visit of the Indian Ambassador to Lhasa; had it been finalized "and if so approximate dates and routes [to be] followed."

Menon added that he had no firm information about visit, apart from 'stray hints' in letters from Ministry about enquiries made by the embassy with the *Watchiaopu* regarding some possible routes. The Consul General needed some advance notice to organize the visit. Some presents were already on their way to present to the Dalai Lama "so that no delay takes place in calls."

It was further explained: "Living conditions in Lhasa being still extremely primitive and harsh I can advise about essential things to be brought from Peking if I know the composition of the party, a period of stay, mode of conveyance [for] journey to Lhasa."

The consul suggested that the Ambassador should fly from Lanzhou to Dam[10]: "since motor journey by either route would be extremely tedious and strenuous. I feel we should ourselves tie up programme instead of relying entirely on Chinese as their arrangements in Tibet will never compare with those they make in China proper."

The Dalai Lama had discreetly enquired about the Ambassador's plans and seemed particularly keen to know "if formal invitation for Buddha Jayanti will be given", during the Ambassador's visit.

---

9 Singh would soon be nominated to replace PN Menon as Consul General in Lhasa; he would not take the post.

10 Damshung, North of Lhasa.

The Chogyal of Sikkim, Indira Gandhi, the Dalai Lama, Jawaharlal Nehru, the Panchen Lama during a banquet in Delhi (end of 1956)

On September 3, Bahadur Singh cabled Kaul about the forthcoming Buddhist celebrations: "We have received six invitations for Buddhist [sic] Jayanti celebrations including one each for Dalai Lama and Panchen Lama."

The invitations for the two leaders were signed by Vice-President Radhakrishnan, while all others were signed by the Prime Minister. Six previous invitations, already given to the Foreign Office, were signed by Jawaharlal Nehru.

The Charge d'Affaires noted that the Chinese authorities were bound to notice this difference: "Would you like us to give some explanation or send fresh letters for Dalai Lama and Panchen Lama by special bag?"

RK Nehru, the Indian Ambassador thought that it would desirable that letters for Dalai Lama and Panchen Lama should also be signed by honorary Chairman as the remaining ten were signed by him.

Gurbachan Singh commented: "Difference in signature has no significance in itself but it might be used by Chinese for their own purpose."

The same day, the Indian Consul wrote to Kaul regarding Taktser Rinpoche, the Dalai Lama's elder brother: "I have discreetly ascertained from *Chikyap Khempo*[11] (another brother of the Dalai Lama), his family's wishes in the matter. They earnestly desire their brother [Taktser] should live in India rather than in America. He particularly emphasized that Dalai Lama's Mother was getting very anxious about the Rinpoche's health and welfare as he has not written to them for a long time."

Menon strongly recommended to the Joint Secretary to grant "an entry visa of unlimited validity to him. He should be persuaded to take up permanent residence in some place like Simla, instead of Darjeeling or Kalimpong which already harbours Gyalo Dhondup and Shakabpa two of the most inveterate opponents of the present regime in Tibet."

The Consul's views were that the continuation of Taktser Rinpoche's stay in US "on American charity seems pointless and only likely to create greater suspicion against the Dalai Lama and family."

**The Ambassador's Visit Again**

On September 4, RK Nehru in Beijing informed Kaul in Delhi that Menon had made some enquiries about the former's visit to Lhasa. The Ministry was requested to inform Lhasa that "while we are hoping to go by air with Chen Yi sometime after Vice President's visit, final decision has not yet been taken."

Menon was asked to check if regular flights were taking place between Beijing and Lhasa: "We have conflicting reports about feasibility of air journey."

RK Nehru added: "Surprised to hear Dalai Lama thinks [my] visit may have something to do with invitation to Buddha Jayanti. I think this speculation should be discouraged."

---

11 See note Chapter 18, Footnote 44.

The Dalai Lama, President Rajendra Prasad, Vice-President Radhakrishnan in Delhi (end of 1956)

The next day, Kaul answered the Consulate in Lhasa about the former Foreign Secretary's hope to visit Lhasa by air with Chen Yi middle of October: "final decision not yet taken."

It was also clarified that RK Nehru could mention to the Dalai Lama that the invitation for the Buddha Jayanti had already been extended to the Chinese: "he will not be handing over any formal invitation himself."

## Gurbachan Singh Posted in Lhasa

On October 5, Kaul informed Menon that Gurbachan Singh, the Chargé d'Affaire in Beijing had been selected to succeed him in Lhasa: "he will leave Delhi on or about 5th November, reach Gangtok 8th or 9th, leave Gangtok 12th, reach Yatung 14th and Lhasa 20th. Suggest you leave Lhasa so as to meet Gurbachan Singh at Yatung on 14th."

Gurbachan Singh was to go to Lhasa without his family.

On the same day, the embassy in China was informed by the Foreign Secretary that "after full consideration Prime Minister has decided that Gurbachan Singh's posting to Lhasa should stand. We are asking Menon to come away by the middle of November."

In another communication the same day, the Consul informed Delhi: "Shall gladly stay on till end October. Grateful if allowed full two months leave in India preferably before proceeding next post. Also, like to report at Delhi prior proceeding on leave. Essential relief reaches here well in time so that departure does not drag into extreme winter in view of family including small child."

The flux of cables continued on the same day; the Foreign Secretary informed Lhasa that it had been reliably informed that "[the] Dalai Lama and the Tibetans in general are greatly disappointed at our not having invited Dalai Lama to participate in the Buddha Jayanti celebrations."

The Foreign Secretary wrote: "some months ago when the names of Dalai Lama and Panchen Lama were suggested by us to the Chinese Government they told us that the two dignitaries would not be able to come to India on account of heavy pre-occupations."

Later formal invitations for both the Dalai Lama and the Panchen Lama were handed over to the Chinese Embassy in Delhi: "We also gave them a note expressing our hope that the two dignitaries would be able to come to India on the occasion of the Buddha Jayanti. We have not yet received any reply to the formal invitations," noted the Foreign Secretary.

The same telegram mentioned again the visit of the Dalai Lama to India: "It does not seem fair that we should be blamed by the Tibetans for our alleged failure to invite Dalai Lama. Obviously, the Chinese Government have not been frank with us in this matter. It is possible that the formal invitation that we have sent will not reach Dalai Lama."

The conclusion was that the Dalai Lama should informally be told that India would be happy to have him in India to participate in the Buddha Jayanti celebrations "and that we have sent formal invitations for him and Panchen Lama to the Chinese Government."

Menon was instructed to let the Dalai Lama's immediate entourage know this.

## The Visit of RK Nehru Does not Materialize.

On October 6, Apa Pant cabled TN Kaul, about Ragashar Shape[12], former Commander-in-Chief of the Tibetan Army and now an official of the PLA stationed in Tibet; the Shape had called on the PO: "He stated that he was taking great risk in coming to meet me without the knowledge of his Chinese escort. He would not have done so but the work for which he is approaching is of vital importance to Tibet."

Ragashar explained to Pant that the Dalai Lama was extremely keen to come to India and would immediately accept an invitation, if it was delivered to him. The Tibetan official added that the Chinese have not so far told anything to the Dalai Lama, "or to any of his officials, including himself that an invitation from Government of India has been extended or was on the way."

According to Ragashar, the Dalai Lama wanted to remove any possible misunderstanding in Nehru's mind "whom he considers to be his elder brother". There was no 'coolness' on the part of the Tibetan leader towards an invitation to visit India and participate in the Buddha Jayanti celebrations.

The Tibetan Minister repeatedly stressed that the Dalai Lama was 'extremely keen' to immediately accept any invitation from India.

Pant told Ragashar that the invitation had been given to the Chinese; the minister wanted Delhi to influence Mao Zedong and Zhou Enlai to forward the invitation to the Dalai Lama; all the monasteries, the Peoples' Parties and officials were anxious to see the Dalai Lama participating in Buddha Jayanti celebrations.

Pant told the Tibetan official that Menon had been approached by people close to the Dalai Lama, who asked whether it was true that an invitation had been extended or not.

---

12 Ragashar had become a minister a month earlier; he was earlier C-in-C. According to Pant, he was not so intelligent and looked very unimpressive; he was a quiet member of the Cabinet. It is spelt 'Raggusar' by Pant.

The same people wanted the invitation to be publicized in Tibet; otherwise "the Chinese may not extend invitation and will give [the] Government of India excuses on behalf of Dalai Lama without even consulting him or his officers."

It was suggested that the Indian Consul General in Lhasa should openly mention the invitation, thereby putting the ball in the Chinese court.

**Flights to Lhasa?**

On October 8, Pant wrote to TN Kaul in Delhi; he did not want to go to Lhasa during the month because the Maharaja of Bhutan was likely to visit Calcutta at that time: "I feel meeting him [in] Calcutta more important than my visit to Lhasa at the moment".

Pant thought that it would be best to postpone his visit to the following year: "Weather in Lhasa likely to be very cold in November." He also suggested that RK Nehru should make his trip to Lhasa in April 1957.

One of the issues, discussed at the end of 1956, was the possibility of using airplanes to fly to/from Lhasa.

The same day, Menon informed Kaul about the trial flights between India and Tibet. General Chen Ming-Yi[13], the 'top communication expert in Tibet' had remarked the previous day at a party in this Consulate that their plane for carrying out trial flights is expected soon from China." The General added that the Chinese Embassy in Delhi was negotiating the establishment of regular air services between China and India via Tibet.

Chen Mingyi wanted the consulate's cooperation: "He was anxious to know about aerial conditions in flight from Dam[14] aerodrome to Bagdogra". The Indian Consul mentioned an Indian plane which flew from Bagdogra to Saugang, near Gyantse in 1954, for dropping medicines for BK Kapur, the PO. The general replied that Chinese Air Force had already made a number of flights "in the direction of

---

13 Maj Gen Chen Mingyi (1917-2002). Chen oversaw the successful completion of the Sichuan-Tibet highway. Credit for the Qinghai-Tibet highway goes to Maj Gen Mu Shengzhong (1910-1994) whose remains rest in a memorial mausoleum in Golmud.

14 Damchung.

The Dalai Lama and the Panchen Lama in India during their visit to India

India [but] their pilots are not familiar with flying near and over east Himalayas."

Menon told Delhi that it was essential to lay down "a specific air route via Phari/Tuna plains over Chumbi Valley and then over Sikkim over the narrowest segment separating West Bengal from Chumbi Valley thus avoiding any flights over Bhutan."

The Chinese had already told, "trusted Tibetan officials that air services between Siliguri and Dam will come into effect very soon."

For Menon, it was important that the Indian planes should carry out trial flights in the direction of Lhasa and Damshung simultaneously with some Chinese flights to India. According to Chen Ming-Yi, the Damshung aerodrome was slightly higher than Lhasa and twin-engine planes had to be used.

Menon wanted to be informed by Delhi of the negotiations with China on the subject: "the extent to which I should try to ascertain details about aerodrome and facilities at [in] Tibet."

Was it only wishful thinking on the part of China?

Was the introduction of flights linked with the Dalai Lama visiting India?

**The Dates of the Celebrations Approach**

On October 10, the Indian Embassy in Beijing returned to the subject of the Buddha Jayanti celebrations: "Both Chinese Foreign office and Mongolian Embassy have been repeatedly reminded of paper for symposium [to be held in India]. Last reminders were given only yesterday. Both have promised to expedite reply."

Regarding the invitation to the Dalai Lama and the Panchen Lama, the Foreign Office was also reminded: "They plead pre-occupation with National Day celebrations and stated they had not heard from authorities to which the matter had been referred."

Beijing had not yet decided.

**The Permission is Granted**

On November 7, RK Nehru informed the Consulate in Lhasa that in the course of a talk with Zhou Enlai two days earlier, the Chinese Premier had said that a telegram had been sent to the Dalai Lama and Panchen Lama enquiring whether they would be ready to go to India. Zhou said that the Lamas had not replied as yet, but he "wanted to convey the impression to our Ambassador[15] that there will be no resistance from the Chinese side to these dignitaries going to India."

Menon in Lhasa was requested to convey the information informally to the Dalai Lama: "You should assure him that we will take every precaution for his security during his journey and stay in India."

The next day, replying to a telegram sent two months earlier[16], the Indian Embassy in Beijing was informed by Delhi that the Chinese

---

15  RK Nehru.
16  On September 6.

Government had no objection to the Dalai Lama visiting India for the Buddhist celebrations. Delhi needed, however, to wait for a formal reply from the Lamas. At that time, it was still thought the Tibetan leader would travel by air: "The trial flight by our aircraft between India and Lhasa was also very satisfactory. On the return journey the aircraft came direct to Delhi."

The Ministry informed the Consulate in Lhasa that the [Chinese] Embassy in Delhi had handed over the invitations for Dalai and Panchen Lamas to the Chinese Foreign Office on September 5: "Deputy Director Asian Division stated invitations will be forwarded to the two dignitaries and their replies communicated to us when received."

Menon was requested to pass on this information. The invitations were signed by Vice-President Radhakrishnan, as Chairman of the All India Buddha Jayanti Committee. It was only while the Vice-President was on tour in Europe and Africa that some invitations had to be issued under the Prime Minister's signature; Nehru was the Honorary Chairman. The Dalai Lama's entourage had to be told that in the Indian protocol, the Vice President had precedence over Prime Minister and came next to President.

The same day, Menon told Kaul in the Ministry, that he had "just been informed by my direct contact with Dalai Lama that General Fan Ming and two other top Chinese leaders handed over our Government's invitation to the Dalai Lama for Buddha Jayanti in November."

They said that the Dalai Lama had to decide about his acceptance, adding that the time was short and that it may be necessary to go by plane.

However, the situation was far from clear.

### The Dalai Lama's Account

In his autobiography, *Freedom in Exile*, the Dalai Lama recounted the weeks preceding his trip to India: "A period of several months went by during which nothing more was said about Buddha Jayanti. Then, sometime about the middle of October, Fan Ming[17] contacted me to

---

17 Gen Fan Ming (December 4, 1914 – February 23, 2010), born Hao Keyong

ask who I wanted to nominate as leader of the delegation: the Indians needed to know. I replied that I would send Trijang Rinpoche, my Junior Tutor, adding that the delegation was ready to go as soon as he gave final clearance. Another two weeks went by and I gradually began to put the whole thing out of my mind when suddenly Chiang Chin-wu[18], who had just arrived back from Peking, came to tell me that the Chinese Government had decided that it would be all right for me to go after all."

The Dalai Lama wrote in his memoirs: "I could hardly believe my ears, so happy was I; 'but be careful,' he [Gen Zhang] warned me. 'There are many reactionary elements and spies in India. If you try to do anything with them, I want you to realise that what happened in Hungary and Poland will happen in Tibet.'" The Tibetan leader said that Gen Zhang was referring to the brutal Russian response to rebellion in those countries.

The Dalai Lama added: "When he had finished speaking, I realised that I should conceal my great joy and instead do my best to appear to be very anxious. I indicated that I was genuinely surprised and concerned at his information about imperialists and reactionaries. This reassured Chiang and he adopted a more conciliatory tone. 'Don't worry too much,' he said. 'If you have any difficulties, our Ambassador will always be there to help you.' With that our meeting ended. The General stood up and, with his customary formality, took leave of me. As soon as he was gone, I rushed off, smiling as if my mouth would reach my ears, to tell my personal attendants the news."

Why the Chinese changed their mind is not clear; but they were now ready to take the 'risk' of letting the two main Tibetan leaders go out of Tibet for a few months.

---

served in PLA during the Battle of Chamdo. He was a senior cadre of the Northwest Bureau and was the representative to the Panchen Lama and later a deputy secretary of the Tibet Work Committee. While in Tibet, Fan became a close associate of the 10th Panchen Lama. A well-educated man, he was responsible for Tibet's social and economic policies while Zhang Guohua, a political rival, assumed command of the PLA armed forces.

18  Gen Zhang Jingwu.

The Dalai Lama had now to formally consult the Kashag, Trungchi, the Tsipons and three big monasteries "but decision to go has been already taken by His Holiness. All consultations are expected to be completed by today."

Menon added: "The story of the last three months' stubborn resistance of all Chinese moves to send representatives in lieu of Dalai Lama and Panchen Lama and mobilization of opinion in favour of acceptance of our invitation as well as the profound keenness of His Holiness to visit India can be reported in person when I am in Delhi end of November."

The Embassy in Beijing was immediately informed of the good news.

From then onwards, the details of the visit could be discussed.

**The Chinese Premier Plans to Visit India**

In the meantime, Zhou Enlai, the Chinese Premier was keen to visit India for the celebrations. An incident worth recounting occurred at the time when the visit to India of the Chinese Premier Zhou Enlai was finalized.

On September 27, the Premier had already informed RK Nehru, the Indian Ambassador in Beijing, that he planned to visit India from November 30 to December 12, 1956; thereafter he wanted to visit Myanmar.

Nehru replied to his homonym ambassador the next day: "Dates suggested broadly suit us. Perhaps if he could come a day or two earlier, it would be better. We should like to know what places in India he would like to visit, such as Bhakra Nangal, Damodar Valley group including Sindri and Chittaranjan; Jamshedpur, Simla, Dehra Dun for [Indian] Military Academy, also Khadakvasala [National Defence Academy] near Poona; Bombay, Bangalore, and Madras. Obviously, he cannot visit every place. Presumably, he will spend three clear days in Delhi."

The Buddha Jayanti Seminar[19] and celebrations were to start on November 24. The Prime Minister added that "a number of distinguished visitors are coming, probably including Prime Ministers

---

19 Called 'symposium' in some dispatches.

**The Dalai Lama with the Chinese Ambassador in Delhi**

of Nepal and Ceylon. This need not interfere with Chou En-lai's visit, but careful arrangements will be necessary to avoid duplication of functions."

Was it a tactic from the Chinese side to create trouble on the border at the time an important visit was in the offing?

The Prime Minister started becoming nervous; he was not happy about a detail in the Dalai Lama's program. The Dalai Lama was scheduled to give a public speech; Nehru told the Education Secretary "the Dalai and Panchen Lamas have accepted the Buddha Jayanti invitations and further that the Dalai Lama has been invited to address a public meeting is extraordinary."

Nehru commented: "It indicates complete ignorance of the political situation in Tibet and China and might well lead to difficulties. As it is, it is very doubtful if the Dalai Lama can come to India. The matter rests not only with him but with others also. To suggest that he is expected to address a public meeting here is to add to these difficulties and make it almost impossible for him to come."

The Prime Minister concluded his note, "in this matter, as indeed in all matters affecting foreign affairs, far more discretion is necessary and reference should be made to the External Affairs Ministry."

Was India getting cold feet?

**Things are Moving**

On November 11, Menon cabled Kaul about his personal program. He would leave the next morning and reach Gyantse on November 13 in the evening. The next day, he would travel to Yatung, reaching Chumbi Valley on November 15 in the morning. He would stay two days in Yatung and then leave for Gangtok where he would be on November 18: "Shall wire from Gangtok date of reaching Delhi."

More detailed information was given regarding Menon's retiring as Consul General of India in Lhasa: "From 12th November till successor reaches Lhasa, Cypher Books and all Top Secret and confidential papers here will be kept sealed in sealed office for security reasons. Communications to me may be made at Gyantse, Yatung and Gangtok."

Menon also noted that he had just received a telegram from the Ministry about Gurbachan Singh's medical condition: "Suggest if Political Sikkim Gangtok also agrees that Chhiber comes up for short period and holds charge here until permanent successor reaches here."

Eventually, Chibber would succeed Menon as India Consul General in Lhasa, a few days later.

The same day, Menon wrote again to Kaul, to inform Delhi that the Dalai and Panchen Lamas "have accepted our invitation and are definitely coming to India. At farewell audience this morning his Holiness made detailed enquiries from me about climate in India."

When he met General Zhang Jingwu, the young Tibetan leader told the PLA officer that the final travelling details would only be finalized later in the day, his tentative programme was the following: "Dalai Lama will be accompanied by entourage of about 40 (30 officials and 10 attendants) and Panchen Lama by entourage of about 20 (details not known) and party will leave by car 16th November reaching Yatung within 5 days."

Zhang had suggested to Beijing that the Tibetan Lama should travel to India by air, the Tibetans "seem to consider road travel up to India much safer."

Menon nevertheless took the opportunity to suggest to Gen Zhang Jingwu that he could recommend to Delhi sending a plane to Tibet for airlifting the party: "Offer of our plane has been separately made to Dalai Lama through [our] contact."

General Zhang stressed his Government's anxiety "about security and comfort of two leaders in India and emphasized the fact that they were visiting a foreign country for the first time in their lives."

Menon gave his personal assurances that this would be taken care of "which seem to have relieved him much."

The outgoing Consul General noted: "We should now be prepared to expect two leaders and their entourage at Sikkim border from 22nd November onwards." He further suggested finalizing all the arrangements for their welcome and onward flight to Delhi from Bagdogra on November 24: "Question of their being State guests at Rashtrapati Bhavan may also be finalized."

He promised more information during the next few days.

**The Programme Finalized**

On November 11, Menon wrote to Kaul, informing him that his contact with the Dalai Lama told him that some decisions had been taken by the Tibetans. The date of Dalai Lama's departure from Lhasa by road had been finalized for November 16. His entourage would consist of his two tutors (Trijang and Ling Rimpoches) and three ministers, Kalond Surkhang, Ragashar[20] and Ngapho[21]. Menon commented "it is a strong team from the Tibetan Kashag (Cabinet)." Altogether the party had 49 officials. In addition, there were 11 interpreters and 40 servants, making a total of 100.

Menon told the Joint Secretary that he had not yet received confirmation from the Chinese "but I may take it as correct."

---

20   Brother of the Maharani of Sikkim.

21   Ngabo Ngawang Jigme.

The party would be further accompanied by 17 members of Dalai Lama's entourage, in addition to the officials mentioned: "I am authorizing my Head Clerk to grant visas when passports are produced here by Foreign Bureau after I leave."

It was not clear on which passports the Dalai Lama's Party would travel.

The Consul General commented: "All Lhasa is jubilant over developments and we should do everything on our part to make visit of these leaders completely successful. Suggest reception for party be arranged at Nathula itself and also provide there guard of honour."

The rest of the arrangements were to be discussed with the PO on radio telephone, while further information received from the Chinese was to be communicated from Gyantse or Yatung.

On the next day, Gangtok gave Delhi more details; the Dalai Lama and his party were to leave Lhasa on November 20 and Yatung on 22. On 23 morning, they were to cross Nathula and reach Changu[22]. A reception would be arranged at the border by the Maharajkumar and the PO would receive the dignitaries at Changu; they would spend the night on the spot. On November 24 in evening, he would reach Gangtok, where the Dalai Lama would give his *darshan,* before flying from Bagdogra on 25 in the forenoon.

Pant said that this programme "would satisfy the Sikkim Raja and Bhutan Raja and Darjeeling, but Kalimpong public would be disappointed if they do not get chance for proper *darshan.*"

The Maharaja of Sikkim would receive the Dalai Lama at 10th mile "as he is physically incapable of going further." The former had expressed his desire to offer hospitality to Dalai Lama during his stay in Sikkkim. Pant remarked: "I could also accommodate him and also part of his entourage in the Residency." The PO requested instructions on the latest proposal, noting that the entire party could be delayed for a day.

---

22 Tsongmo Lake, see Chapter 18, Footnote 16.

## Rumours of Trouble during the Visit

The second part of the cable dealt with rumours that "some elements desire to make trouble during Dalai Lama's visit to India in order to discredit India and also those who are so called rebels or nationalists."

Delhi was told that a news item from Kathmandu said the *Mimang* was contemplating doing harm to the person of Dalai Lama: "I give no thought to such rumours but prefer in principle Chinese insistence on adequate security measures, it is essential that all precautions for security are taken for the journey of the Dalai Lama from Nathula to Bagdogra and further," remarked the PO.

It was however suggested that as the Chinese were providing an escort of nearly 2,000 bodyguards up to Nathula: "suggest at least two companies of Indian Army should meet the party at Nathula itself."

Further, the Bengal and Indian Police would need to take "full security measures in co-operation and co-ordination with Sikkim authorities by bringing in their personnel. Sikkim Darbar are entirely agreeable to this."

Apa Pant noted that there was only one company in Gangtok; it was inadequate "to do this work and instructions should be given to Brigade at Darjeeling or Division Headquarters at Calcutta for necessary action."

Moreover, as some Chinese generals would be accompanying the dignitaries, "feel essential that for security as well as escort work my above suggestion should be considered," wrote the PO.

Regarding the security of the Dalai Lama and his party, Pant wanted the Chinese to be informed that it was India's responsibility "entirely and that their troops or their escort guards should not and need not interfere in our arrangements and are therefore unnecessary. These troops or guards arriving in Sikkim at this juncture would create very bad impression locally both in Sikkim and Bhutan."

The Consul General in Lhasa had informed the PO though wireless that the Dalai Lama would be accompanied by Cabinet Ministers Ngabo, Ragashar and Shashur and …four tutors to which should be added the *Chipkap Khempo*[23], Trijang Rimpoche and about 10 high officials. It meant at least 28 officials: "Besides this there would be 100 persons who will travel as pilgrims independently."

The Panchen Lama would be accompanied by some 22 officials: "Their transport from Bagdogra onwards by plane would require at least 3 Dakotas or one Constellation. Others will travel by train and the heavier luggage also."

That was not a small affair, but it had to be organized in a very short time, due to the last minute decision of the Chinese to clear the leaders' visit.

According to Pant, the Dalai Lama wanted to stay for three to four weeks in India: "Tentative programme of visit to places of pilgrimage and other places should be telegraphed to us and Lhasa *en clair* for definite information of authorities concerned."

The Political Officer in Sikkim affirmed that once Nathu-la was crossed, his office would definitely take charge of the party.

## Menon Appointed Officer on Special Duty

Pant strongly recommended that Menon "should be treated as on duty and asked to act as a liaison officer. His personal acquaintance with the Chinese and Tibetans would be of invaluable help and would avoid all manner of protocol difficulties as especially both Panchen Lama and Dalai Lama would be travelling almost together."

He also suggested that pending Gurbachan's departure for Lhasa, "Menon should be attached to this large and important party."

Pant further advised that, if possible, the Dalai Lama and Panchen Lama should reach Delhi by different planes. He also hoped that their programmes should be drawn separately, if possible: "not only to places of pilgrimage but also to industrial and other development projects."

He noted that in 1954, both Lamas were extensively taken round China where they were impressed with the great changes taking place in that country: "It would be proper for us to show them what is being done in India."

---

23 Or *Jigyab Khenpo*; see Chapter 18, Footnote 44.

Importantly, Pant observed that the visit was of high historic value to people of the border regions; therefore a full-length documentary film on the arrival of the Dalai Lama in Sikkim and of his visit to various places in India needed to be prepared: "Regret lengthy telegram," it concluded.

**Preparations Continue**

On November 12, Pant wrote again to the Ministry about the arrangements to be made: "According to custom Dalai-Lama and Panchen Lama would offer presents to Prime Minister and President and perhaps the Vice-President individually. The approximate prices of these presents would vary from 5,000 to 10,000 rupees each; this would include presents like ancient images thankas and silver-ware which is priceless."

Delhi was asked to suggest "for returning presents to these dignitaries" and if the National Anthem should be played by the guard of honour at the border (Nathu-la).

In the meantime the same day, Kaul answered Pant that in view of the impending visit of Dalai and Panchen Lamas to India, he should postpone his leave from Gangtok: "Please take all arrangements regarding reception of Dalai Lama and party from Nathu-la onwards in your own hands and telegraph detailed suggestions and itinerary."

The Joint Secretary informed the PO that the Ministry was working on a tentative programme for ten days to two weeks stay in Delhi and a month's tour in India: "however, [if] Dalai Lama wishes to stay longer and see more places we shall be very happy."

The PO was reminded that the Buddha Jayanti celebrations started from November 24: "it is desirable that Dalai Lama and party should fly from Bagdogra. Rail journey will be too long and cumbersome and not desirable."

Some special arrangements would be made to fly the Dalai Lama and his party from Bagdogra.

The Indian Embassy in Beijing was to fix a suitable date and time with Chinese Foreign Office for simultaneous announcement of Dalai Lama's visit.

## Another Version

We have another version of the events which were taking shape.

Rinchen Sadutshang[24], a senior Tibetan official wrote in his memoirs, *A Life Unforeseen, A Memoir of Service to Tibet*[25] wrote: "The news that the Dalai Lama had been invited to the Buddha Jayanti festival in India was welcomed by all Tibetans, as it was such an important and holy occasion for Buddhists. However, I learned that once more the Chinese objected to His Holiness going, regardless of how eager he was to participate in this important event."

Sadutshang elaborated: "Their excuse was that it posed a security problem, but such excuses seemed absurd to us Tibetans. Owing to the Chinese objection, it was decided that Trijang Rinpoche, junior tutor to the Dalai Lama, would attend the function as his representative. At that time I was in India on a private visit and suddenly received instructions from our trade mission in Kalimpong that I would have to accompany Trijang Rinpoche as his interpreter and assistant."

The Tibetan official remembered: "Accordingly I went to Nathula Pass in Sikkim in late November to receive Trijang Rinpoche. My family was very pleased that I would have to accompany Rinpoche, as they were his devoted disciples. He rested for a few days in Kalimpong, but before we had even started on our way, we received the joyful news that the Dalai Lama and the Panchen Lama would now both be coming to the Buddha Jayanti festival."

In the meantime, Trijang Rinpoche arrived and he was accompanied by the young Tibetan official to Gangtok where they were joined by the entourage of some twenty officials of the Dalai Lama and the

---

24 Rinchen Sadutshang was born in 1928 near the Tibet-China border to a well-off trading family; educated in a Jesuit school in the Himalayan foothills of British India, he served in the Dalai Lama's government both before and after the 1959 Communist takeover of Lhasa.

One of the only government officials in pre-Communist Tibet to have been educated in English, he recounted the pivotal events that changed his homeland. He played a crucial role in bringing the plight of the Tibetan people to the world's attention.

25 Rinchen Sadutshang, *Life Unforeseen, A Memoir of Service to Tibet*, (London, Wisdom Publications, 2016).

Panchen Lama, as well as five Chinese officials. Saduthsang remarked: "Apa Pant, the political officer in Sikkim, was the liaison assigned to our entourage, and he looked after us for all our engagements."

**Report from the PO Apa Pant**

After the visit, Apa Pant sent a report to the Ministry.

Though we shall study this report in the following chapter, it is worth mentioning it here; it was entitled: "The Visit of His Holiness The Dalai Lama and His Holiness The Panchen Lama to India: A Joint Report by Shri Apa B. Pant, Political Officer in Sikkim, Col PN Luthra, Special Officer (Border Areas), Ministry of External Affairs."

Pant wrote that the visit was a miracle in itself: "No Tibetan could ever hope that the Chinese would allow the two lamas and especially the Dalai Lama to visit India. They were certain that permission for them to visit India would be refused."

In fact, when the Tibetans heard that the Government of India had sent an invitation to the Dalai Lama to visit India, "they all said that such a visit would never be allowed."

Pant remembered: "Often I spoke to some of the Tibetan high officials visiting India as to how friendly the relations between India and China were and as to how great the personal influence of our Prime Minister had been with Mr. Chou En Lai. They all used to shake their heads and say 'Lonchen[26] Pant, you do not know the Chinese. We have lived with them for long'."

The Chinese had openly said that the two Lamas 'were too busy' to visit India, while telling the Tibetan official that "no official invitation had been received from the Government of India".

According to Pant, this made the position of the Indian Government "vis a vis the Tibetans, Bhutanese, Sikkimese and other border people professing the Buddhist faith rather delicate and difficult. They, however, had more faith and trust in us than the Chinese and they were sure that the Chinese were only giving some excuse in order not to allow the Dalai Lama to visit India."

---

26 'Lonchen' is an honorific title for Senior Minister.

Pant continued to describe the months before the visit: "Matters thus languished for nearly six months and as the date approached for the celebrations in Delhi and elsewhere there was gloom and despondency in the Tibetan as well as Sikkimese and Bhutanese circles and our friends from Bhutan and Sikkim indicated to me that all this was another example of how 'powerful and mighty' are the Chinese and as how all the 'good behavior' towards them would lead to no real benefit. This meant that these friends of ours expected us 'to get tough' with the Chinese."

After giving the background of the 'rebellion' in Kham, he further explained "the belief [of the Tibetans] that under these circumstances the Dalai Lama would never be allowed to go. Officially as well as unofficially our Consul General in Lhasa (Shri PN Menon) was approached by the Tibetan officials and I was also sent some 'secret messages' indicating that the Dalai Lama was very keen to visit India and that the Government of India should send as soon as possible their official invitation to him."

The Political Officer gave more details of the behind the scene transaction: "The Dalai Lama also managed to reach me a message stating that if the Chinese were not ready to deliver the invitation cannot the Government of Indian through me invite him directly! I told him that this was, under the present circumstances, not possible. Our attitude in respect of issuing a direct invitation to the Dalai Lama disappointed and disheartened the Tibetan people who felt that we were only afraid of the Chinese."

The description of the events continued; on November 4, Menon had announced openly that the Government of India was still "waiting to know of the reaction of the Dalai Lama and the Panchen Lama to the invitations which were handed over to the Chinese nearly six months ago".

Pant admitted that the open declaration certainly "had its effect on the Chinese and Tibetan circles as people started comparing the reactions to the invitation given by the Chinese to the Dalai Lama to visit China in 1953 and the reactions of the people of Tibet to the invitation given by the Government of India. In 1953 the *Tsongdue Geypa*, the National

Assembly, deliberated for six months over the invitation given by the Chinese and finally advised the Dalai Lama for 'health reasons' <u>not to</u> visit China. The same National Assembly in 1956 within 24 hours unanimously recommended that the Dalai Lama should visit India!"

Pant asserted that the Dalai Lama's mother, his sister Tsering Dolma, who headed the Young Women's League "knew nothing of this visit as late as 6th of November when they left Tibet for India. The Dalai Lama had actually sent a 'special message' with his mother, to me asking me again 'to do something about the invitation'!!"

The Panchen Lama's confidant and adviser, Rimshi Sonam Wongchuk Dillog Rabder also knew nothing on November 7 about the invitation: "All this indicates how suddenly the Chinese made up their mind to allow these two lamas to visit India."

As mentioned, when the invitations were delivered, Gen Fang Ming told the Dalai Lama that he was free to 'accept or reject' it: "The Chinese, however, knew that there was no question of the invitation being refused," commented Pant.

It is in these circumstances that parties of the two Lamas left Tibet for India.

## 22

## In the Land of the Buddha

Coming to the visit of the two Tibetan Lamas to India, we have three fascinating reports of the Tibetan Lamas written by the Indian officials responsible, the PO Apa Pant, PN Menon, then Officer on Special Duty and PN Luthra, Special Officer (Border Areas)[1] in the Ministry of External Affairs.

On January 3, 1957, the PO wrote to the Prime Minister, reporting about his talks with the Tibetans, including the Dalai and the Panchen Lamas. A series of points were made; they are worth mentioning to understand the thinking of the PO at the time of the Tibetan leaders visit to India.[2]

These are, of course, Pant's views, but the social issues raised by the PO will come again and again in the correspondence with Delhi.

1. 'Old Tibet' cannot fight 'new dynamic China'

2. 'Religion' can never mean the maintenance of privileges and power in the hands of a few in a society to the detriment of the many.

3. In Tibet, unless the high monks, thinkers and saints start seriously the reorganizing of the whole social and economic structure which is today based on privileges and is corrupt,

---

1 Or SOBA.

2 All documents in this chapter, except specifically mentioned, are from the Nehru Papers (JN Collection) held at the Nehru Memorial Museum and Library in Delhi. The 'papers' are not indexed.

there is no point in calling Tibet a Buddhist land as the Buddha was a great revolutionary himself who brought not only new learning but the doctrines of social and economic equality to the millions.

4. The monks in the monasteries in Tibet shall have immediately to give up their existence of isolation from the masses and move out into the field of practical action by helping the poor and the ignorant to better their status in society and root out corruption, nepotism and lethargy.

5. The higher spiritual learning shall have to come down to the masses and inspire them to establish a new society which will satisfy the needs and urges of all the people in this modern age.

6. The means and the methods to bring this about shall have to be commensurate with the Dharma, that is they can only work through Truth and Non-violence and for this purpose they should study the life and the works of Mahatma Gandhi in which they are already greatly interested.

7. Even in the expression of their patriotism, they can never take up violence and armed conflict as not only such a course would be suicidal but against the very basic tenets of the Dharma;

8. If they really follow the True Dharma, then the purity and brilliance of their life and actions will impress and even convert those who do not believe in the Dharma and seem to be in opposition to them.

9. The Chinese have also a doctrine of social revolution and change which they are certain will help the common man. The Tibetans shall have to have an equally powerful dynamic policy of social change.

10. Tibet has now, once and for all, joined the stream of modern life and can never go back to its isolation. Railways[3], motorcars

---

3  There was no railway in Tibet at that time. The first railway would reach Lhasa in July 2006. The first plane landed at Damchung, North of Lhasa in 1955.

and jet planes are there to stay and unless the Dharma can answer and solve the problems created by the modern age and unless the Dharma can stand at the bar of modern science it cannot last. If Dharma can last only by remaining isolated in the monasteries and is frightened of the whirr of the machine age, the sooner it dies the better as it never can inspire the people or serve any useful purpose.

11. We are friendly with the Chinese as with everybody else in the world. Just because the Tibetans are now on the war path against the Chinese we cannot get ourselves involved in this conflict though we always wish and are certain that Truth and Dharma will ultimately prevail. To keep up our friendly relations and our religious and cultural ties with Tibet will be our constant endeavour.

12. It is not only in Tibet that this fight for moral and spiritual values is going on though it may seem to be more acute at the moment there. Tibet is not alone therefore in this fight for the re-establishment of the right principles of human endeavour.

13. There are important and valuable contributions from communism in this process of social, scientific and economic advancement of man in society which cannot be overlooked. Power politics and the use of communism to further national or group interests must be separated from the ideological and human aspects of communism. The Tibetans must understand properly this aspect of communism.

Pant concluded, "some in Tibet proper and outside can understand these points and agree with the analysis."

Though nobody can disagree with these points, they were a simplification of a far more complex situation and the colonialist attitude of China towards Tibet was completely omitted.

Pant, however, admitted: "Some of those who see these points and desire to do something to change the social and economic structure inside Tibet find it difficult to do so now as the Chinese will not allow any change to come about except under their own auspices."

Apa Pant was aware that the Dalai Lama himself wanted radical changes …though most of the monks "were most reactionary and adamant."

He continued in the same vein: "Most of the Tibetans are therefore confused and not quite sure whether the Dharma will be able to face and survive such a severe challenge."

His final admission was that "to try and understand all these events, to be friendly and to sympathise and yet to keep completely out of the picture is not a very easy task." And he also mentioned the attraction that "the Tibetans feel towards India and towards you [Nehru], in particular, is often overwhelming and not a little embarrassing."

But the Tibetans felt attracted towards India only in so far as India could defend some higher values. It was not to be the case.

Based on these 'social' views of the unfolding situation on the plateau, the political support to the Tibetans would be practically nil during the two years to come. The strategic angle was totally missing from Pant's analysis.

## Apa Pant's Report of the Visit

It would not serve our purpose to dwell on the 'philosophical' aspects of the PO's report; he noted that his own privilege of travelling "with such a God King and of being on intimate terms with him indicates indeed meritorious work accumulated over thousands of lives! … receiving them on top of the Nathu La, a pass between Sikkim and Tibet, was indeed a unique privilege."

Pant thus described the arrival of the Dalai Lama in Sikkim: "To watch a caravan of over 500 mules winding its way slowly and laboriously from the Chumbi Valley of Tibet towards this pass and the high dignitaries of the Tibetan Government including senior monk officials like the Trichang Rimpoche[4] and the Ling Tsang Rimpoche[5] as well as the members of the Kashag emerging from the swarming mist at this

---

4   Junior Tutor to the Dalai Lama.

5   Senior Tutor to the Dalai Lama.

high altitude into the brilliant sunshine to be followed by the God King himself was an experience never to be forgotten."

The Panchen Lama, the Dalai Lama and Prime Minister Nehru during the visit to a site in December 1956

After giving a long historical background, Apa Pant explained the role and place of the Panchen Lama in the then Tibetan setup: "The Chinese have been since long trying to build up the Panchen Lama as a kind of a counter-check to the position and power of the Dalai Lama in Tibet and outside it. Even the British, when the Dalai Lama was a minor, had tried to recognize the Panchen Lama as the sole authority and had even given him importance as a 'higher incarnation' than the Dalai Lama. This has some basis as the Panchen Lama is the incarnation of the Buddha of Boundless Light, Amitabha or Amita Deva, whilst the Dalai Lama is the incarnation of Bodhisattva, Avalokiteshwara. A Bodhisattva however is and can reach Buddhahood but does not do so willingly in order to help others to tread the Right Path. A Bodhisattva 'renounces' Buddhahood to help others."

A more down-to-earth description of the power struggle between the 13th Dalai Lama and the 9th Panchen Lama followed.

The PO mentioned the fact that there were two candidates to the post: "the Lhasa government 'discovered' another person as the 'true incarnation' of the deceased Panchen Rimpoche[6] in some other part of Tibet." Pant added that the Lama "who travelled in India is the one which some of the monasteries in Tibet would not recognize as the true one."[7]

But whether he was the true incarnation or not "he certainly is a very highly intelligent, courageous, scholarly and extremely efficient as well as a very devout person. He is truly a religious person and spends hours in prayers and meditation," noted Pant.

The PO mentioned that the scenes of jubilation in and around Gangtok as well as in Sikkim, Bhutan, Darjeeling, Kalimpong, Kurseong, were unprecedented in the history of the peoples of these border regions. Gangtok was literally invaded by 20,000 to 30,000 Tibetans, Nepalese, Rais, Lambus, Bhutanese, Tamangs, Gurungs: "The Bhutanese had intimated to me that on this historic occasion more than 6,000 Bhutanese pilgrims would visit India"

All trekked towards Gangtok to catch a glimpse of the divine incarnation of Avalokiteshwara, wrote Pant.

**Crossing over to Sikkim**

At Nathu-la, they had to shiver in the bitingly freezing sub-zero temperatures for nearly nine hours: "by the time the Dalai Lama reached there at 1.30 p.m., snow had started to fall." When the Panchen Lama reached the same day, it was dark.

The first camp was pitched at Chhangu[8]: "The Dalai Lama escorted by the Maharajkumar of Sikkim arrived just as dusk was falling but the

---

6   Now written 'Rinpoche'.

7   The Panchen Lama would later become one of the greatest Tibetan patriots; he would die under mysterious circumstances on January 28, 1989 in his monastery in Tashilhunpo.

8   Changu or Tsomgo Lake; see Chapter 10, Footnote 3.

Panchen Lama's route throughout innumerable twists and turnings of this narrow mountain road was illuminated by ignited pine branches casting weird shadows on the mountain sides and deep down in the valleys." While the camp at Chhangu was prepared for 200 guests, some 500 sought accommodation.

The first incident occurred at a place known as '10 mile'[9] when the Chinese representative tried to put a Chinese flag on the car carrying the Lamas; as a result, Tibetans insisted on the Dalai Lama's own Tibetan flag also being flown on the car: "The swirling crowds and perhaps some mischief makers broke once or twice the standards that flew these flags including the flags of India and Sikkim and thus nearly brought about an international incident".

The PO continued his description of the scenes at Gangtok; it resembled a "great religious fair in India with the addition that in an Indian fair one is always conscious that the idol is made of wood and that the ceremonies have only a symbolic significance whilst in Gangtok it was the God King himself who had descended from his Himalayan heights."

And the crowd was getting two for the price of one.

The next day, the journey from Gangtok to Bagdogra was incident free except for the crowd of nearly 13,000 waiting at Bagdogra "to pick up the dust from the feet of the two lamas. ...The police had great difficulty is keeping the crowds back and the planes escaped damage only due to a miracle."

The Lamas were then flown to Delhi.

## The Dalai Lama's Party

The PO provided a description of the senior members of the Dalai Lama's entourage, starting with the Lama's tutors; Ling Rinpoche and Trichang Rinpoche: "These tutors are not mere religious preceptors but also confidants with definite political views and are political personalities in their own right. They have precedence and seniority over the members of the Cabinet, the Kashag." Pant further noted

---

9 'Das Mile' in Hindi.

that the Tibetan leader had greater faith in the junior tutor, Trichang Rinpoche. This was probably only the personal perception of the PO.

Apart from the two tutors, other important monks, special representatives from the three monasteries of Drepung, Sera and Ganden, travelled with the Dalai Lama. He remarked: "Even the Chinese after having occupied Tibet for nearly seven years have not been able to challenge the influence of these three monasteries and recently the Chinese had to bow down to their wishes when they released Alo Chonjey, the rebel leader."

The two main oracles,[10] used in times of 'crises' or when an important decision needed to be taken, were also present.

The Dalai Lama's brother, the *Chikyap Khempo*[11] as the head of the ecclesiastical department, was one of the main advisors. He eventually had to be operated upon for appendicitis at Nangal: "Of the other monk officials the Dalai Lama trusts *Dronyer Chenmo*[12] most, both in ecclesiastical as well as in political matters. He also consults Khendrung Ta Lama[13] and trusts him."

Then followed the description of the lay officials; the most trusted was Ragashar Shape, the brother of the Maharani of Sikkim: "He is the head of the Tibetan Army and is also Vice-Commander in Chief of the Peoples' Liberation Army." Pant commented that though he was not very energetic "and would rather wait upon events than take any decisive action," the Tibetan Leader still trusted Ragashar.

---

10 Nechung and Gadong oracles.

11 See Chapter 18, Footnote 44.

12 Another senior monk official in the Dalai Lama's secretariat was the *Dronye Chenmo* or Lord Chamberlain. He was the main contact person for private petitions, audiences, etc. He controlled the access to the Dalai Lama; Thubten Woeden Phala was the *Dronye Chenmo* in 1956/57.

13 According to Tsipon Shakabpa: "There were four senior monk officials in the Potala Secretariat Office with general responsibility over all monastic affairs; they determined who should fill monastery posts throughout Tibet, the large and small religious offices, and the monk offices in the government, as well as the steward's offices in the districts. There is a tradition whereby the oldest of the four is given the rank of Ta Lama."

The two other ministers[14] were Surkhang, who, according to Pant, was young and extremely intelligent, and Ngabo Shape, both "had their difficulties in Tibet in carrying conviction to the people about the benefits of the Chinese occupation of Tibet."

Ngabo was the main architect of the Sino-Tibetan Treaty of 1951[15]; he was called a traitor by many and "easily one of the most hated persons today in Tibet. He, however, is very courageous and it has been reported that he is now worried about his part in cooperating with the Chinese in Tibet. …He is, however, a dark horse."

The description continued.

**A Few Words about the Dalai Lama**

Pant came to the main actor, the Dalai Lama; the PO noted that "he is a unique personality. He combines boyish exuberance with grace and dignity and has a sharp irrepressible sense of humour with maturity and clarity of thought. After having lived with him for over two months it can certainly be said that he is a strong nationalist for Tibet and whatever the Chinese may say or do he would try his hardest to gain independence for Tibet. His spiritual attainments also are of no mean order."

The PO then raised a question, the Dalai Lama "realizes that in the present circumstances in Tibet there can and must develop a dynamism that can inspire a new social change and assure progress to the people with a more complete development of man in society based on the true principles of the Dharma."

Pant continued to develop his 'social' views: "Can he thus try to find a way of expressing all that is good and valuable in the ancient history and to modernize it so that the Chinese would not be able to just swamp Tibet and put an end to her culture and also her people."

Further, the Dalai Lama knew that the Chinese communists were well organized and "they are hard fighters and very efficient workers. [The Dalai Lama] also realizes the weakness of his own people. He knows

14 Known as *shapes*.
15 See Volume 1, Chapter 21.

that they are lazy, lethargic and often very corrupt and treacherous to their own cause. …His pilgrimage to India in these circumstances has had a political significance besides the more deeper religious urge."

To complete his description Pant mentioned that, "the Dalai Lama has a sharp clear intellect and has up to date knowledge of world events. He has studied the Marxist doctrines and knows the details of the workings of the administrative and political setups in China and Russia thoroughly. He is keenly interested in mechanical things and loves to take down and put together cameras, clocks and other gadgets. …he grasps the facts quickly and has searching intelligent questions."

This trait remains true more than sixty years later.

**The Panchen Lama**

According to the PO, he was a 'crowd apart', not so worried about the customs and the protocol as the Dalai Lama, as his entourage was much smaller and not having a kingdom to rule, the Panchen Lama "functions more freely and often more forcefully. It would be not right to try and compare his personality with that of the Dalai Lama's."

As Pant put it, "he is younger; in many respects somewhat immature. He, however, has a very sharp intelligence and has had the benefit of continuous instructions from a highly qualified guru, Yongzin Nonchu Trulku Rimpoche."

Being born and brought up in China, the Panchen Lama knew better the Chinese ways (and language), even better than the Tibetan ways and customs, noted Pant: "He is a deeply and genuinely religious person and has been instructed in the *shastras* as well as in various forms of meditation thoroughly."

During his discussions with Pant, he made comparison between Hinduism and Buddhism "both these religions must flourish side by side for the benefit of world peace," the Panchen Lama told the PO: "The Panchen Lama's mind is very alert. He is especially good at grasping new facts about mechanical gadgets and things and has been deeply impressed by India's material progress".

However, the PO added that "his position in Tibet is insecure as he is one of the two incarnates who were chosen for the final choice as the Panchen Lama. …The Panchen Lama thus knows that his position in Tibet depends upon the Chinese power in Tibet."

He told Pant, "with the friendship of India he and [the Tibetan] people will be able to function more freely".

His main advisor was Rimshi Sonam Wangchuk Dilerabden, a strange personality: "a mixture of goodness as well as of acute power consciousness. He is trustworthy to a large extent, but is always conscious of the advantages that he may be able to gain by his contacts in India for the benefit of the position of the Panchen Lama in Tibet."

Both the Panchen Lama and his entourage were keenly interested in business and wanted to establish contacts in Tatanagar, Bombay, Madras, Calcutta and elsewhere. They bought 'outright' ten Tata-Mercedes Benz trucks. Pant believed that the Chinese had given them contracts for running transport vehicles inside Tibet.

After naming other advisors, Pant mentioned Dzasa Che Jigme: "He is highly trusted by the Chinese and the Panchen Lama also seeks his advice. Lately, however he has been somewhat neglected."

We have mentioned Che Jigme in another chapter.[16]

## Some Other Members of the Party

The Dalai Lama had with him three interpreters (Tibetan-English), Kapshopa Se Dhondup, Yuthok Se Jigme and Sadutshang Tsetop. Kapshopa, said Pant, perhaps represented the younger generation who had been "impressed and largely won over" by the Chinese overtures, though they have all been educated in India and "have a kind of cultural, emotional bond with this country," though they never established any contact with the Indian Consulate General at Lhasa: "Since coming to India however they are convinced that they need not be so completely under the Chinese influence. They have expressed often that they feel freer here than in Tibet."

---

16 See Chapter 7, Footnote 23.

Pant noted that it was interesting to see the hopes, fears and reactions of the monks accompanying the Lamas, about India: "They felt that a virtual miracle would take place and somehow or other with the word of command from Pandit Jawaharlal Nehru the Chinese would withdraw from their country proclaiming, as they go away, the independence of Tibet to the outside world!"

Most of them were of course in favour of India giving political asylum to the Dalai Lama: "We have to excuse these rather fantastic notions because after all most of them had no contact with the outside world ever and to say the least are somewhat immature from the point of view of political awareness of events in the outside world."

Some of the Tibetan leaders led by Gyalo Thoundup and Shakabpa wanted to delay the Dalai Lama's return to Tibet in the hope that "[it] will bring sufficient pressure on the Chinese to give a favourable answer to them regarding their fresh negotiations."

Pant commented that these leaders were disappointed: "It is a good thing that they have now understood the true perspective of their actions and their struggle for independence and have further come to understand what it really means to be ushered into the stream of world history."

He added something strange: "The walls of seclusion that surrounded Tibet for centuries have been knocked down and currents of history from China, Russia, India and elsewhere are rushing into this empty vacuum."

Unfortunately for Tibet, the currents of history would only bring destruction and death. A long philosophical lecture followed.

**The Travels in India**

The Government of India had prepared elaborate plans for the visit.

The two parties first went to India's new 'temple', the Bhakra Nangal dam. The PO said that both the Dalai Lama and the Panchen Lama were impressed and were surprised to see so many Europeans working on the project. In their mind, foreigners working in a country were associated with 'foreign domination'.

They had the same perception in Tatanagar and Kolkata. In Dehra Dun, the Tibetan party visited the Indian Military Academy; later, in Mussoorie an incident took place: "the Chinese Counsellor got upset because some of the cadets from the Academy were getting 'too friendly' and were 'frightening' the brother of the Panchen Lama".

They then proceeded to Sanchi: "The arrangements for their visit to Sanchi were perfect and their reception by the Governor at the railway station was impressive and touching. Both the lamas delivered long and fine sermons at Sanchi."

In Agra, the two Tibetan leaders were 'too tired', but they enjoyed watching a movie titled *C.I.D*[17]. The report said that Tibetans loved Indian filmy culture: "If nothing else Indian filmy culture can certainly win over the youth of Tibet for us," remarked Pant.

In Mumbai (at that time Bombay), they visited an atomic reactor, but it was 'too complicated' to understand: "Both the lamas spent a great deal of time in Bombay seeing cinemas and their entourage spent as much time as possible shopping." They spent literally "lakhs of rupees in purchasing jewellery, cloth, cameras and other things."

The trip to the caves in Ajanta was a moving experience for Apa Pant; here the Lamas offered prayers: "After nearly 1,700 years these caves reverberated to the deep sonorous prayers chanted by Buddhist priests."

They then moved to Bangalore where they inspected several factories including the Hindustan Aircraft Factory; in Mysore they were impressed by the cleanliness, friendliness and especially the palaces.

Next halt was in Madras; they went to the Integral Coach Factory and the Buckingham Spinning and Weaving Mills acquainting themselves "with the industrial potential of our country." Everywhere they spent

---

17 *C.I.D.* is a 1956 Indian Hindi film directed by Raj Khosla and produced by Guru Dutt. It stars Dev Anand, Shakila, Johnny Walker, KN Singh and Waheeda Rehman. It is a crime thriller with Dev Anand playing the role of a police inspector investigating a murder case. The music is by Mohammed Rafi and the lyrics by Majrooh Sultanpuri and Jan Nisar Akhtar.

time with the local leaders including Nijalingappa[18], Dr. Bidan Roy[19] and RR Diwakar[20].

Next, the party moved to Nagarjunakonda. The Dalai Lama said that he 'felt that he had been here before': "Nagarjunakonda to the Dalai Lama was a very deeply moving experience," observed the PO in his report: "As I was travelling with these two lamas I suddenly discovered to my great surprise how deeply moving and genuine was their faith and how fresh in their minds were the acts, teachings and life of those sages and saints who tread the path of Lord Buddha nearly 2,000 years[21] ago. To them every stone in these places of pilgrimage was a monument and every building, however decrepit it may be, an epic."

They then moved to Varanasi where both Lamas requested the government to extend their stay there by a day: "They were constantly engaged in either meditation, prayers or sermons, ...thousands of people waiting patiently to seek their blessings or to offer them homage."

Apa Pant noted that the "reactions of the crowds to the Dalai Lama and the Panchen Lama all over India were really remarkable whether in Bombay, Poona, Bangalore or Banaras. They thronged the streets, shouted and cheered without being led by any cheer leaders and just bathed in the light of the glowing personalities of these two lamas".

A small incident took place one day when the Dalai Lama went beyond the time allotted to him for his sermon, "the Panchen Lama who was

---

18 Siddavanahalli Nijalingappa, the Chief Minister of Karnataka between 1956 and 1958 and once again, between 1962 and 1968. He played an important role in the Indian freedom movement as well as in the Karnataka Unification movement.

19 Dr Bidhan Chandra Roy, an eminent Indian physician, educationist, philanthropist, freedom fighter and politician, served as the Chief Minister of West Bengal from 1948 until his death in 1962.

20 Ranganath Ramachandra Diwakar (30 September 1894 – January 1990) was a Congress politician from Karnataka. He served as the President of the Karnataka Pradesh Congress Committee from 1930 to 1942. Later, he became a member of the Constituent Assembly of India; he was the Union Minister of Information and Broadcasting from 1949 to 1952. At the time of the Dalai Lama's visit to India, he was Governor of Bihar. In 1962 he was nominated to the Rajya Sabha where he served till 1968.

21 Infact, 2,500 years.

to follow him got very upset by this encroachment on his time. He refused to give a sermon, but held pooja later in the evening," recounted Pant, who added: "Throughout this trip it has been possible, thanks to the innate good nature and dignity of the Dalai Lama as well as to the efforts of our Liaison Officers, to avoid any unpleasant incidents. Wherever any friction arose it was also possible to express freely and frankly our position to the lamas concerned."

The party left for Gorakpur and Kushinara where they were moved by the stupa: "To all Buddhists Gaya is the most important *Tirth*. It is here that the Lord reached enlightenment and it was here that he announced the four Aryan Truths and demonstrated the glorious Eight-Fold Path."

In Gaya, thousands of pilgrims from "the far flung Indo-Mongoloid people, monks from Mongolia, China, Bhutan, Sikkim, Ladakh, from the region of the Goloks, Amdos, people from Rudok and also from Sinkiang rushed to greet the divine incarnations."

At the time of the Lamas arrival, the news of fresh fighting in Kham broke out, bringing its share of anxiety; even in Lhasa: "fighting had taken place in a Lhasa cinema where four persons were killed and that the Chinese had put up sand-bag barricades around houses where Chinese were staying."

"A contingent of 500 Khampas had arrived to incite the Lhasa people to 'fight' it out now as the Dalai Lama was safe in India," he added.

Then instead of continuing on their journey, the train was 'shunted back to Delhi 700 miles in 24 hours'. The Dalai Lama was called for talks with the Chinese Premier Zhou Enlai.

They just had time to visit Himachal Pradesh, principally Rewalsar, near Mandi where the great tantric master Padmasambhava had performed miracles: "After returning from Rewalsar one found out that the Dalai Lama had again regained his usual peace of mind. ...Critical and difficult situations had to be faced."

## The Need for the Oracle

In the meantime, the oracles were called upon for advice as the Khampa fighters wanted to submit a petition to the Dalai Lama calling upon the Chinese to withdraw from Tibet. The oracle told the Tibetan leader to 'go' to Himachal and instead of [The Dalai Lama] meeting Zhou, the Kashag could speak to him: "the Kashag who are usually more afraid of the Chinese than their own people, this time had to yield to the pressure of the nationalists," said Pant.

During the talks which followed with Zhou, the Kashag made some proposals: "They asked firstly for the removal of the Chinese troops from Tibet," to which the Premier did not reply. They also requested that Lukhangwa, the former Prime Minister of Tibet sacked in 1952, should be re-installed as the Tibetans had faith in him. Apparently, Zhou agreed, admitting that his dismissal was a great mistake.

The Chinese official further told the Kashag that in matters of religion and culture 'Tibet should deal directly with India'. In the future, "in respect of these matters they would correspond with me," noted the PO: "This development would certainly have very far reaching effects specially on the status of Tibet vis-à-vis India and the development of nationalism of the Tibetan people."

It would never be implemented.

During their stay in Delhi, it was decided that the Lamas would not continue their journey to Nepal, but accompany Zhou Enlai to Nalanda where a ceremony was scheduled to bring back some of pilgrim Huan Tsang's relics; quoting the Tibetans, the PO asserted, "the trip to Nepal was cancelled because there were nearly 15,000 Tibetans waiting at Kathmandu to give a tumultuous ovation to the Dalai Lama and that Mr. Chou En Lai did not want to participate in this reception."

## A 'Hysterical' Dream for Independence?

Finally, the two Lamas flew to Nalanda in the Prime Minister's plane; the Dalai Lama remained undecided: should he visit Kalimpong despite the advice to the contrary given by Zhou?

At the same time, he was keen to return to Lhasa as soon as possible: "He was also not quite sure as to how much his visit to India and his contacts with the outside world had achieved for him and was wondering as to what kind of cooperation he should now afford the Chinese when he returns back to Tibet," commented Pant.

Ultimately, the decision to go to Kalimpong "was taken against the express wishes of the Chinese." The Tibetan leader wanted to "talk to the people of Kalimpong and explain to them many matters"; he did not want to 'disappoint them'. Pant observed: "To allow him to go to Kalimpong was a wise decision and certainly enhanced the prestige of India in the eyes of the Tibetans, Bhutanese and Sikkimese."

It would also allow the Dalai Lama to advise some of his most radical followers who "had developed an attitude of acute and somewhat fantastic nationalism; for them, it was good that the Dalai Lama could personally go to them and talk to them."

They were in a kind of "a dream; a hysterical dream, and had to be woken up," said Pant. They wanted Tibet to be independent! It is rather shocking that a senior official of the Government of India, a country which had obtained Independence hardly ten years earlier, could argue against 'Tibetan Independence'. Pant cited their argument: "Why was Indian Government so unhelpful? Do they not know that the Tibetans are fighting now and are ready to die for their freedom?" Many officials in India had already forgotten their own struggle against the British.

In Kalimpong, the Dalai Lama talked "at some length with these people and convinced at least some of them of the futility of their course of action."

The report continued about the visit to Kalimpong, "the atmosphere was tense with various rumours. It was even suggested that the members of the Mimang party may 'abduct' the Dalai Lama!" A few thousand would offer '*satyagraha*' and "forbid the Dalai Lama from returning to Tibet."

Finally, the Dalai Lama "pacified and calmed the violent tempers of his followers and in a few sermons completely quietened them down. It was most wonderful to watch these highly excitable nationalists docile as a lamb eating out of his hand within a few days of his arrival in Kalimpong. The tense atmosphere suddenly changed to a highly sociable happy concourse of friends."

For the Political Officer, it showed the strong character of the Dalai Lama as he went to Kalimpong against the directives of the Chinese government. By this action he proved to himself and to the Chinese government "that he was still a power – which indeed he is. His visit to Kalimpong also proved that India was not standing in the way of Tibetan developments."

The Bhutanese and the Sikkimese were watching with 'great interest' the visit of the Dalai Lama to the hill station.

**Conclusion of the Report**

In conclusion, Pant said that the Tibetan party, including the two Lamas, were 'deeply impressed' with all that they saw in India.

The PO also mentioned "quite a few clever politicians amongst the members of the parties of the two lamas. These persons have been establishing their independent contacts with the Sikkimese, the Bhutanese and other Tibetans in India and perhaps trying to discover in what way in time to come the Tibetans in Tibet and the persons of Tibetan stock outside Tibet could cooperate with each other."

About the Dalai Lama and the Panchen Lama, the PO admitted: "At the present moment there is little common ground between these two but after all ties of blood, custom and common religion can be very strong. The Tibetans on both sides of the Himalayas are not at all conscious of this great mountain as a barrier between them: to them these snowy peaks are indeed their natural habitat and not a dividing line."

He mentioned the 'tricky' idea of 'federating peoples of Tibetan stock': in the past it was "mooted and discussed between most of the leading personalities in these regions," Pant however refrained to give his own opinion, though at the end, he asked: "What of Tibet itself?" Will it be 'sinofised' (sic) and absorbed into the social, political and economic pattern of life of China?

His answer was that economically it would be difficult to absorb too soon and too quickly the whole of Tibet: "Though mineral wealth is being developed in the northern parts of China such as oil in Tsaidan marshes and coal, copper and iron in the Kokonor region and forest wealth is being exploited all along in Tibet the very distance from China would make it difficult for the complete incorporation of Tibet economy into the Chinese."

However, he added that with the settlement of a large number of Chinese migrants "Tibet as we know it today would be annihilated, the process for its complete absorption into China [has] started."

The Chinese authorities had already declared that they would like "to double the population of Tibet within the next five years". Since the invasion, some two lakhs of permanent settlers (officials, workers, farmers, miners) had already settled on the plateau: "It is still however difficult to visualize the arrival suddenly of a few more million Chinese settling down into Tibet within the next five years. Socially even if the Chinese settle down in Tibet it will take some time before they inter-marry amongst the Tibetans and create a new race group of Sino-Tibetans."

Sixty years later, there are hardly any Sino-Tibetans on the plateau, though the population of migrants from the Mainland goes into millions.

The PO asserted: "the Tibetans who acquiesced in the beginning in the utilization of unused land areas in Tibet by the Chinese are now repenting their action." He said that after the revolt in Kham, very large numbers of Chinese settling seems difficult. In conclusion, the key person in these developments was the Dalai Lama: "His word is law and his intervention the final one."

Pant returned to his philosophical best: "India is the land of enlightenment; the land of Lord Buddha. To them [Tibetans] the highest prayer is that they should be 'reborn' in India."

His last comments were for the Chinese; at the beginning of the tour, the Chinese representatives gave an impression as if they were 'greatly upset', in many ways, they tried to 'protect him' from too many contacts with Indians: "They used to suspect every move of ours and get upset by small incidents which were trifling and insignificant in themselves." They thought that Indians were "making too much of these two lamas".

One incident particularly upset them, President Rajendra Prasad called on the Dalai Lama; the Chinese thought, wrote the PO, that "we were trying to steal away the Lamas from them."

It was however explained that the contact between India and Tibet was a religious and spiritual one and that the people of India thought very highly of the Dalai Lama.

Tibet probably missed a chance to be more assertive and bargain for some sort of autonomy at least, but it was difficult in the circumstances, too many Indian officials believed that China's reforms would do good to the Tibetan 'feudal system'. That was the tragedy.

## 23

# A Milestone in the Relations Between India and Tibet?

### The Second Report

Liaison Officer Colonel PN (Pran) Luthra of the Indian Frontier Administrative Service (IFAS) provided another report of the visit. For years, he had served as Advisor to the Governor of Assam for NEFA; he later served as Special Officer (Border Areas) or SOBA[1]; Luthra's views were more strategic, as he was a former Army colonel.[2]

His report covered the period between November 1956 and February 1957. During these two months, as Liaison Officer or LO for the visit, Luthra was in daily contact with the two Lamas; he did not provide a detailed account of their tour "but have confined myself to such impressions and reactions which they themselves had expressed or which I happened to observe."[3]

Luthra's main responsibility was to look after the Panchen Lama's party; he recounted: "At a certain stage of the tour, it became possible to freely and frankly discuss any matter, howsoever delicate, with the Panchen Lama himself or some of his principal associates."

---
1  Some officers had objected to the 'cozy' name, SOFA (Special Officer, Frontier Areas); thereafter, it was changed into SOBA.
2  From the Signal Regiment.
3  All documents in this chapter, except specifically mentioned, are from the Nehru Papers (JN Collection) held at the Nehru Memorial Museum and Library in Delhi. The 'papers' are not indexed.

He also admitted that his contacts with the Dalai Lama "have naturally not been sufficiently deep. ...In the few talks with the Dalai Lama, I considered it fit not to harass him with some of the delicate issues which were causing him anxiety and which were already under discussion by our Prime Minister and other senior officials."

As we have seen in the previous chapter, Apa Pant was directly responsible for the Dalai Lama.

**Eating Tibet Like an Artichoke**

"As far back as the days of Warren Hastings[4], the British realized the importance of Tibet as a buffer State between India and the expansionist menace from Russia. It was not so much an actual military attack on India which the British Government feared as the revolutionary and communist propaganda which might percolate into India through Tibet," noted Luthra at the outset.

In its policy towards Tibet, the British Government vacillated "between aloofness and semi-aloofness." He affirmed that people of the caliber of Sir Charles Bell "prophesied the concern which Tibet's position would cause to India if the Government continued with its neglect of this important region."

Luthra continued by affirming that Tibet was always aware of its weak position: "The 13th Dalai Lama fully realized the defenceless state of his Country, devoted to archaic ecclesiastical feudalism, corruption, nepotism and many other ills which sap the health of a nation. He knew that for its preservation, Tibet would have to lean on a strong outside power. He wanted that power to be the British."

Bell, according to Luthra, did not want China to be that power, because it would "interfere with Tibet's internal life, administration and political ideology."

While China always wanted to absorb Tibet and reduce it to the status of a province, it followed a policy of gradual penetration and integration: "It was eating Tibet like an artichoke, leaf by leaf. Having planned to

---

4 Warren Hastings, Governor of the Presidency of Fort William (Bengal), (28 April 1772 – 20 October 1774).

colonise and assimilate the Eastern part of Tibet and absorb districts such as Batang, Litang, Derge, Golok, etc., it aimed at extending its intensive control in Outer Tibet[5] at a gradual pace."

Once the Communist regime came to power, the days of Tibet as an independent nation were numbered: "in 1950, China marched into Tibet and occupied it through military force. Unlike the previous years, it meant business this time and never before has Tibet been faced with the realistic peril of being absorbed and obliterated as it is today."

Luthra observed that the Chinese "have taken up all the measures which point to the eventual absorption of Tibet. They have posted military forces at key locations. They are guarding the border check posts of Tibet. They are discouraging the dependence of Tibet on neighbouring countries for trade and are in a way meaning to isolate Tibet from any external stimuli."

And they used a 'divide and rule policy' to hasten the country's end.

While Tibet was aware of the necessity for change, of modern scientific techniques replacing age-old methods, "At the same time their way of life and above all their religion was dear to them, for whom the change must grow from within and must not be imposed under the duress of the Chinese Communist regime: the two Lamas stand out as central figures around whom the hopes of Tibet would either prosper or perish," said Luthra.

We have studied this in detail from the Indian point of view in the previous chapters and the first two volumes.

## The Dalai Lama

The colonel first noted that the Dalai Lama and the Panchen Lama were almost in the same age group, the Dalai Lama being 24, and the Panchen Lama 19: "They are both young, impressionable, keen and intelligent."

The Dalai Lama was described as having an unusually sharp intellect, being quick to grasp the essentials of a situation: "He is also more

---

5  Central and Western Tibet.

mature than the Panchen Lama and this may well be because …he has to deal with a greater variety of complicated problems."

Further, he possessed a rare scholarship and deep interest in religious matters: "His active and alert mind is always responsive to new impacts, environments and people. …He never fails to create a hush of sanctity around him."

Once the Dalai Lama told Luthra that left to himself, he would devote his entire time to religion, but he could not escape the traditional responsibility as Head of the State.

The SOBA agreed that the system prevalent in Tibet led to evil practices, however, it was doubtful if Tibetans could introduce reformatory measures by themselves.

According to Luthra, the Dalai Lama displayed "considerable interest in world politics, but is handicapped by lack of personal experience of foreign countries. …When discussing he seems to be cautious and reserved as if there is a repressed side to his being which he is afraid to bring to the surface."

It was also noted that with his large entourage and the diversity of opinion, making a decision was not easy, while his Ministers or other personal staff, "maintain around him a strong girdle of secrecy and exclusiveness."

Luthra's conclusion was that although the Dalai Lama was capable of independent thinking, "he depends on his officials in arriving at a conclusion."

He then analyzed the traits of the second senior-most Lama, the Panchen Lama.

**The Panchen Lama**

The young Panchen Lama definitely showed maturity beyond his years, said the Indian officer: "He is exuberant, outspoken and mirthful. He too is a profound scholar of scriptures and religion." Luthra noted that he seemed to have been carefully indoctrinated in the past history of the Shigatse Government "and the vicissitudes which faced the previous Panchen Lamas from time to time."

The Panchen Lama was not scared to bitterly speak against the Lhasa Government that he held responsible for several high-handed acts: "He is convinced that at one time, one of the Mongol Kings had offered the entire Tibet to Panchen Lama to control and govern. But the Panchen Lama wanted to remain more occupied with religion and was content with the Tsang province and its administration."

He told the SOBA that the Lhasa Government "had always expansionist designs and had usurped nine districts of the Tsang province – five before the Younghusband Expedition and four during the exile of Panchen Lama in China."

Interestingly, the Panchen Lama was resigned to the overlordship of China, simply because China helped to reinstate the Panchen Lama in the Tashilhunpo monastery: "He firmly maintains that the status of the Panchen Lama is equal to that of the Dalai Lama. Although, he is prepared to concede the first priority to Dalai Lama," but it should be confined to the order of precedence or the sequence of seating.

He 'mocked' Lhasa's view that it was the Panchen Lama who facilitated the return of the Chinese to Tibet; Luthra remarked that the young Lama knew that the Chinese had come to stay "and any amount of resentment will not dislodge them from Tibet."

For him, the opposition faced by the Chinese in places such as Batang, Litang and other areas of Kham or Amdo was "not strong enough to overawe the Chinese nor was it likely to assume greater proportions."

He believed that the only factor "which will preserve the Tibetans is their adherence to religion." He was not ready to tolerate any interference from the Chinese in religious affairs; he felt that the "rivalry and antagonism between the Lhasa and Shigatse Governments is inimical to the common interests of both."

Luthra was told by the young Lama that he had often spoken to the Dalai Lama about this: "But the Dalai Lama is very much under the influence of extraneous factors and as a result they do not come sufficiently close to each other."

## The Rift

The 19-year old Lama believed that the rift between the two Governments in Lhasa and Shigatse could only serve the purpose of the Chinese.

For him, the Dalai Lama did not assert himself sufficiently "at the various official conferences held by the Chinese officials such as that of the Preparatory Committee."

Luthra noted that the Panchen Lama was "mechanically-minded and evinces great interest in the working mechanism of aircraft, jet planes, guns."

He added that the Lama had a thorough knowledge of a motor engine and is a good driver. He quickly grasped mechanical things; this was apparent during their visit to the Bangalore Telephone Factory[6].

The Lama was eager to introduce 'development' in Tibet and was looking "forward to the day when railway and motor vehicles will freely ply in his region and the public benefit by water supply and central heating."

Interestingly, despite his young age and the fact that he had been selected and groomed by the Communist Party, he dominated his officials "and I have seen him give orders to his staff in no uncertain manner. In discussions with his officials, he does most of the talking and enunciates conclusions and decisions purpose-fully."

Luthra concluded that he was probably in a better position than the Dalai Lama, with a smaller staff, more devoted to him.

The Indian officials were touched by his good memory for faces and facts; he was "particularly careful to recognize the humbler staff such as motorcar drivers and dispatch-riders."

The fascinating description continued. It was learnt that he did not believe "in the superstitious practices of Tibetan society. [The] Dalai Lama's consultations with his oracles to decide the date of his departure from India, had caused Panchen Lama much amusement."

---

6   Indian Telephone Industries or ITC, a Government of India public undertaking.

For him, action should be taken after thorough study of the past and unbiased deliberation on the present-day implications of a problem: "With such a frame of mind, one can dispense with the oracle."

The Panchen Lama was not consulting his own oracle left in Shigatse.

Luthra recounted that on one occasion, "he eluded his Security Officer and disappeared from a back-door to reach his destination before anybody else!" On several occasions he drove cars 'in a care-free mood': "such actions are indicative of his attempt to unbar the bounds of formalism which encircle him and hamper freedom of movement – the privilege of youth."

He, however, remained deeply religious and was keen to preserve Lamaism and the monastic institutions, "on this point is prepared to take a strong line with the Chinese."

He was at the same time attached to ancient customs and wisdom of Tibet: "He would not like his people to change their dress, although they may have been trained in China." He was against Tibetan medical lore being replaced by modern medical science.

He was keen to open schools teaching new subjects such as modern science, geography, civics, hygiene, side by side with the traditional knowledge contained in the Tibetan scriptures.

Luthra believed that his respect for India had been strengthened during the tour: "He is eager to establish relations with India on the basis of religion, commerce, education, mutual visits, exchange of literature and personal friendship."

He felt that he had been misunderstood in India[7]; he was not a stooge of the Chinese; he regretted that he "never got time or opportunity to express this personally to our Prime Minister." Nehru always gave precedence to the Dalai Lama.

Luthra remembered: "I once asked Panchen Lama what it felt like to be an incarnation of Amitabha. He replied that he had no such consciousness nor does he possess any supernatural powers. He struck me as a man without pretensions."

---

7   Even by Apa Pant, as we have seen in the previous chapter.

This is a rare first-hand description of the young Lama.

## The Relations Between the Two Lamas

Enlightening is the description of the relations between the Dalai and the Panchen Lamas: "There seems to exist personal friendly accord as one would imagine between two youths, who have so much in common," first commented Luthra who recounted: "I have seen them cutting jokes with each other, thumping on each other's backs and exchanging warm greetings."

Unfortunately, the major contending issues were not discussed between the two, as it was considered to be the business of senior officials of each side: "The Lhasa Government officials consider it below their dignity to take the initiative and go to the Shigatse Government officials to discuss any matter."

This division would cost dear to the Tibetan nation, but who was aware of this in the mid-1950s?

Whenever there was a need to discuss a serious issue, "[Lhasa] expects the Shigatse Government People to come to them," noted Luthra; usually the discussions were confined to minor details such as the arrangements of the programme, while on major issues of policy, "they want to maintain complete secrecy, shielding and preserving their information from each other."

Luthra says the 'CID'[8] of each party worked most efficiently: "there is little that comes to pass amongst the Lhasa officials which are not known to Panchen Lama's staff and vice versa."

The sense of competition and rivalry between the two sides was extremely acute; for example, the Dalai Lama's party always expected better accommodation and "would be candidly happy to see Panchen Lama and his party humiliated in some way or the other," wrote Luthra. At the same time, the Panchen Lama entourage was "always at pains to ascertain whether they are getting the same dispensation as the Dalai Lama's party or not."

---

8  Acronym for Criminal Investigations Division.

Luthra remarked that the Panchen Lama often casually walked into the apartments of Dalai Lama, to check if it was more 'commodious or spacious' than his.

The SOBA's conclusion was that, though the Dalai Lama and the Panchen Lama were on individual friendly terms, "they do not discuss major issues amongst themselves," probably due of the power wielded by their officials, particularly in the case of the Dalai Lama.

Perhaps, more seriously, the Dalai Lama's party "looks upon Panchen Lama as an instrument of the Chinese, lacking patriotism and nationalist sentiments," while the Panchen Lama's entourage abhorred the intervention of the Lhasa Government in the affairs of the Shigatse Government.

As a result, "the Shigatse people seem to be taking shelter behind the Chinese, whereas the Lhasa Government people are perhaps itching to wreak their vengeance, were it possible for them to remove the intervening barrier of the Chinese."

The conclusion was that "this state of affairs was regrettable …this has divided Tibet. …In this division, the Chinese have their ideal opportunity to divide and rule," observed the Colonel.

**What are the Personalities Influencing the Lamas**

The Liaison Officer then listed some of the advisors of the two leaders. It is interesting here to have another opinion than Apa Pant.

The Dalai Lama was, according to Luthra under the influence of the Kashag, "whose members, although all veterans do not have a common sense of loyalty or interest for Tibet." The former Army officer had harsh words: "They may discuss an issue amongst themselves but each will do so with a certain reservation in his mind. Each has its own vested interests and the feelings of personal gain and profit dominate each individual mind."

He mentioned Ngabo Ngawang Jigme, "proved to be a collaborator of the Chinese and who thanks to the Chinese wields more and more powers."

Then, Ragashar, 'an honest and guideless person', who was too ineffective to be of any significance.

As for Surkhang, he was capable of "deep manoeuvres but is much concerned about his personal comforts and merriment," noted the LO.

The two tutors of Dalai Lama, Luthra believed that they were very earnest and capable of good advice, while the *Dronyer Chempo*[9] was "perhaps the most honest and upright person. He seems to be in the close confidence of Dalai Lama."

Luthra then mentioned extraneous influences; i.e. his two brothers living in India, "a motley of runaways from Lhasa, who have taken refuge in Kalimpong;" their National movement's objective is to expel the Chinese from Tibet and "the restoration of full-scale control of Tibet to the Dalai Lama."

These leaders obviously did not like the Panchen Lama. To this description should be added other actors such as the royal family of Sikkim, who shared many views with the National Movement, like pushing the Dalai Lama "on extreme lines of taking violent measures against the Chinese to dislodge them by force. They seem to have laid great store on Indian aid and their pattern of plan appears to be the same as during the British days when the Dalai Lama, harassed and cornered by the Chinese, escaped to India time and again to seek refuge and meanwhile waited for an opportune moment to return to his country."

When they were informed of the Nehru's message that India "could not be a partner in any such adventure," they felt let down and betrayed.

Luthra asserted that Gyalo Thondup was particularly bitter and "now ridicules China and India in the same breath. ...Some of his remarks are most obnoxious and certainly not conducive to healthy relations between Tibet and India."

Thondup and Taktse Rinpoche, Dalai Lama's other brother "have a potent influence on Dalai Lama and they harp on every sentimental chord and family tie," said the SOBA.

---

9   Thubten Phala.

As a result of this 'conflicting barrage of opinions', the Dalai Lama was sometime 'bewildered', "his mind is diffused and he is unable to decide upon a course of action through any independent thinking. One cannot but sympathise with him in his dilemma for the problem which faces him is a matter of life and death and never before had a Dalai Lama had to cope with such an intricate and complex situation."

Luthra's conclusion was that the Dalai Lama "deserves India's full measure of advice as a neutral source."

An issue not often mentioned was the 'tulku' system of governance which placed in a pivotal position someone very young without the experience of a more mature leader.

## The Case of Panchen Lama

For the Panchen Lama, the situation was considerably simpler, "There is unity amongst them and they are all eager to make a success of their Government." Their objective was only to maintain a prestige and a position equal to that of Dalai Lama. They want to perpetuate the existence of the Shigatse Government with the aid of the Chinese.

Dzasa Che Jigme, who often lived in China, was a central figure in this scheme: "He is strongly pro-Chinese and very selfish."

Luthra cited an example, at a dinner in the Chinese consulate in Kolkata, Che Jigme proposed a toast to the health of Chairman Mao: "To safeguard his personal position and interests, he would even invite the Chinese to interfere in the internal affairs of his Government." Thankfully, according to the SOBA, the Panchen Lama does not take him too much into confidence.

One person most friendly towards India was the tutor of the Panchen Lama, 'an extremely sensitive and devout person' …[who] was not mingling into politics.

Followed the description of Rimshi Sonam Wangchuk, the Panchen Lama's Trade Agent in India, 'extremely intelligent, diplomatic and shrewd'; he was consulted in all matters: "Wangchuk is capable of giving his earnest and zealous friendship, but at the same time, he can develop a strong antipathy if he is disregarded or shown discourtesy."

The Ta Lama was the Panchen Lama's personal attendant; he could be used to exert significant influence on Panchen Lama, commented Luthra, while the Lama's father, the Tibetan Trade Agent in Shigatse, was "an affable and kindly person but quite ineffective in official matters."

Luthra concluded that the Panchen Lama remained 'a domineering personality': "He is capable of independent thinking and deciding matters according to his own judgment. He does not tolerate much opposition and I have seen him handle his staff including Dzasa Che Jigme most roughly."

For the retired colonel, it was perhaps due to the confidence in "the secure position that he enjoys and the fact that he has accepted the Chinese tutelage unreservedly."

**The Lamas' Hopes and Fears**

According to the liaison officer, while both Lamas were eager to preserve their religion, the Dalai Lama feared that the continued control of the Chinese "may destroy not only the religious and cultural heritage of the Tibetans, but also their nationhood. Though he believed that some steps are necessary for Tibet to maintain its freedom and autonomy, the correct course of action was not clear in his mind," wrote Luthra.

As for the Panchen Lama, he was resigned to the Chinese overlordship, but he felt that it was possible to maintain independence in the religious and cultural spheres: "He would invite the Chinese to assist him in the development and modernization of his area, but, he is prepared to take up cudgels against them, if they interfere with the monastic rights of his land."

It is what he did in the 1980s, it probably cost him his life.

Interestingly, both Lamas were eager to maintain friendly relations with India – the fount of the Tibetan religion; they also saw advantages of a thriving trade with India, added Luthra.

## The Aftermath of the Lamas

During their two-month stay in India, the Tibetan leaders gathered some knowledge about India. In a way, it was a lesson in history and geography: "they had formed some picture in their minds regarding the size and stature of India, and her new aspirations since Independence," asserted Luthra, who added though, at best, their picture was earlier sketchy and incomplete.

Both were much impressed by all that they saw; and the Panchen Lama several times stated that India definitely surpassed China, which probably pleased his Indian hosts.

For them, the visit proved that the Indian people "are earnest and active about their spiritual well-being." They apparently were under the impression that India which gave birth to Buddhism had become more materialistic: "This aspect of the Indian life is a primary factor which would draw the Tibetans towards India more than towards China," reported the SOBA.

They also discovered some identity of aspirations in the religious sphere; similarities between the Tibetan script and the Devanagari script; similar features in the Hindu temples and Luthra added: "they did display considerable veneration for the Hindu Pandits and temples. …The Siva Temple at Madras with its many idols of gods in the Hindu pantheon, particularly impressed Panchen Lama and his tutor."

The colonel observed that the Tibetans had always ascribed supernatural powers to the Indian people: "They were eager to see such cases for themselves, but unfortunately this could not be arranged."

At the end, they expressed the wish to send some scholars and students to India to learn Sanskrit or study the scriptures: "In exchange, they would be only too glad to receive our students in their monasteries or to make available to us any of their religious literature."

Both Lamas were deeply impressed by the gardens in Krishnarajasagar: "The Panchen Lama relaxed in complete abandon as if overwhelmed by the beauty of the surroundings. He said that it was the most beautiful place he had ever imagined or seen," Luthra added that some members of his entourage "were inspired to the point of disrobing themselves to take a bath!"

They were delighted to witness industrial progress: "aimed at improving the standard of life of the Indian people. ...They now understand that India which for so many centuries has supplied to Tibet various commodities and merchandise, would be in a position to play the same role to help develop and modernize Tibet."

It was wishful thinking, as India would be allowed to intervene in Tibet less and less.

Ironically, they showed considerable interest in the factories for the construction of aeroplanes or warlike materials: "the question uppermost in their mind was how self-sufficient India is in her munitions and defence equipment? Whether she had equipment of the same performance as in the Western countries?"

The SOBA summed up the visit as an unqualified success and a new mile-stone in India's relations with the Tibetan people.

**The Chinese Apprehensions**

During the first days, the staff of the Chinese Embassy in Delhi "were acting in a circumspect, narrow and possessive manner. Their attitude displayed a certain immaturity." They were treating the Tibetan parties as their 'preserve', which "must remain in their sphere of influence and friendship and that none of the Indian members should be allowed to cultivate cordial relations with the Tibetans."

In Mussoorie, Yeh Cheng Chang, the Counselor in the Chinese embassy, objected to "a growing friendship between Chung Kushok (brother of the Panchen Lama) and officers of the IMA in Dehra Dun." Luthra had to tell Yeh that he must abandon his suspicious outlook; would he not do so, "it would be very difficult for us to complete the tour successfully," said Luthra.

The Tibetans were India's guests and to look after them, was not to be seen to the detriment of China: "He understood the position and was most penitent during the days that followed." The Panchen Lama had also to speak to the Chinese Counselor: "This incident in a way indicated in a miniature form the entire attitude of the Chinese people," remarked the liaison officer, who also observed that the Chinese were afraid that "India through the sight-seeing tour of the Tibetan parties to places of pilgrimage and industrial and cultural centres, might succeed in winning over the Tibetans and that China might show up disadvantageously."

He added: "India might also be able to demonstrate her commonality and identity with the Tibetan people and this might bring the two closer."

The Chinese were also apprehensive "of certain former citizens of Lhasa who had now taken refuge in Kalimpong and had set up a base of nationalist ideas and aspirations directed against the Chinese."

They were particularly afraid of the two brothers of the Dalai Lama.

Luthra, however, observed that as the tour progressed, "the Chinese took a more liberal and broader view of India's undertaking to show around the Tibetans."

They realized that India had no ulterior motives ....may be that came after "some personal direction from Premier Chou En-lai."

The Chinese explained their presence in the Land of Snows by saying that Tibet "had not progressed one iota during the last thousand years and reforms were now very badly needed in that country."

To conclude, Luthra said that it was important to remember that "if the Chinese get the impression that we are in any way helping the Tibetan people to regain their freedom or indirectly thwarting the Chinese attempts to develop Tibet, they would not only assume stricter control of Tibetan affairs, but perhaps even close the doors of Tibet upon us."

His advice was to be careful "in treading the path of friendship with Tibet for China has an inherently suspicious mind which once aroused, would operate to our mutual disadvantage."

In the following months and years, the doors would slowly close on the Indian activities, irrespective to what India had to offer.

## Suggested Line of Action

From the political viewpoint, India's interest was that Tibet retained its freedom, love for peace and her cultural and religious heritage, said the liaison officer, who understood well the situation on India's borders: "We cannot see our Northern and North-Eastern border in a state of communist turmoil."

From a humane viewpoint also, India wanted Tibet to maintain its freedom and preserve its culture and way of life. It was in the country's long-term interests: "India cannot stand aloof or semi-aloof and see Tibet consumed through the operation of Chinese policies."

His second point was that India's actions should be subtle and tactful "as not to give an impression to the Chinese that we are acting to their detriment." This was, according to him, essential; assistance and support to Tibet, should not be at the cost of friendship with China.

He finally suggested some actions to preserve the Tibetan entity:

a) Although Dalai Lama and some of his officials are earnest to regain their freedom, there is no common bond of loyalty amongst the officials to form a strong and influential group to create and develop a nationalist movement amongst the people. [The] Dalai Lama is subjected to all kinds of advice; sincere and insincere, practical and idealistic, extremist and the most compromising. These are so many pressures working upon him. The burden of initiative principally lies with him. In the first instance, it is essential for him to develop an independent mind which can decide for itself. He must also break away from some of the orthodox sanctity and customary superstitions which hold him in prison. After the example of the 13$^{th}$ Dalai Lama, he should assert himself more powerfully and dispense with the forecasts of his oracles. He must tower over his officials and assume more constitutional powers after the example of the 5$^{th}$ and the 13$^{th}$ Dalai Lamas. He must tour his country and sow the notion of a nationalist movement particularly amongst the peasantry. He might consider a purge in the priestly order to ensure that only the loyal and the honest people are appointed as heads of the monasteries. Socialistic reforms to uplift the down-trodden peasantry and curtailment of privileges and powers of those who stand high in the feudal and priestly order must be devised and implemented. In other words, the entire body-politic of Tibet should be cleansed of evil practices and institutions so that a healthier class with national interests possessing moral strength may emerge. All this should be possible at this stage because of the high religious esteem in which Dalai Lama is held. The Dalai Lama must disregard counsel and influences advising direct action against the Chinese. ...The Dalai Lama needs sincere and sane advice from a neutral well wisher.

b) The Tibetan nationalist base which seems to be gaining ground at Kalimpong has to be handled very tactfully. A good number of the Tibetans there once held important and influential positions in Tibet and even today have a strong influence on the Dalai Lama. They have to be tamed from their plan of declaring a war on the Chinese in Tibet. They should be brought round to a saner and practical viewpoint.

This was perhaps the first time that Delhi had such an insightful view on the main actors on the Roof of the World; the visit to India was indeed a unique occasion.

## Report of the Outgoing Consul General in Lhasa

PN Menon had just retired as Consul General in Lhasa, when the visit of the Dalai Lama was suddenly cleared by Beijing.

He was asked to join the party as Liaison Officer for the Dalai Lama's party. Like Luthra, he wrote a fascinating report; his two-year tenure in Lhasa had helped him "to form certain impressions about the Tibetan political scene and some of the personalities concerned with it."

Like Pran Luthra, Menon believed that the Dalai Lama and the Panchen Lamas "were clearly overwhelmed by the scale of reception accorded to them and by the elaborate arrangements made for their stay, transportation and visits to the important centres of Buddhists pilgrimage, development projects etc."

It was a first for them. It was new and different from what they had seen on a similar trip to China in 1954-55: "While it would be wrong to say that the Tibetan parties were entirely pleased with all that they saw in India, there is no doubt that they have been fairly impressed by the fact that India within a short period of eight or nine years had been able to consolidate her position as an independent country with considerable influence in world affairs while fashioning its internal social, economic and political life on completely democratic lines."

Menon said that his close contact with the Dalai Lama confirmed his earlier appreciation of him: "The Dalai Lama, apart from being a remarkable personality, has I feel matured in many ways as a result of coming into contact with our leaders and institutions."

The former Consul General experienced that "for an average Tibetan material prosperity is not the most important thing in life. Religion and the peculiar social and economic set-up which he has inherited in Tibet as a result of many centuries of isolation from the outside world, still constitute the fundamentals of life."

In his report, Menon also argued that it would be unwise for India "to imagine that the Tibetans have been completely charmed by what they saw in India to the extent that they would hereafter strive to reproduce in their own land the same pattern of life."

However, they realized that many new reforms could be introduced in Tibet.

**India's Material Development**

What appealed the most to the Lamas were the developmental activities such as railways, roads, civil aviation and the efforts made to improve the productive resources, both industrial and agricultural.

At the same time, a young intelligent Tibetan officer told Menon that while they were impressed by India's democratic institutions and individual liberty, "they were also well-aware of the great disparity in wealth that exists in India as compared to the relative lack of inequality in New China."

The reactions varied, the older officials like the Tibetan Cabinet ministers and the senior lamas; though they enjoyed the facilities provided, "seemed to be one of some nervousness about the impact of such a system on their own privileges and old fashioned methods, if introduced in Tibet."

Menon had the impression that they would resist "to the best of their ability Chinese suggestions for modernizing Tibetan lives in some of these directions." At the same time, some of the younger officers were looking for a social revolution.

Like Luthra, Menon analyzed the influence of some members of his entourage on the Dalai Lama. It is interesting to note his views as they slightly vary from Luthra's. Menon witnessed the influence of the monks around the Tibetan leader, "but he was also exposed to the suggestions of his two brothers Gyalo Dhondup and Taktser Rimpoche and the two other Tibetan émigrés in India Tsipon Shagapa[10] and Khenchung[11], all inveterate opponents of the present regime in Tibet."

As there was no unanimity among the Dalai Lama's various advisors: "it was rather disillusioning to discover that even the officials who had come from Tibet were deeply divided amongst themselves."

Menon said that the bane of Tibetan nationalism was "the real lack of a sense of unity and political consciousness in the way we understand it. At times the conflicting advice seemed to make the Dalai Lama rather confused about his ultimate objectives in Tibet and the means of attaining them."

It was often the Tibetan leader's basic common sense which seemed to "guide him away from the pitfalls of some of the advice tendered."

One of the schools of thought was "to seek relatively greater freedom from Chinese control than they would be prepared to concede."

The former Consul General added: "To this extent they represent the genuine national sentiment which desires Tibet's complete independence."

---

10  Shakabpa.
11  See Chapter 9, Footnote 21.

They were aware that Tibet was not in a position to modernize on its own and at the same time, Tibet needed the support of some important neighbouring nations.

From India's side, the stress was on the cultural and religious links between India and Tibet: "they wonder whether this kind of friendship could not be stretched to include a certain amount of political support from us in their struggle to free themselves from complete Chinese absorption."

At the beginning of the tour, some of the prominent officials believed that their leader could "take advantage of his trip to seek political asylum in India and through that exert pressure on the Chinese to secure Tibetan independence," added Menon, who like Luthra thought that this would have been "completely suicidal from every point of view and might have caused [India] grave embarrassment."

As we have seen, the Political Officer in Sikkim was able to dissuade them from such a course of action.

Menon mentioned an undercurrent of "desire to prolong their stay in India to the maximum extent possible, so that the party would be placed in a strong bargaining position vis-à-vis the Chinese, who were becoming quite restive about the delay in the return of two leaders and their entourage to Tibet."

The IFS officer also commented on the Chinese accompanying the parties.

It was composed of the Counselor, his wife, an Attaché (as interpreter to the Counselor), a journalist, some photographers and a few translators: "Right from the start it was clear that the Chinese party were suspicious of our intentions in taking the Lamas on the tour and were anxious to find out whether we had any deep-seated plans behind it."

They did not appreciate that some Indians could strike up a friendship with members of the Tibetan party and "get things done without their intermediary."

Menon remarked that the relations between the Indian officers and the Tibetan party were so good that "throughout the tour, the Tibetans would only approach us for getting things done which normally one would expect them to get done through the Chinese Embassy, which was after all their official Embassy in India."

The Chinese were particularly upset that Tibet was referred to as a nation, while mentioning the cultural and religious links with India: "in all matters concerning Tibet we must keep in mind the extreme suspicion and susceptibilities of the Chinese."

But Menon brought up another point, India's dealings with areas such as Sikkim and Bhutan "which are considered legitimately as within our own orbit"; he pointed out, "we should not do anything to which China can take exception because even if the Chinese do not point it out to us at the time it is quite possible that they may adopt similar tactics."

We have looked at India's relations with Sikkim and Bhutan in previous chapters.

## The Entourage

Among the ministers, the person who impressed Menon the most was Ngabo Shape: "He is clearly the brainiest and most capable member of the Tibetan Cabinet. He is an extremely difficult person to analyze."

In a special report sent from Lhasa during his posting, Menon had commented on Ngabo's personality; his close observation of the Minister during the two-month tour did not change his views: "I am convinced that he is playing an extremely difficult game of trying to balance himself in Tibet without completely falling either into the Chinese net or the alternative net of the Tibetan officialdom."

The Tibetan minister had the confidence of the Chinese, who showed him the highest respect: "He was the one spokesman of the Kashag who seemed to get things done during this tour. He is undoubtedly a personality whose future career would be worthwhile watching."

Surkhang Shape was, according to Menon 'a too slick an operator'. He was not fully trusted by any side: "A man of bad health, brought about largely by his own dissipations, he will not I feel last long as an influence in Tibet. In Kalimpong he let himself go in a big way and it was most difficult even for the members of the Kashag to get hold of him for urgent consultations."

The third Minister, Ragashar Shape, failed to impress Menon: "Silent as a carp, he never seemed to pull much weight in the deliberations of the Kashag. Perhaps this may be an affected pose and the fact that he is trusted by the Dalai Lama may mean that he is considered safe on the point of keeping secrets."

The *Dronger Chenmo* also made an impression on Menon: "Undoubtedly he is one of the brains behind all the resistance to the Chinese in Tibet and possesses in a full measure the confidence of the Dalai Lama."

This was a fact which has been detailed in Melvyn Goldstein's work.[12]

Menon's conclusion: the Tibetans seemed "to be groping for a way out from the present impossible situation which, if allowed to develop on the lines desired by our Chinese friends, would mean their end, both as a class and as a race."

His final remarks were that after the visit to India it may be "easier for Tibetan officials, both lay and monks, to come out to India in future in larger numbers."

Another benefit of the visit was the good influence, "that the hospitality showed to the Dalai Lama and followers will have on our own border populations, drawn from Tibetan ethnic stock."

Menon hoped that the Tibetans would play their cards well and consolidate amongst themselves and try to develop a truly national outlook, "it is possible that they may be able to resist complete absorption by the Chinese."

It was not to happen.

**Independent Tibet, Not a Distinct Possibility**

The former Consul General concluded with these words: "It is only in the event of a global war which will force China to relinquish her physical hold over Tibet or as a result of international Communism

---

12 Melvyn C. Goldstein, *A History of Modern Tibet, Volume 2: The Calm before the Storm: 1951-1955* (Berkeley, University of California Press, 2007).

itself undergoing some startling transformation that the prospect of an independent Tibet emerging can be viewed as a distinct possibility of the future."

Rather ominous?

# 24

# When Men Become Desperate they Consult the Gods

### Talks with Dalai Lama

Before going into the encounters between the Indian Prime Minister and his Chinese counterpart, it is worth spending some time on the first two meetings between Jawaharlal Nehru and the Dalai Lama, which took place on November 26 and 28, 1956.

Unfortunately, from the Prime Minister's side, we have only a few notes kept in the Subimal Dutt Papers[1]; from the Tibetan side, the Dalai Lama's account is extracted from his memoirs, *Freedom in Exile*.

During the first meeting on November 26, the Prime Minister jotted down a few points:

- ➤ Three areas of Tibet: (1) Eastern area liberated by force; (2) Central Tibet under Dalai Lama; (3) Tsang Tibet under Panchen Lama. Originally all these under Dalai Lama, thus limiting Dalai Lama's authority - at present preparation for local self-government in Tibet [the Tibetan Autonomous Region] - creating three parts as autonomous regions.
- ➤ This region to carry out orders of the Chinese Government.
- ➤ Chinese say that Tibet very backward and wanted help to advance.

---
1 The former Foreign Secretary left his personal papers with the Nehru Memorial Museum and Library in New Delhi.

- No present intention but future idea to take lands from monasteries - schools, new educational institutions - equal distribution of land - postpone because of people's opposition.

- State authority must be based on people having faith; otherwise, religion suffers. Hope lies in India.

- Some fighting still going on in Eastern areas. In other areas preparation going on, including Lhasa.

- No definite idea among Tibetans. They have grown desperate, prepared to die.

- Foreign sympathy and aid - majority do not think they can fight out [the] Chinese. Chinese troops about 1,20,000.

- Talks with Chairman Mao in Peking - attempts to convert Dalai Lama to communism. Dalai Lama did not commit himself to communist ideology but expressed objections.[2]

It is difficult to fully decipher these notes, but one can only see that a full background of the situation on the Roof of the World was given to the Prime Minister by the young Tibetan leader.

In his memoirs, the Dalai Lama described the Prime Minister thus: "He was a tall, good-looking man, whose Nordic features were emphasised by his small Gandhi cap. Compared with Mao, he appeared to have less self-assurance, but then there was nothing dictatorial about him. He seemed honest - which was why he was later deceived by Chou En-lai."

During their first formal meeting[3], the Dalai Lama explained "the full story of how the Chinese had invaded our peaceful land, of how unprepared we were to meet an enemy and of how hard I had tried to accommodate the Chinese as soon as I was aware that no one in the outside world was prepared to acknowledge our rightful claim to independence."

It is interesting to note that the Dalai Lama spoke of an 'enemy'.

---

2  For Nehru's jottings of his talks with the Dalai Lama on 26 and 28 November 1956, see, SWJN, Vol. 35, Nehru Memorial Fund; also available in S. Dutt Papers, Nehru Memorial Museum and Library, Sub-File No 6.

3  They had met briefly in Beijing in October 1954.

The long description given by the Tibetan leader corresponds to Nehru's notes. The Dalai Lama also remarked that Nehru listened to him and nodded politely; the Tibetan monk continued: "my passionate speech must have been too long for him and after a while, he appeared to lose concentration, as if he was about to nod off. Finally, he looked up at me and said that he understood what I was saying."

Nehru later asked about the Panchen Lama's views on the situation in Tibet; the Dalai Lama answered that the Panchen Lama was gaining power due to his friendship with Chinese authorities. The Tibetan leader also informed Nehru that the Russians had no representatives in Lhasa; only India, Nepal and 'in a way' Bhutan were represented.

The Indian Prime Minister made it clear to the young Lama that Tibet could no longer remain a forbidden land. Subimal Dutt, the new Foreign Secretary added to Nehru's jotted notes: "PM[4] told me that he had advised Dalai Lama to accept Chinese suzerainty and try to secure the maximum internal autonomy. If he contested Chinese suzerainty, then the Chinese would try to take over Tibet entirely, thereby eliminating any idea of autonomy. Dalai Lama appealed to India for help. PM's reply was that, apart from other considerations, India was not in a position to give any effective help to Tibet; nor were other countries in a position to do so."

Dutt was also informed by the Prime Minister that he had told the Dalai Lama that he should not resist land reforms: "The Chinese Government have not yet started such reforms, but in India and other underdeveloped countries, land reform has been the main plank in the political platform of progressive parties. Dalai Lama himself should take the lead in such reforms. He should be the leader of the people. It is not possible for Tibet to remain isolated from the rest of the world."

According to the Foreign Secretary, Nehru felt that the Dalai Lama was "still thinking in terms of Tibetan independence and looked to India for guidance."

The Dalai Lama was in great dilemma.

---

4    Prime Minister.

## Second Meeting

Another meeting between the Prime Minister and the Dalai Lama took place on November 28, 1955. The Tibetan leader stated that Tibet had "some connection with China externally but having internal autonomy." He further noted: "So long as Chinese suzerainty is there, there would be no internal freedom." Nehru's notes described the points discussed:

- Tibet different country from China - culturally, economically and politically.
- No previous record of being under Chinese suzerainty except for certain periods.
- In 1910-50, complete freedom; then communist intervention.
- In 1951, temporary treaty - internal autonomy under pressure.
- 17 clauses - Tibet[5] returns to its ancestral home (China) - no interference by Chinese on customs, monasteries etc.
- China not following terms of treaty.
- Chinese tightening their grip gradually.
- When Dalai Lama went to China in 1954, public much upset. This time, when he came to India, great hopes and satisfaction.
- For freedom, method not military or force, but peaceful.
- In the past Tibet also conquered parts of China.

The Prime Minister then said that the Dalai Lama should become the leader who started the reforms: "Best way we can help is by maintaining friendly relations with China, otherwise China would fear our [India's] designs on Tibet."

Then, Nehru 'somewhat impatiently' told the young Lama: "But you must realise that India cannot support you."

The Dalai Lama added: "As he spoke in clear, beautiful English, his long lower lip quivered as if vibrating in sympathy with the sound of

---

5  Seventeen-Point Agreement. See Volume 1, Chapter 21.

his voice." The Tibetan leader observed that this was bad, "but not entirely unexpected news."

The meeting continued although Nehru had made his position clear; when the Dalai Lama mentioned that he was considering seeking exile in India, Nehru said: "You must go back to your country and try to work with the Chinese on the basis of the Seventeen-Point Agreement."

The Dalai Lama tried to explain that he had already tried his best: "every time I thought I had reached an understanding with the Chinese authorities, they broke my trust. And now the sinisation in Eastern Tibet was so bad that I feared a massive, violent reprisal which could end up destroying the whole nation. How could I possibly believe that the Seventeen-Point Agreement was workable any longer?"

This was a clear statement that there was no trust anymore between the Tibetans and the Communist regime. At the end, Nehru concluded that he would personally speak to Zhou Enlai: "He would also arrange for me [the Dalai Lama] to meet the Chinese [Prime] Minister."

This would happen during the following weeks.

**Zhou Arrives on the Scene**

Zhou arrived in Delhi the next morning[6]; the Dalai Lama accompanied the Indian Prime Minister to Palam airport to receive him.[7] A meeting between Zhou and the Dalai Lama was arranged the same evening. The Dalai Lama recounted: "When we met again I found my old friend just as I remembered him: full of charm, smiles and deceit. But I did not respond to his artful manners. Instead, I told him quite straightforwardly of my concern about how the Chinese authorities were behaving in Eastern Tibet. I also pointed out the marked difference I had noticed between the Indian Parliament and the Chinese system of government: the freedom of people in India to express themselves as they really felt and to criticise the Government if they thought it necessary."

---

6   November 29, 1955.

7   Because of the Dalai Lama's visit to India, Zhou Enlai came to India at the end of November 1956 for the Buddha Jayanti celebrations; he came again at the end of December 1956 and once again end January 1957. Three official visits in two months, never seen before (or after) in diplomatic annals!

But as usual, Zhou listened carefully before replying "with words that positively caressed the ear." He told the young Tibetan: "You were present in China only at the time of the First Assembly. Since then, the Second Assembly has met and everything has changed immeasurably for the better." The Dalai Lama said that he did not believe him, "but it was useless to argue".

Then Zhou said that he had heard a rumour, the Dalai Lama was considering staying in India: "It would be a mistake," he warned. Tibet needed him: "I left feeling that we had resolved nothing."

Indeed nothing was solved; far from it.

**The Monologue of the Chinese Premier**

On December 31, 1956, during the first meeting between the Indian and Chinese prime ministers, Zhou announced that he wanted to speak about the Tibet question. He then gave a long lecture about the geography and history of Tibet; he explained to his Indian counterpart: "Tibet is a vast territory with only one million population. They are of the same nationality, viz. Tibetan. Throughout history, Tibet has formed a part of China; but, unlike Sinkiang[8] which is also a national minority area, it was never made into a province of China. The religion of the people is Lamaistic. In dealing with Tibet, we take a very careful attitude. In the past, religion and politics were combined into one, that there was the same religious and political leader. But in actuality, political power was vested in the government (Kashag) under the Lama(s), since a new Lama was always an infant (less than one year old) and could not look into political matters till he came of age. Therefore, for more than ten years, political power rested in the hands of the government. Besides, the temples also wielded powers. There are three large ones in Lhasa and there are Living Buddhas there who have power. Therefore, those who have power are the living Buddhas and the persons in government."

One wonders why this long explanation was necessary; except perhaps that the visit of the young Lamas had made Communist China nervous.

---

8   Now spelt as Xinjiang.

Zhou continued his tirade: "Tibet is divided into three parts: Inner Tibet, Outer Tibet, and Chamdo area. In the past, Chamdo was sometimes made a part of Sinkiang [Xikang][9]. Sometimes, it was not a part of Sinkiang [Xikang]. Now, all these three parts are made into one autonomous region. In this area, there has been formed a preparatory committee with Dalai Lama as Head and Panchen Lama as deputy head. Next year, the autonomous area will be formed."

The Premier said: "These three parts still have some distance (differences) among them, because the reactionary governments[10] in the past have created discord among them."

Zhou continued to give his version of the Tibetan history: "We have always advised unity. Our policy has always been to give them an autonomous government under the Central Government, enjoying a large measure of autonomous rights.[11]"

He further briefed a credulous Nehru: "The Central Government consults it on all related matters and local matters are handled by themselves. We fully respect their religion; everyone lives in religion there and every family has to give one or two of its members to the temple. At present, we do not talk of democratic reforms to them; but when other parts of China become economically better and if Tibetans feel the need and agree to it, then we can introduce them."

It was far from the truth as we have seen; the Khampas had started rebelling against the Communists as their religion was suffering a great deal under the new regime: "At present, there is a semi-feudal and semi-slave system in Tibet with compulsory service to government and temples. China can help them in improving their living conditions, but then there is the difficulty of communications. Therefore, it will have to be done slowly," remarked Zhou, commenting on the 'two Lamas'[12] who, according to him were young and able: "They have their

---

9   The note taker meant Xikang or Sikang.

10  In Lhasa.

11  Central Tibet is still called the Tibetan Autonomous Region, though there is not much of 'autonomy'.

12  The Dalai Lama and the Panchen Lama.

own views on subjects. Since their tour of various places in China, they want to improve conditions in Tibet."

Zhou carried on the description in rosy terms (from the Chinese point of view): "We, however, advised them not to go too fast but to take all the government and Lamas with them first. There are bound to be people who are dissatisfied and people who are afraid that their religion would be affected. It is natural because they do not understand the policy of the Central Government. We take an attitude of waiting and seeing."

Then, the Premier brought the issue of 'foreigners' influencing some sections of the Tibetan society. "But there is also a minority under foreign influence which does not like Tibet to be under the Central Government and wants to have an independent Tibet. Their activities are mainly carried out from Kalimpong and these include some Tibetans who have returned from the USA."

There is no doubt that Zhou Enlai referred to the two brothers of the Dalai Lama, first and foremost Gyalo Thondup, but also Tsipon Shakabpa, both based in Kalimpong. The third protagonist was Lobsang Gyentsen[13] who had been referred to by Apa Pant in one of his cables to Delhi.

The speech of the Premier went on and on: "In the past, some trouble was started in Tibet once or twice, but Dalai Lama pacified it. Towards them, we take a mild attitude. We disbanded their organisation, but made no arrests. We let Dalai Lama persuade and educate them. This was the situation in the past."

Zhou then made some more precise accusations: "There is, however, a group in Lhasa which has kept constant contact with Kalimpong and has never stopped its activities. When Dalai Lama went to Peking for People's Conference (and when Your Excellency [Nehru] met him there), these people started rumours that Dalai Lama was not going to return and this caused disturbances. Only when Dalai Lama went back the rumours stopped.[14]"

---

13 See Chapter 9, Footnote 21.
14 One of the persons referred to by Zhou is Thubten Phala, the Lord Chamberlain.

It is quite surprising in bilateral talks to have such a monologue, though one can understand that the Chinese Premier had specially come to brief his Indian counterpart.

Had Nehru nothing to ask or say?

Zhou then justified the last minute permission given to the two Lamas to visit India: "This time, when India invited Dalai Lama and Panchen Lama the Chinese Government knew that some trouble would start in Tibet after they left Lhasa. But, on the other hand, the Chinese Government considered the friendly relations existing with India and they also knew that Dalai Lama would be well received in India and the visit would help religious contacts. Dalai Lama[15] decided to come and also to bring more people with him. Then we also advised Panchen Lama to accept the invitation; because if only Dalai Lama came, it would show disunity between the two Lamas."

The Chinese argument was further developed: "We also knew that when they came to India they would meet many Tibetans who had never returned to Tibet after liberation."

Beijing had decided to take the risk; the visit of the Chinese Premier was meant to mitigate the presence of the Dalai Lama in India and in a way 'control' him.

## The Visit to Kalimpong

The one-sided conversation shifted to Kalimpong: "There are thousands of Tibetans [there]. And although Dalai Lama did not go to Kalimpong, these Tibetans did not give up hope and the US agents have encouraged such and other subversive activities. Dalai Lama's brother, who has recently returned from the US, told Dalai Lama that the United States would support independence movement in Tibet or failing that would welcome him in the United States."

Zhou brought up the issue of the Dalai Lama visiting Kalimpong and Darjeeling area; the Premier cleverly put it: "Now the Kalimpong Tibetans want Dalai Lama to go to Kalimpong in order to preach to them. And it is difficult for him to decide. If he does not go, then it

---

15 The notetaker does not use the article 'the'.

would not be good from the religious point of view. But if he goes, there is bound to be some trouble. At the same time, some of the officers accompanying the Dalai Lama this time have also been influenced in their Indian visit."

He listed the sources of influence:

> Kalimpong Tibetans, including the Dalai Lama's brother. Among those, there are some backward elements who feared reform and were easily susceptible to propaganda.

> Local Indian officers who are quite unfriendly to China. In welcome speeches to the two Lamas, they called Tibet a separate country and made no mention of China at all.

Zhou Enlai cited the example of the Mayor of Mumbai and the Mayor of Madras who apparently referred to Tibet "as a separate country without mentioning China."

In the case of the Mayor of Madras: "he was going to say it but the Chinese Embassy officials came to know about it and protested and therefore that part of the speech was dropped."

Zhou affirmed: "Calling Tibet a different country gives an impression that Tibet could be independent."

Coming back to the Dalai Lama's proposed trip to Kalimpong, Zhou admitted that he was faced with a real problem: "The Chinese Government had advised Dalai [Lama] not to go to Kalimpong; but if he does not go to Kalimpong, it would show that Dalai [Lama] has some prejudice against the Tibetans in Kalimpong. But if he goes to Kalimpong, all sorts of embarrassing questions would arise."

The case of the Panchen Lama was also mentioned, "it would be much more awkward, because Panchen comes from Outer Tibet (Hou Tsang[16]) and there is historically some animosity between the Inner Tibetans and Outer Tibetans. But if Panchen does not go, then also again it would give ground to spread rumours that something is wrong between them or that the Chinese Government is not allowing him to go there."

---

16  U-Tsang, the note-taker has noted the name phonetically.

The Panchen Lama would ultimately be 'advised' to return to Lhasa by plane, which he did.

**Is there a Foreign Influence?**

Zhou also recounted that during the Lama's visit in one of the big temples in India, "something unpleasant between the two Lamas also occurred. Therefore, the matter is very complicated and the chief cause is the instigation of the USA. Taiwan has also a hand in it because another of his brothers (married to a Chinese) has come from Japan."

The Premier referred to Gyalo Thondup, though his information about the Dalai Lama's brother being in Japan was incorrect.

Zhou came back to the situation inside Tibet and pointed a finger at foreigners: "those bent on trouble are preparing for an incident in Lhasa. These people have some armed forces. Some three temples in Lhasa have also armed forces and they want to create an incident with the People's Liberation Army there. If it happened, then there would be bloodshed."

This would happen two years later during the uprising of the Tibetan population in Lhasa.

The Premier then referred to a plot which was discovered "and then an open meeting was called where the representatives of the Central Government declared that they should not try to create an incident; but if they did so, People's Liberation Army would definitely take measures to put it down. People's Liberation Army on its part, would not take any provocative steps. The local government and the People's Liberation Army representatives have formed a committee to handle this matter."

The March 1959 uprising was put down by the PLA in the most brutal manner.

To end the tirade, Zhou noted that for the time being, the matter was over: "but, as long as Dalai Lama is away, something might happen. The Kalimpong people are thinking of keeping Dalai [Lama] as long as possible so that his absence could be taken advantage of."

According to Zhou, this was chiefly instigated by the USA and Taiwan, he threatened: "Since Dalai Lama is in India, if anything happens it will be unfortunate. We will, of course, take measures to put down any incident in Tibet, but still it is not good if something happens."

Zhou observed that he read some newspaper reports saying that Dalai Lama might stay in India: "He can if he wants to as long as he abides by Indian Government's regulations. Whether he wants to go to Kalimpong, he is going to decide tomorrow. He has to consult his Government. This is the whole situation. If anything should happen in Tibet or in Kalimpong, of course the Chinese Government would be directly concerned."

Zhou finally concluded: "Since Dalai Lama is in India, I thought, I should also inform Your Excellency about this. The situation is a complicated one."

The situation was indeed complicated for everybody, including China.

**Nehru Speaks**

Finally, Nehru who had politely waited, started to speak: "Your Excellency has said a good deal." He then unnecessary admitted "Something of what you told me is news to me. I know nothing about Dalai Lama's going to Kalimpong. I am hearing it for the first time. It is a matter primarily for Your Excellency and Dalai Lama to decide. It would be embarrassing for us to say anything either way."

It is rather surprising that the Prime Minister would not have known about the Dalai Lama's intentions to visit Kalimpong.

Nehru also remarked that he was surprised to learn that there were tens of thousands of Tibetans in Kalimpong: "I know that there was a large number but not to this extent. There are many kinds of Tibetans and the people are akin to Tibetans. I have heard also for a long time that Kalimpong has a nest of spies and the spies are probably more than the population."

There was certainly no necessity to mention this to the Chinese Premier, but Nehru carried on in an apologetic manner: "In the past, we have turned out some of the people from Kalimpong, including Americans.

I have not met any of [the] Dalai Lama's brothers [recently]. I have met one eight or nine years ago. And the second time I have met him was when Your Excellency introduced me to him recently. I do not know that his brothers were in Delhi. The Government of India's policy has been not to allow anti-Chinese propaganda to be carried out here."

**Nehru Argues the Chinese case?**

Nehru nevertheless thanked Zhou "for the background material given to me," he, however, admitted "But I do not quite understand what you meant when you said that Tibet in the past had not become a province of China."

Immediately, the Premier answered: "That Tibet is part of China is a fact, but it has never [been] an administrative province of China but kept an autonomous character. Therefore, when we started negotiations for the peaceful liberation of Tibet, …we recognised the autonomous character of the region."[17]

Interestingly, the Chinese leader noted that when he said that India knew more about Tibet, he meant only the past history: "for example, I knew nothing about McMahon Line until recently when we came to study the border problem after liberation of China."

Nehru retorted that historical knowledge was not important but was useful as background information: "History is gone. My impression was that whatever it may be in theory, for all practical purposes Tibet has all along been autonomous."

The Indian Prime Minister argued the Chinese case: "whatever government there might have been in China, Tibet has always been claimed by the Chinese Government. The British tried to create some trouble on account of their fear of Czarist Russia but this is past history."

This statement had serious implications for the border, but Nehru would take a couple of years to realize that; in the meantime, he added: "We recognise that China has, in law and in fact, suzerainty over Tibet even though it may not have been exercised sometime."

---

17 See Volume 1, Chapter 21.

Quoting Zhou's words, the Indian Prime Minister stated: "Tibet has behaved in an autonomous way and was cut off from other countries. The criterion of an independent state is that the state should have independent foreign relations and Tibet had no foreign relations except with England."

The Prime Minister then brought back the issue of the McMahon Line: "[it] was put forward in the 1913 Conference between the Chinese, the Tibetans and the British. That Conference decided not only the McMahon Line but also two other points. The Chinese Government raised objection only to the other two points." Nehru concluded that the Chinese Government surely always knew about the McMahon Line.

Regarding the Dalai Lama's visit to Kalimpong, Nehru observed: "we do not want any incident to take place about Dalai Lama in Kalimpong or while he is in India. We will do as Your Excellency and Dalai Lama decide."

He nevertheless asked Zhou what kind of incident were expected: "If you can give some specific idea about the trouble, we can prevent it."

Zhou Enlai explained that the situation was really very complicated: "it is difficult for me to say as to what specifically might happen. Dalai Lama is also concerned about this matter and he also said that the situation is complicated."

He, however, mentioned two possibilities:

> ➢ We have already raised this matter seriously with the Dalai Lama. Now Dalai Lama will naturally go back and talk to his officials and maybe perhaps nothing would happen except some small quarrels or verbal exchanges and he returns to Lhasa safely.

> ➢ Alternatively, a possibility is that attempts might be made at Kalimpong to detain Dalai Lama. In fact, that is exactly the slogan raised there: 'Won't let Dalai Lama go back'.

It is what the Chinese apprehended the most, the fact that the Dalai Lama would take refuge in India.

Zhou clarified that the Panchen Lama did not want to go to Kalimpong: "If he goes, he might be treated discourteously or some other trouble might be created." It was not what the Premier had said in the morning.

Zhou continued on the possible incidents which might happen: "[the] Indian Government has the power to intervene and check them, because such incidents partake of the nature of anti-Chinese activities or activities designed to create an independent Tibet or espionage or encouragement to subversive activities."

The Chinese leader explained that he was mentioning these possibilities in advance "so that, if anything happens, the Government of India could take preventive measures."

He then came back to the history of Tibet; he observed that even during the Manchu dynasty[18], Tibet was indeed part of China and, "at the end of the 19th century, when China was defeated in war with France and other countries, all Western Powers wanted to divide China; but they could not agree among themselves and so agreed to have separate spheres of influence."

He added that it was especially true after the Boxer Uprising: "That is why Tibet was always kept as a part of China, not only in law but in fact, with a view to keep balance between Powers."

This is a very peculiar interpretation of history; a colonialist one, as far Tibet was concerned.

Zhou Enlai then touched upon the relations of Sikkim and Bhutan with China which differed from those between Tibet and China, he said: "because Sikkim and Bhutan were never under China and even the Imperial Power did not recognise Bhutan and Sikkim as being under them."

He reiterated that the case of Tibet was different as the Manchu Emperor appointed Governors to Tibet and Chinese troops were stationed in Lhasa: "The British wanted to go into Tibet under the pretext that Russia wanted to get into Sikang[19] [Xinjiang]. Russia also made the

---

18 The Qing Dynasty.

19 The note-taker meant Xinjiang or Sinkiang.

same pretext, namely, that Britain was trying to get into Tibet, to get into Sikang [Xinjiang]. Exactly because of this rivalry and balance of power, Sikang [Xinjiang] and Tibet were never taken actually." He admitted that many people are not acquainted with these facts: "Even the Pakistan Prime Minister recently told me that he always thought Tibet to be independent. Even the Simla Conference admitted Chinese suzerainty over Tibet."

The Chinese Premier was clearly in a mission to win India over to its side and avoid that Delhi take the side of the Tibetan independentists. It would be clear with the next topic i.e. the McMahon Line, for which he had conciliatory words.

## The McMahon Line

The clever Zhou explained what he meant when he said that people like him never knew about the McMahon Line till recently. He explained that the Chinese Governments in Beijing and the Kuomintang knew about it: "we studied this question and although this Line was never recognised by us, still apparently there was a secret pact between Britain and Tibet and it was announced at the time of the Simla Conference."

What he said next is interesting more than 60 years later: "And now that it is an accomplished fact, we should accept it. But we have not consulted Tibet so far. In the last agreement which we signed about Tibet, the Tibetans wanted us to reject this Line; but we told them that the question should be temporarily put aside."

He referred to the 1951 Seventeen-Point Agreement.

Zhou had done his homework; he knew about the correspondence between Delhi and Lhasa in 1947-48[20], "Tibetan Government had also written to the Government of India about this matter."

In fact, the correspondence mentioned the lost territories, but never mentioned Tawang specifically. It is only after Maj Bob Khathing took over the administration of Tawang area that some discussions took place between Sumul Sinha, the head of the Indian Mission in Tibet and the Tibetan Kashag.

---

20 See Volume 1, Chapter 1.

The Chinese Premier continued his bluff: "But now we think that we should try to persuade and convince Tibetans to accept it. This question also is connected with Sino-Burmese border and the question will be decided after Dalai Lama's return to Lhasa. So, although the question is still undecided and it is unfair to us, still we feel that there is no better way than to recognise this Line."

Nehru went on his favorite argument: "the border is a high mountain border and sparsely populated." He asserted: "Apart from the major question, there are also small questions about two miles here and two miles there. But if we agree on some principle, namely, the principle of previous normal practice or the principle of watershed, we can also settle these other small points. Of course, this has nothing to do with the McMahon Line."

Zhou answered that the question can be solved "and we think it should be settled early."

## Nehru Answers Some of the Issues

Nehru returned to the Mayor's statement that Tibet was an independent country; the Prime Minister asserted that it had no significance as "he does not know much politically and probably very little about China and Tibet."

He defended the 'ignorant' mayors: "They would generally only know about the great religious significance of Tibet to Indians …that is all that they must be stressing."

Nehru recalled the position of the Government of India and the Treaty on Tibet[21]: "We are naturally interested in what happens in Tibet as one of our near neighbours but we don't want to interfere."

He further stated: "Our main interest is from the point of view of the pilgrims— not only Buddhist pilgrims, but Hindu pilgrims too for whom Kailash and Manasarovar are sacred places and abodes of God."

The Prime Minister philosophically explained: "A Dalai Lama is always a mythical figure and a great deal of mystery is attached to him in the mind of an Indian. So, when Dalai Lama came, the people were

---

21  The 1954 Agreement.

naturally greatly attracted to him. But the only significance is that the people would be interested from a religious point of view."

It was not fully true; the 'masses' in India were aware that Tibet had always been independent before being invaded by China.

**Is Tibet Backward?**

About Zhou's comments on the backwardness and isolation of Tibet, the Prime Minister admitted that it could not remain that way: "They are a deeply religious people and they are naturally afraid that their religion and customs would be upset. I myself personally think that changes are inevitable in Tibet, but I would like Tibetans to feel that they themselves have brought about the changes."

Nehru then cited Zhou: "Tibet is a part of China but with full autonomous powers. Then I don't understand why there should be any trouble in Tibet at all."

This was wishful thinking, but interestingly, for months Nehru would not believe the reports coming from Eastern Tibet, informing him about the dreadful Communist repression, including the bombing of some monasteries.

Zhou agreed with the Indian Prime Minister, but he wanted to clarify 'certain specific matters': "We have always held the view that purely religious contacts should not be limited or restricted by State boundaries. Thus, in Asia, there are many Buddhist countries and they should have more contacts with each other. We have established relations in religious matters even with Thailand."

He then cited Mao Zedong who would have said that there should be more contacts between Chinese Buddhists and Buddhists from other countries; restrictions should be removed: "This would also increase the confidence of Buddhists in Tibet that we respect their religion," Zhou added; it was the reason why Beijing approved of the Dalai Lama's and the Panchen Lama's visit to India, though he clarified: "But purely religious contacts is a difficult matter. Some try to exploit it for political ends, in the West some call themselves Buddhists and try to instigate movement for the independence of Tibet."

Indeed, religion and politics were often mixed in Tibet, but was the aspiration for Independence really linked to religion?

**Discussing the Reforms**

The discussion on Tibet continued.

Answering Nehru who had said that the Tibetans should feel that the reforms were brought about themselves, Zhou stated that it was correct, "but this does not mean that there would be no trouble because there are some who are open to foreign influence and there are some who lack understanding. They feel that since China is a socialist country, religion may be restricted; but actually it is not so."

Zhou added that China respected religion. He said that while the Manchus "used religion to decrease the populations of Tibet and Mongolia, we want to increase population in Tibet without putting any restrictions." Was he speaking of an increase of the Tibetan or the Chinese population?

Again, this was a very doubtful statement which would not be corroborated by the forthcoming events; in the Land of Snows, religion would be more and more monitored by the atheist Communist Party.

The Premier, however, added: "among the Tibetans there are many who are not so progressive. Those who are progressive want quick reforms, but this makes the non-progressive ones suspicious of the progressive elements and they feel that the latter are being influenced by the Hans."

The Khampas, who had already experienced the reforms, had understood that in the long term too, it meant the sinization of the Tibetan plateau.

Zhou cited the example of Sichuan[22]: "the progressive Tibetans wanted early reforms and there was resistance. The backward elements started agitation and an armed lamasery surrounded the People's Liberation Army troops and this People's Liberation Army detachment had to be fed by means of air-dropped food and thus finally they were able to beat back the attack.[23]"

---

22  Zhou meant the Kham province.
23  Zhou probably referred to the massacre of Lithang monastery.

He admitted that some Tibetans later 'ran away to Lhasa': "even if we agree that Tibetans themselves should carry out reforms, such problems and difficulties do arise. If it is a question of internal dissatisfaction alone, we would like to adopt a policy of waiting."

This would be the main outcome of the visit that the 'reforms' would be postponed for …six years. In fact, it would be two years, as 'reforms' would be reintroduced after the March 1959 uprising.

However, the Communist leader added: "But if there is foreign influence in it, then it becomes troublesome. Therefore, we maintain that religious contacts should be developed in Asian countries, but at the same time we should stop subversive activities."

He again complained about some espionage activities which were carried out openly in Kalimpong: "we feel that the Government of India should intervene because these activities will interfere with religious contacts and exchange."

Nehru responded that if any case of espionage came to his notice, the Government would "take steps. But if it is only a vague suspicion and no proof, then it is difficult to take action."

Zhou said that he only sought to inform Government of India beforehand to help the latter "to deal with the situation in case something happens", but for the Dalai Lama's visit to Kalimpong, he promised to discuss the same again with Nehru after having met the Dalai Lama.

## Second Round of Talks

During the next round of talks between Nehru and Zhou, which took place between 2.30 p.m. and 5.00 p.m. on January 1, 1957,[24] Zhou Enlai brought back the issue of Kalimpong; he had discussed the issue with both the Dalai Lama and the Panchen Lama in the morning and told the Lamas about his talk with the Indian Prime Minister the previous day: "[The] Dalai Lama still finds it difficult to decide. The people with him also know the complicated situation; but there are

---

24 File Nos. F 12 (109), NGO/56 and EI2/132/NGO/59, MEA.

over 10,000 people waiting for him at Kalimpong and if he does not go, it may not also look nice."

Zhou told Nehru that the Dalai Lama had not made up his mind and he wanted Zhou to have a talk with his officials "then perhaps something could be decided. Panchen Lama will not be going to Kalimpong. Firstly, it may be embarrassing for him and it may not also be safe because the Tibetans there are mostly from Lhasa and they are hostile."

Zhou said that it was important for the Dalai Lama to decide for himself: "It won't be good for us to tell him. …The Dalai Lama's retinue always makes him waver. If, however, they agree to go directly to Lhasa, then a trial flight to Lhasa will first have to be carried out."

Nehru remarked that the Dalai Lama's party could go to Lhasa from Kolkata: "Perhaps the Tibetans from Kalimpong could come and see him at Bagdogra on the way."

It was an easy way to avoid the issue.

**A Note from the Prime Minister**

In a note addressed to NR Pillai, Secretary General of the Ministry, copied to RK Nehru, India's Ambassador in Beijing and Apa Pant, the Political Officer in Sikkim, the Prime Minister reiterated more or less the same points.

He told the officers: "I had long conversations with Premier Chou En-lai. During his previous visit to Delhi, I also had long talks with him. The present talks were in continuation of those talks."

He had, among other topics, discussed the crisis in Egypt and the Middle East, the Hungarian situation, the Sino-American relations and of course Tibet.

The Prime Minister explained the background of the meetings: "Our talks were through interpreters, the Chinese interpreter and Shri Paranjpe. No one else was present except today when Marshal Ho Lung[25] was a silent witness of them."

---

25  Probably Marshal He Long, then Vice-Premier; see Chapter 4, Footnote 3.

Nehru observed that Paranjpe has taken fairly copious notes and it would be desirable to get a copy of these notes for record in the Ministry, but he added: "I do not want these records to be circulated even in the Ministry and only the persons actually concerned should see them."

Regarding the visit of the two Lamas to Kalimpong, Nehru mentioned that it might be desirable for the two Lamas to go back to Tibet by air: "Premier Chou liked this idea and said that there should be a trial flight before the travel by air. He was going to talk again to the Dalai Lama about this question of going to Kalimpong and let me know more definitely tonight."

The programme of the two Lamas was also discussed; they would go to Mandi in Himachal Pradesh[26] and later to Nalanda and Chittaranjan[27].

Zhou had agreed to this, but Nepal was given up; Nehru pointed out: "it would be better for the Nepal trip to be taken up on some later occasion. I have also indicated that in all the circumstances it would perhaps be better for the two Lamas not to go to Kalimpong during this visit."

The Prime Minister added that the Lamas might go there on some other occasion: "If they fly to Lhasa, their planes would stop at Bagdogra and an opportunity might be given to people to gather there and worship them or take their blessings. This should not be inconvenient for people in Kalimpong which is not far from Bagdogra."

Very few realized that two years later, the Dalai Lama would become a refugee in India and there would be no 'next time' as far as Nepal was concerned at least.

---

26 To Rewalsar or Tso Pema (the Lotus Lake), a holy lake associated with Guru Padmasambhava.

27 Chittaranjan is a town in Paschim Bardhaman district of West Bengal. It is popularly known for the Chittaranjan Locomotive Works located there.

## Fourth Round of Talks[28]

On January 1, 1957, the Indian Prime Minister met the Dalai Lama in the evening; the latter told Nehru that he had not yet decided about his visit to Kalimpong: "He felt that it would be difficult to miss it. I suggested to him to fly back to Lhasa from India. He did not like the idea much and said that he had promised to visit some monasteries in Tibet on the way to Lhasa. Therefore, it was better for him to go by road," noted Nehru.

At least this issue was clear.

During that encounter, Nehru lectured the young Dalai Lama about his brother[29] living in Kalimpong who "often spoke very foolishly and it seemed to me that he was rather unbalanced. I told him that as he had already agreed by a Treaty to Tibet being part of China but autonomous, it was not easy for him to break this agreement."

He referred to the 17-Point Agreement: "any attempt to do so would result in a major conflict and much misery to Tibet. In an armed conflict, Tibet could not possibly defeat China."

Very few realized that an armed conflict would take place two years later.

Nehru reiterated that India also had a treaty with China on Tibet[30]: "Our position all along had been that sovereignty rested with China but Tibet should be autonomous. Therefore, the best course for the Dalai Lama to adopt was to accept this sovereignty but insist on full autonomy in regard to internal affairs. He would be on strong ground on this, and he could build up the Tibetan people under his leadership."

Incidentally, the Tibetans had never been involved, or even informed during the four months of negotiations on the 'Treaty' on Tibet.

Nehru told the Dalai Lama that he was surprised to hear that "some people had advised him to remain in India and not return to Tibet.

---

28 Note to NR Pillai, Secretary General, MEA; RK Nehru, India's Ambassador in Beijing, and Apa Pant, Political Officer in Sikkim on January 1, 1957.

29 Gyalo Thondup.

30 The 'Panchsheel' Agreement of 1954.

That would be the height of folly and it would harm him as well as Tibet. This was not the way to serve the cause of Tibet."

The Prime Minister was adamant: "He [the Dalai Lama] must be in his own country and give a lead to his people." He told the young Lama to listen carefully to his advice.

When Nehru went to accompany Zhou Enlai to the airport[31], the latter told him that no decision had been arrived at about Kalimpong. The Premier had spoken to the Kashag and the Dalai Lama about this: "He had also met the Dalai Lama's two brothers and spoken to them frankly, telling them that they could hold any views they liked but they must not create trouble in Kalimpong or elsewhere."

Nehru noted that the Dalai Lama had promised that he would soon indicate his final decision about Kalimpong to the Chinese Ambassador.

Nehru wrote: "I think it is desirable, whether the Dalai Lama goes to Kalimpong or not, for someone on our behalf to make it clear privately to the brothers of the Dalai Lama that we do not approve of any agitation or trouble in any part of India with regard to Tibet. We sympathise with the people of Tibet and are prepared to help them in any legitimate way. But we cannot tolerate any mischief on the Indian territory."

He further suggested some "special steps should be taken for the prevention of any trouble there," in case the Dalai Lama would decide to visit Kalimpong.

## The Dalai Lama Meets Zhou Again

As he arrived in Delhi, the Chinese Ambassador, who was waiting for him at the station, insisted that the Dalai Lama traveled with him in his car to the Embassy, to meet Zhou Enlai. Amazingly, the Lama's entourage was not informed and the Lord Chamberlain and his security officers became extremely nervous: "Meanwhile, I was having a frank discussion with Chou. He told me that the situation in Tibet had deteriorated, indicating that the Chinese authorities were ready to use force to crush any popular uprising."

---

31 To go to Nalanda?

The Dalai Lama recalled: "At this point I restated bluntly my concern at the way the Chinese were behaving in Tibet, forcing on us unwanted reforms, despite explicit reassurances that they would do no such thing. Again, he replied with great charm, saying that Chairman Mao had announced that no reform should be introduced in Tibet for at least the next six years. And if after that we were still not ready, they could be postponed for fifty years if necessary."

That would be the main outcome of the multiple visits of Zhou Enlai to India: "China was only there to help us, he said". The Dalai Lama answered that still he was not convinced, but Zhou said that he understood that "I was planning to pay a visit to Kalimpong."

The Dalai Lama retorted that it was true: "I had been asked to deliver teachings to the large Tibetan population that lived there."

Zhou strongly advised the young Tibetan leader not to do so "as it was full of spies and reactionary elements." He added that he should be careful of which Indian officials I trusted: "some were good, but that others were dangerous."

When the Dalai Lama changed the topic, Zhou asked him to be the representative of the People's Republic of China at some official function and he presented a cheque and a relic of a Chinese pilgrim[32], who had visited India. The Dalai Lama accepted.

**The Decision to Go Back to Tibet**

The oracle was probably consulted to take the final decision whether or not to return to Tibet. Richen Sadhutshang, a senior official in the Dalai Lama's entourage recounted: "During [a] reception I was abruptly called upon to perform a special duty. I was instructed to go immediately to Kalimpong and bring Nechung Kuten[33], the state oracle, to Delhi by the very next day through whatever means necessary. Nechung Kuten was in Kalimpong being treated for arthritis at the Scottish Mission hospital. I left immediately by train and then traveled by plane from Calcutta to Bagdogra. I made airline reservations for four people—

---

32  Probably Xuanzang, the most celebrated Chinese monk who travelled to India in search of the Dharma.

33  The medium of the State Oracle.

Nechung Kuten, his two attendants, and myself—for the flight from Bagdogra to Calcutta and then for a connecting flight to Delhi, which was scheduled to depart only an hour after we landed. After doing all of this, I still managed to reach Kalimpong that same night."

The presence of the medium of the State Oracle was obviously extremely urgently required: "On arriving in Kalimpong, I immediately made arrangements for discharging Nechung Kuten from the hospital. We left early the next day," recalled Sadutshang.

Unfortunately, his flight from Bagdogra was delayed by two hours, making it impossible for them to take the connecting flight to Delhi: "I talked to the Indian Airlines chief at Bagdogra and explained that I had a VIP with me who must reach Delhi that very day. I made the case that the chief must ask Calcutta to delay the connecting flight. He was very cooperative and did everything I asked for. When we finally arrived in Calcutta and boarded our plane to Delhi, we found all the passengers on board waiting for us with looks of annoyance on their faces!"

The interpreter was able to 'deliver' Nechung Kuten to Hyderabad House in Delhi "that very evening, completing my duty successfully." He sensed that something important was going on: "Earlier I had heard some talk of His Holiness's elder brother Gyalo Thondup, Tsipon Shakabpa, and other senior officials suggesting that His Holiness [should] not return to Tibet for the time being, at least till the situation was more stable."

Apparently, the ministers accompanying the Dalai Lama, Surkhang, Ngabo, and Ragashar supported this idea: "I, therefore, assumed that the Nechung had to be consulted on this matter. Such a decision, however, would not be based solely on the prediction of the state oracle. When His Holiness ultimately made the final decision regarding his return to Tibet, it was based on the specific assurances of Zhou Enlai, who told him that the Chinese authorities in Lhasa would adhere to the proper implementation of the Seventeen-Point Agreement and that changes would be made only as and when the Tibetan people agreed to them."

In his memoirs, the Dalai Lama recounted: "…I consulted the oracle. There are three principal oracles whose advice the Dalai Lama can seek.

Two of them, Nechung and Gadong, were present. Both said that I should return. Lukhangwa came in during one of these consultations, at which the oracle grew angry, telling him to remain outside. It was as if the oracle knew that Lukhangwa had made up his mind. But Lukhangwa ignored him and sat down all the same. Afterwards he came up to me and said, 'When men become desperate they consult the gods. And when the gods become desperate, they tell lies!"

The Dalai Lama's two brothers remained adamant that he should take refuge in India: "Like Lukhangwa, they were both powerful and persuasive men. Neither could understand my hesitation. They believed that with the very existence of the Tibetan people under threat, it was essential to confront the Chinese in any way possible. The best way to do this, they felt, was for me to remain in India," recalled the Dalai Lama.

But the gods had spoken and the Dalai Lama followed their prophesy.

**Religious and Cultural Ties with Tibet**

On February 26, 1957, the Prime Minister dictated a note to the Secretary General of the Ministry of External Affairs; he cited Zhou Enlai who had told him that India and Tibet could have direct relations in regard to religious matters: "I do not remember his wording, nor can I say exactly what he meant. I did not press the matter with him. But, I think, he did say something about Tibetan scholars coming to India to study religion and Sanskrit, and I told him that they would be welcome."

Nehru remarked that any move in this direction should be referred to the Chinese Government: "We should not do anything without their consent. ...Otherwise, this might lead to disillusionment."

He also mentioned a possible visit to Lhasa: "I would indeed like to go there. But I am wholly unable to say anything definitely at this stage about my plans for the summer. Also, of course, if there is any such idea of my going there, I would have to refer it to Premier Chou En-lai first. I would do so rather informally, to begin with."

He then referred to two letters written by the Dalai Lama in which he argued that India being the source of Buddhist Dharma, a strong religious and cultural bond existed between India and Tibet. The

Dalai Lama also quoted Zhou's view about India and Tibet dealing directly in the matters of religion and culture and establishing a permanent relationship. He sought the Indian Government's help for the development of a Tibetan Monastery at Bodh Gaya, and for establishing Tibetan Sanghas[34] and monasteries at different holy places in India. The Dalai Lama also informed him that a new Abbot, "well-versed in spiritual knowledge, would be accredited to Tharpa Choling Monastery at Kalimpong."

Nehru commented: "The various matters referred to in the Dalai Lama's letters might be examined and I can consider sending him an answer." He suggested that the Secretary-General refer to the transcripts of the talks to see if Zhou made such reference the religious contacts with Tibet.

## Another Round of Talks with Zhou Enlai[35]

In the meantime, Zhou Enlai had left for Peking and again returned to India. He was visibly nervous about the Dalai Lama's visit to Kalimpong. A new round of talks took place at the Teen Murti House, Nehru's official residence on January 24, 1957.

The Prime Minister told his Chinese counterpart that he presumed that the latter was aware of the latest programme of the Dalai Lama and Panchen Lama.

At that time, the Dalai Lama was at Kalimpong and was scheduled to attend the Republic Day celebrations at Darjeeling; he would later return to Kalimpong and then proceed to Tibet via Gangtok: "We had taken precautions that there should be no trouble or incident in Kalimpong," explained the Prime Minister.

Zhou Enlai informed Nehru that before Dalai Lama left Delhi, a Tibetan called Shagapa[36] presented a document to the Dalai Lama, "but Shagapa had been spoken to firmly and warned that there must

---

34 Monastic communities.

35 Summary of talks with Chou En-Lai held at New Delhi on 24 January 1957. Jawaharlal Nehru Collection. The talks began at 4.00 p.m. at Teen Murti House in New Delhi.

36 Tsipon W.D. Shakabpa.

be no trouble at Kalimpong," noted the Indian Prime Minister. The Premier nevertheless said that "this Shagapa had left Tibet long ago and was now staying at Kalimpong."

In the end, the Dalai Lama would not stay on in India; though he could see the logic in the arguments of his brothers, he was not going to follow them. About Gyalo Thondup, the Tibetan leader wrote: "He was - and still is - the most fiercely patriotic of my brothers. He has a very strong character and a tendency to be single-minded to the point of stubbornness. But his heart is good and, of all of us, he was the most affected when our mother died. He cried a great deal."

His second brother, Taktser Rinpoche, was described as "milder mannered than Gyalo Thondup, but underneath his calm and jovial exterior there lies a tough and unyielding core. He is good in a crisis, but on this occasion, he too showed signs of exasperation."

At the end, the Dalai Lama had made up his mind to return to Tibet "to give the Chinese one last try, in accordance both with the advice of Nehru and the assurances of Chou En-lai."

After leaving Kalimpong, the Dalai Lama's party had to remain in Gangtok for a month before being able to cross the Nathu la (pass): "But I did not regret this at all and I took the opportunity to give teachings to the local population."

It was the end of an eventful trip which looked visibly benign but had all the portends for the future.

Had the gods become desperate? Had they told the Dalai Lama lies?

The future would speak.

We shall go into this in Volume 4 of this Study.

## 25

# Some Conclusions
# Hoping Against Hope

A major consequence of the Panchsheel Agreement was the advance of the Communist ideology on the Tibetan plateau. A new way of life, less compassionate, less enlightened slowly took over the Roof of the World.

It is interesting to quote from the writings of Apa Pant, the 'philosopher' Political Officer in Sikkim, dealing with Tibet in the Ministry of External Affairs during the period under study.

Though Pant was aware of the strategic importance of the Tibetan plateau, he was often more interested to look at the humane aspects, which could accelerate the fading-out of an ancient civilization.

This is an aspect which should not be neglected, though the loss of a peaceful border would remain in history as the main outcome of this period.

Pant wrote: "With all its shortcomings and discomforts, its inefficiencies and unconquered physical dangers, here was a civilization with at least the intention of maintaining a pattern of life in which the individual could achieve liberation. Without the material conveniences that others have come to expect, the Tibetan as I found him was a cultured, highly developed, intelligent person whose vision, supported by the constant example of the monastic order, was fixed upon the objective of reaching Nirvana. It was a perspective that must make a Tibetan pause and think before accepting communist solutions as the right and only ones for the problems of an ancient society on its way into the modern age."[1]

Pant readily admitted that he always felt "a great admiration for China's culture and civilization, for its long history and indeed for its new revolution". However, he was saddened by the Chinese incapacity to accept (or even understand) a philosophy not fitting in with the Party line. This was, he believed, the main reason for the failure in the relations between China and the Dalai Lama. But this analysis also shows a lack of understanding of Mao's thought process.[2]

Chinese officials in Tibet, like Gen Zhang Jingwu, did not look favorably at the Dalai Lama's aspiration to radically change the Tibetan society, while maintaining his 2000-year old tradition. It could have cast a shadow on the Communist Party.

However, Pant like many of his colleagues, felt that the Tibetans had a lot to learn from the Chinese: "In my travels in Tibet I observed how disciplined the Chinese were. All their activities were directed towards the building of a new culture, a society of new men."

This proved to be a myth; though Pant regretted: "The Chinese could have remedied this warped [social] aspect of [Tibetan] society by helping the Dalai Lama to institute social, political and economic reforms, which he was most eager to do... young as he was, in the hope of Chinese cooperation in a 'modernizing' programme, while retaining what was good and valuable.[3]"

During his visit to Tibet in 1957, Apa Pant had the occasion to discuss these points with the Chinese generals, who could only answer in terms of Marxism and Party discipline. The 'reforms' had then just started.

It is a fact that once the Tibet Agreement was signed in April 1954, the Chinese leadership took a more radical approach towards Tibet, though, for a couple of years, the main factor which determined the

---

1 Pant Apa, *Mandala – An Awakening* (New Delhi: Orient Longman Limited, 1978), p. 112

2 See Volume 1, Chapter 8.

3 Pant, op. cit., p. 114.

Chinese approach was the building of the infrastructure needed to 'stabilize the revolution' on the plateau.

Pant felt that the Chinese officers were not interested "in harmony and compassion but in power and material benefit"; it was an occasion for Pant to ponder upon the confrontation of these two different worlds: "The one so apparently inefficient, so human and even timid, yet kind and compassionate and aspiring to something more gloriously satisfying in human life; the other determined and effective, ruthless, power-hungry and finally intolerant. I wondered how this conflict could resolve itself, and what was India's place in it.[4]"

This last sentence sums up the deeper ramifications of the survival of Tibet as a separate nation. Was it possible to preserve and develop these human qualities in a new Tibet? The future would show that it would not be.

It is true that most of the senior Indian diplomats, educated in 'modern' ideas, thought the 'old Lama hierarchy' should go and Tibet become a 'modern' country; they believed that the Chinese invasion was a chance to make a clean sweep of the old superstitions, beliefs or rituals.

But the Indian border was forgotten in the process.

Pant commented: "In those corridors of power; it often appeared, Tibet, Buddhism, the Dalai Lama, were all regarded as ridiculous, too funny for words; useless illusions that would logically cease to exist soon, thanks to the Chinese, and good riddance"[5].

Pant had some support in the Ministry of External Affairs for his 'philosophical' approach, but few could comprehend the strategic and military aspect of the events unfolding on the Roof of the World.

Whether the Chinese leadership had made up its mind about the 'reforms' or not, their first strategic objective was clear; they needed to build roads across the plateau on a war footing; these roads often leading towards the Indian border.

---

4 Ibid, p. 115.

5 Ibid.

By 1955, the construction of the Tibet-Sinking Highway cutting across Ladakh had started and the roads leading towards the NEFA (today Arunachal Pradesh) and Sikkim had already been completed.

Zhou's words were definitely linked to the development of the communication infrastructure when he proclaimed that the Tibetan society was 'not yet ripe' for socialist changes.

Pant believed that Nehru understood the depth of the conflict; however "the exigencies of power, the feeling that the Chinese must in no circumstances be 'upset' and the needless, nervous and desperate hurry to 'normalize' India-China relations, lost us the larger perspective of action."

These are some of the factors which contributed to the rapid disappearance of one of the planet's most ancient civilizations; it was to be replaced by a more materialistic culture.

Pant was quite clear about the outcome of the situation: the Tibetans were hoping against hope. They did not have the assurance that they would get the benefits brought by the Chinese on the material plane, while maintaining "the old system and the philosophy that taught and practised the path towards liberation of the human mind from turmoil".

It was also true that the Dalai Lama had been quite impressed by the changes he had seen during his visit to China and he certainly had no objection to seeing new communication links being built in Tibet. The zeal, the efficiency and the dedication of new China's leadership had made an impression on the young Dalai Lama and some of his colleagues. Many of these qualities were missing in the large monasteries of Tibet at that time.

The visit of the Dalai Lama and Panchen Lama to India, related in the last three chapters of this Volume, should be seen in this perspective.

This was perhaps one of the most serious consequences of the 'Panchsheel' Agreement: an open support for the forces which led to the complete loss of a 'way of life', based on the eternal values shared with Indian culture. In accepting to put an official seal on the Communist takeover of the Roof of the World, India not only condemned to certain death an old civilisation with its imperfections and its realisations, but made herself somewhat complicit, through her acceptance, to a philosophy of violence and brute force.

**Another Lesson**

Another conclusion of this Volume 3 is that Philosophy is not enough to guard the borders of a nation. Mao Zedong had declared: "The philosophers have so far only interpreted the world, the point is to change it"; without adopting the concept of 'power flowing from the barrel of the gun', the defence of a nation's borders cannot be neglected, at the peril of serious consequences, as was witnessed five years later.

The chapter on the exploration of Tawang by an anthropologist is telling in this perspective, the utter neglect of the preparedness of the defence of the borders for the sake of a romantic theory is something which should never happen again.

During these years, without being able to do anything, India not only lost a good neighbour, which for centuries had deep cultural, economic and emotional exchanges with the Subcontinent, but also a secure border.

Looking at the case of the visit of the Dalai Lama and the Panchen Lama to India, one realizes that India and Tibet no longer had a one-to-one relationship; for every important decision or even small detail, they had to deal through a third party, Communist China. The example of the invitation to the Dalai Lama is typical.

At the same time, the Chinese were rather nervous about the situation developing in Eastern Tibet; this probably explains why Zhou Enlai had to visit India thrice during the two-month stay of the Lamas in India; the Premier had to make sure that the Dalai Lama returned to the Land of Snows. This was not a good omen for anybody.

# Annexure

### The Construction of the Aksai Chin Road

Lakshman Singh Jangpangi, the Indian Trade Agent in Gartok (ITA) made interesting entries in his Diary for the period ending September 30, 1955.[1] The Indian official mentioned several times the rapid development in Western Tibet and the construction of the road between Tibet and Xinjiang.

At that time, it did not occur to anybody that the road would be crossing Indian territory in the Aksai Chin area.

While camping in Gartok, Jangpangi recorded his day-to-day meetings:

**September 12:**

"Mr. Yang Jan-San, Vice-Chief of Foreign Bureau of Ngari (Western Tibet) at Gartok called in the morning. He told me that they would construct [the] Sinkiang[2]-Gartok motor road via Rudok first, as it was easier and shorter than one from Lhasa."

**September 14:**

"I called on Foreign Bureau of Ngari (Western Tibet) on business in connection with lease of site for Agency buildings, wireless facilities and other matters. I also gave my tour programme of Tashigang. The Chinese have now a mule corps of about 80, 50 of which came today from Gargunsa with provisions and clothing, on way to Taklakot. They purchased some of these mules from Tibetan traders at Rs. 1200 to 1500 per mule."

---

1  *Weekly Reports of the Indian Trade Agent, Gartok*; Department: External Affairs, Indian Trade Agency Gangtok; Branch: Western Tibet; File No No. 9(4)-WT/55. Available in The National Archives of India, New Delhi.

2  Xinjiang.

This was a clear indication that the tempo of the occupation of Western Tibet was changing and infrastructure construction, (i.e. the Aksai Chin road), had started start on a war footing.

## September 15:

"The English interpreter of Shu Shuen, of Chinese Foreign Bureau called on business in the morning. Later in the afternoon, I called on Garpon Gyarsipa[3] who returned from Gargunsa last evening, where he had been on an invitation from the Chinese Military Officer, 2nd-in-Command in Western Tibet. He told me that the Chinese were anxious to show him round their headquarters and inquire about new developments in Lhasa, as this Officer had come recently (in August) from Lhasa.

In his estimate, there are about 400 officers and men at Gargunsa and all of whom were engaged in construction of another block of barracks. He was, however, made to understand by the Officer there that they had more men than his estimate, and that some of them were on borders for Check post duties. They also expressed their difficulties in getting timber supply for their houses."

## September 18 and 19:

"The Vice-Chief of Foreign Bureau, Mr. Yang passed us to Gargunsa; he is perhaps also going to Tashigang as he told us at Gartok. Since Chinese have established their headquarters at Gargunsa this village has become a busy place, as PLA personnel are constantly moving up and down."

The setting up of Gargunsa as the main base for the PLA was another indication of what the Chinese were preparing.

## September 20:

"We camped at Marle, 3 miles short of Gargunsa, 17 miles. The village is 1½ miles West of Chinese headquarters which is clearly seen from it. Local inquiries from the villagers reveal that there are about 400 men, but the parties are constantly moving to and fro. They also informed us that a caravan of more than 600 camels brought provisions etc.

---

3   One of the Governors of Western Tibet.

from Sinkiang via Rudok in July. In addition to this small caravans of yaks and mules are bringing in provisions etc. (military stores as well) both from Sinkiang and Lhasa. The local purchases at Trade Marts are additional supply."

There was clearly a change of tempo. Let us not forget that Tashigang was located a few miles from Demchok in Ladakh.

**September 21 to 24:**

"Reached Tashigang on [September] 24. The track is on flat valley on left bank of Gartung, a tributary of Indus. The confluence of these two rivers is about 7 miles above Tashigang. The valley broadens a few miles before Gargunsa and has plentiful of grass and fuel. The locality being warm overgrowth is very thick, but Tashigang itself has less overgrowth and fuel is scarce. Neither the Chinese or Tibetan authorities have so far made any attempt to make a proper road; it is still a beaten track. The Chinese have now surveyed an alignment for motor road and [I] myself saw markings on the route. It is reliably learnt that they have surveyed a possible road alignment from Sinkiang to Gartok via Rudok in July and August 1955. This is further confirmed by Mr. Yang's earlier statement [September 12 entry] that Sinkiang-Gartok road will be given priority."

"They are getting timber from Rongchung (Shipke)[4] and other villages near Himachal Pradesh border) via this place to Gargunsa. There are about 600 yak loads of it and about 300 yak loads have already arrived. They are finding great difficulties in its transportation on yaks. They have also constructed a house at Tashigang, but owing to shortage of timber, it is still unroofed."

**Other Indications of Road Construction**

The Official Report of the 1962 War[5] published by the Indian Ministry of Defence stated: "The Preliminary survey work on the planned Tibet-Sinkiang road having been completed by the mid-1950's, China started constructing motorable road in summer 1955. The highway ran

---

4   Shipki-la in Himachal Pradesh.

5   For Report, see https://www.bharat-rakshak.com/ARMY/history/1962war/266-official-history.html.

over 160 km across the Aksai Chin region of north-east Ladakh. It was completed in the second half of 1957. Arterial roads connecting the highway with Tibet were also laid. On 6 October 1957, the Sinkiang-Tibet road was formally opened with a ceremony in Gartok and twelve trucks on a trial run from Yarkand reached Gartok. In January 1958, the China News Agency reported that the Sinkiang-Tibet highway had been opened two months earlier and the road was being fully utilised."

It is quite clear that the road had started being built during the period covered in Jangpangi's Diary.

**Another Account**

Another interesting account showing how the Indian Army already knew in 1955 that the Chinese were building a road across Indian territory, was published a few years ago in the UK.[6] In 1955, Wignall, a British mountaineer, went on an expedition inside Tibet with the knowledge of Indian Military Intelligence. The Army Chief, General KS Thimayya seriously suspected that the Chinese were building a road on Indian territory; Wignall was asked to get proof of it.

He was eventually caught by the PLA, interrogated and kept as prisoner for several weeks. He was later released in the midst of winter in a high altitude pass. The Chinese thought he would never survive the blizzard or find his way back to India. After an incredible journey, he managed to reach India and was able to report about the road to the army authorities who, in turn, informed the Prime Minister and VK Krishna Menon, the Defence Minister.

Wignall was later told by his Army contact: "Our illustrious Prime Minister Nehru, who is so busy on the world stage telling the rest of mankind how to live, has too little time to attend to the security of his own country. Your material was shown to Nehru by one of our senior officers, who plugged hard. He was criticised by Krishna Menon in Nehru's presence for 'lapping up American CIA agent-provocateur propaganda.' Menon has completely suppressed your information."

6  Sidney Wignall, *Spy on the Roof of the World* (Edinburgh: Canongate, 1997).

'So it was all for nothing?' I [Wignall] asked. 'Perhaps not,' Singh[7] responded. 'We will keep working away at Nehru. Someday he must see the light, and realise the threat communist Chinese occupation of Tibet poses for India.[8]

The Government of India has never acknowledged that it had information about the Aksai Chin road as early as 1954-55, but it is a fact.

The issue would be discussed for the first time in the Lok Sabha only in August 1959.

Why this vital issue was ignored and kept under wraps for so long is a mystery ...and a Himalayan blunder.

---

7   Wignall's Army contact.

8   Wignall, op. cit., p. 250.

# Index

## A

Abor villages 377

Achingmori massacre 302, 303

Aksai Chin 5, 17, 90, 92, 93, 96, 165, 359, 360, 562, 563, 565, 566

Almora-Lipulekh 341

Alo Chantzo 454

Amdo 76, 81, 166, 174, 178, 333, 337, 349, 351, 458, 509

Apa Saheb Bala Saheb Pant 134

Attwood, William H. 58

## B

Bahadur Singh 29, 33, 462, 463

Bajpai, Girja Shankar 55

Bandung Conference 3, 73, 74, 75

Bara Hoti 10, 21, 22, 25, 26, 95

Battle of Chamdo 2, 139, 144, 147, 472

Bhutan Rashtriya Congress 237

Bob Khathing 39, 368, 543

Bomdila 367, 375, 376, 383, 384

Bongdu Trade Market 350

Bumthang Trungyik 454

## C

Central Military Commission (CMC) 385

Chakra Trade Mart 351

Chamoli district 9

Champithang 122, 123, 221, 222

Changu lake 222

Charduar 367

Chen Chia-kang 29

Chiang Kai Shek 87

Chibber, SL 70, 99, 113, 117, 140, 400

Chinghai-Tibet highway 161

Chi Tso Lapta 151

Chorten Karpo 156, 168

Chou Enlai 15, 50, 70, 75, 76, 474, 519, 529, 548, 554, 556

Chumbi Valley 4, 67, 108, 138, 139, 141, 142, 143, 144, 146, 147, 156, 168, 183, 186, 189, 220, 221, 222, 223, 224, 225, 227, 232, 258, 260, 262, 270, 281, 324, 420, 450, 469, 475, 488

Chusul 110

# D

Dalai Lama 136, 141, 145, 163

Darjye Gompa 333

Dayal, Harishwar 39, 55, 223

Demchok village 90

Deng Xiaoping 82, 83, 139

Dhanshiri River 243

Dikyi Lingka 171

Dirang Dzong 367, 368, 371, 373, 374, 375, 376, 379, 381, 382, 384

Doklam incident 282

Dongbra Mart 356

Dorje Namgyel 81

Drepung Monastery 186, 393, 398

Druk Gyalpo 233

Dutt, Subimal 95, 277, 528, 530

Dzasa Samdup Photrang 452

# G

Gandhi, Indira 63, 249

Garhwal-Tibet 9

Gartok 7, 22, 173

Gartok Trade Mart 354

General Zhhang Guohua 449

Ghirti Pass 10

Goshampa House 158

Gothing Pass 10

Gyalo Thondup 44, 153, 154, 183, 216, 230, 514, 535, 538, 550, 553, 556

Gyanima Khargo Trade Mart 350

Gyantse 3, 70, 97, 98, 99, 100, 101, 102, 103, 104, 105, 106, 107, 111, 112, 113, 114, 115, 116, 117, 118, 119, 120, 121, 122, 125, 126, 127, 128, 129, 130, 131, 132, 133, 139, 140, 143, 145, 146, 150, 151, 152, 153, 156, 160, 166, 167, 175, 176, 180, 182, 184, 186, 192, 197, 220, 221, 279, 280, 301, 324, 331, 358, 386, 390, 393, 399, 401, 404, 405, 406, 420, 424, 431, 436, 450, 468, 475, 477

# H

Hermit Kingdom 241

Himmatsinghji Report 86

Hoti Pass 10

Hoti plain 18, 20, 21, 25

# I

Indian Trade Agent 98

Indian Traders in Sikkim 196

Indo-Tibetan Border Police 11

Indo-Tibetan trade 195

Intelligence Bureau (IB) 9, 406

# J

Jamyang Norbu 327

Jelukhaze Pass  27

Jigme Dorji Wangchuck  242

Jokhang Cathedral  143

## K

Kailash-Mansarovar  393

Kaisar Bahadur Thapa  199

Kalimpong  42, 57, 214, 536

Kameng Frontier Division  298, 369, 382

Kang Mao-Chao  30

Kapur, BK  38, 107, 111, 134, 135, 190, 197, 233, 235, 250, 468

Karakoram pass  90

Kaul, TN  16, 20, 21, 25, 27, 30, 36, 47, 70, 109, 113, 197, 208, 216, 246, 247, 288, 383, 388, 395, 459, 467, 468

Khampha Chu valley  140

Kham province  4, 44, 334, 425, 546

Khathing, Maj Bob  39, 543

Kripalani, JB  35

Krishnatry, Maj SM  4, 99, 311, 312

Kumbum monastery  147

Kunwar Singh, Indrajit (KI Singh)  66

Kuomintang  80, 139, 205, 543

Kushok Bakula Rinpoche  4, 93, 387, 388, 392

## L

Labrang Tashi Kyil monastery  148

Lakshman Singh Jangpangi  340

Lall, John  16

Lapchak Mission  388

Leprosy Home at Tawang  377

Lhasa-Chamdo road  139, 151

Li Jue, Maj Gen  160, 281, 366

Liu Wenhui  81

Lohit Frontier Division  91

Luthra, PN  485

## M

Macfarlane, Captain  101, 102

Maharaj Kumar  192, 201, 202, 216, 230, 411, 419, 422, 452, 477

Mahayana Buddhism  213

Manas River  245

Mana Valley  9, 12

Mao Tse-tung  125

Mao Zedong  2, 14, 47, 81, 82, 124, 136, 148, 150, 160, 161, 172, 349, 385, 467, 545, 561

Marshal Chen Yi  280, 366, 446, 447, 448, 450

McMahon Line  50, 51, 57, 85, 298, 299, 301, 313, 314, 325, 371, 384, 386, 425, 540, 541, 543, 544

Menon, Krishna VK  46, 47, 75, 565

Menon, PN  110, 114, 136, 279, 280, 329, 407, 417, 419, 443, 445, 460, 462, 483, 485, 521

Migyitun border settlement  321

Mimang movement  163, 164, 185

Minsar  174, 349, 363

Monlam Festival  413, 454

Mountbatten, Edwina  69

Muja Depon  147, 183

Mukharji, G.  13

Mullik, BN  45

Murty, TS  89, 270, 282

# N

Nabra Trade Mart  352

Nagchuka  143, 145, 158, 180, 408

Namgyal, Tashi  134, 135, 200

Nehru, Jawaharlal  1, 3, 8, 9, 34, 35, 47, 63, 65, 73, 87, 220, 247, 271, 272, 273, 278, 303, 463, 496, 528, 555

Nehru, RK  4, 30, 80, 83, 84, 85, 86, 88, 220, 223, 226, 228, 229, 231, 248, 258, 259, 260, 261, 266, 267, 271, 272, 274, 458, 459, 462, 463, 464, 465, 467, 468, 470, 473, 548, 550

Nepal-Tibet frontier  54

Ngawang Namgyal  238

Nilang-Jadhang area  8, 12

Nilang Valley  4

Niti-Garhwal  341

Niti pass  17

Norbulinka  184

# O

Olaf Caroe  82

# P

Panchen Lama  5, 136, 137, 138, 145, 149, 150, 151, 154, 164, 166, 167, 177, 184, 186, 329, 402, 406, 413, 419, 424, 434, 435, 436, 439, 441, 447, 449, 453, 457, 458, 459, 463, 466, 470, 472, 473, 475, 479, 480, 481, 482, 483, 484, 489, 490, 491, 494, 495, 496, 497, 498, 502, 505, 507, 508, 509, 510, 511, 512, 513, 514, 515, 516, 517, 518, 528, 530, 534, 536, 537, 538, 542, 545, 547, 548, 555, 560, 561

Panchsheel Agreement  2, 5, 8, 14, 16, 23, 557

Panikkar doctrine  7, 58, 95, 296

Panikkar, KM  1, 67, 89, 274, 391

Patel, Sardar  1

Pathania, Brig AS  102

Peking Conference  102

Pemayangtse  202

People's Liberation Army (PLA)  1, 124

Phari Dzong  93, 119, 120

Phu Rapga Pangda Tshang  143

Pillai, NR  9, 15, 63, 66, 548, 550

Political Parties in Sikkim  193

  National Party  193

  Praja Sammelan Party  193

  Sikkim State Congress  193

Praja Sammelan Party  193

Preparatory Committee of the Tibetan Autonomous Region [PCTAR]  178, 445

## Q

Qinghai province  143, 192

Qinghai-Tibet highway  281, 468

## R

Raghavan, N.  50, 61, 65, 108, 113, 458, 459

Ram Chundur Goburdhun  109

Ren Naiqiang  81

Rinpoche, Kushok Bakula  4, 93

Rinpoche, Taktser  147, 464, 556

## S

Sailo, Captain  318

Sangchamalla  8, 9, 292

Saraswati river  9

Sarji Post  18

Sela Pass  367

Senge Dzong  367, 379

Sera monastery  178

Shangtse Trade Mart  353

Shigatse Lhayap  454

Shipki-la  276, 283, 284, 285, 286, 287, 288, 289, 290, 291, 294, 295, 343, 564

Siang Frontier Division  180, 315, 365

Sichuan province  81, 192

Sikkim State Congress  193

Simla-Shipki Pass route  343

Sinha, Nirmal  393, 405, 406, 415, 417

Sinkiang  90

Sino-Indian Agreement  112, 130, 197, 343

Sino-Indian Agreement of April 1954  285

Sino-Tibetan Agreement of 1951  192

Sonam Tsering  199

South-East Asia Organisation [SEATO]  37

Subansiri  4

Subansiri Frontier Division  91, 297, 298, 310

Sumul Sinha  39, 55, 208, 228, 543

## T

Taklakot Mart  346, 347, 360

Tashi Lhumpo monastery  188, 406, 434, 435, 509

Tashi Lhunpo  164, 166, 172

Tawang  4, 367, 368, 376, 384

Tawang Gompa  379

Tension between Nepalese, Lepchas and Bhutias  212

Tharchen Trade Mart  348

The Tibet Agreement  104

Thokar Trade Market  350

Tibetan Autonomous Region  4, 116, 143, 178, 189, 432, 445, 453, 528, 534

Tibetan Trade Agency  216

Tibetan Trade Agent (TTA)  223

Tibet-Qinghai Axis  3

Tibet-Qinghai highway  143

Tibet-Sichuan Axis  3

Trimon Se Kusho  183

Tsangchok-la  10

Tsari Chu valley  299, 313, 320

Tunjun-la  15, 26, 30, 283

## V

Verrier Elwin  4, 366, 375, 383

## W

Wangchuk dynasty  251

Wu-Je  7, 9, 17, 18, 20, 21, 22, 29, 30, 31

## Y

Yang Gongsu  116, 120, 121, 123, 126, 129, 179, 436

Yatung  3, 67, 70, 99, 102, 103, 104, 105, 106, 107, 111, 112, 113, 114, 116, 117, 118, 120, 121, 122, 123, 124, 125, 126, 127, 129, 130, 131, 132, 133, 137, 139, 140, 141, 146, 147, 156, 157, 158, 159, 167, 169, 171, 173, 183, 186, 192, 197, 221, 222, 223, 224, 225, 226, 232, 258, 260, 261, 270, 279, 280, 324, 331, 358, 399, 400, 402, 404, 416, 420, 421, 422, 424, 429, 431, 432, 436, 443, 450, 465, 475, 477

Younghusband  204, 221, 450, 509

## Z

Zhang Jingwu  83, 124, 137, 179, 366, 386, 411, 412, 436, 443, 446, 449, 472, 475, 476, 558

Zhhang Guohua, General  166, 449

Zhou En-lai  3, 5, 7, 8, 9, 32, 38, 46, 47, 48, 50, 51, 55, 61, 65, 66, 67, 71, 74, 80, 87, 210, 295, 323, 337, 385, 439, 450, 467, 470, 473, 499, 500, 532, 535, 537, 541, 542, 547, 551, 552, 553, 554, 555, 561

# Map 1

# Barahoti and Other Passes

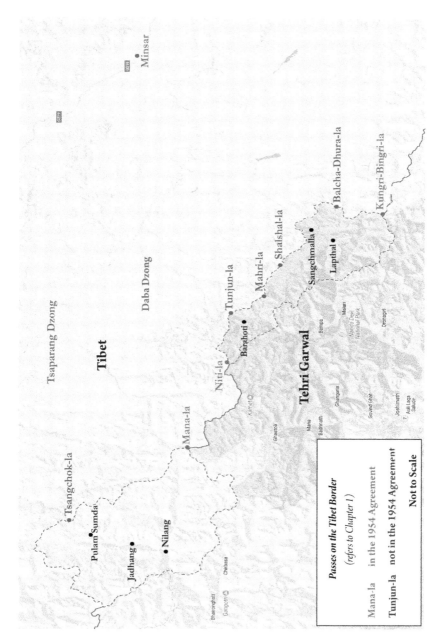

# Map 2

# China's Claim Western Sector

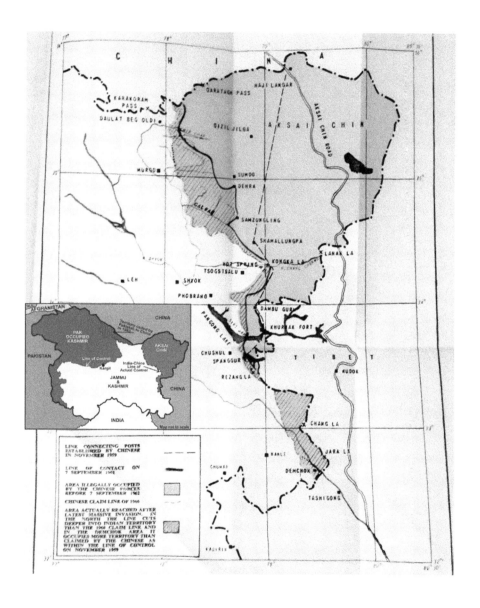

# Map 3

## Chinese Claims in Eastern Sector 1959

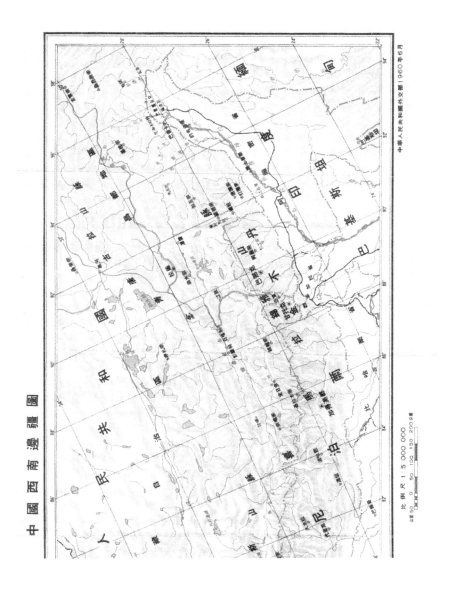

# Map 4

# Dak Bungalows in Tibet

# Map 5

# Tsari Yatra

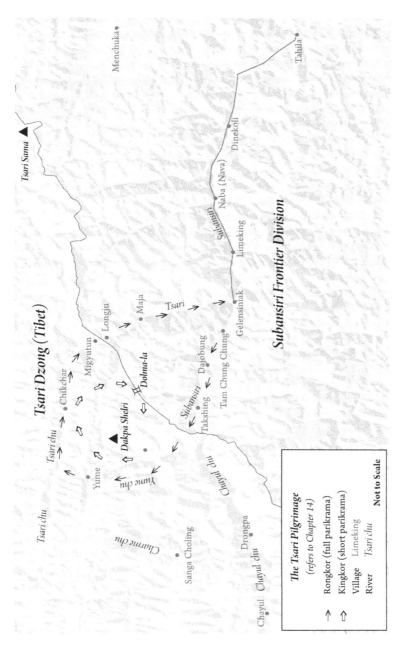

Map 6

# Trade Agency and Marts in Western Tibet

CPSIA information can be obtained
at www.ICGtesting.com
Printed in the USA
BVHW031308250719
554278BV00002B/3/P